W. S. B. Mathews, Emil Liebling

PRONOUNCING and DEFINING DICTIONARY of MUSIC

W. S. B. Mathews, Emil Liebling

PRONOUNCING and DEFINING DICTIONARY of MUSIC

ISBN/EAN: 9783741117640

Manufactured in Europe, USA, Canada, Australia, Japa

Cover: Foto ©Angelika Wolter / pixelio.de

Manufactured and distributed by brebook publishing software (www.brebook.com)

W. S. B. Mathews, Emil Liebling

PRONOUNCING and DEFINING DICTIONARY of MUSIC

PRONOUNCING AND DEFINING

DICTIONARY OF MUSIC

BY

W. S. B. MATHEWS AND EMIL LIEBLING.

PUBLISHED BY
THE JOHN CHURCH COMPANY,
CINCINNATI.   NEW YORK.   CHICAGO.
LEIPSIC.   LONDON.

Copyright, 1896, by THE JOHN CHURCH CO.
International Copyright.

CONTENTS.

SUMMARY OF MUSICAL NOTATION.
    TIME AND METER.
    NOTES.
    RESTS.
    MEASURE NOTATION.
    MEASURE SIGNATURE.
    PITCH NOTATION.
    STAFF AND CLEFS.
    TONES IN KEY.
    SIGNATURES.
    TONIC SOL-FA.
    PATENT NOTES.
    GRACE NOTES AND EMBELLISHMENTS.
    TRILL.
    PEDALS OF THE PIANOFORTE.
    PHRASING AND EXPRESSION
    ABBREVIATIONS.
    SPECIAL SIGNS IN INSTRUMENTAL MUSIC.

CLASSIFICATION OF MUSICAL FORMS.

RULES OF PRONUNCIATION.

PREFACE.

THE book herewith offered the musical public has one aim, which is *utility*—practical use. While there is already a considerable number of small dictionaries, the publishers of the present work believe that there is still room for another, which, as far as possible, should combine the advantages of all the best ones and avoid their prominent defects: such as obsolete and often incorrect phraseology, reduplication of terms, redundancy of obsolete terms, and the like. Accordingly, the work was committed to the present editors, who have agreed upon the selection of terms and information following. Its special points of usefulness are these:

1. The vocabulary, while not so large as two others, is more complete and modern, aggregating nearly 10,000 terms.

2. The definitions have been amended where necessary, and some hundreds of important topics have been entirely rewritten, such as Accent, Consonance, Dissonance, Temperament, and the like.

3. Pronunciations have been affixed to all terms from foreign languages. These are very necessary by reason of the totally different principles of pronunciation which govern terms from the French, German, and Italian, respectively. The pronunciations are approximate only, but they will be found of great assistance.

4. At the beginning, in place of an Introduction, we have placed a general view of Musical Notation, not alone the topics which ordinarily are included under that head, but also those rarer matters of the signs employed in different departments of manuscript music and score-writing. As far as we have been able to collect them, this summary includes every sign liable to be met with by the student, no matter in what department he may work.

5. At one point the work is not consistent with itself. In several of the small works now before the public, long lists of terms are found beginning with the German article *die*, a principle of lexicography as false as would be the inclusion of a series of phrases in an English dictionary beginning with "the." Accordingly these have been relegated to their proper places, under their leading terms. In other cases, however, entire phrases have been included under their leading word, such as those beginning with Allegro, Andante, etc., because these combinations are of constant occurrence, and the complex term possesses an individual significance which is not in all cases exactly the same as the sum of its elements.

6. A large amount of editing has been devoted to rectifying the faulty phraseology of former definitions. We can not hope to have fully succeeded at this point. Careless habits of speech (and of thought as well) retain in colloquial use such erroneous expressions as "note" for tone, "bar" for measure, "time" for measure, "tone" and "semitone" as names of interval, and the like, until scientific musicians pass over such expressions without noticing their defective and misleading form. It is altogether likely that many such examples still remain in the present volume, despite the care that has been taken to remove them.

SUMMARY OF MUSICAL NOTATION.

In writing a piece of music which he has imagined or worked out at the instrument, the composer has mainly to do with two elements in it, the Pitch and the Time. The Expression and Tone-color he leaves for mere suggestion, by means of an occasional $p.$, $f.$, $sf.$, or other incidental mark. Here almost everything is left to the intelligence of the interpretative artist. But in the two provinces first mentioned this is not the case. Everything is set down with exactness. The number and recurrence of tones, their ordering into pulsation and measure, their various relations in pitch, as melody and harmony, all are fully and finally determined. Hence a clear understanding of these parts of musical notation is of the utmost importance to the student, since without it he will never arrive at an exact comprehension of the composer's intention.

NOTATION OF TIME AND METER.

The distinctive sign of musical tone is a character called a Note, which consists essentially of a round or oval head, with or without a stem downward or upward from it.

	Whole.	Half.	Quarter.	Eighth.	16th.	32d.	64th.
NOTES:	𝅝	𝅗𝅥	𝅘𝅥	𝅘𝅥𝅮	𝅘𝅥𝅯	𝅘𝅥𝅰	𝅘𝅥𝅱

There is also a note called a Breve, equal to two Whole notes. This is obsolete in modern music, but occasionally it is found in old music.

A Note indicates Musical utterance, as distinguished from any other kind of utterance. The forms of the notes indicate relative duration. The duration-values correspond to the names given above.

A dot after a note adds one half to its value. A second dot adds half as much as the first. Hence two dots add three fourths to the value of the note.

RESTS.

A Rest is a musical silence, or a rhythmic silence. By this is meant that whereas the term rest in general means merely a cessation from activity, a *musical rest* indicates a temporary cessation from musical activity *while the idea of the music is still going on.* A musical rest is a silence during a certain compass of musical time; *i. e.*, of Rhythm, or Meter. Hence, during rests, the musician is conscious of the rhythmic pulsation and meter. This is the distinction between a musical rest and rest in general. The characters indicating musical rest are also called Rests. They are of forms and denominations corresponding to the notes. Dots are applied to them in the same way as to notes.

Whole Rest.	Half Rest.	Quarter Rest.	Eighth Rest.	16th Rest.	32d Rest.	64th Rest.

A rest of several measures in succession is generally indicated by one of the forms of rest following, together with the figures indicating the length of rest desired, written above the staff.

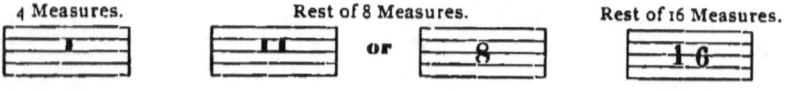

RHYTHMIC PULSATION AND MEASURE NOTATION.

The first step towards music is the recurrence of rhythmic pulsation. All music moves rhythmically, by pulsations of equal value, which are grouped into measures by means of accents. Measures are of two, three, four, six, nine, or twelve pulsations each, and all alike have the strong pulse at beginning. The place of this pulsation is indicated by means of a line across the staff, called a Bar. The strong accent falls upon the tone or time-space immediately following it. Accent is indicated also by means of a little angle ">". In the following examples of measure-forms the accent mark is unnecessary, but is placed there for the guidance of the student. The mere bar, without the extra mark, means exactly the same thing. The bar always shows the place of the strong accent.

MEASURE SIGNATURE.

At the beginning of every piece or movement is placed a Measure Signature, consisting of two figures in the form of a fraction, immediately following the clef. The upper figure denotes the number of pulsations in a measure.

The lower figure tells what kind of note is taken to represent one unit of time. All other notes in the piece are computed with reference to this. The time within the measure may be occupied in any manner the composer pleases. One tone may be prolonged through the entire measure; or every pulse may be subdivided into several parts. All that the measure signature requires is that the unit note or its value shall be present in each pulsation of the measure according to the tables of note-values preceding.

The unit note is generally a quarter or eighth; less frequently a half-note; least often of all a sixteenth or other shorter note.

Now, since the measures run from two pulsations to three, four, six, nine and twelve, each signature appears in several different forms, such as a half-note unit with two, three, four, etc., pulsations; a quarter-note unit with all the varieties of measures, etc. Hence the following forms:

$\frac{2}{1}$ $\frac{3}{1}$ $\frac{4}{1}$ A whole-note unit, and two, three, or four pulsations in a measure.

In all of these forms the value of every note is computed in beats, reckoning from the whole note as one beat.

$\frac{2}{2}$ or ¢ $\frac{3}{2}$ $\frac{4}{2}$ $\frac{6}{2}$

In all these forms the unit is a half note, and all other note forms are computed from that.

$\frac{2}{4}$ $\frac{3}{4}$ $\frac{4}{4}$ or C $\frac{6}{4}$ $\frac{9}{4}$ $\frac{12}{4}$

In all these forms the unit is a quarter, and this is the measure-note from which all are computed.

$(\frac{2}{8})$ $\frac{3}{8}$ $(\frac{4}{8})$ $\frac{6}{8}$ $\frac{9}{8}$ $\frac{12}{8}$

In these forms the measure-note is an eighth, and all forms are computed from that.

$\frac{3}{16}$ $\frac{4}{16}$ $\frac{6}{16}$ etc.

In these forms the measure-note is a sixteenth.

MEASURE FORMS.

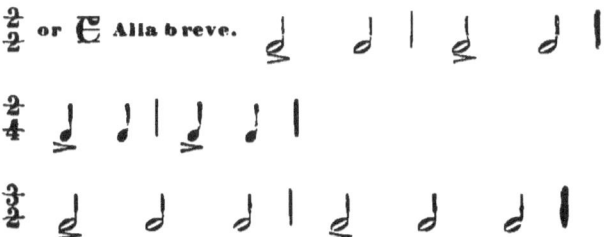

All measures having more than three pulsations are grouped within themselves into twos or threes, thus requiring smaller accents, as indicated approximately in the examples following:

NOTE.—6-8 measure is not at all the same as six-eighths derived from 3-4 measure. The latter is accented as three groups of two:

THE NOTATION OF PITCH.

Musical pitch is noted by means of lines and spaces, grouped into convenient systems called staves, or a staff. In modern music the staff consists of five lines and the appertaining spaces, which number six (those above and below the lines being included). Each of these lines and spaces is called a degree of the staff, and represents a degree of the scale. Therefore, five lines, with the six appertaining spaces, afford places for eleven scale degrees. When more are wanted, short additional lines (called added lines) are written above or below. When these become excessive, the same are repeated with the expression 8vo above or below. The former indicates that the octave above is intended; the latter, the octave below.

Pianoforte music generally employs two such systems of lines, one for the notes to be played by each hand. Organ music employs three staves, the part for the feet requiring an additional staff. Orchestral scores employ as many staves as there are instruments employed. These different staves are distinguished from each other by means of special designations, and by characters called Clefs, or keys. The clefs in use are three in form, and six in variety, according to the manner of applying them. First comes the treble, or G Clef, indicating the place of G above middle C. This is used for the right-hand parts in piano and organ music, the violin, oboe, flute, and instruments of high pitch. The bass, or F Clef, indicates the place of F below middle C. It is used for the basses. The C Clef indicates middle C. It is applied in several different manners.

The following diagram shows the great staff of eleven lines (the line of middle C in the center), with the different clefs applied to the selection of five lines which they serve to identify.

GREAT STAFF OF ELEVEN LINES,

Showing the relation and pitch of the various Clefs and Staves used in Pianoforte and Vocal Music, and in Orchestral Scores; together with the letters indicating absolute pitch.

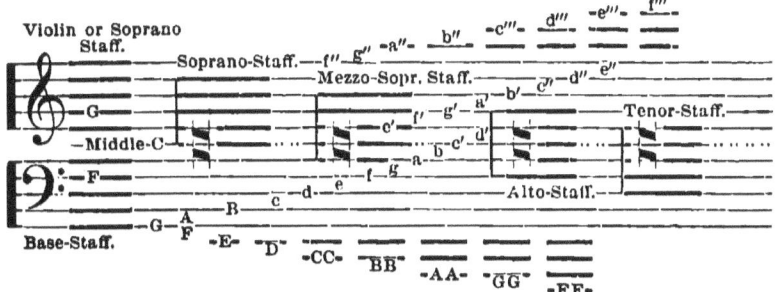

Very high tones, requiring many added lines to properly indicate, are sometimes written an octave lower, with an *8va* over them to show that the passage is to be played an octave higher.

The equivalence of the different clefs is also shown by the following figure, in which the notes which are identical are connected by dotted lines.

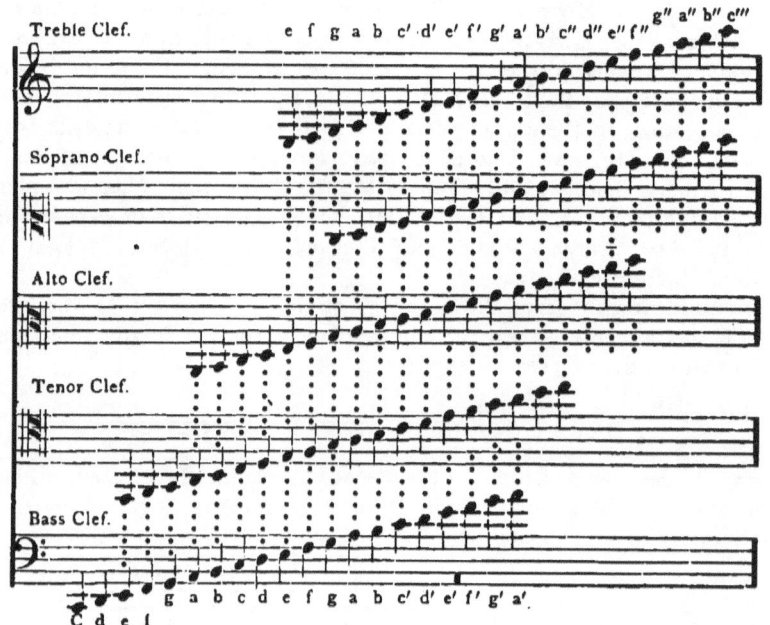

These different clefs, although at first confusing to the student of theory, are later a convenience, since they permit him to represent almost any melody without running off the staff and requiring the addition of added lines.

The staff as above represented may be taken as equivalent to the white keys of the pianoforte, each line and space standing for the tone made by a single key.

NOTATION OF TONES IN KEY.

The staff is adjusted to the representation of the chromatic tones, and the black keys, by means of characters called sharps ♯, flats ♭, and naturals ♮. The sharp, placed upon a staff degree, indicates the next higher tone in the chromatic scale. The flat, the next chromatic tone lower. The natural cancels the flat or sharp, and in certain cases effects adjustments equivalent to either of the former.

Thus, a sharp upon the staff-degree *G*, indicates *G-sharp;* upon *A*, *A-sharp*, etc.

A flat upon *A*, indicates *A-flat;* upon *B*, *B-flat*, etc.

A natural upon *A-sharp*, indicates *A;* upon *B-flat*, *B*, etc.

Double sharps × and double flats ♭♭ are also employed when needed. These indicate a chromatic change of an entire whole step upwards or downwards from the unaffected degree. A double sharp upon *A*, indicates *A-double-sharp*, which is enharmonic with B-natural. *A-double-flat* is equivalent to G-natural, and so on. The double sharps and double flats are employed for indicating chromatic tones in pieces where single sharps or flats are already in use. Thus, to the ear the following two series of tones are not different.

Chromatic signs affect the staff degree upon which they are placed throughout the measure in which they occur, and no further. They affect only the degree upon which they are placed, and not the octaves, except when used as Signatures, in which case they affect not only the degrees to which they are applied, but all octaves of them upon the same staff.

SIGNATURES.

By Signature is meant sharps or flats written after the clef to indicate the adjustment of the staff to key. In this way is indicated whatever modification from the plain staff the key may require, except in the case of the minor mode, which generally requires an accidental sharp or natural upon its seventh degree. Hence, in the following table of signatures, and the names of the staff degrees under them, the minor modes are also shown with this accidental.

THE MUSICAL NOTATION.

Signatures of the Keys, and Relative Minors.

NOTE.—The occurrence of the characteristic accidental above, with a given signature, generally indicates the minor key named.

THE MUSICAL NOTATION.   13

TONES IN KEY. OTHER NOTATIONS.

The Tonic Sol-fa notation consists of the initials of the scale names of tones written in a horizontal line. Digressions into a higher or lower octave are indicated by a short tick above or below the initial. The key is indicated by a direction at beginning.

The bars indicate measure beginnings, and the colons the beats. As many tones are sung in one beat as are represented within the time-space devoted to it. Prolongation of tone is indicated by a — in the spaces through which the tone is to be prolonged. Rests are indicated by leaving the time-space vacant. Example:

Key of G.   COMIN' THRO' THE RYE.

|: s, .,s: s, ,m.—|r .,d: r, m.—|s, .,s,: l, .s,|d :   :|

|s, .,m: d, m.—|r .,d: r, m.—|s .,m: d .s|l : |

|s .,m: f .,r|m .,d: r, m.—|s .,s: l, .s,|d : |

PATENT NOTES.

SOMETIMES CALLED BUCKWHEAT NOTES.

This is a staff notation, much used in the South, with note-heads of peculiar form, indicating the key-name of the tone. All the staff notation (including signatures) is employed, and the characteristic shapes of the note-head additionally.

Do, Ray, Me, Faw, Sol, Law, Se, Do.

SIGNS APPERTAINING TO EXPRESSION AND INTERPRETATION.—MELODIC EMBELLISHMENTS.

THE LONG APPOGGIATURA.

This embellishment consists of a grace note which takes half (*a*), two-thirds (*b*), or even the whole (*c*), of the time of its principal, as shown in the examples following:

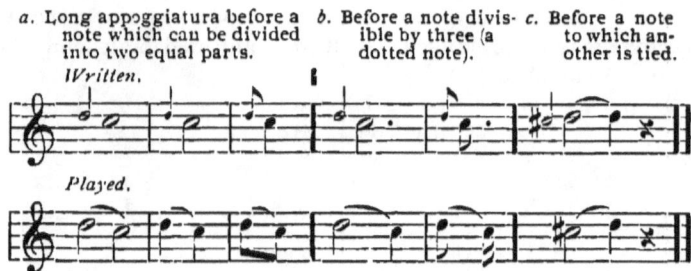

a. Long appoggiatura before a note which can be divided into two equal parts.   *b.* Before a note divisible by three (a dotted note).   *c.* Before a note to which another is tied.

The long appoggiatura is now usually written out in full in large notes.

THE SHORT APPOGGIATURA.

The short appoggiatura is a grace note with a little stroke through its stem. It begins at the time of the principal note, and is played as quickly as possible—(*a, b, c.*)

a. Moderato.   *b. Presto.*   *c. Before double notes.*

AFTER NOTES.

After notes consist of one or more grace notes introduced as passing or changing notes, in passing from one melody note to another. They are generally connected with their principal note by a slur, and never fall on an accent.

DOUBLE APPOGGIATURAS.

Double appoggiaturas consist of two grace notes preceding a melody note. They begin at the proper time of the principal note (and therefore with the corresponding Base note), and are played as quickly as possible, the accent falling on the principal note.

THE TURN, OR GRUPETTO.

The turn consists of a principal note and two auxiliary notes, above and below respectively, which may be a whole step or a half step distant from the principal. Generally, the upper auxiliary is the next tone above in the same key, and the lower a semitone below the principal. When the upper auxiliary is only a semitone above the principal, as in the case of turns on the 3d and 7th degree of the scale, the lower auxiliary is played diatonic, and consequently a whole step below the principal, in order to avoid the misleading chromatic effect which would otherwise be produced. On the 5th degree of the minor scale the lower auxiliary is played chromatic. The turn usually comes at the close of the principal note, as at *a*, *b*, and *c*, in the examples, where also is illustrated the use of accidentals in connection with the turn-sign. Sometimes, however, it comes at the beginning of a note, as at *d*, in which case the turn-sign stands directly over it. With dotted notes the turn comes between the note and the dot, as shown at *e* and *f*.

THE MORDENT AND BOUNDING TRILL.

These two embellishments are precisely alike, except that one is made with the note below the principal, and the other with the note above. The first is distinguished by the vertical stroke through the sign, as at *a*, below. The other, also called Mordent by some, and *Prall Trill* or "Bounding Trill" by others, lacks the vertical stroke through the sign, and is made with the note above. The same embellishment is sometimes written out in small notes, as at *e*. The Prall Trill should be accented on the *first* note, as at *d*. In all cases the embellishment is to be played as rapidly as possible.

THE TRILL.

The trill consists of a rapid vibration or alternation of a principal note and the next above in the same key. A vocal trill should begin somewhat deliberately, but immediately become rapid, as shown at *a* below. It concludes with a turn, which, however, may sometimes be omitted in chain trills. On the pianoforte a long trill, accompanied by a melody in the same hand, may omit the auxiliary note at the moment of sounding the melody, in order to facilitate the passage, as shown at *d*. It is of the greatest importance that the notes of the trill should be of equal power. At the start the auxiliary may be accented. Trills should vibrate at a uniform speed, after the motion is once established, and in some definite ratio to the time of the passage.

The trill begins with the principal note, and not with the auxiliary, although the contrary has been taught by eminent masters, and is sometimes required by a grace note, as at *b* and *c* below.

THE PEDALS OF THE PIANOFORTE.

Modern pianofortes sometimes have two and sometimes three pedals. That upon the right is the *Damper pedal*. (There is no such thing as a loud pedal.)

It is indicated by the abbreviation *Ped.*, and the termination of its use by ※ or ⊕.

In some old music (printed between 1830 and 1850) the use of the pedal is indicated by the character ⊕. This is now obsolete.

Mr. Arthur Foote has proposed the following mark, which indicates that the pedal is to be pressed at the beginning of the line and discontinued at the precise point where the line terminates:

The left-hand pedal is called the *Soft pedal*, and its office is to reduce the volume of sound. Upon upright pianos it does this by bringing the hammers nearer the strings. Upon grand pianos, by shifting the hammers so that they do not strike all the strings of the unison. Hence the origin of the term *Una Corda*, for indicating that the soft pedal should be pressed by the left foot. The term *Tre Corda* indicates its discontinuance. Occasionally these terms are abbreviated to U. C. and T. C., but as a rule they are written out in full.

When there are three pedals the middle one is generally a tone-sustaining pedal. This is a modification of the damper pedal, prolonging whatever tones are actually sounding at the moment when the tone-sustaining pedal is pressed. Meanwhile, others can be taken and left to any extent, the original tone or chord remaining sounding until the vibration of the strings dies away, or until the tone-sustaining pedal is dismissed. There is no mark as yet for this pedal. Its use is advisable in places where there are tones to be prolonged, but where confusion arises from the ordinary damper pedal.

INDICATIONS OF PHRASING AND FORM.

The Slur ⌒ is a curved line drawn over or under several notes, indicating that they are to be closely connected in performance; or that they form a single idea, although the idea itself may contain several smaller ideas.

Cross slur points indicate that the note under them belongs to two ideas, being the end of one and the beginning of the other.

Dots, or pointed specs, over notes indicate Staccato quality. Tones so indicated are disconnected more or less according to the nature of the passage. In older music the dots were sometimes considered to indicate a duration equal to half the value of the notes; and the specs a duration equal to a quarter of the apparent value of the notes. In modern music no distinction of this kind exists.

Short lines over notes indicate emphasis and individuality; occasionally a slight prolonging.

Short lines with a dot, or dots and slur together, indicate a less degree of staccato than the dots alone. Generally considered to equal three fourths of the value of the notes.

∨ Sometimes used to indicate the end of a formal phrase, in pieces edited for elementary instruction. It does not necessarily require separation between the tones, but is intended solely as an aid to the eye in dividing the passage into its constituent parts.

‖ | or | ‖ These are called "reading marks," and indicate the boundaries of subordinate motives. No separation of tones is indicated by these marks. They are solely for aiding the eye.

$\overset{2}{1}$/ $\overset{3}{1}$/ Placed over a bar indicates the strong accent of the great meter, consisting of three or two measures, according to the figure above the little angle.

⌒ Rubato, sometimes employed to indicate a slight emphasis and prolonging of the tone, particularly in suspensions.

, Comma, sometimes indicates a breathing interruption in the flow of tone, similar to that made in melody by the singer taking breath.

   HS. Hauptsatz, Headpiece, or Principal Subject.
   SS. Seitensatz, Sidepiece, or Second Subject.
SCHLS. Schlusssatz, Closingpiece, or Conclusion.
  ZWS. Zwischensatz, Betweenpiece, or Connecting Part, or Interlude.
   MS. Mittelsatz, Middlepiece, or Middle Subject. Often found in the sonatas of Mozart directly after the double bar in the principal movement.

SIGNS APPERTAINING TO EXPRESSION.

    < Gradual increase of intensity.
    > Gradual diminution of intensity.
  <> Swell; increase and diminish.
   pp. As soft as possible.
   ff. As loud as possible.
   > With sudden force.
  sfz. Sforzando. With sudden force.
 rnfz. Rinforzando. Several tones in succession very forcible.
   fp. One tone, or chord, forte, all the rest piano.
  ⌢ Legato. All the tones connected.
  ⸱ ⸱ ⸱ Every tone emphasized, individualized, and slightly separated.
  − − − Every tone strongly individualized.
    , Sometimes used as breathing mark in solfeggi, and in music for wood wind.
    ∧ Tenuto. Hold the tone its full value.

ABBREVIATIONS.

USED MAINLY IN MSS.

* NOTE.—This mark is ambiguous. Rubinstein uses it as a broken tremolo, as at *a*, but generally it is intended as here given. The context will generally determine.

Dotted Bars. Signs of Repetition.
- Sign of repetition of the preceding strain.
- Sign of repetition of the following strain.
- Sign of repetition of the preceding and following strains.

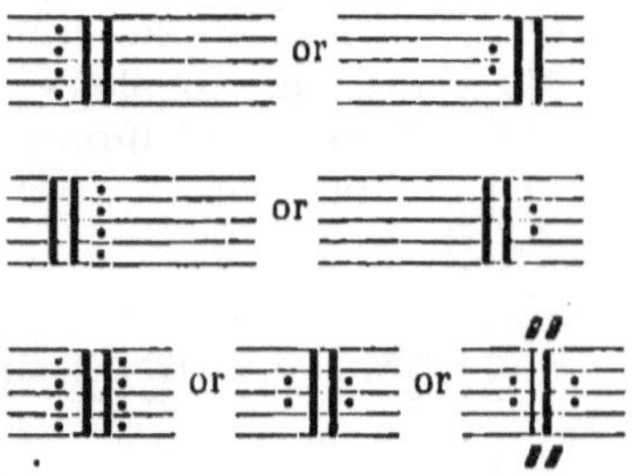

Da Capo Signs. Signs of Repetition

Sign indicating the close of a Repeat, or the end of a Piece.

Sign of Repeat

MUSICAL SIGNS.

A note with two stems belongs to different voices.
Example:

Meaning:
Chords played Arpeggiando.

SPECIAL SIGNS USED IN INSTRUMENTAL MUSIC.

STRINGED INSTRUMENTS PLAYED WITH A BOW.

      ⌐ Down bow.
      ∧ Up bow.
H. B. Half bow.
Sh. St. Short strokes.
W. B. Whole bow.
G. B. Whole length of bow.
M. B. Middle of bow.
Fr. At the nut.
Sp. At the point.
• • • • • • • Short bowing.
– – – – – Long bowing.

MANDOLIN.

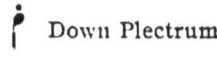

  Down Plectrum.

  Up Plectrum.

BRASS INSTRUMENTS.

0 Open tube.
1, 2, 3. Numbers of the valves.
♩ ♩ ♩ Demi staccato. (Made by tonguing) as if in pronouncing the letter D.

DRUM MUSIC.

V Placed *above* the staff to indicate that the left-hand stick is raised, and *below* the staff to show that the right-hand stick is raised.

⊥ Used to indicate a tap, or a tap beat.

↯ To denote that both sticks drop on the drum-head at the same time.

GUITAR MUSIC.

Signs employed in Guitar music to indicate the fingering.
{
Left hand.	Open string,	0
"	First string,	1
"	Second string,	2
"	Third string,	3
Right hand,	First string,	.
"	Second string,	. .
"	Third string,	. . .
"	Thumb,	+

FLUTE OR FLAGEOLET.

Open hole. ○
Closed hole. ●
Pinched, or partly closed hole. ◉

COMPLETE CLASSIFICATION OF THE MUSICAL FORMS.

THE ELEMENTARY FORMS.

Figure, a musical idea of recognizable peculiarities. In order to embody an idea a tone-succession must possess the following elements: 1, a definite motion and compass in rhythm, extending from some one point in measure to the corresponding point in the next pulsation, measure, or the next measure but one; 2, a melodic figure with a point of accent or emphasis; and 3, a chord-foundation suggested or expressed. In developing a musical idea into larger forms a composer takes one of two courses: Either he retains the rhythm of the motive and modifies the harmony and melody (thematic development), or he retains the harmony and the essential features of the melody and modifies the rhythm (variation).

Motive, a musical idea, taken as a germ or pattern for development. The natural compass of a motive is one measure, which may be from any point within the measure to the corresponding point in the next. A Motive may be a fraction of a measure; or it may run to two measures.

Phrase, a musical symmetry, consisting of two motives, or one motive repeated or sequenced. The natural compass of a Phrase is two measures. But it may extend only to one measure, or be carried to four, or under certain circumstances to a larger number of measures.

Section, a musical symmetry, composed of two phrases. Its natural compass is four measures, but it may be carried to eight. Sections are of two general types: Antecedents, which propose a subject, and Consequents, which answer and complete an Antecedent. These divisions correspond to subjects and predicates in logic.

Period, a completed musical idea, consisting of two sections which answer each other. A Period is like a stanza. Its four phrases may rhyme with each other in almost any manner the composer pleases. Periods arising from motives of a part of a measure might not exceed four measures in compass; and those arising from motives of two measures would naturally reach sixteen measures. Still further variations occur in period-forms through the repetition of some one phrase, or motive, the avoidance or postponement of a cadence, and the like. Periods are to be distinguished also with reference to their character as dependent and independent. A dependent period requires something else to finish it; or devotes itself to finishing something already proposed. Hence a dependent period is either a Consequent of some former antecedent, or the Antecedent of a consequent to occur later. The external indication of dependence in period-forms is the cadence, which, if upon the tonic of the original key, indicates that the period is closed in that direction, at least. If also the period begins in its principal key, it may be taken as independent. But if it begins in some key or chord other than the tonic, there is something implied before it, which may be found in the previous period, or may be merely mental with the composer. Of the latter kind the beginning of the Beethoven sonata, opus 111, may be taken as type.

Period-Group, a succession of periods, which may be developed from the same motives, or may serve as connecting links in a larger work. In the former case the group assumes an independent form, and the Song-form is the result. In the latter case we have modulating periods, passages, and the like.

INDEPENDENT MUSICAL FORMS.

Unitary Forms, containing but one single melodic subject. The simplest type of unitary form is the One-period Song-form, of which the ordinary church tune affords a convenient example. The Two-period Song-form consists of two periods, of which the second is the consequent and complement of the first. The Three-period Song-form consists of three periods, in which the second period is usually in a different key, while the third period is nearly or quite the same as the first. Here we have in miniature a rondo, in which an original subject is brought back again after a digression. The Song-form is the general foundation of all dances, and most popular music, and it furnishes the principal subjects of the slow movements in the classic authors.

The Fugue is a unitary form entirely developed out of a single melodic subject, but its compass is so much extended by the harmonic and contrapuntal transformation of the original subject that the piece, as a whole, often reaches proportions almost symphonic, as in the great organ fugues of Bach.

Variations are also unitary forms, in that they treat of the same melody all through. The original theme in this case is the form, usually a song-form of one or two or three periods. The variations in succession illustrate contrasted manners of treatment, and in their relative order they finally combine to constitute a large form, somewhat suggestive of a rondo or sonata.

An *Etude* is a thematic composition designed to illustrate some difficulty or artistic effect. Occasionally it is of binary order, but generally it is unitary, having but a single subject. The etudes of Chopin illustrate artistic studies in musical effect; and those of Cramer and Clementi those designed for technical purposes.

Canon is a musical form in which one or more voices follow after a leading voice, called the antecedent, singing precisely the same melody. A round is a common example of this form. The canons of Schumann are also good examples.

Canonic Imitation is imitation in the manner of canon, and this art underlies all modern thematic development.

Binary Forms are those in which there are two contrasting melodic subjects, each of which may be, and generally is, a complete song-form of one, two or three periods. The first subject is called the Principal, and when it is repeated it is always in the same key, and generally nearly or quite unchanged, although in some instances it is shortened. The second subject is called Second, and is in a related key to the principal key of the piece. Opinions and practices differ with reference to the relation which should prevail between a Principal and Second, as to tonality. In general, however, in the older practice the Second of a major Principal was in the dominant; and the Second of a minor Principal was in the relative major. Chopin made a very bold departure from this practice when, in his E minor concerto, after a Principal in E minor he introduced a second in E major. The effect is very pleasing.

A Trio is a second subject somewhat milder than the Principal with which it is associated. According to classical practice the trio of a major Principal was in the subdominant, or in the relative minor. These rules are no longer obligatory.

Many *slow movements* of the sonatas and symphonies of Beethoven are binary forms, with a certain amount of passage or modulating work between the Principal and Second. Such movements are concluded with a Coda, or conclusion, and approach the form of the rondo.

A Rondo is a musical form in which a Principal is relieved by a Second and perhaps a Third, the Principal returning from three to five times, with the introduction of more or less connecting matter. This form is more generally a ternary order, wherefore it will be more fully discussed in the next paragraph.

Toccata is a style rather than a form. A Toccata is generally a sort of etude, characterized by rapid motion and brilliancy of effect. Toccatas are generally unitary as to form, but occasionally binary.

Ternary Forms are those in which, besides a Principal and Second, there is also a Third. When three subjects have to be related in this manner, the Second was originally in the dominant or the principal key, or in some key upon the dominant side; while the Third was in the subdominant or in some key upon that side. These rules are no longer followed exactly. The composer is free to follow his fancy, and to place his new subject in any possible key which he conceives best suited to bring out its nature, when taken in connection with the matter and tonality of the accompanying subjects.

The most characteristic of the ternary forms is the *Rondo*, which is defined above. Rondo means *round*, and the frequent return of the Principal is the characteristic trait of this form. The Rondo is primarily lyric in its spirit, and by preference is of a semi-jovial character, wherefore it is never applied to serious purposes; or, if its essential round principle is availed of in more serious forms, the jovial rondo spirit is carefully eliminated. The Berlin theorist, Adolph Bernhardt Marx, was the first to apply the term rondo to slow movements. He called the Adagio of Sonata Pathetique a rondo, which in the return of the Principal it is; but not in spirit of the movement.

The Sonata-Piece is the most conspicuous example of the ternary form. A sonata-piece consists essentially of a Principal, some connecting matter, a Second, and a Conclusion. Here there is a repetition, after which comes a middle part, called an Elaboration, devoted to free fantasia upon the principal themes of the work; after the Elaboration, the first part (Principal, Second, and Conclusion) returns entire, except that the Second is always in the principal key of the work, and the Conclusion is somewhat extended, though this latter is not obligatory. In the older sonata pieces the Principal and the Second are so much more important than the Conclusion that the careless observer may not be inclined to attach much importance to them. The Conclusion, however, is an essential part of this form. The Sonata-Piece is the type of all serious instrumental composition. It forms the principal movement or movements in sonatas and symphonies (including all chamber quartettes and larger works), and many overtures and other works also form themselves upon its general principles.

Complex Forms are forms consisting of two, three, four, or even five, shorter forms, each of which is an independent piece; but all are associated into one Complex form through affinity of tonality, and consecutive qualities of spirit and meaning; or for the sake of contrast. The principal types of Complex forms are Sonata, Suite, Opera, Oratorio, and all forms in which a consecutive musical idea is carried on by means of completed pieces in succession. In all these very large forms, like Opera, for instance, the work is grouped into smaller unities by its division into acts, and each act is generally ended by an elaborate finale, which often reaches great development. As, for instance, the third finale in Mozart's "Marriage of Figaro," and the third finale in Wagner's "Meistersinger."

Sonata. The sonata is the most important of all the complex forms; it is the form of all pieces of that name, as well as of the Symphony, Concerto, Trio, Quartette, Quintet, and nearly all varieties of chamber music. A Sonata consists of from three to four movements. At least one of these movements is a sonata movement (Sonata-piece, *Sonata-satz*) of the form already described in the ternary forms. The first movement usually belongs to this form, and many times the last. Occasionally the same form, somewhat shortened, is employed for the second movement. The first movement of the sonata is generally (almost invariably) thematic. The second movement is generally in some kind of slow movement, lyric and ideal in character. If there are four movements, the third is either a minuet with trio, or a Scherzo with trio (Song-form with trio). The closing movement is either a Rondo or else a Finale, the latter being a sonata-piece. Many sonatas of Beethoven deviate somewhat from this order, such as that in A-flat, opus 26, which begins with an Air and Variations, has a funeral march for second movement, the only sonata-piece being the Finale. The so-called "Moonlight" sonata, opus 27, No. 2, has the slow movement first. The second is a Scherzo, and the Finale is a sonata-piece. The great sonata in C minor, opus 111, begins with a vigorous introduction, leading into a strong sonata-piece, and there is only one other movement, which is an Arietta with variations.

The Symphony is carried out in precisely the same manner as the sonata, except that the development is longer. The Concerto has generally only three movements, the short Scherzo being omitted. In some modern concertos all four movements are condensed into one, or rather the whole is made continuous.

Conditioned Forms are those in which the form is conditioned by extra musical considerations. The prominent types are the *Recitative*, where textual declamation is the primary condition, and emotional coloring the secondary, the purely musical remaining subordinate to both these; all types of *Song* and *Aria*, where the delivery of a text and the intensification of a dramatic moment are the main objects sought. Sometimes these qualities are so accomplished that the musical effect as such is heightened; examples of this are afforded by Schubert's "Erl-King," "Margaret at the Spinning Wheel," "To be sung on the waters," etc. All forms of the conditioned character conform to the general principles of pure form, to as complete an extent as they are able without sacrificing the immediate end sought in their own creation.

Note 1. The principles of form, whether large or small, are the same. Unity, symmetry and contrast are the elements which have to be combined.

Note 2. The above classification of form exhausts the subject, and affords place for every variety of form which can be created.

(For further development of the subject of Musical Form, see "Primer of Musical Forms," by the senior editor of the present work.)

RULES OF PRONUNCIATION.

ITALIAN.

VOWELS.

a is always like ä in *father*.

e has (1) the sound of ĕ in *pen*, and (2) the sound of ā in *fate*.

i is pronounced like ē in *me*, and in short syllables, I in *pin*.

j, at the beginning of a syllable, is like y in *you*. At the end of a word it is like ē in *be*.

o has the sound of ō in *tone*.

u has always the sound of oo in *cool*.

CONSONANTS.

b, d, f, l, n, p, q, v, are the same as in English.

c, before a, o, and u, has the sound of k; before e, i, and y it has the sound of tsh, or that of ch in the word *cheek*. When doubled (cc) and followed by e, i, or y, the first is pronounced like t, and the second takes its usual sound.

ch, before e or i, has the sound of k.

g, before a, o, or u, is hard, as in *go*; before e or i, it has the sound of j or soft g, as in *gem*. When doubled and followed by e or i, it has the sound of dj, or like dg in *lodge*.

gh, followed by e or i, is pronounced like g in *go*.

gl, followed by i, preceding another vowel, pronounced like ll in *million*.

gn, followed by a, e, i, o, or u, is like ni in the English word *minion*.

gua, gue, gui are pronounced gwä, gwā, gwē.

gia, gio, giu are pronounced djiä, djiō, djioo, in one syllable, giving the i a very faint sound, differing almost imperceptibly from the effect of the same combination with the i omitted.

s has (1) the hard sound as in *sis*, and (2) the soft sound as in *ease;* usually the latter when occurring between two vowels.

sc, before e or i, is like sh in *shall;* before a, o, or u, it has the sound of sk.

sch is always like sk, or sch in *school*.

scia, scio, sciu are pronounced shä, shō, shoo.

r, at the beginning of words, is like the English, but at the end of words or syllables, or when combined with another consonant, it should have a rolling sound.

w and **x** are not found in Italian, except in foreign words.

z has usually the sound of ts; it is sometimes pronounced like dz.

Italian words are pronounced exactly as written, there being no silent letter, except h. The vowels always preserve their proper sounds, forming no diphthongs and being uninfluenced by the consonants with which they may be combined.

In words of two or more syllables there is usually a slight emphasis placed on the penult or antepenult, but rarely on the last syllable.

GERMAN.

VOWELS.

a has the sound of ä as in *far*.
au is like ou in *house*.
ai occurs but rarely, and has the sound of ī as in *pine*.
ae or **ä** when long is like ā in *mate*; when short it is like ĕ in *met*.
aeu or **äu** is like oy in *boy*.
e has (1) the sound of ĕ as in *help*, and (2) the sound of ā in *hate*.
ei has always the sound of ī in *pine*.
eu is like oi in *loiter*.
i has the sound of I as in *pin*.
ie takes the sound of ē as in *tree*.
o has the sound of ō as in *tone*.
oe or **ö** has nearly the sound of ĕ as in *fell*.
u has the sound of oo as in *moon*.
ue or **ü** has the sound of the French *u*.
y is used only in foreign words, where it does not differ from I in *pin*.

CONSONANTS.

b and **d** are pronounced as in English.
c is only used in foreign words. Before e, i, and y it is pronounced like ts; before other vowels and consonants it is like k.
ch has nothing corresponding to it in English. It is a guttural sound, produced by pronouncing ahk, but taking care not to close the vocal organs in sounding k. At the beginning of words ch is like k.
chs is pronounced like ks or x.

f, l, m, p, t and **x** are the same as in English.
g has the hard sound as in *go*. In some parts of Germany the unaccented final *g* is softened into something like *ikh*.
h at the beginning of words is aspirated; between two vowels the aspiration is very weak, and before a consonant or at the end of words it is mute; but in this case it makes the preceding vowel long.
j is equivalent to the English y in *you*, and is always followed by a vowel.
k is like the English k, but is never mute before n.
ng sounds like ng in *length*; but in compound words where the first ends in n and the last begins with g, they are separated, and both pronounced distinctly.
q is always joined with u, and together they are pronounced like *kw*.
ph has the sound of f.
pf unites the two letters in one sound uttered with compressed lips.
r has a stronger sound than in English, and is the same at the beginning, middle, or end of a word.
s is like the English s. It is sounded at the end of words, and between two vowels it frequently takes the sound of z.
sch is like the English sh in *ship*.
th takes always the sound of t; h being silent. It has never the sound of th in *thee*.
tz intensifies the sound of z.
v is pronounced like f.
w following a vowel answers to the English v
z is pronounced like ts in *nets*

FRENCH.

VOWELS.

a has two sounds; ă as in *mass*, and ä as in *bar*.
ai is like ā in *fate*.
au is similar to o in English.
e is (1) like ĕ in *met*; (2) like ā in *fate*; (3) similar to ŭ in *bud*, the latter chiefly in monosyllables, as *le*, *de*, etc. It is frequently silent at the end of words.
ei is nearly like ā in *fate*.
eu resembles ŭ in *tub*.
i has the sound (1) of ĭ in *pin*, (2) of ē in *me*.
ia has nearly the sound of ia in *medial*.
ie is like ee in *bee*.
o is pronounced like ŏ in *rob*, and like ō in *rope*.
u has no equivalent in English, but resembles the sound of e in *dew*. By prolonging the sound of *e*, taking care not to introduce the sound of *w*, we get an approximate sound of the French u, or ü as it will be marked in this work.
y, when initial, or coming between two consonants, or standing as a syllable by itself, is the same as the French *i* (I in ill); but between two vowels it is equivalent to double French I (II), the first forming a diphthong with the preceding one and the second with the one following.

CONSONANTS.

Final consonants are almost always silent, except c, f, l, n, and r, which are generally sounded.

b, at the beginning and in the middle of words, is the same as in English.

c has (1) the sound of k before a, o, or u; (2) when written with the cedilla, or before e or i, it has the sound of s. c final is sounded unless preceded by *n*.

ch is pronounced like sh in *she*. In words derived from the Greek, ch is pronounced like *k*.

d is the same as in English. It is silent at the end of words.

f is like the English; when final it is usually sounded.

g, before a, o, or u, is hard, as in *go*; but before e, i, or y it has the sound of z in the English word *azure*. In the combination gue, or gui, the u is silent, but the g takes its hard sound.

gn is pronounced like ni in *union*.

h is mute or slightly aspirated.

j is pronounced like z in *azure*.

k has the same sound as in English.

l has (1) the same sound as in English, and (2) the liquid sound, as in million.

m and n, when not nasal, have the same sound as in English; if preceded by a vowel in the same syllable, they are always nasal unless immediately followed by a vowel in the next syllable.

am, an, em, en are pronounced somewhat like an in *want*.

im, in, ym, aim, ain, eim, ein are pronounced like an in *anger*.

om and on are like on in *song*.

um and un are pronounced like un in *wrung*.

p is generally the same as in English. It is sometimes silent, and always when at the end of a word.

q is usually followed by u, in which case they are together sounded like the letter k.

r is given more roughly than in English. It is often silent when preceded by the vowel e.

s has generally the same sound as in English; between two vowels it has generally the same sound as in the English word *rose*.

se is the same as in English. s final is generally silent.

RULES OF PRONUNCIATION.

t has its hard English sound, but in tial, tiel, and tion it has the sound of s.

th is always the same as t alone. **t** final is usually silent.

v is like the English, only a little softer.

w is found only in foreign words, and is pronounced like v.

x, initial, is pronounced like gz; it occurs but in few words.

ex, at the beginning of words, is sounded like egz. In other places, and between two vowels, it is pronounced like ks.

z is like z in zone.

Final consonants, which would otherwise be silent, are frequently sounded by carrying them over to the next word, when commencing with a vowel.

NOTE.—While the French language does not properly have syllabic emphasis, the rate of speaking is very fast, and the practical result is an emphasis upon the last syllable of words. This rule is almost universal. In some cases we have marked it, in others not.

PRONOUNCING AND DEFINING
DICTIONARY OF MUSIC.

A. 1. Name of a musical pitch produced by from 435 to 450 vibrations per second, and the octaves of the same. French pitch is the former rate and American concert pitch approximately the latter. Also the name of all octaves of these pitches.
2. The name of the staff-degree representing the pitch A or any of its octaves; the name of the key upon the keyboard producing A; the name of open strings producing A. The intonation of the orchestra is adjusted from A of the oboe, the oboe being incapable of modifying its pitch to any practicable extent.
3. Abbr. for Alto (viola).

A (äh), *It.* By, for, to, at, in, etc.

A in alt. The A placed upon the first upper added line.

A in altissimo. An octave above A in alt.

A ballata (ä bäl-lä'tä), *It.* In the style of a ballata.

Abandon (ä-bänh-dônh), *Fr.* Without restraint; with self-abandon; with ease.

A battuta (ä bät-too'tä), *It.* As beaten; strictly in time.

Abb. Abbr. for Abbassamento.

Abbadare (äb-bä-dä'rĕ), *It.* Take care; pay attention.

Abbandonasi (äb-bän-dō-nä'sĭ), *It.* Without restraint; with passionate expression.

Abbandonatamente (äb-bän-dō-nä-tä-měn-tĕ), *It.* Vehemently; violently.

Abbandone (äb-bän-dō'nĕ), *It.* Making the time subservient to the expression; despondingly; with self-abandonment.

Abbandono (äb-bän-dō'nō), *It.* With passionate expression.

Abbassamento di mano (äb-bäs-sä-měn'tō dē mä-nōi, *It.* The down beat, or descent of the hand in beating time.

Abbassamento di voce (äb-bäs-sä-měn'tō dē vō'tshĕ), *It.* Diminishing or lowering of the voice.

Abbassimento (äb-bäs-sĭ-měn'tō), *It.* Under.

Abbellare (äb-běl-lä'rĕ), *It.* To embellish with ornaments.

Abbellimenti (äb-běl-lĭ-měn'tĭ), *It.* Ornaments introduced to embellish a plain melody; grace notes.

Abbellimento (äb-běl-lĭ-měn'tō), *It.* A grace note, or ornament.

Abbellire (äb-běl-lē'rĕ), *It.* To embellish with ornaments.

Abbellitura (äb-běl-lĭ-too'rä), *It.* } Orna-
Abbelliture (äb-běl-lĭ-too'rĕ), *It.* } ments; embellishments.

Abbreviation marks. 1. Oblique strokes which distinguish the *eighth*, *sixteenth*, or *thirty-second* notes; when applied to the stem of the *quarter* or *half note*, signify as many repetitions of the shorter note thus indicated as are equal to the longer note represented. Thus,  is equivalent to ♪♪♪♪ ♪♪♪♪ ,

2. A diagonal stroke with a dot each side signifies a repetition of a group of notes, or sometimes of a complete measure.

3. When the long notes are omitted, the oblique strokes, distinguishing *eighth*, *sixteenth*, etc., notes, are sometimes employed to denote a repetition of such short notes. Thus, ▬ ☰ ☰ indicate a repetition of eighths, sixteenths, thirty-seconds, respectively.

4. A short horizontal line, a row of dots,

ä *arm*, ă *add*, ā *ale*, ĕ *end*, ē *eve*, ĭ *ill*, ī *isle*, ō *old*, ŏ *odd*, oo *moon*, ŭ *but*, ü *Fr. sound*, kh *Ger. ch*, nh *nasal.*

or a waving line is used to express the repetition, or a continuation of the influence, of the preceding character. Thus,

5. A combination of rests so written as to denote a long period of silence. These rests indicate a period of eleven measures' silence.

6. Figures, when placed upon the staff, or over a measure in which rests are written, serve to indicate the number of whole rests or measures of silence.

Abendmusik (ä-bĕnd-moo-sĕk'), *Ger.* Evening music; music of a soft and quiet character.

A bene placito (ä bā'nĕ plä-tshē'tō), *It.* At pleasure.

Abgestossen (äb-ghĕ-stōs's'n), or **Abstossen** (äb-stōs's'n), *Ger.* } Staccato.

Abnehmend (äb-nā'mĕud), *Ger.* Fading away; diminuendo.

Absatz (äb-sätz), *Ger.* Cadence.

Absolute music. Music developed freely, according to its ideal, merely as music. In contradistinction to vocal music, which is restricted by the words; program music, devoted to a series of incidents; and dance music, restricted to the steps of the dance. In short, high art music, loyal to the highest ideal.

Absteigende Tonarten (äb-stī-gĕn-dĕ tōn-är't'n), *Ger.* Descending scales or keys.

Abtönen (äb-tĕh'nĕn), *Ger.* To deviate from the right tone.

Abub (ä-boob), *Heb.* A flute, or hautboy.

Abwechselnd (äb-vĕk's'Ind), *Ger.* Alternating; changing. In organ-playing, alternately, with different manuals; in choir-singing, antiphonally; in dance music, change of movements.

Abyssinian flute. An instrument resembling the German flute, but with mouthpiece like the clarinet, and played upon from the end like an oboe.

Academie de Musique (ä-kä-dĕ-mĕ düh moo-sēēk'), *Fr.* An academy of music, consisting of professors and scholars; a society for promoting musical culture.

Academie Royale de Musique, *Fr.* The name given to the opera-house in Paris.

Academie spirituelle (ä-kä-dĕ-mĕ spī-rī-too-ĕl'), *Fr.* A performance or concert of sacred music.

A cappella (ä käp-pĕl'lä), or **Alla cappella**. *It.* } In the church or chapel style. Without instrumental accompaniment.

A capriccio (ä kä-prī'tshĭō), *It.* In a capricious style; according to the taste of the performer. Especially in the matter of time and phrasing. More commonly the former.

Acatalectic (ä-kä-tä-lĕk'tĭc). *Gr.* A verse having the complete number of syllables without superfluity or deficiency.

Acathistus (ä-kä-this-toos), *Gr.* A hymn of praise sung in the ancient Greek Church in honor of the Virgin.

Academia (ä kä-dĕ-mē'ä), *It.* An academy. The word also means a concert.

Accarezzevole (äk-kä-rĕt-tsä'vō-lĕ), *It.* Blandishing; in a persuasive and caressing manner.

Accarezzevolmente (äk-kä-rĕt-tsĕ-vōl-mĕn'tĕ), *It.* Caressingly; coaxingly.

Accel. (ät-tshĕl), **Acceldo.** (ät-tshĕl-dō), *It.* } Abbreviations of Accelerando

Accelerando (ät-tshĕl-ĕ-rän'dō), *It.* Accelerating the time; gradually increasing the velocity of the movement. An accele an io generally occurs when approaching a climax. The disturbance thus produced in the long rhythms is generally compensated by corresponding retards at the climax.

Acceleratamente (ät-tshĕl-ĕ-rä-tä-mĕn'tĕ), *It.* Speedily.

Accelerato (ät-tshĕl-ĕ-rä'tō), *It.* Accelerated; increasing in rapidity.

Accent. 1. Stress, or emphasis, (a) upon a certain division of measure; (b) a tone in a figure; (c) a chord in an harmonic phrase, and the mark or marks by means of which such stress is indicated. Measure accent falls upon the beginning of the first beat; and in measures having more than three beats, upon the first beat of each aliquot part likewise. (See *Measure*.) Besides the accent upon the beat (the bar indicating the place of the strong accent to be upon the next time-place following) there are subordinate grades of what might be called "molecular" accentuation, upon the beginning of divided beats, and upon the beginning of each aliquot part of a beat when the subdivision extends to quarter-pulse division.

2. The accentuation of a melodic phrase is primarily determined by the measure, but the occurrence of dissonance adds fresh element, every dissonance occurring upon the beginning of a beat, or upon the beginning of a half beat (in quarter-pulse subdivision), receiving an accent of its own, partly due to its rhythmic place, but intensified for the sake of the dissonance. So also dissonant chords, such as appoggiaturas, suspensions, etc., are accented. What is called Syncopation is an accent breaking into the natural order of the measure. (See *Syncopation*.)

3. Also the name applied to the marks indicating accent. The chief of these are the horizontal short angle >, and the abbreviation *sf.* or *sfz*. In old music (from Mozart and before) the expression *fp.* often occurs

indicating that one tone is loud and all the following soft. (See *Forzando*, also *Sforzando*.) The short vertical accent standing upon its base (∧) is not properly an accent, but a mark of tenuto (*q. v.*), but in some French and Belgian music it is occasionally employed where the horizontal mark is intended.

4. Accent is the life of music, and is of multitudinous variety of shading and intensity.

Accento (ät-tshĕn'tō), *It.* Accent or emphasis laid upon certain notes.

Accenti (ät-tshĕn'tē), *It.* } Accents.
Accent (äk-sänh), *Fr.*

Accentuare (ät-tshĕn-too-ä'rĕ), *It.* To accentuate; to mark with an accent.

Accentuation. The act of accenting; the giving to the several notes of a piece their proper emphasis or expression; the art of placing accents.

Accentuato (ät-tshĕn-too-ä'tō), *It.* Distinctly and strongly accented.

Accentuiren (äk-tsĕn-too-ē'r'n), *Ger.* To accent.

Accentus (äk-sĕn'toos), *Lat.* Accent. "Under the name *Accentus* were classed those portions of the ritual song (of the Roman Catholic Church) chanted or intoned by the officiating priest, the deacon, subdeacon, or other sacred ministers at the altar; in contradistinction to *Concentus*, which referred to all that should be sung by the assistants or by a special trained choir." (Rev. F. H. Haberl.) See the next article.

Accentus ecclesiastici, *Lat.* Ecclesiastical accents are melodic forms used in the Roman Catholic Church in chanting, or rather reciting, the collects, epistles, gospels, etc. These melodic inflections which vary the monotone recitation, correspond with the comma, colon, semicolon, period, mark of interrogation, etc. See the preceding article. These variations were of seven kinds, called the *immutabilis*, *medius*, *gravis*, *acutus*, *moderatus*, *interrogatus*, and *finalis*, each of which was practically an upward or downward inflection extending to a particular interval, namely: *immutabilis*, monotone; *medius*, a minor third, sol me; *gravis*, a fifth, sol do; *acutus*, sol mi me sol; *moderatus*, sol la sol; *interrogatus*, sol fa sol; *finalis*, sol la sol fa mi re—thus closing on the ecclesiastical Dorian key.

Accessory notes. Those notes situated one degree above and one degree below the principal note of a turn.

Accessory parts. Accompaniments.

Accessory tones. Harmonics. Tones faintly heard when the principal tone dies away.

Accessory voices. Accompanying voices.

Acciaccare (ät-tshī-äk-kä'rĕ), *It.* A broken and unexpected way of striking a chord.

Acciaccato (ät-tshī-äk-kä'tō), *It.* Violently.

Acciaccatura (ät-tshī-äk-kä-too'rä), *It.* A species of arpeggio; an accessory note placed before the principal note, the accent being on the principal no e. Practically about the same as an appoggiatura.

Accidenti (ät-tshī-dĕn'tē), *It.* } Accidentals.
Accidents (äk-sī-dänh), *Fr.*

Accidentals. 1. The name applied to sharps, flats, naturals, double sharps, and double flats occurring in written music elsewhere than in the signature. (See *Signature*.) The name accidental appertains to the characters only, and not to the tones they help to indicate; many of the tones written by the help of these unforeseen characters being merely the natural diatonic tones of the key into which the passage may have momentarily digressed. (See *Modulation*.) Moreover, minor keys universally require an accidental for the leading tone—always a sharp or a natural.

Accidentals effect the staff-degrees to which they are applied throughout the measure in which they occur; and in strict practice no further. But there have been theorists holding that in certain cases (as when the last tone of the measure is written with an accidental, and this tone is tied over into the next measure) the accidental is continued until some other tone intervenes in the same voice. In consequence of this questionable exception the great majority of composers introduce a natural before again using a staff-degree recently affected by an accidental, even when it occurs in a later measure, but in immediate connection. This practice is precautionary, only. It would be simpler to make the rule inflexible that the influence of the accidental ceases with the measure in which it occurs.

Unlike chromatic signs in the signatures, accidentals do not affect equivalent degrees, but only those to which they are actually applied.

2. This term has also been applied without exception to all chromatic signs originally applied, and to those signs revoking preceding signs—namely, both to those in the signature and those occurring in the course of a piece. The origin of all these signs are the "round B" (*B rotundum*) and "square B" (*B quadratum*), by which in the middle ages B-flat was distinguished from B-natural. By and by the two forms of the letter B became common signs of elevation and depression, being applied not only to B, but also to other notes. The square B assumed various shapes, two of them like our sharp and natural; but no distinction was made between them till towards the end of the seventeenth century—a flat not only flattened a natural note, but also revoked a preceding sharp; a sharp not only sharpened a natural note, but also revoked a preceding flat. Double sharps and flats did not come into use till about 1700. In earlier times, more especially before 1600,

ä *arm*, ă *add*, ā *ale*, ĕ *end*, ē *eve*, ĭ *ill*, ī *isle*, ō *old*, ŏ *odd*, oo *moon*, ŭ *but*, ü *Fr. sound*, kh *Ger. ch*, nh *nasal*.

(35)

composers left it very much to the performers to find out what accidentals were required. For a l ng time, if there was any signature at all, it consisted of a flat only. Before the seventeenth century it was not customary to put more than one flat or one sharp in the signature. Even as late as the first half of the eighteenth century we meet with various anomalies. Bach, Handel, and their contemporaries, for instance, furnish examples of placing one flat and one sharp less in the signature than the key required, accidentals being used in the course of the piece instead of the sharp or flat in the signature. In short, our present system of using sharps, flats, and naturals was not fixed till the second half of the eighteenth century.

Accolade (äk-kō-läd'), *Fr.* The brace which connects two, three, or more staves together.

Accom. } Abbreviations of Accompaniment.
Accomp.

Accom. ad lib. An abbreviation of Accompaniment ad libitum.

Accommodare (äk-kŏm-mō-dä'rĕ), *It.* To tune an instrument.

Accompagnamento (äk-kŏm-pän-yä-mĕn'tō), *It.* Accompaniment; the figured bass or harmony.

Accompagnare (äk-kŏm-pä-nä'rĕ), *It.* To accompany ; to play from the figured bass.

Accompagnato (äk-kŏm-pä-nä'tō), *It.* Accompanied.

Accompagné (äk-kŏmh-pänh-yā), *Fr.* Accompanied.

Accompagnement (äk kŏmh-pänh-yĕ-mänh), *Fr.* An accompaniment.

Accompagner (äk kŏmh-pänh-yā), *Fr.* To accompany.

Accompaniment. A part added to a solo or other principal part, to enhance and enrich its effect. Vocal or instrumental parts in a composition which do not include the principal melody but fill up the harmony, sustain the rhythm, and, by embellishments, heighten the general effect.

Accompaniment ad libitum. Use the accompaniment or not, at pleasure.

Accompaniment obligato. The accompaniment must be used.

Accompanist. The person playing the accompaniment.

Accomp. oblto. An abbreviation of accompaniment obligato.

Accoppiato (äk-kŏp-pī-ä'tō), *It.* Bound, tied; joined together.

Accorciare (äk kŏr-tshī-ä'rĕ), *It.* To contract, to abridge.

Accord (äk-kŏr), *Fr.* A chord; a concord; consonance.

Accordamento (äk-kŏr-dä-mĕn'tō), *It.* Accord of parts; unison.

Accordando (äk-kŏr-dän'dō), *It.* Tuning.

Accordant (äk-kŏr-dänh), *Fr.* In concord, in unison.

Accordare (äk-kŏr-dä'rĕ), *It.* To tune, to cause to accord. Many derivatives occur.

Accordato (äk-kŏr-dä'tō), *It.* Accorded, in tune.

Accordatore (äk-kŏr-dä-tō'rĕ), *It.* One who tunes instruments.

Accordatura (äk-kŏr-dä-too'rä), *It.* System of tuning.

Accordeon. A simple musical instrument, of oblong form, invented by Damian, of Vienna, in 1829. The tone is produced by the inspiration and respiration of a pair of bellows acting upon metallic reeds or tongues. (Free reed.)

The first instruments had only four buttons, or keys, each of which acted on two reeds, making the compass one octave of diatonic scale, but with a separate arrangement, by which these notes might be accompanied with a tonic and dominant harmony. At first it was used only as a toy, but the introduction of a chromatic scale made the accordeon more capable of producing a varied melody and harmony, although the awkwardness of the form was always a hindrance to its use. The German accordeon, or concertina (*q.v.*), of hexagonal form, made the principle of the accordeon more acceptable. The English concertina (*q.v.*) and the harmonium (*q.v.*) are superior instruments constructed upon similar principles.

Accorder (äk-kŏr-dä), *Fr.* To tune an instrument; to sing or play in tune.

Accordeur (äk-kŏr-dŭr'), *Fr.* One who tunes an instrument.

Accordi (äk-kŏr'dē), *It.* Play again as before.

According. An harmonious blending of different parts.

Accordiren (äk-kŏr-dē'r'n), *Ger.* To accord.

Accordo consono (äk-kŏr'dō kŏn'sŏ-nō), *It.* A concord.

Accordo dissono (äk-kŏr'dō dīs'sŏ-nō), *It.* A discord.

Accordoir (äk-kŏr-dwä'). *Fr.* A tuning-key, tuning-hammer

Accresciuto (äk-krē-shīoo'tō), *It.* Increased, superfluous, augmented in respect to intervals.

Acceleratamente (ät-tshĕl-ĕ-rä-tä-mĕn'tĕ, *It.* speedily, swiftly.

A cemb. An abbreviation of A cembalo.

A cembalo (ä tshĕm'bä-lō), *It.* For the harpsichord or cembalo.

Acetabulum (ä-tsĕ-tä'boo-loom), *Lat.* An ancient instrument of music.

Achromatic music. Simple music in which modulations seldom occur, and few accidental flats and sharps are used.

ä *arm*, ä *add*, ā *ale*, ĕ *end*, ē *eve*, ĭ *ill*, ī *isle*, ŏ *old*, ō *odd*, oo *moon*, ŭ *but*, ü *Fr.sound*, kh *Ger. ch*, nh *nasal.*

Acht (äkht), *Ger.* Eight.
Achtel (äkh't'l), *Ger.* Eighth, quaver or eighth note.
Achtelnote (äkh't'l-nō'tĕ), *Ger.* A quaver, an eighth note.
Achtelpause (äkh't'l-pou'sĕ), *Ger.* A quaver or eighth-note rest.
Achtfusston (äkht-foos-tōn), *Ger.* Eight-foot tone. A tone which sounds as written, in contradistinction from a sixteen-foot tone, which sounds an octave lower; or a four-foot tone, sounding an octave higher than written.
Achtstimmig (äkht'stĭm-mĭg), *Ger.* For eight voices.
A cinque (ä tshĭn-kwĕ), *It.*, or (ä sänhk), *Fr.* For five voices or instruments.
Acolytes. Persons, usually boys, employed in the musical services of the Catholic Church, or as assistants to the priest at the altar.
Acolythi (ä-kō-lē'thĭ), *Gr.* Acolytes.
Acolythia (ä-kō-lē'thĭ-ä), *Gr.* The order of service observed in the Greek Church.
Acousmate (ä-koos-mät), *Fr.* The sound of instruments or voices heard in the air.
Acoustics. The science which treats of the nature and properties of sounds.
Acoustique (ä-koos-tĕk), *Fr.* Acoustics.
Acte (ăkt), *Fr.* An act; a part of an opera.
Acte de cadence (äkt dŭh kä-dänhs), *Fr.* A cadence; a final part.
Acteur (ăk-tūr'), *Fr.* An actor; an operatic performer.
Action. The mechanism of a keyboard instrument, by means of which the performer produces tones. Hence includes the keys, connecting levers, and everything else between the fingers of the performer and the actual opening of the pipe or reed, or the vibration of the strings. In an organ-action the principal parts are the keys, trackers, rollers, pull-downs, and valves. In the pianoforte, the keys, jacks, under hammers and hammers, dampers.
Acts. Parts of an opera or theatrical entertainment.
Acuite (äk-weet'), *Fr.* Acuteness.
Acustica (ä-kooz'tĭ-kä), *It.* Acoustics; the doctrine of sounds.
Acustik (ä-koos'tĭk), *Ger.* Acoustics.
Acustisch (ä-koos'tĭsh), *Ger.* Acoustic.
Acuta (ä-koo'tä), *It.* Acute, shrill; also, a shrill-toned organ-stop of two-foot pitch.
Acute. High, shrill, sharp as to pitch.
Acuteness. Refers to the pitch of sounds. The greater the number of vibrations, the higher or more acute does the sound become.
Ad (äd), *Lat.* At, to, for, by.
Adag. An abbreviation of Adagio.

Adagietto (ä-dä'jĭ-ĕt-tō), *It.* Slow, but not quite so slow as adagio.
Adagio (ä-dä'jĭ-ō), *It.* A slow rate of movement, slower than andante, but not so slow as lento, grave, or largo. Often employed as the name of a movement in a symphony or sonata.
Adagio assai (ä-dä'jĭ-ō äs-sä'ē), *It.* Very slow and with much expression.
Adagio cantabile e sostenuto (ä-dä'jĭ-ō kän-tä'bĭ-lĕ ā sōs-tĕ-noo'tō), *It.* Slow, in a singing style and sustained.
Adagio con gravita (ä-dä'jĭ-ō kōn grä'vĭ-tä) *It.* Slow, with gravity and majesty.
Adagio molto (ä-dä'jĭ-ō mōl'tō), *It.* Very slow and expressive.
Adagio non troppo (ä-dä'jĭ-ō nōn trōp'pō), *It.* Not too slow.
Adagio patetico (ä-dä'jĭ-ō pä-tĕ'tĭ-kō), *It.* Slowly and pathetically.
Adagio pesante (ä-dä'jĭ-ō pĕ-zäu'tĕ), *It.* Slowly and heavily.
Adagio poi allegro (ä-dä'jĭ-ō pō-ē äl-lä'grō), *It.* Slow, then quick.
Adagio quasi una fantasia (ä-dä'jĭ-ō kwä-sē oo nä fäu-tä-sē'ä), *It.* An adagio similar to a fantasia.
Adagio religioso (ä-dä'jĭ-ō rĕ-lĭ-jĭ-ō'sō), *It.* Slowly, and in a devotional manner.
Adagissimo (ä-dä-jĭs'sĭ-mō), *It.* Extremely slow.
Adaptation. A union of sentiment between the words and the music.
Adattare (ä-dät-tä'rĕ), *It.* Adapted.
Adattazione (ä-dät-tä-tsĭ-ō'nĕ), *It.* Adaptation.
Ad captandum (äd cäp-tän'doom), *Lat.* In a light and brilliant style.
Added lines. Short lines, either above or below the staff; ledger lines.
Added sixth. A sixth added to a fundamental chord.
Additato (äd-dĭ-tä'tō), *It.* Fingered.
Additional keys. Those keys of a pianoforte which extend above F in Alt.
Additional accompaniments. Accompaniments or parts added to a choral work by a later hand than that of the composer, in order to bring the instrumentation more nearly to the later standard of fullness and sonority; or to introduce instruments of later invention. Parts of this ki d have been added to "The Messiah" by Mozart, Robert Frauz, and others.
Addolorato (äd-dō-lō-rä'tō), *It.* With sad and melancholy expression.
Addottrinante (äd-dōt-trē-nän'tĕ), *It.* Teacher, professor.
À demi-jeu (ä dĕ-mĭ-zhŭ), *Fr.* } With half
À demi-voix (ä dĕ-mĭ-vwä), the voice or tone. See *Mezza Voce.*

ä *arm,* ă *add,* ā *ale,* ĕ *end,* ē *eve,* ĭ *ill,* ī *isle,* ŏ *old,* ō *odd,* oo *moon,* ŭ *but,* ü *Fr. sound,* kh *Ger. ch.* nh *nasal.*

Adept. A thorough composer, performer, or singer.

À deux (ä düh), *Fr.* For two voices or instruments.

À deux temps (ä düh tänh), *Fr.* In two time; two equal notes in a measure.

Adiaponon (ä-dĭ-ä-pō-nŏn), *Gr.* A species of pianoforte with six octaves; invented in 1820 by Lahuster, a watchmaker of Vienna. The tone was produced from metal bars. In a later adaptation of the same idea, called the *Adiaphone*, the tones were produced from tuning-forks. Both these forms were of permanent tune.

Adiratamente (ä-dĭ-rä-tä-měn'tě), **Adirato** (ä-dĭ-rä'tō), *It.* } Angrily; sternly.

A dirittura (ä dĭ-rĭt-too'rä), *It.* Directly; straight.

Adjuvant (äd'yoo-vänt), *Ger.* The deputy master of the choristers; assistant to an organist.

Ad lib. An abbreviation of Ad libitum.

Ad libitum (äd lĭb-ĭ-toom), *Lat.* At will, at pleasure; changing the time of a particular passage at the discretion of the performer.

Adonia (ä-dō'nĭ-ä), *Ger.* A solemn feast of the ancients at which hymns and odes were sung.

Adonic verse. A verse consisting of one long, two short, and two long syllables.

Adornamente (ä-dōr-nä-měn'tě), *It.* Gaily, neatly, elegantly.

Adornamenti (ä-dōr-nä-měn'tĭ), *It.* Embellishments.

Adornamento (ä-dōr-nä-měn'tō), *It.* An ornament, an embellishment.

Adoucir (ä-doo-sēr), *Fr.* To soften, to flatten.

A due, or, **A 2** (ä doo'ě), *It.* For two voices or instruments; a duet.

A due clarini ä doo'ě klä-rē'nĭ), *It.* For two trumpets.

A due corde (ä doo'ě kōr'dě), *It.* Upon two strings.

A due cori (ä doo'ě kō'rě), *It.* For two choirs.

À deux mains (ä düh mänh), *Fr.* } For two
A due mani (ä doo'ě mä-uě), *It.* } hands.

A due soprani (ä doo'ě sō-prä'nē), *It.* For two trebles.

A due stromenti (ä doo'ě strō-měn'tĭ), *It.* For two instruments.

A due voce (ä doo'ě vō'tshě), *It.* For two voices.

A-dur (ä-door), *Ger.* The key of A major.

Ædophone. A musical instrument invented in the eighteenth century.

Æolian. One of the ancient Greek modes answering to the diatonic succession, *i*n si do re mi fa sol la; referring to the winds; played upon by the wind.

Æolian, the. An automatic instrument of the reed organ class, with many sets of reeds, and mechanism enabling it to perform overtures and much pretentious music.

Æolian harp. An instrument invented by Kircher about the middle of the seventeenth century. The tones are produced by the strings being so arranged that the air causes vibration among them when it passes through.

The box of the Æolian harp should be long enough to exactly fit the window where it is proposed to place it, and about five or six inches deep. There should be at least six strings of silk or gut, tuned in unison, passing over bridges about three fourths of an inch high, near each end. Under the influence of the wind the strings vibrate in sweetly harmonious chords, changing with every variation in the current of the wind. Of course all the tones produced are necessarily partial tones of the vibrating string; but the varying intensity of the wind makes so many changes in the combinations of tones produced as to give at times much the effect of mysterious intelligence.

Æolian lyre. The Æolian harp.

Æolian mute. A combination of the Æolian pitch-pipe and the mute for the violin.

Æolian pianoforte. A pianoforte with reed attachment, invented and manufactured by the firm of T. Gilbert & Co., Boston, about 1850. The piano, of the small pattern of square then universally manufactured, was provided with a set of free reeds and a bellows operated by a pedal at the right of the regular pedals of the piano. The reed instrument was of the old-fashioned "melodeon" pattern, the reeds being practically unvoiced, and the bellows of the pressure variety. The design of the addition was that of giving the piano a sustaining power, which up to that time had not been secured. The effect of the two tones in combination was agreeable in passages where a stennto was desired. But the instrument had only a temporary currency in consequence of the practical impossibility of keeping the strings in tune with the reeds.

Æolodicon (ä-ō-lō'dĭ-kŏn), *Gr.* A keyed instrument, the tone of which resembles that of the organ, and is produced by steel springs, which are put in vibration by means of bellows.

Æolodion (ä-ō-lō'dĭ-ŏn), *Gr.* An æolodicon.

Aeolsharfe (ä'ōls-här'fě), *Ger.* An Æolian harp.

Æolus modus. The Æolian, or fifth. Authentic mode of the Greeks, nearly allied to the Phrygian mode. The scale is the same as the old scale of A minor without any accidentals. (See *Greek Modes*.)

Æotana (ä-ō-tä'nä), *Gr.* A very small musical instrument made of several short metallic reeds fastened in a frame and played upon by the breath of the performer. Perhaps the ancestor of the modern "jew's-harp."

Aequal (ā-kwāl) Ger., from Lat. Generally applied to organ-stops, in which use it signifies "8 ft."

Aeolsklavier (ā-ōls-klä-veer'), Ger. Æolian piano. An obsolete keyboard wind instrument, invented in 1825 by Schortmann, of Buttlestedt. It had reeds of wood instead of metal, by the vibration of which a soft, pleasing tone was produced.

Æquisonans (ā-quī-sō'näns), Lat. A unison; of the same or like sound.

Æquisonus. Sounding in unison; concordant.

Ære recurvo (ā-rē rē-coor'vō), Lat. A military wind instrument resembling a trumpet; the bucena.

Ærophone (ĕ'rō-fōn). A French reed instrument of the melodeon class.

Æsthetics (ĕs-thĕt'Iks), Gr. The principles or laws of the beautiful. The chief writers upon this department of philosophy have been Germans, the foremost being Winkelmann, Herder, and Hegel. The latter made the most ambitious attempt to discover the principles of the musically beautiful. Among recent writers, Schopenhauer is to be mentioned as having gone into this subject more deeply and in a more successful manner than any of the others.

Aeussserste Stimmen (ois'sĕrs-tĕ stĭm'mĕn), Ger. pl. The extreme parts.

Ævia (ā'vī-ä), It. An abbreviation of the word Alleluia.

Affabile (äf-fä'bĭ-lĕ), It. In a courteous and pleasing manner.

Affabilita (äf-fä-bē'lī-tä), It. } With ease
Affabilmente (äf-fä-bīl mĕn'tĕ), } and elegance; with freedom; in a pleasing and agreeable manner.

Affanato (äf-fä-nä'tō), It. Sad, mournful, distressed.

Affanoso (äf-fä-nō'sō), It. With mournful expression.

Affectation. An attempt to assume or exhibit what is not natural or real.

Affectirt (äf-fĕk-tĭrt'), Ger. With affectation.

Affectueux (äf-fĕk-tü-üh), Fr. Affectionate.

Affet. An abbreviation of Affettuoso.

Affettatamente (äf-fĕt-tä-tä-mĕn'tĕ), It. Very affectedly.

Affettazione (äf-fĕt-tä-tsī-ō'nĕ), It. An artificial style.

Affettivo (äf-fĕt-tē'vō), It. Affecting, pathetic.

Affetto (äf-fĕt'tō), It. Feeling, tenderness, pathos.

Affettuosamente (äf-fĕt-too-ō-zä-mĕn'tĕ), It. With tenderness and feeling.

Affettuosissimo (äf-fĕt-too-ō-sĕs'sī-mō), It. With pathos; with tender expression. Superlative of Affettuoso.

Affettuoso (äf-fĕt-too-ō'zō), It. With tender feeling or emotion.

Affettuoso di molto (äf-fĕt-too-ō'zō dē mōl'tō), It. With much feeling.

Affiche de comèdie (äf-fĭsh düh kō-mĕ-dē), Fr. A playbill.

Affilas (or **ilas**) il tuono (äf fē-läs ĭl too-ō'nō), It. To sustain a sound with steadiness.

Affinity. A quality possessed by those chords that admit of an easy and natural progression from one to the other.

Afflitto (äf-flēt'tō), } Sorrowfully,
Afflizione (äf-flē-tsī-ō'nĕ), It. } with mournful expression.

Affreto. An abbreviation of Affrettando.

Affrettando (äf-frĕt-tän'dō), It. } Hurrying,
Affrettate (äf-frĕt-tä'tĕ) } quickening, accelerating the time.

Affrettoso (äf-frĕt-tō'zō), It. Quick, accelerated, hurried.

A fofa (ä fō-fä), Por. A Portuguese dance resembling the fandango.

After note. A small note occurring on an unaccented part of the measure, and taking its time from the note preceding it.

After notes, double. Two after notes taking their time from the preceding note.

Agevole (ä-jā'vō-lĕ), } Lightly,
Agevolmente (ä-jĕ-vōl-mĕn'tĕ), It. } easily, with agility.

Agevolezza (ä-jĕ-vō-lĕt'tsä), It. Lightness, ease, agility.

Aggiustamente (äd-joos-tä-mĕn tĕ), It. In strict time.

Aggiustare (äd-joos-tä'rĕ), } Adjusted, ar-
Aggiustato (äd-joos-tä'tō), It. } ranged, adapted.

Aggraver la fugue (äg-grä-vä lä füg), Fr. To augment the subject of fugue.

Agilita (ä-jē'lī-tä), It. Lightness. agility.

Agilita, con. It. With agility, with lightness. with rapidity

Agilmente (ä-jĕl-mĕn'tĕ), It. Nimbly gay.

Agiren (ä-ghē'r'n), Ger. To act to mimic.

Agitamento (ä-jī-tä-mĕn'tō), It. Agitation, restlessness, motion.

Agitato (ä-jī-tä'tō), It. Agitated, hurried, restless.

Agitato allegro (ä-jī-tä'tō äl lä'grō), It. An allegro which is not steadily held, but is nervous, unsteady, and unreposeful.

Agitato con passione (ä-jī-tä'tō kōn päs-sī-ō'nĕ), It. Passionately agitated.

Agite (ä-zhēt), Fr. Agitated.

Agli (äl'yē), *It. pl.* See *Alla.*

Agnus Dei (äg'noos dā-ē), *Lat.* "Lamb of God." Last movement in the Mass.

Agoge (ä-gō'ghĕ). *Gr.* Used by the ancient Greeks to signify melodic motion of different kinds necessary to musical expression. In modern use restricted to accent and expression. (Not sanctioned by authoritative usage.)

Agoge rhythmica (ä-gō'ghĕ rĭth-mĭ-kä), *Gr.* Rhythmical movement.

Agogik (ä-gō'ghĭk), *Ger.* The art of expressive nuance (variety) in tempo. (Rubato, accelerando, etc.)

À grand chœur (kür), *Fr.* For the entire chorus.

À grand orchestre (ŏr-kĕstr), *Fr.* For the full or complete orchestra.

Agreménts (ä-grā-mänh), *Fr. pl.* Embellishments, ornaments.

Ai (ä-ē), *It.* To the; in the style of.

Aigre (ägr), *Fr.* Harsh, sharp.

Aigrement (ā-gr-mänh), *Fr.* Sharply, harshly.

Aigu (ā-gü), *Fr.* Acute, high, sharp, shrill.

Air. A short song, melody, or tune with or without words. A series of tones bearing a certain relation to each other by their symmetry and regularity, producing a unity of effect, which is called "a tune."

Air à boire (ȧr ˈ bwȧˈ), *Fr.* A drinking-song.

Air à reprises (är ˈ rŭh-prēz), *Fr.* A catch.

Air chantant (är shänh-tänh), *Fr.* An air in graceful, melodious style.

Air détaché (är dā-tä-shā), *Fr.* A single air or melody extracted from an opera or larger work.

Air ecossais (är ā-cōs-sā), *Fr.* A Scotch air.

Air irlandais (är ēr-länh-dā), *Fr.* Irish air.

Air italien (är I-tä-lī-änh), *Fr.* An Italian air.

Air rapide - är rü-pĕd), *Fr.* A flourish.

Airs des bateliers vénétiens (är dĕ bä-tĕ-lēr vĕ-nä-sĭ-änh), *Fr.* Melodies sung by the Venetian gondoliers and boatmen.

Airs français (är fränh-sā), *Fr.* French airs.

Air russes (är rūs), *Fr.* Russian airs.

Airs tendres (är tänh-dr), *Fr.* Amatory airs; love songs.

Air varié (är vä-rī-ā), *Fr.* Air with variations; an air embellished and ornamented.

Ais (äis), *Ger.* The note A♯.

Als-dur (äis-door), *Ger.* The key of A♯ major. This key is not in use, being represented by B♭ major.

Ais-moll (äis-mōll), *Ger.* The key of A♯ minor. Not in use, being represented by B♭ minor.

Aisé (ā zā), *Fr.* Glad, joyful; also, easy, facile, convenient.

Aisément (ā-zā-mänh), *Fr.* Easily, freely.

Ajakti-keman (ä-yäk-lē kä-män), *Tur.* A Turkish instrument resembling the violin.

Akkord (äk-kŏrd'), *Ger.* See *Accord,*

Akromat (ä-krō-mät'), *Ger.* A musician, a singer.

Akromatisch (ä-krō-mä'tĭsh), *Ger.* See *Achromatic.*

Akustik (ä-koos'tĭk), *Ger.* See *Acoustics.*

Al (äl), *It.* To the; in the style of.

À l'abandon (ä lä-bänh-dōnh), *Fr.* Without restraint; with passionate expression.

À la chasse (ä lä shäss), *Fr.* In hunting style.

À la française (ä lä fränh-sā'), *Fr.* In the French style.

À la grecque (ä lä grĕk), *Fr.* In the Greek style.

À la mesure (ä lä mä-zür), *Fr.* In time; synonymous with A tempo.

À la militaire (ä lä mĭl-ĭ-tär'), *Fr.* In military or march style.

À l'antique (ä länh-tēk), *Fr.* Antique, in the style of the ancients.

Alamoth (ä'lä-mōt), *Heb.* This word occurs in Psalm lxviii. 25. "First go the *sharim* (singers), then follow the *neginim* (kinnors), in the midst are *alamoth* (damsels playing on the timbrels)" Gesenius and others understand the word to signify treble music, "vox clara et acuta, quasi virginum." But, on the other hand, in I. Chron. xv. 20, the names of *men* are given as players of "nebels on alamoth." It is one of the many obscure musical terms which are met with in the Bible. It, however, seems to have been associated with *nebels*, much as the expression *sheminith* is with *kinnors*, and may, therefore, be supposed to refer to the pitch or method of playing on those instruments.

A la polacca (ä lä pō-läk'kä), *It.* In the style of the polacca.

Alarum, All' armi, *It.* A call to arms.

"Alarums sounded and ordnance shot off."
—*Shakspeare.*

Originally a general shout; afterwards, a recognised signal by trumpets and drums.

A la savoyarde (ä lä sä-vwä-yärd), *Fr.* In the style of the airs of Savoy.

Albada (äl-bä'dä), *Sp.* A morning serenade.

Alberti bass. A bass consisting of *arpeggios* or *broken harmony, e. g.*:

 &c.

So called after its reputed inventor, Domenico Alberti, who died in 1739.

Albogue (äl-bō-gä'), *Sp.* An instrument belonging to the flute species.

Alcaics. Several kinds of verse, so called from Alcaeus, a lyric poet and their inventor.

Alemanian. Pertaining to Alcman, a lyric poet.

Alemanian verse. A verse consisting of six anapests or their equivalents, with the exception of the last two syllables, which are omitted.

Aleluya (ä-lĕ-loo'yä), *Sp.* Hallelujah.

Alemana (ä-lĕ-mü'nä), *Sp.* An old Spanish dance.

Alexandrian verse. A verse consisting of twelve syllables, or twelve and thirteen alternately.

Al fine (äl fē'nĕ), *It.* To the end.

Al fine e poi la coda (äl fē'nĕ ă pō-ē lä kō'dä), *It.* "After playing to where the *fine* is marked, go on to the *coda*."

Aliquot tones. Accessory or secondary sounds; tones indistinctly heard, which are always produced with the principal tone, at harmonic intervals above it. See *Partial Tones.* The flageolet tones of the violin.

A l'italiénne (ä lī-tä-lī-änh), *Fr.* In the Italian style.

A livre ouvert (ä lē-vr oo-vär), *Fr.* At the opening of the book. To play a piece at first sight.

Al (äl),
All' (äll),
Alla (äl-lä),
Alle (äl-lĕ),   *It.*
Agli (äl-yĕ),
Allo (äl-lō),
} = *a il*, "up to;" e. g., *accel. al presto*, increase the speed up to presto. Also, in the style or manner of.

Alla breve (äl-lä brä'vĕ), *It.* A quick species of measure, marked ¢ equivalent to 2-2, two counts in a measure. This measure is to be distinguished from 4-4 measure, marked ₵ which has four beats and is generally slower. Each contains the value of a breve—equal to two semibreves, or four minims. Modern composers often subdivide these measures into two parts, each containing two halves, and this is called Alla Cappella time to distinguish it from the Alla Breve, from which it is derived.

Alla caccia (äl'lä kät'tshī-ä), *It.* In the style of hunting music.

Alla camera (äl'lä kä'mĕ-rä), *It.* In the style of chamber music.

Alla cappella (äl'lä käp-pĕl'lä), *It.* In the church or sacred style; derived from Alla Breve style, the bar being subdivided. See *Alla breve.*

Alla diritta (äl'lä dī-rīt'tä), *It.* In direct ascending or descending style. With the right hand.

Alla francese (äl'lä frän-tshä-zĕ),
Alla franzese (äl'lä frän-tsä-zĕ),   *It.* } In the French style.

Alla hanacca (äl'lä hä-näk'kä), *It.* A kind of dance resembling the polonaise.

Alla madre (äl'lä mä'drĕ), *It.* To the Virgin Mary. Songs and hymns addressed to the Virgin Mary.

Alla maniera turka (äl'lä mä-nī-ä'ra toor'kä), *It.* In the Turkish style.

Alla marcia (äl'lä mär'tshī'ä), *It.* In the style of a march.

Alla mente (äl'lä měn'tě), *It.* Extemporaneous. (*V. Contrapunto alla mente.*)

Alla militare (äl'lä mī'lī-tä'rĕ), *It.* In the military style.

Alla moderna (äl'lä mō-děr'nä), *It.* In the modern style.

Alla moresco (äl'lä mō-rĕs'kō), *It.* In the Moorish style.

Alla Palestrina (äl'lä pä-lĕs-trē'nä), *It.* In the style of Palestrina; in the ecclesiastical style.

Alla polacca (äl'lä pō-läk'kä), *It.* In the time and style of a polonaise or Polish dance.

Alla quinta (äl'lä kwīn-tä), *It.* At, or in, the fifth.

Allargando (äl-lär-ghän'dō), *It.* Gradually slower and louder; in broader style; "widening."

Alla riversa (äl'lä rĕ-vĕr'sä), *It.* In an opposite direction.

Alla rovescio (äl'lä rō-vĕ'shō), *It.* In a reverse or contrary movement.

Alla russe (äl'lä roos-sĕ), *It.* In Russian style.

Alla scozzese (äl'lä skō-tsä'zĕ), *It.* In Scotch style.

Alla siciliana (äl'lä sē-tshī-lī-ä'nä), *It.* In the style of the Sicilian shepherd's dance.

Alla stretta (äl'lä strĕt'tä), *It.* Increasing the time; accelerating the movement. In close, compressed style.

Alla tedesca (äl'lä tĕ-děz'kä), *It.* In the German style.

Alla turka (äl'lä toor'kä), *It.* In the Turkish or Oriental style.

Alla unisono (äl'lä oo-nē'sō-nō), *It.* See *All' unisono.*

Alla veneziana (äl'lä vĕ-nĕ-tsī-ä'nä), *It.* In the Venetian style.

Alla zingara (äl'lä tsĕn'gä-rä), *It.* In the style of gipsy songs.

Alla zoppa (äl'lä tsŏp'pä), *It.* In a constrained and limping style.

Alla 3za,-*It.* A sign which, when placed above the staff, indicates that with each note played, a note a third higher must be played, and when placed below the staff, a note a third lower.

Alla 6ta. A sign, which, when placed above the staff, indicates that with each note played, a note a sixth higher must be played, and when placed below the staff, a note a sixth lower.

ä *arm*, ă *add*, ā *ale*, ĕ *end*, ē *eve*, ĭ *ill*, ī *isle*, ō *old*, ŏ *odd*, oo *moon*, ŭ *but*, ü *Fr. sound*, kh *Ger. ch*, nh *nasal.*

(41)

All' antica (äl-län-tē'kä), *It.* In the ancient style.

All' espagnuola (äl-lĕss-pän-yoo-ō'lä), *It.* In the Spanish style.

All' improviso (äl-lĕm-prō-vē'zō), *It.* } With-
All' improvista (äl-lĕm-prō-vēs'tä), *It.* } out previous study; extemporaneously.

All' inglese (äl-lĕn-glä'zē), *It.* In the English style.

All' italiana (äl-lē-tä-ll-ä'nä), *It.* In the Italian style.

All' ongarese (äl-lōu-gä-rä'zē), *It.* In the Hungarian style.

All' ottava (äl-lōt-tä'vä), *It.* At the octave. (1) A direction to play an octave higher or lower. In the former case the words are placed above the note or notes; in the latter case below them. The word *bassa* ("low")—at the low octave) is sometimes added. Instead of *all' ottava* the abbreviations *all' 8va* and *8va* are often used. (2) This expression is also used in scores to indicate that one instrument has to play with another in octaves.

All' ottava alta (äl-lōt-tä-vä äl-tä), *It.* In the octave above.

All' ottava bassa (äl-lōt-tä-vä bäs-sä), *It.* In the octave below.

All' unisono (äl-loo-nē'sō-nō), *It.* In unison; a succession of unisons or octaves.

All' 8va. An abbreviation of All' ottava.

Alle (äl-lĕ), *It.* To the; in the style of.

Alle (äl'lĕ), *Ger.* All: *alle Instrumente*, all the instruments; the whole orchestra.

Allegramente (äl-lĕ-grä-mĕn'tĕ), *It.* } Gaily,
Allégrement (äl-lā-grĕ-mänh), *Fr.* } joyfully, quickly.

Allegrante (äl-lĕ-grän'tĕ), *It.* Joyous, mirthful.

Allegrativo (äl-lĕ-grä-tē'vo), *It.* Gladdening, cheering, blithe.

Allegrettino (äl-lĕ-grĕt-tē'nō), *It.* A diminutive of Allegretto, and rather slower.

Allegretto äl-lĕ-grĕt'tō , *It.* Rather light and cheerful, but not as quick as allegro.

Allegretto scherzando (äl-lĕ grĕt'to skĕr-tsan'dō), *It.* Moderately playful and lively.

Allegrezza (äl-lĕ-grĕt'zä), *It.* } Joy, gladness,
Allegria (äl-lĕ-grē'ä), *It.* } cheerfulness, gaiety.

Allegrezza, con, *It.* With cheerfulness, joy, animation.

Allegri di bravura (äl-lĕ-grē dē brä-voo'rä), *It.* Compositions written in a brilliant and effective style.

Allegrissimamente (äl-lĕ-gri-sĭ-mä-mĕn'tĕ), *It.* Very joyfully; with great animation.

Allegrissimo (äl-lĕ-grĭs'sĭ-mō), *It.* Extremely quick and lively; the superlative of Allegro.

Allégro (äl-lā'grō), *Fr. and It.* Quick, lively; a rapid, vivacious movement, the opposite to the pathetic, but it is frequently modified by the addition of other words that change its expression.

Allegro agitato (äl-lā'grō ä-jĭ-tä-tō), *It.* Quick, with anxiety and agitation.

Allegro appassionato (äl-lā'grō äp-päs-sĭ-ō-nä'tō), *It.* Quick and passionate.

Allegro assai (äl-lā'grō äs-sä'ē, *It.* Very quick.

Allegro brillante (äl-lā'grō brĕl-län'tĕ), *It.* Requiring a brilliant style of execution.

Allegro comodo (äl-lā'grō kŏ'mō-dō), *It.* With a convenient degree of quickness, "convenience" here determined according to the best effect of the pass ge, in its details and spirit, and not with reference to the convenience of the performer.

Allegro con brio (äl-lā'grō kŏn brē'ō), *It.* Quick, with brilliancy.

Allegro con brioso (äl-lā'grō kŏn brē-ō'zō), *It.* Joyful and bold.

Allegro con fuoco (äl-lā'grō kŏn foo-ō'kō), *It.* Quick, with fire and animation.

Allegro con moltissimo moto (äl-lā'grō kŏn mŏl-tēs'sĭ-mō mō'tō), *It.* A very quick allegro; as fast as possible.

Allegro con moto, *It.* Quick, with more than the usual degree of movement.

Allegro con spirito (äl-lā'grō kŏn spē'rĭ-tō), *It.* Quick, with much spirit.

Allegro di bravura (äl-lā'gro dē brä-voo'rä), *It.* Quick, with brilliant and spirited execution.

Allegro di molto (äl-lā'grō dē mōl'tō), *It.* Exceedingly quick and animated.

Allegro fuocoso (äl-lā'grō foo-ō-kō'zō), *It.* With a great deal of fire and animation.

Allegro furioso (äl-lā'grō foo-rĭ-ō'zō), *It.* Quick, with fury and impetuosity.

Allegro gajo (äl-lā'grō gä'yō), *It.* In a gay and spirited style.

Allegro giusto (äl-lā'grō joos'tō), *It.* Quick, with exactness; in steady and precise time.

Allegro ma grazioso (äl-lā'grō mä grä-tsĭ-ō'zō), *It.* Quick, but gracefully.

Allegro ma non presto (äl-lā'grō mä nōn prĕs-tō), *It.* Quick, but not too fast.

Allegro ma non tanto (äl-lā'grō mä nōn tän-tō), *It.* Quick, but not too much so.

Allegro ma non troppo (äl-lā'grō mä nōn trōp-pō), *It.* Quick and lively, but not too fast.

Allegro moderato (äl-lā'grō mō-dĕ-rä'tō), *It.* Moderately quick.

Allegro molto (äl-lā'grō mōl-tō), *It.* Very quick and animated.

Allegro non molto (äl-lā'grō nŏn mōl'tō), *It.* Not very fast.

Allegro non troppo (äl-lā'grō nŏn trōp'pō), *It.* Quick, not too fast.

ā *arm*, ă *add*, ä *ale*, ĕ *end*, ē *eve*, ĭ *ill*, ī *isle*, ō *old*, ŏ *odd*, oo *moon*, ŭ *but*, ü *Fr. sound*, kh *Ger. ch*, nh *nasal*.

Allegro risoluto (äl-lā′grō rē-zō-loo′tō), *It.* Quick, with vigor and decision.

Allegro veloce (äl-lā′grō vē-lō′tshē), *It.* Quick, with extreme velocity.

Allegro vivace (äl-lā′grō vē-vä′tshe), *It.* With vivacity, very rapidly.

Allegro vivo (äl-lā′grō vē-vō), *It.* With great life and rapidity.

Allegrusio (äl-lē-groo′zī-ō), *It.* Good-humored, sprightly.

Allein (äl-līn′), *Ger.* Alone, single.

Alleinsang (äl-līn′säng), *Ger.* A solo.

Alleinsänger (äl-līn′säng-ĕr), *Ger.* A solo-singer.

Alleinspieler (äl-līn′spē-lĕr), *Ger.* One who plays a solo.

Alleluia (äl-lē-loo-yä), *Fr.* Praise the Lord; Hallelujah.

Allelujah (äl-lē-loo-yü), *Heb.* An ascription of praise; Hallelujah.

Allemande (äll-mäuhd), *Fr.* A German air. Also an obsolete dance form in common measure, beginning upon the last beat. The measure was slow, and the steps were made in a rapid, sliding manner, as in the modern waltz, but there was no turning, only a peculiar entwining and unloosening of the arms of the dancers in the various steps. It is said by some that the Allemande was invented in the lesser provinces of Germany or Switzerland, but its antiquity is unknown. Scarlatti, Corelli, Bach, Handel, and other composers of the period they represent, incorporated the measure of this dance in their suites, sonatas, and lessons, in which it was written in common time of four crotchets in a measure. But many peasant dances of this name are in 3-4 or 3-8 measure.

Allentamento (äl-lĕn-tä-mēn′tō), } *It.* } Relaxation, giving way, slackening of the speed.
Allentato (äl-lĕn-tä′tō),

Allentando (äl-lĕn-tän′dō), *It.* Decreasing the movement until the close.

Allied tones. Accessory tones.

Allmälich (äl′mä-līkh), *Ger.* Little by little.

Al′ loco (äl-lō′kō), *It.* To the previous place; a term of reference.

Allonger (äl-lōnh-zhā), *Fr.* To lengthen, prolong, delay.

Allonger l'archet (äl-lōnh-zhā lär-shā), *Fr.* To lengthen or prolong the stroke of the bow in violin music.

Alma (äl-mä), *Ara.* The name given in the O lent to singing and dancing girls, who are hired to furnish amusement at public entertainments and to sing dirges at funerals, etc.

Almain. } The name of an old slow dance
Alman. } of a dignified character.
Almand. }

Almanes, *pl.* See *Alman*.

Alma Redemptoris (äl-mä rē-dĕm-tō-rīs), *Lat.* A hymn to the Virgin.

Almees (äl-mās), *Ara.* Arabian dancing girls.

Almehs (äl-mās), *Tur.* Turkish singing and dancing girls.

Alpenhorn (äl-p′n-hōrn), *Ger.* The Alpine or cowhorn.

Al piacere (äl pē-ä-ishā′rē), *It.* At pleasure. *See A piacere.*

Al piu (äl pē′oo), The most.

Alphabet. The seven letters used in music, A, B, C, D, E, F, G. When more are required, either ascending or descending, the letters are repeated in the same order.

Alpine horn. An instrument made of the bark of a tree, and used by the Alpine shepherds for conveying sounds a long distance.

Al rigore di tempo (äl rē-gō′rē dē tĕm′pō), *It.* In very rigorous and strict time.

Al rigore del tempo (äl rē-gō′rē dĕl tĕm′pō), *It.* In very rigorous and strict time.

Al riverso (äl rē-vĕr′sō), *It.* Reverse, backward motion.

A la russe (ä lä rüss), *Fr.* In the Russian style.

Al seg. An abbreviation of Al segno.

Al segno (äl sān′yō), *It.* To the sign; meaning that the performer must return to the sign :S: in a previous part of the piece and play from that place to the word *fine*, or the mark ⌢ over a double bar. The sign itself :S: is sometimes used in place of the direction *al segno*.

Alt (ält), *It.* High. This term is applied to the notes which lie between f on the fifth line of treble staff and g on the fourth added line below.

Alta (äl′tä), *It.* High, or higher; *Ottava alta*, an octave higher.

Alta (äl′tä), *Sp.* A dance formerly used in Spain.

Alta-viola (äl′tä-vē-ō′lä), *It.* A counter tenor viol.

Altclarinet (ält′klä-rĭ-nĕt′), *Ger.* A large clarinet, a fifth deeper than the ordinary clarinet.

Al tedesco (äl tē-dĕs′kō), *It.* In the German style.

Altera prima donna (äl′tē-rä prē′mä dōn′nä). *It.* One of two principal female singers.

Alteratio (äl-tē rī′tsi-ō), *Lat.* } Changed, aug-
Alterato (äl-tē rä′tō), *It.* } mented. In
Altéré (äl-tē-rā′), *Fr.* } composition it means doubling the value of a note.

Altered notes. Notes changed by accidentals.

Alternamente (äl-tĕr-nä-mĕn′tē), *It.* Alternating, by turns.

Alternando (äl-tĕr-nän′dō), *It.* See *Alternamente*.

Alternations. Melodies composed for bells.

Alternativo (äl-tĕr-nä-tē'vō), *It.* A movement alternating with another. A sort of trio, of less importance than the movement with which it alternates.

Altgeige (ält'ghī-ghĕ), *Ger.* The viola, or tenor violin.

Ait horn. A cornet in E-flat.

Alti (äl'tē), *It.* High; the plural of alto.

Altieramente (äl-tē-ər-ä-měn'tē), *It.* With grandeur; haughtily.

Altisonante (äl-tī-sō-nän'tō), *It.* Loud-sounding.

Altisono (äl-tē'sō-nō), *It.* Sonorous.

Altisonous. High-sounding. A term formerly used to denote the highest part intended for the natural adult male voice.

Altiso (äl-tē'zō), *It.* An abbreviation of Altissimo.

Altissimo (äl-tis'sī-mō), *It.* The highest; extremely high as to pitch. It is applied to all the high treble notes which are more than an octave above F, on the fifth line of the treble staff.

Altist. An alto singer.

Altista (äl-tēs'tä), *It.* } One who has an alto
Altiste (äl-tēst), *Fr.* } voice.

Alto, äl'tō), *It.* High. (1) One of the four chief classes of the human voice; the deeper of the two classes of the female voice, which in England is more commonly called *contralto*. There are to be distinguished three different kinds of alto voices: those of women, boys, and men. Among the latter are again to be distinguished those of the *castrati* and of the *alti naturali*, *tenori acuti*, or *falsetti*. The last-mentioned male altos, in England also called counter tenors, make use of a developed *falsetto* (head voice). The English music written for this kind of voice demands a compass from g to c''. The *alti naturali*, who, till the introduction of the *castrati*, sang in the churches of Italy and elsewhere the soprano and alto parts, are said to have sung up to a''. For the compass of the female alto see Contralto. (2) Alto is also one of the names of the stringed instruments, which is a little larger and a fifth lower in pitch than an ordinary violin. *Viola*, *Tenor*, and *Bratsche* are synonyms. The three upper strings of the viola correspond with the three lowest of the violin. The question very naturally arises why the term alto (high) should be applied to the lowest voices and a low-pitched instrument. The reason is probably to be found in the fact that this part was formerly sung by very high male voices, and the notes representing its usual range were written by means of the C clef, which brought them upon the highest lines of the staff and upon added lines above.

Alto basso (äl-tō bäs'sō), *It.* A primitive instrument formerly in use in northern Italy, consisting of a wooden box, over which were stretched a few gut strings, which the performer struck with a stick held in his left hand, while he played on a flageolet held in his right hand.

Alto clef. The C clef on the third line, which makes the note on that line c'. It is used for the alto voice, viola, etc.

Alto concertina. A concertina having the compass of a viola.

Alto flauto (äl-tō flä-oo'tō), *It.* An alto flute; used in bands.

Alt' ottava (ält- ōt-tä'vä), *It.* The same notes an octave higher.

Alto primo (äl-tō prē'mō), *It.* The highest alto.

Alto secondo (äl-tō sĕ-kōn'dō), *It.* The lowest alto.

Alto tenore (äl-tō tĕ-nō'rĕ), *It.* The highest tenor.

Alto trombone. A trombone with the notation on the alto clef. Its compass is from the small c or e to the one-lined a or two-lined c.

Alto viola (äl-tō vē ō'lä), *It.* The viola, or tenor violin.

Alto violino (äl tō vē ō-lē'nō), *It.* Small tenor violin on which the alto may be played.

Altposaune (ält-pō-sou'ně), *Ger.* Alto trombone.

Altra (äl'trä), *It.* } Other, another.
Altro (äl'trō), *It.* }

Altri (äl'trē), *It.* Others.

Altro modo äl'trō mō'dō), *It.* Another mode or manner.

Altsänger (ält'säng-ĕr), *Ger.* Alto singer, counter tenor singer.

Altschlüssel (äl 'shlüs-s'l), *Ger.* The alto clef; the C clef on the third line.

Altus (äl'toos), *Lat.* The alto or counter tenor.

Altviole (ält'fī-ō-lĕ), *Ger.* The viola, or tenor violin.

Altzeichen (ält'tsī-k'n), *Ger.* See *Altschlüssel*.

Alzamento (äl-tsä-měn'tō). *It.* An elevating of the voice; lifting up.

Alzamento di mano (äl-tsä-měn'-tō dē mä'nō), *It.* To elevate the hand in beating time.

Alzando (äl-tsäu'dō), *It.* Raising, lifting up.

Al. zop. An abbreviation of Alla zoppa.

Amabile (ä-mä'bī-lĕ), *It.* Amiable, gentle, graceful.

Amabilita (ä-mä-bī-lī-tä'), *It.* Tenderness, aihinbility.

Amabilita, con. With amiability.

Amabilmente (ä-mä-bīl-měn'tĕ), *It.* Amiably, gently.

A major. The major mode founded on it.

Amarezza (ä-mä-ret'zä), *It.* Bitterness, sadness.

Amarezza, con, *It.* With bitterness; with sorrow.

Amarissimamente (ä-mä-rĭs-sĭ-mä-měn'tĕ), *It.*
Amarissimo (ä-mä-rĭs'sĭ-mō),
Very bitterly in a mournful, sad, and afflicted manner.

Amaro (ä-mä'rō), *It.* Grief, bitterness, affliction.

Amateur (ăm-ä-tŭr), *Fr.* One who has taste and proficiency in music, but does not practice it as a profession. As compared with an artist, an amateur is one who has learnt nothing thoroughly. Distinguished from *Dilettanti,* one who toys with art, and *Cognoscenti,* one who knows an art, but does not practice it.

Amati. A name applied to violins made by the brothers Amati, in Italy, in the middle of the seventeenth century. They are smaller than the ordinary violin, and distinguished for their peculiar sweetness of tone.

Ambitus (äm'bĭ-toos), *Lat.* Compass or range of sounds; also, the distance between the highest and lowest sounds.

Ambo (äm'bō), *Lat.* The desk at which the canons were sung in the middle ages.

Ambon (änh-bŏnh), *Fr.* The ambo.

Ambrosian chant. A series of sacred melodies or chants collected and introduced into the Church by St. Ambrose, Bishop of Milan, in the fourth century, and supposed to have been borrowed from the ancient Greek music.

Ambrosianus cantus (äm-brō-sĭ-ä'noos kän'-toos), *Lat.* Ambrosian chant.

Ambubaje (äm-boo-bä'yĕ), *Gr.* The name of a society of strolling flute-players among the ancient Greeks.

Ambulant (änh-bü länh), *Fr.* Wandering; an itinerant musician.

Ame (äm), *Fr.* The soundpost of a violin, viola, etc.

Amen (ä'měn), *Heb.* "So be it." A word used as a terminati u to psalms, hymns, and other sacred music.

Amen chorus. A chorus in which the word amen forms the principal language.

Ameno (ä-mä'nō), *It.* Charming, pleasing, sweet.

American fingering. That style of fingering in which the sign x is used to indicate the thumb in piano-playing, in distinction from the German or foreign fingering, in which the thumb is called the first finger.

American organ. A reed instrument of the harmonium kind, differing from harmoniums in the method of the bellows (which sucks the air through the reeds, instead of expelling it through them). Also differing in tone quality, which is broader and less thin and nasal—merits due in part to the suction-bellows, in part to superior voicing of the reeds, and in part to resonance added by the hollow spaces within the case. The American organ owes its suction-bellows to the late Jeremiah Carhart, and its name and resonant cases to Mason & Hamlin. All makes of this instrument now, however, partake of its characteristic excellencies.

A mezza aria (ä mět'sa ä'rĭ-ä), *It.* An air partly in the style of a recitative; between speaking and singing.

A mezza voce (ä mět'sä vō'tshĕ),
A mezza di voce (ä mět'sä dē vō'tshe), *It.* In a soft, subdued tone; with half the power of the voice. The term is also applied to instrumental music.

A mezza manico (ä mět'sä mä-nē'kō), *It.* In violin-playing, the placing the hand near the middle of the neck.

A-moll (ä-mŏll), *Ger.* The key of A minor.

A molto cori (a mōl'tō kō'rē), *It.* Full choruses; a collection of choruses.

A monocorde (ä mŏnh-ō-kŏrd), *Fr.* On one string only.

Amore (ä-mō'rĕ), *It.* Tenderness, affection, love.

Amore, con, *It.* With tenderness and affection.

A moresco (ä mō-rěs'kō), *It.* In the Moorish style; in the style of a moresco or Moorish dance.

Amorevole (ä-mō-rä'vō-le), *It.* Tenderly, gently, lovingly.

Amorevolmente (ä-mō-rĕ-vōl-měn'tĕ), *It.* With extreme tenderness.

Amorosamente (ä-mō-rō-zä-měn'tĕ), *It.* In a tender and affectionate style.

Amoroso (ä-mō-rō'zo), *It.* See *Amorosamente.*

Amphibrach (äm'fĭ-bräkh), *Ger.* A musical foot, comprising one short, one long, and one short note or syllable, accented and marked thus, ⌣ ‒ ⌣

Amphimacer (äm'fĭ-mä-tsěr), *Gr.* A musical foot, comprising one long, one short, and one long note or syllable, accented and marked thus, ‒ ⌣ ‒

Amphion (äm'fĭ-ōn), *Gr.* The most ancient Greek musician. He played upon the lyre.

Ampollosamente (äm-pŏl-lō-zä-měn'tĕ), *It.*
Ampolloso (äm-pŏl-lō'zō),
In a bombastic and pompous manner.

Ampoulé (änh-poo-lä), *Fr.* High-flown, bombastic.

Amusement (ä-müz-mänh), *Fr.* A light and pleasing composition introduced as an exercise in a course of piano studies.

Anabasis (ä-nä'bä-sĭs), *Gr.* A succession of ascending tones.

Anacreontic (ä-nä-krē-ŏn'tĭk), *Gr.* In the Bacchanalian or drinking style.

Anafil (ä-nä-fēl'), *Sp.* A musical pipe used by the Moors.

ä *arm,* ă *add,* ā *ale,* ĕ *end,* ē *eve,* ĭ *ill,* ī *isle,* ō *old,* ŏ *odd,* oo *moon,* ŭ *but,* ü *Fr. sound,* kh *Ger. ch,* nh *nasal.*

Anafilero (ä-nä-fĕ'lĕ-rō), *Sp.* A player on the anafil.

Anagaza (ä-nä-gä'thä), *Sp.* A bird-call.

Anakara (ä-nä-kä'rä), *It.* The kettledrum.

Anakarista (ä-nä-kä-rĭs'tä), *It.* A tympanist, or kettledrum-player.

Anakrusis (ä-nä-kroo'sĭs) The up stroke in conducting or beating time.

Analisi (ä-nä'lĭ zē), *It.*
Analyse (ä-nä-lēz), *Fr.* } An analysis.

Analyzation. The resolution of a musical composition into the elements which compose it, for the sake of ascertaining its construction.

Anapest (ä'nä-pĕst), *Gr.* A metrical foot, containing two short notes or syllables, and a long one, accented and marked thus, ‿ ‿ ―

♫ | ♩ or two unaccented tones followed by an accented tone, thus, ♩ ♩ | ♩

Anche (änhsh), *Fr.* The reed, or mouthpiece, of the oboe, bassoon, clarionet, etc.; also the various reed-stops in an organ.

Anche d'orgue (änhsh d'õrg), *Fr.* A reed-stop of an organ.

Ancia (än-tshē'ä), *It.* A reed.

Ancient flute. An instrument of the oboe kind, composed of two tubes, with a mouthpiece attached, then called *double-flute*. It is not certain whether both tubes were sounded together, but probably not.

Ancora (än-kō'rä), *It.* Once more, repeat again; also, yet, still, etc.

Ancor piu mosso (än-kōr pē-oo mōs'sō), *It.* Still more motion, quicker.

Andacht (än'däkht), *Ger.* Devotion.

Andächtig än'däkh-tĭg), *Ger.* Devotional.

Andamento (än dä-mĕn'tō), *It.* A rather slow movement; also, an accessory idea or episode introduced into a fugue to produce variety.

Andante (än-dän'tĕ), *It.* A movement in moderate time, but flowing steadily, easily, gracefully. This term is often modified, both as to time and style, by the addition of other words; as,

Andante affettuoso (än-dän'tĕ äf-fĕt-too-ō'zō), *It.* Moderately, and with much pathos.

Andante amabile (än-dän'tĕ ä-mä'bĭ-lĕ), *It.* An andante expressive of affection.

Andante cantabile (än-dän'tĕ cän-tä'bĭ-lĕ), *It.* Andante, and in a singing and melodious style.

Andante con moto (än-dän'tĕ kŏn mō'tō), *It.* Moving easily, with motion or agitation; rather lively.

Andante grazioso (än-dän'tĕ grä-tsĭ-ō'zō), *It.* Moderately slow in time, and in graceful, easy style.

Andante largo (än-dän'tĕ lär'gō), *It.* Slow, broad, distinct, and exact.

Andante maestoso (än-dän'tĕ mä-ĕs-tō'zō), *It.* Moving rather slowly and in majestic style.

Andante ma non troppo, e con tristezza (än-dän'tĕ mä nŏn trŏ'pō, ā kŏn trĕs-tĕt'sä), *It.* Not too slow, and with pathos.

Andante non troppo. Moving slowly, but not too much so.

Andante pastorale (än-dän'tĕ päs-tō-rä'lĕ), *It.* Moderately slow and in simple, pastoral style.

Andante piu tosto allegretto (än-dän'tĕ pē'oo tōs-tō äl lĕ-grĕt'tō), *It.* Andante, or almost allegretto.

Andante quasi allegretto, *It.* An andante nearly as rapid as allegretto.

Andantemente (än-dän-tĕ-mĕn'tĕ), *It.* See *Andante.*

Andantino (än-dän-tē'nō), *It.* Diminutive of andante. Opinions are divided as to whether it denotes a slower or faster movement than andante. But the general idea makes andantino a little faster than andante, shading toward allegretto. Italian lexicographers take the latter view, but non-Italian composers do not seem so unanimous.

Andantino sostenuto e simplicemente, Il canto e poco piu forte (än-dän-tē'nō sŏs-tĕ-noo'tō ā sĭm-plē-tshĕ-mĕn'to, ĕl kän-tō ā pō-kō pē'oo fōr'tĕ). In a sustained and simple manner, with the melody a little louder than the other tones.

Andno. An abbreviation of Andantino.

Andar diritto (än-där' dĭ-rĕt'tō), *It.* To go straight on.

Andare a tempo (än-dä'rĕ ä tĕm'pō). *It.* To play or sing in time.

Anelantemente (ä-nĕ-län-tĕ-mĕn'tĕ), *It.* Anxiously, ardently.

Anelanza (ä-nĕ-län'tsä), *It.*
Anelito (ä-nĕ-lē-tō) } Shortness of breath.

Anemochord. A species of Æolian harp.

Anemometer. A windgauge, or machine for weighing the wind in an organ.

Anfang (än'fäng), *Ger.* Beginning.

Anfänger (än'fĕng-ĕr), *Ger.* A beginner.

Anfangsgründe (än-fängs-grün'dĕ), *Ger.* Rudiments, elements, principles.

Anfangsritornell (än'fängs-rē-tōr-nĕl'), *Ger.* Introductory symphony to an air.

Anführer (än'fü-rĕr), *Ger.* A conductor, director, leader.

Angeben (än'gä-b'n), *Ger.* To give a sound; to utter a tone; *den Ton angeben,* to give out the tone.

Angelica (än-gä'lĭ-kä), *Ger.* } An organ-stop;
Angélique (änh-zhä-lēk), *Fr.* } also an angelot.

Angelot. An old musical instrument, somewhat similar to the lute.

Angelus (än'gĕ-loos), *Lat.* "The Angel of the Lord." The angelic annunciation. Also, the prayer-time of the *Angelus,* namely, morning, noon and evening.

ä *arm,* ă *add,* ā *ale,* ë *end,* ē *eve,* ĭ *ill,* ī *isle,* ō *old,* ŏ *odd,* oo *moon,* ŭ *but,* ü *Fr. sound,* kh *Ger. ch.* nb *nasal.*

Angemessen (än'ghĕ-mĕs's'n), *Ger.* Conformable, suitable, fit.

Angenehm (än'ghĕ-nām'), *Ger.* Agreeable, pleasing, sweet.

Angkloung (änk-loong), *Jav.* A rude instrument of the Javanese, made of different lengths of bamboo fastened to a strip of wood. A sort of xylophone.

Anglaise (änh-zläz). *Fr.* } In the English
Anglico (än'glĕ-kō). *It.* } style; a tune adapted for an English air or country dance.

Angore (än-gō'rĕ), *It.* Distress, anguish, passion, grief.

Angoscevole (än-gō-shĕ'vō-lĕ), *It.* Sad, sorrowful.

Angoscia (än-gō'shä), }
Angosciamente (än-gō-shä-měn'tĕ), *It.* } Anxiety, anguish, grief.

Angosciosamente (än-gō-shō-zä-měn'tĕ), *It.* Apprehensively, anxiously, sorrowfully.

Angoscioso (än-gō-shō'zō), *It.* Afflicted, distressed.

Ängstlich (ängst'lĭkh), *Ger.* Uneasy, timid, anxious.

Anhaltend (än'häl-těnd), *Ger.* Continuous, constant, holding out.

Anhaltende Cadenz (än'häl-těu-dĕ kä-děnts'), *Ger.* A pedal note or organ point; a protracted cadence.

Anhang (än'häng), *Ger.* A postscript, an appendix, a coda.

Anima (ä'nĭ-mä), *It.* Soul, feeling; animated, lively.

Animato (ä-nĭ-mä'tō), *It.* Animated; with life and spirit.

Animazione (ä-nĭ-mä-tsĭ-ō'nĕ), *It.* Animation.

Animé (änh-ĭ-mā), *Fr.* } Animated, lively,
Animo (ä'nĭ-mō), *It.* } spirited.

Animo, con, *It.* With boldness.

Animo corde (ä'nĭ-mō kŏr'dĕ), *Lat.* An instrument invented in 1789 by Jacob Schnell, of Paris. The tone is produced by wind passing over the strings.

Animosamente (ä-nĭ-mō-zä-měn'tĕ), *It.* Boldly; resolutely.

Animoso (ä-nĭ-mō'zō), *It.* In an animated manner; lively, energetic.

Anklang (än'kläng), *Ger.* Accord, harmony, sympathy.

Anlage (än'lä-ghĕ), *Ger.* The plan or outline of a composition.

Anlaufen (än'lou-f'n), *Ger.* To increase in sound, to swell.

Anleitung (än'lī-toong), *Ger.* An introduction, a preface.

Anmuth (än'moot), *Ger.* Sweetness, grace.

Anmuthig (än'moo-tĭg), *Ger.* Agreeable, pleasant, sweet.

Anonner (än-nŏnh-nā), *Fr.* To hesitate, blunder or stammer.

Anpfeifen (än'pfī-f'n), *Ger.* To whistle at; to hiss at.

Ansatz (än'säts), *Ger.* The position of the vocal parts (glottis, etc.) in singing. The embouchure of a wind instrument.

Anschlag (än'shläg), *Ger.* Touch; manner of striking the keys. 2. Obsolete term for a peculiar kind of appoggiatura.

Anspielen (än'spē-l'n), *Ger.* To play first.

Anstimmung (än'stĭm-moong), *Ger.* Intonation, tuning.

Answer. A term used in fugue.

Anteludium (än-tĕ-loo'dĭ-oom), *Lat.* A prelude, or introduction.

Antecedent. The subject of a fugue or of a point of imitation.

Anthem. A vocal composition in the sacred style, set to words generally taken from the Bible. There are anthems with and without accompaniment. The forms in which this kind of composition presents itself are very varied. "There are five species of anthems," says Dr. Busby. "(1) The *Verse and Chorus* anthem, consisting of verse and chorus, but beginning in verse; (2) the *Verse* anthem, containing verse and chorus, but beginning in verse; (3) the *Full* anthem, consisting wholly of chorus; (4) the *Solo* anthem, consisting of solos and choruses, but without verse; and (5) the *Instrumental* anthem." *Verses* are those portions of an anthem that are meant to be performed by a single voice to each part.

Anthema. An ancient Greek dance with song.

Anthem, choral. An anthem in a slow, measured style, after the manner of a choral.

Anthem, full. An anthem consisting wholly of chorus.

Anthem, solo. An anthem consisting of solos and choruses.

Anthologie (än-tō-lō-ghee'), *Fr. and Ger.* Anthology, a collection of choice compositions. Lit., "a gathering of flowers."

Anthologium (än-thō-lō'gĭ-oom), *Gr.* The name of a book in which are collected the hymns, prayers, and lections of the Greek Church.

Anthropoglossa (än-thrō-pō-glōs'sä), *Gr.* The vox humana, an organ-stop somewhat resembling the human voice.

Antibacchius (än'tĭ-bäk-kĭ-oos). A musical foot of three syllables, the first two long or accented and the last short or unaccented, thus, — — ⌣.

Antica (än-tē'kä), *It.* Ancient.

Anticipamento (än-tē-tshĭ-pä-měn'tō), *It.* Anticipation.

Anticipation. The taking of a note or chord before its natural and expected place.

ä *arm*, ă *add*, ā *ale*, ĕ *end*, ē *eve*, ĭ *ill*, ī *isle*, ō *old*, ŏ *odd*, oo *moon*, ŭ *but*, ü *Fr. sound*, kh *Ger. ch.* nh *nasal*.

Anticipation. The introduction of a note previous to the entrance of the harmony to which it belongs. The anticipations are indicated in the illustrations by *.

Anticipazione (än-tē-tshī-pä-zī-ō'nĕ), *It.* See *Anticipation*.

Antico (än-tē'kō), *It.* Ancient.

Antico, all' (än-tē'kō, äll'), *It.* In the ancient style.

Antienne (än-tī-ĕn'), *Fr.* An anthem.

Antifona (än-tīf'ō-nä), *It. and Sp.* An anthem.

Antifonal (än-tī-fō-näl), *Sp.*) A book of
Antifonario (än-tī-fō-nä'rī-ō), *It.*) anthems; an anthem-singer.

Antifonero (än-tī-fō-nä'rō), *Sp.* A precentor.

Antiphon. The chant or alternate singing in churches and cathedrals.

Antiphona (än-tīf'ō-nä), *Gr.* An anthem.

Antiphonaire (änh-tē-fō-nār'), *Fr.* A book of anthems, responses, etc.

Antiphonarium (än-tī-fō-nä'rī-oom), *Gr.* The collection of antiphons used in the Catholic Church; they are sung responsively by the priest and congregation.

Antiphonary. Book of anthems, responses, etc., in the Catholic Church.

Antiphone (än-tīf-ō-nĕ), *Gr.* The response made by one part of the choir to another, or by the congregation to the priest in the Roman Catholic service; also, alternate singing.

Antiphonon (än-tīf'ō-nōn), *Gr.* In ancient Greek music, accompaniment in the octave.

Antiphony. The response of one choir to another when an anthem or psalm is sung by two choirs; alternate singing or chanting.

Antistrofa (än-tī-strō'fä), *Sp.* An ancient Spanish dance.

Antistrophe.) The second couplet of each
Antistrophy.) period in the ancient Greek odes sung in parts; that part of a song or dance which was performed by turning from left to right, in opposition to the *strophe*, which turns from right to left.

Antithesis. Counter subject. In fugues this term is applied to the *answe.*; it generally signifies contrast.

A parte (ä pär-tĕ), *It.* On the side of.

A parte equale (ä pär-tĕ ä-kwä'lĕ), *It.* A term applied to a musical performance where the voices or instruments sustain an equally prominent part; where two or more performers sustain parts of equal difficulty.

A passo a passo (ä päs-sō ä päs-sō), *It.* Step by step; regularly.

Apertus (ä-pĕr'toos), *Lat.* Open; as, open diapason, open canon, etc.

Apfelregal (äp'fĕl-rĕ-gäl), *Ger.* Apple-register, a reed-stop in old organs; no longer in use.

Aphonie (ä-fō-nē), *Fr.* Aphony, want of voice.

Aphonous. Being destitute of voice.

Aphony. Dumbness, loss of voice.

A piacere (ä pē-ä-tshä'rĕ), *It.* At pleasure.

A piacimento (ä pē-ä-tshē-mĕn'tō), *It.* At the pleasure or taste of the performer.

A piena orchestra (ä pē-ā'nä ŏr-kĕs'trä), *It.* For full orchestra.

A plomb (ä plŏmh), *Fr.* Firm, in exact time, with precision.

A poco (ä pō'kō), *It.* By degrees, gradually.

A poco a poco (ä pō'kō ä pō'kō), *It.* By little and little.

A poco piu lento (ä pō'kō pē'oo lĕn-tō), *It.* A little slower.

A poco piu mosso (ä pō'kō pē'oo mōs-sō), *It.* A little quicker.

Apollo, *or*, **Apollon.** An instrument of the lute class, with twenty strings, invented in 1678 by Prompt, a musician of Paris.

Apollino (ä-pōl-lē'nō), *Gr.* An harmonic invention or contrivance combining the different qualities and powers of several kinds of instruments, and capable of playing them separately or all together.

Apollo. In ancient mythology, the god of music, and said to be the inventor of the lyre.

Apollo lyra. An instrument shaped like a lyre, with a brass mouthpiece like a horn; now obsolete.

Apollonicon. An organ, invented by John Henry Völler in 1800. It had immense self-acting machinery, bringing the whole power of the instrument into operation at once, producing the effect of a full orchestra. It had six keyboards, and could be played upon by six performers at the same time. Was exhibited in London.

Apotome (ä'pō-tō-mĕ), *Gr.* That portion of a major tone that remains after deducting from it an interval less, by a comma, than a major semitone.

Appassionatamente (äp-päs-sī-ō-nä-tä-mĕn'tĕ),
Appassionatamento (äp-päs-sī-ō-nä-tä-mĕn'tō), } *It.*
Appassionato (äp-päs-sī-ō-nä'tō),
Passionately, with intense emotion and feeling.

Appeau (äp-pō), *Fr.* Tones which resemble the singing of birds.

Appel (äp-pĕl), *Fr.* Call of the drum.

Appenato (äp-pĕ-nä'tō), *It.* Grieved, distressed; an expression of suffering and melancholy.

Applaudissement (äp-plō-dĕss-mŏnh), *Fr.* }
Applauso (äp-plü-oo'zō), *It.* }
Applause.

ä *arm*, ă *add*, ā *ale*, ĕ *end*, ē *eve*, ĭ *ill*, ī *isle*, ō *old*, ŏ *odd*, oo *moon*, ŭ *but*, ü *Fr. sound*, kh *Ger. ch*, nh *nasal*.

Applicatur (äp-plĭ-kă-toor'), *Ger.* The art of fingering.

Appoggiando (äp-pōd-jän'do), *It.* } Leaning
Appoggiato (äp-pōd-jä'tō), upon, dwelt upon, drawn out.

Appoggiatura (äp-pōd-jä-too'rä), *It.* Leaning note, grace note, note of embellishment. An accessory tone, or grace note, situated one degree from the principal tone. The appoggiatura is sometimes written as a grace note, and sometimes is written out in full. It is struck upon the beat, in the time of its own principal tone, and is longer or shorter according to the nature of the passage. See Introduction, page 14.

Appoggiatura, compound. An appoggiatura, consisting of two or more grace notes or notes of embellishment.

Appoggiatura, inferior. An appoggiatura situated one degree below its principal note.

Appoggiatura, superior. An appoggiatura situated one degree above its principal note.

Appoggiature (äp-pōd-jä-too'rĕ), *It.* See *Appoggiatura*.

Apprestare (äp-prĕs-tä'rĕ), *It.* To prepare, or put in a condition to be played.

Appretiren (äp-prĕ-tē'-r'n), *Ger.* To set in order.

À premiére vue (ä prĕ-mĭ-är vü), *Fr.* } At first
A prima vista (ä prē'mä vēz'tä), *It.* } sight.

Âpre (äpr), *Fr.* Harsh.

Âprement (äpr-mŏnh), *Fr.* Harshly.

Âpreté (äp-rĕ-tä), *Fr.* Harshness.

A punta d' arco (ä poon'tä där'kō), *It.* With the point of the bow.

A punto (ä poon'tō), *It.* Punctually, exactly, correctly.

À quatre mains (ä kätr mänh), *Fr.* } For
A quattro mani (ä kwät'trō mä'nē), *It.* } four hands. For two performers on one pianoforte.

A quattro, or, **a 4,** *It.* For four voices or instruments; a quartette.

A quattro parti (ä kwät'trō pär-tē), *It.* In four parts.

À quatre voix (ä kätr vwä), *Fr.* } For
A quattro voci (ä kwät'trō vō'tshē), *It.* } four voices.

À quatre seuls (ä kätr söl), *Fr.* } For four
A quattro soli (ä kwät'trō sō-lē), *It.* } solo voices or instruments.

A quattro tempo staccati e vivace (ä kwät'trō tĕn'pō stäk-kä'tē ā vē-vä'tshĕ), *It.* The measure in four time to be taken with spirit and animation.

Ar (är), *Por.* Air.

Arbitrii (är-bĭt'rĭ-ē), *Lat.* Certain points or embellishments which a singer introduces or improvises at pleasure while singing an aria or tune.

Arbitrio (är-bē'trĭ-ō), *It.* At the will or pleasure of the performer.

Arc (ärk), *It.* The bow; an abbreviation of Arco.

Arcata (är-kä'tä), *It.* Manner of bowing.

Arcato (är-kä'tō), *It.* Bowed, played with the bow.

Arche (är'khĕ), *Ger.* The sounding-board of an organ.

Arcicembalo (är-tshĭ-tshĕm'bä-lo), *It.* A cembalo, or harpsichord, invented in the sixteenth century, having an enharmonic scale. Little is known about it.

Archeggiare (är-kăd-jä'rĕ), *It.* To use the bow, to fiddle.

Archet (är-shä), *Fr.* } A violin-bow.
Archettino (är-kĕt-tē'nō), *It.* }

Archetto (är-kĕt'tō), *It.* } A little bow.
Arcicello (är-tshĭ-tshĕl'lō), *It.* }

Archiluth (är-shē-lüt), *Fr.* } See *Archlute*.
Arciliuto (är-tshēl-yoo'tō), *It.* }

Archlute. A theorbo or lute with two nuts and sets of strings, one for the bass. The strings of the theorbo were single, but in the archlute the bass strings were doubled with an octave and the small strings with a unison.

Arco (är'kō), *It.* With the bow (after *pizzicato*).

Ardente (är-dĕn'tĕ), *It.* With fire, glowing, vehement.

Ardentemente (är-dĕn-tĕ-mĕn'tĕ), *It.* Ardently, vehemently.

Ardentissimo (är-dĕn-tĭs'sĭ-mō), *It.* Very ardently.

Arditamente (är-dē-tä-mĕn tĕ), *It.* Boldly, with ardor.

Arditezza (är-dĭ-tĕt'sä), *It.* Boldness.

Ardito (är-dē'tō), *It.* Bold, with energy.

Ardito di molto (är-dē'tō dē mōl'tō), *It.* Passionately, with much force.

Aretinian syllables. The syllables ut, re, mi, fa, sol, la, introduced by Guido d' Arezzo for his system of hexachords, or six notes.

Argentin (är-zhän-tän), *Fr.* Silver-toned.

Arghool (är-ghool), *Tur.* A musical instrument of the Turks, of the flute species.

Aria (ä'rĭ-ä), *It.* An air; a song; a vocal composition for a single voice, with instrumental accompaniment. The aria, such as we find it in the opera, oratorio, cantata, etc., in the structure of which it forms one of the most important elements, was developed in the seventeenth century. Of the varieties of the aria form none is historically more noteworthy than the aria with *da capo*—that is, a composition consisting of a more or less extended first part, a shorter second part, and a repetition of the first part. For a long period it was the prevalent type. Most of the other varieties of the aria form sprang out of this one. For instance, that in which a free, modified repetition took the place of the *da capo*; or that in which the repetition was altogether dispensed with; or that in which the center of gravity was to be found in the second part, and so forth. Arias, however, have often been written in the rondó form, and also in what we may call the abridged sonata form. Since Mozart, the great masters have departed more and more from the conventional pattern, and have taken for their guides, as regards form as well as sentiment, the character and mood of the person for whom, and the nature of the situation for which, the aria is intended. See *Air*.

Aria buffa (ä'rĭ-ä boof'fä), *It.* A comic or humorous air.

Aria cantabile (ä'rĭ-ä kän-tä'bĭ-lĕ), *It.* An air in a graceful and melodious style.

Aria concertata (ä'rĭ-ä kŏn-tshĕr-tä'tä). *It.* An air, with orchestral accompaniments, in a concertante style; a concerted air.

Aria concertante, *It.* An aria with *obligato* instrumental accompaniment—*i. e.*, an aria in which one or more instruments vie with the voice.

Aria d' abilita (ä'rĭ-ä dä-bĕl-lĭ-tä'), *It.* A difficult air, requiring great skill and musical ability in the singer.

Aria di bravura (ä'rĭ-ä dē brä-voo'rä), *It.* A florid air in bold, marked style, and permitting great freedom of execution.

Aria di cantabile, *It.* See *Aria cantabile.*

Aria fugata (ä'rĭ-ä foo-gä'tä), *It.* An air accompanied in the fugue style.

Aria d' ostinazione (ä'rĭ-ä dŏs-tĭ-nä-tsĭ-ō'nĕ), *It.* An aria all parts of which are essentially counterpoints to the same bass figure (called *basso ostinato*) repeated over and over.

Aria parlante (ä'rĭ-ä pär-län'tĕ), *It.* An air in the declamatory style; a recitative *a tempo*.

Aria tedesca (ä'rĭ-ä tĕ-dĕs'kä), *It.* An air in the German style.

Aria und Chor (ä'rĭ-ä oond kōr), *Ger.* Air and chorus.

Arie (ä'rĭ-ä), *It. pl.*
Arien (ä'rĭ-ĕn), *Ger. pl.* } Airs or songs.

Arie aggiunte (ä-rĭ-ä äd-joon'tĕ), *It.* Airs added to or introduced into an opera or other large work.

Arietta (ä-rĭ-ĕt'tä), *It.*
Ariette (ä-rĭ-ĕt), *Fr.* } A short air or melody.

Arietta alla veneziana (ä-rĭ-ĕt'tä äl'lä vĕ-nä-tsĭ-ä'nä), *It.* A short air in the style of the Venetian barcarolles.

Ariettina (ä-rĭ-ĕt-tē'na), *It.* A short air or melody.

A rigore del tempo (ä rĕ-gō'rĕ dĕl tĕm'pō), *It.* In strict time.

Arigot (ä-rĭ-gō), *Fr.* A fife.

Ariosa (ä-rĭ-ō'zä), *It.* In the movement of an aria, or tune.

Ariose cantate (ä-rĭ-ō'zĕ kän-tä'tĕ), *It.* Airs in a style between a song and recitative, introducing frequent changes in time and manner.

Arioso (är-ĭ-ō'zō), *It.* In style of an air; melodious. Historically considered, the aria marks a single moment in the course of a dramatic action. The text often consists of but a few words, many times repeated (as we find in Handel's oratorios, etc.), and the musical development is the main thing. The opposite of aria is *recitative* (*q. v.*), in which the declamation of the syllables is the main thing, colored, perhaps, by means of clever orchestration. The arioso stands between these extremes. In modern practice it has had a great development, especially at the hands of Wagner. An arioso declaims the text about as carefully as a recitative; it accentuates the emotional moment of the drama about as consistently as the aria; but it is of a more flexible character, and, being less bound by conditions of symmetry, is free to follow the delicate emotional transitions or shadings of the text in a way impracticable for an aria in classical form. The problem of the composer in composing an arioso for an important moment of a work is to indulge himself in free fantasy to the extreme extent needed for dramatically representing the text, and at the same time not depart from symmetry, or, at least, a quasi symmetry, and a unity of key satisfactory to the musical ear.

Arm. A small piece of iron at the end of the roller of an organ.

Armer la clef (är-mä' lä klā), *Fr.* The signature; or, the flats and sharps placed immediately after the clef.

Armoneggiare (är-mō-nĕd-jä'rĕ), *It.* To sound in harmony.

Armonia (är-mō'nĭ-ä), *It.* Harmony, concord.

Armoniaco (är-mō-nĭ-ä'kō), *It.* Harmonized.

Armoniale (är-mō-nĭ-ä'lĕ), *It.* Harmonious, concordant.

Armoniato (är-mō-nĭ-ä'tō), *It.* See *Armoniaco.*

Armonica (är-mō'nĭ kä), *It.* The earliest form of the accordion; a collection of musical glasses, so arranged as to produce exquisite effects.

Armonica guida (är-mō'nĭ-kä gwē-dä), *It.* A guide to harmony.

Armonici (är-mō-nē'tshĭ), *It.* Harmonic.

Armonico (är mō'nĭ-kō), *It.* Harmonious.

Armoniosamente (är-mō'nĭ-ō-zä-mĕn'tĕ), *It.* Harmoniously.

Armonioso (är-mō-nĭ-ō'zō), *It.* Concordant, harmonious.

Armure (är-mür), *Fr.* The signature of the key.

Arpa (är'pä), *It.*
Arpe (är'pĕ), } The harp.

Arpa d' eolo (är'pä dä-ō'lō), *It.* An Eolian harp.

ä *arm*, ă *add*, ā *ale*, ĕ *end*, ē *eve*, I *ill*, ī *isle*, ŏ *old*, ō *odd*, oo *moon*, ŭ *but*, ü *Fr. sound*, kh *Ger. ch*, nh *nasal*

Arpa doppia (är'pä döp'pī-ä), *It.* The double-action harp; it meant formerly a harp with two strings to each note.

Arpanetta (är-pä-nĕt'tä), *It.* } A small harp or
Arpinella (är-pī-nĕl'lä), } lute.

Arpeg. An abbreviation of Arpeggio.

Arpegement (är-pâzh-mänh), *Fr.* An arpeggio.

Arpeggi (är-pĕd'jē), *It.* Arpeggios.

Arpeggiamento (är-pĕd-jä-mĕn'tō), *It.* In the style of the harp; arpeggio.

Arpeggiando (är-pĕd-jän'dō), *It.* } Music
Arpeggiato (är-pĕd-jä'tō), } played arpeggio, in imitation of the harp; harp music.

Arpeggiare (är-pĕd-jä'rĕ), *It.* To play upon the harp.

Arpeggiatura (är-pĕd-jä-too'rä), *It.* Playing arpeggio, or in the style of the harp.

Arpeggio (är-pĕd-jō'), *It.* Playing the notes of a chord quickly, one after another, in the harp style, thus.

Arpeggio accompaniment. An accompaniment which consists chiefly of chords played in arpeggio style.

Arr. } Abbreviations of Arrangement.
Arrang. }

Arrangement. The selection and adaptation of a composition or parts of a composition to instruments for which it was not originally designed, or for some other use for which it was not at first written.

Arranger (är-ränh zhä), *Fr.* } To ar-
Arrangiren (är-ränh-ghē'r'n), *Ger.* } range music for particular voices or instruments; to arrange orchestral music for the pianoforte.

Arsis (är'sĭs), *Gr.* The up stroke of the hand in beating time.

Ars musica (ärs moo'sĭ-kä), *Lat.* The art of music.

Art (ürt), *Ger.* Species, kind, quality.

Art de l'archet (ärt dŭh lär-shä), *Fr.* The art of bowing.

Articolare (är-tĭ-kō-lä'rĕ), *It.* } To pronounce
Articuler (är-tĭ-kü-lā), *Fr.* } the words distinctly; to articulate each note.

Articulate. To utter distinct separate tones; to sing with a distinct and clear enunciation.

Articulation. A distinct and clear utterance; clear and exact rendering of every syllable and tone.

Articolato (är-tĭ-kō-lä'tō), *I'.* Articulated, distinctly enunciated.

Articolazione (är-tĭ-kō-lä'tsĭ-ō'nĕ), *It.* Exact and distinct pronunciation.

Artikuliren (är-tĭk-oo-lē'r'n), *Ger.* To articulate.

Artista (är-tĭs'tä), *It.* } An artist; one who
Artiste (är-tĭst'), *Fr.* } excels in the composition or performance of music.

As (äs), *Ger.* The note A♭.

Asas (äs-äs), *Ger.* A-double-flat.

Ascoltatore (äs-kōl-tä-tō'rĕ), *It.* An auditor, a hearer.

As-dur (äs-door), *Ger.* The key of A♭ major.

Asheor (ä'shĕ-ŏr), *Heb.* A ten-stringed instrument of the Hebrews.

As-moll (äs-mŏll), *Ger.* The key of A♭ minor.

Asperges me (äs-pär'gĕs mā), *Lat.* The opening of the Mass in the Catholic service.

Aspirare (äs-pĭ-rä'rĕ), *It.* To breathe loudly; to use too much breath in singing.

Asprezza (äs-prĕt'tsä), *It.* Roughness, dryness, harshness.

Assai (äs-sä'ē), *It.* Very, extremely, in a high degree. In composition with other terms it intensifies everything, as, Allegro assai, Very allegro, etc.

Assai piu (äs-sä'ē pē'oo), *It.* Much more.

Assemblage (äs-sänh-bläzh), *Fr.* Double-tonguing on the flute; executing rapid passages on wind instruments.

Assez (äs-sä), *Fr.* Enough, sufficiently.

Assez lent (äs-sä länh), *Fr.* Rather slowly.

Assoluto (äs-sō-loo'tō, *It.* Absolute, free, alone, one voice.

Assonant. Having a resemblance of sounds.

Assonante (äs-sō-nän'tĕ), *It.* Harmonious, consonant.

Assonanz (äs-sō-nänts'), *Ger.* } Similarity, or
Assonanza (äs-sō-nän'tsä), *It.* } consonance of tone.

Assourdir (äs-soor-dēr'), *Fr.* To muffle, to deaden, to stun.

Assourdissant (äs-soor-dĭs-sänh), *Fr.* Deafening, stunning.

A suo arbitrio (ä soo'ō är-bĭ'trĭ-ō),
A suo bene placito (ä soo'ō bä-nĕ plä'-tsĭ-tō), *It.*
A suo comodo (ä soo'ō kŏ'mō-dō),
At pleasure, at will, at the inclination or discretion of the performer; synonymous with Ad libitum.

A suo bene placimento (ä soo'ō bä-nĕ plä'tshĭ-mĕn'tō), *It.* An old term, signifying At the will or pleasure of the performer.

Atabal. A kind of tabour used by the Moors.

A tem. } Abbreviations of A tempo.
A temp. }

A tempo (ä tĕm'pō), *It.* In time. A term used to denote that, after some deviation or relaxation of the time, the performers must return to the original movement.

A tempo comodo ä tĕm'pō kō-mō-dō), *It.* In convenient time; an easy, moderate time.

A tempo dell' allegro (ä tĕm'pō dĕl lül-lä'grō), *It.* In allegro time.

ä *arm*, ă *add*, ā *ale*, ĕ *end*, ē *eve*, ĭ *ill*, ī *isle*, ō *old*, ŏ *odd*, oo *moon*, ŭ *but*, ü *Fr. sound*, kh *Ger. ch*, nh *nasal*.

A tempo di gavotta (ä těm'pō dē ga-vŏt'tä), *It.* In the time of a gavot; moderately quick.

A tempo giusto (ä těm'pō joos'tō), *It.* In just, strict, exact time.

A tempo ordinario (ä těm'pō ŏr-dĭ-nä'rĭ-ō), *It.* In ordinary, moderate time.

A tempo rubato (ä těm'pō roo-bä'tō), *It.* Irregular time; deviation in time so as to give more expression, but so that the time of each bar is not altered on the whole. See *Rubato.*

Athem (ä'těm), *Ger.* Breath, breathing, respiration.

Athemholen (ä-těm-hōl'n), *Ger.* To breathe, to respire.

Athemzug (ä-těm-tsoog), *Ger.* Act of respiration, breathing.

Athmen (ät'měn), *Ger.* To blow softly.

A ton basse (ä tŏnh bäss), *Fr.* In a low tone of voice.

A tre, *or,* **a 3** (ä trä), *It.* For three voices or instruments; a trio, or terzetto.

A tre corde (ä trä kŏr'dě), *It.* For three strings; with three strings. Discontinue the soft pedal.

A tre mani (ä trä mä'nĭ), *It.* For three hands.

A tre parti (ä trä pär'tĭ), *It.* In three parts.

A tre soli (ä trä sō'lĭ), *It.* For three solo voices.

A tre soprani (ä trä sō-prä'nĭ), *It.* For three soprano voices.

A tre voci (ä trä vō'tshĭ), *It.* For three voices.

Atril (ä-trēl'), *Sp.* A missal-stand.

À trois, *or,* **a 3** (ä trwä), *Fr.* For three voices or instruments.

À trois mains (ä trwä mänh), *Fr.* For three hands.

À trois parties (ä trwä pär-tē), *Fr.* In three parts.

À trois voix (ä trwä vwä), *Fr.* For three voices.

Attacca (ät-täk'kä),
Attacca subito (ät-täk'kä soo'bĭ-tō), *It.* } Attack or commence the next movement immediately.

Attacca l' allegro (ät-täk'kä läl-lä'grō), *It.* Commence the allegro immediately.

Attaccare (ät-täk-kä'rě), *It.* } To attack or commence the performance.
Attaquer (ät-tä-kä), *Fr.*

Attendant keys. Those keys having most sounds in common with any given key; the relative keys. In C major the attendant keys are its relative minor A, the dominant G, and its relative minor E, the subdominant F and its relative minor D.

Atto (ät'tō), *It.* An act of an opera or play.

Atto di cadenza (ät'tō dē kä-děn'tsa), *It.* The point in a piece where a cadence may be introduced.

Atto primo (ät-tō prē'mō), *It.* The first act.

Attore (ät-tō'rě), *It.* An actor or singer in an opera or play.

Attori (ät-tō'rě), *It.* The principal actors or singers in an opera.

Atto secondo (ät'tō sě-kōn'dō), *It.* The second act.

Atto terzo (ät-tō těr'tsō), *It.* The third act.

Attrice (ät-trē'tshě), *It.* An actress or singer.

Aubade (ō-bäd), *Fr.* A morning serenade.

Audace (ä-oo-dä'tshě), *It.* Bold, spirited, audacious.

Auf (ouf), *Ger.* On, upon, in, at, etc.

Aufblasen (ouf'blä-z'n), *Ger.* To sound a wind instrument.

Auf dem Oberwerk (ouf děm ō'běr-wärk), *Ger.* Upon the *upper work,* or highest row of keys in organ-playing. Generally indicates the swell organ.

Auffassung (ouf'fäs-soong), *Ger.* Conception, reading of a work.

Aufführung (ouf'fü-roong), *Ger.* Performance.

Aufgeregt (ouf'ghě-rěght), *Ger.* Excited, agitated.

Aufgeweckt (ouf'ghě-wěkt), *Ger.* Sprightly, lively, cheerful.

Aufgewecktheit (ouf'ghě-wěkt'hīt), *Ger.* Liveliness, cheerfulness.

Aufhalten (ouf'häl-t'n), *Ger.* To stop, to retard, to keep back.

Aufhaltung (ouf'häl-toong), *Ger.* Keeping back; a suspension.

Auflage (ouf'lä-ghě), *Ger.* Edition.

Auflösung (ouf'lě-zoong), *Ger.* The resolution of a discord. Also, a natural (♮).

Aufs (oufs), *Ger.* To the, on the.

Aufschlag (ouf'shläg), *Ger.* Up beat; the unaccented part of a bar.

Aufsteigende Tonarten (ouf'stī-ghěn-dě tōn'-är-t'n), *Ger. pl.* Ascending scales or keys.

Aufstrich (ouf'strīkh), *Ger.* An up bow.

Auftakt (ouf'täkt), *Ger.* The unaccented part of a bar; especially the commencement of a piece, or division of a piece, when it does not open with a note on the first accented part of the bar, but on a later unaccented one.

Auftritt (ouf'trĭtt), *Ger.* A scene

Aufzug (ouf'tzoog), *Ger.* Act of a play or opera.

Augmentatio (oug-měn-tä'tsĭ-ō), *Lat.* Augmentation.

Augmentation. Applied to intervals which are chromatically enlarged beyond the compass of the corresponding perfect or major intervals. (2) In canon, the repetition of a subject in notes of greater value, as halves for quarters, etc.

Augmenté (ōg-mänh-tä'), *Fr.* Augmented.

ä *arm,* ă *add,* ā *ale,* ĕ *end,* ē *eve,* ĭ *ill,* ī *isle,* ŏ *old,* ō *odd,* oo *moon,* ŭ *but,* ü *Fr. sound,* kh *Ger. ch,* nh *nasal.*

Augmentazione (oug-měn-tä-tsǐ-ō'nĕ), *It.* Increase.

Augmented. An epithet applied to such intervals as are more than a major or perfect.

Augmented fifth. A fifth containing four whole tones, or steps.

Augmented fourth. A fourth equal to three whole steps.

Augmented intervals. Those which include a semitone more than major, or perfect, intervals; as, A perfect fifth Augmented fifth

Augmented octave. An interval equal to five whole tones, or steps, and two semitones, or half steps.

Augmented second. An interval equal to one whole and one half step, equal to three half steps.

Augmented sixth. An interval equal to four whole tones, or steps, and one semitone, or half step.

Augmented unison. A semitone, or half step.

Augmento (ä-oog-měn'tō), *It.* Augmentation.

Auletes (ou-lā'tĕs),*Gr.* A flute-player, a piper.

Auletic. Pertaining to a pipe; (little used).

Au lever du rideau (ō lĕ-vä düh rē-dō),*Fr.* At the rising of the curtain.

Aulo (ä-oo'lō), *It.* } A species of ancient
Aulos (ou'lōs), *Gr.* } flute.

Aulodia (ä-oo-lō'dǐ-ä), *It.* Singing, accompanied by the flute.

Aumentazione (ä-oo-měn-tä-tsǐ-ō'nĕ), *It.* Augmentation.

A una corda (ä oo'nä kōr'dä), *It.* On one string.

Aus (ous), *Ger.* From, out of.

Ausarbeitung (ous'är-bī-toong),*Ger.* The last finish or elaboration of a composition.

Ausdehnung (ous'dā-noong),*Ger.* Expansion, extension, development.

Ausdruck (ous'drook), *Ger.* Expression.

Ausdrucksvoll (ous'drooks-fōll), *Ger.* Expressive.

Ausführung (ous'fü-roong),*Ger.* Performance.

Ausfüllung (ous'fül-loong), *Ger.* The filling up, the middle parts.

Ausgabe (ous'gä-bĕ), *Ger.* Edition.

Ausgang (ous'gäng), *Ger.* Going out, exit, conclusion.

Ausgehalten (ous'ghĕ-häl-t'n), *Ger.* Sostenuto.

Ausgeigen (ous'ghī-g'n), *Ger.* To play to the end.

Ausgelassen (ous'ghĕ-läs's'n),*Ger.* Wild, ungovernable.

Ausgelassenheit (ous'ghĕ-läs's'n-hīt),*Ger.* Extravagance, wantonness.

Aushalten (ous'häl-t'n), *Ger.* To hold on, to sustain a note.

Aushaltung (ous'häl-toong), *Ger.* The sustaining of a note.

Aushaltungszeichen(ous'häl-toongs-tsī'kh'n), *Ger.* A pause (⌒).

Auslösung (ous'lĕ-zeong), *Ger.* A mechanism which permits the hammer of the pianoforte to immediately drop away from the string while the finger yet remains upon the key.

Ausweichen (ous'wī-kh'n), *Ger.* To make a transition from one key to another.

Ausweichung (ous'wī-khoong), *Ger.* A transient modulation, or change of key.

Autentico (ä-oo-těn'tǐ kō), *It.* Authentic.

Auteur (ō-tür), *Fr.* An author, a composer.

Authentic. A name given to those church modes whose melody was confined within the limits of the tonic, or final, and its octave.

Authentic cadence. The old name for a perfect cadence; the harmony of the dominant followed by that of the tonic, or the progression of the dominant to the tonic. See *Cadence.*

Automatic musical instruments. Those which are played by mechanism, such as the orchestrion, music-boxes, the æolian, etc.

Autor (ou-tor'), *Sp.* } An author, a com-
Autore (ä-oo-tō'rĕ), *It.* } poser.

Auxiliary notes. Tones not belonging to the chord, but accessory to it, standing one degree above or below the true harmonic tone. They are *appoggiaturas* on the beat, *passing tones* on the half beat, *suspensions* held over out of a previous chord, and *changing notes*. See *Dissonances.*

Avant-scene (ä-vänh-sän), *Fr.* Before the opening of the opera or scene.

Ave (ä-vĕ), *Lat.* Hail!

Avec (ä-vĕk), *Fr.* With.

Avec allegresse (ä-vĕk äl-lĕ-gräs), *Fr.* Lively, sprightly.

Avec ame ou gout (ä-vĕk äm oo goo), *Fr.* With feeling or grace.

Avec douleur (ä-vĕk doo-lür), *Fr.* With grief, with sadness.

Avec feu (ä-vĕk fü), *Fr.* With spirit.

Avec force (ä-vĕk fôrss), *Fr.* With power.

Avec gout (ä-vĕk goo), *Fr.* With taste.

Avec grande expression (ä-vĕk gränh dex-prä-sǐ-ônh), *Fr.* With great expression.

Avec lenteur (ä-vĕk länh-tür), *Fr.* With slowness, lingering.

Avec les pieds (ä-vĕk lĕ pē-ä), *Fr.* With the feet, in organ-playing.

Avec liaison (ä-vĕk lǐ-ä-sônh), *Fr.* With smoothness.

ä *arm*, ă *add*, ā *ale*, ĕ *end*, ē *eve*, ĭ *ill*, ī *isle*, ŏ *old*, ŏ *odd*, oo *moon*, ŭ *but*, ü *Fr. sound*, kh *Ger. ch*, un *nasal.*

Avec mouvement (ä-vĕk moov-mônh), *Fr.* With movement.

Ave Maria (ä'vĕ mä-rē'ä). *Lat.* "Hail Mary." A hymn or prayer to the Virgin Mary.

Avena (ä-vā'nä), *It.* A reed, a pipe.

A vicenda (ä vē-tshĕn'dä), *It.* Alternately, by turns.

A vide (ä vēd), *Fr.* Open.

A vista (ä vī'stä), *It.* At sight.

A voce sola (ä vō'tshĕ sō'lä), *It.* For one voice alone.

Avoir du retentissement (ä-vwär dü rä-tänh-tĕss-mônh), *Fr.* To be repeated.

Avoir le vois haut (ä-vwär' lūh vwü sō), *Fr.* To have a loud voice.

A voix forte (ä vwä fŏrt), *Fr.* With a loud voice.

A volonté (ä vŏ-lônh-tā), *Fr.* At will, at pleasure.

A vue (ä vü), *Fr.* At sight.

Azione sacra (ä-tsī-ō'nĕ sä'krä), *It.* An oratorio; a sacred musical drama.

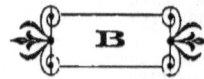

B. The name of a pitch one whole step higher than A. Also of the staff-degrees, representing B and its octaves. In Germany the name B is applied to the pitch B flat, B-natural being called H. This usage is gradually becoming obsolete.

Baazas (bä-zä), *Fr.* A species of guitar.

Babara (bä-bä'rä), *Sp.* A Spanish country dance.

Bacchanalian songs. Drinking songs; songs pertaining to drunkenness and revelry.

Bacchia. A Kamschatka dance in 2-4 time.

Bacchius (bäk'kī-oos), *Gr.* A musical foot, consisting of one short, unaccented, and two long, accented notes or syllables, marked ◡ — —.

Bacchuslied (bäkh'oos-lēd), *Ger.* A Bacchanalian song.

Bacciocolo (bät-tshī-ō-kō'lō), *It.* A musical instrument of the guitar kind, common in some parts of Tuscany.

Bachelor of Music. The first musical degree taken at the English universities. It is not conferred by German or continental universities.

Badinage (bä-dī-näzh), *Fr.* Playfulness, sportiveness.

Bagatelle (bäg-ä-tĕl'), *Fr.* A trifle, a toy, a short, easy piece of music.

Bagpipe, or, **bagpipes.** An ancient wind instrument, still in use in many countries, consisting of a leathern bag (into which the wind is conveyed through a tube, one end of which the player holds in his mouth), and from two to five pipes (on the shortest of them, the *chanter,* which has several finger-holes, the performer plays the tune; the others, the *drone,* produce each only one note, which they sustain throughout). The form and structure of this instrument vary in different countries, and even in one and the same country. Bagpipes with more than one drone pipe have the smaller drone pipes generally tuned a fifth or an octave, or one a fifth and another an octave, above the fundamental note produced by the longest pipe, two of the smaller pipes being often tuned in unison.

Baguette (bä-ghĕt'), *Fr.* A drumstick.

Baguettes de tambour (bä-ghĕt dŭh täm-boor), *Fr.* Drumsticks.

Baile (bä-ē'lĕ), *Sp.* The national dances of Spain.

Baisser (bäs-sä), *Fr.* To lower or flatten the pitch or tone.

Baisser le rideau (bäs-sä lŭh rē-dō), *Fr.* To drop the curtain.

Balalaika (bä-lä-lä'kä), *Rus.* A rude, guitar-like instrument of the Ukraine. It has three strings.

Balancé (bä-länh-sä), *Fr.* A step, or figure, in dancing.

Balancement (bäl-änhs'mänh), *Fr.* Quivering motion, a tremolo. Corresponding to the *Bebung,* a trembling of the finger, which was communicated to the strings of the violin or clavier.

Balcken, or, **Balken** (bäl'k'n), *Ger.* The bass bar placed under the fourth string in a violin.

Baldamente (bäl-dä-mĕn'tĕ), *It.* Boldly.

Baldanza (bäl-dän'tsä), *It.* } Audacity, boldness.
Baldezza (bäl-dĕt'sä),

Balg (bälgh), *Ger.* The bellows of the organ.

Bälgtreter (bälg'trĕ-tĕr), *Ger.* Organ-blower, or bellows-treader, in old German organs.

Balgzug (bälg'tsoog), *Ger.* In an organ, the bellows-stop.

Balken (bäl'k'n), *Ger.* See *Balcken.*

Ballabile (bäl-lä'bī-lĕ), *It.* In the style of a dance.

Ballad. This word is derived from *ballata* (dancing-song), which in its turn is derived from *ballare* (to dance). The popular meaning of *ballad,* in English, is "a simple song;"

the specific and more widely accepted meaning is "a lyrico-narrative poem, or the music to such a poem." Ballads have been composed for a single voice (which is the most reasonable course), for several voices, for chorus with and without accompaniment, and also for single instruments with and without accompaniment, and for orchestra.

Ballade (bäl-lä′dĕ), *Ger.* } A dance, dancing;
Ballata (bäl-lä′tä), *It.* } also a ballad.

Balladenmässig (bäl-lä d'n-mäs-sĭgh), *Ger.* After the manner of a ballad.

Balladensänger (bäl-läd'n'säng-ĕr), *Ger.* A ballad-singer.

Balladist. A writer of ballads.

Ballad of Ballads. The designation given in an old version of the Bible to Solomon's Song.

Ballad opera. Light opera; an opera in which ballads and dances predominate.

Balladry. The subject or style of ballads.

Ballad-singer. One whose employment is to sing ballads.

Ballad style. In the manner or style of a ballad.

Ballare (bäl-lä-rĕ), *It.* To dance.

Ballatella (bäl-lä tĕl′lä), } A short ballata.
Ballatetta (bäl-lä-tĕt′tä), *It.* }

Ballerina (bäl-lĕ-rē′nä), *It.* A dancing-mistress, a female dancer.

Ballerino (bäl-lĕ-rē′nō), *It.* A dancing-master, a male dancer.

Ballet (bäl-lā), *Fr.* } (1) An artistic, as
Balletto (bäl-lĕt′tō), *It.* } distinguished from a social dance, performed by several persons. (2) A kind of opera, in which there was not much of a plot, but a great deal of dancing. (3) The representation of an action by pantomime and dancing. (4) A sprightly kind of composition for several voices, which became popular at the end of the sixteenth century. As many of them had a *Fa la* burden, they were, in England, commonly called *Fa las*.

Ballet-master. The person who superintends the rehearsals of the ballet, and who frequently invents the fable and its details.

Ballete. A ballet.

Balletti (bäl-lĕt′tē), *It.* Dance airs.

Ball' (bäl′lē), *It. pl.* Dances.

Balli della stiria (bäl′lē dĕl-lä stĭ′rĭ-ä), *It. pl.* Styrian dances, resembling waltzes.

Ball' ungaresi (bäl′loon-gä-rä′zĕ), *It. pl.* Hungarian dance in 2-4 time, generally syncopated, or accented on the weak part of the measure.

Ballo (bäl′lō), *It.* A dance, or dance tune.

Ballonchio (bal-lŏn′kĭ-ō), *It.* An Italian country dance.

Band. A number of instrumental performers playing in concert on their respective instruments.

Band, brass. A band where only brass instruments are played.

Band, chamber. A band whose performances consist only of chamber music.

Band, choral. Orchestral performers.

Band, full. Where all the instruments proper to a band are employed.

Bandmaster. The leader or conductor of a band.

Bandola (bän-dō′lä), *Sp.* An instrument resembling a lute.

Bandora (bän-dō′rä), *It.* } An ancient string-
Bandore (bän-dō′rĕ), } ed instrument of the lute or zither species.

Band, reed. A band with only reed instruments.

Band, regimental. A band belonging to a regiment; a military band.

Band, string. A band with only stringed instruments.

Bandurria. (bän-door-rĭ′ä), *Sp.* A species of Spanish guitar; a bandora.

Banjo. A long-necked stringed instrument, the body of which consists of a broad hoop with a skin stretched over it. The strings, from five to nine, are variously tuned. Of great antiquity.

Bänkelsänger. (bän′k'l-säng-ĕr), *Ger.* A ballad-singer.

Bar. Lines drawn perpendicularly across the staff to show that the strong pulse immediately follows. Hence, the bar shows where the measure begins. The term bar is also inelegantly used in place of measure.

Barbarism. In music it relates to false harmony or false modulation.

Barbiton (bär′bĭ-tŏn), *Gr.* A name formerly applied to the viol and violin.

Barbitos (bär′bĭ-lōs). *Lat.* An ancient instrument of the lyre species.

Barcarola (bär-kä-rō′lä), *It.* } A song or air
Barcarolle (bär-kä-rōl′), *Fr.* } sung by the Venetian gondoliers, or boatmen, while following their avocations.

Barcaruola (bär′kä-roo-ō′lä), *It.* The song of the gondolier. A barcarole.

Bard. A poet and singer among the ancient Celts. The bard was a person of great importance, and received great attention from high and low.

Bardd alan (bärd ä-län), *Wel.* A professor of music.

Bardone (bär-dō′nĕ), *It.* See *Bourdon.*

Bar. A line drawn across the staff to show the place of the strong accent, which is always upon the time-space immediately following, and hence to show the division of measures. The measure itself, and the space between the bars, is sometimes called

ä *arm,* ă *add,* ā *ale,* ĕ *end,* ē *eve,* ĭ *ill,* ī *isle,* ō *old,* ŏ *odd,* oo *moon,* ŭ *but,* ü *Fr. sound,* kh *Ger. ch,* nh *nasal.*

a bar, but improperly. The name bar means simply the line, and its office is to indicate the place of the strong accent. A very heavy mark called Double Bar is used in psalmody to indicate the end of phrases and lines of poetry, and in instrumental music sometimes to indicate the end of a strain. When accompanied by dots upon the left or right, the strain upon that side is to be repeated. Double bars sometimes serve to mark the measure, and sometimes are inserted in the middle of a measure. There is no rule upon this subject. Bars did not come into more general use till about the middle of the seventeenth century. In scores they are to be met with centuries before that time, but for the most part only in theoretical books, as it was not then the custom to print compositions in score. With the rise of the monodic style in Italy, towards the end of the sixteenth century, bars came to the fore, as the publications with a *basso continuo* prove. The systems of notation called Tablature have almost always made use of bars.

Barem (bä-rĕm′), *Ger.* A stopped register, of soft 8 or 16 feet tone, in German organs.

Bärentanz (bär′ĕn-tăntz), *Ger.* Bear dance. Imitating the primitive music of the peasant, with shrill piccolo and drum.

Bari. An abbreviation of Baritone.

Baribasso. A deep baritone voice.

Bariolage (bär-ĭ-ō-läzh), *Fr.* A passage for the violin, etc., in which the open strings are more especially used.

Baritenor. The deeper sort of tenor voice.

Bariton (bä-rĭ-tônh′), *Fr.* } (1) The
Baritono (bä-rē′tō-nō), *It.* } male
Baritone, *or,* **baryton,** *or,* **barytone.** } voice
which is higher in pitch than the bass and lower than the tenor, and participates to some extent in the character of both. Its usual compass is from a to f′. (2) A brass instrument with valves, having a compass of three octaves, from b♭ to b′♭, or from c to c″. (3) The *viola di bordone* (or *bardone*), a stringed instrument which went out of use in the second half of the eighteenth century. It had six or seven catgut strings above the fingerboard, which were played with the bow, and from eight to twenty-seven wire strings below the fingerboard, which were plucked and sounded sympathetically with the upper ones. (4) The word *barytone* is often used as an epithet to indicate an instrument related to other instruments as the barytone voice to other voices.

Baritone clef. The F clef on the third line of the stave. It is now no longer used.

Baritono (bä-rĭ-tō′nō), *It.* Baritone.

Barocco (bä-rŏk′kō), *It.* } A term applied to
Baroque (bä-rōk), *Fr.* } music in which the harmony is confused and abounding in unnatural modulations.

Bärpfeife (bär′pfī-fĕ), *Ger.* Bear pipe; an obsolete reed-stop of soft intonation.

Barra (bär′rä), *It.* A bar line; a bar.

Barrage (bär-räzh′), *Fr.* See *Barré*.

Barre (bär), *Fr.* A bar in music.

Barré (bär-rä), *Fr.* In guitar-playing, a temporary nut, formed by placing the forefinger of the left hand across some of the strings.

Barred C. C with a bar across it; one of the marks of alla breve measure, thus, ₵

Barre de luth (bär dŭh loot), *Fr.* The bridge of the lute.

Barre de mesure (bär dŭh mĕ-zür), *Fr.* A bar line.

Barre de répétition (bär dŭh rā-pā-tĭ-sĭ-ônh), *Fr.* A dotted double bar; also, a thick line used as an abbreviation to mark the repetition of a group of notes.

Barrel. The body of a bell.

Barrel chime. The cylindrical portion of the mechanism sometimes used for the purpose of ringing a chime of bells.

Barrel organ. An organ in which the keys which give the wind access to the pipes are acted upon by pins (staples) fixed on a cylinder, which is made to revolve by turning a handle. This turning of the handle also sets the wind-producing mechanism in motion. The same principle has also been applied to small church organs, for the advantage of small parishes unable to hire an organist. The cylinders, each pegged for a certain number of tunes, are bought and renewed as wanted.

Barrer. The act of employing the forefinger of the left hand as a nut in guitar-playing.

Barrer, great. The act of pressing all the strings of the guitar at the same time, with the forefinger of the left hand.

Barrer, small. The act of pressing two or three strings of a guitar with the forefinger of the left hand.

Barrure (bär-rür), *Fr.* The bar of a lute, etc.

Baryphonus (bä-rĭ-fō′noos). A man with a very deep or very coarse voice.

Barz (bärz), *Wel.* A poet-musician, a bard.

Bas (bäh), *Fr.* Low.

Bas dessus (bäh dŭs-sĕ), *Fr.* A mezzo-soprano, or second-treble voice.

Base. } The lowest, or deepest, male voice;
Bass. } the lowest part in a musical composition.

Basilica (bä-zēl′ĭ-kä), *It.* A cathedral.

Bassa (bäs′sä), *It.* Low, deep; 8va bassa, play the notes an octave lower.

Bass alberti. A bass formed by taking the notes of chords in arpeggios.

Bassanello (bäs-sä-nĕl′lō), *It.* An obsolete musical instrument.

Bassa ottava (bäs′sä ōt-tä′vä), *It.* Play the passage an octave lower than written.

Bass beam. A thin strip of wood glued inside the viol, nearly under the bass string.

Bassbläser (bäss′blä-z'r), *Ger.* A bassoonist.

Bass chantante (bäs shänh-tänht), *Fr.* The vocal bass.

Bass clarinet. A clarinet an octave lower than the B-flat clarinet.

Bass clef. The bass, or F clef, placed upon the fourth line.

Bass concertina. A concertina having the compass of a violoncello.

Bass, continued. Bass continued through the whole piece; the figured bass.

Basse (bäss), *Fr.* The bass part.

Basse chantante (bäss shänh-tänht), *Fr.* Vocal bass. See *Bass chantante*.

Basse chiffree (bäss shēf-frā), *Fr.* A figured bass.

Basse continue (bäss kônh-tē-nü), *Fr.* Thorough bass. Figured bass.

Basse contrainte (bäss kônh-tränht), *Fr.* The constrained, or ground bass.

Basse contre (bäss kôntr), *Fr.* Bass counter, double bass; also, the deep bass voice, called by the Italians *basso profondo*.

Basse de cromorne (bäss dŭh krō-morn) (also written **cremorne**), *and* **Basse de hautbois** (bäss dŭh hō-bwä), *Fr.* Old French names for the bassoon, but also the names of the lowest members of the oboe and cromorne families.

Basse figurée (bäss fī-gü-rā), *Fr.* The figured bass.

Basse fondamentale (bäss fônh-dä-mänh-täl), *Fr.* The fundamental bass.

Basse taille (bäss tällyĕ), *Fr.* Baritone voice; low tenor voice.

Basset horn. A variously bent and constructed instrument of the clarinet family, no longer used by composers. It is said to have been invented in 1770. Its compass extends from f to c‴.

Bassett. A little bass, generally somewhat higher than the usual bass.

Bassetto (bäs-sĕt′tō), *It.* The little bass; also an obsolete instrument with four strings; also an 8 or 16-feet reed-stop in an organ.

Bass, figured. A bass figured, or accompanied by numerals, denoting the harmony to be played by the other parts of the composition.

Bass, first. High bass.

Bassflöte (bäss flĕ-tĕ), *Ger.* } An old instrument of the bassoon species; also the name of an organ stop on the pedal, of 8-feet tone.
Bass flute.

Bass, fundamental. The bass which contains the roots of the chords only. This bass is not intended to be played, but serves as a test of the correctness of the harmony.

Bassgeige (bäss′ghī-ghĕ), *Ger.* Bass viol; the contrabasso.

Bass, given. A bass to which harmony is to be placed.

Bass, high. A baritone, a voice midway between bass and tenor.

Bass horn. An instrument resembling the ophicleide, formerly much used in bands.

Bassi (bäs′sē), *It.* A term implying the entrance of the brass instruments.

Bassist (bäs-sĭst′), *Ger.* } A bass-singer.
Bassista (bäs-sĭs′tä), *It.* }

Bass, low. Second bass.

Basso (bäs′sō), *It.* The bass part.

Basso buffo (bäs′sō boof′fō), *It.* The principal bass-singer in the comic opera.

Basso cantante (bäs′sō kän-tän′tē), *It.* The vocal bass part; also the principal bass-singer in an opera.

Basso comico (bäs′sō kō′mĭ-kō), *It.* A comic bass-singer in an opera.

Basso concertante (bäs′sō kŏn-tshĕr-tän-tĕ), *It.* The principal bass; also the lighter and more delicate parts performed by the violoncello, or bassoon.

Basso construtto (bäs′sō kōn-stroot′tō), *It.* Ground bass, constrained bass.

Basso continuo (bäs′sō kōn-tē′noo-ō), *It.* The continued bass; a bass that is figured to indicate the harmony.

Basso contra (bäs′sō kōn-trä), *It.* } A double bass viol;
Basso contro (bäs′sō kōn′trō), *It.* } the lowest or gravest part of a musical composition.

Bass oder F Schlüssel (bäss ō′dĕr F shlüs′s'l), *Ger.* The bass, or F clef.

Basso d' accompagnamento (bäs′sō däk-kŏm-pän-yä-mĕn′tō), *It.* An accompanying bass.

Basso figurato (bäs′sō fī-goo-rä′tō), *It.* The figured bass.

Basso fondamentale (bäs′sō fōn-dä-mĕn-tä′lĕ), *It.* The fundamental bass.

Basson (bäs-sônh), *Fr.* Bassoon.

Basson quart (bäs′sônh kär), *Fr.* An instrument whose tones are a fourth lower than the ordinary bassoon.

Basson quinte (bäs′sônh kănht), *Fr.* A small bassoon of the same compass as the ordinary bassoon, but the tones are a fifth higher.

Basso numerato (bäs′sō noo-mĕ-rä′tō), *It.* Figured bass.

Bassoon. A wind instrument with a double-reed mouthpiece, invented about 1539, and since then much improved. The Italian name, *fagotto* (fagot, bundle of sticks), describes somewhat its outward appearance. Its usual compass extends from b♭ to b′♭; its extreme upper limit is e″♭. Music for the bassoon is written in the bass and tenor clefs, the latter clef being used for the higher notes. It is not very agreeable as a solo instrument, but indispensable in full orchestra. The lower tones are strong and rough, but the middle rich and pleasing.

Bassoonist. A performer on the bassoon.

Bassoon stop. A reed-stop in the organ which imitates the tones of the bassoon.

Basso ostinato (bäs'sō ōs-tĭ-nä'tō), *It.* A constantly recurring bass theme, forming the foundation of a polyphonic composition (chaconne, passacaglia, etc.).

Basso primo (bäs'sō prē'mo), *It.* The first bass.

Basso ripieno (bäs'sō rĭ-pĭ-ā'nō), *It.* A bass part only intended to be played in the full or tutti passages.

Basso rivoltato (bäs'sō rĭ-vōl-tä'tō), *It.* An inverted bass.

Basso secondo (bäs'sō sĕ-kōn'dō), *It.* The second bass. The lower bass.

Basso tenuto (bäs'sō tĕ-noo'tō), *It.* Continued bass.

Basso violino (bäs'sō vē-ō-lē'nō), *It.* A small bass viol.

Basspfeife (bäss pfī-fĕ), *Ger.* Basspipe, bassoon.

Basspommer (bäss'pŏm-m'r), *Ger.* The lowest member of the pommer family. See *Pommer*.

Bassposaune (bäss'pō-zou-nĕ, *Ger.* Bass trombone, sackbut.

Basssaite (bäss'sī-tĕ), *Ger.* Bass string.

Bassschlüssel (bäss'shlüss-s'l), *Ger.* The bass clef.

Bass staff. The staff marked with the bass clef.

Bassstimme (bäss'stĭm-mĕ), *Ger.* Bass voice, bass part.

Bass string. The string of any instrument upon which the lowest note is sounded.

Bass trombone. A trombone having a compass from the great c to the one-lined c, and noted in the F clef.

Bass tuba (bäss too-bä), *Lat.* See *Tuba*.

Bass viol. An old name for the viol da gamba, now often given to the violoncello.

Bass viol, double. A stringed instrument, the largest and deepest toned of its class.

Bass voice. The lowest or deepest of male voices.

Basszeichen (bäss'tsī-kh'n), *Ger.* The bass clef.

Basta (bäs'tä), *It.* } Enough, sufficient;
Bastante (bäs-tän'tĕ), *It.* } proceed no further unless directed by the conductor.

Bastardilla (bäs-tär-dēl'yä), *Sp.* A species of flute.

Batillus (bä-tĭl'loos), *Lat.* An instrument used by the Armenians in their church service in the place of bells. A board struck with a hammer.

Battement (bät-mŏuh'), *Fr.* } An old name
Battimento (bät-tĭ-měn'tō), *It.* } for that kind of short shake called a beat.

Battere (bät'tĕ-rĕ), *It.* The down stroke in beating time.

Batterie (bät-trē), *Fr.* The roll of the drum; also, a particular way of playing the guitar by striking the strings instead of pulling them.

Baton (bä-tōnh'),
Baton de mesure (bä-tōnh' dŭh mĕ-zür), *Fr.* } The stick used by the conductor in beating time.

Battre (bätr), *Fr.* To beat.

Battre la caisse (bätr lä käss),
Battre le tambour (bätr lŭh tämboor), *Fr.* } To beat the drums.

Battre la mesure (bätr lä mĕ-zür), *Fr.* To beat time; to mark the time by beating with the hand or with a stick.

Bau (bou), *Ger.* The structure, the fabric, the construction of musical instruments.

Bäuerisch (by'ĕr-ish), *Ger.* Rustic, coarse.

Bauernflöte (bou'ĕrn-flĕ-tĕ), *Ger.* Rustic flute; a stopped register in an organ.

Bauernlied (bou'ĕrn-lēd), *Ger.* A rustic ballad.

B cancellatum (B kän-tsĕl-lä'toom), *Lat.* The old name for a sharp (♯).

B, double. The b below G gamut; the twelfth below the bass-clef note.

B-dur (Bā-door), *Ger.* The key of B♭ major.

B durum (B doo'room), *Lat.* B *hard* or B major.

Bearbeitet (bĕ-är'bī-tĕt), *Ger.* Adapted, arranged.

Bearbeitung (bĕ-är'bī-toong), *Ger.* Adaptation.

Bearing notes. In tuning instruments those erroneous, or falsely tempered fifths, on which "the wolf" is said to be thrown.

Bearpipe. See *Bärpfeife*.

Beat. The rise or fall of the hand or baton in marking the divisions of time in music. These motions, in the different varieties of measure, take the following directions: *Double*, down, up; *Triple*, down, left, up; *Quadruple*, down, left, right, up; *Sextuple*, down, down, left, right, up, up. An important musical embellishment, consisting of the principal note and the note *below* it, resembling a short trill; also the pulsation arising from the interference of two series of vibrations slightly differing in pitch. The number of beats per second will be equal to the number of vibrations in which one series exceeds the other.

Beatings. Regular pulsations produced in an organ by pipes of the same key when they are not exactly in unison.

ä *arm*, ă *add*, ā *ale*, ĕ *end*, ē *eve*, ĭ *ill*, ī *isle*, ō *old*, ŏ *odd*, oo *moon*, ŭ *but*, ü *Fr. sound*, kh *Ger. ch*, nh *nasal*.

Beating time. Marking the divisions of the bar by means of the hand, foot, or baton.

Beben (bā'b'n), *Ger.* To tremble, to shake, to vibrate.

Bebende Stimme (bā'bĕn-dĕ stim'mĕ), *Ger.* A trembling voice.

Bebung (bā'boong), *Ger.* A shaking, a vibration. On the clavier, a tremolo made by vibrating the finger upon the key. (Impracticable upon the pianoforte.) Also, a German organ-stop.

Bec (bĕk), *Fr.* The mouthpiece of a clarinet.

Bécarre (bā-kăr), *Fr.* The mark called a natural (♮).

Becco (bĕk'kō), *It.* The mouthpiece of a clarinet, flageolet, etc.

Becco polacco (băk'kō pō-lăk'kō), *It.* A species of large bagpipe used in some parts of Italy.

Becken (bĕk'n), *Ger.* A cymbal.

Bedeckt (bĕ-dĕkt), *Ger.* Covered, stopped. Said of strings, in contradistinction to *leer*, open. Also of stopped pipes.

Bedon (bĕ-dŏuh'), *Fr.* An old name for a tabret, or drum.

Be (bā), *Ger.* Flat, B♭.

Beffroi (bĕf-frwä'), *Fr.* The frame that supports the bell in a belfry; a belfry. The tamtam.

Begeisterung (bĕ-ghis'tĕ-roong), *Ger.* Inspiration, animation, enthusiasm.

Begl. An abbreviation of Begle tung.

Begleiten (bĕ-gli't'n), *Ger.* To accompany.

Begleitende Stimmen (bĕ-gli'tĕn-dĕ stim'měn), *Ger. pl.* The accompanying parts.

Begleitung (bĕ-gli'toong), *Ger.* An accompaniment.

Beharrlich (bĕ-härr'lĭkh), *Ger.* Perseveringly.

Beherzt (bĕ-härtst'), *Ger.* Courageous.

Beisp. An abbreviation of Beispiel.

Beispiel (bi'spĕl), *Ger.* Example.

Beisser (bīs's'r), *Ger.* A mordent.

Beitöne (bi'tĕ-nĕ), *Ger.* Accessory tones.

Beizeichen (bi'tsi-kh'n), *Ger.* An accidental.

Belfry. A tower in which a bell or bells are hung.

Belieben (bĕ-lē'b'n), *Ger.* Pleasure; at pleasure.

Beliebig (bĕ-lē'bĭg), *Ger.* To one's liking, or pleasure.

Béliere (bā-lĭ-ār'), *Fr.* The tongue of a bell.

Bell. A vessel, or hollow body, of cast metal, used for making sounds. It consists of a barrel, or hollow body, enlarged or expanded at one end, an ear, or cannon, by which it is hung to a beam, and a clapper inside. (2) A hollow body of metal, perforated, and containing a solid ball to give sounds when shaken. (3) The wide, circular opening at the end of a trumpet, horn, and similar instruments.

Bella (bĕl'lä), *Sax.* A bell.

Bell-chamber. That portion of the tower or steeple in which the bell hangs; the belfry.

Bell diapason (di-ä-pā'sŏn). An organ diapason stop of clear and sonorous voice.

Bellezza (bĕl-lĕt'sä), *It.* Beauty of tone and expression.

Bellezza della voce (bĕl-lĕt'sä dĕl'lä vō'tshĕ). *It.* Beauty or sweetness of voice.

Bell gamba. A gamba stop in an organ, the top of each pipe spreading out like a bell.

Bell harp. An old instrument, probably the lyra or cithera of the ancients. (2) A stringed instrument, so named from its being swung like a bell when played.

Bellicosamente (bĕl-lĭ-kō-zä-mĕn'tĕ), *It.* In a martial and warlike style.

Bellicoso (bĕl-lĭ-kō-zō),

Bellicum (bĕl'lĭ-koom), *Lat.* The sound of a trumpet calling to battle.

Bell metronome. A metronome with a small bell that strikes at the beginning of each bar.

Bellows. A pneumatic appendage for supplying organ-pipes with air.

Bellows, exhaust. A kind of bellows used on organs and other reed instruments; the air, when the chamber is exhausted, being drawn in through the reeds.

Bell-ringers. Performers who, with bells of different sizes, ranging from smallest to largest, are able to produce very pleasing and effective music.

Bell-scale. A diapason with which bell-founders measure the size, thickness, weight, and tone of their bells.

Belly. The soundboard of an instrument, that part over which the strings are distended.

Bel metallo di voce (bĕl mĕ-täl'lō dĕ vō'tshĕ), *It.* A clear and brilliant voice.

Bemerkbar (bĕ-märk'bär), *Ger.* Observable, marked; to be played in a prominent manner.

Bémol (bā-mŏl), *Fr.* The mark called a

Bemolle (bā-mŏl'lĕ), *It.* flat (♭).

Bemolise (bā-mō-lēz), *Fr.* Marked with a flat.

Bemolisée (bĕ-mō-lĭ-zä'), *Fr.* A note preceded by a flat.

Bemoliser (bĕ-mō-lĭ-zä'), *Fr.* To flat.

Bemollizzare (bĕ-mŏl'lĭ-tsä'rĕ), *It.* ten notes; to lower the pitch by putting a flat before them.

Ben (bĕn), *It.* Well, good.

Bene (bā'nĕ),

Benedicite (bĕn-ĕ-dī'tsĭ-tĕ), *Lat.* A canticle used at morning prayer, in the church, after the first lesson.

Benedictus (bĕn'ĕ'dĭc'toos), *Lat.* "Blessed is He that cometh." Second part of the Sanctus, which forms the fourth part of the Mass.

Bene placito (bā'nĕ plā'tshī-tō), *It.* At will, at pleasure, at liberty to retard the time and ornament the passage.

Ben marcato (bĕn mär-kä'tō), } *It.* Well
Bene marcato (bā-nĕ mär-kä'tō), } marked, in a distinct and strongly accented manner.

Ben marcato il canto (bĕn mär-kä'tō Il kün'tō), *It.* Mark well the melody.

Ben moderato (bĕn mŏ-dĕ-rä'tō), *It.* Very moderate time.

Ben pronunciato (bĕn prō-noon-tshä'tō), } *It.*
Ben pronunziato (bĕn prō-noon-tsī-ä'tō), } Pronounced clearly and distinctly.

Ben tenuto (bĕn tĕ-noo tō), *It.* Held on; fully sustained.

Be quadro (bā kwä'drō), *It.* } The mark called
Bé quarré (bā kär-rā), *Fr.* } a natural (♮).

Bequem (bĕ-quäm'), *Ger.* Convenient.

Berceuse (bĕr-süss), *Fr.* A cradle-song.

Bergamasca (bĕr-gä-mäs'kä), *It.* A kind of rustic dance.

Bergeret (bĕr-jĕ-rĕt'), *It.* An old term signifying a song.

Bergomask. A rustic dance. See *Bergamasca.*

Bergreigen (bärg'rī-ghĕn), *Ger.* Alpine melody.

Berlingozza (bĕr-lĭn-gōt'sä), *It.* A country dance.

Berloque (bĕr-lōk), *Fr.* In military service, the drum calling to meals.

Bes (bĕs), *Ger.* The note B-double-flat, B♭♭.

Besaiten (bĕ-sī't'n), *Ger.* To string an instrument.

Beschleunigend (bĕ-shloi'nĭ-gĕnd), *Ger.* Hastening.

Beschreibung (bĕ-shrī'boong), *Ger.* A description.

Befiedern (bĕ-fĕ'dĕrn), *Ger.* To quill a harpsichord.

Besingen (bĕ-sĭng'ĕn), *Ger.* To sing, to celebrate in song.

Bestimmt (bĕ-stĭmt), *Ger.* Distinct.

Bestimmtheit (bĕ-stĭmt'hīt), *Ger.* Precision, certainty.

Betglocke (bĕht'glŏk-ĕ), *Ger.* Prayer-bell.

Betonend (bĕ-tō'neud), *Ger.* } Accented.
Betont (bĕ-tōut), *Ger.* }

Betonung (bĕ-tō'noong), *Ger.* Accentuation.

Betrübniss (bĕ trüb'nĭss), *Ger.* Grief, sadness.

Betrübt (bĕ-trübt'), *Ger.* Afflicted, grieved.

Beweglich (bĕ-wä'glĭkh), *Ger.* Movable.

Bewegt (bĕ-wägt), *Ger.* Moved, rather fast.

Bewegung (bĕ-wä'goong), *Ger.* Motion, movement.

Beyspiel (bī'spĕl), *Ger.* An example.

Bezeichnung (bĕ-tsīkh'noong), *Ger.* Mark, accentuation.

Bezifferte Bass (bĕ-tsĭf'fĕr-tĕ bäss), *Ger.* The figured bass.

B-flat. The flat seventh of the key of C.

Bianca (bē-än'kä), *It.* A minim, or half note.

Bichord (bē'kŏrd), *Lat.* A term applied to instruments that have two strings to each note.

Bien attaquer une note (bī-änh ät-täk-ä ün nŏt), *Fr.* To strike a note firmly.

Bimmolle (bĭm-mŏl'lĕ), *It.* The mark called a flat (♭).

B in alt (bē ĭn ält), *It.* The third in alt; the tenth above the treble-clef note.

B in altissimo (bē ĭn äl-tĕs'sĭ-mō), *It.* The third note in altissimo; the octave above b in alt.

Binary measure (bī-nä-ry). Common time of two in a bar.

Bind. A tie uniting two notes on the same degree of the staff.

Binde (bĕn'dĕ), *Ger.* A tie or bind.

Binding notes. Notes held together by the tie or bind.

Bindung (bĭn'doong), *Ger.* Connection.

Bindungszeichen (bĭn'doong-tsī'kh'n), *Ger.* A tie, or bind.

Biquadro (bĕ-kwä'drō), *It.* A natural (♮).

Bird organ. A small organ used in teaching birds to sing.

Birne (bēr'nĕ), *Ger.* The mouthpiece of the clarinet.

Bis (bĭs), *Lat.* Twice; indicating that the passage marked is to be repeated.

Biscanto (bĭs-kän'tō), *It.* A kind of duet; where two are singing.

Bischero (bĭs'kĕ rō), *It.* A peg of a violin, violoncello, or similar instrument; the pin of any instrument.

Biscroma (bĭs-krō'mä), *It.* } A semi-quaver,
Biscrome (bĭs krōm'), *Fr.* } or sixteenth note.

Bis diapason (bĭs dī-ä-pä'sŏn), *Lat.* A double octave, or fifteenth; a compass of two octaves.

Biseau (bī-zō'), *Fr.* The stopper of an organ-pipe to make the tone sharper or flatter.

Bisinia (bī-sē'nĭ-ä), *Lat.* A term applied to a pianoforte passage where the notes played by one hand are regularly repeated by the other.

Bisinium (bī-sē'nĭ-oom), *Lat.* A composition in two parts; a duet, or two-part song.

Bis unca (bĭs oou'kä), *Lat.* An old name for a semiquaver.

Risser (bis-sĕ), *Fr.* To redemand.

Bissex (bĭs sĕx'), *Lat.* A species of guitar, with twelve strings.

Bitterkeit (bĭt'tĕr-kīt), *Ger.* Bitterness.

Bizzarramente (ĕt-sär-rä-mĕn'tĕ), *It.* Oddly, in a whimsical style.

Bizzarria (bĕt-sär-rē'ä), *It.* Written in a capricious, fantastic style; sudden, unexpected modulations.
Bizzarro (bĕt-sar'ro), *It.* Whimsical, odd, fantastical.
Bianche (blänsh), *Fr.* A minim, or half note.
Blanche pointée (blänsh pwänh-tā'), *Fr.* 𝄾. A dotted half note.
Blasebalg (blä'sĕ-bälg), *Ger.* The bellows of an organ.
Blasehorn (blä'zĕ-hōrn), *Ger.* Bugle horn, hunter's horn.
Blasemusik (blä'zĕ-moo'zĕk'), *Ger.* Music for wind instruments.
Blasen (blä'z'n), *Ger.* To blow; to sound.
Bläser (blä'z'r), *Ger.* A blower; an instrument for blowing.
Blasinstrument (bläz'in-stroo-ment'), *Ger.* A wind instrument.
Blast. The sudden blowing of a trumpet or other instrument of a similar character.
Blatant. Bleating, bellowing.
Blatt (blätt), *Ger.* A leaf; a reed. The single reed of the clarinet and of the basset horn.
Blechinstrumente (blĕkh'in-stroo-mĕn'tĕ), *Ger.* The brass instruments, as trumpets, trombones, etc.
Blockflöte (blŏk'flŏ-tĕ), *Ger.* An organ-stop, composed of large scale-pipes, the tone of which is full and broad.
Blower, organ. One who works the bellows of an organ.
Bluette. A short, brilliant piece.
B-mol (bā-mōl), *Fr.* The character called a flat (♭). See *Bemol*.
B-moll (bē-mōl), *Ger.* The key of B♭ minor.
Board. A term applied to several different members among musical instruments, as, Fingerboard, upon which the fingers act; Soundboard, which vibrates in the pianoforte, or upon which the pipes are placed in the organ; Keyboard, the keys, etc.
Boat-songs. Gondolier-songs.
Bocal (bō'käl), *Fr.* } The mouthpiece of a
Bocca (bŏk'kä), *It.* } horn, trumpet, trombone, and similar instruments.
Bocca ridente (bŏk'kä rī-ren'tĕ), *It.* "Smiling mouth." A term in singing, applied to a peculiar opening of the mouth, approaching to a smile, believed to be conducive to the production of a pure tone.
Bocchino (bŏk-kē'nō), *It.* Mouthpiece of a horn.
Bocina (bō-thē'nä), *Sp.* A species of large trumpet; a bugle horn.
Bocina de cazador (bō-thē'nä dĕ kä-thä-dōr'), *Sp.* A huntsman's horn.
Bockpfeife (bŏk'pfī-fĕ), *Ger.* A bagpipe.
Bockstriller (bŏks'trĭl-lĕr), *Ger.* A bad shake, with false intonation.

Boden (bō'd'n), *Ger.* The back of a violin, viola etc.
Boehm Flöte. A flute of improved mechanism, invented in 1834 by Theobald Boehm. The improvement consists of a series of keys by means of which the fingering is simplified and the different tonalities are more nearly equal in facility. The same system has also been applied to the oboes and clarinets.
Bogen (bō'g'n), *Ger.* The bow of a violin, etc.
Bogenführung (bō'g'n-fü-roong), *Ger.* The management of the bow; the act of bowing.
Bogeninstrumente (bō'g'n-in-stroo-mĕn-tĕ), *Ger.* Bow instruments; instruments played with a bow.
Bogenstrich (bō'g'n-strĭkh), *Ger.* A stroke of the bow.
Bolero (bō-lā'rō), *Sp.* A lively Spanish dance, in 3-4 time, with castanets.
Bomb. A stroke upon a bell; to sound.
Bombarde (bŏnh-bärd'), *Fr.* } A powerful
Bombardo (bŏm-bär'dō), *It.* } reed-stop in an organ of 16-feet scale; also an old wind instrument of the hautboy species.
Bombardon (bŏm-bär'dŏn), *Ger.* A large bass wind instrument of brass, with valves something like the ophicleide. The bombardon was originally a very deep bassoon, now obsolete. The name is also applied to an organ-stop, a 16-feet reed.
Bombix (bŏm'bĭx), *Gr.* An ancient Greek instrument, formed of a long reed or tube.
Bonang (bō-näng'), *Jav.* A Javanese instrument, consisting of a series of gongs placed in two lines on a frame.
Bones. A name sometimes given to castanets; castanets made of bone.
Bons temps de la mesure (bŏnh tŏnh dŭh lä mĕ-sür'), *Fr.* The accented parts of a measure.
Bora (bō'rä), *Tur.* A tin trumpet used by the Turkish military.
Bordone (bōr-dō'nĕ), *It.* } An organ-stop.
Bourdon (boor-dŏnh), *Fr.* } the pipes of which are stopped or covered, and produce the 16-feet, and sometimes the 32-feet tone; also a drone bass. A stopped diapason.
Bordun. See *Bourdon*.
Bordone falso (bōr-dō'nĕ fäl-zō), *It.* A term formerly used for harmony having a drone bass, or one of the other parts continuing in the same pitch.
Bordun Flöte (bōr'doon flŏ'tĕ), *Ger.* An organstop. See *Bordone*.
Bourdon de cornemuse (boor-dŏnh dŭh kōrnmüz), *Fr.* The drone of a bagpipe.
Bourdon de musette (boor-dŏnh dŭh mü-zĕt), *Fr.* The drone of a bagpipe.
Boudoir piano (boo-dwär). An upright piano.
Bouffe (boof), *Fr.* A buffoon.

ă *arm*, ă *add*, ā *ale*, ĕ *end*, ē *eve*, ĭ *ill*, ī *isle*, ō *old*, ŏ *odd*, oo *moon*, ŭ *but*, ü *Fr. sound*, kh *Ger. ch*, nh *nasal*.

Bourree (boor-rā), *Fr.* A step in dancing. A lively old French dance in 4-4 or 2-4 time. The second and fourth quarters of the measure divided.

Boutade (boo-täd), *Fr.* An instrumental piece like a caprice or fantasia. (2) An old French dance. (3) A kind of short ballet, which was performed as if the performers set about it impromptu.

Bow. An instrument consisting of an elastic wooden rod and a number of horsehairs stretched from the bent head to the movable nut. It is used in playing on the violin and many other stringed instruments which are made to sound by friction, the bow being drawn over the strings and setting them in vibration. Its present length is from twenty-seven to thirty inches, but formerly it was shorter.

Bowhair. Hair used in making the bows of violins, violoncellos, etc.; it is usually horsehair.

Bowhand. The right hand; the hand which holds the bow.

Bowing. The art of using the bow, playing with the bow.

Bow instruments. All instruments whose tones are produced by the bow.

Boyaudier (bŏ-yō-dĭ-ā′), *Fr.* A maker of violin-strings.

Boy choir. A choir of boys, from eight to fourteen years of age. Such organizations are confined mostly to Episcopal and Catholic churches.

B quadratum (bā kwä-drü′toom), *Lat.*
B quadrum (bā kwä′droom), } An old name for the natural (♮); formerly this was applied to the note b.

Brace. A character, curved or straight, used to connect the different staves.

Brachygraphy, musical. The art of writing music in shorthand, by means of signs, characters, etc.

Braccio (brü′tshĭ-ō), *It.* A term applied to the violin and other instruments of a similar character that are held up to the neck with the left hand and played with a bow.

Branches. Those parts of a trumpet that conduct the wind.

Bran de Inglaterra (brän dĕ ĕn-glä-tĕr′rä), *Sp.* An old Spanish dance. Evidently the English Brawl.

Branle (bränhl), *Fr.* A lively old dance, performed in a circle.

Bransle (bränhsl), *Fr.* An old dance, slow, and resembling the Alman.

Brass band. A number of performers whose instruments are exclusively brass.

Brass instrument. Wind instruments made of brass, and used chiefly for field service.

Bratsche (brä′tshĕ), *Ger.* The viola, or tenor violin.

Bratschen (brä′tshĕn), *Ger.* Violas.

Bratschenspieler (brä′tshĕn-spē′lĕr), *Ger.* Violist; one who plays on the viola.

Bratschenstimme (brä′tshĕn-stĭm′mĕ), *Ger.* The viol part of any composition.

Brautlied (brout′lēd), *Ger.* A bridal hymn, a wedding-song.

Brautmesse (brout′mĕs-sĕ), *Ger.* Music before the wedding ceremony; the ceremony itself.

Brava (brä′vä), *fem.*
Bravi (brä′vē), *pl.* } An exclamation of approval, often
Bravo (brä′vō), *mas.* } used in theaters; excellent, very good, etc.

Bravissima (brä-vĭs′sĭ-mä), *fem.*
Bravissimi (brä-vĭs′sĭ-mē), *pl. It.* } Exceedingly
Bravissimo (brä-vĭs′sĭ-mō), *mas.* } good, exceedingly well done.

Bravour-arie (brä-voor′ä′rĭ-ō), *Ger.* An aria di bravura.

Bravura (brä-voo′rä), *It.* Spirit, skill, requiring great dexterity and skill in execution.

Bravura, con (brä-voo′rä kōn), *It.* With spirit and boldness of execution.

Bravura mezza (brä-voo′rä mĕt-sä), *It.* A song requiring a moderate degree of skill.

Brawl. } A shaking or swinging motion.
Brawle. } (2) An old round dance in which the performers joined hands in a circle; the balls were usually opened with it.

Bray. The harsh sound of a trumpet or similar instrument.

Brazen instruments. Brass instruments.

Brazzo (brät′sō), *It.* Instruments played with a bow.

Breit (brīt), *Ger.* Broad.

Breloque (brĕ-lŏk′), *Fr.* In military service, the call of a drum for breakfast or dinner.

Bretador (brā-tä-dōr), *Sp.* A bird-call.

Brettgeige (brĕt′ghī-ghĕ), *Ger.* A small pocket fiddle.

Breve (brā′vĕ), *It.* Short; formerly the breve was the shortest note. The notes then used were the large, the long, and the breve. The breve is now the longest note; it is equal to two semibreves, or whole notes. (2) A double note. *Alla breve*, to the breve, i. e., a half-note to each beat. A rather quick movement, formerly much used in church music.

Breve rest. A rest equal in duration to a breve, or double note.

Breviario (brĕ-vĭ-ä′rĭ-ō), *It.* A breviary.

Breviary. A book containing the matins, lauds, and vespers of the Catholic Church.

Brevis (brĕ′vĭs), *Lat.* A breve.

Bridge. A piece of wood on which the strings of stringed instruments rest, and which it self rests on the resonance-box or resonance-board (soundbox or soundboard), to which it transmits the vibrations of the strings.

Brief. An upright piece of wood, over which the strings of a bass viol are drawn.

Brill. An abbreviation of Brillante.

Brillante (bril-län'tē), *It.* } Bright, spark-
Brillante (brē-yäubt'), *Fr.* } ling, brilliant.
Brillare (bril-lä'rē), *It.* To play or sing in a brilliant style.
Brillenbässe (bril-l'n bäs-se), *Ger.* Lit., "spectacle basses." A kind of bass called thus on account of its resemblance to a pair of spectacles.
Brimbaler (brănh-bă-lā'), *Fr.* To ring.
Brindisi (brĭn-dē'sĭ), *It.* A drinking-song.
Brio (brē'ō), *It.* Vigor, animation, spirit.
Brioso (brī-ō'zō), *It.* Lively, vigorously, with spirit.
Brisé (brī-zā'), *Fr.* Split; broken into an arpeggio.
Broach. An old musical instrument, played by turning a handle.
Broderies (brō-dŏ-rē'), *Fr.* Ornaments, embellisuments.
Broken cadence. See *Interrupted cadence.*
Broken chords. Chords whose notes are not taken simultaneously, but in a broken and interrupted manner.
Brokking. An old term, signifying quavering
B rotundum (bā rō-toon'doom), *Lat.* The character called a flat (♭); formerly this was applied only to the note b.
Bruit (brü-ē'), *Fr.* Noise, rattle, clatter.
Brummeisen (broom'mī-z'n), *Ger.* A jew's-harp.
Brummen (broom'měn), *Gr.* To hum, to drum.
Brummton (broom'tōn), *Ger.* A humming sound.
Brusquement (brüsk-mōnh), *Fr.* Brusque, rough, rude.
B-sharp. The sharp seventh of the diatonic scale of C; in keyed instruments the same as C-natural.
Buccina (boot'tshī-nä), *It.* An ancient wind instrument of the trumpet species.
Buccinal (book'sĭ-năl), *Lat.* Sounding like a horn or trumpet.
Buccinateur (bük-sĭ-nä-tür'), *Fr.* A trumpeter.
Buccino (book'sĭ-nō', *Lat.* To sound a trumpet.
Buccinum (book'sĭ-noom), *Lat.* A trumpet.
Buccolica (book-kō'lĭ-kä), *It.*}
Bucolic (boo-kŏ'lĭk), *Lat.* } Pastoral songs or verses.
Bucolique (bü-kō-lēk'), *Fr.* }
Buffa (boof'fä), *It.* } Comic, humorous, in the
Buffo (boof'fō), *It.* } comic style; also a singer who takes comic parts in the opera.

Buffa caricata (boof'fä kä-rī-kä'tä), *It.* } A
Buffo caricato (boof'fō kä-rī-kä'tō), *It.* } comic character in Italian opera.
Buffet organ. A very small organ.
Buffo burlesco (boof'fō boor-lĕs'kō), *It.* A buffo-singer and caricaturist.
Buffone (boof-fō-nē), *It.* Comic singer in an opera.
Buffonescamente (boof-fō-nĕs-kä-měn'tē), *It.* In a burlesque and comical manner.
Buffo opera (boof'fō ō'pĕ-rä), *It.* A comic opera, a burletta.
Bugle. A hunting-horn. (2) An instrument of copper or brass, similar to the French horn, but higher and more piercing. There are different kinds, one furnished with keys, and another kind with pistons or cylinders.
Bugle horn. A hunting-horn.
Bunge (boon'ghē), *Ger.* A drum; a kettledrum.
Bungen (boon'ghěn), *Ger.* To drum.
Buon (boo-ōn), *It.* Good.
Buonaccordo (boo-ō-näk'kŏr'dō), *It.* An instrument resembling a pianoforte, but smaller, to accommodate children.
Buona nota (boo-ō-nä nō'tä), *It.* Accented note.
Buona mano (boo-ō'nä mä'nō), *It.* A good hand, a brilliant performer.
Buon gusto (boo-ōn goos'tō), *It.* Good taste; refinement of style.
Burden. A regular return of the theme in a song at the close of each verse; the chorus.
Burla (boor'lä), }
Burlando (boor-län'dō), } *It.*
Burlesco (boor-lĕs-kō), }
Burlescamente (boor-lĕs-kä-měn-tě), }
Facetious, droll, comical; in a playful manner.
Burlesque music. A musical composition or performance, in which light and trifling matters are treated with great gravity and solemnity, and serious matters turned into ridicule.
Burletta (boor-lĕt'tä), *It.* A comic operetta; a light musical and dramatic piece, somewhat in the nature of the English farce.
Burasca (boor-räs'kä), *It.* A composition descriptive of a tempest.
Burre (bür), *Fr.* A dance melody.
Burthen. See *Burden.*
Busna (boos'nä), *It.* A species of trumpet.
Buzz. A low, humming noise.

ŭ *arm*, ă *add*, ā *ale*, ĕ *end*, ē *eve*, ĭ *ill*, ī *isle*, ō *old*, ŏ *odd*, oo *moon*, ŭ *but*, ü *Fr. sound*, kh *Ger. ch*, nh *nasal*.

(63)

C. The first note of the modern scale, called by the French *ut*, and by the Italians *do*. The major scale of C is called the natural scale, because it has no flats or sharps.

C C. The lowest note on the manuals of an organ, and is called an 8-feet note, that being the length of the open pipe required to produce it.

C C C. This note is an octave below C C, and requires a 16-feet pipe.

C C C C. A note an octave below C C C; it requires a 32-feet pipe.

C with *one stroke*; the German method of indicating middle C. The six notes above it are marked in the same manner.

C with *two strokes*; an octave above C with one stroke.

C with *three strokes*; an octave above C with two strokes.

C with *four strokes*; an octave above C with three strokes.

₵ Indicates common time of four crotchets, or quarter notes, in a bar.

₵ This character indicates alla breve or alla capella time.

C. A. The initials of Col arco; sometimes used in abbreviation.

Cabaletta (kä-bä-lĕt′tä), *It.* A simple melody of a pleasing and attractive character; an operatic air, like the rondo in form; a cavaletta. Literally, "a little horse," a descriptive term based on the characteristic movement of the accompaniment, which is generally in triplets, like a horse cantering.

Cabinet d'orgue (käb-ĭ-nä d'ŏrg), *Fr.* The case, or cabinet, in which the keys of an organ are sometimes placed.

Cabinet pianoforte. An upright pianoforte.

Caccia (kät′tshä), *It.* A hunt. *Alla caccia*, in hunting style; *i. e.*, hearty, free, offhand.

Caccia, alla (kät′tshä äl′lä), *It.* In the hunting style.

Cachucha (kä-tchoo′tchä), *Sp.* A popular Spanish dance, in triple time.

Cacofonia (kä-kō-fō-nī′ä), *It.* } Want of harmony, cacophony.
Cacofonie (kăk-ō-fō-nē), *Fr.* }

Cacofonico (kä-kō-fō′nĭ-kō), *It.* Cacophonous, discordant.

Cacophony (kä-kŏf′ō-ny). A combination of discordant sounds, false intonation, bad tones.

Cad. An abbreviation of Cadenza.

Cadence (kä-dänhs), *Fr.* A shake, or trill; also, a close in harmony.

Cadence. A close. Lit., "a fall." The term applies to melody as well as to harmony; (1) to the last melodic step of a strain (not necessarily a "fall" as regards pitch, but always a subsidence of motion into relative rest), and to a shake or brilliant passage of more or less extent, which leads up to the close of a piece, or part of a piece (*v. Cadenza*); (2) to two chords which form a close, mark a point of rest, complete or incomplete.

The *harmonic cadences* may be divided into four classes. (1) The chords of the dominant and tonic form a *full*, or *authentic*, cadence, which is *perfect* when the bass has the fundamental note of the first and of the second chord, and the highest part the octave of the fundamental note of the second chord (a), but otherwise is *imperfect* (aa). (2) The chords of the subdominant (major or minor) and tonic form the *plagal* cadence. According to some theorists it is, like the authentic, a full close; according to others it is not (b). (3) The chord of the tonic (c), or any other chord (cc), and that of the dominant form a *half close*, or *semicadence*. Some writers, however, call this cadence imperfect. Indeed, the nomenclature is very unsettled. (4) An *interrupted*, *deceptive*, or *false* cadence occurs where the chord of the dominant is followed by any chord except that of the tonic (d).

ä *arm*, ă *add*, ā *ale*, ĕ *end*, ē *eve*, ĭ *ill*, ī *isle*, ŏ *old*, ō *odd*, oo *moon*, ŭ *but*, ü *Fr. sound*, kh *Ger. ch*, nh *nasal*.

Cadence, authentic. A perfect, or final, cadence; the harmony of the dominant, followed by that of the tonic, or the progression of the dominant to the tonic.

Cadence brisee (cä-dens brō-sā'), *Fr.* An abrupt shake, beginning with the auxiliary tone.

Cadence, church. The plagal cadence.

Cadence evitee (ĕv-ē-tā), *Fr.* "Avoided cadence." A dominant chord followed by another dissonance, or by an unexpected resolution.

Cadence, half. A cadence that is imperfect; a close on the dominant.

Cadence imperfaite (ănh-pĕr-fā), *Fr.* An imperfect cadence.

Cadence, imperfect. Half cadence.

Cadence interrompue (änh-tĕr-rŏnh-pü), *Fr.* An interrupted cadence.

Cadence-marks. Short lines placed perpendicularly to indicate the cadence-notes in chanting.

Cadence parfaite (pär-fāt), *Fr.* A perfect cadence.

Cadence perlée (pĕr-lā), *Fr.* A brilliant cadence.

Cadence rompue (rŏnh-pü), *Fr.* A broken, or interrupted, cadence.

Cadence, suspended. Where the cadence passes through several modulations from the dominant to the tonic chord.

Cadencia (kä-dĕn'thĭ ä), *Sp.* }
Cadens (kä'dĕns), *Lat.* } Cadence.

Cadenz (kä-dĕnts), *Ger.* } A cadence; an ornamental passage
Cadenza (kä-dĕn'tsä), *It.* } introduced near the close of a song or solo, either by the composer or extemporaneously by the performer, a cadence (*q. v.*). In English the word *cadenza* is used in the sense of a short, or a more or less extended flourish, which does not form part of the rhythmical structure of a composition, but is a mere intercalation. Such flourishes may be met with anywhere in the course of vocal and instrumental compositions, more especially, however, at the end of the last solo of pieces for solo voices or instruments. In the aria and kindred forms the cadenza was a prominent feature. It assumed, however, the greatest importance in the concerto; there the flourish expands often into a brilliant fantasia on themes of the composition into which it is introduced—a fantasia either improvised by the performer or written out in full by the composer. These long concerto cadenzas occur in the first and last movements, at the end of the last solo, and begin usually on the chord of the fourth and sixth, preceding the full close (dominant, tonic).

Cadenza d' inganno (kä-dĕn'tsä dĕn-gän-nō), *It.* An interrupted, or deceptive, cadence.

Cadenza fiorita (kä-dĕn'tsä fē-ō-rē'tä), *It.* An ornate, florid cadence, with graces and embellishments.

Cadenza sfuggita (kä-dĕn-tsä sfoog-ghē'tä), *It.* An avoided, or broken, cadence.

Cadenza sospesa (kä-dĕn'tsä sŏs-pā'zä), *It.* A suspended cadence.

Cæsure (sĕ-sür), *Fr.* } (1) A pause in
Cæsura (tshĕ'soo-rä), *It.* } verse, so introduced
Cæsura (tsā-soo'rä), *Lat.* } as to avoid the recital and make the versification in reproductions. (2) A cut. The break at the end of a phrase. (3) The rhythmic termination of any passage consisting of more than one musical foot. (4) The last accented note of a phrase, section, or period.

Cæsural (tsä-soo'räl), *Lat.* Relating to the cæsura, or to the pause, in the voice.

Caisse (käss), *Fr.* A drum.

Caisse roulante (käss roo-länht), *Fr.* The side drum, the body being of wood and rather long.

Caisses claires (käss klär), *Fr.* The drums.

Cal. An abbreviation of Calando.

Calamus (kä'lä-moos) *or*, **Calamus pastoralis** (kä-lä'moos päs-tō-rä'lĭs), *Lat.* A reed, or pipe, used by shepherds.

Caland (kä-länd'), *It.* } Gradually dimin-
Calando (kä-län'dō), *It.* } ishing the tone and retarding the time; becoming softer and slower by degrees.

Calascione (kä-lä-shĭ-ō'nĕ), *It.* A species of guitar.

Calathumpian music. A discordant combination of sounds. A low and grotesque performance upon instruments, unmusical and out of tune.

Calata (kä-lä'tä), *It.* An Italian dance in 2-4 time.

Calcando (käl-kän'dō), *It.* Pressing forward and hurrying the time.

Calcant (käl-känt), *Ger.* The bellows-treader in old German organs.

Call. The beat of a drum.

Call, adjutant's. A drumbeat directing the band and field music to take the right of the line.

Calliope (kăl-lē'ŏ-pĕ). In pagan mythology the muse that presided over eloquence and heroic poetry. (2) An instrument formed of metal pipes, with keys like an organ; they are placed on steam engines sometimes, and the tones are produced by currents of steam instead of air.

Calma (käl'mä),
Calmate (käl-mä'tē), *It.* } Calmness, tranquillity, repose.
Calmato (käl-mä'tō),

Calo. An abbreviation of Calando.

Calore (kä-lō'rĕ), *It.* Warmth, animation.

Caloroso (kä-lō-rō'zo), *It.* Very much animation and warmth.

Calumeau (käl'ü-mō). A reed, or pipe.

Cambiare (käm-bĭ-ä'rĕ), *It.* To change, to alter.

Camera (kä'mĕ-rä), *It.* Chamber; a term applied to music composed for private performance or small concerts.

Camera musica (kä-mĕ-rä moo'zĭ-kä), *It.* Chamber music.

Caminando (kä-mĭ-nän'dō), *It.* Flowing, with easy and gentle progression.

Campana (käm-pä'nä), *It.* A bell.

Campanada (käm-pä-nä'dä), *It.* Sound of a bell.

Campanarum concentus (käm-pä-nä'-room kōn-sĕn'toos),
Campanarum modulatio (käm-pä-nä'-room mō-doo-lä'tsĭ-ō), } *Lat.*
Ringing of bells or chimes; chiming of bells.

Campanarum pulsator (käm-pä-nä'room poolsä'tor), *Lat.* A ringer of bells.

Campanella (käm-pä-nĕl'lä),
Campanello (käm-pä-uĕl'lō), *It.* } A little bell.

Campanetta (käm-pä-nĕt'tä), *It.* A set of bells tuned diatonically, and played with keys like a pianoforte.

Campanile (käm-pä-nē'lĕ), *It.* A belfry.

Campanology (käm-pä-nŏl'ŏ-gy). The art of ringing bells.

Campanone (käm-pä-nō'nĕ), *It.* A great bell.

Canarder (kȧ-när-dä'), *Fr.* To imitate the tones of a duck.

Canarie (kȧ-nä-rē'), *Fr.* } An old dance, in
Canaries (kȧ-nä'rĕs), *En.* } lively 3-8 or 6-8, and
Canario (kä-nä'rĭ ō), *It.* } sometimes 12 8, time of two strains. It derives its name from the Canary Islands, from whence it is supposed to have come.

Cancan (kän-kän). A vulgar kind of dance.

Cancellen (kän'sĕl-l'n), *Ger.* Grooves. The small channels in an organ windchest, conducting air to the pipes.

Cancelling sign. A natural (♮) employed to remove the effect of a previous flat or sharp.

Cancrizans (kän-krē'tsäns), *It.* } Retrograde
Cancrizante (kän krĭ-tsän-tĕ), movement; going backward.

Canere (kä'nĕ-rĕ), *Lat.* To sing; to play upon an instrument.

Canevas (kȧn-ĕ-vä'), *Fr.* Unconnected words set to music. (2) The rough sketch, or draft, of a song, indicating the measure of the verses required.

Cangiare (kän-jī-ä'rĕ), *It.* To change, to alter.

Canna (kän'nä), *It.* A reed, or pipe.

Cannon. The portion of a bell by which it is suspended.

Cannon-drum. The tomtom used by the natives of the East Indies.

Canon (kăn'ŏn). In ancient music, a rule, or method, for determining the intervals of notes. A musical composition for two or more voice-parts, in which the essential thing is that each of the parts in turn sings the very same melody (called the subject), note for note, while the other voices make harmony with it. The simplest form of canon is the old form called a Round, so called from the voices following each other round and round through the very same notes, but at intervals producing harmony.

A canon may have one subject or more than one, and it may be for two voices or more than two. Hence such names as "2 in 1," meaning that two voices have a single subject; "4 in 2," meaning that four voices have two subjects, etc.

Canons are further named from the interval in which the second voice begins. For instance, at a) below, the second voice enters in the octave of the same phrase as given out by the first voice. It is, therefore, a canon "2 in 1" at the octave. At b) the second voice enters in the under fifth, and at c) in the over sixth. See, also, *Imitation*.

Canone (kä'nō-nĕ),
Canonico (kä-nō-nĭ-kō), *It.* } A canon.

Canone al sospiro (kä'nō-nĕ äl sōs-pē'rō), *It.* A canon whose different parts commence at the distance of a crotchet rest from each other.

Canone aperto (kä'nō-nĕ ä-pär'tō), *It.* An open canon; a canon of which the solution or development is given.

ä *arm*, ȧ *add*, ā *ale*, ĕ *end*, ē *eve*, ĭ *ill*, ī *isle*, ŏ *odd*, ō *old*, oo *moon*, ŭ *but*, ü *Fr. sound*, kh *Ger. ch.* nh *nasal*.

Canone chiuso (kä'nō-nĕ kē-oo'zō), *It.* A close or hidden canon, the solution or development of which must be discovered; also an enigmatical canon.

Canone in corpe (kä'nō-nĕ ĭn kōr'pä), *It.* A perpetual fugue.

Canone partito (kä'nō-nĕ pär'tī-tō), *Lat.* A perpetual fugue, in which all the parts are written in partitions, or different lines, or in separate parts, with the proper pauses which each is to observe.

Canone sciolto (kä'nō-nĕ shē-ōl'tō), *It.* A free canon, not in the strict style.

Canon, free. A canon not in strict conformity to the rules, the melody of the first part not being followed throughout.

Canon, hidden. A close canon. See *Canone chiuso*.

Canonical mass. A mass in which the different parts of the musical service are in strict canonical order.

Canonical hours. The daily offices of devotion prescribed to the Roman Catholic clergy. They are: (1) Matins and Lauds; (2) Prime; (3) Tierce; (4) Sext; (5) None; (6) Vespers; (7) Compline. Of these, Matins and Lauds, Vespers, and Compline are called the greater hours, and the others the lesser hours.

Canonic imitation. Imitation in which a second voice more or less closely follows the melody previously given out by another voice, and at a certain interval above or below, and with more or less close exactness. See *Canon* and *Imitation*.

Canon, infinite. A canon, the end of which leads to the beginning; a perpetual fugue.

Canon perpetuus (kä'uōn pär-pā'too-oos), *Lat.* See *Canon, infinite*.

Canon, mixed. A canon of several voices, beginning at different intervals.

Canon, strict. A canon in which the rules of this form of composition are strictly followed.

Canore (kā-nōr), *Fr.* ⎫
Canoro (kä-nō'rō), *It.* ⎬ Musical, tuneful, harmonious.
Canorus (kä-nō'rous), *Lat.* ⎭

Cant. An abbreviation of Canto and Cantate.

Cantab. An abbreviation of Cantabile.

Cantabile (kän-tä'bĭ-lĕ), *It.* That can be sung; in a melodious, singing, and graceful style, full of expression.

Cantabile ad libitum (kän-tä'bĭ-lĕ ăd lĭb-ĭ-toom), *It.* In singing style, at pleasure.

Cantabile con molto portamento (kän-tä'bĭ-lĕ kōn mōl'tō pōr-tä mĕn'tō), *It.* In singing style, with a great deal of portamento; in a melodious style, with embellishments at pleasure, but few and well chosen.

Cantajuolo (kän-tä-yoo ō'lō), *It.* ⎫ A street
Cantambanca (kän-täm-bän'kä), ⎬ singer; an itinerant musician; a contemptuous name for a singer.

Cantamento (kän-tä-mĕn'tō), *It.* Tune; air.

Cantando (kän-tän'dō), *It.* In a melodious, singing style.

Cantans (kän-täns), *Lat.* Singing.

Cantante (kän-tän'tĕ), *It.* A singer; also a part intended for the voice.

Cantante ariose (kän-tän'tĕ ä-rĭ-ō'zĕ), *It.* A species of melody which, by its frequent changes of measure and conversational style, first served to mark the distinction between air and recitative.

Cantar a la almohadilla (kän-tär' ä lä äl'mō ä-dēl'yä), *Sp.* To sing alone, and without being accompanied by instruments.

Cantare (kän-tä'rĕ), *It.* To sing, to celebrate, to praise.

Cantare manierata (kän-tä-rĕ mä-nĭ-ĕ-rä'tä), *It.* To sing with too many embellishments, without taste or judgment.

Cantarina (kän-tä-rē'nä), *Sp.* A woman who sings in public.

Cantata (kän-tä'tä), *It.* ⎫ The word originally meant something
Cantate (käub-tät), *Fr.* ⎬ sung, in contradistinction to something played (sonata). So varied are the innumerable exemplifications of the cantata that it is impossible to define its character. Now this name is given to a vocal composition of some extent, consisting of recitatives, arias, choruses, etc., with orchestral accompaniments in most cases; formerly it often signified a short vocal composition for one voice, with organ, harpsichord, or some other simple accompaniment. Indeed, the range of the cantata may be said to extend from an elaborate song to a short oratorio, and an opera not intended for the stage.
Cantate (kän-tä'tĕ, *Ger.* ⎭

Cantata amorose (kän-tä'tä ä-mō-rō'zĕ), *It.* A cantata having love for its subject.

Cantata morali o spirituali (kän-tä'tä mō-rä'lĕ ō spē-rĭ-too-ä'lĕ), *It.* A cantata designed for the church.

Cantatilla (kän-tä-tĭl'lä), *It.* ⎫ A short cantata; an air preceded by a recitative.
Cantatille (käub-tä tēl), *Fr.* ⎬
Cantatina (kän-tä-tē'nä), *It.* ⎭

Cantator (kän-tä'tōr), *Lat.* A singer, a chanter.

Cantatore (känh-tä-tō'rĕ), *It.* A male singer.

Cantatorium (kän-tä-tō'rĭ-oom), *Lat.* The book from which the priests in the Roman Catholic service chant or recite the responses.

Cantatrice (kän-tä-trē'tshĕ), *It.* A female singer.

Cantatrice buffa (kän-tä-trē'tshĕ boof'fä), *It.* ⎫ A female singer; a woman who sings in comic opera.
Cantatrix (kän-tä'trĭx), *Lat.* ⎭

Cantazzare (kän-tä-tzä'rĕ), *It.* To sing badly.

Cantellerando (kän-tĕl-lĕ-rän'dō), *It.* Singing with a subdued voice; murmuring, trilling.

Canterellare (kän-tĕ-rĕl-lä'rĕ), *It.* To chant, or sing.

Canterino (kän-tĕ-rē'nō), *It.* A singer; a chanter.
Cantica (kän'tĭ kä), *It.* ⎫ Canticles; the
Canticæ (kän't.-ĭsä), *Lat.* ⎬ ancient *laudi*, or
Cantici (kän'tĭ t-hē), *It. pl.* ⎩ sacred songs of
Cantico (än-tē'kō), *Sp.* the Roman Catholic Church.
Canti carnascialeschi (kän'tē cär-näs-tsĭ-ä-lĕs kē), *It.* ⎫
Canti charnevali (kä-"tē l·är-nĕ-vä'lē), ⎬ Songs of the carnival week.
Canticle. A sacred hymn, or song. (2) A canto, a division of a song.
Cantico (kän'tĭ-kō), *It.* ⎫ A canticle.
Canticum (kän'tĭ-koom), *Lat.* ⎭
Cantillate (kän'tĭl-lā e). To chant, to recite with musical tones.
Cantillation. A chanting, a recitation with musical modulations.
Cantillatio (kän-tĭl-lä-tsĭ'ō), *Lat.* A singing style of declamation.
Cantilena (kän-tĭ-lā'nä), *It.* The melody, air, or principal part in any composition; generally the highest vocal part.
Cantilena scotica (kän-tĭ-lā'nä skō'tĭ-kä), *It.* A Scotch air or tune.
Cantilene (kän-tĭ-lā'nĕ), *It.* A cantilena.
Cantino (kän-tē'nō), *It.* The smallest string of the violin, guitar, etc.
Cantio (kän'tsĭ-ō), *Lat.* A song.
Cantique (känh-tĕk'), *Fr.* A canticle, or hymn of praise.
Cantique des cantiques (känh-tĕk' dĕ känh-tĕk'), *Fr.* Solomon's Song.
Canto (kän'tō), *It.* (1) A song, a melody. (2) The art of singing. (3) The highest part in concerted music. (4) The soprano voice (5) The highest string of an instrument. (*V. Cantino.*)
Canto a cappella (ä käp-pĕl'lä), *It.* Vocal church music without instrumental accompaniment.
Canto Ambrosiano (äm-brō-zĭ-ä'nō), *It.* Ambrosian chant.
Canto armonico (kän'tō är-mō'nĭ-kō), *It.* A part-song for two, three, or more voices.
Canto clef. The C clef when placed on the first line.
Canto concertante (kän'tō kŏn-tshĕr-tän'tĕ), *It.* The treble of the principal concerting parts.
Canto cromatico (kän'tō krō-mä'tĭ-kō), *It.* Chromatic vocal music.
Canto fermo (kän'tō fär'mō), *It.* A chant or melody. (2) Choral singing in unison on a plain melody. (3) Any subject consisting of a few long, plain notes, given as a theme for counterpoint.
Canto figurato (kän'tō fē-goo-rä'tō), *It.* A figured melody.
Canto fioritto (kän'tō fē-ō-rēt'tō), *It.* A song in which many ornaments are introduced.

Canto funebre (kän'tō foo-nā'brē), *It.* A funeral song.
Canto Gregoriano (kän'tō grĕ-gō-rĭ-ä'nō), *It.* The Gregorian chant.
Canto llano (kän'ō l·ä'nō), *Sp.* ⎫ The plain
Canto piano (kän'tō pĭä-nō), *It.* ⎭ chant or song.
Canto necessario (kän'tō nä-tchĕs-sä'rĭ-ō), *It.* A term indicating those parts that are to sing through the whole piece.
Canto primo (kän'tō prē'mō), *It.* The first treble or soprano.
Cantor (kän-tōr'), *It.* A singer, a chanter.
Cantor (kän'tōr), ⎫
Cantor choralis (kän'tŏr kō-rä'lĭs), *Lat.* ⎬ A precentor; a leader of the choir.
Cantorate (kän-tō-rä'tĕ), *It.* A leading singer of a choir.
Cantore (kän-tō'rĕ), *It.* A singer, a chanter, a poet.
Canto recitativo (kän-tō rä-tshĭ-tä-tē'vō), *It.* Recitative, declamatory singing.
Cantorei (kän-tō-rī'), *Ger.* The dwelling-house of the cantor. (2) A class of the choristers in the public school.
Cantoren (kän-tō'r'n), *Ger.* Chanters, a choir of singers.
Canto ripieno (kän'tō rē-pĭ-ā'nō), *It.* The treble of the grand chorus; the part that sings or plays only in the grand chorus.
Cantoris (kän-tō'rĭs), *Lat.* A term used in cathedral music to indicate the passages intended to be sung by those singers who are placed on that side of the choir where the cantor or precentor sits. This is usually on the left-hand side on entering the choir from the nave.
Canto rivoltato (kän'tō rē-vōl-tä'tō), *It.* The treble changed.
Canto secondo (kän'tō sĕ-kōn'dō), *It.* The second treble.
Canto simplice (kän'tō sĭm-plē'tshĕ), *It.* A plain song.
Cantrice (kän-trē'tshĕ), *It.* ⎫ A female singer
Cantrix (kän'trĭx), *Lat.* ⎭ a songstress.
Cantus (kän'toos), *Lat.* A song, a melody; also the treble, or soprano part.
Cantus Ambrosianus (kän'toos äm-brō-sĭ-ä'noos), *Lat.* The four chants, or melodies, introduced into the Church by St. Ambrose, Bishop of Milan, in the fourth century, and which are supposed to be derived from ancient Greek melodies.
Cantus figuratus (kän'toos fē-goo-rä'toos), *Lat.* Embellished or figurative chants or melodies.
Cantus firmus (kän'toos fīr'moos), *Lat.* The plain song or chant. See *Canto fermo.*
Cantus Gregorianus (kän'toos grĕ-gō-rĭ-ä'noos), *Lat.* Those four chants, or melodies, introduced into the Church by St. Gregory, and which, with the Ambrosian chants, formed a series of eight modes, or tones, as they were called.

Cantus mensurabilis (kän'toos mēn-soo-rä'bĭ-lĭs), *Lat.* A regular, or measured, melody.

Cantus mollis (kän'toos mŏl'lĭs), *Lat.* A song written in the minor key.

Canum (kä'nŭm), *Tur.* A Turkish musical instrument, on which the ladies play.

Canzona (kän-tsō'nä), *It.* } Song, ballad, can-
Canzone (kän-tsō'nō), } zonet. (2) A graceful and somewhat elaborate air, in two or three strains, or divisions. (3) An air in two or three parts, with passages of fugue and imitation, somewhat similar to the madrigal.

Canzonaccea (kän-tsō-nät'tshē-ä), *It.* A low, trivial song, a poor canzone.

Canzoncina (kän-tsōn-tshē'nä), *It.* A short canzone, or song.

Canzone sacra (kän-tsō'nĕ sä'krä), *It.* A sacred song.

Canzonet. A short song, in one, two, or three parts.

Canzonnetta (kän-tsō'nĕt'tä), *It.* A short canzone.

Canzoni (kän-tsō'nĭ), *It.* A sonata; in connection with a passage of music it has the same meaning as allegro.

Canzoniere (kän-tsō-nĭ-ā'rĕ), *It.* A songbook.

Canzonina (kän-tsō-nē'nä), *It.* A canzonet.

Capelle (kä pĕl'lĕ), *Ger.* A chapel, a musical band.

Capellmeister (kä'pĕl'mĭs'tĕr), *Ger.* The director, composer, or master of the music in a choir.

Capo (kä'pō), *It.* The head, or beginning; the top.

Capodastro (kä pō-däs'trō), *It.* See *Capotasto*.

Capo d' Instrumenti (kä'pō dĭn-ĕs-troo-mĕn'-tĭ), *It.* The leader, or director, of the instrumental performers.

Capo d' orchestra (kä'pō dŏr-kĕs'trä), *It.* The leader of the orchestra.

Capona (kä-pō'nä), *Sp.* A Spanish dance.

Capotasto (kä-pō-täs'tō), *It.* The nut, or upper part, of the fingerboard of a violin, violoncello, etc. (2) A small instrument used by guitar-players to form a temporary nut upon the fingerboard to produce certain effects.

Capo violino (kä'pō vē-ō-lē'nō), *It.* The first violin.

Cappella (käp-pĕl-lä). *It.* A chapel, or church. (2) A band of musicians that sing or play in a church.

Cappella musica (käp-pĕl'lä moo'zĭ-kä), *It.* Chapel or church music.

Capriccietto (kä-prēt-shĭ-ĕt'tō), *It.* A short capriccio.

Capriccio (kä-prēt'shĭ-ō), *It.* A fanciful and irregular species of composition; a species of fantasia; in a capricious and free style.

Capricciosamente (kä-prēt-shĭ-ō-zä-mĕn'tĕ), *It.* Capriciously.

Capriccioso (kä-prēt-shĭ-ō'zō), *It.* In a fanciful and capricious style.

Capricci (kä-prēt'shĭ), *It.* } A caprice. See
Caprice (kü prēs), *Fr.* } *Capriccio*.

Caprice. A whimsical, fanciful style of composition. See *Capriccio*.

Capricieusement (kä-prē-süs-mŏnh'), *Fr.* Capriciously.

Capricieux (kä-prē-sü), *Fr.* In a fanciful and capricious style.

Car. (kär), *It.* An abbreviation of *Carta*.

Caracteres de musique (kär-äk-tār' dŭh mü-zĕk') *Fr.* A term applied to musical signs; all the marks or symbols belonging to musical notation.

Caramillo (kä-rä-mēl'yō), *Sp.* A flageolet, a small flute.

Caressant (kä-rĕs-sänh), *Fr.* Caressing, tenderly.

Carezzando (kä-rĕt-tsän'dō), *It.* } In a caress-
Carezovole (kä-rĕt-sō-vō'lĕ), } ing and tender manner.

Caricato (kä-rĭ-kä'tō), *It.* Exaggerated, caricature.

Caricatura (kä-rĭ-kä-too'rä), *It.* A caricature, an exaggerated representation.

Carillon (kä-rĭl-yōnh), *Fr.* Chime. See *Carillons*.

Carillon a clavier (kä-rĭl-yōnh ä klä-vĭ-ā), *Fr.* A set of keys and pedals, acting upon the bells.

Carillonement (kä rĭl-yōnh-mänh), *Fr.* Chiming.

Carillonner (kä-rĭl-yō-nä'), *Fr.* To chime or ring bells.

Carillonneur (kä-rĭl-yo-nŭr'), *Fr.* A player, or ringer, of bells or carillons.

Carillons (kä-rĭl-yōnh'). *Fr. pl.* Chimes; a peal or set of bells, upon which tunes are played by the machinery of a clock, or by means of keys, like those of a pianoforte. (2) Short, simple airs, adapted to such bells. (3) A stop in an organ, to imitate a peal of bells.

Carita (kä-rē'tä), *It.* Tenderness, feeling.

Carita, con (kä-rē'tä kōn), *It.* With tenderness.

Carmagnole (kär-män-yōl'), *Fr.* A famous French revolutionary song. It came into vogue in 1792, and derives its name from the Piedmontese town Carmagnola.

Carmen (kär'mĕn), *Ger.* } A tune, a song, a
Carmen (kär'mĕn), *Lat.* } poem.

Carmen natalitium (kär'mĕn nä-tä lē'tsĭ-oom), *Lat.* A carol.

Carol. A song. (2) A song of joy and exultation, a song of devotion. (3) Old ballads sung at Christmas and Easter.

Carola (kä-rō'lä), *It.* A ballad, a dance with singing.
Carolare (kä-rō lä'rĕ), *It.* To sing in a warbling manner, to carol.
Caroletta (kä-rō-lĕt'tä), *It.* A little dance.
Carolle (kä-rōl'), *Fr.* A carol.
Carrure des phrases (kär-rūr dĕ fräz), *Fr.* The quadrature, or balancing, of the phrases.
Cartel (kär-tĕl), *Fr.* The first sketch of a composition, or of a full score. (Obsolete.)
Cartellone (kär-tĕl-lō'nĕ), *It.* A large playbill; the printed catalogue of operas to be performed during the season.
Cassa (käs'sä), *It.* The drum.
Cassa grande (käs'sä grän'dĕ),
Cassa militare (käs'sä mī-lī-tä'rĕ), } *It.* } The great drum in military music.
Cassatio (käs-sä'tsĭ-ō), *Lat.*
Cassazione (käs-sä-tsĭ-ō'nĕ), *It.*
Cassation (käs-sä'tsĭ-ōn), *Ger.* } Lit., "dismissal." Originally the concluding piece of a musical performance, afterwards a kind of serenade consisting of several instrumental pieces.
Castagnet. Castanet.
Castagnetta (käs-tän-yĕt'tä), *It.*
Castagnettes (käs-tänh-yĕt'), *Fr.*
Castagnole (käs-tän-yō'lĕ), *Sp.*
Castanetas (käs-tän-yä'täs), *Sp.* } Snappers; castanets, used in dancing.
See *Castanets*.
Castanets. Snappers used to accompany dancing; an instrument of music formed of small, concave shells of ivory or hard wood, shaped like spoons. Castanets are used by dancers in Spain and other southern countries to mark the rhythm of the bolero, cachucha, etc.
Castanheta (käs-tän-ā-tä), *Por.*
Castanuelas (käs-täu-yoo-ā'läs), *Sp.* } Castanets.
Castrato (käs-trä'tō), *It.* A eunuch. A male singer with a soprano voice.
Catch. A humorous composition for three or four voices, supposed to be of English invention, and dating back to the Tudors. The parts are so contrived that the singers catch up each other's words, thus giving them a different sense from that of the original reading.
Catena di trilli (kä-tä'nä dē trēl'lē), *It.* A chain, or succession of shakes.
Catgut. A small string for violins and other instruments of a similar kind, made of the intestines of sheep and lambs, and sometimes cats.
Catling. A lute-string.
Cauda (kou'dä), *Lat.* Coda.
Cavalletta (kä-väl-lĕt'tä),
Cavalletto (kä-väl-lĕt'tō), } *It.* } A cabaletta.
Cavalquet (käv-äl-kā'), *Fr.* Trumpet signal for the cavalry.
Cavata (kä-vä'tä), *It.* Production of tone; also a small song, sometimes preceded by a recitative; a cavatina.

Cavatina (kä-vä-tē'nä), *It.*
Cavatine (käv-ä-tēu'), *Fr.* } An air of one strain only, of dramatic style, sometimes preceded by a recitative.
C. B. The initials of Col basso and Contra basso.
C barré (bär-rā, *Fr.*
C barred. } The character 𝄵 used to indicate alla breve or alla capella time.
C clef. The tenor clef. It is called the C clef because on whatever line it is placed it gives to the notes of that line th · name and pitch of middle C. Is used also for Sop. and Alt.
C-dur (tsā-door), *Ger.* The key of C major.
Cebell. The name of an old air in common time, characterized by a quick and sudden alternation of high and low notes.
Celebrer (sä-lĕ-brā'), *Fr.* To celebrate, to extol, to praise.
Celeramente (tshä-lĕ-rä-mĕn'tĕ), *It.* Quickly, fast.
Celere (tshä'lĕ-rĕ), *It.* Quick, rapid, with velocity.
Celeridad (ihä-lä-rī-däd'), *Sp.*
Celerita (thä-lä-rī'tä), *It.*
Célérité (sä-lä-rī-tā), *Fr.* } Celerity, velocity, rapidity.
Céleste (sä-lĕst'), *Fr.* Celestial, heavenly; in some passages it indicates the employment of the pedal which acts on the celestina, or soft stop. Also a tremolo stop, or a stop consisting of a set of reeds or pipes a very little sharp, giving rise to a moderately quick beat or waving.
Celestial music. Among the ancients, the harmony of sounds supposed to result from the movements of the heavenly bodies.
Celestina (tshä-lĕs-tē'nä), *It.* An organ stop of small 4-feet scale, producing a very delicate and subdued tone. Also a tremolo stop in reed organs.
'Celli (tshĕl'lĕ). An abbreviation of Violoncelli.
'Cellist (tshĕl'lĕst). An abbreviation of Violoncellist; one who plays the 'Cello.
'Cello (tshĕl'lō). An abbreviation of Violoncello.
Cemb. An abbreviation of Cemballo.
Cembalista (tshĕm-bä-lēz'tä), *It.* A player on the harpsichord; also a player on the cymbals.
Cembalo (tshĕm'bä-lō),
Cembolo (tshĕm'bō-lō), } *It.* } A harpsichord; also the name for a cymbal.
Cenobites. Monks of a religious order, who live in a convent and perform the services of the choir.
Cento (tsĕn-tō), *Lat.* A composition formed by one hundred verses and passages from other authors, and disposed in a new order.
Centone (tsĕn-tō'nĕ), *Lat.* A cento, or medley of different tunes or melodies.
Ces (tsĕs), *Ger.* The note C♭.

ä arm, ă add, ā ale, ĕ end, ē eve, ĭ ill, ī isle, ŏ old, ō odd, oo moon, ŭ but, ü *Fr. sound*, kh *Ger.* ch, uh *nasal*.

Ces-dur (tsĕs-door), *Ger.* The note of C♭ major.

C. espr. An abbreviation of Con espressione.

Cesura. } A pause in verse introduced to aid
Cesure. } the recital and render the versification more melodious. See *Cæsura*.

Cetera (tshā'tĕ-rä), *It.* A cittern, a guitar.

Cetera tedesca (tshā'tĕ-rä tĕ-dĕs'kä), *It.* The German zither, a ten-stringed instrument of the lute class.

Ch. An abbreviation of Choir and Chorus.

Cha chi (kü kē). A Chinese instrument, similar to the kin, but having the chromatic scale.

Chacona (tshä-kō'nä),*Sp.* } A chaconne, a slow,
Chaconne (shä-kŏnh),*Fr.* } graceful Spanish movement, in 3-4 time, and composed upon a ground bass. It is usually stated that the chaconne is in the major mode, and that passacaille, which is somewhat similar to it in rhythm, is in the minor. This is not the case, as the following theme, on which Bach's celebrated Ciaccona for violin solo is founded, will show:

Chacoon. A dance like a saraband. See *Chacona*.

Chair organ. Found in old organ music. See *Choir organ*.

Chal. An abbreviation of Chalumeau.

Chalil (kä-lēl'), *Heb.* An old Hebrew instrument, similar to a pipe or flute.

Chalmey. See *Chalumeau*.

Chalotte. A tube of brass, made to receive the reed of an organ-pipe.

Chalmeau (shǎl-mō'), } An ancient rus-
Chalumeau (shä-lü-mō), *Fr.* } tic flute, resembling the hautboy, and blown through a calamus, or reed. The term is also applied to some of the low notes of the clarinet.

Chamber music. Music composed for private performance, or for small concerts before a select audience, such as instrumental duets, trios, quartets, etc.

Chamber voice. A voice especially suited to the execution of parlor music.

Changeable. A term applied to chants which may be sung either in the major or minor mode of the key or tonic in which they are written.

Changer de jeu (shănh-zhā dŭh zhü), *Fr.* To change the stops or registers in an organ.

Changes. The various alternations and different passages produced by a peal of bells.

Changing notes. German," wechseln Tönen," dissonant tones occurring upon the unaccented part of the beat. *Changing* tones differ from *passing* tones in this, that whereas passing tones lead across from one consonant tone to another, changing tones return again to the consonant tone from which they "changed." For instance, upon the chord of do in the progression do re mi, re would be a passing tone; but in the progression do re do, the re would be a changing tone.

Chans. An abbreviation of Chanson.

Chanson (shänh-sŏnh), *Fr.* A song.

Chanson bachique (shänh-sŏnh bǎk-ĕk'), *Fr.* A drinking-song.

Chanson des rues (shänn-sŏnh dĕ rü'), *Fr.* A street song; a vaudeville.

Chansonner (shänh-sŏnh-nā'), *Fr.* To make songs.

Chansonnette (shänh-sŏnh-nĕt'), *Fr.* A little or short song, or canzonet.

Chansonniere (shänh-sŏnh-ni-ār'), *Fr.* A female song-writer.

Chansons de geste (shänh-sŏnh dŭh zhĕst), *Fr.* The romances formerly sung by the wandering minstrels of the middle ages. Literally, "Songs of Deeds." These were great national epics of France, which had their origin from about A. D. 800 to 1300. Among the most famous were "The Song of Roland" and the "Song of Antioch." These epics appear to have grown up out of the detached labors of several generations of minstrels, each adding something of his own to the store, as he had received it from his master.

Chant. A simple melody, generally harmonized in four parts, to which lyrical portions of the Scriptures are set, part of the words being recited *ad libitum* and part sung. A "single" chant consists of only two strains. A "double" chant consists of four. (2) To recite musically, to sing.

Chant (shänh), *Fr.* The voice part; a song or melody, singing.

Chant amoureux (shänh-tä-moo-rŭh), *Fr.* A love-song, an amorous ditty.

Chantant (shänh-tänh), *Fr.* Adapted to singing; in a melodious and singing style.

Chantante (shänh-tänht), *Fr.* Singing.

Chantante bass (shänh-tänht bäss), *Fr.* Vocal bass.

Chant d' eglise (shänh d'ē-glēz'), *Fr.* Church singing.

Chant de Noel (shänh dŭh nō-ĕl'),*Fr.* A Christmas carol.

Chant des oiseaux (shänh dĕ swä-zō'),*Fr.* Singing of the birds.

Chant de triomphe (shänh dŭ trē-ŏnhf), *Fr.* A triumphal song, a song of victory.

Chant du soir (shänh dü swär), *Fr.* Evening chant.

Chantée (shän-tā), *Fr.* Sung.

Chanter. One who chants. (2) The pipe that sounds the treble or tenor in a bagpipe.

Chanter (shänh-tā'), *Fr.* To sing, to celebrate, to praise.

ă *arm,* ă *add,* ā *ale,* ĕ *end,* ē *eve,* ĭ *ill,* ī *isle,* ŏ *old,* ŏ *odd,* oo *moon,* ŭ *but,* ü *Fr. sound,* kh *Ger. ch,* nh *nasal.*

Chanter à livre ouvert (shänh-tā' ä lĕvr oo-vār'), *Fr.* To sing at sight.

Chanter à pleine voix (shänh-tā' ä plăn vwä), *Fr.* To be in full voice.

Chanter, arch. The chief chanter, the leader of the chants.

Chanterelle (shänh-tĕ rĕl), *Fr.* Treble string; the smallest string of the violin.

Chanterres (shänh-tĕ-rē), *Fr.* The singers of songs and ballads in the tenth and following centuries.

Chanteur (shänh-tŭr'), *Fr.* A singer.

Chanteur des rues (shänh-tŭr dĕ rü'), *Fr.* A street singer.

Chanterie (shänh-trē'), *Fr.* } Institutions es-
Chantry. } tablished and endowed for the purpose of singing the souls of the founders out of purgatory. A church or chapel endowed with revenue for the purpose of saying mass daily for the souls of the donors.

Chant pastorale (shänht päs-tō-räl'), *Fr.* A pastoral song.

Chantry priests. Priests selected to sing in the chantry.

Chanteuse (shänh-tüs'), *Fr.* A female vocalist.

Chant funebre (shänh fü-năbr), *Fr.* Dirge, a funeral song.

Chant sur le livre (shänh soor lŭh lĕvr), *Fr.* A barbarous kind of counterpoint, or descant, as it was termed, performed by several voices, each singing extempore. An extemporaneous counterpoint added by one or more singers to the *canto fermo* sung by others. It is identical with *contrapunto alla mente*.

Chant, Phrygian. A chant intended to excite the hearers to fury and rage.

Chant, Roman. The Gregorian chant.

Chant sacre (shänh tsŭkr), *Fr.* Sacred music.

Chantor. A singer in a cathedral choir.

Chantre (shäntr), *Fr.* A chorister, a chanter, a singing boy.

Chapeau chinois (shä-pō' shĕ-nwä'), *Fr.* A crescent, or set of small bells, used in military music.

Chapelle (shäp-ĕl'), *Fr.* A chapel. See *Cappella*.

Characteristic chord. The leading, or principal, chord.

Characteristic note. A leading note. The fourth and seventh from the tonic.

Characters. A general name for musical signs.

Charakterstücke (kä-räc-t'r stük'ĕ), *Ger.* Characteristic pieces. Pieces descriptive of moods, impressions, and events.

Charivari (shä-rĭ-vä'rĭ), *Fr.* Noisy music, made with tin dishes, horns, bells, etc.; clatter; a mock serenade.

Charlatan (shär-lä-tänh'), *Fr.* A quack; an imposter; a superficial artist who makes great pretensions, which are not justified in performance.

Chasse (shäss), *Fr.* Hunting; in the hunting style.

Chatsoteroth (kăt-sō'tĕ-rōth), *Heb.* } The
Catzozerath (kăt-zō-zē'räth), } silver trumpet of the ancient Hebrews.

Che (kā), *It.* Than, that, which.

Che chi (kā kē). One of the eight species into which the Chinese divide their musical sounds.

Chef (shäf), *Fr.* Leader, chief.

Chef-d'attaque (shä-dät-täk), *Fr.* The leader, or principal first-violin performer; also the leader of the chorus.

Chef-d'œuvre (shä-doovr), *Fr.* A masterpiece, a capital performance; the principal, or most important, composition of an author.

Chef-d'orchestre (shä-dōr-kĕstr), *Fr.* The leader of an orchestra.

Cheipour, *Per.* A Persian trumpet used in military service.

Chelys (kā-lĭs), *Gr.* A species of lute, or viol.

Cheng chi (kĕng kē). One of the eight species into which the Chinese divide their musical sounds.

Cherubical hymn. A hymn of great importance in the service of the Holy Communion. "Holy, holy, holy," etc.

Chest of viols. An old expression applied to a set of viols, two of which were basses, two tenors, and two trebles, each with six strings. These instruments were particularly adapted to those compositions called fantasias.

Chest tone. } The lowest register of the voice.
Chest voice. }

Chest, wind. A reservoir in an organ for holding the air, which is conveyed from thence into the pipes by means of the wind trunks and channels.

Chevalet (shĕv-ä-lä'), *Fr.* The bridge of a violin, viola, etc.

Cheville (shĕ-vĕl'), *Fr.* The peg of a violin, viola, etc.

Chevrotement (shĕ-vrōt-mŏnh), *Fr.* A tremor or shake in singing.

Chevroter (shĕ-vrō-tā'), *Fr.* To sing with a trembling voice; to make a bad or false shake.

Chiara (kē-ä'rä), } *It.* Clear, brilliant, pure
Chiaro (kē-ä'rō), } as to tone.

Chiaramente (kē-ä-rä-mĕn'tĕ), *It.* Clearly, brightly, purely.

Chiarentana (kē-ä-rĕn-tä'nä), *It.* An Italian country dance.

Chiarezza (kē-ä-rĕt'sä), *It.* Clearness, neatness, purity.

Chiarina (kē-ä-rē'uä), *It.* A clarion.

ä *arm*, ă *add*, ā *ale*, ĕ *end*, ē *eve*, ĭ *ill*, ī *isle*, ō *old*, ŏ *odd*, oo *moon*, ŭ *but*, ü *Fr. sound*, kh *Ger. ch.* nh *nasal.*

(72)

Chiaroscuro (kē-ä-rŏs'koo-rō), *It.* Light and shade; the modifications of piano and forte.
Chiave (kē-ä'vē), *It.* A clef, or key.
Chiave maestro (kē-ä'vě mä-äs'trō), *It.* The fundamental key or note.
Chickera (kē'kĕ-rä), *Hin.* An instrument used in India, having four or five strings and played with a bow.
Chiesa (kē ä'zä), *It.* A church.
Chiffres (shěfr), *Fr.* Figures used in harmony and thorough bass.
Chifla (tshě'flä),
Chifladera (tshē-flä'dĕ-rä), *Sp.* } A whistle.
Chifladura (tshē-flä-doo'rä), *Sp.* Whistling.
Chiflar (tshē-flär'), *Sp.* To whistle.
Chime. A set of bells tuned to a musical scale; the sound of bells in harmony; a correspondence of sound.
Chime-barrel. The cylindrical portion of the mechanism sometimes used for ringing a chime of bells.
Chimney. In an organ, a small tube passing through the cap of a stopped pipe.
Chinese flute. An instrument used by the Chinese, made of bamboo.
Chinese musical scale. A scale consisting of five notes without semitones, the music being written on five lines in perpendicular columns, and the elevation and depression of tones indicated by distinctive names.
Chinnor (also **Kinnor**) (kĕn-nōr),
Chinor (kē-nōr), *Heb.* } An instrument of the harp or psaltery species, supposed to have been used by the ancient Hebrews. See *Kinnor.*
Chirimia (tshē-rē'mĭ-ä), *Sp.* The hautboy.
Chirogymnast (kē'rŏ-ghĭm'näst), *Gr.*
Chirogymnaste (kē'rŏ-gĭm-näs'tĕ), *It.* } A square board, on which are placed various mechanical contrivances for exercising the fingers of a pianist.
Chiroplast (kē'rŏ-pläst), *Gr.* A small machine invented by Logier, to keep the hands and fingers of young pianoforte-players in the right position.
Chitarone (kē-tä-rō'nĕ), *It.* A large, or double, guitar.
Chitarra (kē-tär'rä), *It.* A guitar, a cithara.
Chitarrista (kē-tär-rēs'tä), *It.* One who plays on the guitar.
Chittarra coll' arco (kē-tär'rä kŏl lär-kō), *It.* A species of guitar played with a bow like a violin.
Chittarrina (kĕt-tar-rē'nä),
Chittarrino (kĕt-tär-rē'nŏ), *It.* } The small Neapolitan guitar.
Chiuso (kē-oo'zō), *It.* Close.
Cho. Abbreviation of Chorus.
Chœur (kŭr), *Fr.* The choir or chorus.

Choice notes. Notes placed on different degrees in same measure, either or all of which may be sung.
Choir. That part of a cathedral or church set apart for the singers. (2) The singers themselves, taken collectively.
Choir, boy. A choir formed of boys from eight to fourteen years of age. These choirs are confined mostly to the Episcopal Church.
Choir, grand. In organ-playing, the union of all the reed stops.
Choir organ. In a large organ, the lowest row of keys is called the choir organ, which contains some of the softer and more delicate stops, and is used for accompanying solos, duets, etc.
Chor (kōr), *Ger.* (*pl. Chöre.*) Choir, chorus choir of a church.
Choragus (kō-rā'goos), *Lat.* The leader of the chorus in the Greek and Roman drama.
Choral. Belonging to the choir; full, or for many voices.
Choral (kō-räl'), *Ger.* Psalm or hymn tune; choral song or tune.
Choral anthem. An anthem in a simple, measured style, in the manner of a choral.
Choral-book. A collection of choral melodies either with or without a prescribed harmonic accompaniment.
Choralbuch (kō-räl'bookh), *Ger.* Choral-book; a book of hymn tunes.
Chöräle (kō-rä'lĕ), *Ger. pl.* Hymn tunes.
Choral hymn. A hymn to be sung by a chorus.
Choralist. Chorister, choir singer.
Choraliter (kō-räl'ī-tĕr),
Choralmässig (kō-räl'mäs-sĭg), *Ger.* } In the style or measure of a psalm tune or choral.
Choral service. A form of religious service in which the priest sings in response to the choir, and the entire liturgy is intoned or chanted instead of being read.
Choraltar (kōr'äl-tär'), *Ger.* The high, or great, altar.
Choramt (kōr'ämt), *Ger.* Cathedral service, choral service.
Chorautus (kō-rou'toos), *Lat.* The name given by the ancient Romans to the bagpipe.
Chord. Two or more tones sounding together harmonically. With reference to their musical quality, chords are divided into *harmony*, or *natural chords* (all the tones of which are partials of the fundamental), and *combination* chords (imitations of the former but composed of elements belonging to different fundamentals). To the former belong the major triad and the chord of the dominant seventh. In the key of C, these:

Combination chords are of every kind.

ä *arm*, ă *add*, ā *ale*, ĕ *end*, ē *eve*, ĭ *ill*, ī *isle*, ŏ *odd*, ō *old*, oo *moon*, ŭ *but*, ü *Fr. sound*, kh *Ger. ch.* nh *nasal.*

from the least appealing of all, the minor triad, to the most dissonant of sevenths and ninths. According to another view, all chords are triads (three tones), sevenths (four tones), or ninths (five tones). And all are derived from forms like the following:

Chorda (kŏr'dä), *Lat.* A string of a musical instrument.

Chord, accidental. A chord produced either by anticipation or suspension.

Chorda characteristica (kŏr'dä kä'räk-tē-rĭs'tĭ-kä), *Lat.* The leading, or characteristic, note or tone.

Chorda, dominant septima. The dominant chord of the seventh.

Chordæ essentiales (kŏr'dä ĕs-sĕn'tsĭ-ä'lĕs), *Lat.* These are the tonic, third and fifth of each diatonic mode or scale.

Chordæ vocales (kŏr'dä vō-kä'lĕs), *Lat.* Vocal chords.

Chord, anomalous. A chord in which one or more of the intervals are greater or less than of those of the fundamental chord.

Chordaulodian. } The name given to a musical instrument resembling a large barrel organ, self-acting. It was invented by Kaufmann, of Dresden.

Chord a vido (kŏrd ä vē dō), *It.* A name formerly given to a sound drawn from the open string of a violin, violoncello, or similar instrument.

Chord, characteristic. The principal chord; the leading chord.

Chord, chromatic. A chord that contains one or more chromatic tones.

Chord, common. A chord consisting of a fundamental note, together with its third and fifth.

Chord, dominant. A chord that is found on the dominant of the key in which the music is written. (2) The leading, or characteristic chord.

Chord, equivocal. A name sometimes given to the diminished seventh.

Chordienst (kŏr'dĕnst), *Ger.* Choir or choral service.

Chord, imperfect common. A chord founded on the leading tone. It has a minor third and diminished fifth.

Chord, inverted. A chord whose lowest tone is not the fundamental but the third, fifth, or seventh from the true fundamental.

Chordirector (kŏr'dĭ-rĕc-tŏr'), *Ger.* The director who trains the chorus at the opera-house.

Chord, leading. The dominant chord.

Chord nona. Chord of the ninth.

Chord of the eleventh. A chord founded on the chord of the ninth by adding the interval of the eleventh.

Chord of the fifth and sixth. ($^6_5$) The first inversion of the chord of the seventh, formed by taking the third of the original chord for the bass, and consisting of that together with its third, fifth, and sixth.

Chord of the fourth and fifth. ($^4_5$) Chord of the eleventh, with the seventh and ninth omitted.

Chord of the fourth and sixth. ($^6_4$) The second inversion of the common chord.

Chord of the ninth. (9) A chord consisting of a third, fifth, seventh, and ninth with its root.

Chord of the second and fourth. ($^4_2$) The third inversion of the seventh.

Chord of the seventh. (7) A chord consisting of the root, together with the third, fifth, and seventh.

Chord of the sixth. (6) The first inversion of the common chord.

Chord of the third, fourth, and sixth. ($^6_4_3$) The second inversion of the chord of the seventh.

Chord of the thirteenth. Founded on the chord of the ninth by adding the eleventh and the thirteenth.

Chord of the critone. Third inversion of the dominant seventh containing a superfluous fourth.

Chordometer. An instrument for measuring strings.

Chords, derivative. Chords derived from the fundamental chords.

Chords, diminished. Chords having minor thirds and diminished fifths and sevenths.

Chords, imperfect. Those which do not contain all the intervals belonging to them.

Chords, relative. Chords containing one or more tones in common.

Chords, small threefold. A common chord with a minor third.

Chord, threefold. The common chord.

Chord, transient. A chord in which, in order to smooth the transition from one chord to another, notes are introduced which do not form any component part of the fundamental harmony.

Chöre (kō'rĕ), *Ger. pl.* Choirs, choruses.

Chorea (kō'rĕ-ä), *Lat.* A dance in a ring; a dance.

Choree (kō'rā), *Gr.* In ancient poetry a foot of two syllables, the first long, the second short; the trochee.

Choreus (kō'rĕ-oos), *Lat.* The choree, or trochee.

Choriambus. A musical foot, accented thus:

Chorion (kō'rĭ-ŏn), *Gr.* A hymn in praise of Cybele.

Chori præfectus (kō'rē prä-fĕk'toos), *Lat.* A chanter.

ä *arm*, ă *add*, â *ale*, ĕ *end*, ē *eve*, ĭ *ill*, ī *isle*, ō *old*, ŏ *odd*, oo *moon*, ŭ *but*, ü *Fr. sound*, kh *Ger. ch*, nh *nasal*.

Chorist (kŏ-rĭst'), *Ger.* } A chorister, a choral-
Choriste (kŏ-rēst), *Fr.* } singer.
Chorister. A leader of a choir; a singer.
Chorknabe (kŏr'knä-bĕ), *Ger.* Singing-boy.
Chorocitharistæ (kŏ-rō-tsĭ-tä-rĭs'tä), *Lat.* A concert of instruments and voices; those who play to dancing.
Chorsänger (kŏr'säng-ĕr), *Ger.* } A chorister.
Chorschüler (kŏr-shū'lĕr), } a choral-singer; a member of the choir.
Chorton (kŏr'tōn), *Ger.* Choral tone; the usual pitch or intonation of the organ, and, therefore, of the choir. A choral tune.
Chorus. A company of singers; a composition intended to be sung by a number of voices. (2) Among the ancient Greeks the chorus was a band of singers and dancers who assisted at the performance of their dramas, and occupied that part of the theater answering to the present parquet.
Chorus, cyclic (sē'klĭk). The chorus among the ancient Athenians which performed at some of their dramatic representations, dancing in a circle around the altar of Bacchus.
Choruses, martial. Choruses in commemoration of warlike deeds.
Chorus-tone. See *Chorton.*
Christe eleison (krĭs-tĕ ā-lī'sŏn), *Gr.* O Christ, have mercy; a part of the Kyrie, or first movement, in a mass.
Christmas carols. Light songs, or ballads, commemorating the birth of Christ, sung during the Christmas holidays.
Christmesse (krĭst'mĕs-sĕ), *Ger.* } Christmas
Christmette (krĭst'mĕt-tĕ), } matins.
Chroma (krō'mä), *Gr.* The chromatic signs; a sharp (♯) or flat (♭).
Chroma diesis (krō'mä dī-ā'sĭs), *Gr.* A semitone, or half tone.
Chroma duplex. The double sharp, marked by the sign × or ♯♯.
Chromameter (krō-mä-mĕ'tĕr). A tuning-fork.
Chromatic. This word, derived from the Greek *chroma*, color, has a twofold meaning. (1) In modern music, progressing by semitones, chromatic in distinction from diatonic (*q. v.*). Chromatic notes are notes of the diatonic scale altered by sharps, flats, or naturals. A chromatic scale is one which proceeds throughout by semitones. (*V. Diatonic scale.*) A chromatically altered chord is a chord which contains one or more notes foreign to the key to which it belongs, one or more notes proper to the key being sharpened or flattened a semitone. (2) In the musical genus called by the ancient Greeks chromatic, the tetrachord (a series of four notes, a division of the scale) ascended by two semitones and a tone and semitone; for instance, b c d♭ e.
Chromatic depression. The lowering a note by a semitone.

Chromatic elevation. The elevation of a note by a semitone.
Chromatic instruments. All instruments upon which chromatic tones and melodies can be produced.
Chromatic keyboard. An attachment applied to the ordinary keys of a piano, for the purpose of enabling players of moderate skill to execute with greater facility the simple chromatic scale, chromatic runs, cadenzas, etc.
Chromatic keys. The black keys of a pianoforte. (2) Every key in the scale of which one or more chromatic tones occur. Not sanctioned by good usage.
Chromatic melody. A melody the tones of which move by chromatic intervals.
Chromatic scale. A scale which consists of twelve semitones, or half steps, in an octave.
Chromatic signs. Accidentals; sharps, flats, and naturals.
Chromatic tuning-fork. A tuning-fork sounding all the tones and semitones of the octave.
Chromatici suoni (krō-mä'tĭ-tshē soo-ō'nĭ), *It.* Chromatic sounds.
Chromatics, accidental. Chromatics employed in preparing the leading note of the minor scale; chromatics incidentally employed.
Chromatique (krō-mä'tĕk), *Fr.* } Chromatic,
Chromatisch (krō-mät'ĭsh), *Ger.* } moving by semitones.
Chromatiquement (krō-mä-tĕk'mŏnh), *Fr.* Chromatically.
Chromatisches Klanggeschlecht (krō-mä-tĭ'shĕs kläng-ghĕ-shlĕkht'), *Ger.* The chromatic genus or mode.
Chromatische Tonleiter (krō-mä'tĭ-shĕ tōn'lī'tĕr), *Ger.* The chromatic scale.
Chronometer (krō-nō-mä'tĕr), *Gr.* The name given to any machine for measuring time.
Chronometer, Weber. An invention of Godfrey Weber, similar to a metronome, but simpler in construction, consisting of a chord marked with fifty-five inch spaces, and having a weight attached to its lower end. The rate of motion is varied by the length of the cord.
Chrotta (krŏt'tä), *It.* The primitive fiddle, differing from the modern in the absence of a neck; the crowle.
Church cadence. Another name for the plagal cadence.
Church modes. See *Gregorian modes.*
Chute (shūt), *Fr.* Obsolete mark of embellishment, equivalent to a long appoggiatura.
Ciaccona (tshē-äk-kō'nä), *It.* } A slow Span-
Ciacconne (tshē-äk-kōn'nĕ), } ish dance, generally constructed on a ground bass. See *Chaconne.*
Ciaramella (tshē-ä-rä-mĕl'lä), *It.* A bagpipe.

---

a arm, *ă* add, *ā* ale, *ĕ* end, *ē* eve, *ĭ* ill, *ī* isle, *ŏ* old, *ō* odd, *oo* moon, *ŭ* but, *ü* *Fr.* sound, *kh Ger.* ch, *nh nasal.*

Cicuta (tsē-koo'tä), *Lat.* A pipe or flute made from the hollow stalks of the hemlock; a shepherd's pipe.

Cicutrenna (tshē-koo-trĕn'nä), *It.* A musical pipe.

Cimbale. See *Cimbel*.

Cimbali (tshĕm-bä'lē), *It. pl.* } Cymbals; military instruments used to mark the time.
Cimballes (sĭm-bäl), *Fr. pl.* }

Cimbalello (thĕm-bä-lä'yō), *Sp.* A small bell.

Cimbel (tsĭm'bĕl), *Ger.* A mixture stop of acute tone.

Cimbelstern (tsĭm'bĕl-stärn), *Ger.* Cymbal star. An organ-stop consisting of five bells, and composed of circular pieces of metal cut in the form of a star, and placed at the top of the instrument in front.

C in alt. The eleventh above the G, or treble, c of note; the fourth note in alt.

C in altissimo. The octave above C in alt; the fourth note in altissimo.

Cinelle, *Tur.* } A cymbal; a Turkish musical instrument, more noisy than musical.
Cinellen, }

Cink (tsĭnk), *Ger.* A small reed-stop in an organ. See *Kinkhorn*.

Cinnara (tshĕn'nä-rä), *It.* The harp of the Romans.

Cinq (sănkh), *Fr.* } Five; the fifth voice or part in a quintet.
Cinque (tshĕn'kwĕ), *It.* }

Cinyra (sĭn'ē-rä). An old name for the harp.

Ciphering (sī'fĕr-ĭng). The sounding of the pipes of the organ when the keys are not touched; due to leakage in the valves.

Circular canon. A canon which goes through the twelve major keys.

Circle of fifths. A method of modulation which conveys us round through all the scales back to the point from which we started.

Circular scale. The row of tuning-pins and the wrest-plank of a piano, made in a curved form, in order to throw the strings farther apart.

Cis (tsĭs), *Ger.* The note C♯.

Cis-cis (tsĭs-tsĭs), *Ger.* The note C-double-sharp, C♯♯, C✕.

Cis-dur (tsĭs-door'), *Ger.* The key of C♯ major.

Cis-moll (tsĭs-mŏll), *Ger.* The key of C♯ minor.

Cistella (tsĭs-tĕl'lä), *Lat.* A small chest or box, triangular in shape, and strung with wires, which are struck with little rods. See *Dulcimer*.

Cistre (sĕstr), *Fr.* A cithern, a small harp.

Cistrum. See *Cittern*.

Citara (tshē-tä-rä), *It.* A cittern, a guitar.

Citaredo (tshē-tä-rä'dō), *It.* } A minstrel, a player upon the harp or cittern.
Citarista (tshē-tä-rĕs'tä), }

Cithar (tsĭth'är), *Dan.* A cittern.

Cithara (tsē'tä-rä), *Lat.* } The lute, an old instrument of the guitar kind.
Cithara (thĕt'ä-rä), *Sp.* }

Cithara bijuga (tsē'tä-rä bī-yoo'gä), *Lat.* A cithara, so called from its having two necks which determine the length of the strings.

Cithara hispanica (thĕt'ä-rä hĭs-pän'ĭ-kä), *Sp.* The Spanish guitar.

Cithara, keyed. The clavicitherium.

Citharodia (tsĭ-thä-rō'dĭ-ä), *Gr.* The art of singing to the lyre or cithara.

Citharn. See *Cithern*.

Citharœdus (tsĭ-tä-rē'doos), *Lat.* He who plays upon a harp or cithara.

Cither. } An old instrument of the lute or guitar species; the oldest on record had three strings, which were afterward increased to eight, nine, and up to twenty-four. The cither was very popular in the sixteenth century. The cittern and guitar seem to be derived from the same Greek word.
Cithera. }
Cithern. }
Cittern. }
Cythorn. }

Citole (tsī-tō'lĕ), *Lat.* An old instrument of the dulcimer species, and probably synonymous with it.

Cittam. The ancient English name of the guitar.

Civetteria (tshē-vĕt-tä'rĭ-ä), *It.* Coquetry; in a coquettish manner.

Clair (klăr), *Fr.* Clear, shrill, loud.

Claircylindre (klăr-sĭ-länbdr). An instrument invented by Chladni in 1787, for the purpose of experimenting in acoustics.

Clairon (klă-rônh), *Fr.* Trumpet; also the name of a reed-stop in the organ.

Clamor. In bell-ringing, a rapid multiplication of strokes.

Clang. A sharp, shrill noise. See *Klang*.

Clango (klăn'gō), *Lat.* To clang, to sound.

Clangor (klän'gŏr), *Lat.* A sound, noise; the clang of the trumpet when blown powerfully.

Clapper. The tongue of a bell.

Claquebois (klăk-bwä), *Fr.* A three-stringed viol.

Clar. An abbreviation of Clarinet.

Clara voce (klä'rä vō'tsĕ), *Lat.* A clear, loud voice.

Clarabella (klä'rä-bĕl'lä), *Lat.* } An organ-stop of eight-feet scale, with a powerful, fluty tone; the pipes are of wood and not stopped.
Claribella (klä'rĭ-bĕl'lä), }

Claribel flute. An organ-stop of the flute species.

Clarichord. See *Clavichord*.

Clarichorde (klär-ĭ-kŏrd), *Fr.* The clarichord, or clavichord.

Clarin (klä'rēn), *Ger.* A clarion; also the name of a four-feet reed-stop in German organs.

Clarinblasen (klä-rēn'blä-zĕn), *Ger.* Soft notes or tones upon the trumpet.

Clarinet. One of the most important wood wind instruments. It is said to have been invented about 1700 by J. C. Denner, of Nuremberg. It consists of a cylindrical tube, with finger-holes and keys, which terminates in a bell, and has a beak-like mouthpiece with a single beating reed. Its extreme compass extends from e to a'''. There are clarinets of different pitch; those commonly used in the orchestra are the clarinets in C, in B♭, and in A. The clarinets in D, E♭, F, A♭, etc., are rarely used except in military bands. All clarinets, the one in C excepted, are transposing instruments; that is to say, they do not sound the notes which are written. For instance, the B♭ clarinet sounds them a tone lower, and the A clarinet a minor third lower. Music for the clarinet is written in the G clef. (*V. Chalumeau.*) Besides the above-mentioned clarinets, there are a bass clarinet and a baritone clarinet. Now clarinets are also made of ebonite. Also an organ-stop, voiced like a clarinet.

Clarinet, alto. A large clarinet, curved near the mouthpiece, and a fifth deeper than the ordinary clarinet.

Clarinet, bass. A clarinet whose tones are an octave deeper than those of the C or B♭ clarinet.

Clarinettista (klä-rĭ-nĕt-tēs'tä), *It.* } A performer
Clarinettiste (klär-ĭ-nĕt-test), *Fr.* } former upon the clarinet.

Clarinetto (klä-rĭ-nĕt'tŏ), *It.* A clarinet.

Clarinetto d'amore (klä-rĭ-nĕt'tŏ dä-mō'rĕ), *It.* A species of clarinet a fifth lower than the C clarinet. An alto clarinet.

Clarinetto dolce (klä-rĭ-nĕt'tŏ dōl'tshĕ), *It.* A species of clarinet a fifth lower than the C clarinet.

Clarinetto secondo (klä-rĭ-nĕt'tŏ sĕ-kŏn'dŏ), *It.* The second clarinet.

Clarino (klä-rē'nŏ), *It.* } A small, or octave,
Clarion. } trumpet; also the name of a 4-feet organ-reed stop, tuned an octave above the trumpet-stop. The term is also used to indicate the trumpet parts in a full score.

Clarion harmonique (klä-rĭ-ōnh här-mōnh-nĭk'), *Fr.* An organ-reed stop. See *Harmonique.*

Clarionet-flute. An organ-stop of a similar kind to the stopped diapason.

Clarone (klä-rō'nĕ), *It.* A clarinet.

Clarus (klä'roos), *Lat.* Loud, clear, bright.

Clarté de voix (klär-tā dŭh vwä), *Fr.* Clearness of voice.

Classic, or, **Classical.** These words are used in music, as in the other arts and in literature, in various sens s, which often more or less overlap. (1) "Of the first class, of the first rank;" more especia'ly applied to the older, universally acknowledged, masters and their wo ks, those of the best epoch of the art. (2) Having, or resembling, the style and temper of these masters and their works —their perfectness of form, and sobriety, and ideal beauty of contents. The opposite of "classical" in this sense is "romantic" (*q. v.*). Also in popular use to designate serious music in general, as distinguished from the merely *ad captandum* and ephemeral.

Classical music. Standard music; music of first rank, written by composers of the highest order.

Clause. A phrase.

Clausel (klou'z'l), *Ger.* } A close, a ca-
Clausula (klou'sū-lä), *Lat.* } dence, a concluding musical phrase.

Clav. An abbreviation of Clavecembalo, Clavichord, and Clavecin.

Clavecin (kläv-ĕ-sănh), *Fr.* The harpsichord.

Clavecin acoustique (kläv-ĕ-sănh ä-koōz-tĕk), *Fr.* An instrument of the harpsichord or pianoforte class, now obsolete.

Clavicymbalum (klä-vĭ-tsĭm'bä-loom). *Lat.* The harpsichord; spinet.

Ciavicymbel (klä-vĭ-tsĭm'b'l), *Ger.* A clavichord.

Claveciniste (klä-vĕ-sănh-ĕst'), *Fr.* A harpsichord-player, or maker.

Clavessin (kläv-ĕ-sănh'), *Fr.* The harpsichord. See *Clavecin.*

Claviatur (klä-vĭ-ä-toor'), *Ger.* The keys of a harpsichord, piano, etc.

Clavicembalo (klä-vĭ-tshĕm'bä-lō), *It.* }
Clavicembalum (κlä'-vĭ-tsĕm-bä'loom), *Lat.* } The harpsichord.

Clavichord. A small, keyed instrument like the spinet, and the forerunner of the pianoforte. The tone of the clavichord was agreeable and impressive but not strong. The strings were made to vibrate by means of a small brass upright, called a tangent, fixed in the key. The tangent "stopped" the string (like a violinist's finger) and caused it to sound at the same time.

Clavicytherium (klä-vĭ-tsĭ-tā'rĭ-oom), *Lat.* A species of upright harpsichord, said to have been originally in the form of a harp or lyre. It was invented in the thirteenth century, and was the earliest approach to the modern pianoforte.

Clavicylinder. An instrument exhibited in Paris in 1806. It was supposed to consist of a series of cylinders, which were operated upon by bows set in motion by a crank and brought in contact with the cylinders by means of the keys of a fingerboard.

Clavier (klä-vēr), *Fr.* } The keys or key-
Clavier (klä-fēr'), *Ger.* } board of a pianoforte, organ, etc. Also an old name for the clavichord.

Clavierauszug (klä-fēr'ous'tsoong), *Ger.* An arrangement of a full score for the use of pianoplayers.

Clavieren (klä-fē'rĕn), *Ger. pl.* The keys. See *Clavier.*

Clavierlehrer (klä-fēr'lā'rĕr), *Ger.* A pianoforte-teacher.

Clavierschule (klä-fēr-shoo'lĕ), *Ger.* A pianoforte instruction book.

Clavierspieler (klä-fēr'spē'lĕr), *Ger.* A pianoforte-player.

Clavierstimner (klä-fēr'stĭm'mĕr), *Ger.* A pianoforte-tuner.

Clavierübung (klä-fēr'ü'boong), *Ger.* Exercises for the clavichord.

Clavierunterricht (klä-fēr'oon'tĕr-rĭkht), *Ger.* Lessons or instruction on the pianoforte.

Clavis (klä'vĭs), *Lat.*}
Clavis (klä'vĭs), *Ger.* } A key; a clef.

Clear flute. An organ-stop of 4-feet scale, the tone of which is very clear and full.

Clé (klā), *Fr.* } A key: a character used to
Clef (klā), determine the name and pitch of the notes on the staff to which it is prefixed.

Clef, alto. The C clef on the third line of the staff.

Clef, baritone. The F clef when placed on the third line.

Clef, bass. The character at the beginning of the staff, where the lower or bass notes are written, and serving to indicate the pitch and name of those notes. The F clef.

Clef, C. So called because it gives its name to the notes placed on the same line with itself.

Clef, counter tenor. The C clef when placed on the third line in order to accommodate the counter tenor voice.

Clef d'accordeur (klā däk-kŏr-dŭr), *Fr.* A tuning-hammer.

Clef de fay (klā dŭh fā), *Fr.* The F, or base, clef.

Clef descant. The treble, or soprano, clef.

Clef d'ut (klā doot), *Fr.* The C clef.

Clef, F. The base clef.

Clef, French treble. The G clef on the bottom line of the staff; formerly much used in French music for the violin, flute, etc.

Clef, German soprano. The C clef placed on the first line of the staff for soprano

Clef, mean. The tenor clef or

Clef, mezzo-soprano. The C clef when placed on the second line of the staff.

Clef note. The note indicated by the clef.

Clef sol (klā sol), *Fr.* The G, or treble, clef.

Clef, soprano. The C clef placed on the first line. (Obsolete.)

Clef, tenor. See *Mean clef*.

Clef, treble. The G clef; soprano clef.

Cloche (klōsh), *Fr.* A bell.

Clochette (klŏ-shĕt'), *Fr.* A little bell; a hand bell.

Clocks, musical. Clocks containing an arrangement similar to a barrel organ, moved by weights and springs, and producing various tunes.

Clorone. A species of clarinet which is a fifth lower than the clarinet; alto clarinet.

Close. A cadence; the end of a piece or passage.

Close harmony. Harmony in which the notes or parts are kept as close together as possible.

C major. The diatonic scale or key of C without flats or sharps.

C minor. The diatonic scale or key of C with minor third and sixth.

C-moll (tsä-mŏll), *Ger.* The key of C minor.

C natural. C without flat or sharp.

C. O. An abbreviation of Choir organ.

Co (kō),
Coi (kō ē), *It.* } With; with the.
Col (kōl),

Coalottino (kō-ä-lŏt-tē'nō), *It.* See *Concertino*.

Cocchina (ko-kē'-nä), *It.* An Italian country dance.

Coda (kō'dä), *It.* The end; a few measures added to the end of a piece of music to make a more effective termination.

Coda brillante (kō'dä brĭl-län'tē), *It.* A brilliant termination.

Codetta (kō-dĕt'tä), *It.* A short coda or passage added to a piece, or serving to connect one movement with another.

Coffre (kŏfr), *Fr.* The frame of a lute, guitar, etc.

Cogli (kōl'yē), *It.* With the.

Cogli stromenti (kōl'yē strō-mĕn'tē), *It. pl.* With the instruments.

Cognoscente (kōn-yō-shĕn'tē), *It.* One well versed in music; a connoisseur.

Coi bassi (kō'ē läs'sē), *It.* With the basses.

Coi fagotti (kō-ē fä-gŏt-tē), *It.* With the bassoons.

Coi violini (kŏr vē-ō-lē'nē), *It.* With the violins.

Colachon (kō-lä-shōnh), *Fr.* An Italian instrument, much like a lute, but with a longer neck.

Col arco (kōl är'kō), *It.* With the bow. See *Coll' arco*.

Colascione (kō-läs-shĭ-ō'nē), *It.* An instrument like the guitar, with two strings only.

Col basso (kōl bäs-sō), *It.* With the bass.

Col C. An abbreviation of Col canto.

Col canto (kōl kän'tō), *It.* With the melody, or voice. See *Colla voce*.

Coll (kōl),
Colla (kōl'lä), *It.* } With the.
Collo (kōl'lō),

ä *arm,* à *add,* ā *ale,* e *end,* ē *eve,* ĭ *ill,* ī *isle,* ŏ *old,* ŏ *odd,* oo *moon,* ŭ *but,* ü *Fr. sound,* kh *Ger. ch,* nh *nasal.*

Colla destra (kōl'lä däs'trä), *It.* With the right hand.

Colla massima discrezione (kōl'lä mäs'sĭ-mä dĭs-krĕ tsĭ-ō'nĕ), *It.* With the greatest discretion.

Colla parte (kōl'lä pär'tĕ), *It.* With the part; indicating that the time is to be accommodated to the solo singer or player.

Colla piu gran forza e prestezza (kōl'lä pē'oo grä · fŏr'zä ā prĕs-tĕt'zä), *It.* As loud and as quickly as possible.

Colla punta d'arco (kōl'lä poon'tä där'kō), *It.* With the point, or tip, of the bow.

Colla sinistra (kōl'lä sĭ-nĭs'trä), *It.* With the left hand.

Colla voce (kōl'lä vŏ'tshĕ), *It.* With the voice, implying that the accompanist must accommodate and take the time from the singer.

Coll'arco (kōl lär'kō), *It.* With the bow; the notes are to be played with the bow, and not pizzicato.

College songs. Songs for the use of, and sung by, college students; usually of a convivial and spirited character.

Col legno (kōl län'yō), *It.* With the bow-stick.

Col legno dell' arco (kōl län' yō dĕl lär'kō), *It.* With the bow-stick; strike the strings with the wooden side of the bow.

Colla parti (kōl'lē pär'tĕ), *It.* With the principal parts.

Colle trombe (kōl'lĕ trŏm'bĕ), *It.* With the trumpets.

Coll' ottava (kōl lŏt-tä-vä), *It.* With the octave.

Colofane (kōl-ō-fäne), *Fr.*
Colofonia (kōl-lō-fō'nĭ-ä), *It.*
Colophane (kōl-ō-fäne), *Fr.*
Colophon (kōl-ō-fŏnh), *Fr.*
Colophonium (kō-lō-fō'nĭ-oom), *Ger.*
Colophony, *Eng.*
Resin; used for the hair in the bow of a violin, etc., to enable the performer to get a better hold upon the strings.

Coloratura (kō-lō-rä-too'rä), *It.* } Orna-
Colorature (kō-lō-rä-too'rĕ), *It.* } mental
Coloraturen (kō-lō-rä-too'rĕn), *Ger.*) passages, roulades, embellishments. etc., in vocal music. This word, the plural form of which, in Italian, is colorature, is, less properly, but very conveniently, used also in connection with instrumental music.

Combination, *or,* **Combinational tones.** See *Resultant tones.*

Combination pedals. See *Composition pedals.*

Come (kō'mĕ), *It.* As, like, the same as.

Comédie (kŏm-ä-dē), *Fr.* Comedy, play.

Comédien (kŏm-ä-dĭ-änh'), *Fr.* } A come-
Comediante (kō-mä-dĭ-än'tĕ), *Sp.* } dian, an actor.

Comédienne (kŏm-ä-dĭ-änh'), *Fr.* An actress.

Comedy, lyric. A comedy specially adapted for singing.

Come il primo tempo (kō'mĕ ĕl prē'mŏ tĕm'pō), *It.* In the same time as the first.

Come prima (kō'mĕ prē'mä), *It.* As before, as at first.

Comes (kō'mĕs). *Lat.* The companion, or answer, to the *dux* (guide), or subject, of a fugue.

Come sopra (kō'mĕ sō'prä), *It.* As above; as before; indicating the repetition of a previous, or similar, passage.

Come sta (kō'mĕ stä), *It.* As it stands; perform exactly as written.

Come tempo del tema (kō'mĕ tĕm'pō dĕl tā'mä), *It.* In the same time as the theme.

Comico (kō'mĭ-kō), *It.*) Comic; also a
Comique (kō-mēk'), *Fr.* j comic actor, and a writer of comedies.

Comic opera. Burlesque opera; an opera interspersed with light songs, dances and jests.

Comic song. A song set to comical, humorous words.

Comiquement (kō-mēk'mänh), *Fr.* Comically, jocosely.

Cominciante (kō-mĭn-tshĭ-än'tĕ), *It.* A beginner in music, etc.

Cominciata (kō mĭn-tshĭ-ä'tä), *It.* The beginning, the commencement.

Comma (kom'mä), *It.* This is the name of various small intervals not used in practical music, forming the difference between two notes of nearly the same pitch. Two of these small intervals are: (1) The *comma syntonum*, or the comma of Didymus, which is the difference between a major and a minor tone, equal to the ratio 80:81. (2) The *comma ditonicum*, or comma of Pythagoras, which is the difference between the twelfth fifth (just intonation, not tempered) and the seventh octave above a given note.

Commedia (kŏm-mä'dĭ-ä), *It.* A play, a comedy; also a theater.

Comme il faut (kŏm ēl fō), *Fr.* As it should be.

Commencant (kŏm-mänh-sänh), *Fr.* A beginner in music, etc.

Commencer (kŏm-mänh-sä), *Fr.* To begin, to commence.

Commodamente (kŏm-mō-dä-mĕn'tĕ), *It.* With ease and quietude.

Commodo (kŏm-mō'dō), *It.* Quietly, composedly.

Common chord. A chord consisting of a bass note with its third and fifth, to which its octave is usually added.

Common chord, imperfect. A chord consisting of a bass, accompanied by its minor third and imperfect fifth.

Common hallelujah meter. A stanza of six lines of iambic measure, the syllables of each being in number and order as follows: 8, 6, 8, 6, 8, 8.

Common measure. Four-pulse measure.

Common meter. A verse, or stanza, of four lines in iambic measure, the syllables of each being in number and order, thus, 8, 6, 8, 6.

Common particular meter. A stanza of six lines in iambic measure, the number and order of syllables as follows: 8, 8, 6, 8, 8, 6.

Common time. Common measure.

Common turn. A turn consisting of the principal note, the note above it, and the note below it.

Comodamente (kō-mō-dä-mĕn'tĕ), *It.* }
Comodo (kō'mō-dō), } Conveniently, easily, quietly, with composure.

Compass. The range of notes or sounds of which any voice or instrument is capable.

Compiacevole (kōm-pī-ä-tshä'vō-lĕ), } *It.*
Compiacimento (kōm-pī-ä-tshī-mĕn'tō), } Agreeable, pleasing, attractive.

Compiacevolmente (kōm-pī-ä-tshŏ-vōl-mĕn'tĕ), *It.* In a pleasant and agreeable style.

Complainte (kōm-plänht'), *Fr.* A religious ballad.

Complement. That quantity which is wanting to any interval to fill up an octave.

Complementary part. That part which is added to the subject and counter subject of a fugue.

Complete cadence. A full cadence.

Complin (kōm'plĭn), *Lat.* Evening service during Lent in the Catholic Church.

Componiren (kōm-pō-nē'r'n), *Ger.* To compose music.

Componista (kōm-pō-nēs'tä), *It.* A composer, an author.

Composer (kŏnh-pō-zä), *Fr.* To compose music.

Composer. One who composes; one who writes an original work.

Compositeur (kōm-pō-sī-tûr'), *Fr.* } A composer of
Compositore (kōm-pō-sī-tō'rĕ), *It.* } poser of
Componist (kōm-pō-nĭst'), *Ger.* } music.

Compositeur de fugues (kōm-pōs-ĭ-tûr' dūh füg), *Fr.* A composer of fugues.

Composition. Any musical production; the art of inventing or composing music according to the rules of harmony.

Composition, free. That which deviates somewhat from the rules of composition.

Composition, erotic. That which has love for its subject.

Composition, strict. A composition that adheres rigidly to the rules of art.

Composition pedals. Pedals connected with a system of mechanism for arranging the stops of an organ Invented by J. C. Bishop.

Compositor, music. A person who sets music type.

Compositura (kōm-pō-sī-too'rä), } *It.* } A com-
Composizione (kōm-pō-sī-tsī-ō'nĕ), } position, or musical work.

Composizione di tavolino (kōm-pō-sī-tsī-ō'nĕ dē tä-vō lē'nō), *It.* Table music, music sung at table, as glees, catches, rounds.

Composso (kōm-pōs'sō), } *It.* } Composed, set
Composto (kōm-pōs'tō), } to music.

Compound intervals. Those which exceed the extent of an octave; as a ninth, tenth, etc.

Compound stops. Where three or more organ-stops are arranged so that by pressing down one key they all sound at once.

Compound measures. Those which include, or exceed, six parts in a measure, and contain two, or more, principal accents, as, 6-4, 6-8, 9-4, 9-8, 12-8, etc.

Con (kōn), *It.* With.

Con abbandono (kōn äb-bän-dō'nō), *It.* With passion, with ardent feeling.

Con abbandono ed espressione (kōn äb-bän-dō'-nō ĕd ĕs-präs-sī-ō'nĕ), *It.* With passionate feeling and self-abandon.

Con affetto (kōn äf-fĕt'tō), } *It.* } In an
Con affezione (kōn äf-lĕt'tsī-ō'nĕ), } affecting manner, with warmth

Con afflizione (kōn äf-flē-tsī-ō'nĕ), *It.* With affliction, mournfully.

Con agilita (kōn ä-jĭl-ĭ-tä'). *It.* With agility, neatly.

Con agitazione (kōn ä-jĭ-tä-tsī-ō'nĕ), *It.* With agitation, hurriedly.

Con alcuna licenza (kōn äl-koo'nä lē-tshĕn-tsä), *It.* With a certain degree of license as regards time and expression.

Con allegrezza (kōn äl-lĕ-grĕt'tsä), *It.* With lightness, cheerfully.

Con alterezza (kōn äl-tĕ-rĕt'tsä), *It.* With an elevated and sublime expression.

Con amabilita (kōn ä-mä-bĭl'ĭ-tä), *It.* With gentleness and grace.

Con amarezza (kōn ä-mä rĕt'tsä), *It.* With affliction, with a sense of grief.

Con amore (kōn ä-mō'rĕ), *It.* With tenderness and affection.

Con anima (kōn ä'nĭ-mä), } *It.* } With anima-
Con animo (kōn ä'nĭ-mō), } tion and boldness.

Con animazione (kōn ä-nĭ-mä-tsī-ō'nĕ), *It.* With animation, decision, boldness.

Con audace (kōn ä-oo-dä'tshĕ), *It.* With boldness, audacity.

Con bellezza (kōn bĕl-lĕt'tsä), *It.* With beauty of tone and expression.

Con bizarria (kōn bē-tsär'rī-ä), *It.* Capriciously, at the fancy of the player or composer.

Con bravura (kōn brä-voo'rä), *It.* With bravery, with boldness.

Con brio (kōn brē'ō), *It.* With life, spirit, brilliancy.

Con brio ed animato (kōn brē'ō ĕd ä-nĭ-mä'tō), *It.* With brilliancy and animation.

Con calma (kōn käl'mä), *It.* With calmness and tranquillity.

Con calore (kŏn kä-lō'rĕ), *It.* With warmth, with fire.

Con carita (kŏn kä-rē'tä), *It.* With tenderness.

Con celerita (kŏn tshä-lĕ-rĭ-tä'), *It.* With celerity, with rapidity.

Concento (kŏn-tshĕn'tō), *It.* Concord, agreement, harmony of voices and instruments.

Concentrare (kŏn-tshĕn-trä'rĕ), *It.* To concentrate the sounds. It also means to veil the sounds in mystery.

Concentus (kŏn-tsĕn'toos), *Lat.* Harmonious blending of sounds; concord.

Concert. A performance in public of practical musicians, either vocal or instrumental, or both. (2) Harmony, unison.

Concert, amateur. A concert of nonprofessional musicians.

Concertando (kŏn-tshĕr-tän'dō), *It.* A concertante.

Concertant (kŏnh-sĕr-tänh'), *Fr.* Performer in a concert, a musician.

Concertante (kŏn-tshĕr-tän'tĕ), *It.* A piece in which each part is alternately principal and subordinate, as in a duo concertante. (2) A concerto for two or more instruments, with accompaniments for a full band. (3) A female concert singer.

Concertato (kŏn-tshĕr-tä'tō), *It.* In an irregular and extemporaneous manner. See, also, *Concertante.*

Concerted music. Music in which several voices or instruments are heard at the same time; in opposition to solo music.

Concertgeber (kŏn-tsĕrt'gä'bĕr), *Ger.* One who gives a concert.

Concertina (kŏn-tshĕr-tē'nä), *It.* A small musical instrument, hexagonal in form, which, as regards construction, is somewhat similar to the accordion (*q. v.*). The English treble concertina has a compass of about three and a half or four octaves (from g to g'''') with all the intermediate semitones, and is a double-action instrument—that is, on expanding and compressing the bellows the same note is produced. The tenor, bass, and double-bass concertina are, like the accordion, single-action instruments, producing different notes on expanding and compressing the bellows. Charles Wheatstone patented the concertina in 1829. The German concertina is a less perfect instrument than the English concertina; it is a single-action instrument, and its scale is not chromatic.

Concertina, alto. A concertina having the compass of the viola.

Concertina, bass. A concertina having the compass of the violoncello.

Concertina, soprano. A concertina having the compass of the violin.

Concertino (kŏn-tshĕr-tē'nō), *It.* A small concerto. (2) The opposite of *ripieno*—namely, principal, or *concertante;* for instance, *violino concertino,* principal violin. (5) The name concertino is sometimes applied to a first-violin part in which are entered the obligato passages of the other parts. (*V. Concerto grosso.*)

Concertiren (kŏn-tsĕr-tē'r'n), *Ger.* To accord, to agree in sound; also a soli movement where each instrument or voice has in its turn the principal part.

Concertmeister (kŏn-tsĕrt' mīs'tĕr), *Ger.* The leader of the orchestra, the first of the first violins.

Concerto (kŏn-tshĕr'tō), *It.* (1) A concert. (2) A composition consisting generally of three, rarely of four, movements, for one or more solo instruments, with orchestral accompaniment. Its form is, on the whole, that of the sonata; its distinctive features are the tutti (the orchestral ritornelli) and certain peculiarities arising from the intention to display the solo instrument and the powers of the player. As one of these peculiarities may be mentioned the cadenzas played by the performer of the solo part just before the concluding tutti of the first and the last movement. (*V. Sonata* and *Cadenza.*) The customary tutti, which, for instance, in Mozart's concertos, appear in diffusive fullness, are in more modern times often curtailed or altogether omitted. This is especially the case with the long introductory tutti, which generally presented both the first and the second subject, afterwards taken up by the solo part or solo parts. Also the cadenzas have lost much of their former importance. In other words, the concerto, at one time a show-piece, has more and more become a tone-poem. Concertos without orchestral accompaniment need hardly be mentioned; they are exceptional, and of very rare occurrence.

In its earliest application the word "concerto" was synonymous with "concent," signifying not a definite form, but a composition in parts, either purely vocal or vocal and instrumental. Giuseppe Torelli, who died in 1708, is regarded as the inventor of the modern concerto. The development of the concerto runs parallel, one may say is identical, with that of the sonata. The earlier exemplifications of these forms differ indeed often only in name. With Mozart (1756-1791) the concerto reached, so to speak, maturity. (See the following articles):

Concerto, a solo. A concerto written for the purpose of displaying the powers of a particular instrument, without accompaniment.

Concerto da camera (kŏn-tshĕr'tō dä kä'mĕ-rä), *It.* Chamber concerto. Contra to *Concerto grosso.*

Concerto di chiesa (kŏn-tshĕr'tō dē kē-ä'zü), *It.* A concerto for church use.

Concerto doppio (kŏn-tshĕr'tō dōp'pĭ-ō), *It.* A concerto for two or more instruments.

Concerto grande (kŏn-tshĕr'tō gränd), *Fr.*
Concerto grosso (kŏn-tshĕr'tō grōs-sō), *It.*
A grand orchestral composition for many instruments; a grand concert.

Concerto spirituale (kŏn-tshĕr'tō spē-rē-too-ä'lĕ), *It.* A miscellaneous concert, consisting chiefly of sacred or classical music.

Concert, operatic. A performance of music selected from operas.

Concertsaal (kŏn-tsĕrt'säl), *Ger.* Concert-hall.

Concertspieler (kŏn-tsĕrt'spē-lĕr), *Ger.* A solo player, concerto player.

Concert spirituel (kŏn-tsĕrt' spē-rē-too-âl'), *Fr.* See *Concerto spirituale.*

Concertstück (kŏn-tsĕrt'stük), *Ger.* A concert-piece; a concerto.

Concert pitch. The pitch adopted by general consent for some one given note, and by which every other note is governed. The so-called French normal diapason is now generally adopted, computed from A—435 vibrations per second. This is nearly a half step lower than the concert pitch in use by American piano-makers previous to about 1885.

Concitato (kŏn-tshī-tä'tō), *It.* Agitated, perturbed.

Conclusione (kŏn-kloo-zī-ō'nĕ), *It.* The conclusion, or winding up.

Con comodo (kŏn kŏ'mō-dō), *It.* With ease, in convenient time.

Concord. A harmonious combination of sounds; the opposite to a discord.

Concordant. Agreeing, correspondent, harmonious. Concord depends upon the frequency of coincidences between vibrations of the different tones composing the concord. Hence the most agreeable concord is that of the octave, of which the ratio is 1:2, a coincidence occurring with every vibration of the lower tone. The next is that of the fifth, in which the ratio is 2:3, a coincidence occurring with every second vibration of the lower tone. And so the concords shade off through the intervals of the harmonic series, which follow the ratios 1:2:3:4: 5:6:7:8:9:10, etc.

Concordanza (kŏn-kŏr-dän'tsä), *It.*
Concorde (kŏn-kŏrd), *Fr.*
Concordia (kŏn-kŏr'dĭ-ä), *It.*
} Concord, harmony.

Con delicatezza (kŏn dĕl-ĭ-kä-tĕt'sä), *It.* With delicacy and sweetness.

Con desiderio (kŏn dā-zĭ-dā'rĭ-ō), *It.* With desire and ardent longing.

Con devozione (kŏn dā-vō-tsī-ō'nĕ), *It.* With devotion, devoutly.

Con diligenza (kŏn dĭ-lĭ-jĕn'tsä), *It.* With care and diligence.

Con discrezione (kŏn dĭs-krā-tsī-ō'nĕ), *It.* With discretion; at the discretion of the performer.

Con disperazione (kŏn dĭs-pĕ-rä-tsī-ō'nĕ), *It.* With despair, violence of expression.

Con divozione (kŏn dĕ-vō-tsī-ō'nĕ), *It.* With religious feeling; in a devotional manner.

Con dolce maniera (kŏn dŏl'tshĕ mä-nĭ-ä'rä), *It.* } In a simple, delicate manner; with softness, sweetness, delicacy.
Con dolcezza (kŏn dŏl-tsĕt'sä), }

Con dolore (kŏn do-lō'rĕ), *It.* Mournfully, with grief and pathos.

Conductor. The master, or chief, of an orchestra, who directs the time and performance of every piece with his baton.

Conductus (kŏn-dook'toos), *Lat.* A very old species of descant, which, instead of being founded upon some popular melody, was entirely original, both descant and harmony, and entirely independent of everything but the imagination of the composer.

Con duolo (kŏn doo-ō'lō), *It.* Mournfully, with grief.

Conduttore (kŏn-doot-tō'rĕ), *It.* A conductor.

Con eleganza (kŏn ā-lĕ-gän'tsä), *It.* With elegance.

Con elevatezza (kŏn ā-lĕ-vä-tĕt-tsä), *It.* }
Con elevazione (kŏn ā-lĕ-vä tsī-ō'nĕ), *It.* }
With elevation of style; with dignity.

Con energia (kŏn ā-nĕr-jē'ä), *It.* } With energy and emphasis.
Con energico (kŏn ā-nĕr'jī-kō), *It.* }

Con entusiasmo kŏn ĕn-too-zī-äs'mō), *It.* With enthusiasm.

Con equalianza (kŏn ā-kwä-lī-än'tsä), *It.* With smoothness and equality.

Con e senza stromenti (kŏn ā sĕn-tsä strō-mĕn'tĕ), *It.* With and without instruments.

Con esp. } An abbreviation of Con espressione.
Con espres. }

Con espressione (kŏn ās-prĕs-sĭ-ō'nĕ), *It.* With expression.

Con facilita (kŏn fä-tshē-lī-tä'), *It.* With facility and ease.

Con espressione dolorosa (kŏn ās-prĕs-sī-ō'nĕ dō-lō-rō'zä), *It.* With a sad expression.

Con estro poetico (kŏn ās'trō pō-ä'tī-kō), *It.* With poetic fervor.

Con fermezza (kŏn fĕr-mĕt'sä), *It.* With firmness.

Con festivita (kŏn fĕs-tĕ'vĭ-tä), *It.* With festive gayety.

Con fiducia (kŏn fē-doo'tshĭ-ä), *It.* With hope, with confidence.

Con fierezza (kŏn fē-ĕ-rĕt'sä), *It.* With fire, fiercely.

Con flessibilita (kŏn flĕs-sī-bē'lī-tä), *It.* With freedom, flexible.

Con forza (kŏn fŏr'tsä), *It.* With force; with vehemence.

Con freddezza (kŏn frĕd-dĕt'sä), *It.* With coldness and apathy.

Confrérie de St. Julien (kŏn-frā'rē dŭh sä̈nh jü-lĭ-änh'), *Fr.* An ancient French association, or club, of ballad-singers and itinerant fiddlers.

ä *arm,* ă *add,* ā *ale,* ĕ *end,* ē *eve,* ĭ *ill,* ī *isle,* ŏ *old,* ō *odd,* oo *moon,* ŭ *but,* ü *Fr. scund,* kh *Ger. ch.* nh *nasal.*

(82)

Con fretta (kŏn frĕt'tä), *It.* Hurriedly, with an increase of time.
Con fuoco (kŏn foo-ō'kō), *It.* With fire and passion.
Con furia (kŏn foo'rĭ-ä), *It.* } With fury,
Con furore (kŏn foo-rō'rĕ), *It.* } rage, vehemence.
Con garbo (kŏn gär'bō), *It.* With simplicity and elegance.
Con gentilezza (kŏn jĕn-tĭ-lĕt'tsä), *It.* With grace and elegance.
Con giustezza (kŏn joos-tĕt'tsä), *It.* With justness and precision.
Con giustezza dell' intonazione (kŏn joos-tĕt'tsä dĕl lĕn-tō-nä-tsĭ-ō'nĕ), *It.* With just and correct intonation.
Con gli (kŏn glē), *It. pl.* With the.
Con gli stromenti (kŏn glē strō-mĕn'tĕ), *It.* With the instruments.
Con gradazione (kŏn grä-dä-tsĭ-ō'nĕ), *It.* With gradual increase and decrease.
Con grande espressione (kŏn grän'dĕ ĕs-prĕs-sĭ-ō'nĕ), *It.* With much expression.
Con grandezza (kŏn grän-dĕt'tsä), *It.* With dignity and grandeur.
Con gravita (kŏn grä-vĭ-tä'), *It.* With gravity.
Con grazia (kŏn grä'tsĭ-ä), *It.* With grace and elegance.
Con gusto (kŏn goos'tō), *It.* With taste.
Con impeto (kŏn ĕm'pĕ-'ō), *It.* }
Con impetuosita (kŏn ĕm-pĕ-too-ō-sĭ-tä'), *It.* } With impetuosity and vehemence.
Con impeto doloroso (kŏn ĕm'pĕ-tō dō-lō-rō'zō), *It.* With pathetic force and energy.
Con indifferenza (kŏn ĭn-dĭf-fĕ-rĕn'tsä), *It.* In an easy and indifferent manner.
Con innocenza (kŏn ĭn-nō-tshĕn'tsä), *It.* In a simple, artless style.
Con intimissimo sentimento (kŏn ĭn-tĭ-mĭs'-sĭ-mō sĕn-tĭ-mĕn'tō), *It.* With very much feeling; with great expression.
Con intrepidezza (kŏn ĭn-trĕ-pĭ-dĕt'tsä), *It.* With intrepidity, boldly.
Con ira (kŏn ē'rä), *It.* With anger.
Con isdegno (kŏn ĕs-dän'yō), *It.* With anger, angrily.
Con ismania (kŏn ĕs-mä'nĭ-ä), *It.* In a frenzied style.
Con istrepito (kŏn ĕs-trä'pĭ-tō), *It.* With noise and bluster.
Conjoint degrees. Two notes which immediately follow each other in the order of the scale.
Conjunct (kŏn-yoonkt'), *Lat.* A term applied by the ancient Greeks to tetrachords, or fourths, when the highest note of the lower tetrachord was also the lowest note of the tetrachord next above it.
Conjunct succession. Where a succession of tones proceed regularly upward or downward through successive scale degrees.

Con leggerezza (kŏn lĕd-jĕ-rĕt'tsä), *It.* }
Con leggierezza (kŏn lĕd-jĭ-ĕ-rĕt'tsä), *It.* } With lightness and delicacy.
Con lenezza (kŏn lĕ-nĕt'tsä), *It.* With mildness, sweetness.
Con lentezza (kŏn lĕn-tĕt'tsä), *It.* With slowness, lingering.
Con maesta (kŏn mä'ĕs-tä'), *It.* With majesty and grandeur.
Con malanconia (kŏn mä-län-kō-nē'ä), }
Con malenconia (kŏn mä-lĕn-kō-nē'ä), *It.* }
Con malinconia (kŏn mä-lĭn-kō-nē'ä), }
With an expression of melancholy and sadness.
Con mano destra (kŏn mä'nō dĕs'trä), *It.* }
Con mano dritta (kŏn mä'nō drĕt'tä), *It.* }
With the right hand.
Con mano sinistra (kŏn mä'nō sĕ-nĭs'trä), *It.* With the left hand.
Con misterio (kŏn mĭz-tä'rĭ-ō), *It.* With mystery, with an air of mystery.
Con moderazione (kŏn mō-dĕ-rä-tsĭ-ō'nĕ), *It.* With a moderate degree of quickness.
Con molto espressione (kŏn mōl'tō ĕs-prĕs-sĭ-ō'nĕ), *It.* With much expression.
Con molto carattere (kŏn mōl'tō kä-rät'tĕ-rĕ), *It.* With much character and emphasis.
Con molto passione (kŏn mōl'tō päs-sĭ-ō'nĕ), *It.* With much passion and feeling.
Con molto sentimento (kŏn mōl'tō sĕn-tĭ-mĕn'tō), *It.* With much feeling or sentiment.
Con morbidezza (kŏn mōr-bĭ-dĕt'tsä), *It.* With excess of feeling or delicacy.
Con moto (kŏn mō'tō), *It.* With motion; not dragging.
Connecting note. A note held in common by two successive chords.
Con negligenza (kŏn näl-yĭ-jĕn'tsä), *It.* In a negligent manner, without restraint.
Con nobilita (kŏn nō-bĕ-lĭ-tä'), *It.* With nobility.
Connaisseur (kŏn-nä-sŭr), *Fr.* } One skilled
Connoisseur (kŏn-wä sŭr), *Fr.* } in music; a good judge and critic of musical composition and performance.
Con ottava (kŏn ōt-tä'vä), *It.* } With the oc-
Con 8va. } tave; to be played in octaves.
Con passione (kŏn päs-sĭ-ō'nĕ), *It.* In an impassioned manner, with great emotion.
Con piacevolezza (kŏn pĕ-ä-tshĕ-vō-lĕt'tsä), *It.* With pleasing and graceful expression.
Con piu moto (kŏn pē'oo mō'tō), *It.* With increased motion.
Con precipitazione (kŏn prĕ-tshĭ-pĭ-tä-tsĭ-ō'nĕ), *It.* With precipitation; in a hurried manner.
Con precisione (kŏn prĕ-tshĕ-zĭ-ō'nĕ), *It.* With exactness and precision.
Con prestezza (kŏn prĕs-tĕt'tsä), *It.* With precision and exactness.

ä *arm*, ă *add*, ā *ale*, ĕ *end*, ē *eve*, ĭ *ill*, ī *isle*, ŏ *odd*, ō *old*, oo *moon*, ŭ *but*, ü *Fr. sound*, kh *Ger.*, ch, nh *nasal*.

Con rabbia (kŏn răb'bĭ-ä), *It.* With rage, with fury.

Con rapidita (kŏn rä-pē-dī'tä'), *It.* With rapidity.

Con replica (kŏn rä'plĭ-kä), *It.* With repetition.

Con risoluzione (kŏn rē-zō-loo-tsĭ-ō'nŏ), *It.* With firmness and resolution.

Con scioltezza (kŏl shē-ōl-tĕt'tsä), *It.* Freely, disconnectedly.

Con sdegno (kŏn sdän'yō), *It.* With wrath; in an angry and scornful manner.

Consecutive. A term chiefly applied to progressions of perfect fifths and octaves, which are permissible only under certain conditions or for special purposes. They are most objectionable when the parts which thus offend are extreme parts. Consecutive unisons are likewise prohibited. But the prohibition of consecutive octaves and unisons applies only to individual parts, not to the doubling, reinforcing, of one part by another. Hidden consecutives are discussed in the article *Hidden Fifths and Hidden Octaves*.

Consecutive fifths. Two or more perfect fifths, immediately following one another in similar motion. Consecutive fifths are disagreeable to the ear, and forbidden by the laws of harmony.

Consecutive octaves. Two parts moving in unison or octaves with each other.

Con semplicita (kŏn sĕm-plē-tshĭ-tä'), *It.* With simplicity.

Con sensibilita (kŏn sĕn-sĭ-bē-lĭ-tä'), *It.* With sensibility and feeling.

Con sentimento (kŏn sĕn-tĭ-mĕn'tō), *It.* With feeling and sentiment.

Consequent (kŏn-sē-kwĕnt), *Lat.*
Consequente (kŏn sē-kwĕn'tĕ), *It.* } An old term, meaning the answer in a fugue, or of a point of imitation.

Conservatoire (kŏn-sĕr-vä-twär'), *Fr.*
Conservatoria (kŏn-sĕr-vä-tō'rĭ-ä), *It.*
Conservatorio (kŏn-sĕr-vä-tō'rĭ-ō)), *It.*
Conservatorium (kŏn-sĕr-fä-tō'rĭ-oom) *Ger.*
Conservatory.
A school or academy of music in which every branch of musical art is taught and an art-standard maintained.

Con severita (kŏn sĕ-vä'rī-tä), *It.* With strict and severe style.

Consolante (kŏn sō-län'tĕ), *It.* In a cheering and consoling manner.

Consolatamente (kŏn-sō-lä-tä-mĕn'tĕ), *It.* Quietly, cheerfully.

Con solennita (kŏn sō-lĕn-nĭ-tä'), *It.* With solemnity.

Con somma espressione (kŏn sŏm'mä ĕs-prĕs-sĭ-ō'uĕ), *It.* With very great expression.

Consonance. An accord of sounds agreeable and satisfactory to the ear; the opposite to a discord or dissonance. See *Concord*.

Consonant. Accordant, harmonious.

Consonantamente (kŏn-sō-nän-tä-mĕn'tĕ), *It.* Accordantly.

Consonantia (kŏn-sō-nän'tsĭ-ä), *Lat.* Accord, agreement of voices.

Consonant sixths. The major and minor sixths.

Consonant thirds. The major and minor thirds.

Consonanz (kŏn-sō-nänts'), *Ger.* } A consonance, a concord.
Consonanza (kŏn-sō-nän'tsä), *It.* }

Consoniren (kŏn sō-nē'r'n), *Ger.* To harmonize; to agree in sound.

Con sonorita (kŏn sō-nō-rī-tä'), *It.* With a sonorous, vibrating kind of tone.

Con sordini (kŏn sŏr-dē'nĭ), *It. pl.* With the mutes. This indicates: (1) in pianoforte playing that the soft pedal has to be used; (2) in violin, viola, etc., playing, that a mute has to be placed on the bridge; (3) in horn, trumpet, etc., playing, that a mute has to be inserted into the bell. *Sordini* is the plural of *Sordino*. (*V. Sordino.*)

Con spirito (kŏn spē'rĭ-tō), *It.* With spirit, life, energy.

Con strepito (kŏn strä'pĭ-tō). *It.* In a boisterous manner, with impetuosity.

Con stromenti (kŏn strō-mĕn'tĭ), *It. pl.* }
Con strumenti (kŏn stroo-mĕn'tĭ), *It. pl.* } With the instruments; meaning that the orchestra and voices are together.

Con suavezza (kŏn soo-ä-vĕt'tsä), *It.* } With
Con suavita (kŏ soo-ä'vī-tä), *It.* } sweetness and delicacy.

Cont. An abbreviation of Contano.

Contadina (kŏn-tä-dē'nä), *It.* A country dance.

Contadinesco (kŏn-tä-dĭ-nĕs'kō), *It.* Rustic, in a rural style.

Contano (kŏn-tä'nō), *It.* To count, or rest; a term applied to certain parts not played for the time being, while the other parts move on.

Con tenerezza (kŏn tĕ-nĕ-rĕt'tsä), *It.* With tenderness.

Con timedezza (kŏn tē-mē-dĕt'tsä), *It.* With timidity.

Con tinto (kŏn tĕn'tō), *It.* With various shades of expression.

Continuato (kŏn-tē-noo-ä'tō), *It.* Continued, held on, sustained.

Continued bass. See *Basso continuo*.

Continued harmony. A harmony that does not change, though the bass varies.

Continued rest. A rest continuing through several successive measures, the number of measures being indicated by a figure over a whole rest.

Continuo (kŏn-tē'noo-ō), *It.* Without cessation.

Continuous horizontal line. A line indicating that the passages are to be played as unisons.
Contra (kŏn'trä), *It.* Low, under.
Contrabassist. A double-bass player.
Contrabass (kŏn'trä-bäs), *It.* } The
Contrabbasso (kŏn'träb-bäs-sŏ), *It.* } double
Contrabass viol. } bass.
Contraddanza (kŏn-träd-dän'tsä), *It.* A country dance.
Contra-fagotto (kŏn'trä-fäg-gŏt'tŏ), *It.* The double bassoon; also the name of an organ-stop of 16- or 32-feet scale.
Contr' alti (kŏn-träl'tē). The higher male voices, usually called counter tones.
Contralto (kŏn-träl'tō) *It.* The deepest species of female voice.
Con tranquillezza (kŏn trän-kwĭl'lĕt-tsä), *It.* }
Con tranquillita (kŏn trän-kwĭl-lĭt-tä') } With tranquillity; with calmness.
Contraposaune (kŏn'trä-pō-zou'nĕ), *Ger.* Double trombone; a 16- or 32-reed stop in an organ.
Contrappuntista (kŏn-träp-poon-tēz'tä), *It.* One skilled in counterpoint.
Contrappunto (kŏn-träp-poon'tŏ), *It.* Counterpoint.
Contrappunto alla decima (kŏn-träp-poon'tŏ äl'lä dā'shĭ-mä), *It.* A species of double counterpoint, where the principal counterpoint may rise a tenth above, or fall as much below, the subject.
Contrappunto alla mente (kŏn-träp-poon'tŏ äl'lä mĕn'tĕ), *It.* See *Chant sur le livre*.
Contrappunto doppio (kŏn-träp-poon'tŏ dŏp'pĭ-ō), *It.* Double counterpoint.
Contrappunto doppio alla duo decima (kŏn-träp-poon'tŏ dŏp'pĭ-ō äl'lä duo-ō dā'tshĭ mä), *It.* Double counterpoint in the twelfth.
Contrappunto sciolto (kŏn-träp-poon'tŏ shē-ōl'tō), *It.* A free counterpoint.
Contrappunto sopra il soggetto (kŏn-träp-poon'tŏ sō'prä el sŏd-jĕt'tō), *It.* Counterpoint above the subject.
Contrappunto sotto il soggetto (kŏn-träp-poon'tŏ sŏt'tō el sŏd'jĕt-tō), *It.* Counterpoint below the subject.
Contrappunto syncopato (kŏn-träp-poon'tŏ sĕn-kō-pä'tō), *It.* The syncopation of one part for the purpose of producing discord.
Contrapunkt (kŏn'trä-poonkt'), *Ger.* Counterpoint.
Contrapunctum floridum (kŏn-trä-poonk'-toom flō'rĭ-doom), *Lat.* Ornamental counterpoint.
Contrapunctum in decima gravi (kŏn-trä-poonk'toom in dā'i-mä grä've), *Lat.* A term given to double counterpoint when the parts move in tenths or thirds below the subject.
Contrapuntal. Relating to counterpoint.
Contrapuntist.
Contrappuntista (kŏn-träp-poon-tēz'ta), *It.* } One skilled in counterpoint.

Contrapuntus simplex (kŏn-trä-poon'toos sĭm'plĕx), *Lat.* Simple counterpoint.
Contr' arco (kŏn-trär'kō), *It.* Bowing an instrument in a manner contrary to rule.
Contrario (kŏn-trä'rĭ-ō), *It.* Contrary.
Contrary bow. A reversed stroke of the bow.
Contrary motion. Motion in an opposite direction to some other part; one rising as the other falls.
Contrassoggetto (kŏn-träs-sŏd-jĕt'tō), *It.* The counter subject of a fugue.
Con trasporto (kŏn träs-pōr'tō), *It.* With anger, excitement, passion.
Contra tempo (kŏn-trä tĕm'pō), *It.* Against the time; syncopation, one part moving in a slower progression than the other parts.
Contra tenor. See *Counter tenor*.
Contratöne (kŏn'trä-tö-nĕ), *Ger.* A term applied to the deeper tones of the bass voice.
Contra violone (kŏn-trä vē-ō-lō'nĕ), *It.* } The
Contre-basse (kŏntr-bäss), *Fr.* } double bass.
Contredance (kŏntr-dänhs), *Fr.* A country dance, a dance in which the parties engaged stand in two opposite ranks.
Contre partie (kŏntr pär-tē), *Fr.* The second part.
Contrepoint (kŏntr-pwänh), *Fr.* Counterpoint.
Contre-sujet (kŏntr-sü-zhā). *Fr.* The counter subject, or second subject in a fugue.
Contre-temps (kŏntr-tänh), *Fr.* Syncopation, driving notes, notes tied and accented contrary to the natural rhythmic flow of the measure.
Contretenour (kŏntr-tĕ-noor'), *Fr.* Counter tenor.
Con tristezza (kŏn trĕz-tĕt'tsä). *It.* With sadness, with heaviness.
Contro (kŏn-trō), *It.* Counter, low.
Con tutta forza (kŏn toot-tä fōr'tsä), *It.* }
Con tutta la forza (kŏn toot-tä lä fōr'tsä), *It.* } With all possible force, with the whole power, as loud as possible.
Con variazone (kŏn vä-rĭ-ä-tsĭ-ō'nĕ), *It.* With variations.
Con veemenza (kŏn vä-ā-mĕn'tsä), *It.* With vehemence, force.
Con velocita (kŏn vĕ-lō-tshĭ-tä'), *It.* With velocity.
Conversio (kŏn-vĕr'sĭ-ō), *Lat.* Inversion in counterpoint.
Con vigore (kŏn vē-gō'rĕ), *It.* With vigor, sprightliness, strength.
Con violenza (kŏn vē-ō-lĕn'tsä), *It.* With violence.
Con vivacita (kŏn vē-vä-tshĭ-tä'), *It.* } With
Con vivezza (kŏn vē-vĕt'tsä), *It.* } liveliness, vivacity, animation.
Con voce rauca (kŏn vō'tshĕ rä'oo-kä), *It.* With a hoarse or rough voice.

ä *arm*, ă *add*, ā *ale*, ĕ *end*, ē *eve*, ĭ *ill*, ī *isle*, ō *old*, ŏ *odd*, oo *moon*, ŭ *but*, ü *Fr. sound*, kh *Ger. ch.* nh *nasal*

Con volubilita (kŏn vō loo-bē-lĭ-tä'), *It.* With volubility, with fluency and freedom of performance.

Con zelo (kōn tsā'lō), *It.* With zeal.

Con 8va. An abbreviation of Con ottava.

Con 8va ad libitum. With octaves at pleasure.

Coperto (kō-pĕr'tō), *It.* Covered, muffled.

Coppelflöte (kōp'p'l-flö-tĕ), *Ger.* Coupling-flute; an organ-stop of the clarabella or stopped diapason species, intended to be used in combination with some other stop.

Copula (kŏ'poo-lä), *It.* } A coupler. An arrangement by which two rows of keys can be connected together, or the keys connected with the pedals.
Copule (kō-pūl'), *Fr.*

Copyright. The exclusive right of an author or his representative to print, publish, or sell his work during a specified term of years.

Cor. An abbreviation of Cornet.

Cor (kŏr), *Fr.* A horn, commonly called the French horn.

Corale (kō-rä'lĕ), *It.* Choral; the plain chant.

Cor anglais (kōr änh-gläs), *Fr.* "English horn." This instrument is a large-sized oboe, with a compass from e to a″. But as the cor anglais is a transposing instrument, and sounds a perfect fifth lower than the notes written for it, these latter extend from b to e‴.

Corante (kō-rän'tĕ), } *It.* A slow dance in 3-2 or 3-4 time.
Coranto (kō-rän'tō),

Corda (kŏr'dä), *It.* A string; *una corda*, one string. Used to denote the soft pedal on the piano, as against *tre corde*, three strings, or the full power of the instrument.

Cordatura (kŏr-dä-too'rä), *It.* The scale or series of notes by which the strings of any instrument are tuned.

Corde (kŏrd), *Fr.* A string.

Corde à boyau (kŏrd ä bwä-yō), *Fr.* Catgut; strings for the violin, harp, etc.

Corde à jour (kŏrd ä zhoor), *Fr.* } An open string on the violin, viola, etc.
Corde à vide (kŏrd ä vēd),

Cor de chasse (kŏr dŭh shäss), *Fr.* The hunting horn; the French horn.

Corde de luth (kŏrd dŭh loot), *Fr.* A lute-string.

Corde fausse (kŏrd fōss), *Fr.* A false or dissonant string.

Cor de postillon (kŏr dŭh pōs-tēl-yōnh), *Fr.* Postillion's horn.

Cordes de Naples (kŏrd dŭh Nä-pl), *Fr.* The strings imported from Naples for the violin, harp, etc.

Cor de signal (kŏr dŭh sēn-yäl), *Fr.* A bugle.

Cor de vaches (kŏr dŭ vä-shä), *Fr.* The cowboy's horn.

Corde vuide (kŏrd vwēd), *Fr.* An open string on the violin, viola, etc.

Cordiera (kŏr-dĭ-ā'rä), *It.* The tailpiece of a violin, viola, etc.

Cordon de sonnette (kŏr-dōnh dŭh sŏn-nāt), *Fr.* A bellrope.

Coreografia (kō-rĕ-ō-grä-fē'ä), *It.* The method of describing the figures of a dance.

Coriambus (kō-rĭ-äm'boos), *Gr.* In ancient poetry, a foot consisting of four syllables, the first and last long and the others short.

Corifeo (kō-rĭ-fä'ō), *It.* The leader of the dances in a ballet.

Corista (kō-rēs'tä), *It.* A chorister.

Cormorne. A soft-toned horn; also a reed-stop in English organs. See *Cremona*.

Corn (kŏrn), *Wel.* A horn.

Cornamusa (kŏr-nä-moo'zä), *It.* A species of bagpipe.

Cornamute. A wind instrument, a species of bagpipe.

Cornare (kŏr-nä'rĕ), *It.* To sound a horn or cornet.

Corne (kŏrn), *Fr.* A horn.

Corne de chasse (kŏrn dŭh shäss), *Fr.* See *Cor de chasse*.

Cornemuse (kŏr-nŭh-mŭz), *Fr.* Bagpipes.

Cornet. (1) An obsolete wind instrument, generally made of wood, of which there were several kinds, of different sizes. (*V. Cornetto.*) (2) The name of several organ-stops, generally mixtures of 3 to 5 ranks. (3) A brass instrument of the trumpet family. (*V. Cornet à pistons.*)

Corneta. } A name sometimes applied to a reed-stop in an organ of 16-feet scale.
Cornetto.

Cornet à bouquin (kŏr-nĕt ä boo'känh), *Fr.* Cornet; bugle horn.

Cornet à pistons (kŏr-nĕt ä pēs-tōnh), *Fr.* A brass instrument of the trumpet family with valves (*q. v.*), by means of which a chromatic scale can be produced. It is usually in the key of B♭, and has one or more crooks (A, A♭, G), and, therefore, the notes written for it (from f♯ to c‴) sound a tone, minor third, major third, or perfect fourth lower. The soprano cornet is in the key of E♭. Cornets in other keys are also to be met with, but are less common than those above mentioned.

Cornet dreifach (kŏr-nĕt' drī'fäkh), *Ger.* Cornet with three ranks, in German organs.

Cornett (kŏr-nĕt'), *Ger.* } A cornet.
Cornetta (kŏr-nĕt'tä), *It.*

Cornetica (kŏr-nā'tĭ-kä), *Sp.* } A small cornet.
Cornettino (kŏr-nĕt-tē'nō), *It.*

Cornetto (kŏr-nĕt'tō), *It.* A cornet.

Corni (kŏr'nē), *It. pl.* The horns.

Cornist. } A performer on the cornet or horn.
Corneter.

Corniste (kŏr-nĕst'), *Fr.* A player upon the horn.

Corno (kŏr'nō), *It.* A horn.

ă *arm*, ă *add*, ā *ale*, ĕ *end*, ē *eve*, ĭ *ill*, ī *isle*, ŏ *old*, ŏ *odd*, oo *moon*, ŭ *but*, ü *Fr. sound*, kh *Ger. ch*, nh *nasal*.

(86)

Corno alto (kōr′nŏ ăl′tō), *It.* A horn of a high pitch. See *Horn.*

Corno basso (kōr′nō băs′sō), *It.* A bass horn, a horn of a low pitch.

Corno cromatico (kōr′nō krō-mä-tĭ-kōi, *It.* The chromatic horn.

Corno di bassetto (kōr′nō dē băs-sĕt′tō), *It.* The basset horn. A species of clarinet a fifth lower than the C clarinet. (2) A delicate-toned reed-organ stop of 8-feet scale.

Corno di caccia (kōr′nō dē kät′tshĭ-ä), *It.* The hunting, or French horn.

Corno dolce (kōr′nō dōl′tshē), *It.* Soft horn; an organ-stop, occurring both in the manuals and pedals.

Corno in B basso, *It.* A low B horn.

Corno inglese (kōr′nō ĕn-glä′zĕ), *It.* The English horn, an alto oboe.

Cornopean. An organ-reed stop of 8-feet pitch and broad scale; also a wind instrument of the trumpet species. See *Cornet à pistons.*

Corno primo (kōr′nō prē′mō), *It.* The first horn.

Corno quarto (kōr′nō kwär′tō), *It.* The fourth horn.

Corno quinto (kōr′nō kwĭn′tō), *It.* The fifth horn.

Corno secondo (kōr′nō sĕ-kōn′dō), *It.* The second horn.

Corno sordo (kōr′nō sōr′dō), *It.* A horn with da‐pers.

Corno ventile (kōr′nō vĕn-tē′lĕ), *It.*
Cor omnitonique (kōr ŏmh-nĭ-tō-nĕk), *Fr.*
Chromatic horn, with valves or keys for producing the semitones.

Coro (kō′rō), *It.* } A choir, a chorus, a piece
Coro (kō′rō), *Sp.* } for many voices.

Corona (kō-rō′nä), } *It.* } A pause or
Coronata (kō-rō-nä′tä), hold (𝄐).

Coro primo (kō-rō prē′mō), *It.* The first chorus.

Corps (kōr), *Fr.* The body of a musical instrument. (2) A band of musicians.

Corps de ballet (kōr dŭh băl-lā), *Fr.* A general name for the performers in a ballet.

Corps de voix (kōr dŭh vwä), *Fr.* Body or fulness of tone.

Corrente (kōr-rĕn′tĕ), *It.* An old dance tune in ⁶⁄₄ v triple time. See *Coranto.*

Corrépétiteur (kōr-rā-pä-tĭ-tūr′), *Fr.* } A mu-
Corripetitore (kōr-rĭ-pĕ-tĭ-tō′rĕ), *It.* } sician who instructs the chorus singers of the opera.

Coryphæus (kō-rĭ-fā′oos), *Gr.* The conductor of the chorus. See *Corifeo.*

Coryphée (kō-rĭ-fā), *Fr.* The leader or chief of the group of dancers in a ballet.

Cosaque (kō-săk), *Fr.* The Cossack dance.

Cotil. An abbreviation of *Cotillon.*

Cotilion (kō-tēl-yŏnh), *Fr.* Lit., "petticoat." "A social game in form of a dance." The cotillon has no characteristic music. A waltz, galop, or any other dance tune is used for the purpose.

Couac (kwăk), *Fr.* The "quack" of the clarinet, oboe, and bassoon, caused by a bad reed or reeds, deranged keys, wearied lips, etc., which in English is also called the "goose."

Coulé (koo-lā′), *Fr.* (1) Slurred, legato. (2) A grace consisting of two or three ascending or descending notes, forming, as it were, a double or triple appoggiatura.

Counter. A name given to an under part, as, counter tenor.

Counter bass. A second bass.

Counter dance. See *Contredanse.*

Counterpart. The part to be applied to another, as, the bass is the counterpart of the treble.

Counterpoint. Point against point. (1) The art of adding one or more parts to a given part. (2) A part or parts added to a given part.
The contrapuntal style is distinguished from the harmonic in this, that whilst the latter consists of a melody accompanied by chords, the former is a simultaneous combination of several melodies, or melodic parts. The supreme contrapuntal forms are Canon and Fugue.
In teaching counterpoint, theorists assume generally five species; (a) Note against note—a semibreve against a semibreve; (b) two notes against one—two minims against a semibreve; (c) four notes against one—four crotchets against a semibreve; (d) syncopated counterpoint—the second minim of one bar tied to the first of the following bar against a semibreve entering on the first part of each bar; (e) florid counterpoint—a mixture of the three preceding species.
Further, counterpoint is divisible into simple and double counterpoint. The latter differs from the former in this, that its parts are invertible, i. e., may be transposed an octave, or ninth, tenth, twelfth, etc., above or below one another. Counterpoint is called triple when three, and quadruple when four parts are mutually invertible.

Counterpoint, double. A counterpoint that admits of an inversion of the parts.

Counterpoint, equal. Where the notes are of equal duration.

Counter subject. (1) The second theme in double fugues and fugues with two subjects in distinction from the principal subject. (2) The subject accompanying the answer (the resumption by one part of the subject proposed by another) of a fugue. But the accompaniment of the answer gets this name only when it is retained throughout the fugue. (3) A melody forming a counterpoint against a cantus firmus.

Counter tenor. Male alto voice. (*V. Alto.*)

Counter tenor. High tenor; the highest male voice. It is generally a falsetto.

ä *arm*, ă *add*, ā *ale*, ĕ *end*, ē *eve*, ĭ *ill*, ī *isle*, ŏ *old*, ō *odd*, oo *moon*, ŭ *but*, ü *Fr. sound*, kh *Ger. ch*, nh *nasal*.

Counter tenor clef. The C clef, when placed on the third line.

Counter theme. See *Counter subject*.

Country dance. Whether "country" means here simply "rustic," or has to be regarded as a corruption of "contra," is still a matter of controversy. But whatever the right interpretation may be, a country dance is a contra dance. One writer defines it as "a dance in which partners are arranged opposite to each other." Another writer, after remarking that at the commencement the gentlemen are arranged on one side and the ladies on the other, proceeds thus in his description of the dance: "In its figures the dancers are constantly changing places, leading one another back and forward, up and down, parting and uniting again. The numerous different figures, which give an interest to this dance, are generally designated with a particular name. The music is sometimes in 2-4 and sometimes in 6-8 time" ("Chambers's Encyclopædia"). To this has, however, to be added that these are the most common, but not the only times in which country-dance tunes have been composed.

Coup de baguette (koo düh bä-gwĕt), *Fr.* Beat of the drum.

Coup de cloche (koo düh klōsh), *Fr.* Stroke of the clock.

Couper le sujet (koo-pā lüh soo-jā'), *Fr.* To curtail or contract the subject or theme.

Coupler. See *Copula*.

Couplet (koo-plā), *Fr.* } A stanza, or verse;
Couplet. } two verses or lines of poetry forming complete sense.

Coups d'archet (koo där-shā), *Fr.* Strokes of the bow; ways or methods of bowing.

Courante (koo-ränht), *Fr.* Running; an old dance in triple time. The second part of a suite, usually in passage work.

Courtal (koor-täl), } An old instrument;
Courtaud (koor-tō), *Fr.* } a species of short
Courtaut (koor-tō), } bassoon.

Covered consecutives. Implied consecutives.

Covered octaves. Consecutive octaves that are implied in the movement of the voices.

C. P. Abbreviation of Colla parte.

Cr. }
Cres. } Abbreviations of Crescendo.
Cresc. }

Cracovienne (krä-kō'vē-ĕun'), *Fr.* A Polish dance in 3-4 time. Similar to the mazurka.

Cravicembalo (krä-vĭ-tshĕm-bä'lō). *It.* A general name for all instruments of the harpsichord species.

Credo (krā'dō), *Lat.* I believe. Third part of the Catholic mass.

Crembalum (krĕm-bä-loom), *Lat.* A jew's-harp.

Cremona (krĕ-mō'nä), *It.* An organ-stop; the name of a superior make of violins from the place where the violin was perfected—Cremona, in Italy.

Cremorn. A reed-organ stop of 8-feet scale.

Cres. al forte, *or,* **al ff.** Increasing as loud as possible.

Cres. al fortissimo. Increasing to very loud.

Crescendo (krĕ-shĕn'dō), *It.* A word denoting a gradually increasing power of tone; it is often indicated by the sign ⊏.

Crescendo al fortissimo (krĕ-shĕn'dō äl för-tĕs'sĭ-mō), *It.* Increase the tone until the greatest degree of power is obtained.

Crescendo al diminuendo (krĕ-shĕn'dō äl dē-mē-noo-ĕndō), *It.* }
Crescendo e diminuendo (krĕ-shĕn'dō ā dē-mē-noo-ĕn-dō), *It.* }
Crescendo poi diminuendo (krĕ-shĕn'dō pō-ē dē-mē-noo-ĕn-dō), *It.* }
Increase and then diminish the tone; indicated often by the sign ⊏⊐.

Crescendo e incalcando poco a poco (krĕ-shĕn'dō ā ēn-käl-kän-dō pō'kō ä pō'kō), *It.* Increasing the tone and hurrying the time by degrees.

Crescendo il tempo (krĕ-shĕn'dō ĕl tĕm'pō), *It.* Increase the time of the movement.

Crescendo nel tempo e nella forza (krĕ-shĕn'dō nĕl tĕm'pō ā nĕl'lä fŏr'tsä), *It.* Increase in time and power.

Crescendo poco a poco (krĕ-shĕn-dō pō'kō ä pō'kō), *It.* Increasing the tone by little and little.

Crescent. A Turkish instrument made of small bells hung on an inverted crescent.

Cres. dim. An abbreviation of Crescendo e diminuendo.

Cres. e legato (krĕs. ā lĕ-gü'tō), *It.* Crescendo and legato.

C, reversed. A sign in old music of a diminution of one half the value of the notes.

Croche (krōsh), *Fr.* A quaver, or eighth note.

Croche double (krōsh doo-b'l), *Fr.* A semiquaver, or sixteenth note.

Croche pointee (krōsh pwän-tā), *Fr.* A dotted quaver.

Croche quadruple (krōsh kwä-drü-pl), *Fr.* A hemidemisemiquaver, or sixty-fourth note.

Croche triple (krōsh trē-pl), *Fr.* A demisemiquaver, or thirty-second note.

Crochet (krō-shā), *Fr.* The hook of a quaver, semiquaver, etc.

Croma (krō'mä), *It.* A quaver, or eighth note.

Cromatica (krō-mä'tĭ-kä) } *It.* Chromatic, re-
Cromatico (krō-mä'tĭ-kō) } ferring to intervals and scales.

Crome (krō'mĕ), *It. pl.* Quavers; when written under crotchets or minims, it shows that those notes are to be divided into quavers.

Cromhorn (krŏm'hŏrn), *Ger.* A reed-stop in an organ.
Crommo (krŏm'mō), *It.* A choral dirge or lamentation.
Cromorne (krō-mōrn), *Fr.* The name of a family of obsolete reed wind instruments. In Germany it was called *Krummhorn* (crooked horn). Cromorne is said to be a corruption of *cormorne* (*cor*, horn; *morne*, dim, gloomy).
Crooked flute. An Egyptian instrument in the shape of a bull's horn.
Crooked horn. } The buccina; a wind
Crooked trumpet. } instrument of the ancients.
Crooks. Curved tubes which are inserted into horns, trumpets, etc., for the purpose of altering the key. The A crook, for instance, in making the tube of an instrument in B♭ longer, makes its pitch also a semitone lower.
Cross. The head of a lute; a mark for the thumb, placed over a note.
Cross flute. A transverse flute, a German flute, so called in distinction from the flageolet, played from the end, like a clarinet.
Crotale (krō-täl'), *Fr.* } An ancient mu-
Crotalo (krō'ä-lō), *It.* } sical instrument,
Crotalum (krō-tä'loom), *Gr.* } used by the priests of Cybele. From the reference made to it by different authors it seems to have been a small cymbal or a species of castanet.
Crotales. Little bells.
Crotchet. A note equal in value to half a minim.
Crotchet rest. A rest equal in duration to a crotchet.
Crowd, *Eng.*, **Crwth** (krooth), *Wel.* A more or less lyre-shaped instrument, the strings of which were originally twanged; afterwards it was also played upon with a bow, modifications of structure being consequently introduced.
Crowle. An old English wind instrument of the bassoon species.
Crowther. See *Crowder.*
Crucifixus (kroo-tsī-fix'oos), *Lat.* Part of the *Credo* in a mass.
Cruit (kru-īt), *Iri.* An ancient musical instrument of the Irish. See *Crwth.*
Crupezia (kroo-pā'zǐ-ä), *Gr.* Wooden clogs worn by the Greek musicians in beating time.
Crutchetam. Name originally given to the crotchet.
Crwth (krooth), *Wel.* An old Welsh instrument, having six strings, resembling the violin.
C. S. The initials of *Con sordino.*
Csárdás (tsär-däs), *Magyar.* A Hungarian (Magyar) dance in 2-4 or 4-4 time. Triple time is very exceptional, and not true to the national character. The Csárdás (from *Csárda*, inn on the heath) is often preceded by a moderate movement called *Lassu* (from *Lassan*, slow). The quick movement is called *Fris* (from the German *Frisch*, fresh, brisk, lively).
C-Schlüssel (tsä'shlüs-s'l), *Ger.* The C clef.
Cto. Abbreviation of Concerto.
Cuclear (koo-klä-är'), *Sp.* To sing as the cuckoo.
Cue. The tail, the end of a thing. The last words of an actor on a stage, serving as an intimation to the one who follows, when to speak and what to say.
Cum cantu (koom kän'too), *Lat.* With song, with singing.
Cum Sancto Spiritu (koom sänk'tō spē'rǐ-too), *Lat.* Part of the Gloria in a mass.
Currendaner (koor-rĕn-dä'nĕr), *Ger.* } School-
Currende (koor-rĕn'dĕ), } boys, or young choristers, chanting in procession through the streets.
Custo (koos-tō), *It.* } A direct ∽. A
Custos (koos'tōs), *Lat.* } mark sometimes placed at the end of a staff to indicate the note next following.
Cylinder. Part of the horn. (Ventil, piston.)
Cymbales (sänh-bäl), *Fr.* } Circular metal
Cymbals. } plates used in bands, usually in combination with the great drum; they are clashed together, producing a ringing, brilliant effect.
Cymbalum (tsǐm-bä-loom), *or,* **Cimbalum.** *Lat.* Instrument of the dulcimer kind, used by the gypsies.
Cymbale (sänh-bäl), *Fr.* } A mixture organ-
Cymbel (tsǐm'b'l), *Ger.* } stop of a very acute quality of tone.
Cypher system. An old system of musical notation, in which the notes were represented by numerals.

ɷ n, ā *add*, ä *ale*, ĕ *end*, ē *eve*, ĭ *ill*, ī *isle*, ŏ *old*, ō *odd*, oo *moon*, ū *but*, ü *Fr. sound*, kh *Ger. ch*, nh *nasal.*

D. The second note in the diatonic scale of C.
Da (dä), *It.* By, from, for, through, etc.
Dabbuda (däb-boo-dä'), *It.* A psaltery, a species of harp.
Da capo (dä kä'pō), *It.* From the beginning; an expression placed at the end of a movement to indicate that the performer must return to the first strain.
Da capo al fine (dä kä'pō äl fē'nĕ), *It.* Return to the beginning and conclude with the word Fine.
Da capo al segno (dä kä'pō äl sän'yō), *It.* Repeat from the sign $.
Da capo fin al segno (dä kä'pō fēn äl sän'yō), *It.* Return to the beginning and end at the sign $.
Da capo e poi la coda (dä kä'pō ā pō'ē lä kō'dä), *It.* Begin again and then play to the coda.
Da capo senza repetizione, e poi la coda (dä kä'pō sĕn-tsä rā-pā-tī-tsī-ō'nĕ, ā pō'ē lä kō'dä), *It.* Begin again, but without repetition, and then proceed to the coda.
Da capo sin' al segno (dä kä'pō sēn äl sän'yō), *It.* Return to the beginning and conclude at the sign $.
D' accord (däk-kōrd'), *Fr.* } In tune, in
D' accordo (däk-kōr-dō), *It.* } concord, in harmony.
Dach (däkh), *Ger.* Lit., "roof." The upper part of the sound-box of a stringed instrument. The belly of a violin, etc.
Da chiesa (dä kē-ā'zä), *It.* For the church.
Dactyl (däk'tĭl), *Lat.* A metrical foot, consisting of one long syllable, followed by two short ones, marked thus, — ⌣ ⌣.
Dactylion (däk-tĭl'ĭ-ŏn), *Gr.* An instrument invented by H. Herz, with a view to assist pianists in making their fingers independent and of equal strength and suppleness. It consists of ten rings that hang above the keyboard and are fastened to steel springs.
Dactylus (däk'tĭ-loos), *Lat.* See *Dactyl.*
Dada. A term used in drum music to indicate the left hand.
Daina (dä-ē'nä). } A kind of Lithuanian
Dainos (dä-ē'nōs). } folksong that has love and friendship for its subject. *Dainos* is the plural of *daina.*
Daire. The tambourine, or hand drum.
Daktylus (däk'tĭ-loos), *Gr.* A dactyl.

Dagli (däl'yī), } Contractions of the
Dai (däl), } preposition *da*, and the
Dall' (däll'), } *It.* } masculine and femi-
Dalla (däl'lä), } nine, singular and plu-
Dalle (däl'lĕ), } ral, forms of the defi-
Dallo (däl'lō), } nite article *il, lo* (m. sing.), *i, gli* (m. plur.), *la* (f. sing.), *le* (f. plur.). From the, by the, of the, etc.
Da lontano (dä lōn-tä'nō), *It.* "At a distance; the music is to sound as if far away.
Dal segno (däl sän'yō), *It.* From the sign $. A mark directing a repetition from the sign.
Dal segno alla fine (däl sän'yō äl-lä fē'nĕ), *It.* From the sign to the end.
Dal segno fin al segno (däl sän'yō fēn äl sän'yō), *It.* From sign to sign.
Dal teatro (däl tā-ä'trō), *It.* In the style of theater music.
Damenisation. The syllables da, me, ni, po, tu, la, be, which Graun employed in his solmization.
Damper. A little cushion of felt connected with the piano-key in such a manner that, being raised when the key is depressed, it permits the string to vibrate. When the key is released the damper falls upon the string and stops the vibration. (2) The mute of brass instruments.
Damper-pedal. That pedal in a pianoforte which raises the dampers from the strings and allows them to vibrate freely. Its use is indicated by the abbreviation *ped.*
Dämpfen (dăm'pfĕn), *Ger.* To muffle, or deaden, the tone of an instrument.
Dämpfer (dăm'pfĕr), *Ger.* A mute, or damper.
Dance, morrice. } A dance in imitation of
Dance, morris. } the Moors, usually per-
Dance, morriske. } formed by young men dressed in loose frocks, adorned with bells and ribbons, and accompanied by castanets, tambours, etc.
Dances. Certain tunes composed especially for dancing.
Danklied (dänk'lēd), *Ger.* A thanksgiving song.
Danse (dänhs), *Fr.* A dance tune.
Danse contre (dänhs kōntr), *Fr.* A country dance, a quadrille.
Danse de matelot (dänhs dŭh mät-ā-lō), *Fr.* A dance resembling the hornpipe.
Danza (dän'tsä), *It.* A dance.

ä *arm,* ă *add,* ä *ale,* ĕ *end,* ē *eve,* ĭ *ill,* ī *isle,* ō *old,* ŏ *odd,* oo *moon,* ŭ *but,* ü *Fr. sound,* kh *Ger. ch,* nh *nasal.*

(90)

Danzetta (dän-tsĕt'tä), *It.* A little dance, a short dance.

Da prima (dä prē'mä), *It.* At first; from the beginning.

Darabukkeh (dä-rä-boo'kĕh). A small Arabian drum, made in various forms.

Dar la voce (där lä vō'tshĕ), *It.* To strike, or give, the keynote.

Darmsaite (därm'sī-tĕ),
Darmsaiten (därm'sī-t'n), } *Ger.* } Gut strings used for the harp, violin, guitar, etc.

Darsteller (där'stĕl-lĕr), *Ger.* A performer.

Da scherzo (dä skärt'sō), *It.* In a lively, playful manner.

Das (däs), *Ger.* The; neuter form of definite article.

Dasselbe (däs-sĕl'bĕ), *Ger.* The same.

Dauer (dou'ĕr), *Ger.* The length, or duration, of notes.

Daum (doum), *Ger.* The thumb.

Daumenklapper (dou'mĕn-kläp-pĕr), *Ger.* Castanet, snapper.

D. C. The initials of Da capo.

D-dur (dā'door), *Ger.* D major; the key of D major.

Début (dā'bü), *Fr.* First appearance; the first public performance.

Débutant (dā'bü-tänh),
Débutante (dā'bu-tänht), } *Fr.* } A singer or performer who appears for the first time before the public.

Decachord (dĕk'ä-kŏrd),
Decachordon (dĕk ä-kŏr'dŏn), *Lat.*
Decacordo (dĕk-ä-kŏr'dō), *It.* } An ancient musical instrument of the harp or guitar species, with ten strings. It was called by the Hebrews *Ilasur*.

Decamerone (dĕk-ä-mĕ-rō'nĕ), *It.* A period of ten days; a collection of ten musical pieces.

Decani (dĕ-kā'nī), *Lat. pl.* In cathedral music this term implies that the passages thus marked must be taken by the singers on the side of the choir where the dean usually sits.

Décidé (dĕ-sē-dā),
Décidément (dĕ-sē-dā-mänh), } *Fr.* } With decision, with resolution.

Decima (dā'tsī-mä), *Lat.* A tenth; an interval of ten degrees in the scale, also the name of an organ-stop sounding the tenth.

Décime (dā-sēm), *Fr.* A tenth See *Decima*.

Decimole. A musical figure formed out of the division of any note or chord into ten parts, or notes, of equal value.

Décisif (dā-sē-sīf), *Fr.* Decisive, clear, firm.

Decisione (dä-tshē-zī-ō'nĕ), *It.* Decision, firmness.

Décisivement (dā-sē-zēv-mönh), *Fr.* Decisively.

Decisivo (dā-tshī-zē'vō),
Deciso (dä-tshē'zō), } *It.* } In a bold and decided manner.

Decke (dĕk'ĕ), *Ger.* The soundboard of a violin, violoncello, etc.; also the cover or top in those organ-stops which are covered or stopped.

Declamando (dĕk-lä-män'dō), *It.* With declamatory expression.

Declamatio (dĕk-lä-mä'tī-ō), *It.* Declamation, recitative.

Declamation. Dramatic singing. The art of rendering words with the proper pronunciation, accentuation, and expression. The mastery of this art is as necessary to the singer as to the speaker.

Declamazione (dĕk-lä-mä-tsī-ō'nĕ), *It.* Declamation.

Decorative notes. Notes of embellishment, appoggiaturas, etc.

Decr.
Decres. } Abbreviations of Decrescendo.

Decrescendo (dā-krĕ-shĕn'dō), *It.* Gradually diminishing in power of tone ⟹.

Decuplet. A group of ten equal notes, to be played in an aliquot part of a measure.

Dedicato (dĕd-ī-kä'tō), *It.*
Dédié (dā-dī-ā), *Fr.* } Dedicated.

Deficiendo (dä-fē-tshī-ĕn'dō), *It.* Dying away.

Degli (dāl'yē), *It.* Of the.

Degré (dĕ-grā'), *Fr.* A degree of the staff.

Degree. A line or space of the staff.

Del (dĕl), *It.* Of the.

Délassement (dā-läss-mänh'), *Fr.* An easy and agreeable composition.

Deliberatamente (dĕ-lē-bĕ-rä-tä-mĕn'tĕ),
Deliberato (dĕ-lē bĕ-rä'tō), } *It.* } Deliberately.

Delicatamente (dĕl-ī-kä-tä-mĕn'tĕ), *It.* Delicately, smoothly.

Délicatesse (dā-lī-kä-tĕss), *Fr.*
Delicatezza (dĕl-ī-kä-tĕt'zä), *It.* } Delicacy, refined execution.

Delicatissimamente (dĕl-ī-kä-tēs-sī-mä-mĕn'tĕ),
Delicatissimo (dĕl-ī-kä-tīs'sī-mō), } *It.* } With extreme delicacy.

Delicato (dĕl-ī-kä'tō), *It.* Delicately, smoothly.

Delie (dĕ-lē), *Fr.* Loose, light, easy.

Delirio (dē-lē'rī-ō), *It.* Frenzy, excitement.

Deliziosamente (dē-līt-sī-ō-zä-mĕn'tĕ), *It.* Deliciously, sweetly.

Dell' (dĕll),
Della (dĕl'lä),
Delle (dĕl'lĕ), } *It.* } Of the, by the, etc
Dello (dĕl'lō),

Dem (dĕm), *Ger.* To the. Dative form of the definite article.

Démancher (dā-mänh-shā), *Fr.* To change or alter the position of the hand; to shift on the violin, etc.; to cross hands on the pianoforte, making the left hand play the part of the right, and vice versa.

Demande (dĕ-mänhd'), *Fr.* The question, or proposition, of a fugue; called also *dux*, or leading subject.

Demi (dŏ-mē'), *Fr.* Half.

Demi=baton (dŏ-mē'bä'tŏnh), *Fr.* A breve rest.

Demi=cadence (dŏ-mē'kä-dänhs'), *Fr.* A half cadence, or cadence on the dominant.

Demi=staccato (dā-ĭnē'stäk-kä'tō), *Fr.* Half staccato. The tones slightly separated, but not so much as in staccato. Demi-staccato differs from non legato in that the former is positive and the latter is merely negative, the tones failing to connect, but not being purposely separated.

Demi=mesure (dĕ-mē'mĕ-zür'), *Fr.*
Demi=pause (dĕ-mē'pōz), } A minim or half rest.

Demi=quart de soupir (dĕ-mē'kär dŭh soo-pēr), *Fr.* A demisemiquaver rest.

Demisemiquaver. A short note, equal in duration to one half the semiquaver, made thus, ♫ or thus, ♫

Demisemiquaver rest. A mark of silence, equal in duration to a demisemiquaver, made thus,

Demi=soupir (dĕ-ĭnē'soo-pēr, *Fr.* A quaver rest.

Demi=ton (dĕ-mē tŏnh), *Fr.* } An interval of a
Demitone (dĕ-mē'tŏn). } half-tone.

Dénoument (dā-noo-mänh), *Fr.* Conclusion, the catastrophe of an opera, play, etc.

De plus en plus vite (dŭh plü zänh plü vēt), *Fr.* More and more quickly.

Depressio (dĕ-prĕs'sĭ-ō), *It.* The fall of the hand in beating time.

Depression, chromatic. Depression by a chromatic sign.

De profundis (dĕ prō-foon'dĭs), *Lat.* " Out of the depths. O Lord." One of the seven penitential psalms.

Der (där), *Ger.* The singular masculine form of the definite article, and genitive feminine form of same. 2) Of the.

Dergleichen (dĕr-glī'kh'n), *Ger.* The like.

Dérivé (dĕ-rē-vā), *Fr.* Derivative.

Derivative chords. Chords derived from others by inversion.

Des (dĕs), *Ger.* The note D♭. Also genitive form of definite article. From the, of the.

Désaccordé (däz-äk-kŏr-dā), *Fr.* Untuned; put out of tune.

Désaccorder (däz-äk-kŏr-dā), *Fr.* To untune, to put out of tune.

Descant. Harmony, extemporaneous or otherwise, sung or played to a given melody or theme. See *Discant.*

Descant clef. The treble, or soprano, clef.

Descend. To pass from a higher to a lower tone.

Descendant (dĕ-sänh-dänh), *Fr.* Descending.

Deschant (dĕ-shänh), *Fr.* Discant.

Des=dur (dĕs'door), *Ger.* D♭ major.

Design. A design, or plan. Sometimes used in place of motive, but more generally to indicate the plan of a larger part of a composition.

Des=moll (dĕs-mŏll), *Ger.* The key of D♭ minor.

Desperazione (dĕs-pĕ-rä-tsĭ-ō'nĕ), *It.* See *Disperazione.*

Dessauer Marsch (dĕs'sou-ĕr märsh), *Ger.* A famous instrumental march, one of the national airs of Germany.

Dessin (dĕs-sänh), *Fr.* The design, or sketch, of a composition.

Dessus (dĕs-süs), *Fr.* The treble, or upper, part.

Desto (dĕs'tō), *It.* Brisk, sprightly.

Destra (dĕs'trä), *It.* Right; *destra mano*, the right hand.

Détaché (dā-tü-shā), *Fr.* Detached, staccato.

Determinatissimo (dā-tĕr-mĭ-nä-tĕs'sĭ-mō), *It.* Very determined, very resolutely.

Determinato (dā-tĕr-mĭ-nä'tō). *It.* Determined, resolute.

Determinazione (dā-tĕr mĭ-nä-tsĭ-ō'nĕ), *It.* Determination, resolution.

Detto (dĕt'tō), *It.* The same.

Deutlich (doit'lĭkh), *Ger.* Distinctly.

Deutsche Flöte (doit'shĕ flö'tĕ), *Ger.* A German flute.

Deux (dü), *Fr.* Two.

Deuxieme (dü-zĭ-ăm'), *Fr.* Second.

Deuxieme position (dü-zĭ-ăm' pō-zē'sĭ-onh), *Fr.* The second position of the hand or fingers in playing the violin, etc.

Devoto (dā-vō'tō), *It.* Devout, religious.

Devozione (dā-vō-tsĭ-ō'nĕ), *It.* Devotion, religious feeling.

Dextra (dĕx-trä), *Lat.* }
Dextre (dĕxtr), *Fr.* } The right hand.

Di (dē), *It.* Of, with, for, etc.

Dialogue. A composition in which two parts, or voices, respond alternately to each other.

Dialogo (dē-ä-lŏ'gŏ), *It.* }
Dialogue (dē-ä-lŏg'), *Fr.* } A dialogue.

Diana (dē-ä'nä), *It.* } The reveille; the beat
Diane (dĭ-än-nh), *Fr.* } of drums at daybreak.

Diap. An abbreviation of Diapason.

Diapason (dĕ-ä-pä'sŏn), *Gr.* } The whole oc-
Diapason (dĭ-ä-pä'sŏn), *Eng.* } tave. (1) An octave. (2) The compass of a voice or instrument. (3) Pitch; as the diapason normal of the French. (4) The English name of the organ-stops which the Italians and Germans call characteristically "principal" (Principale, Principal). The diapasons are the most important foundation stops of the organ.

Diapason, open. An organ-stop the pipes of which are open at the top, and made of metal.

Diapason, stopped. An organ-stop, generally of wood, having its pipes closed at their upper end with a wooden plug by which it is tuned.

Diapente (dē-ä-pĕn'tĕ), *Gr.* A perfect fifth; also an organ-stop.

Diapente col ditono (dē-ä-pĕn'tĕ kŏl dī-tō'nō), *Gr.* A major seventh.

Diaphonie (dē-ä-fō'nĕ). (1) Clear, transparent; two sounds heard together. (2) In Greek music it meant dissonance, as symphony meant consonance. (3) One of the earliest attempts at simultaneous combination of notes in the middle ages. It preceded discant, which in its turn was followed by counterpoint.

Diaphony (dē-äf-ō-ny).

Diaphonics (dē-ä-fŏn'ĭks). The science of refracted sounds.

Diaschisma (dē-ä-skĭs'mä), *Gr.* This term is to be met with in mathematical calculations of the ratios of intervals. It is the name of various small intervals not used in practical music.

Diastema (dē-äs'tĕ-mä), *Gr.* An interval.

Diatonic (dī-ä-tŏn'ĭk). (1) Through the tones. In modern music, as distinguished from chromatic. A diatonic scale is one consisting of the tones belonging to the three principal harmonies of the key, and of no others; that is to say, of tonic, subdominant, and dominant, whether the mode be major or minor. (2) The Greeks distinguished their modes as diatonic, enharmonic, and chromatic, which differed from each other in the nature of intervals composing them. See *Key, mode.*

Diatonic flute. A flute capable of producing the various shades or differences of pitch of the major and minor . . . es.

Diatonic melody. A me' / in which no tones foreign to the key are u..ed.

Diatonico (dē-ä-tō'nĭ-kō), *It.*
Diatonique (dē-ä-tōnh-nēk'), *Fr.* } Diatonic.
Diatonisch (dē-ä-tōn'ĭsh), *Ger.*

Diatoniquement (dē-ä-tōnh-nĕk'mänh), *Fr.* Diatonically.

Di bravura (dē brä-voo'rä), *It.* In a brilliant, florid style.

Di chiaro (dē kē-ä'rō), *It.* Clearly.

Dichord (dī-kŏrd), *Gr.* (1) A two-stringed instrument. (2) An instrument the strings of which are tuned in pairs.

Dichten (dĭhk't'n), *Ger.* To compose metrically.

Dichter (dĭhk'tĕr), *Ger.* A poet, a minstrel.

Di colto (dē kōl'tō), *It.* At once, instantly, suddenly.

Didactic. That which is calculated to instruct.

Die (dē), *Ger.* The plural form of the definite article. Also feminine singular.

Diesare (dē-ä-zä'rĕ), *It.*
Diéser (dĭ-ä-zä), *Fr.* } To raise the pitch of a note, either at the signature or in the course of a composition, by means of a sharp.

Diese (dī-āz), *Fr.* A sharp (♯).

Dies iræ (dī'ĕz ē'rä), *Lat.* "Day of vengeance," a venerable hymn of the Church. Second movement of the Requiem.

Diesis (dē-ā'sĭs), *Gr. and It.*
Diesis (dī-ā'sĭs), *Fr.* } A quarter of a tone; half a semitone. A term which has been applied to various small intervals, mostly to intervals smaller than a semitone. (2) The name given to the sharp in Italy, and also in France.

Dies, music. Steel punches for the purpose of stamping music-plates.

Diese, double. A double sharp (𝄪).

Die zeugmenon (dē tsĭg'mĕ-nŏn), *Gr.* The third tetrachord disjoined from the second.

Difference tones. See *Resultant tones.*

Difficile (dĭf-fē'tshĭ-lĕ), *It.* Difficult.

Digitorium. A small, portable, dumb instrument, with five keys, for exercising the fingers.

Digital exercises. Exercises for strengthening the fingers and rendering them independent of each other.

Dignita (dĕn-yĭ-tä'),
Dignitade (dĕn-yĭ'tä'dĕ), *It.* } Dignity, grandeur, greatness.
Dignitate (dĕn-yĭ-tä'tĕ),

Di grado (dē grä'dō), *It.* By degrees; step by step; in opposition to di salto.

Digressione (dē-grĕs-sĭ-ō'nĕ), *It.* A deviation from the regular course of a piece.

Diletant (dē-lĕ-tänh'), *Ger.* } A lover of
Dilettante (dē-lĕt-tänh'tĕ), *It.* } art; an amateur who composes or performs without making music a profession.

Dilettosamente (dē-lĕt-tō-zä-mĕn'tĕ), *It.* Pleasantly, agreeably.

Dilicatamente (dē-lĭ-kä-tä-mĕn'tĕ), *It.* Delicately, softly. See *Delicatamente.*

Dilicatezza (dē-lĭ-kä-tĕt'sä), *It.* Delicateness, softness, neatness.

Dilicatissimamente (dē-lĭ kä-tĕs-sĭ-mä-mĕn'tĕ), *It.* With extreme softness and delicacy.

Dilicatissimo (dē-lĭ-kä-tĕs'sĭ-mō), *It.* With extreme softness and delicacy.

Dilicato (dē-lĭ-kä'tō), *It.* Soft, delicate.

Diligenza (dē-lĭ-jĕn'tsä), *It.* Diligence.

Diligenza, con (dē-lĭ-jĕn'tsä kŏn), *It.* In a diligent and careful manner.

Diludium (dĭ-loo'dĭ-oom), *Lat.* An interlude.

Diluendo (dī-loo-ĕn'dō), *It.* Diminishing; a gradual dying away of the tone until it is extinct.

Dim.
Dimin. } Abbreviations of Diminuendo.

ä *arm*, ă *add*, ā *ale*, ĕ *end*, ē *eve*, ĭ *ill*, ī *isle*, ō *old*, ŏ *odd*, oo *moon*, ŭ *but*, ü *Fr. sound*, kh *Ger. ch*, nh *nasal*.

(93)

Diminished. This word is applied to intervals or chords which are less than minor or perfect intervals.

Diminished chords. Chords that contain diminished intervals.

Diminished fifth. An interval equal to two whole tones and two semitones.

Diminished fourth. One whole tone and two semitones.

Diminished imitation. A style of imitation in which the answer is given in notes of less value than that of the subject.

Diminished intervals. Those which are one chromatic semitone less than minor or perfect intervals.

Diminished octave. One chromatic semitone less than a full octave.

Diminished seventh. One chromatic semitone less than a minor seventh.

Diminished sixth. One chromatic semitone less than a minor sixth.

Diminished third. One chromatic semitone less than a minor third.

Diminished triad. A chord composed of the minor third and the diminished or imperfect fifth.

Diminué (dĭ-mĕn-oo-ā'), *Fr.* Diminished.

Diminuendo (dē-mē-noo-ăn'dō), *It.* Diminishing gradually the intensity or power of the tone.

Diminuer (dĭ-mē-noo-ā'), *Fr.* To diminish.

Diminution. In counterpoint this means the imitation of a given subject, or theme, in notes of shorter length or duration; in opposition to augmentation.

Diminuzione (dē-mĭ-noo-tsĭ-ō'nĕ), *It.* Diminution.

Di molto (dē mōl'tō), *It.* Very much; an expression which serves to augment the meaning of the word to which it is applied.

D in alt, *It.* The fifth note in alt; the twelfth above the G, or treble-clef note.

D in altissimo, *It.* The fifth note in altissimo; the twelfth above G in alt.

D'inganno (dēn-gün'nō), *It.* An unexpected ending.

Di nuovo (dē noo-ō'vō), *It.* Anew, once more, again.

Dioxia. A perfect fifth; the fifth tone, or sound.

Di peso (dē pā'zō), *It.* At once.

Diphonium. A vocal duet.

Di posta (dē pōs'tü), *It.* At once.

Di quieto (dē kwē-ā'tō), *It.* Quietly.

Direct. A mark sometimes placed at the end of a staff to indicate the note next following (∿). To beat time for a musical performance, and to direct the interpretation.

Directeur (dĭ-rĕk-tŭr'), *Fr.* The director, or conductor, of a musical performance.

Direct motion. Similar, or parallel, motion; the parts rising or falling in the same direction.

Director. The conductor, or manager, of a musical performance.

Direct turn. A turn consisting of four notes, viz., the note above that over which the sign is placed, the principal note, the note below it, and ending with the principal note.

Direttore (dē-rĕt-tō'rĕ), *It.* A director. See *Directeur.*

Dirge. A musical composition, either vocal or instrumental, designed to be performed at a funeral, or in commemoration of the dead.

Diritta (dĕ-rĕt'lä), *It.* Direct; straight on, in ascending or descending intervals.

Dis (dēz), *Ger.* The note D♯.

Di salto (dē säl'tō), *It.* By leaps or by skips; in opposition to di grado.

Disarmonia (dēz-är-mō'nĭ-ä), *It.* Discord, want of harmony.

Discant. Lit., " diverse song." (1) One of the early phases of counterpoint. The term signified at first the addition of a melody to a melody. Afterwards, however, the number of the parts was not limited. According to the number of parts employed the discant was double, triple, or quadruple. (2) The highest kind of the human voice, the soprano, or treble. Also the highest member of a family of instruments, the highest register of an instrument, and the highest part of a composition.

Discantschlüssel (dĭz-känt'shlü-s'l), *Ger.* The soprano; the C clef placed upon the first line, the note upon that line being called C. It is seldom used now.

Discantstimmen (dĭz-känt-s'tĭm'm'n), or, **Discantregister** (dĭz-känt'rā-ghĭs'tĕr), *Ger.* The organ-stops which comprise only the treble, not the bass notes. They are also called *Halbe Stimmen,* half-stops.

Discantgeige (dĭs'känt-ghī'ghĕ), *Ger.* An obsolete term for the violin.

Discantist (dĭs-kän-tĭst'), *Ger.* Treble, or soprano singer.

Discantsaite (dĭs-känt'sī'tĕ), *Ger.* Treble string.

Discantsänger (dĭs-känt'säng'ĕr), *Ger.* Treble or soprano singer.

Discantus (dĭs-kän'toos), *Lat.* Discant.

Discendere (dē-shän'dā-rĕ), *It.* To descend.

Discepola (dē-shā'pō-lä), *It.* A female pupil.

Discepolo (dē-shā'pō-lō), *It.* Disciple, pupil, scholar.

Disciolto (dē-shē-ōl'tō), *It.* Skillful, dexterous.

Discord. A dissonant interval, an interval that does not satisfy the ear, but causes unrest. The opposite of a discord is a concord. (2) A chord which contains one or more dis sonant intervals, and which, on account of its unsatisfying and disquieting effect, requires to be resolved into a consonant chord. (*V. Introduction.*) The foregoing are the uses of this term, as popularly employed. Properly speaking, however, discord is an unmusical, inharmonious effect, which may go far beyond the limits of the permissible. Any inharmonious combination. A *Dissonance* is a discordant combination musically employed. Inasmuch as consonance depends upon appreciable relations between the tones so related, dissonance and discord depend upon the clashing of vibrations and the inability of the ear to find a common measure or principle of unity. These clashings take place in dissonance (*q. v.*), but the manner in which a dissonance is used suggests to the ear the resolution, the later entrance of the concordant tone which the dissonance had temporarily displaced.

Discordant. A term applied to all discordant or inharmonious sounds.
Discordante (dĭs-kŏr-dän'tĕ), *It.* Discordant.
Discordantemente (dĭs-kŏr-dän-tĕ-mĕn'tĕ), *It.* Discordantly.
Discordare (dĭs-kŏr-dä'rĕ), *It.* } To be out of
Discorder (dĭs-kŏr-dā·), *Fr.* } tune.
Discorde (dĭs-kŏrd), *Fr.* } Discord.
Discordia (dĭs-kŏr'dĭ-ü), *Lat.* } Discord.
Discreto (dĭs-krā'tŏ), *It.* Discreetly.
Discrezione (dĭs-krät-tsĭ-ō'nĕ), *It.* Discretion, judgment, moderation.
Dis-dur (dĭs-door), *Ger.* The key of D♯ major.
Disharmonie (dĭs-här-mō-nē'), *Ger.* Disharmony.
Disharmonisch (dĭs-här-mō'nĭsh), *Ger.* Unharmonious.
Disharmony. Discord, want of harmony.
Disinvolto (dĭs-ĭn-vŏl'tŏ), } *It.*
Disinvolturato (dĭs-ĭn-vŏl-too-rä'tŏ), }
Off-hand, bold, not forced, naturally.
Disis (dēs-ĕs), *Ger.* D-double-sharp.
Disjunct. Disjoined. A term applied by the Greeks to those tetrachords where the lowest sound of the upper one was one degree higher than the acutest sound of the one immediately beneath it.
Disjunct succession. A succession by skips.
Dis-moll (dĭs-mŏl), *Ger.* The key of D♯ minor.
Disonanza (dĭs-ō-nänt'sä), *It.* Dissonance.
Disonare (dĭs-ō-nä'rĕ), *It.* To sound discordantly.
Di sopra (dē sō'prä), *It.* Above.
Disperato (dĭs-pĕ-rä'tŏ), *It.* Despaired of; with desperation.
Disperazione (dĭs-pĕ-rä-tsĭ-ō'nĕ), *It.* Despair, desperation.
Dispersed harmony. Harmony in which the notes forming the various chords are separated from each other by wide intervals. Strictly, chord positions in which the upper voices exceed the compass of an octave.

Disposition. The arrangement of the stops in an organ, disposing them according to power, quality of tone, etc. (2) Estimate as to cost and appointment of an organ.
Dissonance. The inharmonious relation of tones. (See *Discord.*) Strictly speaking, dissonance is the musical employment of discord. All harmonic combinations are dissonant in greater or less degree, except the unison, octave, major and minor thirds and sixths, the perfect fifth, and harmonic seventh. All dissonances are employed as temporary substitutes for consonants, in order to render the harmonic motion more emphatic and appealing. The disappearance of the dissonance is generally effected by the voice having it progressing one degree to the consonant tone displaced. Most dissonances are either *Suspensions*, held over out of a previous chord, *Appoggiaturas*, struck free upon the beat but resolved upon the half beat, *Passing tones*, introduced in passing by degrees from one chord tone to another, or *Changing tones*, where a voice skips off to a dissonant tone and immediately returns.
Dissonant chords. All the chords except the perfect concord and its derivatives.
Dissonant (dĭs-sō-nänh), *Fr.* } Dissonant,
Dissonante (dĭs-sō-nän'tĕ), *It.* } out of tune, discordant.
Dissonanz (dĭs-sō-nänts'), *Ger.* } Dissonance;
Dissonanza (dĭs-sō-nänt'sä), *It.* } discord.
Dissonare (dĭs-sō-nä'rĕ), *It.* } To sound
Dissoner (dĭs-sō-nā'), *Fr.* } out of tune;
Dissoniren (dĭs-sō-nē'r'n), *Ger.*) to be discordant.
Dissoni suoni (dĭs-sō nē soo-ō'nĭ), *It.* Inharmonious sounds; discords.
Distico (dĭs-tē-kŏ), *Sp.* A distich.
Distinti suoni (dĭs-tēn'tĭ soo-ō'nĭ), *It.* Distinct sounds.
Distinto (dĭs-tēn'tŏ), *It.* Clear, distinct.
Distonare (dĭs-tō-nä'rĕ), *It.* To be out of tune.
Distoniren (dĭs-tō-nē'r'n), *Ger.* To get out of tune; to produce discord either in singing or playing.
Di testa (dē tĕs'tä), *It.* Of the head, in speaking of the voice.
Dithyrambe (dē-tĭ-rähmb), *Fr.* } A song or
Dithyrambe (dē-tĭ-räm'bĕ), *Ger.* } ode sung in ancient times in honor of Bacchus; a wild, rhapsodical composition.
Dithyrambic (dē-thĭ-räm'bĭk), *Gr.* In style of a dithyrambe.
Ditirambica (dē-tē-räm'bĭ-kä), } *It.* } Dithyram-
Ditirambico (dē-tē-räm'bĭ-kŏ), } *It.* } bic.
Ditirambo (dē-tē-räm'bŏ), *It.* See *Dithyrambe.*
Dito (dē'tŏ), *It.* The finger.
Dito grosso (dē'tŏ grŏs'sŏ), *It.* The thumb
Diton (dē-tōnh), *Fr.* } Of two parts or
Ditone (dē-tō-nĕ), *Gr.* } tones; a major
Ditono (dē'tō-nō), *It.* } third or interval of
Ditonus (dĭ-tō-noos), *Lat.* } two whole tones.

Ditty. A song, a sonnet; a little poem to be sung.

Div. Abbreviation of Divisi, divided.

Divan (dē'văn), *Per.* Among the Persians a term applied to a series of poems with the distichs ending in every letter successively; a collection of the writings of a single author.

Diverbia (dĭ-vĕr'bĭ-ä), *Lat.*} A musical dialogue, often used by the ancients to enrich their drama.
Diverbio (dē-vär'bĭ-ō), *It.*

Divertimento (dē-vĕr-tĭ-mĕn'tō), *It.* A short, light composition, written in a pleasing and familiar style.

Divertissement (dĭ-vĕr-tĕss'mänh), *Fr.* (1) A light, entertaining composition, consisting of a series of pieces, which may be in any form. (2) A composition consisting of a number of movements or simple tunes loosely strung together. A potpourri. (3) Formerly the name of a series of dances or songs inserted in the acts of operas, ballets, and plays. (4) Now a short ballet with little or no action, often a mere medley of dances.

Divisi (dē-vē'zī), *It.* Divided, separated. In orchestral parts this word implies that one half the performers must play the upper notes and the others the lower notes. The term has a similar meaning when it occurs in vocal music.

Division. (1) A variation of a simple theme. (2) A long note divided into short notes. A series of notes forming a chain of sounds, and in vocal music sung to one syllable. To run a division is to execute such a series of notes.

Division (dĭ-vē-zē ōnh), *Fr.* A double bar.

Division du temps (dĭ-vē-zē-ōnh dü tänh), *Fr.* Time-table.

Division-marks. Figures with a curved line above them, showing the number of equal parts into which the beats are divided in a group of notes, $\overline{3}$, $\overline{5}$, $\overline{7}$, $\overline{9}$, etc.

Divotamente (dē-vō-tä-mĕn'tĕ), *It.*} Devoutly, in a solemn style.
Divoto (dē-vō'tō),

Divozione (dē-vot-tsĭ-ō'nĕ), *It.* Devotion, religious feeling.

D. M. The initials of Destra mano.

D-moll (dä-mōll), *Ger.* The key of D minor.

Do (dō), *It.* A syllable applied to the first note of a scale in sol-faing. In France the "fixed Do" system prevails, whereby the name Do is always applied to C or its derivatives (C-sharp, C-flat) in all keys.

Doctor of Music. The highest musical degree conferred by the universities. It is conditioned upon presenting an extended and meritorious composition, lasting forty minutes or more, for soli, chorus, and orchestra, together with a satisfactory demonstration in musical history, theory, etc.

Doglia (dōl'yĭ-ä), *It.* Grief, affliction, sadness.

Doigt (dwä), *It.* Finger.

Doigté (dwä-tä), *Fr.* Fingered.

Doigter (dwä-tä), *Fr.* To finger; the art of fingering any instrument.

Doigts fixes.(dwä fĕk-sĕ), *Fr.* Fixed fingers.

Dol. An abbreviation of Dolce.

Dolcan. Obsolete name for Dulciana, an organ-stop (*q. v.*).

Dolce (dōl'tshĕ), *It.* Sweetly, softly, delicately.

Dolce con gusto (dōl'tshĕ kŏn goos'tō), *It.* Softly, sweetly, with taste and expression.

Dolce e cantabile (dōl'tshĕ ā kän-tä'bĭ-lĕ), *It.* Sweet, soft, in singing style.

Dolce e lusingando (dōl'tshĕ ā loo-sĕn-gän'dō), *It.* In a soft and insinuating style.

Dolce e piacevolmente espressivo (dōl'tshĕ ā pē-ä'tshĕ-vōl-mĕn'tĕ ĕs-prĕs-sē'vō), *It.* Soft and with pleasing expression.

Dolce ma marcato (dōl'tshĕ mä mär-kä'tō), *It.* Soft and delicate, but marked and accented.

Dolce maniera (dōl'tshĕ mä-nĭ-ā'rä), *It.* A delicate and expressive manner of delivery.

Dolcemente (dōl-tshĕ-mĕn'tĕ), *It.* Sweetly, gently, softly.

Dolcezza (dōl-tshĕt'zü), *It.* Sweetness, softness of tone.

Dolciano (dōl-tshī-ä'nō), *It.* } A small bassoon, formerly much used as a tenor to the hautboy.
Dolcino (dōl-tshē'nō),

Dolciss. An abbreviation of Dolcissimo.

Dolcissimo (dōl-tshĕs'sĭ-mō), *It.* With extreme sweetness and delicacy. A very soft organ-stop of the dulciana quality.

Dolemment (dō-lĕm-mänh), *Fr.* Dolefully, mournfully.

Dolent (dō-länh), *Fr.* } Sorrowful, mournful, pathetic.
Dolente (dō-lĕn'tĕ), *It.*

Dolentemente (dō-lĕn-tĕ-mĕn'tĕ), *It.* Sorrowfully, mournfully.

Dolentissimo (dō-lĕn-tĕs'sĭ-mō), *It.* With extreme sadness; with very pathetic and mournful expression.

Dolore (dō-lō'rĕ), *It.* Grief, sorrow.

Dolorosamente (dō-lō-rō-zä mĕn'tĕ), *It.* }
Doloroso (dō-lō-rō'zō),
Dolorously, sorrowfully, sadly.

Dom (dŏm), *Ger.* A cathedral.

Domchor (dŏm'kōr), *Ger.* The cathedral choir.

Dominant. The name applied by theorists to the fifth note of the scale.

Dominant chord. A chord found on the dominant, or fifth, note of the scale, so called from its establishing the key and requiring the tonic to follow it.

Dominante (dŏm-ĭ-nänht), *Fr.* } The dominant.
Dominante (dō-mĭ-nän'tĕ), *Ger.*

Dominant harmony. Harmony on the dominant or fifth of the key.

Dominant section. A section terminating on the common chord of the dominant.

Dominicali psalmi (dō-mĭ-nĭ-kä'lē säl'mē), *Lat.* Certain psalms of the Roman Catholic Church, sung in the Vespers.

Domkirche (dŏm'kĕr'khĕ), *Ger.* A cathedral.

Dona nobis pacem (dō'nä nō'bĭs pä'tsĕm), *Lat.* "Grant us Thy peace." The concluding movement of the Mass.

Donna (dŏn'nä), *It.* Lady; applied to the principal female singers in an opera.

Dopo (dō'pō), *It.* After.

Doppel (dŏp'p'l), *Ger.* Double.

Doppel-be (dŏp'p'l-bä), *Ger.* A double flat (♭♭), equal to a depression of two half-steps.

Doppelflöte (dŏp'p'l-flö'tĕ), *Ger.* Double flute; a stop in an organ the pipes of which have two mouths.

Doppelfuge (dŏp-p'l-foo'ghe), *Ger.* Double fugue.

Doppelflügel (dŏp'p'l - flü-g'l), *Ger.* Double grand pianoforte. (1) An instrument invented in the last century, also called Dinplasion and Vis-à-vis. It had at both ends one or two keyboards, which acted upon two separate sets of strings. (2) Piano à claviers renversés (*q. v.*).

Doppelgedeckt (dŏp'p'l-gĕ-dĕkt'), *Ger.* Double-stopped diapason.

Doppelgeige (dŏp'p'l-ghī'ghĕ), *Ger.* An organ-stop. See *Viola d'Amour.*

Doppelgriffe (dŏp-p'l-grĭf'fĕ), *Ger.* Double stop on the violin, etc.

Doppelkanon (dŏp'p'l-kä-nōn), *Ger.* A canon with two subjects.

Doppelkreuz (dŏp'p'l-kroitz), *Ger.* A double sharp (♯♯ or X), raising a note two semitones.

Doppelpunkt (dŏp-pĕl-poonkt), *Ger.* Double dot after a note.

Doppelschlag (dŏp'p'l-shlägh), *Ger.* A mordent, a turn.

Doppelschritt (dŏp'p'l-shrĭt), *Ger.* A quick march.

Doppelt (dŏp-p'lt), *Ger.* Double.

Doppelte Noten (dŏp'p'l-tĕ nō't'n), *Ger.* Double notes.

Doppelter Trillerlauf (dŏp'p'l-tĕr trĭl'lĕr-louf), *Ger.* Double cadence.

Doppelt gestrichene Note (dŏp'pĕlt ghĕ-strĭ'kh'nĕ nō'tĕ), *Ger.* A semiquaver.

Doppia lyra (dŏp-pĭ-ä lē'rä), *It.* A double lyre.

Doppio (dŏp'pĭ-ō), *It.* Double, twofold; sometimes indicating that octaves are to be played.

Doppio movimento (dŏp'pĭ-ō mō-vĭ-mĕn-tō). *It.* Double movement or time; that is, as fast again.

Doppio pedale (dŏp'pĭ-ō pĕ-dä'lĕ), *It.* Playing a bass passage on the organ with the pedals moving in octaves, etc.; that is, using both feet at the same time.

Doppio tempo (dŏp'pĭ-ō tĕm'pō), *It.* Double time, as fast again.

Doppo (dŏp'pō), *It.* After. See *Dopo.*

Dorian (dō-rĭ-än), *Gr.* } The name of one of
Dorien (dō-rĭ-änh), *Fr.* } the ancient modes or scales. (1) In the ancient Greek system, the octave species c͡ f g a b c d e, and one of the transposition scales. (2) In the ecclesiastical system, the octave species d e f g͡ a b c d, the first (authentic) mode.

Doric mode. Dorian.

Dossologia (dŏs-sŏ-lō'jĭ-ä), *It.* Doxology.

Dot. (1) A point placed after a note increases its duration one half. (2) A point placed above or below a note indicates that the latter has to be played staccato (detached). If there is at the same time a slur, the notes thus marked are played mezzo staccato (lit., "half detached"). (3) A series of two or four dots placed by a double bar indicate that the strain upon that side is to be played twice through. See *Repeat.*

Dot, double. Two dots placed after a note to increase its duration three fourths of its original value.

Double (doo'b'l), *Fr.* Variation. Doubles may be defined as repetitions of a song, dance tune, or instrumental air, ornamented with figures, graces, diminutions, runs, etc. The term is obsolete.

Double A, or, AA. In England the term double is applied to all those bass notes from G to F inclusive. In Germany the rule is different. See *Double G.*

Double-action harp. A harp with pedals, by which each string can be shortened two semitones.

Double afternote. Two afternotes, taking their time from the previous note.

Double appoggiatura. A union of two short appoggiaturas.

Double B, or, BB. See *Double G.*

Double bar. Two thick strokes drawn down through the staff to divide one strain or movement from another. In many editions these are incorrectly placed.

Double bass. This instrument, the largest member of the violin family, and the fundamental part of the orchestra, has generally either three or four strings. In Germany the double bass is tuned as under (*a*), in England most frequently as under (*b*), and in Italy and France as under (*c*). The double bass sounds the notes an octave lower than they are written.

Double bassoon. This instrument is an octave lower in pitch than the bassoon. Its extreme compass extends from the double contra B♭ to the small F (B♭♭ to f). The compass of a double bassoon designed by Dr. W. H. Stone, and made by Haseneir, of Coblentz, extends from C, to c'. Also a 16- or 32-feet organ reed-stop, of smaller scale and softer tone than the double trumpet.

Double bemol (bā-mōl), *Fr.* Double flat.

Double C, *or,* **CC.** See *Double G.*

Double chant. A simple harmonized melody in four strains or phrases, and extending to two verses of a psalm or canticle.

Double chorde (doobl kŏrd), *Fr.* Playing one and the same note on the violin upon two strings at once.

Double counterpoint. A counterpoint which admits of the parts being inverted.

Double croche (doobl krŏsh), *Fr.* Double-hooked; a semiquaver.

Doubled. A term applied when one of the notes of a chord is repeated in a different part of the same chord.

Double D, *or,* **DD.** See *Double G.*

Double demisemiquaver. A note equal in duration to one half of a demisemiquaver; a sixty-fourth note. It is written thus:

Double descant. Where the treble or any high part can be converted into the bass, and vice versa.

Double diapason. An organ-stop tuned an octave below the diapasons. It is called a 16-feet stop on the manuals; on the pedals it is a 32-feet stop.

Double diese (doobl dī-āz), *Fr.* A double sharp (## or ×).

Doubled letters. Capital letters doubled, indicating that the tone is an octave lower than where the letters stand single.

Double drum. A large drum used in military bands and beaten at both ends.

Double dulciana. An organ-stop of small 16-feet scale and delicate tone.

Double E, *or,* **EE.** See *Double G.*

Double F, *or* **FF.** See *Double G.*

Double flageolet. A flageolet consisting of two tubes, blown through one mouthpiece, and producing two sounds at one time.

Double flat. A character (♭♭) which, placed upon a staff degree, indicates a depression of a whole step.

Double flute. A flute so constructed that two tones may be produced from it at the same time; a stop in an organ. See *Doppelflöte.*

Double fugue. A fugue on two subjects.

Double G. The octave below G gamut; the lowest G on the pianoforte. In England the term Double is applied to all those bass notes from G to F inclusive.

Double grand pianoforte. An instrument with a set of keys at each end, invented by James Pierson, of New York.

Double hautboy. A 16-feet reed-organ stop of small scale.

Double lyre. The lyria doppia, an old instrument of the viol kind.

Double note. A breve; a note twice the length of a whole note.

Double octave. An interval of two octaves; a fifteenth; the bisdiapason of the ancient Greeks.

Double quartet. A composition written for eight instruments or voices; eight singers.

Double reed. The mouthpiece of the hautboy, bassoon, etc., formed of two pieces of cane joined together.

Double shake. Two notes shaken simultaneously; they must form sixths or thirds.

Double sharp. A character which, when placed upon a staff degree, indicates an elevation of a whole step. It is usually written as follows: ## or ×.

Double-stopping. In violin-playing, two tones at once.

Double-stopped diapason. An organ-stop of 16-feet tone on the manuals; the pipes are stopped or covered at the top.

Double suspension. A suspension that retards two notes and requires a double preparation and resolution.

Double tierce. An organ-stop tuned a tenth above the diapasons, or a major third above the octave.

Double time. Inelegant for Double Measure. A movement in which every measure is composed in two equal parts. It is marked by letting the hand fall and rise alternately.

Double-tongueing. A method of articulating quick notes used by flute-players.

Double trill. See *Double shake.*

Double triplet. The union of two triplets; a sextole, thus:

Double trumpet. An organ-stop of 16-feet scale; sometimes the lowest octave of pipes is omitted, and it is then called the Tenoroon trumpet.

Double twelfth. An organ-stop sounding the fifth above the foundation stops; it is generally composed of stopped pipes.

Doublette (doob-lĕt'), *Fr.* An organ-stop tuned an octave above the principal; in England it is called the fifteenth. A mixture of two ranks.

Doucet (doo-sā'), *Fr.* Sweet, soft, gentle.

Doucement (doos'mänh), *Fr.* Sweetly, softly, pleasingly.

Douleur (doo-lŭr'), *Fr.* Grief, sorrow, pathos.

Douloureusement (doo-loor-ŭs-mänh), *Fr.* Plaintively, sorrowfully.

Douloureux (doo-loor-üh), *Fr.* Sorrowful, tender, plaintive.
Doux (dooz), *Fr.* Sweet, soft, gentle.
Douzieme (doo-zhĭ-ām'), *Fr.* A twelfth.
Downbeat. The accented part or parts of a bar at which in beating time the hand or foot falls. (*V. Thesis.*)
Downbow. The drawing of the bow in playing a stringed instrument from the nut to the head.
Downbow-sign. A sign used in violin music indicating that the bow is to be drawn down; thus, ⊓.
Doxologia (dŏx-ō-lŏ′gĭ-ä), *Lat.* } Doxology.
Doxologie (dŏx-ŏl′ō-zhē), *Fr.*
Doxology, *Gr.* A form or expression of praise and honor to God, but more especially the "Gloria in excelsis Deo" ("Glory to God in the highest") and the "Gloria Patri et Filio et Spiritui Sancto" ("Glory be to the Father, and to the Son, and to the Holy Ghost.") The former is called the Greater Doxology (*Doxologia major*), the latter the Lesser (*Doxologia minor.*) Also versified forms of the same.
Drag. A digore in drum music.
Drahtsaite (drät′sŏi′tĕ), *Ger.* Music wire; wire string.
Drama. A poem accompanied by action; a play, a tragedy or comedy.
Dramatic. A term applied to music written for the stage and to all other music representing passion.
Dramaticamente (drä-mä-tĭ-kä-měn′tĕ), *It.* }
Dramatiquemente (drä-mä-těk-mänht), *Fr.* Dramatically.
Dramatique (drä-mä-těk′), *Fr.* } Dramatic.
Dramatisch (drä-mä′tĭsh), *Ger.*
Dramatis personæ (drä-mä′tĭs pěr-sō′nä), *Lat.* The characters of an opera or play.
Dramaturge (drăm-ä türzh), *Fr.* } A dramatist.
Dramaturgo (drä-mä-toor′gŏ), *It.*
Drame (dräm), *Fr.* } A drama.
Dramma (dräm′mä), *It.*
Dramma burlesca (dräm′mä boor-lēs′kä), *It.* A comic or humorous drama.
Dramma lirico (dräm′mä lē′rĭ-kō), }
Dramma per musica (dräm-mä pěr moo′zĭ-kä), *It.*
An opera or musical drama.
Drammaticamente (dräm-mä-tĭ-kä-měn′tĕ), *It.* Dramatically, in a declamatory style.
Drammatico (dräm-mä′tĭ-kō), *It.* Dramatic.
Drawstops. The knobs or buttons by means of which the organist brings on or takes off certain "stops" or sets of pipes. See *Stop.*
Drehorgel (dra′org′l), *Ger.* Barrel organ.
Drehsessel (drä′sěs-s′l), *Ger.* } A music-stool.
Drehstuhl (drä′stool),
Dreher (drä′ĕr), *Ger.* A slow waltz, or German dance.

Drei (drī), *Ger.* Three.
Dreiachtel (drī-äkh′t′l), *Ger.* Three quavers, or eighth-notes.
Dreiachteltact (drī-äkh′t′l-täkt), *Ger.* Measure in 3-8 time.
Dreihändig (drī′hän-dĭg), *Ger.* For three hands.
Dreiangel (drī′an-g′l), *Ger.* Triangle.
Dreichörig (drī′kör-ĭgh), *Ger.* Three-choired. Applied to any piano having three strings to each note. Nearly all upright pianos, as well as grands, belong to this class. Also applied to compositions for three choirs.
Dreigesang (drī′ghĕ-säng′), *Ger.* Trio for three voices.
Dreiklang (drī′kläng), *Ger.* A triad, a chord of three sounds.
Dreimal (drī′mäl), *Ger.* Thrice.
Dreisang (drī′säng), } *Ger.* } A trio.
Dreispiel (drī′spēl),
Dreist (drīst), *Ger.* Brave, bold, confident.
Dreistigkeit (drīs′tĭg-kīt), *Ger.* Boldness, confidence, resolution.
Dreistimmig (drī′stĭm-mĭgh), *Ger.* Three-voiced.
Dreivierteltact (drī-fĕr′t′l-täkt), *Ger.* Measure in 3-4 time.
Dreizweiteltact (drī-tswī′t′l-täkt), *Ger.* Measuring 3-2 time, or a measure of three minims.
Dringend (drĭng′ĕnd), *Ger.* Pressing.
Dritta (drĕt′tä), } *It.* } Right; *mano dritta,* the right hand.
Dritto (drĕt′tō),
Dritte (drĭt′tĕ), *Ger.* Third.
Droite (drwät), *Fr.* Right; *main droite,* the right hand.
Drommete (dröm-mä′tĕ), *Ger.* A trumpet.
Drone. The two or three pipes of the bagpipes which furnish the fixed and unvarying accompaniment to the melody of the chanter, the third or fourth pipe. A drone bass is often found in orchestral and other instrumental works. (*V. Bagpipe.*)
Drönen (drö′nĕn), *Ger.* To give a low, dull sound; to drone.
Drücker (drē′k′r), *Ger.* A sticker in organ action.
Drum. An instrument of percussion consisting of one or two skins stretched over a frame, frequently cylindrical in form and always circular at the top. There are a great many kinds of drums—the Tambourine, Sidedrum, Bass, or Big, Drum, Kettledrum, etc., the most important of which will be noted in their places.
Druma (droo-mä), *Iri.* A drum.
Drum, bass. A large drum used in military bands. See *Double drum.*
Drum bass. A term applied to the mere use of the tonic and dominant in playing upon the double bass.

ä arm, ă add, ā ale, ĕ end, ē eve, I ill, ī isle, ŏ old, ŏ odd, oo moon, ŭ but, ü *Fr. sound,* kh *Ger. ch,* nh *nasal.*

(99)

Drum major. The principal drummer in a military band; the officer directing the band.

D. S. The initials of Dal Segno.

Ductus (dook'toos), *Lat.* Melodic movement, or order of successive notes, which may be: (1) *rectus*, direct, *i. e.*, ascending; (2) *reversus* or *revertens*, reversed, *i. e.*, descending; or (3) *circumcurrens*, circumcurrent, *i. e.*, ascending and descending.

Dudeler (doo'dlĕr), *Ger.* One who plays or sings badly.

Dudelkasten (doo'd'l-käs-t'n), *Ger.* Barrel organ; a hurdygurdy.

Dudelsack (doo'd'l-säk), **Dudelkastensack** (doo'd'l-käs-t'n-säk), *Ger.* A bagpipe, a cornamuse, a hornpipe.

Due (doo'ĕ), *It.* Two; in two parts.

Due clarini (doo'ĕ klä-rē'nē), *It.* Two trumpets.

Due corde (doo'ĕ kōr-dĕ), *It.* Two strings. See *A due corde*.

Due cori (doo'ĕ kō-rī), *It.* Two choirs or choruses.

Due pedali (doo'ĕ pĕ-dä'lī), *It.* The two pedals a.e to be used.

Duet. A composition for two voices or instruments, or for two performers upon the same instrument.

Due trombe (doo'ĕ trōm'bĕ), *It.* Two trumpets.

Duett (doo-ĕt'), *Ger.* A duet.

Duette (doo-ĕt'tĕ), *Ger. pl.* } Duets.
Duetti (doo-ĕt'tī), *It. pl.* }

Duettino (doo-ĕt-tē'nō), *It.* A short and easy duet.

Duetto (doo-ĕt'tō), *It.* A duet.

Due volte (doo'ĕ vōl'tĕ), *It.* Twice.

Dulcet. Soft, sweet, musical; an organ-stop.

Dulcian (dül-sē-änh'), *Fr.* A small bassoon. See *Dolciano*. A dulciana stop.

Dulciana stop. An 8-feet organ-stop; of a soft and sweet quality of tone.

Dulciana principal. A 4-feet organ-stop of delicate tone.

Dulcimer. A very ancient instrument whose principal parts are a wooden frame, a soundboard with one or several soundholes, two bridges, and appliances for the fastening and tuning of the wire strings with which it is strung. A dulcimer is played upon with two hammers.

Dumb spinnet. Another name for the clavichord.

Dumpf (doompf), **Dumpfig** (doomp'fīg), *Ger.* } Of a dull, hollow, muffled sound.

Dumpfigkeit (doomp'fīg-kīt), *Ger.* Hollowness, dullness of sound.

Duo (doo'ō), *It.* Two; in two parts; a composition for two voices or instruments; a duet.

Duo concertante (doo'ō kōn-tshĕr-tän'tĕ), *It.* A duo in which each part is alternately principal and subordinate.

Duodecima (doo-ō-dā'tshī-mä), *It.* } The
Duodecimo (doo-ō-dā'tshī-mō), } twelfth; the twelfth note from the tonic; the name is also applied to an organ-stop tuned a twelfth above the diapasons.

Duodecima acuta (doo-ō-dā'tsī-mä ä-koo'tü), *Lat.* A twelfth above.

Duodecima gravi (doo-ō-dā'tsī-mä grä'vē), *Lat.* A twelfth below.

Duodecimole (doo-ō-dā-tshī-mō'lĕ), *It.* A musical phrase, formed by a group of twelve notes.

Duodramma (doo-ō-dräm'mä), *It.* Duodrama. A dramatic piece for two performers; more especially a spoken drama with musical accompaniments, a kind of melodrama (*q. v.*).

Duoi (doo-ō'ē), *It.* Two.

Duole. A group of two notes to fill the time of three of the same denomination, as in 6-8 measure two eighth-notes with a figure 2 to occupy the time of three eighth-notes:
$\frac{6}{8}$ ♪♪₂ equal to ♪♪♪

Duolo (doo-ō'lō), *It.* Sorrow, sadness, grief.

Duomo (doo-ō'mō), *It.* A cathedral.

Dupla (doo-plä), *Lat.* Double.

Duple time. Double time.

Duplex longa (doo'plĕx lōn'gä), *Lat.* Maxima, one of the notes in the old system of music.

Duplication. Doubling; where one or more of the intervals of a chord are repeated in different parts.

Duplo (doo-plō), *It.* Double.

Dur (door), *Ger.* Major, in speaking of keys and modes; as, *C-dur*, C major.

Dur (dür), *Fr.* Hard, harsh of tone. Major, as distinguished from minor.

Duramente (doo-rä-mĕn'tĕ), *It.* Harshly, roughly; also meaning that the passage is to be played in a firm, bold style, and strongly accented.

Durate (doo-rä'tĕ), *It.* Hard, rough; also implying false relations in harmony.

Durchcomponiren (doorkh'kŏm-pŏ-nē'r'n), *Ger.* Lit., "to compose through." A *durchcomponirtes Lied*, "a through-composed song," is a song of which each verse has a setting of its own, whilst in other songs one setting serves for all verses.

Durchdringend (doorkh-drīng'ĕnd), *Ger.* Penetrating, piercing.

Durchdringende Stimme (doorkh-drīng'ĕn-dĕ stīm'mĕ), *Ger.* A shrill voice or tone.

Durchführung (doorkh'fü-roong), *Ger.* Development. Generally applied to the free fantasia serving for middle part of the main movement in sonatas and other serious movements.

Durchgangstöne (doorkh'gängs-töu-ĕh), *Ger.* Passing tones.
Durchgehend (doorkh'gä-ĕnd), *Ger.* Passing, transient; passing through.
Durée (dü-rā'), *Fr.* Length, duration of notes.
Durement (dür-mänh), *Fr.* Hard, harsh.
Dureté (dü-rĕ-tā'), *Fr.* See *Durate*.
Durezza (doo-rāt'zä), *It.* Hardness, harshness of tone or expression.
Duro (doo'rō), *It.* Rude, harsh.
Düster (düs'tĕr), *Ger.* Gloomy.
Duten (doo-t'n), *Ger.* } A contemptuous
Düten (dü-t'n), *Ger.* } term, meaning to toot or blow on a horn.
Dux (doox), *Lat.* Leader, guide; the subject, or leading melody, of a fugue.
Dynamics. This term in music has reference to expression and the different degrees of power or intensity to be applied to notes.

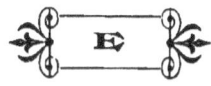

E, called in France and Italy *mi*; the third note of the modern scale of Guido d'Arezzo.
E, Ed (ād), *It.* And.
E. The smallest and most acute string on the violin and guitar.
Ebollimento (ā-bŏl-lĭ-mĕn'tō), *It.* Ebullition. Boiling.
Eccedente (ĕt-tshĕ-dĕn'tĕ), *It.* Augmented, in speaking of intervals.
Ecclesia (ĕk-klā'zĭ-ä), *It. and Lat.* Church.
Ecclesiastical. A term applied to all music written for the Church.
Ecclesiastical modes. See *Church modes*.
Ecclesiastico stilo (ĕk-klā-zĭ-äs-tĭ-kō stē'lō), *It.* In the church or ecclesiastical style.
Ecco (ĕk'kō), *It.* Behold.
Echappement (ā-shäp-mänh), *Fr.* Release. *Double Echappement*, repeating-mechanism in a piano.
Echeggiare (ā-kĕd-jĭ-ä'rĕ), *It.* To echo, to resound.
Echelle (ā-shĕll), *Fr.* The scale, or gamut.
Echelle chromatique (ā-shĕll krō-mät-ēk'),*Fr.* The chromatic scale.
Echelle diatonique (ā shĕll dĭ-ä-tōnh-ēk'), *Fr.* The diatonic scale.
Echo (ā-kō), *Fr.* In organ music this term means a repetition or imitation of a previous passage, with some striking modification in regard to tone. An echo.
Echo cornet. An organ-stop the pipes of which are of small scale, with a light, delicate tone. It is usually placed in the swell.
Eclat (ā-klä'), *Fr.* A burst of applause, expressions of approbation.
Eclatante (ā-klä-tänht'), *Fr.* Piercing, loud.
Eclisses (ā-klĕss), *Fr.* The sides or hoops of a violin, guitar, etc.
Eclogue (ĕk-lŏg), *Gr.* A pastoral song or poem.
Eco (ā'kō), *It.* An echo.

Ecole (ĕ-kōl), *Fr.* A school, a method or course of instruction, a style formed by some eminent artist.
Ecole de chant (ā-kōl düh shänh), *Fr.* A singing-school.
Ecossais (ā-kŏs-sā'), *Fr.* } Scotch; a dance,
Ecossaise (ā-kŏs-sāz), *Fr.* } tune, or air in the Scotch style. (2) An old dance of Scotch origin. It was of a grave character, and either in 3-2 or 3-4 time. (3) The modern écossaise is a lively contredanse in 2-4 time, formerly popular in France, Germany, and other countries.
Ecossäse (ā-kŏs-sā'zĕ), *Ger.* See *Ecossaise*.
Ecoutants (ā-koo-tänh), *Fr.* Auditors, listeners.
Ed (ād), *It.* And.
Edel (ā'd'l), *Ger.* Noble.
Editeur (ā-dĭ-tŭr), *Fr.* Editor, publisher.
E=dur (ā door), *Ger.* The key of E major.
Effet (ĕf-fā). *Fr.* } Effect; the effect of mu-
Effetto (ĕf-fā'tō), *It.* } sic upon an audience.
E-flat. The black key of the piano or organ next to the left of E. The flat of E. The flat seventh of F, and the second flat introduced in modulating by fourths from the natural diatonic scale.
Egalement (ā-gŭl-mänh), *Fr.* Equally, evenly, smoothly.
Egalité (ā-gŭl-ĭ-tā'), *Fr.* Equality, evenness.
Eglise (ā-glēz), *Fr.* Church.
Egloga (āl'yō gä), *It.* } An eclogue; a pas-
Eglogue (ā-glŏg'), *Fr.* } toral poem.
Eguale (ĕ-goo-ä'lĕ), *It.* Equal, even, alike; also applied to a composition for several voices or instruments of one kind, as, male voices only; female voices only.
Egualezza (ā-goo-ä-lĕt'zä), *It.* Equality, evenness.
Egualmente (ā-goo-äl-mĕn'tĕ), *It.* Equally, evenly, alike.
Eighth. An octave.

ä *arm*, ă *add*, ā *ale*, ĕ *end*, ē *eve*, ĭ *ill*, ī *isle*, ō *old*, ŏ *odd*, oo *moon*, ŭ *but*, ü *Fr. sound*, kh *Ger. ch*, nh *nasal*.

Eighth-note. A quaver.

Eilend (ī'lĕnd), *Ger.* Hurrying.

Ein (īn), **Eine** (ī'nĕ), *Ger.* } A; an; one.

Einchörig (īn'kör-ĭgh), *Ger.* One-choired. This term is applied (1) to any instrument which has but one string to each note; (2) to a composition for one choir, to distinguish it from a composition for two or more distinct choirs.

Einfach (īn'fäkh), *Ger.* Simple, plain, unornamented.

Eingang (īn'gäng), *Ger.* Introduction, preface, prelude.

Eingestrichen (īn'ghĕ-strī-kh'n), *Ger.* Note of the treble marked with one stroke. This refers to the octave from middle C to the B above. Called also "once-marked octave."

Einheit (īn'hīt), *Ger.* Unity.

Einhelfen (īn'hĕl-f'n), *Ger.* To prompt.

Einigen (ī'nī-ghĕn), *Ger.* Some, any.

Einigkeit (ī'nīgh-kīt), *Ger.* Unity, concord, harmony.

Einklang (īn'kläng), *Ger.* Unison.

Einleitung (īn'lī-toong), *Ger.* Introduction, prelude.

Einleitungssatz (īn'lī-toongs-sätz), **Einleitungsspiel** (īn'lī-toongs-spēl), *Ger.* } Introductory movement; overture, prelude.

Einmal (īn'mäl), *Ger.* Once.

Einsang (īn'säng), *Ger.* A solo.

Einschnitt (īn'shnīt), *Ger.* A phrase, or incomplete musical sentence.

Einsatzzeichen (īn'sätz-tsī-kh'n), *Ger.* (1) The sign which the leader gives to the various performers to commence. (2) In a canon, the mark which signifies the commencement of the imitating voice.

Einstimmen (īn'stĭm-m'n), *Ger.* To agree in tune, to be concordant.

Einstimmigkeit (īn'stĭm-mĭgh-kīt), *Ger.* A concord, agreement. Literally, one-voiced.

Eintönig (īn'tö-nīgh), *Ger.* Monotonous.

Eintretend (īn'trĕ-tĕnd), *Ger.* Entering, beginning.

Eintritt (īn'trīt), *Ger.* Entrance, entry, beginning.

Eis (īs), *Ger.* The note E♯.

Eisteddfod (ĕs'tĕd-fŏd), *Welsh.* A bardic congress. An assemblage of bards first held in 1078.

Electric piano. A piano invented in 1851, the wires of which were vibrated by hammers actuated by electro-magnetism. Several attempts of this kind have been made, but all have failed.

Elégamment (ĕl-ā-gäm-mänh), *Fr.* **Elegantemente** (ĕl-ĕ-gän-tĕ-mĕn'tĕ), *It.* } Elegantly, gracefully.

Elegante (ĕl-ĕ-gän'tĕ), *It.* Elegant, graceful.

Eleganza (ĕl-ĕ-gän'tsä), *It.* Elegance, grace.

Elegia (ĕl-ĕ-jē'ä), *It.* An elegy, or monody; music of a mournful or funereal character.

Elegiac. Plaintive, mournful, sorrowful.

Elegiaco (ĕl-ĕ-jī-ä'kŏ), *It.* **Elégiaque** (ĕl-ā-zhī-ák), *Fr.* } Mournful, plaintive, elegiac.

Elegy. A mournful or plaintive poem, or a funeral-song.

Elementary music. Exercises and studies specially adapted to beginners in the study of music.

Elements. The first or constituent principles or parts of anything; the principles or rudiments of musical science.

Elevamento (ĕl-ĕ-vä-mĕn'tŏ), **Elevatezza** (ĕl-ĕ-vä-tĕt'zä), *It.* } Grandeur, sublimity, loftiness of expression.

Elevato (ĕl-ĕ-vä'tŏ), *It.* Elevated, exalted, sublime.

Elevazione (ĕl-ĕ-vä-tsī-ŏ'nĕ), *It.* Elevation, grandeur.

Elevatio (ĕl-ĕ-vä'tsī-ŏ), *Lat.* Elevation. (1) The upbeat in beating time. (2) The unaccented part of a bar. (3) The rising of a melody beyond the ambitus (compass) of the mode. (4) A motet or any other vocal or instrumental composition performed during the elevation of the Host.

Elevation. To the four meanings given in the preceding article is to be added this: (5) The obsolete English name of two ornaments. As one of the "smooth graces," it is synonymous with an ascending double appoggiatura; as one of the "shaked graces" it is more complicated.

Elève (ā-lāv), *Fr.* A pupil.

Eleventh. An interval comprising an octave and a fourth.

Elf (ĕlf), *Ger.* Eleven.

Elfte (ĕlf'tĕ), *Ger.* Eleventh.

Eloge (ā-lŏzh'), *Fr.* Praise, eulogy.

Elogy. See *Eulogy.*

Embellir (änh-bĕl-lēr'), *Fr.* To embellish, to adorn, to ornament.

Embellissement (änh-bĕl-lĕss-mŏnh), *Fr.* Embellishment.

Embellishment. Ornament, decoration, notes added for the purpose of heightening the effect of a piece.

Embouchure (änh-boo-shoor), *Fr.* The mouthpiece of a flute, hautboy, or other wind instrument; that part to which the lips are applied to produce the sound. It also refers to the position which the mouth must assume in playing the instrument.

E-moll (ā-mŏll), *Ger.* The key of E minor.

Empâter les sons (önh-pä-tā lĕ sŏnh), *Fr.* To sing or play in a masterly manner, without defects or imperfections.

Empfindung (ĕmp-fĭn'doong), *Ger.* Emotion, passion, feeling.

Empfindungsvoll (ĕmp-fĭn′doongs-fŏll), *Ger.* Full of expression.

Emphase (ĕm-fä′zĕ), *Ger.* Emphasis.

Emphatique (änh-fä-tēk′), *Fr.* } Emphatical.
Emphatisch (ĕmp-fä′tĭsh), *Ger.* }

Emphatiquement (än-fä-tĕk′mänh), *Fr.* Emphatically.

Emphasis. Marked expression; particular stress or accent on any note, indicated thus: > *fz.*, *sf.*, etc.

Emphasize. To sing with marked accent.

Empìto (ĕm-pē′tŏ), *It.* Impetuosity.

Empituosamente (ĕm-pē-too-ŏ-zä-mĕn′tĕ), *It.* Impetuously.

Emporté (änh-pŏr-tā), *Fr.* Passionate, hurried.

Emportement (änh-pŏrt-mänh), *Fr.* Passion, transport.

Empressé (änh-prĕss-sā), *Fr.* In haste, eager, hurried.

Empressement (änh-prĕss-mänh), *Fr.* Eagerness, zeal.

En (änh), *Fr.* In.

Enarmonico (ĕn-är-mō′nĭ-kŏ), *It.* Enharmonic.

Encore (änh-kōr′), *Fr.* Again, once more; demand for the repetition of a piece.

Ende (ĕnd′ĕ), *Ger.* End, conclusion, concluding piece.

Energia (ĕn-ĕr-jē′ä), *It.* } Energy, force, emphasis.
Energie (ĕn-ĕr-zhē), *Fr.* }

Energicamente (ĕn-er-jē-kä-mĕn′tĕ), *It.* Energetically, forcibly.

Energico (ĕn-är′jĭ-kŏ), *It.* Energetic, vigorous, forcible.

Energique (ĕn-ĕr-zhĕk′), *Fr.* } Energetic, with emphasis.
Energisch (ĕu-ä′ghĭsh), *Ger.* }

Energiquement (ĕu-ĕr-zhĕk-mänh), *Fr.* Energetically, forcibly.

Enfant de chœur (änh-fänh dŭh kür), *Fr.* Singing boy.

Enfasi (ĕn-fä′zī), *It.* Emphasis, earnestness.

Enfaticamente (ĕn-fä-tĭ-kä-mĕn′tĕ), *It.* Emphatically.

Enfatico (ĕn-fä′tĭ-kŏ), *It.* Emphatical, with earnestness.

Enflatamente (ĕn-fī-ä-tä-mĕn′tĕ), *It.* Proudly, pompously.

Enfler (änh-flā′), *Fr.* To swell, to increase the tone.

Enge (ĕng-ĕ), *Ger.* Close, condensed, compressed; this term is applied to the stretto in a fugue. In speaking of organ-pipes, it means narrow, straight.

Enge Harmonie (ĕng-ĕ här-mō-nē′), *Ger.* Contracted or close harmony, the intervals or sounds being close together.

Engelstimme (ĕng′ĕl-stĭm′mĕ), *Ger.* Angel voice. Angelica. A full-reed stop in an organ.

Engführung (ĕng′für-oong), *Ger.* "Narrow working." The condensed canonic treatment of a theme in fugue. A stretto.

English fingering. In pianoforte music the use of a sign (×) to designate the thumb, in distinction from the German fingering, where the thumb is designated as the first finger.

English horn. A species of oboe, a fourth or a fifth lower than the instrument usually designated by that name.

Enguichure (änh-ghē-shür′), *Fr.* The mouthpiece of a trumpet.

Enharmonic (ĕn-här-mŏn′ĭk). (1) In our present system of music, with its twelve equal semitones in the octave, those notes, intervals, and scales are called enharmonic which differ in notation but not in pitch. Enharmonic chords are chords which have in common one or several tones the same in pitch but different in notation. An enharmonic modulation is one by means of such chords. (2) With the ancient Greeks the word "enharmonic" had an entirely different meaning. In their enharmonic genus the tetrachord presented itself as a progression of two quarter-steps and a major third; for instance, e $e+$ f a (a development from the trichord $e\ f\ a$).

Enharmonic intervals. Such as have only a nominal difference; for instance, the minor third, C, E♭, and the extreme second, C, D♯; or, the extreme fifth, C, G♯, and the minor sixth, C, A♭, etc.

Enharmonic organ. An organ in which the octave, instead of being limited to a division of twelve intervals, contains from seventeen to twenty-four. An organ capable of playing in perfect tune within limits of the diatonic modes.

Enharmonicus (ĕn-här-mō′nĭ-koos), *Lat.* }
Enharmonique (änh-här-mŏnh-ēk′), *Fr.* }
Enharmonisch (ĕu-här-mō′nĭsh), *Ger.* }
Enharmonic.

Enoncer (ā-nōnh-sā), *Fr.* To enunciate, to proclaim.

Ensayo (ĕn-sä′yō), *Sp.* Rehearsal of a piece.

Enseignement (änh-sān-mänh), *Fr.* Instructions.

Enseigner (änh-sänh′yä), *Fr.* To instruct, to teach.

Ensemble (änh-sänh′bl), *Fr.* Together. Taken substantively this word signifies: (1) Perfect harmony between different parts of a whole; (2) mutual understanding and entire agreement between the performers in rendering a composition. A morceau d'ensemble is a composition for two or more parts, more especially quintets, sextets, septets, etc., in an opera, oratorio, or similar work.

Entgegen (ĕnt-gā′gh'n), } *Ger.*
Entgegengesetzt (ĕnt-gä′g'n-ghĕ-sĕtzt), }
Contrary, opposite, speaking of motion.

ä *arm*, ă *add*, ā *ale*, ĕ *end*, ē *eve*, ĭ *ill*, ī *isle*, ŏ *old*, ŏ *odd*, oo *moon*, ŭ *but*, ü *Fr. sound*, kh *Ger.*, ch, nh *nasal.*

(103)

Enthousiasme (änh-too-zī-äsm), *Fr.* }
Enthusiasmus (ĕn-too-zī-äs'moos), *Ger.* } Enthusiasm.

Enthusiastisch (ĕn-too-zī-äs'tĭsh), *Ger.* Enthusiastically.

Entr'acte (änh-tr'-äkt), *Fr.* Between the acts; music played between the acts of a drama.

Entrante (ĕn-trän'tĕ), }
Entrata (ĕn-trä'tä), *It.* } An entrance, introduction, prelude.
Entrada (ĕn'trä'dä), }

Entrée (änh-trā'), *Fr.* Entry, entrance, beginning. A pompous introduction in march form.

Entscheidung (ĕnt-shī'doong), *Ger.* Decision, determination.

Entschieden (ĕnt-shē'd'n), *Ger.* Decided, in a determined manner.

Entschlafen (ĕnt-shlä'f'n), *Ger.* To die away, to diminish.

Entschlossen (ĕnt-shlŏs's'n), *Ger.* Determined, resolute.

Entschluss (ĕnt-shlooss'), *Ger.* Resolution.

Entusiasmo (ĕn-too-zī-äs'mŏ), *It.* Enthusiasm.

Entwurf (ĕnt-woorf'), *Ger.* Sketch, outline of a composition.

Enunciato (ā-noon-tshī-ä'tŏ), *It.* Enunciated, proclaimed.

Envoy. The postscript, or ending, of a ballad.

Eolia (ā-ŏ'lĭ-ä), }
Eolian (ā-ŏ'lĭ-än), *It.* } See *Æolian*.

Epic. A poem in the narrative style, dealing with heroic incidents upon a large scale.

Epicedio (ĕp-ī-tshā'dĭ-ŏ), *It.* } An elegy,
Epicedium (ĕp-ī-sē'dĭ-ŭm), *Eng.* } dirge, funeral-song, or ode.

Epigonion (ĕp-ī-gŏ'nĭ-ŏn) *Gr.* } An ancient
Epigonium (ĕp-ī-gŏ'nĭ-oom), *Lat.* } Greek instrument with forty strings, so named from Epigonius, its inventor.

Epilogue. A speech or short poem addressed to the spectators by one of the actors after the conclusion of the play.

Epigone. An imitator.

Epinette (ā-pē-nĕt'), *Fr.* A spinet.

Epinicion (ĕp-ī-nē'sī-ŏn). A triumphal song, a song of victory.

Episode. An incidental narrative or digression; a portion of a composition not founded upon the principal subject or theme.

Episodio (ĕp-ī-sō'dĭ-ŏ), *It.* Episode, digression.

Episodisch (ĕp-ī-sō'dĭsh), *Ger.* In the manner of an episode.

Epistrophe (ĕp-ī-strŏ'fĕ), *Gr.* A repetition of the concluding melody.

Epitalamio (ĕp-ī-tä-lä'mĭ-ŏ), *It.* } Epithala-
Epithalme (ĕp-ī-täl-mĕ), *Fr.* } mium.

Epithalamion (ĕp-ī-thä-lä'mĭ-ŏn), *Gr.* }
Epithalamium (ĕp-ī-thä-lä-mĭ-oom), *Gr.* }
Epithalamium, *Eng.* }
Epithalamy, *Eng.* }
A marriage-song; a nuptial-song or ode.

Epode (ĕ-pŏ'dĕ), *Gr.* Conclusion of a chorus; a short lyric poem.

Epode. In lyric poetry, the third or last part of the ode; that which follows the strophe and antistrophe. The word is now used for any little verse or verses that follow one or more great ones; thus a pentameter after a hexameter is an epode.

E poi (ā pŏ'ē), *It.* And then.

E poi la coda (ā pŏ'ē lä kŏ'dä), *It.* And then the coda.

Epopee (ĕ-pŏ'pā), *Gr.* An epic poem.

Eptacorde (ĕp-tä-kŏrd), *Fr.* A heptachord, a lyre with seven strings.

Equábile (ĕ-kwä'bĭ-lĕ), *It.* Equal, alike, uniform.

Equabilmente (ĕ-kwä-bĭl-mĕn'tĕ), *It.* Equally, smoothly, evenly.

Equal counterpoint. A composition in two, three, four, or more parts, consisting of notes of equal duration.

Equal temperament. That equalization or tempering of the different sounds of an octave which renders them all of an equal degree of purity, the imperfection being divided among the whole. See *Temperament*.

Equal voices. Compositions in which either all male or all female voices are employed.

Equisonant. Of the same or like sound; a unison. In guitar music the term is used to express the different ways of stopping the same note.

Equisono (ā-kwē'zō-nō), *It.* Having the same sound.

Equivocal. Such chords as may by a slight change in the notation belong to more than one key.

Ergriffen (ăr-grĭf'f'n), *Ger.* Struck, affected, moved.

Erhaben (ăr-hä'b'n), *Ger.* Elevated, sublime, in a lofty and exalted style.

Erheben (ăr-hā'b'n), *Ger.* To raise, to elevate, to lift up the hand in beating time.

Erhöhen (ăr-hö'ĕn), *Ger.* See *Erheben*.

Erhöhung (ăr-hö'oong), *Ger.* An elevation.

Erhöhungszeichen (ăr-hö'oongs-tsī'kh'n), *Ger.* Sharps or double sharps.

Erniedrigung (ăr-nē'drĭ-ghoong), *Ger.* The depression of a note by means of a flat or natural.

Erniedrigungszeichen (ăr-nē-drĭ-ghoongs-tsī'kh'n), *Ger.* A flat, or other sign, for lowering a note a semitone.

Ernst (ărnst), }
Ernsthaft (ărnst'häft), } *Ger.* Earnest, serious; in a grave and earnest style.

ä *arm*, ă *add*, ā *ale*, ĕ *end*, ē *eve*, ĭ *ill*, ī *isle*, ŏ *old*, ŏ *odd*, oo *moon*, ŭ *but*, ü *Fr. sound*, kh *Ger. ch.* nh *nasal*

Ernsthaftigkeit (ärnst'häf-tĭg-kĭt), *Ger.* Earnestness, seriousness.

Ernstlichkeit (ärnst'lĭkh-kĭt), *Ger.* Earnestness.

Ernst und mit steigender Lebhaftigkeit (ärnst oond mĭt stī'ghĕn-dĕr läb'häf-tĭgh-kĭt), *Ger.* Earnestly, and with increasing vivacity.

Erntelied (ärn'tĕ-lēd), *Ger.* Harvest-song.

Eröffnung (är-öf'noong), *Ger.* Opening, beginning.

Eröffnungsstück (är-öf'noongs-stük), *Ger.* Overture.

Eroico (ĕ-rō'ĭ-kō), *Gr.* Heroic.

Erotic (ĕr-ŏt'ĭc). An amorous composition or poem.

Erotical (ĕr-ŏt'ĭ-kăl). Pertaining to love.

Erotica (ĕ-rō'tĭ-kä), *It.* Love-songs, amatory ditties.

Erotic songs. Love-songs.

Erst (ärst), *Ger.* First.

Erstemal (ärs'tĕ-mäl), *Ger.* First time.

Ertönen (är-tö'nĕn), *Ger.* To sound, to resound.

Erweckung (är-wĕk'oong), *Ger.* Animation, excitement.

Erweitert (är-wī'tĕrt), *Ger.* Expanded, developed.

Es (ĕs), *Ger.* The note E♭.

Esacordo (ĕ-zä-kōr'dō), *It.* Hexachord.

Esatta (ĕ-zät'tä), *It.* Exact, strict.

Esatta intonazione (ĕ-zät'tä ĭn-tō-nät-sĭ-ō'nĕ), *It.* Exact intonation.

Es-dur (ĕs-door), *Ger.* The key of E♭ major.

Esecuzione (ĕz-ĕ-koot-sĭ-ō'nĕ), *It.* Execution, facility of performance.

Esempio (ĕ-zĕm'pĭ-ō), *It.* Example.

Esercizio (ĕ-zär-tshē'tsĭ-ō), *It.* An exercise, a study.

Es-es (ĕs-ĕs), *Ger.* The note E-double-flat (E♭♭).

Esitamento (ĕ-zĭ-tä-mĕn'tō), *It.* }
Esitazione (ĕ-zē-tät-sĭ-ō'nĕ), *It.* } Hesitation.

Es-moll (ĕs-mŏll), *Ger.* The key of E♭ minor.

Esonare (ĕ-zō-nä'rĕ), *It.* To adorn, to embellish.

Espace (ĕs-päs), *Fr.* A space; the interval between two lines of the staff.

Espagnol (ĕs-pän-yŏl), *Fr.* } Spanish,
Espagnuolo (ĕs-pän-yoo-ō'lō), *It.* } in the Spanish style.

Esperto (ĕs-pār'tō), *It.* Skillful, expert.

Espirando (ĕs-pē-rän'dō), *Sp.* Diminishing to the end.

Espirando (ĕs-pē-rän'dō), *It.* Breathing deeply; with great endeavor.

Espr. }
Espress. } Abbreviations of Espressivo.

Espressione (ĕs-prĕs-sĭ-ō'nĕ), *It.* Expression, feeling.

Espressivo (ĕs-prĕs-sē'vō), *It.* Expressive, to be played or sung with expression.

Espringale (ĕs'prĭn-gä-lĕ), *It.* Spring dance.

Essempio (ĕs-sĕm'pĭ-ō), *It.* See *Esempio*.

Essential harmonies. The three harmonies of the key: tonic, dominant, and subdominant.

Essential notes. The real, component notes of a chord; in contradistinction to all merely accidental, passing, or ornamental notes.

Estemporale (ĕs-tĕm-pō-rä'lĕ), }
Estemporaneo (ĕs-tĕm-pō-rä'nĕ-ō), *It.* } Extemporaneous.

Estinguendo (ĕs-tĭn-goo-ĕn'dō), } Becom-
Estinte (ĕs-tĕn'tĕ), *It.* } ing ex-
Estinto (ĕs-tĕn'tō), } tinct, dying away gradually in time and strength of tone.

Estravagante (ĕs-trä-vä-gän'tĕ), } Extrav-
Estravaganza (ĕs-trä-vä-gän'tsä), *It.* } agant.

Estremamente (ĕs-trā-mä-mĕn'tĕ), *It.* Extremely.

Esultazione (ĕs-ool-tät-sĭ-ō'nĕ), *It.* Exultation.

Et (ĕt), *Lat.* And.

Eteinte (ĕ-tänht), *Fr.* See *Estinte*.

Etendre (ĕ-tänhdr), *Fr.* To extend, to spread.

Etendue (ĕ-tänh-dü), *Fr.* The extent or compass of an instrument or voice.

Et incarnatus (ĕt ĭn-kär-nä'toos), *Lat.* "And was born," etc. A portion of the Credo.

Etouffé (ā-toof-fā), *Fr.* Stifled, smothered; a word used in harp-playing to signify a deadening of the tones, extinguishing the vibration by touching the strings; in pianoforte music it means an exceedingly soft style of playing.

Etouffer (ā-toof-fā), *Fr.* To stifle, to deaden the tone.

Etouffoirs (ā-too-fwär), *Fr. pl.* The dampers.

Etre en repetition (ātr änh rĕp-ĕ-tē'sĭ-ōnh), *Fr.* To be in rehearsal.

Et resurrexit (ĕt rĕ-soor-rĕx'ĭt), *Lat.* "And rose again." A part of the Credo.

Etta (ĕt'tä), *It.* } Little; an Italian final
Etto (ĕt'tō), } diminutive; as, *troxbetta*, a little trumpet.

Ettachordo (ĕt-tä-kōr'dō), *It.* Instruments having seven strings.

Etude (ā-tüd), *Fr.* A study. Strictly speaking, a composition for practice in which the overcoming of some one technical difficulty is aimed at. There are, however, also études which are studies in expression or in phrasing. Further, during the last half century it has been the fashion to write études de concert, concert studies, *i. e.*, studies intended not merely for private practice, but also, perhaps chiefly, for public display. Not a few of these études de concert are indeed works of imagination and exquisite musicianship.

Etudier (ā-tü-dē-ā), *Fr.* To study, to practice.

Et vitam (ĕt vē'tăm), *Lat.* "And life everlasting." A part of the Credo, in the Mass.

Etwas (ĕt'vŭs), *Ger.* Some, somewhat, a little.

Etwas langsamer (ĕt'vŭs lăng'să-mĕr), *Ger.* A little slower.

Eufonia (ā-oo-fō-nē'ĭ), *It.* Euphony; an agreeable sound.

Eufonico (ā-oo-fō'nĭ-kō), *It.* Harmonious, well-sounding.

Euphone (üh-fōn), *Fr.* A reed-stop in an organ, of 16-feet scale.

Euphonie (üh-fō-nē'), *Fr.* } Euphony, sweetness of tone.
Euphonie (oi-fō-nē'), *Ger.* }
Sounds agreeable to the ear.

Euphony. Agreeable sound; an easy, smooth enunciation of sounds.

Euharmonic. Producing harmony or concordant sounds.

Euharmonic organ. An ingenious instrument of American origin, invented by H. W. Poole about the year 1848. It contains three or four times the usual number of distinct sounds within the compass of an octave, furnishing the precise intervals for every key. The name was wrongly chosen, in place of enharmonic.

Euouae. A collocation of the vowels contained in and indicative of the words "Seculorum, Amen." According to the old form of the letters, *Erovae*.

Euphon (yoo-fŏn). A kind of glass harmonica with a compass from c to f''', invented by the great physicist, E. F. F. Chladni, about 1790. The tone of this instrument is produced by rubbing with moistened fingers strips of glass, which communicate their vibrations to rods of metal.

Euphoniad (yoo-fō'nĭ-ăd). An instrument of American origin, containing thirty keys with their semitones, and combining in its tones those of the organ, horn, bassoon, clarinet, and violin.

Euphonious (yoo-fō'nĭ-ŭs). Smooth and melodious.

Euphonium. A bass wind instrument of modern invention, used in military bands. It has two tubes, played at will from a single mouthpiece.

Euterpe (oi-tăr'pĕ), *Gr.* The seventh muse, celebrated for the sweetness of her singing.

Eveillé (ā-vā-yā), *Fr.* Lively, gay, sprightly.

Evirati (ĕ-vē-rä'tŏ), *It.* Men with soprano voices among the Italians, who formerly took the treble parts in the church and theater. They are now nearly, if not quite, extinct.

Evolutio (ĕ-vō-loo'tsĭ-ō), *Lat.* Inversion of the parts in double counterpoint.

Exécutant (ĕx-ā-koo-tänh), *Fr.* A performer, either vocal or instrumental.

Exequiæ (ĕx-ā'kwĭ-ā), *Lat.* Dirge.

Exequien (ĕx-ā'kwĭ-ĕn), *Ger.* Masses for the dead.

Exercice (ĕx-ĕr-sĕss'), *Fr.* Exercise.

Exercice de l'archet (ĕx-ĕr-sĕss' düh l'är-shā), *Fr.* Practice of the bow in violin-playing.

Exercise. A musical composition calculated to improve the voice or fingers of the performer.

Explosive tone. A tone produced by sounding a note suddenly and with great emphasis, and suddenly diminishing; indicated thus: >, or *Sf.*

Expressif (ĕx-präs-sēf'), *Fr.* Expressive.

Expression. That quality in a composition or performance which appeals to our feelings; taste or judgment displayed in rendering a composition and imparting to it the sentiment of the author.

Expressivo (ĕx-prĕs-sē'vō), *It.* See *Espressivo*.

Extemporaneous. Without premeditation.

Extempore (ĕx-tĕm'pō-rē), *Lat.* Unpremeditated, improvised.

Extemporize. To perform extemporaneously, without premeditation.

Extended harmony. See *Dispersed harmony*.

Extended phrase. Whenever, by repeating one of the feet, or by any other variation of the melody, three measures are employed instead of two, the phrase is termed extended, or irregular.

Extended section. A section containing from five to eight measures.

Extraneous. Foreign, far-fetched, belonging to a remote key.

Extraneous modulation. A modulation into some remote key, far distant from the original key and its relatives.

Extravaganza (ĕx-trä-vä-gänt'sä), *It.* A dence or ornament which is in bad taste; an extravagant and eccentric composition.

Extreme. A term referring to the most distant parts, as the treble and bass. Relating also to intervals in an augmented state; as extreme sharp sixth, etc.

---

arm, ă add, ā ale, ĕ end, ē eve, ĭ ill, ī isle, ō old, ŏ odd, oo moon, ŭ but, ü *Fr.* sound, kh *Ger.* ch. nh nasal.

F, The name of the fourth note in the natural diatonic scale of C. A perfect fourth above C.

Fa. A syllable applied in sol-faing to the fourth degree of every scale.

Fa bémol (fä bā-mŏl), *Fr.* The note F♭.

Fa-burden. A term applied by the old English musical writers to a certain species of counterpoint, consisting of thirds and sixths added by ear to a cantus firmus. Later it signified any kind of improvised accompaniment. See *Falso bordone*.

Faces d'un accord (fäss d'ŭn ăk-kŏr), *Fr.* The various positions of a chord.

Fach (fäkh), *Ger.* Ranks; thus, *fünffach*, five ranks.

Facile (fä-sēl'), *Fr.* }
Facile (fä-tshĕ'lĕ), *It.* } Light, easy.

Facilita (fä-tshē'lĭ-tä), *It.* } Facility; an easier
Facilité (fä-sēl-ĭ-tā), *Fr.* } arrangement or adaptation.

Facilement (fä-sēl-mänh), *Fr.* } Easily, with
Facilmente (fä-tshēl-měn'tĕ), *It.* } facility.

Fackeltanz (fäk'l-tänts), *Ger.* Dance with flambeaux.

Facture (fäk-tür), *Fr.* The composition, or workmanship, of a piece of music.

Fa dièse (fä dĭ-āz), *Fr.* The key of F♯.

Fa dièse majeur (fä dĭ-āz' mä-zhŭr'), *Fr.* The key of F♯ major.

Fa dièse mineur (fä dĭ-āz' mĭ-nŭr'), *Fr.* The key of F♯ minor.

Fa diesis (fä dĕ-ā'zĭs), *It.* Fa-sharp. F♯.

Fagott (fä-gŏtt'), *Ger.* A bassoon.

Fagottino (fä-gŏt-tē'nō), *It.* A small bassoon.

Fagottist (fä-gŏt-tĭst'), *Ger.* } A performer
Fagottista (fä-gŏt-tĕs'tä), *It.* } on the bassoon.

Fagotto (fä-gŏt'tō), *It.* A bassoon, also an organ-stop.

Fagotto contro (fä-gŏt'tō kōn'trō). *It.* A large bassoon, an octave, a fifth, or a fourth lower than the common bassoon.

Fagottone (fä-gŏt'tō-nĕ), *It.* A large bassoon formerly in use, an octave lower than the fagotto.

Fahnenmarsch (fä'něn-märsh), *Ger.* The march or tune that is played when the colors are lodged.

Faible (fā'bl), *Fr.* Weak, feeble, thin.

Faiblement (fā'bl-mänh), *Fr.* Feebly, weakly.

Faire (fār), *Fr.* To do, to execute.

Faites bien sentir la mélodie (fāt bĭ-änh' sänh-tēr' lä mā'lō-dē), *Fr.* Play the melody very distinctly.

Fa, la. The burden, chorus, or refrain of many old songs. Fa, la, etc., were much in fashion in the seventeenth century, and are to be found in the works of some eminent composers.

Falalella (fä-lä-lĕl'lä), *It.* A nonsensical song.

Fall (fäl), *Ger.* A cadence.

Falsa (fäl'sä), *It.* } False, wrong, inharmo-
Falsch (fälsh), *Ger.* } nious.

Falsch singen (fälsh sĭng'ĕn), *Ger.* To sing out of tune.

False. Those intonations of the voice that do not truly express the intended intervals are called false, as well as all ill-adjusted combinations. The term false is applied in music to any violation of acknowledged or long-established rules, or to anything imperfect or incorrect.

False accent. When the accent is removed from the first beat of the bar to the second or fourth, it is called false accent.

False cadence. An imperfect or interrupted cadence.

False fifth. An old term for an imperfect or diminished fifth; a fifth containing only six semitones, as C, G♭.

False relation. The principal and most objectionable kind of false relation arises where a note which has appeared in one part reappears immediately after in another part chromatically altered—*i. e.*, a semitone flattened or sharpened (a). As numerous examples in our best composers show, such progressions have by no means always a bad effect. Another kind of false relation is the occurrence of the tritonus (an augmented fourth or diminished fifth) between the first note of the one and the second note of the other of two progressive parts. Hence the strict prohibition by the old theorists of the progression of two major thirds (b). The practice and teaching of more modern times deals with this matter in a high-handed way.

(a)   (b)

False triad. The diminished triad, formerly so called on account of its having a false fifth.

ä *arm*, ă *add*, ā *ale*, ĕ *end*, ē *eve*, ĭ *ill*, ī *isle*, ō *old*, ŏ *odd*, oo *moon*, ŭ *but*, ü *Fr. sound*, kh *Ger. ch*, nh *nasal*.

Falsett (fäl-sĕt'), *Ger.* } **Falsetto.** (1) The
Falsetto (fäl-sĕt'tō), *It.* } head voice, as distinguished from the chest voice. (2) A singer who sings soprano or alto parts with such a voice. *Falsetti* must not be confounded with *castrati*.

Falsette. } A false or artificial voice; that
Falsetto. } part of a person's voice that lies above its natural compass.

Falso (fäl'sō), *It.* False.

Falso bordone (fäl'sō bŏr-dō-nĕ), *It.* What the French call *Faux-bourdon* and the English *Fa-burden*. There are several kinds of falso bordone. The most important are: (1) The early manner of accompanying a melody (cantus firmus) in thirds and sixths, with the exception of the first and last note, with which the highest part took the octave and the middle part generally the fifth of the tenor—*i. e*, the part which "holds" the cantus firmus. Or the melody (cantus firmus) was in the highest part, and was accompanied by fourths and sixths below, except at the close, where the lowest part took the octave. (2) Rhythmically unmeasured vocal compositions in simple counterpoint, consisting of progressions of consonant chords, whose even course, however, is interrupted at the cadences by prepared suspensions.

Fa majeure (fä mä-zhŭr'), *Fr.* } The key of F
Fa majore (fä mä-zhōr'), } major.

Fa mineur (fä mĭ-nŭr'), *Fr.* Key of F minor.

Fanatico (fä-nä'tĭ-kō), *It.* A fanatic or passionate admirer.

Fancies. An old name for little lively airs or tunes. See *Fantasia*.

Fandango (fän-dän'gō), *Sp.* A dance much used in Spain, in 3-4, 3-8, and also 6-8 measure, generally accompanied with castanets and having a strong emphasis upon the second beat of each bar. Its characteristic rhythm is this:

|: 𝅘𝅥𝅭 𝅘𝅥 𝅘𝅥𝅰 𝅘𝅥𝅮𝅘𝅥𝅮𝅘𝅥𝅮 | 𝅘𝅥𝅮𝅘𝅥𝅮𝅘𝅥𝅮 𝅘𝅥 :|

Fanfare (fänh-fär), *Fr.* A short, lively, loud, and warlike piece of music, composed for trumpets and kettledrums. Also short, lively pieces performed on hunting-horns in the chase.

Fantaisie (fän-tä-zē), *Fr.*} Fantasy, fancy,
Fantasia (fän-tä-zē'ä), *It.* } caprice, whim. (1)
Fantasie (fän-tä-sē'), *Ger.*} The name of Fantasia is given to various kinds of composition—to preludes consisting of a few arpeggios and runs, to lengthy works full of thought and learning, to potpourris of operatic tunes, etc., which, however, all agree in being free in style, not restricted by any definite form. (2) An improvisation. (3) The instrumental pieces called Fantasias (also written Fantazias and Phantasias), Fancies (or Funsies), etc., were at first mostly of a fugal nature. Those which Dr. Burney had in his possession were for viols, and "consisted more of motets, madrigals, and *in nomines* (*q. v.*), originally designed for voices, than of fantasie made expressly for instruments." Christopher Simpson writes in 1667 that "this kind of music is now much neglected, by reason of the scarcity of auditors that understand it; their ears being better acquainted and more delighted with light, airy music." He names as "the best composers of Fancies in England, Alfonso Ferabosco, Coperario, Lupo, Mico, White, Ward, Dr. Colman, and Jenkins. (4) We find the term Fancies also applied to vocal compositions and to short, lively tunes.

Fantasioso (fän-tä-zĭ-ō'zō), *It.* Fantastic, capricious.

Fantasiren (fän-tä-zē'r'n), *Ger.* To improvise, to play extemporaneously.

Fantasticamente (fän-täs-tĭ-kä-mĕn'tĕ), *It.* In a fantastic sty.e.

Fantastico (fän-täs'tĭ-kō), *It.* } Fantastical,
Fantastique (fän-täs-tēk'), *Fr.* } whimsical, capricious in relation to style, form, modulation, etc.
Fantastisch (fän-täs'tĭsh), *Ger.* }

Farandole (fä-ränh-dōl'), *Fr.*} A lively
Farandoule (fä-ränh-dool), } dance in 6 8 time, peculiar to Provence.

Farce. A short, extravagant comedy, interspersed with airs or songs with instrumental accompaniments.

Farsa (fär'sä), *It.* } Farce.
Farsa (fär'sä), *Sp.* }

Farsa in musica (fär'sä in moo'zĭ-kä), *It.* Musical farce; a species of little comic opera, in one act.

Fascie (fäs'tshĭ-ĕ), *It. pl.* The sides, or hoops, of a violin, viola, etc.

Fastosamente (fäs-tō-zä-mĕn'tĕ), *It.* Pompously, proudly.

Fastoso (fäs-tō'zō), *It.* Proud, stately, in a lofty and pompous style.

Faucette (fō-sĕt'), *Fr.* } Falsetto.
Fausset (fō-sä'), }

Faux (fō), *Fr.* False, out of tune.

Faux accord (fō zäh-kōrd'), *Fr.* A dissonance.

Faux bourdon (fō boor-dōnh), *Fr.* See *Fa-burden*.

F clef. The bass clef; a character placed on the fourth line of the staff so that the two dots are in the third and fourth spaces.

F-dur (ĕf-door), *Ger.* The key of F major.

Feathering. A term sometimes applied to a particularly delicate and lightly detached manner of bowing certain rapid passages on the violin.

Feeders. Small bellows sometimes employed to supply th large bellows of an organ with wind.

Feier (fī'ĕr), *Ger.* Festival, celebration.

Feiergesang (fī'ĕr-ghō-säng), *Ger.* Solemn hymn, anthem.

Feierlich (fī'ĕr-līkh), *Ger.* Solemn, festive.
Feierlichkeit (fī'ĕr-līkh-kīt), *Ger.* Solemnity, pomp.
Feigned voice. A falsetto voice.
Feine Stimme (fī'nĕ stīm'mĕ), *Ger.* A fine voice.
Feint. A figure in drum music.
Feinte. An old name for a semitone; an accidental.
Feldflöte (fĕld-flö'tĕ), *Ger.* A peasant flute.
Feldkunstpfeifer (fĕld koonst'pfī-fĕr), *Ger.* A military musician.
Feldmusik (fĕld'moo-zīk), *Ger.* Military music.
Feldrohr (fĕld'rōr), *Ger.* A rural pipe of oboe order.
Feldton (fĕld'tōn), *Ger.* The tone or keynote of the trumpet and other military wind instruments.
Feldtrompete (fĕld-trōm-pā'tĕ), *Ger.* Military trumpet.
Ferma (fār'mä), *It.* Firm, resolute, steady.
Fermamente (fār-mä-mĕn'tĕ), *It.* Firmly, steadily.
Fermata (fār-mä'tä), *It.* } A pause or hold
Fermate (fār-mä'tĕ), *Ger.* } marked thus, ⌢.
Fermate (fār-mä'tĕ), *It.* } Firmly, steadily,
Fermato (fār-mä'tō), } resolutely.
Fermement (fār-mĕ-mäuh), *Fr.* Firmly, resolutely.
Fermo (fār'mō), *It.* Firm, resolute.
Ferne (fār'nĕ), *Ger.* Distance.
Fernwerk (fĕrn'wĕrk), *Ger.* Distant, or remote, work; term applied to a particular row of keys in German organs.
Feroce (fā-rō'tshĕ), } Fierce,
Ferocemente (fā-rō tshĕ-mĕn'tĕ), *It.* } with an expression of ferocity.
Ferocita (fā-rō-tshī-tā'), *It.* Fierceness, roughness.
Fertig (fĕr'tīgh), *Ger.* Quick, nimble, dexterous.
Fertigkeit (fĕr'tīgh-kīt), *Ger.* Quickness, dexterity.
Fervemment (fār-vä-mäuh), *Fr.* Fervently, vehemently.
Fervente (fār-vĕn'tĕ), *It.* Fervent, vehement.
Ferventemente (fār-vĕn-tĕ-mĕn'tĕ), *It.* } Fer-
Fervidamente (fār vē-dä mĕn'tĕ), } vently, vehemently.
Fervido (fār'vī dō), *It.* Fervent, vehement.
Fes (fĕs), *Ger.* The note F♭.
Feses (fā'sĕs), *Ger.* F-double-flat.
Fest (fĕst), *Ger.* Feast, festival; also firm, steady.
Festigkeit (fĕs'tīg-kīt), *Ger.* Firmness, steadiness.
Festivamente (fĕs-tĕ-vä-mĕn'tĕ), *It.* Gaily, brilliantly.

Festivita (fĕs-tĕ-vī-tä'), *It.* Festivity, gayety.
Festivo (fĕs-tē'vo), *It.* Merry, cheerful, gay.
Festlich (fĕst'līkh), *Ger.* Festive, solemn.
Festlichkeit (fĕst'līkh-kīt), *Ger.* Festivity, solemnity.
Festlied (fĕst'lēd), *Ger.* A festive song.
Festoso (fĕs-tō'zō), *It.* Merry, cheerful, gay.
Festouvertüre (fĕst'ō-vĕr-tü'rĕ), *Ger.* Festival overture; an overture in a vigorous, brilliant style.
Festzeit (fĕst'tsīt) *Ger.* Festival-time.
F. F. Fortissimo; very loud.
F. F. F. Very fortissimo; as loud as possible.
Feuer (foi'ĕr), *Ger.* Fire, ardor, passion.
Feurig (foi'rīgh), *Ger.* Fiery, ardent, passionate.
Fiacca (fē-äk'kä), } Feeble, weak, languish-
Fiacco (fē-äk'kō), *It.* } ing, speaking of the tone.
Fiasco (fē-äs'kō), *It.* The technical term for a failure; a complete breakdown in a musical performance.
Fiato (fē-ä'tō), *It.* The breath, the voice.
Fiddle. A common name for violin.
Fiddler. A common name for violinist, usually applied to a poor player.
Fiddlestick. A violin-bow.
Fides (fē'dĕs), *Lat.* (1) A catgut string; (2) A stringed instrument.
Fidicen (fē'dī-tsĕn), *Lat.* A harper; one who plays upon a stringed instrument.
Fidicina (fē'dī-tsē'nä), *Lat.* A woman who plays upon a stringed in-trument.
Fidicula (fē-dĭ'koo-lä), *Lat.* A small lute or guitar.
Fiducia (fī-doo'tshī-ä), *It.* Confidence.
Fiedel (fē'd'l), *Ger.* A fiddle, a violin.
Fiedelbogen (fē'd'l-bō'g'n), *Ger.* A fiddlestick, a violin-bow.
Fiedelbrett (fē'd'l-brĕt), *Ger.* A squeaking fiddle.
Fiedler (fēd'lĕr), *Ger.* A fiddler.
Fiel. An old name for the fiddle, or violin.
Field music. Music for military instruments; martial music.
Fier (fē-ā'), *Fr.* Proud, haughty.
Fieramente (fē-ĕr ä-mĕn'tĕ), *It.* Fiercely, vehemently, boldly.
Fière (fī-ār), *Fr.* Proud, lofty, fierce.
Fièrement (fī-ār-mäuh), *Fr.* In a fierce manner.
Fieramente assai (fē-ä-rä-mĕn'tĕ äs-sä'ī), *It.* Very bold and energetic.
Fiero (fē-ā'rō), *It.* Bold, energetic, lively.
Fierté (fĕr-tā'), *Fr.* Fierceness, boldness.
Fife. A simple cross flute (*v. Flute*), generally either in the key of F or B♭, and chiefly used in military music in combination

Fifer. One who plays on the fife.

Fiffaro (fē'fä-rō), *It.* A fife.

Fifre (fēfr), *Fr.* A fife, also a fifer; the name is also applied to one of the stops in a harmonium.

Fifteenth. An interval of two octaves; also the name of an organ-stop, tuned two octaves above the diapasons.

Fifth. The interval from any tone of the scale to the fifth above or below, the extreme tones themselves being counted.

Fifth, augmented. An interval containing four whole steps.

Fifth, diminished. An interval containing two whole steps and two half-steps.

Fifth, perfect. An interval containing three whole steps and one half-step.

Fifths, consecutive. Two or more perfect fifths immediately following one another in two parallel parts of the score.

Fifth, sharp. An interval consisting of eight semitones.

Figur (fī-goor'), *Ger.* A musical figure, phrase, or idea.

Figura (fē-goo-rä'), *It.* Note employed as an ornament.

Figuralgesang (fī-goo-räl'ghĕ-säng'), *Ger.* Varied and ornamented chant, as opposed to plain chant.

Figurantes (fē-gü-ränht'), *Fr.* Those dancers in a ballet who do not dance singly, but in groups and many together. In the drama, people who figure without having anything to say.

Figuration. An ornamental treatment of a passage, by introducing passing tones, appoggiaturas, etc., in one or more of the voices.

Figurato (fē-goo-rä'tō), *It.* } Figured, florid,
Figuré (fī-gü-rä'), *Fr.* } embellished.

Figured. Free, florid; a term applied to an air which, instead of moving note by note with the bass, consists of a free and florid melody. It also means indicated or noted by figures.

Figured bass. A shorthand system of noting harmonies. It consists of a bass part with figures which indicate the principal intervals of the intended chords. In the case of triads, unless they are inverted, the bass is generally left without figures. Accidentals affect the corresponding intervals of the figures beside which they stand. An accidental standing by itself affects the third above the bass note. A stroke through a figure shows that the interval is sharpened a semitone. An oblique stroke under or above a bass note indicates that not the note thus marked, but the following one, is the basis of the harmony to be taken; horizontal lines indicate that a harmony has to be continued whilst the bass proceeds, and the words *tasto solo* or the sign o indicate that nothing but the bass notes is to be played.

Figures of diminution. Numerical characters which diminish the duration of the notes over which they are placed. The notes with a figure three are called triplets, where there are two triplets a figure six is used.

Filar la voce (fē-lär lä võ'tshĕ), *It.* To spin out, to prolong the tone, gradually augmenting and diminishing the sound of the voice.

Filarmonico (fē-lär-mō'nĭ-kō), *It.* Philharmonic, music-loving.

Filer (fĭ-lā), *Fr.* To spin, to draw out.

Filer le son (fĭ-lā lŭh sōnh), *Fr.* See *Filar la voce.*

Filet de voix (fĭ-lā dŭh vwä), *Fr.* A very thin voice.

Fileur (fĭ-lŭr), *Fr.* A spinner; a stringmaker.

Filum (fĭ-loom), *Lat.* A name formerly given to the stem of a note.

Fin (fănh), *Fr.* The end.

Fin al (fēn äl), *It.* End at; play as far as.

Final. The final is in the church modes what the tonic is in our modern musical system. In the authentic modes the final is on the first degree, in the plagal modes on the fourth degree of the scale. Besides these regular finals (*i. e.*, "concluding notes") there are also irregular ones (confinals), which occur frequently in the endings of the Psalms and in the sections of the Responsories, Graduals, and Tracts.

Final close. Final cadence.

Finale (fē-nä'lĕ), *It.* (1) The concluding movement of a sonata, symphony, etc., and the concluding divisions of the acts of an opera. This latter kind of finale is a culminating ensemble piece, many-membered in movement and matter, and generally with chorus. (2) A final (*q. v.*).

F in alt. The seventh above G in alt; the seventh note in alt.

F in altissimo. The octave above F in alt the seventh note in altissimo.

Fin a qui (fēn ä kwē), *It.* To this place.

Fine (fē'nĕ), *It.* The end, the termination.

Fine del aria (fē'nĕ dĕl ä'rĭ-ä), *It.* The end of the air.

Fine del atto (fē'nĕ dĕl ät'tō), *It.* The end of the act.

Finement (fănh-mänh), *Fr.* Finely, acutely.

Fingerboard. That part of a stringed instrument on which the fingers press; the keyboard, or manual, of a pianoforte, organ, etc.

Fingered. A term applied to piano music, signifying that figures or other characters are applied to the notes to show the method of fingering.

Fingering, American. The use of the sign (X) to indicate the thumb in pianoforte-playing, in distinction from the German or foreign fingering, in which the thumb is called the first finger.

Fingering, foreign. } A method of fingering piano music which designates the thumb as the first finger.
Fingering, German. }

Fingerleiter (fĭng'ĕr-lī'tĕr), *Ger.* Finger-guides.

Fingern (fĭng'ĕrn), *Ger.* To play, to finger.

Fingersatz (fĭng'ĕr-sätz), *Ger.* Fingering.

Finished. A term applied to those vocal or instrumental performers who have attained an advanced and artistic execution.

Finita (fē-nē'tä), } Finished, ended, concluded.
Finito (fē-nē'tō), } *It.*

Finite canon. A canon which is not repeated.

Fino al (fē'nō äl), *It.* Play as far as, stop at, end at.

Fin qui (fēn kwē), *It.* To this place.

Fint (fēnt), } Feigned, false, interrupted, in respect to cadences; a feint, or deceptive, close.
Finto (fēn'tō), }

Fioca (fē-ō'kä), } Hoarse, faint, feeble.
Fioco (fē-ō'kō), } *It.*

Fiochezza (fē-ō-kĕt'zä), *It.* Hoarseness.

Fioreggiante (fē-ō-rĕd-jī-än'tĕ), *It.* Too ornate, decorated with roulades, cadences, etc.

Fioretti (fē-ō-rĕt'tē), *It.* Little graces, or ornaments, in vocal music.

Fioriscente (fē-ō-rī-shĕn'tĕ), } Florid, abounding with ornaments.
Fiorito (fē-ō-rē'tō), } *It.*

Fiorita cadenza (fē-ō-rē'tä kä-dĕnt'sä), *It.* A cadenza whose last note but one is divided into many notes.

Fioritezza (fē-ō-rī-tĕt'sä), *It.* Embellishment. A florid style of performance.

Fioritura (fē-ō-rī-too'rä), *It.* Literally, "a flowering." A florid melodic ornament. *Fioreggiare*, the corresponding verb, signifies to ornament (flower) a melody by solving its principal elements into a multiplicity of shorter notes of varied pitch. *Fioriture* is the plural of *fioritura*.

First. A word applied to the upper part of a duet, trio, quartet, or any other composition, vocal or instrumental; such parts generally express the air.

First bass. High bass.

First inversion. A term applied to a chord when the bass takes the third. See *Inversion*.

First soprano. The high soprano.

First tenor. The high tenor.

Fis (fĭs), *Ger.* The note F♯.

Fis-dur (fĭs-door), *Ger.* The key of F♯ major.

Fis-fis (fĭs-fĭs) *Ger.* The note F-double-sharp.

Fis-moll (fĭs'moll), *Ger.* The key of F♯ minor.

Fistel (fĭs'tel), *Ger.* Feigned voice; falsetto.

Fistola (fĭs'tō-lä), *It.* } A reed, a pipe.
Fistula (fĭs'too-lä), *Lat.* }

Fistula dulcis (fĭs'too-lä dool'tsĭs), *Lat.* This was once a common flute, and was blown at the end. See *Flûte à bec*.

Fistula Germanica (fĭs'too-lä gĕr-mä'nĭ-kä), *Lat.* German flute.

Fistula Panis (fĭs'too-la pä'nĭs), *Lat.* The Pandean pipes; wind instruments of the ancients.

Fistula pastoralis (fĭs'too-lä päs-to-rä'lĭs), *Lat.* The Pandean pipes; wind instruments of the ancients.

Fistula pastorica (fĭs'too-lä päs-tō-rī-kä), *Lat.* Name given by Cicero and other classical writers to the oaten pipe used by the audience in the Roman theaters to express their disapprobation.

Fistulator (fĭs'too-lä'tŏr), *Lat.* } A piper, a player on a flute or flageolet.
Fistulatore (fĕs'too-lä-tō'rĕ), *It.* }

Fistuliren (fĭs-too-lē'r'n), *Ger.* (1) To sing or speak with the head voice. (2) In speaking of organ-pipes, to overblow, *i. e.* to sound one of the upper partial notes instead of the fundamental note.

Fithele. The old English name for the fiddle.

Fixed syllables. Syllables which do not change with the change of key. The Italians use fixed syllables.

Flachflöte (fläkh-flö'tĕ), *Ger.* Shallow flute; flageolet; also an organ-stop of rather thin tone.

Flageolet (flä-zhĕ-ō-lä'), *Fr.* } A small flûte à bec, that is, a straight flute, with a plug in the mouthpiece which leaves only a narrow slit for the breath to pass through. (2) An organ-stop. (3) Flageolet tones are those ethereal sounds produced on stringed instruments (violin, harp, etc.) by lightly touching a string in certain places with a finger, and then setting it in vibration by drawing the bow over it or plucking it. (*V. Harmonics*.)
Flageolet (flä-ghĕ-ō-lĕt'), *Ger.* }

Flageolet, double. A flageolet having two tubes.

Flagioletta (flä-jĭ-ō-lĕt'tä), *It.* (See *Flageolet*.)

Flam. In drum music a grace note or stroke corresponding with the appoggiatura in other compositions. There are two flams, the open and the close. The latter is made as rapidly as possible, so that the two notes are almost together. The open flam is not so close.

Flaschinett (fläsh'ĭ-nĕt), *Ger.* The flageolet.

Flat. A character which lowers a note one semitone (♭).

Flat, double. A character composed of two flats, indicating a depression of two semitones (♭♭).

Flatter la corde (flät-tä lä kŏrd), *Fr.* To play the violin, etc., in a soft, expressive manner.

ă arm, ă add, ā ale, ĕ end, ē eve, ĭ ill, ī isle, ō old, ŏ odd, oo moon, ŭ but, ü *Fr. sound*, kh *Ger. ch.* nh *nasal.*

(111)

Flautando (flä-oo-tän'dō), *It.* } Flute-like tone;
Flautato (flä-oo-tä'tō), } that quality of tone obtained by drawing the bow smoothly and gently across the strings over that end of the fingerboard nearest the bridge.

Flautina (flä-oo-tē'nä), *It.* } A small flute, an
Flautino (flä-oo-tē'nō), } octave flute; a piccolo.

Flautista (flä-oo-tēs'tä), *It.* A performer on the flute.

Flauti nisoni (flä'oo-tē oo-nē'sō-nē), *It.* The flutes in unison.

Flauto (flä'oo-tō), *It.* A flute.

Flauto a becco (flä-oo-tō ä bĕk'kō), *It.* A beaked flute. A flute having a mouthpiece like a flageolet.

Flauto ad libitum (flä'oo-tō), *It.* The flute part may be played or omitted.

Flauto alto (flä'oo-tō äl'tō), *It.* A tenor flute used in bands.

Flauto amabile (flä'oo-tō ä-mä'bī-lē), *It.* The name of an organ-stop of soft and delicate tone.

Flauto amoroso (flä'oo-tō ä-mō-rō'zō), *It.* A 4-feet organ-stop of delicate tone.

Flauto dolce (flä'oo-tō dōl'tshĕ), *It.* An organ-stop of soft, agreeable tone.

Flauto piccolo (flä'oo-tō pĕk'kō-lō), *It.* An octave flute, a small flute of very shrill tone; a flageolet.

Flauto tacere (flä-oo-tō tä-tshä'rĕ), *It.* The flute is not to play.

Flauto tedesco (flä'oo-tō tĕ-dĕs'kō), *It.* A German flute.

Flauto terzo (flä'oo-tō tĕrt'sō), *It.* The third flute.

Flauto transverso (flä'oo-tō träns-vĕr'sō), *It.* }
Flauto traverso (flä'oo-tō trä-vĕr-sō), }
The transverse flute—thus named because it is held across, and blown at the side, contrary to the flûte à bec; it is also often called the German flute. The name is also applied to an organ-stop.

Flebile (flä'bĭ-lĕ), *It.* Mournful, sad, doleful.

Flebilmente (flä-bĭl-mĕn'tĕ), *It.* Mournfully, dolefully.

Flessibile (flĕ-sē'bĭ-lĕ), *It.* Flexible, pliant.

Flessibilita (flĕ-sĭ-bē-lĭ-tä'), *It.* Flexibility.

F-Löcher (ĕf-lökh'ĕr), *Ger.* The f holes, or soundholes, of a violin, etc.

Flon-flon (flōn-flōn), *Fr.* Bad music; trash. Also the burden of certain old vaudevilles.

Florid. Ornamental, figured, embellished.

Florid counterpoint. Figured counterpoint.

Flötchen (flöt'khĕn), *Ger.* A little flute, a pipe, a flageolet.

Flöte (flö'tĕ), *Ger.* A flute.

Flöten (flö't'n), *Ger.* To play upon the flute.

Flötenspieler (flö't'n-spē'lĕr), *Ger.* A flute-player.

Flötenstimme (flö't'n-stĭm'mĕ), *Ger.* A soft, sweet voice; the part for the flute.

Flötenzug (flö't'n-tsoog), *Ger.* A flute-stop in an organ.

Flöte traverso (flö'tĕ trä-vĕr'sō), *Ger.* The German flute; also an organ-stop. See *Flauto traverso*.

Flötist (flö-tĭst'), *Ger.* A flute-player.

Flourish. An appellation sometimes given to the decorative notes which a performer adds to a passage, with the double view of heightening the effect and showing his own dexterity and skill.

Flüchtig (flükh'tĭgh), *Ger.* Lightly, nimbly.

Flüchtigkeit (flükh'tĭgh-kīt), *Ger.* Lightness, fleetness.

Flügel (flü'g'l), *Ger.* A wing; a harpsichord, a grand piano.

Flügel (flü'g'l), *Ger.* Lit., "wing." A grand pianoforte. Formerly a harpsichord.

Flügelhorn (flü'g'l-hörn), *Ger.* (1) A bugle. (2) A keyed brass instrument which is made in various keys and forms. The Kenthorn, Klappenhorn, and Cornet belong to the genus Flügelhorn.

Fluit (floit), *Dut.* } A flute.
Fluta (floo'tä), *Lat.* }

Fluepipes. Those organ-pipes (metal as well as wooden) which are made to sound by forcing the wind through a slit (the windway) at the top of the foot, and against a sharp edge (the upper lip, which divides the wind, part of which only enters the body of the pipe. The *fluework* is the aggregate of such pipes.

Flute. An organ-stop of the flue species, the tone of which resembles that of the flute.

Flute. There are two kinds of flute: the flûte à bec (beak flute), or direct flute, and the flûte traversière, or cross flute: the former has a plugged mouthpiece at one end of the tube, the latter is blown through a lateral hole. Excepting the flageolet, the flûte à bec has entirely disappeared, at least among the art-producing European nations. The instrument understood when we now speak of the flute is the cross flute, also called German flute. It is generally made of wood, sometimes of metal, and consists of a conical tube, stopped at its wider end, and provided with six fingerholes and a number of keys. As improved by Boehm, it has a compass from c' to c''''. Music for this instrument, which is one of the most important members of the orchestra, is written as it sounds. A small, or octave, flute, the flauto piccolo (with a compass from d'' to a''''; written $d'—a'''$) is also sometimes used in the orchestra. In military bands flutes in E♭ and in F, and small flutes an octave higher, are to be met with. Now flutes are also made cylindrical and of ebonite. The so-called flute of ancient Greek music was not a true flute, but a sort of imperfect oboe. Of the same nature, probably, were the double flutes,

ä *arm*, ă *add*, ā *ale*, ĕ *end*, ē *eve*, ĭ *ill*, ī *isle*, ō *old*, ŏ *odd*, oo *moon*, ŭ *but*, ü *Fr. sound*, kh *Ger. ch*, nh *nasal*.

figured upon ancient monuments, consisting of two tubes, diverging from each other at an acute angle. It is not certainly known whether both tubes were sounded simultaneously, and if so, whether the resulting effect was that of a melody with harmony or a melody with a drone bass, but the latter is regarded as more probable from the circumstance of similar flutes being still extant in Abyssinia and elsewhere.

Flute, *Fr.* The same as flautando and flautato (*q. v.*).

Flute à bec (floot ä běk), *Fr.* "Beak flute." A direct flute. It has a beak-shaped mouthpiece with a plug which leaves only a narrow aperture for the breath to pass through. There was a whole family of flûtes à bec, bass, tenor, alto, etc. (*V. Flute.*)

Flute allemande (floot äl-mänhd), *Fr.* The German flute.

Flute, Boehm (bōm). A perfected flute, invented by M. Boehm, of Germany, in 1832. It differs from the common flute in having the size and location of the holes arranged in their natural order with keys.

Flute conique (floot kŏn-ēk), *Fr.* Conical flute; an organ-stop.

Fluted. A term applied to the upper notes of a soprano voice when they are of a thin and flutelike tone.

Flute d'allemande (flute d'äl-mänhd), *Fr.* A German flute.

Flute d'amour (floot d'ä-moor), *Fr.* A flute the compass of which is a minor third below that of the German flute; the name is also applied to an organ-stop of 8- or 4-feet scale.

Flute, diatonic. A flute capable of producing all the different tones of the major and minor diatonic scales.

Flute dolce (floo'tĕ dōl'tshĕ), *It.* A flute with a mouthpiece like that of a flageolet.

Flute douce (floot doos), *Fr.* Soft flute; the flûte à bec; there were four kinds, the treble, alto, tenor, and bass.

Flutée (floo-tä), *Fr.* Soft, sweet.

Flute harmonique (floot här-mŏnh-ēk), *Fr.* See *Harmonic flute.*

Flute, octave. A flute the tones of which range an octave higher than the German flute.

Flute octaviante (floot ŏk-tä-vĭ-änht), *Fr.* Octave flute, an organ-stop.

Flute ouverte (floot oo-vär), *Fr.* An organ-stop of the diapason species.

Flute, pastoral. } A flute shorter than the
Flute, shepherd's. } transverse flute and blown through a lip piece at the end.

Fluter (floo-tā), *Fr.* To play the flute.

Flute traversière (floot träv-ĕr-sĭ-ār), *Fr.* The transverse, or German, flute.

F-moll (ĕf-mŏll), *Ger.* The key of F minor.

Foco (fō-kō), *It.* Fire, ardor, passion.

Focosamente (fō-kō-zä-měn'tĕ), *It.* Ardently, vehemently.

Focosissimo (fō-kō-zē'sĭ-mō), *It.* Very ardently, with a great deal of passion.

Focoso (fō-kō'zō), *It.* Fiery, passionate.

Foglietto (fōl-yē ĕt'tō), *It.* A name given to a first-violin part which contains all the obligato passages of the other parts. A foglietto is used by the player who assists at the rehearsals of ballets, sometimes by conductors instead of a score, and also by the leader of the orchestra.

Fois (fwä), *Fr.* Time.

Fois première (fwä prěm-ĭ-ār), *Fr.* The first time.

Fois deuxième (fwä dü-zĭ-äm), *Fr.* The second time.

Folia (fō'lĭ-ä), *Sp.* A species of Spanish dance.

Folio, music. A case for holding loose sheets of music; a wrapper used in a music-store for the convenience of classifying the music.

Follia di spagna (fōl'yĭ-ä dē spän-yä), *Sp.* A species of composition invented by the Spaniards, consisting of variations on a given air.

Fondamentale (fŏn-dä-měn-tä'lĕ), *It.* Fundamental; fundamental bass.

Fondamento (fŏn-dä-měn'tō), *It.* The fundamental bass; the roots of the harmony.

Fond d'orgue (fōnh d'ŏrg), *Fr.* The most important stop in an organ, called in England the open diapason, 8-feet scale. In Germany this is called the 8-feet principal.

Foot. A certain number of syllables constituting a distinct metrical element in a verse. In very old English music it was a kind of drone accompaniment to a song which was sustained by another singer.

Form. The arrangement of material in a tone poem into symmetrical and effective order. The plan of a music-piece with reference to its verses, cantos, and division; in short, its metrical structure. The laws of musical form have in view clearness and comprehensibility in musical works, as well as symmetry pure and simple. There are certain typical forms which are used oftener than others, and which are often approximated closely by forms apparently novel and free. These are the Fugue Song, Song-form with Trio, Variation, Rondo, and Sonata-piece. (See Introduction.)

Forlana (fōr-lä'nä), *It.* } A lively Venetian
Forlane (fōr-län'), *Fr.* } dance in 6-8 time.

Fort (fŏr), *Fr.* } Loud, strong.
Forte (fŏr'tĕ), *It.* }

Fortement (fŏrt'mänh), *Fr.* } Loudly,
Fortemente (fŏr-tĕ-měn'tĕ), *It.* } powerfully, vigorously.

Fortezza (fōr-tĕt'zä), *It.* Force, power, strength.

ä *arm,* ă *add,* ā *ale,* ĕ*'end,* ē *eve,* ĭ *ill,* ī *isle,* ō *old,* ŏ *odd,* oo *moon,* ŭ *but,* ü *Fr. sound,* kh *Ger. ch,* nh *nasal.*

8 . (113)

Forte=piano (fôr-tĕ-pē-ä'nō), *It.* ⎫ The piano-
Forte=pianó (fôrt-pĭ-ä'nō), *Fr.* ⎬ forte; a key-
Fortepiano (fôr' ĕ-pĭ-ä'nō), *Ger.* ⎭ ed instrument of German invention, so called from its capability of expressing different degrees of power or intensity of tone.

Forte possibile (fôr'tĕ pōs-sĕ'bĭ-lĕ), *It.* As loud as possible.

Fortiss. An abbreviation of Fortissimo.

Fortissimo (fôr-tēs'sĭ-mo), *It.* Very loud.

Fortissimo quanto possibile (fôr'tēs'sĭ-mō kwän-tō pōs-sĕ'bĭ-lĕ), *It.* As loud as possible.

Fortschreitung (fôrt'shrī-toong), *Ger.* Progression (in harmony).

Fortsetzung (fôrt'sĕt-soong), *Ger.* A continuation.

Forza (fôrt'sä), *It.* Force, strength, power.

Forzando (fôr-tsän'dō), *It.* ⎫ Forced; laying a
Forzato (fôr-tsä'tō), *It.* ⎬ stress upon one note or chord; sometimes marked V ∧ >.

Forzar la voce (fôrt'sär lä vŏ'tshĕ), *It.* To force the voice.

Forzare (fôr-tsä'rĕ), *It.* To strengthen.

Fourchette tonique (foor-shĕt tōnh-ĕk), *Fr.* A tuningfork.

Four-part song. A song arranged for four parts.

Fourth. A distance comprising three diatonic intervals; that is, two tones and a half.

Fourth flute. A flute sounding a fourth higher than the concert flute.

Fourth shift. The last shift in violin-playing.

Française (fränh-säz'), *Fr.* A graceful dance in 3-4 time.

Franchezza (frän-kĕt'zä), *It.* Freedom, confidence, boldness.

Française (frän-säz'), *Fr.* ⎫ French; in
Franzese (frän-tsä'zĕ), *It.* ⎬ the French
Französisch (frän-tsö'zĭsh), *Ger.* ⎭ style.

Frappe (fräp), *Fr.* Stamping, striking; a peculiar manner of beating time or striking notes with force.

Frapper (fräp-pā), *Fr.* To beat the time; to strike.

Frase (frä-zĕ), *It.* A phrase; short musical passage.

Frasi. Phrases.

Fraseggiare (frä-sĕd-jĭ-är'ĕ), *It.* To phrase; to deliver a melody or idea properly, *i. e.*, with expression.

Frauenstimme (frou'ĕn-stĭm'mĕ), *Ger.* A female voice.

Freddamente (frĕd-dä-mĕn'tĕ), *It.* Coldly, without animation.

Freddezza (frĕd-dĕt'tsä), *It.* Coldness, frigidity.

Freddo (frĕd'dō), *It.* Cold, devoid of sentiment.

Fredon (frĕ-dōnh), *Fr.* Trilling; a flourish or other extemporaneous ornament.

Fredonnemente (frĕ'dōn-mänh), *Fr.* Humming.

Fredonner (frä-dōnh-nā'), *Fr.* To trill, to shake; also to hum, to sing low.

Free composition. In a free style; a composition not in strict accordance with the rules of musical art.

Freemen's songs. Little compositions for three or four voices, in use about 1600.

Free reed. A reed-stop in an organ, in which the tongue by a rapid vibratory motion to and fro produces the sound. The tone of a free reed is smooth and free from rattling, but not usually so strong as that of the striking reed.

Fregiare (frä-jī-ä'rĕ), *It.* To adorn, to embellish.

Fregiatura (frä-jī-ä-too'rä), *It.* An ornament, an embellishment.

Frei (frī), *Ger.* Free.

Frémissement (frä'mĕss-mänh), *Fr.* Humming, singing in a low voice.

French horn. See *Horn.*

French sixth. One form of an augmented sixth; a chord composed of a major third, extreme fourth, and extreme sixth.

French treble clef. The G clef on the bottom line of the staff, formerly much used in French music for violin, flute, etc.

Fresco (frĕs'kō), ⎫ Freshly,
Frescamente (frĕs-kä-mĕn'tĕ), *It.* ⎬ vigorously, lively.

Fretta (frĕt'tä), *It.* Increasing the time; accelerating the movement.

Frets. Thin strips of wood, metal, or ivory, inserted transversely in, and slightly projecting from, the fingerboard of various stringed instruments—the old viols, lutes, theorboes, and the still flourishing guitar—in order to facilitate correct stopping. Catgut frets, too, are found on old instruments. Strings bound round the necks of instruments were, indeed, the earliest frets.

Freude (froy'dĕ), *Ger.* Joy, rejoicing.

Freudengesang (froy'd'n-gĕ-säng'), *Ger.* A song of joy.

Freudig (froy'dĭgh), *Ger.* Joyfully.

Freudigkeit (froy'dĭgh-kīt), *Ger.* Joyfulness, joyousness.

Fr i (frī), *Ger.* Free, unrestrained as to style.

Freie Schreibart (frī'ĕ shrīb'ärt), *Ger.* Free style of composition.

Friedensmarsch (frē'd'ns-märsh), *Ger.* A march in honor of peace.

Frisch (frĭsh), *Ger.* Freshly, briskly, lively.

Friska. The quick movement in the Hungarian national dances called Czárdás. (See C.)

ä *arm*, ă *add*, ā *ale*, ĕ *end*, ē *eve*, ĭ *ill*, ī *isle*, ō *old*, ŏ *odd*, oo *moon*, ŭ *but*, ü *Fr. sound*, kh *Ger. ch*, nh *nasal*.

(114)

Frivolo (frē'vō-lō), *It.* Frivolous, trifling, trashy.

Frohgesang (frō'ghĕ-säng'), *Ger.* A joyous song.

Fröhlich (frö'lĭkh), *Ger.* Joyous, gay.

Fröhlichkeit (frö'lĭkh-kīt), *Ger.* Joyfulness, gayety.

Frohnamt (frōn'ämt), *Ger.* High Mass.

Frosch (frŏsh), *Ger.* The lower part, or nut, of a violin-bow.

Frottola (frōt'tō-lä), *It.* A ballad, a song, generally of erotic sentiment. Musically it was between the artistic madrigal and the entirely simple folksong called Villanella. Current in Italy during the fifteenth and sixteenth centuries.

Frühlingslied (irü'lĭngs-lēd), *Ger.* Spring-song.

Frühmesse früh'mĕs-sĕ), *Ger.* { Matins, early
Frühstück (irü'stük), } Mass.

F-Schlüssel (ĕf-shlüs's'l), *Ger.* The F or bass clef.

Fuga (foo'gä), *It.* A flight; a chase. See *Fugue*.

Fuga authentica (foo'gä ou-tĕn'tĭ-kä), *Lat.* A fugue with an authentic theme or subject.

Fuga canonica (foo'gä kä-nŏ'nĭ-kä), *Lat.* A canon.

Fuga contraria (foo'gä kŏn-trä'rĭ-ä), *Lat.* A fugue in which the answer is generally inverted.

Fuga doppia (foo'gä dŏp'pĭ-ä), *It.* A double fugue.

Fuga irregularis (foo'gä ĭr-rĕg-oo-lä'rĭs), *Lat.* An irregular fugue.

Fuga libera (foo'gä lĭb'ē-rä), *Lat.* A free fugue.

Fuga mixta (foo'gä mĭx'tä), *Lat.* A mixed fugue.

Fuga obligata (foo'gä ŏb-lĭ-gä-tä), *Lat.* A strict fugue.

Fuga partialis (foo'gä pär-tsĭ-ä'lĭs), *Lat.* The common form of the fugue intermixed with passages of a different character.

Fuga propria (foo'gä prō'prĭ-ä), *Lat.* A regular fugue strictly according to rule.

Fuga plagale (foo'gä plä-gä'lĕ), *It.* A fugue with a plagal theme or subject.

Fuga ricercata (foo'gä rē-tshĕr-kä'tä), *It.* An artificial fugue.

Fuga sciolta (foo'gä shē-ŏl'tä), *It.* } A free
Fuga soluta (foo-gä sō-loo'tä), *Lat.* } fugue.

Fuga totalis (foo'gä tō-tä'lĭs), *Lat.* A canon.

Fugara (foo-gä'rä), *Lat.* An organ-stop of the bomba species, of 4-feet tone.

Fugato (foo-gä'tō), *It.* In the style of a fugue.

Fuge (foo'ghĕ), *Ger.* A fugue.

Fuge galante (foo'ghĕ gä-län'tĕ), *Ger.* A free fugue in the style of chamber music.

Fugha (foo'gä), *It.* A fugue.

Fughetta (foo'gĕt'tä), *It.* A short fugue.

Fugirtes (foo-gĕr'tĕs), *Ger.* { In the fugue
Fugirt (foo-gērt), } style; *fugirt* is also applied to the ranks of a mixture stop in an organ.

Fugitive pieces. Ephemeral, short-lived compositions.

Fugue. This word is derived from the Latin *fuga*, flight, and a certain kind of musical composition has been called thus because "one part, as it were, tries to flee and escape from the others; but it is pursued by them, until they afterwards meet in an amicable way, and finally come to a satisfactory understanding." The technical description must necessarily be less simple than this poetical one.

There are fugues for instruments, for voices and for instruments and voices combined. A fugue may be in two, three, four, five, and more parts. The word fugue had not always the same meaning as in our time and since the days of J. S. Bach and Handel, the masters of masters; but it always signified an imitative form—a canon or something more or less like what we call a fugue. Various kinds of fugues are enumerated under *fuga* with its accompanying epithets. A fugue, in its final evolution, consists of an exposition and two or more developments, which generally are connected by episodes. In a fugue in four parts the exposition is somewhat like this: One part proposes the subject; a second part follows with the answer (*i. e.*, the imitation of the subject at the fifth above or fourth below); a third part resumes the subject an octave higher or lower than the part which commenced; and a fourth part brings up the rear with the answer an octave higher or lower than the part which was second in the order of succession. The counterpoint with which the part that first enunciates the subject accompanies the answer is called countersubject, but it is properly so called only when it recurs as an accompaniment with the subsequent enunciations of the subject and answer. Sometimes the subject and countersubject are simultaneously introduced. When after an episode, short or long, the first development begins, the subject is taken up and answered by the parts in another order of succession. Supposing the alto to have begun before, the tenor or soprano or bass will begin now. Further, the imitations will be at different intervals of pitch and time. The drawing closer together of the subject and its answer, so that the latter begins before the former has completed its course, is called the stretto. This contrivance is especially resorted to in the last development. Other contrivances that may be utilized are the augmentation, diminution, inversion, and retrogression of the subject. The stretto is frequently followed by a pedal-point, on which the subject is piled up in various layers, so as to form a striking conclusion to the whole. The matter out of which the episodes are wrought may be new, but oftener (in order to insure unity) is derived

---

ā *arm*, ă *add*, ä *ale*, ĕ *end*, ē *eve*. ĭ *ill*, ī *isle*, ō *old*, ŏ *odd*, oo *moon*, ü *but*, ü *Fr. sound*, kh *Ger. ch*, nh *nasal*.

(115)

from the subject, countersubject, or other accompaniments of the subject.

An important division of fugues remains yet to be noticed, namely, that into real and tonal fugues. A real fugue is one in which the answer is an exact transposition of the subject; a tonal fugue is one in which the answer is an imitation of the subject slightly modified for the purpose of keeping within the same key.

Two words often heard in connection with fugues may be here explained. Coda, or codetta, is the name given to the notes which are appended to the subject when at its conclusion the answer does not strike in at once. R-percussion is the reappearance of the subject and answer in a new order with regard to succession and pitch in the various developments of a fugue.

Double, triple, and quadruple fugues are fugues with two, three, and four subjects. Two kinds of double fugue have to be distinguished: (1) That in which two subjects are first separately worked out and only subsequently combined. (2) That in which the second subject enters at once with the first subject as a constant countersubject. See, also, under *Fuga*.

Fugue, counter. A fugue in which the subjects move in contrary directions.

Fugue, double. A fugue on two subjects.

Fugue renversée (füg rănh-vĕr-sā'), *Fr.* A fugue, the answer in which is made in contrary motion to that of the subject.

Fugue, strict. A fugue in which the fugal form and its laws are strictly observed.

Fugue, perpetual. A canon so constructed that its termination leads to its beginning, and hence may be continually repeated.

Fugue, simple. A fugue containing but a single subject.

Fuguist. A composer or performer of fugues.

Führer (füh'rĕr), *Ger.* Conductor, director; also the subject or leading theme in a fugue.

Full. For all the voices or instruments.

Full anthem. An anthem in four or more parts, without verses or solo passages; to be sung by the whole choir in chorus.

Full band. A band in which all the instruments are employed.

Full cadence. See *Perfect cadence*.

Füllflöte (fül'flö-tĕ), *Ger.* Filling-flute; a stopped organ-register of 4-feet tone.

Full orchestra. An orchestra in which all the stringed and wind instruments are employed.

Full organ. An organ with all its registers or stops in use.

Full score. A complete score of all the parts of a composition, vocal or instrumental, or both combined, written on separate staves placed under each other.

Full service. A service for the whole choir in chorus.

Füllstimmen (füll'stĭm-mĕn), *Ger.* "Filling voices." Parts added for giving resonance and fullness to the chords, without character as independent voices.

Fundamental. Properly speaking, the root of a series of partial tones. The tone of which all tones in a harmony chord are partials. The root of a chord.

Fundamental tones. A name sometimes applied to the three root-tones of a key, namely, the tonic, subdominant, and dominant.

Funèbre (fü-nĕbr'), *Fr.* } Funereal,
Funerale (foo-nĕ-rä'lĕ), *It.* } mournful.
Funereo (foo-nā'rĕ-ō), *It.*

Fünf (fünf), *Ger.* Five.

Fünffach (fünf'fäkh), *Ger.* Fivefold; five ranks, speaking of organ-pipes.

Fünfstimmig (fünf'stĭm-mĭg), *Ger.* For five voices.

Fünfte (fünf'tĕ), *Ger.* Fifth.

Fünfzehnte (fünf'tsăn-tĕ), *Ger.* Fifteenth.

Funzioni (foon-tsĭ-ō'nĕ), *It. pl.* Oratorios, masses, and other sacred musical performances in the Roman Catholic Church.

Fuoco (foo-ō'kō), *It.* Fire, energy, passion.

Fuocoso (foo-ō-kō'zō), *It.* Fiery, ardent, impetuous.

Für (für), *Ger.* For.

Für beide Hände zusammen (für bī'dĕ hăn'dĕ tsoo-zäm'men), *Ger.* For both hands together.

Für das ganze Werk (für dăs gän'tsĕ wărk), *Ger.*
Für das volle Werk (für dăs föl'lĕ wărk), *Ger.* } For the full organ.

Für die linke Hand allein (für dĕ lĭn'kĕ hănd äl-līn'), *Ger.* For the left hand alone.

Für die rechte Hand allein (für dĕ rĕkh'tĕ hănd äl-līn'), *Ger.* For the right hand alone.

Fureur (fü-rŭr'), *Fr.* } Fury, passion, rage.
Furia (foo'rĭ-ä), *It.* }

Furiant (foo'rĭ-änt), *Ger.* A quick Bohemian dance with sharp accents and changing varieties of measure. Called also Furie.

Furibondo (foo-rĭ-bŏn'dō), *It.* Furious, mad, extreme vehemence.

Furie (fü-rē), *Fr.* Fury, passion.

Furieusement (fü-rüz-mänh), *Fr.* } Furiously, madly.
Furiosamente (foo-rĭ-ō-zä-mĕn'tĕ), *It.* }

Furioso (foo-rĭ-ō'zō), *It.* Furious, vehement, mad.

Furlandò (foor-län'dō), *It.* } An antiquated dance.
Furlano (foor-lä'nō), *It.* }

Furniture stop. An organ-stop, consisting of several ranks of pipes, of very acute pitch. A mixture stop.

Furore (foo-rō'rĕ), *It.* Fury, rage, passion.

Für zwei Manuale (für tswī' mä-noo-ä'lĕ), *Ger.* For two manuals, in organ-playing.

Fusa (foo'sä), *Lat.* A quaver.

Fusée (fü-zā), *Fr.* A very rapid roulade or passage; a skip, etc.

Fusella (foo-sĕl'lä), *Lat.* Name formerly applied to the demisemiquaver.

Fuss (foos), *Ger.* Foot; the lower part of an organ-pipe.

Füsse (füs'sĕ), *Ger. pl.* Feet.

Füssig (füs'sig), *Ger.* Footed; 8-*füssig*, or, *achtfüssig*, of 8-feet size, or scale.

Fusston (foos-tōn), *Ger.* The tone or pitch; as, 8-*Fusston*, or, *Achtfusston*, a pipe of 8-feet tone.

Fut (fooe), *Fr.* The barrel of a drum.

Fz. An abbreviation of Forzando.

G. The name of the fifth note in the natural diatonic scale of C, to which is applied the syllable sol; it is also one of the names of the highest, or treble, clef. Abbreviation of *gauche*, left hand.

Gabel (gä'b'l), *Ger.* A fork.

Gagliarda (gäl-yĭ-är'dä), *It.* A galliard.

Gagliardamente (gäl-yĭ-är-dä-mĕn'tĕ), *It.* Briskly, gaily.

Gagliardo (gäl-yĭ-är'dō), *It.* Brisk, merry, gay.

Gai (gä), *Fr.* Gay, merry.

Gaiement (gā-mänh), *Fr.* Merrily, lively, **Gaiment** (gā-mänh), gay.

Gaillarde (gā-yärd'), *Fr.* Merry, brisk; also a galliard.

Gaillardement (gā-yärd'mänh), *Fr.* Merrily, briskly.

Gaio (gä'ī-ō), *It.* With gayety and cheerfulness.

Gaita (gä-ē-tä), *Sp.* A bagpipe; also a kind of flute; a street organ.

Gaja (gī'yä), *It.* Gay, merry, lively.
Gajo (gä'yō),

Gajamente (gä-yä-mĕn'tĕ), *It.* Gaily, cheerfully.

Galante (gä-län'tĕ), *It.* Gallantly, **Galantemente** (gä-län-tĕ-mĕn'tĕ), boldly.

Galanteriefuge (gä-län-tĕ-rē'foo-ghĕ), *Ger.* A fugue in the free style.

Galanterien (gä-län-tĕ-rē'ĕn), *Ger. pl.* The ornaments, turns, trills, etc., with which the old harpsichord music was embellished.

Galanteriestücke (gä-län-tĕ-rē'stü'kĕ), *Ger. pl.* Pieces in the free ornamental style.

Galanterstyl (gä-länt'ĕr-stēl), *Ger.* Free style, ideal style.

Galliard. A lively old dance in triple time, formerly very popular. Of Italian origin.

Galop (gäl'ō), *Fr.* A quick round dance, in 2-4 time.

Galopade (gäl-ō-päd'), *Fr.*
Galopp (gä-lŏp'), *Ger.* A galop.
Galoppo (gä-lŏp'pō), *It.*

Galoubé (gä-loo-bā), *Fr.* A small flute
Galoubet (gä-loo-bā), with three holes, sometimes to be met with in France, especially in Provence.

Gamba (gäm'bä), *It.* The viol di gamba, or bass viol. See that term.

Gamba-bass. A 16-feet organ-stop, on the pedals.

Gamba major. A name given to a 16-feet organ-stop, or double gamba.

Gambe (gäm'bĕ), *Ger.* Viol di gamba.

Gambeta (gäm-bĕ-tä'), *Sp.* An ancient Spanish dance.

Gambette (gäm-bĕt'tĕ), *Ger.* A small, or octave, gamba stop in an organ.

Gambviole (gämb-fē-ō'lĕ), *Ger.* An instrument resembling the violoncello.

Gamma (gäm'mä), *It.* The Greek name of
Gamme (gäm), *Fr.* the letter G (Γ). In musical terminology the word gamma has been employed variously. (1) As the name of the lowest note (G) of the Guidonian scale. (2) As the name of that scale. (3) In the sense of scale, or gamut, generally. (4) In the sense of compass of a voice or instrument, the succession of notes from the lowest to the highest. See following.

Gamma ut, *or,* **Γ ut.** The name of the note G, the lowest note in the old solmisation. From this name is derived the English word gamut.

Gamme chromatique (gäm krō-mä-tĕk'), *Fr.* The chromatic scale.

Gamme descendante (gäm dĕ-sänh-dänht), *Fr.* Descending scale.

Gamme de sol majeur (gäm düh sŏl mä-zhür), *Fr.* Scale of G major.

Gamme d'ut majeur (gäm d'üt mä-shür), *Fr.* Scale of C major.

Gammes en bemols (găm sänh bă-mŏl), *Fr.* Scales with flats.

Gamme majeure montante (găm mä-zhür' mŏnh-tänht'), *Fr.* An ascending major scale.

Gammes. Exercises on the scale.

Gamut. The scale of notes belonging to any key.

Gamut G. That G which is on the first line of the bass staff.

Gamut, Guido's. The table or scale introduced by Guido, and to which he applied the syllables ut, ra, mi, fa, sol, la. It consisted of twenty notes, namely, two octaves and a major sixth, the first octave distinguished by the capital letters, G, A, B, etc., the second by the small letters, g, a, b, etc., and the major sixth by double letters, gg, aa, bb, etc.

Ganascione (gä-nä-shĭ-ō'nĕ), *It.* An Italian lute.

Gang (gäng), *Ger.* Pace, rate of movement or motion.

Ganiles (gä'nĭ-lĕs), *Sp.* Fauces, organs of the voice.

Ganz (gänts), *Ger.* Whole, entire; also all, very.

Ganz langsam (gänts läng'säm), *Ger.* Very slowly.

Ganze Note (gän'tsĕ nō'tĕ), *Ger.* A whole note, or semibreve.

Ganzer Ton (gän'tsĕr tōn), **Ganzton** (gänts-tōn), *Ger.* } A whole tone. Improper expression for "a whole step." The interval of a major second.

Ganzes Werk (gän'tsĕs wärk), *Ger.* The full organ.

Ganzschluss (gänz shloos), *Ger.* Real close of a piece as opposed to the *Halbschluss*, or half close.

Ganzverhallend (gänts'fĕr-häl'lĕnd), *Ger.* Entirely dying away.

Garbatamente (gär-bä-tä-mĕn'tĕ), *It.* Gracefully.

Garbato (gär-bä'tō), *It.* Graceful.

Garbo (gür'bō), *It.* Simplicity, grace, elegance.

Garibo (gä'rĭ-bō), *It.* A dance, a ball.

Gariglione (gä-rĕl-yĭ-ō'nĕ), *It.* Chime, musical bells.

Garnir un violin de cordes (gär-nēr' ûnh vē-ō-länh dŭh kŏrd), *Fr.* To string a violin.

Garrire (gär-rē'rĕ), *It.* To chirp, to warble like a bird.

Gastrollen (gäst'rōl-l'n), *Ger.* A term applied to a singer or actor on a starring expedition.

Gauche (gōzh), *Fr.* Left.

Gauche main (gōzh mänh), *Fr.* The left hand.

Gaudente (gä-oo-dĕn'tĕ), *It.* Blithe, merry, sprightly.

Gaudentemente (gä-oo-dĕn-tĕ-mĕn'tĕ), *It.* Joyfully, merrily.

Gaudioso (gä-oo-dĭ-ō'zō). *It.* Merry, joyful.

Gavot (gă-vŏt'), *Eng.* **Gavotta** (gă-vŏt'tä), *It.* **Gavotte** (gä-vŏt), *Fr.* } A dance consisting of two light, lively strains in common time.

Gaymente (ghĕ-mĕn'tĕ), *Sp.* Gayly, briskly, lively.

Gaytero (ghĕ-tä'rō), *Sp.* One who plays on a bagpipe; a piper.

Gazzarra (gät'zär-rä), *It.* Rejoicings with music and cannon.

G clef. The treble clef; a character composed of the letters G and S, for the syllable sol, which in modern music invariably turns on the second line of the staff. It was formerly used upon other degrees.

G doubl , *or*, **Double G.** The octave below G gamut.

G-dur (gä'door), *Ger.* The key of G major.

Geberdenspiel (ghĕ-bĕr'd'n-spēl), *Ger.* Pantomime.

Gebläse (ghĕ-blä'sĕ), *Ger.* Bellows, apparatus for blowing.

Gebrochen (ghĕ-brō'kh'n), *Ger.* Broken.

Gebrochene Akkorde (ghĕ-brō'kh'-nĕ äk-kōr'dĕ), *Ger.* **Gebrochener Accord** (ghĕ-brō'kh'-nĕr äk-kōrd), *Ger.* } Broken chords, chords played in arpeggio.

Gebrochene Stimme (ghĕ-brō'kh'-nĕ stĭm'mĕ), *Ger.* A broken voice.

Gebunden (ghĕ-boon'd'n), *Ger.* Connected, syncopated, in regard to the style of playing or writing.

Gebundene Note (ghĕ-boon'dĕ-nĕ nō'tĕ), *Ger.* A tied note, a note which is to be held and not repeated.

Gebundener Styl (ghĕ-boon'dĕ-nĕr stēl), *Ger.* Style of strictly connected harmony; style of counterpoint.

Geburtslied (ghĕ-boorts'lēd), *Ger.* Birthday-song.

Gedackt (ghĕ-däkt'), **Gedeckt** (ghĕ-dĕkt'), *Ger.* } Stopped, in opposition to the open pipes in an organ.

Gedacktflöte (ghĕ-däkt-flō'tĕ), *Ger.* Stopped flute, in an organ.

Gedact. See *Gedackt*.

Gedeckte Stimmen (ghĕ-dĕk'tĕ stĭm'mĕn), *Ger. pl.* Stops with covered pipes, as the stopped diapason.

Gedehnt (ghĕ-dänt'), *Ger.* Lengthened.

Gedicht (ghĕ-dĭkht'), *Ger.* A poem, tale, fable.

Gefährte (ghĕ-fär'tĕ), *Ger.* The answer in a fugue.

Gefällig (ghĕ-fäl'lĭg), *Ger.* Pleasingly, agreeably.

Gefiedel (ghĕ-fē'd'l), *Ger.* Fiddling, playing on the fiddle.

ä *arm*, ă *add*, ā *ale*, ĕ *end*, ē *eve*, ĭ *ill*, ī *isle*, ō *old*, ŏ *odd*, oo *moon*, ŭ *but*, ü *Fr. sound*, kh *Ger. ch*, nh *nasal*.

Gefühl (ghĕ-fül'), *Ger.* Sentiment, expression.

Gegen (ghä'g'n), *Ger.* Against, contrasted with, opposed to.

Gegenbewegung (gĕ'g'n-bĕ-wĕ'goong), *Ger.* Contrary motion.

Gegengesang (gĕ'g'n-gĕ-säng'), *Ger.* Antiphony.

Gegenhall (gĕ'g'n-häll'), *Ger.* } Resonance,
Gegenschall (gĕ'g'n-shäll'), echo.

Gegenpunkt (gĕ'g'n-poonkt'), *Ger.* Counterpoint.

Gegenstimme (gĕ'g'n-stĭm'mĕ), *Ger.* Counter tenor, or alto, part.

Gegenstimmig (gĕ'g'n-stĭm'mĭg), *Ger.* Dissonant, discordant.

Gegensubject (gĕ'g'n-soob-yĕkt'), *Ger.* Countersubject, in a fugue.

Gehend (gä'ĕnd), *Ger.* A word referring to movement, and having the same meaning as andante.

Gehörlehre (ghĕ-hör'lä-rĕ), *Ger.* Acoustics.

Gehörspielen (ghĕ-hör'spēl'n), *Ger.* To play by ear.

Geige (gī'ghĕ), *Ger.* The violin.

Geigen (gī'ghĕn), *Ger.* To play on the violin.

Geigenblatt (gī'ghĕn-blätt), *Ger.* The fingerboard of a violin.

Geigenbogen (gī'ghĕn-bō'g'n), *Ger.* Violin-bow.

Geigenclavicymbel (gī'ghĕn-clä-vĭ-tsĭm'bĕl), *Ger.* An instrument similar to a harpsichord or pianoforte.

Geigenförmig (gī'ghĕn-för'mĭg), *Ger.* Having the form of a violin.

Geigenfutter (gī'ghĕn-foot'tĕr), *Ger.* Case for a violin.

Geigenhals (gī'ghĕn-häls), *Ger.* The neck of a violin.

Geigenharz (gī'ghĕn-härts), *Ger.* Spanish resin, hard resin.

Geigenholz (gī'ghĕn-hölts), *Ger.* The wood used in making violins.

Geigenmacher (gī'ghĕn-mä'khĕr), *Ger.* A violin-maker.

Geigenprincipal (gī'ghĕn-prĭn-tsī-päl'), *Ger.* A German organ diapason stop, with a tone like that of the gamba, but fuller.

Geigensaite (gī'ghĕn-säī'tĕ), *Ger.* Violin string.

Geigensattel (gī'ghĕn-sät't'l), *Ger.* } The
Geigensteg (gī'ghĕn-stägh), bridge of a violin.

Geigenschule (gī'ghĕn-shoo'lĕ), *Ger.* A violin-school, or method of instruction.

Geigenstrich (gī'ghĕn-strĭkh), *Ger.* A stroke of the violin-bow.

Geigenstück (gī'ghĕn-stük), *Ger.* A tune for the violin.

Geigenwerk (gī'ghĕn-wärk), *Ger.* The celestina, an organ-stop of 4-feet scale.

Geigenwirbel (gī'ghĕn-wĭr'b'l), *Ger.* A violin-peg.

Geigenzug (gī'ghĕn-tsoog), *Ger.* A violin-stop.

Geiger (gī'ghĕr), *Ger.* Violin-player.

Geistlich (gīst'lĭkh), *Ger.* Ecclesiastical, clerical.

Geistliche Gesänge (gīst'lĭ-khĕ gĕ-sän'gĕ), }
Geistliche Lieder (gīst-lĭ-khĕ lē'dĕr), *Ger.* } Psalms, hymns, spiritual songs.

Geistreich (gīst'rīkh), *Ger.* } Spirited, full of
Geistvoll (gīst'fŏl), life and animation.

Geklingel (ghĕ-klĭng''l), *Ger.* Tinkling, ringing of a bell.

Gelassen (ghĕ-läs's'n), *Ger.* Calmly, quietly.

Gelassenheit (ghĕ-läs's'n-hīt), *Ger.* Calmness, tranquillity.

Geläufe (ghĕ-loy'fĕ), *Ger.* } Running pas-
Geläufen (ghĕ-loy'fĕn), sages, scale passages, rapid movements.

Geläufig (ghĕ-loy'fīgh), *Ger.* Easy, fluent, rapid.

Geläufigkeit (ghĕ-loy'fīgh-kīt), *Ger.* Fluency, ease.

Geläut (ghĕ-loyt), *Ger.* A peal of bells, ringing of bells.

Gelinde (ghĕ-lĭn'dĕ), *Ger.* Softly, gently.

Gelindigkeit (ghĕ-lĭn'dĭgh-kīt), *Ger.* Softness, gentleness, sweetness.

Gellen (gĕl'l'n), *Ger.* To sound loudly.

Gellenflöte (gĕl'l'n-flō'te), *Ger.* Clarionet.

Geltung (gĕl'toong), *Ger.* The value or proportion of a note.

Gemächlich (ghĕ-mäkh'lĭkh), *Ger.* } Quietly;
Gemachsam (ghĕ-mäkh'säm), in a calm, slow manner.

Gemählig (ghĕ-mä'lĭg), *Ger.* Gradually, by degrees.

Gemässigt (ghĕ-mäs'sĭgt), *Ger.* Moderate, moderato.

Gemisch (ghĕ-mĭsh'), *Ger.* Mixed; mixture, or compound, stops in an organ.

Gemsenhorn. An instrument formed of a small pipe made of the horn of a chamois, or wild goat.

Gemshorn (ghĕms'hōrn), *Ger.* An organ-stop with conical pipes. The tone is light, but very clear.

Gemshornquint (ghĕms'hōrn-kwĭnt), *Ger.* An organ-stop with conical pipes, sounding a fifth above the foundation stops.

Gemüth (ghĕ-müt'), *Ger.* Mind, soul.

Gemüthlich (ghĕ-müt'lĭkh), *Ger.* Agreeable, expressive.

Genera (gĕ-nä'rä), *Lat.* } A term used by the
Genus (gä'noos), ancients to indicate the modes according to which they divided

their tetrachords. The different methods of dividing the octave: When both tones and semitones are employed, according to the natural arrangement of the diatonic scale, it is called the diatonic or natural genus; when it is divided by semitones only, it is called the chromatic genus, and the enharmonic genus when quarter tones also are used.

Generalbass (ghĕn'ĕr-äl-bäs), *Ger.* Thorough bass.

General pause, A general cessation or silence of all the parts.

Generalprobe (ghĕn'ĕr-äl-prō'bĕ), *Ger.* A general rehearsal.

Generateur (zhă nĕ-rä-tŭr'), *Fr.* The fundamental note of the common chord.

Generator. The principal sound or sounds by which others are produced; the fundamental note of the common chord.

Genere (jā'nĕ-rĕ), *It.* See *Genera*.

Generoso (jă-nĕ-rō'zō), *It.* Noble, in a dignified manner.

Genialia (gă-nĭ-ä'lĭ-ä), *Lat.* The name given by the ancient Romans to cymbals, because they were used in the celebration of weddings.

Génie (zhă'nĕ), *Fr.* } Genius, talent, spirit.
Genis (jă'nĭs), *It.*

Genre (zhänhr), *Fr.* Style, manner.

Genre chromatique (zhänhr krō-mä-tēk'), *Fr.* The chromatic genus.

Genre diatonique (zhänhr dĭ-ä-tŏnh-ēk'), *Fr.* The diatonic, or natural, genus.

Genre enharmonique (zhänhr änh-här-mŏnh-ĕk'), *Fr.* The enharmonic genus.

Genre expressif (zhänhr ĕs-prĕs-sēf'), *Fr.* The expressive style.

Gentil (zhän-tēl'), *Fr* } Pleasing, graceful, elegant.
Gentile (jĕn-tē'lĕ), *It.*

Gentilezza (jĕn-tēl lĕt'zä), *It.* Grace, elegance, refinement of style.

Gentilmente (jĕn-tēl-mĕn'tĕ), *It.* Gracefully, elegantly.

Genus (gā'noos), *Lat.* See *Genera*.

Genus chromaticum (gā'noos krō-mä'tĭ-koom), *Lat.* The chromatic genus or mode.

Genus diatonicum (gā'noos dī ä-tō'nĭ-koom), *Lat.* The diatonic genus or mode.

Genus enharmonicum (gā'noos ĕn-här-mō'nĭ-koom), *Lat.* The enharmonic genus or mode.

Genus inflatile (gā'noos ĭn-flä'tĭ-lĕ), *Lat.* Wind instruments.

Genus percussibile (gā'noos pĕr-koos-sē'bĭ-lĕ), Instruments of percussion.

Genus tensile (gā'noos tĕn'sĭ-lĕ), *Lat.* Stringed instruments.

Gerade Bewegung (ghĕ-rä'dĕ bĕ-vä'goong), *Ger.* Similar motion.

Gerade Taktart (ghĕ-rä'dĕ täkt'ärt), *Ger.* Common time.

Geriesel (ghĕ-rē'z'l), *Ger.* A soft, murmuring sound.

German fingering. A method of fingering piano music which designates the thumb as the first finger, in distinction from the English or American mode, which indicates the use of the thumb by a sign.

German flute. See *Flauto traverso*.

German scale. A scale of the natural notes, consisting of A, H, C, D, E, F, G, instead of A, B, C, etc., the B being always reserved to express B♭.

German sixth. A name given to a chord composed of a major third, perfect fifth, and extreme sixth, as,

German soprano clef. The C clef placed on the first line of the staff for soprano, instead of the G clef on the second line of that part.

Ges (ghĕs), *Ger.* The note G♭.

Gesang (ghĕ-säng'), *Ger.* Singing; the art of singing; a song, melody, air.

Gesangbuch (ghĕ-säng'bookh), *Ger.* Song-book, hymn-book.

Gesang der Vögel (ghĕ-säng' dĕr fö'g'l), *Ger.* Singing of birds.

Gesänge (ghĕ-säng'ĕ), *Ger. pl.* Songs, hymns.

Gesangsgruppe (ghĕ-sängs'groop-pĕ), *Ger.* Song group; the second subject of a sonata movement, so called in contradistinction from the leading subject, which is thematic.

Gesangsweise (ghĕ-sängs'wī-zĕ), *Ger.* In the style of a song.

Gesangverein (ghĕ-säng'fĕr-īn), *Ger.* A choral society.

Gesangweise (ghĕ-säng'wī-zĕ), *Ger.* Melody, tune.

Gesause (ghĕ-sou'zĕ), *Ger.* Humming, whistling.

Geschick (ghĕ-shĭk'), *Ger.* Skill, dexterity.

Geschlecht (ghĕ-shlĕkht'), *Ger.* Genus.

Geschleift (ghĕ-shlīft'), *Ger.* Slurred, legato.

Geschmack (ghĕ-schmäk'), *Ger.* Taste.

Geschwanzte Noten (ghĕ-shwänts'tĕ nō'tĕn), *Ger.* A quaver, or flag notes.

Geschwind (ghĕ-shwĭnd'), *Ger.* Quick, rapid.

Geschwindigkeit (ghĕ - shwĭnd'ĭg - kīt), *Ger.* Swiftness, rapidity, speed.

Geschwindmarsch (ghĕ-shwĭnd'märsh), *Ger.* A quickstep.

Ges-dur (ghĕs-door), *Ger.* The key of G♭ major.

Geses (ghĕs-ĕs), *Ger.* G-double-flat.

Gesinge (ghĕ-sĭng'ĕ), *Ger.* Constant singing, bad singing.

Gestossen (ghĕ-stōs's'n), *Ger.* Separated, detached.

Gestrichene (ghĕ-strĭ'khĕ-nĕ), *Ger.* A quaver.

Getern. } Old names for the cittern.
Getron.

ä *arm*, ă *add*, à *ale*, ĕ *end*, ē *eve*, ĭ *ill*, ī *isle*, ŏ *old*, ŏ *odd*, oo *moon*, ŭ *but*, ü *Fr. sound*, kh *Ger. ch*, nh *nasal*.

(120)

Getheilt (ghĕ-tīlt'), *Ger.* Divided. *Getheilte Violinen*, the same as *violini divisi*.

Getön (ghĕ-tön'), *Ger.* Repeated sounds, clamor.

Getragen (ghĕ-trä'gh'n), *Ger.* Well sustained, carried.

Getrost (ghĕ-trōst'), *Ger.* Confidently, resolutely.

Geübtere (ghĕ-üb'tĕ-rĕ), *Ger.* Expert performers.

Gewirbel (ghĕ-wĭr'b'l), *Ger.* The roll of drums.

Gewiss (ghĕ-wĭs'), *Ger.* Firm, resolute.

Gewissheit (ghĕ-wĭs'hīt), *Ger.* Firmness, resolution.

Geziert (ghĕ-tsērt), *Ger.* With affectation.

G-flat. The flat seventh of A♭; the fifth flat introduced in modulating by fourths from the natural diatonic mode.

G gamut. The G on the first line of the bass staff.

Ghiighe. An old name for the fiddle. See *Gigue*.

Ghiribizzi (ghĕ-rĭ-bēt'zĭ), *It.* Unexpected intervals; eccentric, fantastical passages.

Ghiribizzoso (ghĕ-rĭ-bĕ-tsō'zo), *It.* Fantastical, whimsical.

Ghironda (ghĕ-rŏn'dä), *It.* A hurdygurdy.

Ghittern. An old name for the cittern.

Gicheroso (jĕ-kĕ-rō'zŏ), *It.* Merry, playful.

Giga (jē'ʁä), *It.*
Gigue (zhĕg), *Fr.*
Gigue(gē'gĕ), *Ger.*
A jig. A very lively old dance in duple, or quadruple, ternary time—as 12-8 (or 4-4 with quaver triplets), 6-8, 6-4, and also in 12-16 and 24-16. Examples in simple ternary time (3-8) are comparatively rare, and a jig in 𝄵 with triplets is something exceptional. Nothing certain can be said about the origin of this dance. The name is supposed to be derived from the German word Geig, or Geige, meaning a fiddle, as the music is particularly adapted to instruments of that class.

Gigelira (jē-jä-lī'rä), *It.* A xylophone, or Strohfiedel (*q. v.*).

Gighardo (jē-gär'dō), *It.* A sort of jig.

G in alt. The first note in alt; the octave above the G, or treble clef note.

G in altissimo. The first note in altissimo; the fifteenth above the G or treble clef note.

Ginglarus. A small Egyptian flute.

Giochevole (jō-kā'vŏ-lĕ), *It.* Merry, sportive, gay.

Giochevolmente (jō-kā-vŏl-měn'tě),
Giocolarmente (jō-kō-lär-měn'tě), *It.*
Merrily, sportively.

Giocondamente (jō-kŏn-dä-měn'tě), *It.* Merrily, joyfully, gayly.

Giocondo (jō-kŏn'dō), *It.* Cheerful, merry, gay.

Giocosamente (jō-kō-zä-měn'tě), *It.*
Giocoso (jō-kō'zō), *It.*
Humorously, sportively.

Gioja (jō'yä), *It.* Joy, gladness.

Giojante (jō-yän'tě), *It.*
Giojoso (jō-yō'zō), *It.*
Blithe, joyful, gay.

Giojosamente (jō-yō-zä-měn'tě), *It.* Joyfully, merrily.

Gioviale (jō-vī-ä'lĕ), *It.* Jovial.

Giovialita (jō-vī-ä-lī-tā'), *It.* Joviality, gaiety.

Giraffe (jĭ-räff'). A species of ancient spinet.

Gis (ghīs), *Ger.* The note G♯.

Gis-moll (ghīs-mōll), *Ger.* The key of G♯ minor.

Gittana (jē-tä'nä), *It.* A Spanish dance.

Gittern (jĭt'tĕrn). A species of cittern.

Gitteth (jĭt'teth), *Heb.* An instrument which David brought from Gath, of the harp kind.

Giubbiloso (joob-bī-lō'zo), *It.* Jubilant, exulting.

Giubilazione (joo-bī-lät-sī-ō'nĕ),
Giubilio (joo-bī-lē'ō), *It.*
Giubilo (joo'bī-lō),
Jubilation, rejoicing.

Giucante (joo-kän'tĕ),
Giuchevole (joo-kä-vō'lĕ), *It.*
Merry, joyful. See *Giojante*.

Giulivamente (joo-lī-vä-měn'tĕ), *It.* Joyfully, lively.

Giulivissimo (joo-lī-věs'sī-mō), *It.* Very joyful.

Giulivo (joo-lē'vō), *It.* Cheerful, joyful.

Giullari (jool-lä'rē), *It.* Bands of dancers, actors, or singers.

Giuocante (joo-ō-kän'tĕ), *It.* With sport and gaiety.

Giuoco (joo-ō'kō), *It.* An organ-stop.

Giuocoso (joo-ō-kō'zō), *It.* See *Giocoso*.

Giustamente (joos-tä-měn'tĕ), *It.* Justly, with precision.

Giustezza (joos-tět'zä), *It.* Precision.

Giusto (joos'tō), *It.* A term signifying that the movement indicated is to be performed in an equal, steady, and just time.

Given bass. A bass given, to which the harmony is to be added.

Giving out. The prelude by which the organist announces to the congregation the tune they are to sing.

Glais (glä), *Fr.* The passing bell.

Glais funèbre (glä fü-uäbr), *Fr.* A funeral-knell.

Glapissant (glä-pīs-säṅh), *Fr.* Shrill, squeaking.

Glasses, musical. An instrument formed of a number of glass goblets shaped like finger-glasses, tuned by filling them with more or less water, and played upon with the fingers moistened.

ä *arm*, ă *add*, ā *ale*, ĕ *end*, ē *eve*, ĭ *ill*, ī *isle*, ŏ *odd*, ō *old*, oo *moon*, ŭ *but*, ü *Fr. sound*, kh *Ger. ch.* nh *nasal*.

Glatt (glät), *Ger.* Smooth, even.

Glätte (glät'tĕ), *Ger.* Smoothness, evenness.

Glee. A vocal composition in three or four parts, generally consisting of more than one movement, the subject of which may be grave, tender, or gay and bacchanalian. The glee in its present form first appeared in the middle of the eighteenth century, and is a composition peculiar to England.

Gleemen. An ancient name for minstrels.

Gleich (glīkh), *Ger.* Equal, alike, consonant.

Gleichklang (glīkh'kläng), *Ger.* Consonance of sound, unison.

Gleichschwebende Temperatur (glīkh-shwā-běn-dĕ těm-pĕ-rä-toor'), *Ger.* Equal temperament. The division of the octave into twelve equal parts in such a way as to afford the nearest possible approximation to correct intervals with the imperfections equally distributed in all keys.

Gleichstimmig (glīkh'stĭm-mĭg), *Ger.* Harmonious, accordant.

Gleiten (glī't'n), *Ger.* To slide the fingers.

Gli (glē), *It. pl.* The.

Glide. Portamento.

Gliding. In flute-playing, a sliding movement of the fingers for the purpose of blending the tones.

Glied (glēd), *Ger.* Link; the term is used to express a chord, as, *Einglied*, one chord; *Zweiglied*, two chords.

Glissade (glĭs-säd'), *Fr.* Gliding; the act of passing the fingers in a smooth, unbroken manner over the keys or strings.

Glissando (glēs-sän'dō), -*It.* } Slurred,
Glissato (glēs-sä'tō), *It.* } smooth,
Glissement (glēs-mŏuh), *Fr.* } in a gliding manner, by sliding the fingers along the keys.

Glisser (glēs-sā'), *Fr.* An embellishment which is executed by turning the nail and drawing the thumb or finger rapidly over the keyboard.

Glissez le pouce (glēs-sā' lŭh poos), *Fr.* Slide the thumb.

Glissicando (glēs-sī-kän'dō), *It.* } Slurred,
Glissicato (glēs-sī-kä'tō), *It.* } smooth, in a gliding manner. See, also, *Glisser*.

Gli stromenti (glē strŏ-měn'tē), *It.* The instruments.

Glitschen (glĭt'shĕn), *Ger.* To glide the finger. See *Glisser*.

Glöckchen (glŏk'kh'n), *Ger.* A little bell.

Glocke (glŏk'ĕ), *Ger.* A bell.

Glöckeln (glŏ'kĕln), *Ger.* To ring little bells.

Glockengeläute (glŏ'k'n-gĕ-loy'tĕ), *Ger.* The ringing or chiming of bells.

Glockenist (glŏk'ĕn-ĭst), *Ger.* } Player on
Glöckner (glŏk'nĕr), *Ger.* } the chimes, or bell-ringer.

Glockenklang (glŏk'ĕn-kläng), *Ger.* The sound of bells.

Glockenspiel (glŏk'ĕn-spĕl), *Ger.* Chimes; also a stop in imitation of bells in German organs.

Glöckleinton (glŏk'līn-tōn), *Ger.* An organ-stop of very small scale and wide measure.

Gloria (glō'rĭ-a), *L.* " Glory be to God on high." A principal movement in the Mass.

Glottis (glŏt'tĭs), *Gr.* The narrow opening at the upper part of the trachea, or windpipe, which by its dilation and contraction contributes to the modulation of the voice. The name is also applied to a kind of reed used by the ancient flute-players, which they held between their lips and blew through in performance.

Glühend (glü'ĕnd), *Ger.* Ardent, glowing.

G-moll (gā-mōl), *Ger.* The key of G minor.

Gnacchera (näk-kā'rä), *It.* A tambourine, a tabor.

Gnugab (noo-gäb'), *Ger.* The name given by the ancient Hebrews to the organ.

Gola (gō'lä), *It.* The throat; also a guttural voice.

Goll trompo. A trumpet used by the ancient Irish, Danes, Normans, and English.

Golpe de musica (gŏl-pĕ dä moo'zī-kä), *Sp.* A band of music.

Gondellied (gŏn'd'l-lēd), *Ger.* A gondolier-song.

Gondoliera (gōn-dō-lē-ā'rä), *It.* A gondola-song; a song with an easy-rocking motion, à la the movement of a gondola.

Gondolier-songs. Songs composed and sung by the Venetian gondoliers, of a very graceful and pleasing style; barcarolles.

Gong. A Chinese instrument of the pulsatile kind, consisting of a large circular plate of metal, which, when struck, produces an exceedingly loud noise.

Gorgheggiamento (gŏr-gād-jī-ü-měn'tō), *It.* Trilling, quavering.

Gorgheggiare (gŏr-gād-jī-ä'rĕ), *It.* To trill, to shake.

Gorgheggio (gŏr-gād'jī-ō), *It.* A trill, a shake of the voice in singing.

Gout (goo), *Fr.* Taste, style, judgment.

Governing key. The principal key; that key in which a piece is written.

Grabgesang (gräb'gĕ-säng), *Ger.* } Dirge;
Grablied (gräb'lēd), *Ger.* } funeral song.

Grace note. Any note added to a composition as an embellishment.

Graces. Ornamental notes and embellishments, either written by the composer or introduced by the performer. The principal embellishments are the appoggiatura, the turn, and the shake or trill.

Gracieux (grä-sĭ-üh), *Fr.* Graceful.

Gracile (grä'tshī-lĕ), *It.* Thin, weak, small; referring to the tone.

Grazioso (grä-thī-ō'zō), *Sp.* Graceful.

ă *arm*, ā *add*, ä *ale*, ĕ *end*, ē *eve*, ĭ *ill*, ī *isle*, ō *old*, ŏ *odd*, oo *moon*, ŭ *but*, ü *Fr. sound*, kh *Ger. ch*, nh *nasal*.

Grad (gräd), *Ger.* Steps, degree. See *Grado*.

Gradare (grä-dä'rĕ), *It.* To descend step by step.

Gradatamente (grä-dä-tä-mĕn'tĕ), *It.* } By degrees, a gradual increase or diminution of speed or intensity of tone.
Gradation (grä-dä-sĕ-ŏnh), *Fr.*
Gradazione (grä-dä-tsĭ-ŏ'nĕ), *It.*

Gradevole (grä-dā'vō-lĕ),
Gradevolmente (grä-dä-vōl-mĕn'tĕ), *It.* } Gracefully, pleasingly.

Gradire (grä-dē'rĕ), *It.* To ascend step by step.

Graditamente (grä-dĭ-tä-mĕn'tĕ), *It.* In a pleasing manner.

Graditissimo (grä-dĭ-tēs'sĭ-mō), *It.* Very sweetly, most gracefully.

Gradleiter (gräd'lī-tĕr), *Ger.* A scale.

Grado (grä'dō), *It.* A degree, or single step, on the staff; di grado means that the melody moves by degrees, ascending or descending, in opposition to di salto, by skips of greater intervals.

Grado ascendente (grä'dō ä-shĕn-dĕn'tĕ), *It.* A descending degree.

Grado descendente (grä'dō dä-shĕn-dĕn'tĕ), *It.* A descending degree.

Grados (grä-dōs), *Sp.* Musical intervals.

Gradual. That part of the Roman Catholic service that is sung between the Epistle and the Gospel, and which was anciently sung on the steps of the altar.

Gradualmente (grä-doo-äl-mĕn'tĕ),
Graduatamente (grä-doo-ä-tä-mĕn'tĕ), *It.* } Gradually, by degrees or steps.

Gradus ad Parnassum (grä'doos äd pär-näs'-soom), *Lat.* The road to Parnassus. This name was applied by the contrapuntist Fux to his elaborate textbook in counterpoint. Also by Clementi to his collection of 100 pieces for the higher art of piano-playing. The latter work is very important.

Gradual modulation. Modulation in which some chord is taken before the modulating chord, which may be considered as belonging to the original key or the new key.

Graduare (grä-doo-ä'rĕ), *It.* To divide into degrees.

Graduazione (grä-doo-ä-tsĭ-ŏ'nĕ), *It.* See *Graduzione*.

Graduellement (grä-dwäl'mänh), *Fr.* } Gradually, by degrees.
Gradweise (gräd'wī-zĕ), *Ger.*

Grail (grāl). The Gradual.

Graillement (grä-mänh), *Fr.* A hoarse sound.

Grammar, musical. The rules by which musical compositions are governed.

Grammatical accent. The common-measure accent, marked by the length of the words, and a regular succession of strong and weak parts.

Gran (grän),
Grande (grän'dĕ), *It.* } Great, grand.

Gran cantore (grän kän-tō'rĕ), *It.* A fine singer.

Gran cassa (grän käs'sä), *It.* The great drum.

Grand-barré (gränh-bär-rä'), *Fr.* In guitar-playing this means laying the first finger of the left hand upon all the six strings of the guitar at once.

Grand bourdon. Great or double bourdon, an organ-stop of 32-feet tone in the pedal.

Grand chantre (gränh shäntr), *Fr.* A precentor.

Grand chœur (grän kür), *Fr.* Full organ; all the stops.

Grand choir. In organ-playing, the union of all the reed-stops.

Grand cornet. This name is sometimes given to a reed-stop of 16-feet scale on the manuals of an organ.

Grande messe (gränhd mäss), *Fr.* High Mass.

Grande mesure a deux temps (gränhd mäzhür ä dü tänh), *Fr.* Common time of two beats in a bar, marked 2-2, or sometimes 4-4, or ₵. See, also, *Alla cappella*.

Grandezza (grän-dĕt'sä), *It.* Grandeur, dignity.

Grandioso (grän-dĭ-ō'zō), *It.* Grand, noble.

Grandisonante (grän-dĭ-zō-nän'tĕ), *It.* Very sonorous, full-sounding.

Grand jeu (grän zhüh), *Fr.* Full organ. Applied to harmoniums. Also the name of a stop which brings on all the reeds at once.

Grand opera. Italian opera; a full opera with an intricate plot and full cast of performers.

Grand orgue (gränh dŏrg), *Fr.* Great organ.

Grand pianoforte. A pianoforte in which nearly all the octaves have three strings to each tone, tuned in unison, and struck at once by the same hammer.

Grand sonata. An extended sonata, consisting generally of four movements.

Gran gusto (grän goos'ŏ), *It.* In a lofty, elevated manner, a full, rich, high-wrought composition. The manner of a fine and great singer is said to be in the gran gusto.

Gran prova (grän prŏ'vä), *It.* The last rehearsal.

Gran tamburo (grän täm-boo'rō), *It.* The great drum.

Grappa (gräp'pä), *It.* The brace, or character, used to connect two or more staves.

Gratias agimus (grä'tsĭ-äs ä'gĭ-moos), *Lat.* Part of the Gloria in a mass. "We give thanks to Thee."

Grave (grä'vĕ), *It.* A slow and solemn movement; also a deep, low pitch in the scale of sounds.

Gravement (gräv-mänh), *Fr.* } With gravity, in a dignified and solemn manner.
Gravemente (grä-vĕ-mĕn'tĕ), *It.*

Gravezza (grä-vĕt'tsä), *It.* Gravity, solemnity.

Gravicembalo (grä-vĕ-tshĕm'bä-lō), *It.* } An
Gravicembolo (grä-vĕ-tshĕm'bō-lō), old name for the harpsichord.

Gravis (grä'vĭs), *Lat.* Heavy, ponderous. The name of one of the accentus ecclesiastici.

Gravisonante (grä-vĭ-zō-nän'tĕ), *It.* Loud-sounding.

Gravita (grä-vĭ-tä'), *It.*
Gravität (grä-fĭ-tät'), *Ger.* } Gravity, majesty.
Gravité (grä-vĭ-tā'), *Fr.*

Gravity. That modification of any sound by which it becomes deep or low in respect to some other sound. The gravity of sounds depends in general on the mass, extent, and tension of the sonorous bodies. The larger and more lax the bodies, the slower will be the vibrations and the graver the sounds.

Grazia (grä'tsĭ-ä), *It.* } Grace, elegance.
Grazie (grä'tsĭ-ĕ), *Ger.*

Graziosamente (grä-tsĭ-ō zä-mĕn'tĕ), *It.* Gracefully, smoothly.

Grazioso (grä-tsĭ-ō'zō), *It.* In a graceful style.

Greater scale. Major scale.

Greater sixth. A name sometimes given to the major sixth.

Greater third. A name sometimes given to the major third.

Great octave. The name given in Germany to the notes between C and B inclusive. These notes are expressed by capital letters.

Great organ. In an organ with three rows of keys, usually the middle row, so called because containing the greatest number of stops, and having its pipes of large scale and voiced louder than those in the swell, or choir, organ.

Great sixth. The appellation given to the chord of the fifth and sixth when the fifth is perfect and the sixth major.

Greek modes. The ancient Greek modes or scales were twelve in number; of these, six were authentic and six plagal. The sounds are supposed to have been somewhat similar to those in the scale of C, and the differences in mode due to the selection of a point of repose.

Gregorian chant. A style of choral music, according to the eight celebrated church modes introduced by Pope Gregory in the sixth century.

Gregorianisch (grĕ-gō-rĭ-än'ĭsh), *Ger.* Gregorian.

Gregorianischer Gesang (grĕ-gō-rĭ-än'ĭsh-ĕr), *Ger.* The Gregorian chant.

Gregorian modes. } The eight tunes, or
Gregorian tones. } tones, authorized by St. Gregory for use in intoning the religious offices. Part of them are still in the plain song (*q. v.*).

Gregoriano (grä-gō-rĭ-ä'nō), *It.* } Gregorian.
Gregorien (grä-gō-rĭ-änh), *Fr.*

Grell (grĕll), *Ger.* Shrill, acute.

Grellheit (grĕl'hīt), *Ger.* Sharpness, shrillness.

Grelot (grä-lō), *Fr.* A small bell.

Griffbret (grĭff'brĕt), *Ger.* The fingerboard of a violin, violoncello, etc.

Grifflloch (grĭf'lōkh), *Ger.* The holes of a flute and like instruments.

Grillig (grĭl'lĭg), *Ger.* Capricious, fanciful.

Gringotter (gränh-gō-tā'), *Fr.* To quaver, to warble.

Grisoller (grē-zō-lā'), *Fr.* To sing like a lark.

Grob (grōb), *Ger.* Deep, low voice, bass.

Grobgedackt (grōb'ghĕ-däkht'), *Ger.* Large stopped diapason of full tone.

Groppetto (grōp-pĕt'tō), *It.* See *Gruppetto*.

Groppo (grōp'pō), *It.* A group of notes, a rapid vocal passage.

Gros-fa. A name formerly given to old church music in square notes, semibreves, and minims.

Grossartig (grōs'är-tĭg), *Ger.* Grand.

Grosse (grōs'sĕ), *Ger.* Major, speaking of intervals; also grand in respect to style.

Grosse caisse (grōs käss), *Fr.* The great drum.

Grosse Nazard (grōs'sĕ nä-tsärd'), *Ger.* An organ-stop, sounding a fifth above the diapasons.

Grosse Quinte (grōs'sĕ quĭn'tĕ),
Grosses Quintenbass (grōs'sĕs quĭn't'n-bäss), } *Ger.*
An organ-stop in the pedals sounding a fifth or twelfth to the great bass of 32 feet or 16 feet.

Grosse Sonate (grōs'sĕ sō-nä'tĕ), *Ger. pl.* Grand sonatas.

Grosses Principal (grōs'sĕs prĭn-tsĭ-päl'), *Ger.* An organ-stop of 32-feet scale of the open diapason species.

Grosse Terz (grōs'sĕ tärtz), *Ger.* Great third. The major third.

Grosse Tierce (grōs'sĕ tĕr'sĕ), *Ger.* Great third sounding-stop in an organ, producing the third or tenth, above the foundation stops.

Grosse Trommel (grōs'sĕ trŏm'm'l), *Ger.* The great drum.

Grossgedackt (grōs'ghĕ-däkt'), *Ger.* Double-stopped diapason of 16-feet tone in an organ.

Grosso (grōs'sō), *It.* Full, great, grand.

Grossvatertanz (grōs'fä-tĕr-tänts'), *Ger.* Grandfather's dance; an old-fashioned dance.

Gros tambour (grō tänh-boor), *Fr.* The great drum.

Grottesco (grŏt-tĕs'kō), *It.* Grotesque.

Ground bass. A bass consisting of a few simple notes, intended as a theme, on which, at each repetition, a new melody is con-

Group. Several short notes tied together.

Grundakkord (groond'äk-kŏrd), *Ger.* An uninverted chord.

Grundstimme (groond'stĭm-mĕ), *Ger.* The bass part.

Grundton (groond-tōn), *Ger.* The bass note; fundamental, or principal, tone.

Gruppetto (groop-pĕt'tō), *It.* A turn; also a small group of grace, or ornamental, notes.

Gruppe (groop'pĕ), *Ger.* } A group of notes;
Gruppo (groop'pō), *It.* } formerly it meant a trill, shake, or turn.

G-Schlüssel (gā'shlüs-s'l), *Ger.* The G, or treble, clef.

Guaracha (gwä-räk'ä), *Sp.* A Spanish dance.

Guaranita (gwä rä-nē'tä), *Sp.* A variety of the Spanish guitar.

Guarnerius (gwar-nā'rĭ-ŭs). A make of violin highly prized, so called from the name of the manufacturer.

Guddok (goo-dōk), *Rus.* A rustic violin with three strings, used among the Russian peasantry.

Guerriero (goo-ĕr-rĭ-ā'rō), *It.* Martial, warlike.

Guet (gā), *Fr.* A military trumpet piece.

Guia (ghē-ä), *Sp.* Fugue, conductor, leader.

Guida (gwē'dä), *It.* Guide; also the mark called a direct ⁓.

Guide. That note in a fugue which leads off and announces the subject.

Guide-main (ghēd mänh), *Fr.* The hand-guide, an instrument invented by Kalkbrenner for assisting young players to acquire a good position of the hands on the pianoforte.

Guidon (ghē-dŏnh), *Fr.* The mark called a direct.

Guidonian hand. The figure of a left hand used by Guido, and upon which was marked the names of the sounds forming his three hexachords.

Guidonian syllables. The syllables ut, re, mi, fa, sol, la, used by Guido d'Arezzo, and called the Aretinian scale.

Guido's gamut. The table, or scale, introduced by Guido Aretinus about 1050, and to the notes of which he applied the syllables ut, re, mi, fa, sol, la. It consisted of twenty notes, viz., two octaves and a major sixth, the first octave being distinguished by capital letters, the second by small letters, and the sixth by double small letters.

Guigue (goo-ē'ghĕ), *It.* See *Giga*.

Guiltern. See *Gittern*.

Guimbarde (ghĕm-bärd'), *Fr.* A jew's-harp.

Guion (ghē-ōn), *Sp.* A sign indicating that the piece or passage is to be repeated.

Guitar. A long-necked instrument which in modern times has been strung generally with six strings, and whose fingerboard is provided with frets. The strings, which are plucked with the fingers of the right hand, are tuned in E A d g b e', but as guitar music is written an octave higher than it sounds, their notation is as follows:

Guitare (ghĭ-tär'), *Fr.* }
Guitarre (ghĕ-tär'rĕ), *Sp.* } A guitar.
Guitarre (ghĭ-tär'rĕ), *Ger.* }

Guitare d'amour (ghĕ-tär d'ä-moor), *Fr.* An instrument (invented by Georg Staufer, of Vienna, in 1823) with six strings, tuned like those of the guitar, but played with a bow. In some of its features it resembles the guitar in others the violoncello. It has, not inaptly, been described as a viola bastarda. The Germans call it, also, Bogenguitarre (bow-guitar), Knieguitarre (knee-guitar), and Violoncelliguitarre (violoncello-guitar).

Guitare d'amour (ghē-tär d'ä-moor'), *Fr.* A modification of the German guitar.

Guitarre lyre (ghĕ-tär lērh), *Fr.* A French instrument having six strings and formed somewhat like an ancient lyre.

Guiterne (ghē-tärn'), *Fr.* An ancient species of lute or guitar.

Gunst (goonst), *Ger.* Grace, tenderness, favor.

Guracho (goo-rä-kō), *Sp.* See *Guarache*.

Gusto (goos'tō), *It.* Taste, expression.

Gustosamente (goos-tō-zä-měn'tĕ), *It.* Tastefully, expressively.

Gustoso (goos-tō'zō), *It.* Expressive, tasteful.

G ut. A name applied by Guido to the tone large G, because this tone was the lowest of the whole system of tones.

Gutdünken (goot'dün-k'n), *Ger.* At pleasure, according to the taste of the performer.

Guttural. Formed in the throat, pertaining to the throat.

Gutturalmente (goot-too-räl-měn'tĕ), *It.* Gutturally.

ä *arm*, ă *add*, ā *ale*, ĕ *end*, ē *eve*, ĭ *ill*, ī *isle*, ō *old*, ŏ *odd*, oo *moon*, ŭ *but*, ü *Fr. sound*, kh *Ger. ch*, nh *nasal*.

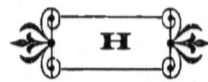

H. This letter is used by the Germans for B-natural, which note is called by the French and Italians si. Abbreviation for Haud.

Habanera (hä-bä'nĕ-rä), *Sp.* A slow Spanish dance in 3-4 time; a dance.

Haberrohr (hä'bĕr-rōr), *Ger.* Shepherd's flute.

Hackbrett (häk'brĕt), *Ger.* The dulcimer.

Halb (hälb), *Ger.* Half.

Halbcadence (hälb-kä-dĕn'tsĕ), *Ger.* Half-cadence.

Halbgedackt (hälb'gĕ-däkt), *Ger.* Half-covered. Applied to the rohrflöte and clarinet-flute stops in organs.

Halbnote (hälb-nō'tĕ), *Ger.* A minim, or half-note.

Halbprincipal (hälb'prĭn-tsĭ-päl'), *Ger.* An organ-stop of four-feet pitch, and consequently an octave higher than the pitch of the open diapason.

Halbton (hälb'tōn), *Ger.* Half-tone, semitone.

Half=cadence. An imperfect cadence, a close on the dominant.

Half=note. A minim.

Half=note rest. A pause equal in duration to a half-note.

Half=shift. The first shift on a violin; that on the fifth line.

Half=step. The smallest interval used in music.

Hall (häll), *Ger.* Sound, clangor, clang.

Halle (häl'lĕ), *Ger.* Hall.

Hallelujah (häl-lĕ-loo'yah), *Heb.* "Praise ye the Lord"; a song of thanksgiving.

Hallelujah meter. A stanza in six lines of iambic measure, the syllables of each being in number and order as follows: 6, 6, 6, 6, 8, 8.

Hallen (häl'l'n), *Ger.* To sound, to clang.

Halltrompete (häll'trŏm-pĕ'tĕ), *Ger.* A powerful trumpet.

Halmpfeife (hälm-pfī'fĕ), *Ger.* Shepherd's pipe.

Hals (häls), *Ger.* Neck of a violin, viola, etc.

Halt (hält), *Ger.* A pause; a hold.

Hammer. That part of the action or mechanism of a pianoforte which strikes the strings and thus produces the sound.

Hammer, tuning. An instrument by which pianos and harps are tuned, by tightening or loosening the strings.

Hammerklavier (häm'mĕr-klä-fēr'), *Ger.* The modern piano.

Hanakische (hä-na'kĭ-shĕ), *Ger.* A hanacca. A Moravian dance in 3-4 measure, somewhat resembling a polonaise, but quicker.

Hände (hän'dĕ), *Ger.* Hands.

Handlage (händ-lä'gĕ), *Ger.* The position of the hand.

Handleiter (händ-lī'tĕr), *Ger.* Handguide. See *Guide*.

Hand organ. A portable instrument consisting of a cylinder, on which by means of wires, pins, and staples are set the tunes, the revolution of the cylinder causing the pins, etc., to act on the keys and also to give admission to the wind.

Handstücke (händ'stü-kĕ), *Ger.* Hand pieces, exercises for training the fingers in piano-playing.

Hardiment (här-dĭ-mäuh), *Fr.* Boldly, firmly.

Harfe (här'fĕ), *Ger.* A harp.

Harfen (här'f'n), *Ger.* To play on the harp.

Harfenbass (här'fĕn-bäss), *Ger.* A bass like a harp; broken chords.

Harfensaite (här'fĕn-sāi'tĕ), *Ger.* Harp-string.

Harfenspieler (här-f'n-spē'lĕr), *Ger.* Harp-player.

Harmonia (här-mō'nĭ-ä), *Lat.* A daughter of Mars and Venus. Her name was first used to indicate music in general.

Harmonic. Concordant, musical.

Harmonica. A musical instrument invented by Benjamin Franklin, consisting of glasses, sometimes globular and sometimes flat. The tone is produced by rubbing the edge of the globular glasses with a moistened finger, or striking the flat ones with small hammers. The name is also applied to an organ-stop of delicate tone.

Harmonica=ätherisch (här-mō'nĭ-kä-ā'tĕr-ĭsh), *Ger.* A mixture stop of very delicate scale in German organs.

Harmonical trumpet. An instrument very much like a trumpet, except that it is longer and consists of more branches; the sack-but.

Harmonic figuration. The progression from one tone to another of the same chord by means of passing tones, thence passing in the same manner through successive different chords.

Harmonic flute. An open metal organ-stop, of 8- or 4-feet pitch; the pipes are of double length, that is, 16 or 8 feet, and the bodies have a hole bored in them midway between the foot and the top; the tone is exceedingly full, fluty, and powerful.

Harmonichord. An instrument having the form of an upright piano, but a tone something like that of a violin, produced by the friction of a cylinder covered with leather upon the strings. It was invented in 1785 by Fr. Kaufman.

Harmonici (här-mō′nĭ-tshē), *It. pl.* Harmonics in violin music.

Harmonic mark. A sign used in violin, harp music, etc., to indicate that certain passages are to be played upon such parts of the open strings as will produce the harmonic sounds, O.

Harmonicon. A small instrument held in the hand, the sounds being produced from small metal springs set in motion by blowing from the mouth.

Harmonics. (1) The sounds produced by the vibrations of divisions (aliquot parts) of a string, column of air, etc. Simple sounds are very rare. What we regard as one sound is in reality a compound of a multiplicity of sounds produced by a multiplicity of various simultaneous vibrational forms. If, for instance, an impact is given to a string, it vibrates not only in its full length but at the same time also in divisions. The vibrations of the full length of the string give the fundamental tone, the doubly-quick vibrations of the halves of the string give the octave above the fundamental tone, the trebly-quick vibrations of the string the fifth above the octave, and so on. The several tones which make up the compound sound are called partial tones, or partials; the lowest of them is called fundamental tone, prime, or principal tone; those above the fundamental tone are called the upper partial tones, upper partials, overtones, or harmonics. The fundamental tone is generally the loudest of the partial tones, and with it the upper partials blend so as to be indistinguishable, or only in part distinguishable under certain conditions. The number and relative strength of the partial tones vary in the different classes of instruments and voices and in the different individuals of the same class; it is on the number and the relative strength of the partials that the timbre (quality, character of tone) of instruments and voices chiefly depends. In the following illustration, which shows the first sixteen partial tones of the sound C, the figures indicate the sequence of the partials in the series, and also the relative number of their vibrations in a given time. As the actual sounds of the 7th, 11th, 13th, 14th, and 15th partials can only be approximately represented, they have been distinguished by asterisks.

(2) Harmonics is also the name given to certain tones produced on the violin, harp, and other stringed instruments, tones which owe another name—flageolet tones—to their peculiar character. By touching a vibrating string very lightly in the middle, or at a point a third, fourth, fifth, etc., of its length distant from one of its ends (*i. e.*, from the nut or the bridge) it is made to vibrate in two, three, four, five, etc., divisions, and the result are notes respectively an octave, twelfth, fifteenth, seventeenth, nineteenth, etc., higher than the tone obtained from the open string—*i. e.*, by its full-length vibration.

Harmonic stops. Organ-stops whose pipes, owing to greater pressure of wind, do not produce their fundamental tones, but the first harmonic—*i. e.*, the tone an octave above the fundamental tone. Such stops are the Flûte octaviante and Flûte harmonique.

Harmonic triad. The common chord, consisting of a fundamental note, its third and fifth.

Harmonie (här-mō-nē′), *Fr.* } Harmony.
Harmonie (här-mō-nē′), *Ger.* }

Harmoniemusik (här-mō-nē′moo-zēk′), *Ger.* A military band consisting of brass instruments. The brass in the orchestra. Music for wind instruments only.

Harmonieusement (här-mō-nĭ-ŭs-mänh), *Fr.* Harmoniously.

Harmonieux (här-mō-nĭ-ŭh′), *Fr.* Harmonious.

Harmonious. A term applicable to any two or more sounds which form a consonant or agreeable union.

Harmoniphon. A small instrument with a keyboard like a pianoforte, invented in 1837, and intended to supply the place of hautboys in an orchestra. The sounds are produced from small metal tongues acted upon by a current of air through a flexible tube.

Harmonique (här-mō-nēk), *Fr.* Harmonic; the relation of sounds to each other; also applied to organ-pipes of double length.

Harmoniquement (här-mō-nēk-mänh), *Fr.* Harmonically.

Harmoniren (här-mō-nē′r′n), *Ger.* To harmonize, to be in unison.

Harmonisch (här-mō′nĭsh), *Ger.* Harmonious, harmonical.

Harmonische Theilung (här-mō′nĭ-shē tī-loong), *Ger.* Harmonical division.

Harmonist. One acquainted with the science of harmony.

Harmonium. A keyboard wind instrument of the reed-organ kind, the tones of which are produced by the vibration of free reeds. (*V. Reeds.*) The bellows are worked, except in very large harmoniums, by the performer by means of two pedals (treadles). Small harmoniums have only one set of reeds, *i. e.*, one reed to each note; larger harmoniums have several sets. These different sets of reeds, varied in tone, are brought into play by drawing out corresponding stops. The "expression-stop" closes a valve which shuts off the wind-reservoir, and thus the whole management of the wind is given into the hands (literally, to the feet) of the performer, who, by the greater or lesser quantity of wind furnished by him, can play more or less loud, increase and decrease the tone at pleasure. The harmonium differs from the reed organ in having a pressure-bellows, forcing the air out through the reeds.

Harmonize. To combine two or more parts according to the laws of harmony.

Harmonized. A melody is said to be harmonized when additional parts are subjoined in order to give it more fullness.

Harmonometre (här-mŏ-nŏ-mātr'), *Fr.* An instrument to measure the proportion of sounds; a species of monochord.

Harmony. The agreement or consonance of two or more united sounds. The art of combining sounds into chords and treating those chords according to certain rules.

Harmony, figured. Harmony in which, for the purpose of melody, one or more of the parts of a composition move, during the continuance of a chord, through certain notes that do not form any of the constituent parts of that chord.

Harmony, natural. The harmonic triad of common chord.

Harmony, suspended. One or more notes of a chord retained in the following chord.

Harp. One of the most ancient stringed instruments, the tones of which are produced by plucking the strings (mainly of catgut) with the fingers of the right and left hands. The harp has a diatonic scale. On account of the absence of the chromatic tones the performer was, of course, unable to modulate. To remedy this defect various contrivances have been resorted to. The most perfect instrument hitherto constructed is Erard's "double-action pedal harp," a development of the single-action pedal harp. It has seven pedals by which the strings may be raised either a semitone or a whole tone, and thus all the keys become practicable. This double-action harp has a compass of more than six and a half octaves—from C♭ to f''''♭, and, as each string can be raised two semitones, even to f''''♯. The seven pedals act respectively throughout all the octaves, each on one of the seven degrees of the C♭ major scale, this being the key in which the harp is tuned. The single-action harp was in the key of E♭, and its compass extended from F, to d''''. The harp of the ancient Egyptians was without a "pillar" for supporting the pull of the strings. It was simply a bow, patterned after the hunting-bow, and in the earliest times had only five strings.

Harp, Æolian. An instrument consisting of wire or catgut drawn in parallel lines over a box of thin wood and placed so that a current of air may cause the strings to vibrate.

Harp, couched. Name originally given to the spinet.

Harp, double=action. A harp with pedals that can be used in two positions, the first raising the instrument a half-step, and the second a whole step.

Harpe (härp), *Fr.* A harp.

Harpechorde (härp-kŏrd), *Fr.* An old French name for the harpsichord.

Harpe Eolienne (härp ā-ŏ-li-ĕnn), *Fr.* Æolian harp.

Harpeggiate (här-pĕd-ji-ä'tĕ), *It.* In the style of a harp, arpeggiately.

Harpeggiato (här-pĕd-ji-ä'tō), *It.* Causing the sounds of a chord to be played not together but distinctly one after another. See *Arpeggiato*.

Harpeggiren (här-pĕ-ghē'r'n), *Ger.* Arpeggiate.

Harper. } A performer upon the harp.
Harpist. }

Harpicordo (här'pĭ-kŏr-dō), *It.* A harpsichord.

Harp, Jew's. A small instrument made of brass, or steel, with a flexible metal tongue, played upon by placing it between the teeth and vibrating the tongue by striking it with the finger; the action of the breath determines the power of the tone. Known in the music trade as the "Irish harp."

Harp lute. An instrument having twelve strings, and resembling the guitar.

Harp pedal. The pedal of a pianoforte, sometimes called the soft pedal.

Harpsecol. See *Harpsichord*.

Harpsichord. A keyboard instrument, one of the predecessors of the pianoforte. The strings, instead of being struck by tangents, as in the clavichord, or by hammers, as in the pianoforte, were plucked by quills or pieces of hard leather. (*V. Jack.*) The spinet and virginal are varieties of the harpsichord, differing from it in size and form. The form of the harpsichord is indicated by the German name of the instrument—*Flügel*, wing, the same as the modern grand piano. The harpsichord has often more than one keyboard, and also was provided with stops by which the tone could be modified.

Harpsichord, double. A harpsichord with two unison strings and an octave.

Harpsichord, harmonica. A harmonica, the sounds of which are produced by means of keys similar to the pianoforte, invented at Berlin.

Harpsicon. An old name for the harpsichord.

Harp, single=action. A harp whose pedals can be used in one position only, raising the sounds of the instrument a half-step.

Harp style. In the arpeggio style.
Harp, triangular. An ancient instrument of Phrygian invention.
Harsur (här-soor), *or*, **Hasur** (hä-zoor). *Heb.* An instrument of ten strings, used by the Hebrews.
Harte (här'tĕ),*Ger.* Major, in respect to intervals and scales.
Hartklingend (härt'klĭng'ĕnd), *Ger.* Hardsounding; harsh.
Hate (hawt), *Fr.* Haste, speed.
Hautbois (hō-bwä), *Fr.* An oboe.
Haupt (howpt), *Ger.* Head, principal.
Hauptgesänge (howpt'ghĕ-säng-ĕ), *Ger.*
Hauptmelodie (howpt'měl-ō-dē),
The principal melody.
Hauptkirche (howpt'kĭr-khĕ),*Ger.* Cathedral.
Hauptmanual (howpt'mä-noo-al), *Ger.* The great, or principal, manual; the great organ.
Hauptnote (howpt'nō'tĕ), *Ger.* The principal note in a shake or turn; that note over which the ᴧᴧᴧ or the *tr.* is placed.
Hauptperiode (howpt'pĕ-rī-ō'dĕ), *Ger.* Principal period; the principal period in a musical phrase.
Hauptprobe (howpt'prō-bĕ),*Ger.* The final, or general, rehearsal.
Hauptsatz (howpt'sätz), *Ger.* The principal theme, or subject; the motive, or leading idea.
Hauptschluss (howpt'shloos),*Ger.* A final cadence.
Hauptstimme (howpt'stĭm'mĕ), *Ger.* Principal voice; principal part.
Hauptthema (howpt'tä-mä), *Ger.* The principal theme.
Hauptton (howpt'tōn),*Ger.* Fundamental, or principal tone; the tonic.
Haupttonart (howpt'tōn-ärt), *Ger.* The principal key of a composition.
Hauptwerk (howpt'wärk), *Ger.* Chief work, or manual; the great organ.
Hausse (hōss), *Fr.* The nut of a bow.
Hausser (hōs-sä'), *Fr.* To raise, or sharpen, the pitch.
Haut (hō), *Fr.* Acute, high, shrill.
Hautb. An abbreviation of Hautboy.
Hautbois (hō-bwä), *Fr.* The oboe, or hautboy.
Hautbois d'amour (hō-bwä d'a-moor'), *Fr.* A species of hautboy, with a pleasing tone, but difficult to play in tune, and now nearly obsolete; also an organ-stop.
Hautboy (hō'boy). Oboe. A portable wind instrument of the reed kind, with a double reed, consisting of a tube gradually widening from the top toward the lower end, and furnished with keys and circular holes for modulating its sounds; the tone is penetrating and slightly nasal, and peculiarly adapted to express soft and plaintive passages. The name is also given to an 8-feet organ reed-stop, the tone of which resembles that of the hautboy.
Hautboy-clarion. See *Octave hautboy.*
Haute-contre (hōt-kōntr), *Fr.* High or counter tenor.
Haute-dessus (hōt-děs-sü), *Fr.* High treble, first treble.
Hautement (hōt-mänh), *Fr.* Haughtily, in a dignified manner.
Haute-taille (hōt-tä-yŭh), *Fr.* High tenor.
H-bes (hü-běs), *Ger.* B-double-flat.
H-dur (hü-door), *Ger.* B major.
Head. That part of a note which determines its position on the staff, and to which the stem is joined.
Head tones. Tones produced by the upper register of the voice.
Head voice. The upper or highest register of the voice; the falsetto in men's voices.
Heerhorn (hār'hōrn), *Ger.* A military trumpet.
Heerpauke (hār'pow-kĕ), *Ger.* Kettledrum, tymbal.
Heerpauker (hār'pow-kĕr), *Ger.* Kettledrummer, military drummer.
Heftig (hĕf'tĭg), *Ger.* Vehement, boisterous.
Heftigkeit (hĕf'tĭg-kīt), *Ger.* Vehemence, impetuosity.
Heimlich (hīm'lĭkh), *Ger.* Secret, furtive, stealthy.
Heiss (hīss), *Ger.* Hot, ardent.
Heiter (hī'tĕr), *Ger.* Serene, bright.
Heldenlied (hĕl'd'n-lēd), *Ger.* Heroic song.
Heldenmüthig (hĕl'd'n-mü'tĭg), *Ger.* Heroic.
Hell (hĕl), *Ger.* Clear, bright.
Helle Stimme (hĕl'lĕ stĭm'mĕ), *Ger.* A clear voice.
Hemi (hā'mī), *Gr.* Half.
Hemidemisemiquaver. A sixty-fourth note.
Hemidemisemiquaver rest. A sixty-fourth rest.
Hemidiapente (hĕm'ī-dē-ä-pĕn'tĕ), *Gr.* Diminished, or imperfect, fifth.
Hemiditonos (hĕm-ī-dē-tō'nōs), *Gr.* Lesser or minor third.
Hemiope (hä-mē'ō pĕ), *Gr.* An ancient flute, consisting of a tube with three holes.
Hemiphrase. A member of a phrase consisting of only one bar.
Hemitonium (hā-mĭ-tō'nĭ-ŭm), *Gr.* A semitone or half-tone.
Heptachord. A scale or system of seven sounds. In ancient poetry verses sung or played on seven chords or different notes; a lyre or cithera having seven strings.
Heptachordon (hĕp'tä-kŏr'dōn), *Gr.* The major seventh.

Heptameris (hĕp-tä-mā'rĭs), *Gr.* In ancient music the seventh part of a meris, or forty-third part of an octave.

Herabstrich (här-äb'strĭkh), *Ger.* } A downbow.
Herstrich (här'strĭkh),

Heraufgehen (här-ouf'gä'n), *Ger.* To ascend.

Heroisch (hā-rō'ĭsh), *Ger.* Heroically.

Herunterstrich (hĕr-oon't'r-strĭkh), *Ger.* A downbow upon the violin.

Hervorgehoben (här-fōr'ghĕ-hō'b'n), }
Hervorhebend (här-fōr'hä'bĕnd), *Ger.*
Hervortretend (här-fōr'trä-tĕnd),
Play the notes very prominently and distinctly.

Herzlich (härts'lĭkh), *Ger.* Tenderly, delicately.

Hes (hĕs), *Ger.* B♭. Used when the tone is supposed to come from B natural, or H, as the Germans call it.

Hexachord (hĕx'ä-kōrd), *Gr.* A scale, or system, of six sounds; an interval of a sixth; a lyre having six strings.

Hexachorde (hĕx-ä-kōrd'), *Fr.* A hexachord. See that word.

Hexameron (hĕx-äm'ĕ-rŏn), *Gr.* Set of six musical pieces, or songs.

Hexameter. In ancient poetry a verse of six feet, the first four of which may be either dactyls or spondees, the fifth always a dactyl, and the sixth a spondee.

Hexaphonic. Composed of six voices.

Hiatus (hī-ä'toos), *Lat.* A gap, imperfect harmony.

Hibernian melodies. Irish melodies.

Hidden canon. A close canon.

Hidden fifths and **Hidden octaves.** In the article "Consecutives" it has been stated that progressions of perfect fifths and octaves are prohibited. Hidden fifths and octaves—which occur when the second of two intervals formed by two parts progressing in similar motion is a perfect fifth or octave—are likewise prohibited, but not so strictly. Many of these progressions are indeed quite harmless. They are, barring some exceptions, least objectionable when the upper of the two parts proceeds a degree upward or downward, and the lower takes a leap of a third, fourth, or fifth. The more or less of their innocuousness depends upon the closeness of the harmonic connection and the progression of the other parts. Much, moreover, is permissible in the middle parts which would incur censure in the extreme parts. These progressions are prohibited and called hidden because the ear fills up, as it were, the gap or gaps between the actual sounds, and hears fifths or octaves which otherwise are not obvious. For instance, if the actual sounds are as at (a), the ear hears as at (b).

Hiefhorn (hēf'hŏrn), *Ger.* Bugle-horn, hunting-horn.

Hief (hēf), *Ger.* } Sound given by
Hiefstoss (hēf'stōss), the bugle or hunting-horn.

Hierophon (hē'rō-fŏn), *Gr.* A singer of sacred music.

Higgaion selah (hĭg-gä'ŏn sä-läh), *Heb.* A term employed in ancient Hebrew music to indicate the use of stringed instruments with the trumpet.

High. Acute in pitch, speaking of sounds.

High bass. A voice between bass and tenor, a baritone.

Higher rhythm. A rhythmical form composed of several smaller ones.

High Mass. The Mass celebrated in the Roman Catholic churches by the singing of the choristers, distinguishing it from the low Mass in which the canticles are read without singing.

High soprano. The first soprano.

High tenor. Counter tenor voice; the highest male voice.

High treble clef. In old French music the G clef placed on the first line.

Himno (hĭm-nō), *Sp.* A hymn.

Hinaufstrich (hĭn-owf'strĭkh), *Ger.* } An upbow.
Hinstrich (hĭn'strĭkh),

Hirtenflöte (hĭr't'n-flö'tĕ), *Ger.* Shepherd's flute.

Hirtengedicht (hĭr't'n-gĕ-dĭkht'), *Ger.* Pastoral poem, idyl.

Hirtenlied (hĭr't'n-lēd), *Ger.* A pastoral song.

Hirtlich (hĭrt'lĭkh), *Ger.* Pastoral, rural.

Hirtenpfeife (hĭr't'n-pfī'fĕ), *Ger.* Rural pipe, pastoral pipe.

His (hĭs), *Ger.* The note B♯.

Hisis (hĭs'ĭs), *Ger.* B-double-sharp.

H-moll (hä'mŏl), *Ger.* The key of B minor.

Hoboe (hō'bō-ĕ), *Ger.* } Oboe, hautboy.
Hoboy (hō'boy),

Hoboen (hō'bō-ĕn), *Ger. pl.* Oboe, hautboys.

Hoboist (hō-bō-ĭst), *Ger.* Hautboy-player.

Hoch (hōkh), *Ger.* High.

Hochamt (hōkh'ämt), *Ger.* High Mass.

Hochfeierlich (hōkh-fī'ĕr-lĭkh), *Ger.* Exceedingly solemn.

Hochgesang (hōkh'gĕ-säng), *Ger.* Ode, hymn.

Hochhorn (hōkh'hŏrn), *Ger.* Hautboy.

Hochlied (hōkh'lēd), *Ger.* Ode, hymn.

Hochmuth (hōkh'moot), *Ger.* Haughtiness elevation, pride.

Höchsten (hökh-stĕn), *Ger.* Highest.

Hochzeitsgedicht (hōkh'tsĭts-gĕ-dĭkht'), *Ger.*
Hochzeitslied (hōkh'tsĭts-lēd),
Epithalamium; nuptial poems; wedding-song.

Hochzeitsmarsch (hōkh'-tsĭts-märsh), *Ger.* Wedding-march.

Hocket. A name formerly given to a rest; or, cutting short a note without accelerating the time. It corresponds to the term staccato. It is no longer used.

Hofcapelle (hōf-kä-pĕl'lĕ), *Ger.* Court chapel.

Hofconcert (hōf-kŏn-tsĕrt'), *Ger.* Court concert.

Hofdichter (hōf-dĭkh'tĕr), *Ger.* Poet laureate.

Hofkirche (hōf-kĭrkh'ĕ), *Ger.* Court church.

Höflich (hŏf'lĭkh),
Höflichkeit (hŏf'lĭkh-kīt), *Ger.* In a pleasing and graceful style.

Hofmusikant (hōf'moo-zĭ-künt'), *Ger.* Court musician.

Hoforganist (hōf-ŏr-gä-nĭst'), *Ger.* Court organist.

Höhe (hō'hĕ), *Ger.* Height, elevation, acuteness.

Hoheit (hō'hīt), *Ger.* Dignity, loftiness.

Hohelied (hō'hĕ-lēd), *Ger.* The Song of Solomon.

Hohen (hō'ĕn), *Ger.* High, upper.

Hohle und heisere Stimme (hō'le oond hī'zĕ-rĕ stĭm'mĕ), *Ger.* Hollow and hoarse voice.

Hohlflöte (hōl'flō-tĕ), *Ger.* Hollow-toned flute; an organ-stop producing a thick and powerful hollow tone. Each pipe has two holes in it, near the top and opposite each other.

Hohlquinte (hōl'kwĭn-tĕ), *Ger.* A quint stop of the hohl-flute species.

Hold (hōld), *Ger.* Pleasing, agreeable.

Hold. A character (𝄐) indicating that the time of a note or rest is to be prolonged.

Holding. The burden or chorus of a song. (Found in Shakespeare.)

holding-note. A note that is sustained or continued while the others are in motion.

Holzbläser (hŏlts'blä-zĕr), *Ger.* Players upon wood wind instruments.

Holzflöte (hŏlts'flö-tĕ), *Ger.* Wood flute; an organ-stop.

Homophone. A letter or character expressing a like sound with another.

Homophonie (hō-mō-fō-nē), *Fr.* Homophony.

Homophonoi suoni (hō-mō-fō'nō-ē soo-ō'nē), *It.* Unisons.

Homophonous. Of the same pitch, in unison.

Homophony. Unison; two or more voices singing in unison.

Hopswalzer (hŏps' wäl' tsĕr), *Ger.* Quick waltzes.

Horæ (hō'rä),
Horæ regulares (hō'rä rĕg-oo-lä'rĕs), *Lat.*
Hours; chants sung at prescribed hours in convents and monasteries.

Horizontal lines. Used in connection
Horizontal strokes. with the figured bass, they usually show the continuation of the same harmony, the bass note being unchanged, but they are sometimes used to abbreviate the expression of figures, in which case, if the bass part moves, the harmony must necessarily be changed.

Horn. A wind instrument chiefly used in hunting.

Horn, alpine. A narrow wooden tube, or trumpet, about eight feet long, widening to a bell at the larger end. Played by means of a cup-shaped mouthpiece. The tone is very penetrating, but it is very difficult to blow. It gives the natural harmonics of its own fundamental.

Horn, basset. An instrument resembling the clarinet, but of greater compass, embracing nearly four octaves.

Horn, bassetto. A species of clarinet a fifth lower than the C clarinet.

Hörner (hör'nĕr), *Ger. pl.* The horns.

Hörnerschall (hör'ner-shäll), *Ger.* Sound of horns.

Horn, French. A brass wind instrument consisting of a long, twisted tube terminating in a wide, outspreading bell. There are two kinds of horns: the natural horn, and the valve horn. The following natural harmonic series can be obtained by the modification of the position of the lips and the force of air blown into the tube:

The first of these notes is, however, not practicable, and the notes marked as crotchets are not in tune. By inserting the hand more or less far into the bell the natural (or open) notes may be more or less flattened, and thus all the other notes obtained, at least from F♯, below the first G, upward. But these stopped (or closed) notes are not so clear as the natural ones, especially those more than a semitone below the latter. The length of the tube, and, consequently, the key of the instrument, can be altered by crooks (*q. v.*). The notation for the horn is always in the key of C. Only the horn in C alto, however, sounds the notes as they are written, whereas the one in B♭ basso sounds them a major ninth lower, the one in C an octave lower, the one in D a minor seventh lower, the one in E♭ a major sixth lower, the one in E a minor sixth lower, the one in F a perfect fifth lower, the one in G a perfect fourth lower, the one in A a minor third lower, the one in B♭ alto a major second lower, etc. On the valve horn can be produced all the semitones, from the F♯ below the second C upward, as open notes. The horn with three valves comprises in fact seven natural horns. (*V. Valves.*) Music for the horn is noted in the G clef, with the exception, however, of the lowest notes, which are written in the F clef, and an octave lower than the rest.

Hornpipe. An old dance, in triple time, peculiar to the English nation. It is supposed to have received its name from the instrument played on during its performance. Modern hornpipes are usually in common time, and of a more lively character than the ancient hornpipe.

Hosanna (hō-zän'nä), *Lat.* Part of the Sanctus in a Mass.

Houl (howl), *Per.* A common drum of the Persian soldiery.

Hreol (wrä'ōl), *Dan.* A Danish peasant dance, similar to the reel.

H. S. Abbreviation for Hauptsatz.

Huchet (hü-shā), *Fr.* A huntsman's or postman's horn.

Huer (hwä), *Fr.* To shout.

Hüfthorn (hüft'hōrn), *Ger.* Bugle-horn.

Huggab (hoog-gäb), *Heb.* An organ of the Hebrews; Pan's pipes.

Huitain (hwē-tänh), *Fr.* A strnza of eight lines.

Huitpied (hwēt-pī-ā), *Fr.* Eight feet, of organ-stops.

Hülfslinien (hülfs'lē-nī-ĕn), *Ger.* Ledger lines.

Hülfsnote (hülfs'nō-tĕ), *Ger.* } Auxiliary note,
Hülfston (hülfs'tōn), } accessory note, a note standing one degree above, or below, the principal note.

Hülfsstimme (hülfs'stĭm'mĕ), *Ger.* Obligato voice.

Hummel (hoom'mĕl), } *Ger.* } A sort of
Hummelchen (hoom'mĕl-khĕn), } bagpipe; in organs the thorough bass drone.

Hummen (hoom'm'n), *Ger.* Humming, singing in a low voice.

Humor (hoo-mōr'), *Ger.* Caprice, humor, whim.

Humoreske (hoo'mō-rĕs'kĕ), *Ger.* A fancy piece, a humorous or whimsical piece.

Humorous songs. Songs full of mirth and humor.

Hunting-horn. A bugle, a horn used to cheer the hounds.

Hunting-song. A song written in praise of the chase.

Hurdygurdy. An old instrument consisting of four strings, which are acted upon by a wheel rubbed in resin powder, which serves as a bow. Two of the strings are affected by certain keys which stop them at different lengths and produce the tune, while the others act as a drone bass.

Hurtig (hoor'tĭg), *Ger.* Quick, swiftly; same meaning as allegro.

Hurtigkeit (hoor'tĭg-kīt), *Ger.* Swiftness, agility, quickness.

Hydraulicon (hī-draw'lĭ-kŏn), *Gr.* An ancient instrument whose tones were produced by the action of water.

Hydraulic organ. An organ whose motive power was water, and the invention of which is of much greater antiquity than the pneumatic, or wind, organ. It is supposed to have been invented by Ctesibius, a mathematician of Alexandria. It is not certainly known precisely what use water served in this instrument, but it is believed to have aided in preserving the wind, somewhat after the manner of water upon a plate upon which a vessel is inverted and the air exhausted. The water aids in preserving the vacuum.

Hymeneal (hī'mĕ'nĕ-ăl). } A marriage-song,
Hymenean (hī-mē'nē-ăn). } or appertaining thereto.

Hymn. A song of praise or adoration to the Deity; a short, religious lyric poem intended to be sung in church. Anciently, a song in honor of the gods or heroes.

Hymnal. } A compilation, or collection,
Hymn-book. } of hymns.

Hymne (ĕmn), *Fr.* } A hymn, sacred song,
Hymne (hĭm'nĕ), *Ger.* } an anthem.

Hymnologie (ĕmn-nōl-ō-jē), *Fr.* Hymnology.

Hymnologist. A writer, or composer, of hymns.

Hymnology. Information concerning hymns.

Hymns, theurgic. Songs of incantation; the first hymns of Greece.

Hymnus (hĭm'noos), *Lat.* A hymn.

Hymnus Ambrosianus (hĭm'noos äm-brō-zĭ-ä'uoos), *Lat.* The Ambrosian chant.

Hymn, Vesper. A hymn sung in the Vesper service of the Catholic Church.

Hypate, *Gr.* The first or most grave string in the lyre; the lowest of the Greek tetrachords.

Hypathoides. The lower sounds in the ancient Greek scale.

Hyper (hī'pĕr), *Gr.* Over, above. Applied to the names of intervals this word signifies "super," or "upper"; applied to the names of the Greek transposition scales and ecclesiastical octave species it signifies "a fourth higher"; applied to the Greek octave species it signifies "a fifth higher," or, when (with regard to the names of the notes and the succession of the intervals) comes to the same thing, "a fourth lower."

Hyperæolian (hī'pĕr-ē-ō'lĭ-ăn), *Gr.* (1) The authentic Æolian mode. (2) In the ancient Greek system the name of one of the transposition scales. (3) In the mediæval ecclesiastical system the octave species b c d e f g a b, the eleventh (sixth authentic) mode. (*V. Church modes.*)

Hyperdiapason (hī'pĕr-dī-ä-pä'son), *Gr.* The upper octave.

Hyperditonos (hī'pĕr-dī-tō'nŏs), *Gr.* The third above.

Hyperdorian (hī'pĕr-dō'rī-ăn), *Gr.* The authentic Dorian mode. In the ancient Greek system the name of the octave species b c d e f g a b, also called Mixolydian, and of one of the transposition scales.

Hyperionian (hī'pĕr-ē-ō'nī-ăn), *Gr.* The authentic Ionian mode.

Hyperlydian (hī'pĕr-lī-dī-ăn), *Gr.* The authentic Lydian mode. The name of the octave species g a b c d e f g, and of one of the transposition scales.

Hypermixolydian (hī'pĕr-mĭx'ō-lĭd'ī-ăn), *Gr.* The authentic Mixolydian mode.

Hyperphrygian (hī'pĕr-frĭj'ī-ăn), *Gr.* (1) The authentic Phrygian mode. (2) In the ancient Greek system the name of the octave species a b c d e f g a, also called Locrian, and of one of the transposition scales. (3) In the mediæval ecclesiastical system the name of the octave species f g a b c d e f, the twelfth (sixth plagal) mode. (*V. Church modes.*)

Hypo. Below, under. Applied to intervals this word signifies "sub," or "lower"; applied to the names of the Greek transposition scales and ecclesiastical octave species it signifies "a fourth below"; applied to the names of the Greek octave species it signifies "a fifth below," or, what (with regard to the names of the notes and the succession of the intervals) comes to the same thing, "a fourth above."

Hypoæolian (hī'pō ē ō'lī-ăn), *Gr.* (1) The plagal Æolian mode. (2) In the ancient Greek system the name of one of the transposition scales. (3) In the mediæval ecclesiastical system the name of the octave species e f g a b c d e, the tenth (fifth plagal) mode.

Hypocritic (hĭp-ō-krĭt'ĭc), *Gr.* An epithet applied by the ancients to the art of gesticulation, which was prominent in their public vocal performances.

Hypocritic music. Among the ancient Greeks all music intended for the stage or theater; in modern times all music adapted to pantomimic representation.

Hypodiapason (hī'pō-dē-ä-pä-sŏn), *Gr.* The lower octave.

Hypodiapente (hī'pō-dī-ă-pĕn'tĕ), *Gr.* The fifth below.

Hypoditonos (hī'pō-dē-tō'nŏs), *Gr.* The third below.

Hypodorian (hī'pō-dō'rī-ăn), *Gr.* (1) The plagal Dorian mode. (2) In the ancient Greek system the name of the octave species a b c d e f g a, also called Æolian, and of one of the transposition scales. (3) In the mediæval ecclesiastical system the octave species a b c d e f g a, the second (first plagal) mode.

Hypoionian (hī'pō-ē-ō'nī-ăn), *Gr.* (1) The plagal Ionian mode. (2) In the ancient Greek system the name of one of the transposition scales. (3) In the mediæval ecclesiastical system the name of the octave species g a b c d e f g, the fourteenth (seventh plagal) mode. (*V. Church modes.*)

Hypolydian (hī'pō-lĭd'ī-ăn), *Gr.* (1) The plagal Lydian mode. (2) In the ancient Greek system the name of the octave species f g a b c d e f, also called Syntonolydian, and of one of the transposition scales. (3) In the mediæval ecclesiastical system the name of the octave species c d e f g a b c, the sixth (third plagal) mode.

Hypomixolydian (hī'pō-mĭx'ō-lĭd'ī-ăn), *Gr.* (1) The plagal Mixolydian mode. (2) In the mediæval ecclesiastical system the name of the octave species d e f g a b c d, the eighth (fourth plagal) mode.

Hypophrygian (hī'pō-frĭj'ī-ăn), *Gr.* (1) The plagal Phrygian mode. (2) In the ancient Greek system the name of the octave species g a b c d e f g, also called Ionian, and of one of the transposition scales. (3) In the mediæval ecclesiastical system the name of the octave species b c d e f g a b, the fourth (second plagal) mode.

Hypoproslambanomenos, *Gr.* The note below the Proslambanomenos—namely, G.

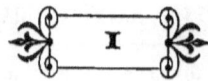

Iambe (ĕ-änh-būh), *Fr.* Iambus.
Iambic, ⎫ A poetical and musical foot, consisting of one short, unaccented, and one long, accented, note or syllable.
Iambus. ⎭
Iambics. Certain songs, or satires, which are supposed to have been the precursors of the ancient comedy; they were of two kinds, one for singing and one for recitation, accompanied by instruments.
Iastian (ē-ăs'tĭ-ăn), *Gr.* One of the ancient Greek modes. The Ionian.
Ictus (ĭk'tŭs), *Gr.* A stroke of the foot, marking the point of emphasis in music.
Idillio (ē-dēl'lĭ-ō), *It.* An idyl.
Idyl. A short poem in pastoral style; an eclogue.
Idylle (ē-dĭll'), *Fr.* ⎫ An idyl.
Idylle (ĭ-dĭl'lĕ), *Ger.* ⎭
Il (ēl), *It.* The.
Ilarita (ē-lä-rī-tä'), *It.* Hilarity, cheerfulness, mirth.
Il piu (ēl pē'oo), *It.* The most.
Il piu forte possibile (ēl pē'oo fōr'tĕ pŏs-sē'-bĭ-lĕ), *It.* As loud as possible.
Il piu piano possibile (ēl pē'oo pē-ä'nō pŏs-sē'bĭ-lĕ), *It.* As soft as possible.
Im (ĭm), *Ger.* In the.
Imboccatura (ĕm-bŏk-kä-too'rä), *It.* Mouthpiece, embouchure.
Imbroglio (ĕm-brŏl'yō), *It.* Confusion, want of distinct ideas.
Imitando (ĭm-ĭ-tän'dō), *It.* Imitating.
Imitando la voce (ĭm-ĭ-tän'dō lä vō'tshĕ), *It.* Imitating the inflections of the voice.
Imitatio (ĭm-ĭ-tä'tsĭ-ō), *Lat.* Imitation, in counterpoint.
Imitation. The more or less exact repetition of a musical figure in another voice. (See also *Canon.*) Imitation is strict when the melodic intervals and resulting harmonies are exactly imitated; free when not even the melody and rhythm are exactly repeated. (See also subordinate titles below.) A sequence is an imitation, but in the same voice.
Imitation, augmented. A style of imitation in which the answer is given in notes of greater value than those of the subject.
Imitation, diminished. A style of imitation in which the answer is given in notes of less value than those of the subject.
Imitation, freely inverted. Where the order of successive notes is not strictly retained.

Imitation, in contrary motion. That in which the answers invert the subject so that the rising intervals descend, and the falling intervals ascend.
Imitation, in different divisions. That in which the subject is answered in a different division of the bar; for instance, the subject beginning on the accented division is answered on the unaccented.
Imitation, in similar motion. Where the answer retains the same order of notes as the subject.
Imitation, retrograde. A form of imitation in which the subject is commenced backwards in the answer.
Imitation, reversed retrograde. A form of imitation in which the subject is commenced backwards in the answer, and in contrary motion.
Imitation, simple. A simple imitation.
Imitation, strictly inverted. That form of imitation in which half and whole tones must be precisely answered in contrary motion.
Imitative music. Music written to imitate some of the operations of nature, art, or human passion, as the firing of cannon, the rolling of thunder; love, joy, grief, etc.
Imitato (ĭm-ĭ-tä'tō), *It.* Imitation.
Imitazione (ĭm-ĭ-tä-tsĭ-ō'nĕ), *It.* Imitation, referring to counterpoint.
Immer (ĭm'mĕr), *Ger.* Always, ever.
Imparfait (änh-pär-fä'ĭ, *Fr.* Imperfect.
Impaziente (ĭm-pä-tsĭ-ĕn'tĕ), *It.* Impatient, hurried.
Impazientemente (ĭm-pä-tsĭ-ĕn-tĕ-mĕn'tĕ), *It.* Impatiently, hurriedly.
Imperfect. Not perfect; less than perfect, in speaking of intervals and chords.
Imperfect cadence. A cadence which ends on a triad of the dominant; the preceding chord may be either that of the tonic or subdominant or in minor keys the sixth of the scale: the triad of the dominant always being major.
Imperfect close. Imperfect cadence.
Imperfect concords. Thirds and sixths are called imperfect concords because they are liable to change from major to minor, or the contrary, still remaining consonant.
Imperfect consonances. The major and minor third and the major and minor sixth.
Imperfect intervals. A defective name for diminished intervals.

ä *arm*, ă *add*, ā *ale*, ĕ *end*, ē *eve*, ĭ *ill*, ī *isle*, ō *old*, ŏ *odd*, oo *moon*, ŭ *but*, ü *Fr. sound*, kh *Ger. ch*, nh *nasal*.

Imperfect measure. An old term for twofold measure.

Imperfect time. A term by which the ancients designated common time, indicated by the letter C or a semicircle.

Imperfect triad. The chord of the third, fifth, and eighth, taken on the seventh of the key, consisting of two minor thirds.

Imperfetto (ĭm-pĕr-fĕt'to), *It.* Imperfect.

Imperiosamente (Im-pā-rĭ-ō-zä-mĕn'tĕ), *It.* Imperiously, pompously.

Imperioso (Im-pā-rĭ-ō'zō), *It.* Imperious, pompous.

Imperturbabile (im-pĕr-toor-bä'bĭ-lĕ), *It.* Quietly, easily.

Impeto (ĭm'pĕ-tō), *It.* Impetuosity, vehemence.

Impeto doloroso (ĭm'pĕ-to dō-lō-rō'zō), *It.* Pathetic force and energy.

Impetuosamente (Im-pā-too-ō-zä-mĕn'tĕ), *It.* Impetuously.

Impetuosita (Im-pā-too-ō-zĭ-tä'), *It.* Impetuosity, vehemence.

Impetuoso (Im-pā-too-ō'zō), *It.* Impetuous, vehement.

Imponente (Im-pō-nĕn'tĕ), *It.* Imposingly; haughtily.

Impresario (Im-prĕ-sä'rĭ-ō), *It.* A term applied by the Italians to the manager or conductor of operas or concerts.

Impromptu (ănh-prōmp'too), *Fr.* An extemporaneous production.

Improvisare (Im-prō-vĭ-zä'rĕ), *It.* To compose, or sing, extemporaneously.

Improvisateur (ănh-prō-vĭ-zä-tŭr), *Fr.* } See
Improvisator (Im-prō-fĭ-zä'tŏr), *Ger.* } *Improvvisatore.*

Improvisation. The act of singing, playing, or composing music without previous preparation; extemporaneous performance.

Improvisatrice (ănh-prō-vĭ-zä-trĕss), *Fr.* A female who plays or sings extemporaneously.

Improvise. To sing or play without premeditation.

Improvisé (ănh-prō-vĭ-zā), *Fr.* Extemporaneous.

Improviser (ănh-prō-vĭ-zā'), *Fr.* To improvise.

Improvvisamente (Im-prō-vĭ-zä-mĕn'tĕ), *It.* Extemporaneously.

Improvvisare (Im-prō-vĭ-zä'rĕ), *It.* To improvise.

Improvvisata (Im-prō-vĭ-zä'tä), *It.* An extempore composition.

Improvvisatore (Im-prō-vĭs-sä-tō-re), *It.* One who sings or declaims in verse extemporaneously.

Improvviso (Im-prōv-vĭ-zō), *It.* Extemporaneous.

In (ĕn), *It. and Lat.* In, into, in the.

Inbrunst (ĭn-broonst), *Ger.* Fervor, ardor, warmth of passion.

Inbrünstig (ĭn'brüns-tĭg), *Ger.* Ardent, fervent, passionate.

Incalzando (In-käl-tzän'dō), *It.* Spurring on, hastening.

Incantation. Enchantment; a form of words pronounced or sung in connection with certain ceremonies, for the purpose of enchantment.

Incantazione (In-kän-tä-tsĭ-ō'nĕ), *It.* Songs of incantation.

Incarnatus (In-kär-nä'toos), *Lat.* "Was born of the Virgin Mary.". Part of the Credo in the Mass.

Inconsolato (in-kōn-sō-lä'tō), *It.* In a mournful style.

Incordare (In-kōr-dä'rĕ), *It.* To string an instrument.

Incrociamento (In-krō-tshä-mĕn'tō), *It.* Crossing.

Indeciso (ĭn-dĕ-tshĕ'zō), *It.* Undecided, wavering, hesitating; slight changes of time and a somewhat capricious value of the notes.

Indegnatamente (ĭn-dän-yä-tä-mĕn'tĕ), *It.* }
Indegnato (In-dän-yä'to), Angrily, furiously, passionately.

Index. A direct ∿; also the forefinger.

Indications sceniques (ănh-dĕ-kä'sĭ-ouh sä-nĕk'), *Fr.* Stage directions.

Indifferente (In-dĕf-fĕ-rĕn'tĕ), }
Indifferentemente (In-dĕf-fĕ-rĕn-tĕ-mĕn'tĕ), }
It. Coldly, with indifference.

Indifferenza (In-dĕf-fĕ-rĕn'tsä), *It.* Indifference.

In disparte (In dĕs-pär'tĕ), *It.* A term used in operatic music, signifying that the part is to be addressed to someone aside or not taking part in the performance.

In distanza (In dĕs-tän'tsä), *It.* A distance.

Infantile (ĭn-fän-tē'lĕ), *It.* Childlike, infantine; the thin quality of tone in the upper notes of some female voices.

Infernale (In-fĕr-nä'lĕ), *It.* Infernal, diabolic.

Infervorato (In-fĕr-vō-rä'tō), *It.* Fervent, impassioned.

Infiammatamente (In-fē-äm-mä-tä-mĕn'tĕ), *It.* Ardently, impetuously.

Infinite canon. An epithet given to those canons which are so constructed that the end leads to the beginning, and the performance may be indefinitely repeated; also called circular, or endless, canon.

Infinito (In-fĭ-nē'to), *It.* Perpetual.

Inflatile. An epithet applied to wind instruments, as a hautboy or flute.

Inflection. Any change or modification in the pitch or tone of the voice.

Infra (In'frä), *Lat.* Beneath.

In fretta (In frĕt-tä), *It.* In haste, hastily.

ärm, ă add, ä ale, ē end, ĕ eve, ī ill, ĭ isle, ō old, ŏ odd, oo moon, ŭ but, ü Fr. sound, kh Ger. ch, nh nasal.

Infuriante (ĭu-foo-rĭ-än'tĕ), *It.* } Furious, rag-
Infuriato (ĭu-foo-rĭ ä'tŏ),   ing.

Inganni (ĭn-gän'nĕ), *It. pl.* See *Inganno*.

Inganno (ĭu-gän'nŏ), *It.* A deception; applied to a deceptive, or interrupted, cadence; also to any unusual resolution of a discord, or an unexpected modulation.

Inhalt (ĭn'hält), *Ger.* Contents.

Inharmoniously. Discordantly.

In lontananza (ĭu lŏn-tä-nänt'zä), *It.* In the distance.

Inner parts. The alto and tenor, as distinguished from outer parts, the bass and soprano.

Inner pedal. A sustained or holding note in an inner part.

Inni (ĭu-nĕ), *It. pl.* Hymns.

Innig (ĭn-nĭg), *Ger.* Sincere, cordial.

Inno (ĭn-nŏ), *It.* A hymn, canticle, ode.

Innocente (ĭn-nŏ-tshĕn'tĕ), *It.* }
Innocentemente (ĭn-nŏ-tshĕn-tĕ-mĕn'tĕ),
Innocently, in an artless and simple style.

Innocenza (ĭn-nŏ-tshĕn-tsä), *It.* Innocence.

In partito (ĭn pär-tē'tŏ), *It.* In score.

Inquieto (ĭn-quĭ-ā'tŏ), *It.* Restless, uneasy, agitated.

Insensibile (ĭn-sĕn-sē'bĭ-lĕ), *It.* }
Insensibilmente (ĭn-sĕn-sĭ-bĭl-mĕn'tĕ),
Insensibly, by small degrees, by little and little.

Inständig (ĭn-stän'dĭg), *Ger.* Urgent, pressing.

Instante (ĭn-stän'tä), *It.* Urgent, pressing.

Instantemente (ĭn-stän-tĕ-mĕn'tĕ), *It.* Vehemently, urgently.

Instrument. A musical instrument is any sonorous body artificially constructed for the production of musical sounds.

Instrument à cordes (änh-strü-mänh ä kŏrd), *Fr.* A stringed instrument.

Instrumental. A term applied to music composed for or performed on instruments.

Instrument a l'archet (änh-strü-mänh ä lär-kä), *Fr.* Instrument played with a bow.

Instrumentale (ĭn-stroo-mĕn-tä'lĕ), *It.* Instrumental.

Instrumentalist. One who plays on an instrument.

Instrumental 'score. A score in which the instrumental parts are given in full.

Instrument à percussion (änh-strü-mänh ä pär-koos-sē-ŏn), *Fr.* Instruments of percussion.

Instrumentare (ĭn-stroo-mĕn-tä'rĕ), *It.* To compose instrumental music.

Instrumentation. The act of writing for an orchestra, with a practical knowledge of each instrument, and of the distribution of harmony among the different instruments.

Instrument à vent (änh-strü-mänh ä vänh), *Fr.* A wind instrument.

Instrumentazione (ĭn-stroo-mĕn-tä-tsĭ-ŏ'nĕ), *It.* Instrumentation.

Instrumentenmacher (ĭn - stroo - mĕnt' ĕn mäkh'ĕr), *Ger.* An instrument-maker.

Instrumentiren (ĭn-stroo-mĕn-tē'r'n),
Instrumentirung (ĭn-stroo-mĕn-tē'roong), *Ger.* Instrumentation.

Instrumento (ĭn-stroo-mŏn'to), *It.* An instrument.

Instrumento da arco (ĭn-stroo-mĕn'tŏ dä är kŏ), *It.* A stringed instrument.

Instruments, bow. All instruments whose tones are produced by means of a bow.

Instruments, brass. Wind instruments formed of brass and used chiefly for military purposes.

Instruments, inflatile. Wind instruments.

Instruments, keyed. All instruments the sounds of which are produced by the pressure of the fingers upon the keys.

Instruments,mechanical. Instruments which produce tunes by the means of some mechanical contrivance, as crank, springs weights, etc.

Instruments, percussive. } Instruments
Instruments, pulsatile.   whose sound are produced by being struck.

Instruments, pneumatic. Instruments, the tones of which are produced by the action of the wind.

Instruments, reed. Instruments whose tone are produced by the action of air upon reed of metal or wood.

Instruments, stringed. Instruments whose tones are produced by striking or drawing strings or the friction of a bow.

Instruments, tensile. A general name for all instruments dependent upon the tension of strings for their tone.

Instrument vent (änh-strü-mänh vänh), *Fr* A wind instrument.

Intavolare (ĭn-tä-vŏ-lä'rĕ), *It.* To write notes to copy music.

Intavolatura (ĭn-tä-vŏ-lä-too'rä), *It.* Musical notation.

In tempo (ĭn tĕm'pŏ), *It.* In time.

In tempore justo (ĭn tĕm'pō-rĕ yoos-tŏ), *Lat.* direction to sing or play in equal, just, an exact time.

Intendant (änh-tänh-dänh), *Fr.* } Director,
Intendente (ĭn-tĕn-dĕn'tĕ), *It.*   conductor
See *Impresario*.

Interlude. A short musical representation introduced between the acts of any drama or between the play and afterpiece; an intermediate strain or movement played between the verses of a hymn.

Interludium (ĭn-tĕr-loo'dĭ-oom), *Lat.* }
Intermede (änh-tĕr-mād'), *Fr.*
Intermedio (ĭn-tĕr-mā'dĭ-ŏ), *It.*
Intermezzo (ĭn-tĕr-mĕt'sŏ), *It.*
An interlude; intermediate, placed between two others; detached pieces introduced between the acts of an opera.

ä *arm*, ă *add*, ā *ale*, ĕ *end*, ē *eve*, ĭ *ill*, ī *isle*, ō *old*, ŏ *odd*, oo *moon*, ŭ *but*, ü *Fr. sound*, kh *Ger. ch.* nh *nasal*

Intermediate. A term applied to those flats and sharps which do not form any part of the original key of a composition, and which are also called accidentals.

Intermedietto (In-tĕr-mä-dĭ-ĕt'tö), *It.* A short interlude, or intermezzo.

Intermezzi (In-tĕr-mĕt'tsĕ), *It. pl.* Interludes, detached pieces or dances.

Interrotto (In-tĕr-rŏt'tö), *It.* Interrupted, broken, speaking of cadence, accent, or rhythm.

Interrupted cadence. A cadence in which the triad of the dominant is followed by some chord which changes the progression of the harmony.

Interruzione (In-tĕr-root-sĭ-ō'nĕ), *It.* Interruption.

Interval. The distance, or difference, of pitch between tones. Intervals are reckoned by the degrees of the scale included, counting the tone of beginning and that of ending. Intervals are represented upon the staff according to their essential nature, an augmented fourth, for instance, arising and resolving differently from a diminished fifth, which would be commensurate with it. Intervals are always reckoned upwards from a given tone, unless the contrary is expressly stated.

Interval, augmented. An interval which is a chromatic semitone, or half-step, greater than a major or perfect interval.

Interval, diminished. An interval less than a perfect interval by a chromatic half-step or semitone.

Intervall (In-tĕr-väll'), *Ger.* }
Intervalle (änh-tĕr-väll'), *Fr.* } An interval.
Intervallo (In-tĕr-väl'lō), *It.* }
Intervallum (In-tĕr-väl'loom), *Lat.* }

Intervalle (In-tĕr-väl'lĕ), *Ger. pl.* Intervals.

Intervalli vietati (In-tĕr-väl-lē vē-ä-tä'tī), *It.pl.* Forbidden intervals.

Intervals, consecutive. Intervals passing in the same direction in two parallel parts.

Intervening subject. An intermediate subject of a fugue.

Intimissimo (In-tĭ-mĕs'sĭ-mō), *It.* Very expressive, with great feeling.

Intimo (In'tĭ-mō), *It.* Inward feeling, expressive.

Intonare (In-tō-nä'rĕ), } *It.* } To pitch the
Intuonare (In-too-ō-nä'rĕ), } voice, to sound the keynote, to begin.

Intonation. (1) The act and art of producing sound from the voice or an instrument, both as regards quality and pitch. (2) A voice's or instrument's capacity of yielding sound. (3) The initial phrase sung alone by the officiating priest or leading chorister of the antiphon and other portions of the divine service in Roman Catholic churches. (4) The opening notes, those before the reciting note, of the Gregorian chant.

Intonation, false. A variation in pitch from what is understood to be the true tone.

Intonato (In-tō-nä'-tō), *It.* Tuned, set to music.

Intonatura (In-tō-nä-too'rä), } *It.* } Intona-
Intonazione (In-tō-nä-tsĭ-ō'nĕ), } tion.

Intoniren (In-tō-nī'r'n), *Ger.* To intone, to sound.

Intrada (In-trä'dä), *It.* } A short prelude or
Intrade (In-trä'dĕ), *Ger.* } introductory movement.

Intrepidamente (In-trĕ-pĭ-dä-mĕn'tĕ), *It.* Boldly, with intrepidity.

Intrepidezza (In-trĕ-pĭ-dĕt'sä), *It.* Intrepidity, boldness.

Intrepido (In-trä'pĭ-dō), *It.* Intrepid, bold.

In triplo (In trĕp'lō), *It.* An old term, signifying a composition in three parts.

Introduction. That movement in a composition, the design of which is to prepare the ear for the movements which are to follow.

Introduzione (In-trō-doo-tsĭ-ō'nĕ), *It.* An introduction.

Introduzione marziale (In-trō-doo-tsĭ-ō'nĕ mär-tsĭ-ä-lĕ), *It.* An introduction in martial style.

Introit (In-trō'It), *Eng.* } Entrance; a
Introit (änh-trwä), *Fr.* } hymn, or an-
Introito (In-trō-ē'tō), *It.* } them, sung
Introito (In-trō-ē'tō), *Sp.* } while the
Introitus (In-trō'ĭ-toos), *Lat.* } priest enters within the rails at the communion-table; also the commencement of the Mass.

Inventio (In-vĕn'tsĭ-ō), *Lat.* A name sometimes given to a tricinium.

Invention (änh-vänh-sĭ-ōnh), *Fr.* An old name for a species of prelude or short fantasia.

Invenzione (In-vĕn-tsĭ-ō'nĕ), *It.* Invention, contrivance.

Inversio (In-vär'sĭ-ō), *Lat.* Inversion; see that word.

Inversio cancrizans (In-vär'sĭ-ō kän krĭ-zäns'), *Lat.* Retrograde, or crab-like inversion, or imitation; because it goes backwards.

Inversio in octavam acutam (In-vär'sĭō In ŏc-tä-väm ä-koo'täm), *Lat.* Inversion in the octave above, the transposition of the lower part an octave above.

Inversio in octavam gravem (In-vär'sĭ-ō In ŏk-tä-väm grä'vĕm), *Lat.* Inversion in the octave below; the transposition of the upper part an octave below to form the bass, while the other part remains stationary.

Inversion. (1) An interval is inverted by transposing the lower of two notes an octave higher or the upper an octave lower. (2) A chord is inverted by placing the third, fifth, seventh, or ninth in the bass instead of the fundamental note. (3) A subject is inverted when its motion is contrary to that of the original, when the notes that before ascended descend, and the notes

Inversion. (4) In double counterpoint inversion is the placing of an upper part under a lower part, or a lower part above a higher one, by transposing them an octave, tenth, or other interval higher or lower.

Inversion, retrograde. An inversion made by commencing on the last note of the subject and writing it backwards to the first note.

Invert. To change the position either in a subject or chord.

Inverted. Changed in position.

Inverted chord. A chord whose fundamental tone is not its lowest.

Inverted turn. A turn which commences with the lowest note instead of the highest.

Invitatorio (In-vī-tä-tō'rī-ō), *Sp.* Psalm or anthem sung at the beginning of the matins.

Invitatorium (In-vī-tä-tō'rī-oom), *Lat.* A verse sung in the Roman Catholic Church at the beginning of matins, alternately with two verses of the 94th Psalm. The concluding words are generally "Venite adoremus."

Invitatory. A part of the service sung in the Roman Catholic Church; a psalm or anthem sung in the morning.

Ionian (I-ō'nĭ-ăn), *Gr.* (1) In the ancient
Ionic (I-ŏn'ĭk), Greek system, the name of the octave species (in later times called Hypophrygian) g a b c d e f g, and of one of the transposition scales. (*V. Iastian.*) (2) In the mediæval ecclesiastical system, the name of the octave species c d e f g a b c, the thirteenth (seventh authentic) mode. (*V. Church modes.*)

Ionic music. A light, airy style of music.

Ira (ē'rä), *It.* Anger, wrath.

Irata (ē-rä'tä), } Angrily,
Irato (ē-rä'tō),   *It.* } passion-
Iratamente (ē-rä-tä-měn-tě), } ately.

Irish harp. An instrument having more strings than the lyre, yet for a long time only used for playing a simple melody or a single part. Also the music-trade name for the toy instrument known as "jew's-harp."

Irish tunes. Tunes peculiar to the Hibernians, generally of a sweet, mellow character.

Irlandais (ēr-länh-dā'), *Fr.* } An air or dance
Irländisch (ēr'län-dĭsh), *Ger.* } tune in the Irish style.

Ironicamente (ō-rō-nĭ-kä-měn'tě), *It.* Ironically.

Ironico (ē-rō'nĭ-kō), *It.* Ironical.

Irregular cadence. An imperfect cadence.

Irregolare (ēr-rä-gō-lä'rě), *It.* Irregular.

Irresoluto (ēr-rä-zō-loo'tō), *It.* Irresolute, wavering.

Isdegno, con (ēs-dān'yō kōn), *It.* With indignation.

Ismania, con (ēs-mä'nĭ-ä kōn), *It.* With wildness, with madness.

Isochronal, *Gr.* } Uniform in time; per-
Isochronous. } formed in equal time.

Isotonic system. A system of music consisting of intervals in which each concord is tempered alike, and in which there are twelve equal semitones.

Istesso (ĕs-těs'sō), *It.* The same.

Istesso tempo (ĕs-těs'sō těm'pō), *It.* The same time.

Istrepito, con (ēs-trä-pě'tō kōn), *It.* With noise and bluster.

Istrionica (ēs-trī-ō'nĭ-kä), *It.* Histrionic; the theatrical art.

Istrumentale (ēs-troo-měn-tä'lě), *It.* Instrumental.

Istrumentazione (ēs-troo-měn-tä-tsī-ō'ně), *It.* Instrumentation.

Istrumento (ēs-troo-měn'tō), *It.* An instrument.

Italian mordent. A short shake, or trill, consisting of the alternation of a tone with the next tone above it.

Italiano (ō-tä-lī-ä'nō), *It.* }
Italienisch (ē-tä-lĭ-ā'nĭsh), *Ger.* } Italian.
Italienne (ē-tä-lĭ ěnu), *Fr.* }

Italian sixth. A name sometimes given to a chord composed of a major third and an augmented sixth.

Ite missa est (ē'tä 'mĭs-sä ĕst), *Lat.* The termination of the Mass: sung by the priest to Gregorian music.

I trovatori (ē trō-vä-tō'rē), *It.* The troubadours.

ä *arm*, ă *add*, ā *ale*, ĕ *end*, ē *eve*, ĭ *ill*, ī *isle*, ō *old*, ŏ *odd*, oo *moon*, ŭ *but*, ü *Fr. sound*, kh *Ger. ch*. nh *nasal*.

J

Jack. (1) In the harpsichord the upright slip of wood on the back end of the key-lever to which is attached a crow-quill or piece of hard leather, projecting at right angles. The quill or piece of leather serves as a plectrum with which the corresponding string is plucked. (2) A part of the action of the pianoforte, the escapement-lever, which is also called "hopper."

Jaegerchor (yā'ghĕr-kōr), *Ger.* Hunting chorus.

Jagdhorn (yägd'hōrn), *Ger.* } Hunting-horn,
Jagdzink (yägd'tsĭnk), } bugle-horn.

Jagdruf (yägd'roof), *Ger.* Sound of the bugle or hunting-horn.

Jagdsinfonie (yägd'sĭn-fō-nē'), *Ger.* Hunting symphony.

Jagdstück (yägd'stük), *Ger.* A hunting-piece.

Jägerchor (yā'ghĕr-kōr), *Ger.* See *Jaegerchor*.

Jägerhorn (yā'ghĕr-hōrn), *Ger.* Hunting-horn, bugle-horn.

Jailtage (yăl-tāj). The only musical instrument of Tartary, consisting of a box of fir about four feet long and three inches wide, the upp. r part of which is open, over which six wire strings are stretched. It is played on with both hands, but chiefly with the left, and produces both treble and bass.

Jaleo (hä-lā'ō), *Sp.* A national Spanish dance.

Jambico (ĕ-äm'bĭ-kō), } *It.* } An iambic.
Jambo (ĕ-äm'bō),

Jangle. To sound discordantly or inharmoniously.

Janitscharenmusik (yä-nĭt-shä'r'n-moo-zĭk'), *Ger.* The music introduced into Europe by the Janizaries; military music, consisting of wind instruments and instruments of percussion, such as drums, cymbals, triangles, etc.

Jargon. The union of several discordant notes.

Jauchzend (yowkh'tsĕnd), *Ger.* Shouting, joyful.

Jeu (zhŭh), *Fr.* Play; the style of playing on an instrument; also a register in an organ or harmonium.

Jeu céleste (zhŭh sā-lĕst), *Fr.* The name of a soft stop in a harmonium; also an organ-stop of French invention, formed of two dulciana pipes, the pitch of one being slightly raised, giving to the tone a waving, undulating character.

Jeu d'anche (zhŭh d'änsh), *Fr.* A reed-stop in an organ.

Jeu d'anges (zhŭh d'änzh), *Fr.* Soft stops.

Jeu d'échos (zhŭh d'ā-kō), *Fr.* Echo stop.

Jeu de flutes (zhŭh dŭh floot), *Fr.* Flute stop.

Jeu d'orgues (shŭh d'ōrg), *Fr.* Register, or row of pipes, in an organ.

Jeux (zhŭh), *Fr. pl.* Stops, or registers, in an organ or harmonium.

Jeux forts (zhŭh fōr), *Fr.* Loud stops; forte stops.

Jew's-harp. A small instrument of brass or steel, and shaped somewhat like a lyre; when played it is placed between the teeth and struck with the forefinger. Known in the music trade as "Irish harp."

Jewstrump. A term applied by old writers to the jew's-harp.

Jig. A light, brisk movement; an old species of dance in 6-8 or 12-8 time; the name is supposed to have been derived from *Gieig*, a fiddle.

Jingles. Loose pieces of metal placed around a tambourine to increase the sound.

Jodeln (yō'd'ln), *Ger.* A style of singing peculiar to the Tyrolese peasants, the natural voice and the falsetto being used alternately.

Joie (zhwä), *Fr.* Joy, gladness.

Jongleurs (zhŏnh-gloor), } *Fr. pl.* } Thus were
Jonglours (zhŏnh-glūr), } called in the time of the troubadours and trouvères the professional minstrels and players on instruments who either were in the service of the former or traveled about the country independently. Their performances were not confined to singing, playing, and recitation, but comprised — especially in later times — legerdemain, tumbling, rope-dancing, etc.

Jota (hō'tä), *Sp.* A Spanish national dance.

Jouer (zhoo-ā), *Fr.* To play upon an instrument.

Jovialisch (yō-fĭ-ä'lĭsh), *Ger.* Jovial, joyous, merry.

Jubelflöte (yoo'b'l-flō'tĕ), *Ger.* An organ-stop of the flute species.

Jubelgesang (yoo'b'l-ghĕ-zäng), } *Ger.* } Song of
Jubellied (yoo'b'l-lēd), } jubilee.

Jubeind (yoo'belnd), *Ger.* Rejoicing.

Jubilant. Joyful, triumphant.

Jubilee. A season of great public joy and festivity. Among the Jews every fiftieth year was a jubilee.

Jubiloso (yoo'bĭ-lō'zō), *It.* Jubilant, exulting.

Just. A term applied to all consonant intervals, and to those voices, strings, and pipes that give them with exactness.

Juste (zhüst), *Fr.* Accurate in time, tone, harmony, and execution.

Justesse (zhüs-tăss'), *Fr.* Exactness, correctness, or purity, of intonation.

ă arm, ă add, ā ale, ĕ end, ē eve, ĭ ill, ī isle, ŏ old, ŏ odd, oo moon, ŭ but, ü Fr.sound, kh Ger. ch, nh nasal.

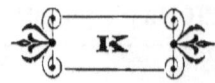

Kabaro (kä-bä′rō). A small drum used in Egypt and Abyssinia.

Kalamaika (kăl-ä-mä′kä). A lively Hungarian dance in 2-4 time, full of animation and passion.

Kammer (käm′mĕr), *Ger.* Chamber.

Kammercantate (käm′mĕr-kän-tä′tĕ), *Ger.* Chamber cantata.

Kammercompònist (käm′mĕr-kōm-pō-nĭst), *Ger.* "Chamber composer." A composer who has to furnish compositions required for the private concerts of a prince.

Kammerconcert (käm′mĕr-kōn-tsĕrt), *Ger.* Chamber concert.

Kammerduet (käm′mĕr-doo-ĕt′), *Ger.* Chamber duet. A duet for chamber performance.

Kammermusic (käm′mĕr-moo-zĭk′), *Ger.* Chamber music; music for private performance.

Kammermusikus (käm′mĕr-moo′zĭ-koos), *Ger.* Chamber musician; member of a prince's private band.

Kammersängerin (käm′mĕr-säng-ĕr-ĭn), *Ger.* Private singer to a prince or king.

Kammerspiel (käm′mĕr-spĕl), *Ger.* See *Kammermusik*.

Kammerstyl (käm′mĕr-stĕl), *Ger.* Style of chamber music, as opposed to the ecclesiastical and theatrical styles.

Kammerton (käm′mĕr-tōn), *Ger.* The pitch, or lower tuning of the instruments in chamber music, opposed to the higher tuning of the organ in church music.

Kammervirtuose (käm′mĕr-fīr-too-ō′zĕ), *Ger.* A chamber virtuoso. A virtuoso in the service of a prince.

Kampoul (käm-pool). A gong of small dimensions used by the Malays.

Kandele (kän-dā′lĕ). Ancient minstrel's harp, of the Finns.

Kanon (kä′nōn), *Ger.* A rule. (1) An instrument formerly employed for measuring intervals; it was a monochord with a movable bridge. Sometimes it had also a second string in unison with the first, thereby permitting the effect of the intervals to be observed by sounding both tones at once. The mathematical character of the intervals was ascertained by observing the string-lengths producing the several tones. (2) A canon. A musical form in which several voices repeat the same melody successively, in the style of a round.

Kanoon (kän-ōn), *Gr.* Musical instrument of the dulcimer variety, used in Arabia.

Kantate (kän-tä′tĕ), *Ger.* Cantata.

Kanzellied (kän′tsĕl-lēd), *Ger.* Hymn before the sermon.

Kapelle (kä-pĕl′lĕ), *Ger.* A chapel. A musical establishment—consisting of a choir of singers, of a band of instrumentalists or of both—connected with a church or a court, or in the pay of a nobleman. Now the expression is generally applied to a band of instrumentalists.

Kapellknaben (kä-pĕl′knä′bĕn), *Ger.* Choir boys.

Kapellmeister (kä-pĕl′mĭs-tĕr), *Ger.* Chapelmaster; musical director.

Kapellstyl (kä-pĕl′stĕl), *Ger.* A cappella; unaccompanied vocal composition in strict style.

Karfreitag (kär-frī′täg), *Ger.* Good Friday

Keck (kĕk), *Ger.* Fresh.

Keckheit (kĕk′hīt), *Ger.* Boldness, vigor.

Keeping time. An inelegant form of expression. Keeping time means that the pulsation is evenly observed, the accentuation upon the proper points of the measure, and all the tones brought in with their proper time-relation.

Kehle (kā′lĕ), *Ger.* The voice, the throat.

Kehllaut (kāl′lout), *Ger.* A guttural sound.

Kemangeh (kĕ-män-gäh′), *Tur.* A stringed instrument of the Turks, played with a bow.

Kenet (kĕn′ĕt). An Abyssinian trumpet.

Kenner (kĕn′nĕr), *Ger.* A connoisseur; a professor.

Kent bugle. A bugle having six keys, four of which are commanded by the right hand and two by the left.

Kerana (kĕ-rä′nä), *Per.* A Persian horn, which is sounded at sunset and at midnight.

Keraulophon (kĕ-rou′lō-fōn), *Ger.* An 8-feet organ-stop, of a stringy and pleasing quality of tone, its peculiar character being produced by a small round hole bored in the pipe near the top, promoting the formation of overtones.

Keren (kĕr-ĕn), *Heb.* A horn; an instrument first used by the Hebrews, formed of a ram's-horn, and subsequently made of metal.

Kern (kĕrn), *Ger.* The languid, or langward, in organ-pipes.

Kernstimmen (kĕrn′stĭm-m′n), *Ger.* The fundamental, or 8 feet, stops of an organ.

Keron-jebel (kĕr′ōn-yä-b′l), *Heb.* Jubilee horn.

Kerrena (kĕr-rä′nä), *It.* An Indian trumpet.

Kesselpauke (kĕs′s′l-pow′kĕ), *Ger.* Kettledrum.

Ketch. Name applied by old writers to a catch.

ä *arm*, ă *add*, ā *ale*, ĕ *end*, ē *eve*, ĭ *ill*, ī *isle*, ō *old*, ŏ *odd*, oo *moon*, ŭ *but*, ü *Fr. sound*, kh *Ger. ch*, nh *nasal*.

(140)

Kettentriller (kĕt′t'n-tril′lĕr), *Ger.* Chain of shakes.

Kettledrum. This instrument consists of a brass or copper kettle, more or less hemispherical, over the top of which is stretched a skin. In the orchestra two kettledrums are generally employed, sometimes more. Each has a compass of a fifth: the lower may be tuned to any note from F to c, and the higher to any note from B-flat to f. Kettledrums are made to sound by means of two sticks, which have a soft knob at one end.

Key. (1) A family of chords (and the tones composing them) bearing a fixed relation to a central tone, called a keytone, or tonic. (2) Once applied to what is now called clef. (3) A mechanical lever for controlling the tone on many musical instruments, such as the organ, piano, flute, horn, accordion, clarinet, etc. Keys are of many forms, according to the service required of them. (4) The instrument by means of which the tuning-pins of the pianoforte are moved. This instrument is now commonly called a tuning-key, or a tuning-hammer.

Keyboard. The rows of keys of a pianoforte, organ, or similar instrument.

Keyboard, chromatic. An attachment applied to the keys of a piano for the purpose of enabling players of moderate skill to execute chromatic scales and passages with facility and correctness.

Key bugle. A Kent bugle.

Keyed. Furnished with keys.

Keyed harmonica. An instrument with keys, the hammers striking upon plates of glass.

Keyed instruments. All instruments whose tones are produced by the pressure of the fingers upon keys.

Keyed-stop violin. An arrangement which may be attached to a violin, consisting of a fingerboard made of ebony, with thirty-three stops, called keystops, which stand above the strings and act upon them perpendicularly.

Keyed violin. An instrument having forty strings, arranged like those of a piano, and acted upon by horsehair bows, under the pressure of keys like those of an organ.

Key harp. An instrument of recent invention, resembling a piano externally, with a similar arrangement of keys and pedals. It consists of an adjustment of tuning forks of various pitches, over cavities of sonorous metal.

Keynote. The tonic, or repose, note of a scale.

Keytone. The keynote.

Khasan (khä′zăn), *Heb.* The principal singer in a synagogue.

Kin chi (kĭn kē). A Chinese musical instrument possessing a body of thin wood, with five strings of silk, of different sizes. The scholar's lute. A kind of dulcimer.

King chi (king kee). A Chinese instrument consisting of a frame of wood with pendent stone, graduated through sixteen notes and struck with a hammer.

Kinnor (kĭn-nōr′), *Heb.* A small harp, or lyre, held in the hand and played upon while dancing. David played the kinnor.

Kirche (kĭr′khĕ), *Ger.* Church.

Kirchencantate (kĭr′kh'n-kän-tä′tä), *Ger.* A cantata for use in church services. Bach produced a large number of works of this kind. Generally they consist of a biblical text set for chorus and solos, with accompaniment of orchestra and organ.

Kirchencomponist (kĭr′kh'n-kŏm-pō-nĭst′), *Ger.* Composer of church music.

Kirchendienst (kĭr′kh'n-dēnst), *Ger.* Church service; form of prayer.

Kirchenfest (kĭr′kh'n-fĕst), *Ger.* Church festival.

Kirchengesang (kĭr′kh'n-ghĕ-säng′), *Ger.* }
Kirchenlied (kĭr′kh'n-lēd),
Spiritual song, canticle, psalm, or hymn.

Kirchenmusik (kĭr′kh'n-moo-zĭk′), *Ger.* Church music.

Kirchenschluss (kĭr′kh'n-shloos), *Ger.* An ecclesiastical, or plagal, cadence; the chord of the subdominant followed by the tonic.

Kirchenstyl (kĭr′kh'n-stēl), *Ger.* Church style, ecclesiastical style.

Kirchentöne (kĭr′kh'n-tön-ĕ), *Ger.* The church, or ecclesiastical, modes.

Kit. The name of a small pocket violin used by dancing-masters. Its length is about sixteen inches, and that of the bow about seventeen.

Kitar (kĭ-tär). A musical instrument of the Arabs. Our word "guitar" is derived from this.

Kithara (kĭth′ä-rä), *Gr.* A cithara, or lyre, of the Greeks.

Klage (klä′ghĕ), *Ger.* Lamentation.

Klagend (klä′g'nd), *Ger.* Plaintive.

Klagegedicht (klä′ghĕ-gĕ-dĭkht′), *Ger.* }
Klagelied (klä′ghĕ-lēd),
Elegy, mournful song, lamentation

Klageton (klä′ghĕ-tōn), *Ger.* Plaintive tune, or melody.

Klang (kläng), *Ger.* Sound; tune; ringing.

Klangboden (kläng-bō-d'n), *Ger.* Soundboard.

Klänge (kläng′ĕ), *Ger. pl.* Sounds, melodies.

Klangfarbe (kläng′fär-bĕ), *Ger.* Sound-color; the quality, or timbre, of sounds.

Klanggeschlecht (kläng′ghĕ-shlĕkht′), *Ger.* A genus, or mode.

Klanglehre (kläng′lä-rĕ), *Ger.* Acoustics.

Klanglos (kläng′lōs), *Ger.* Soundless.

Klappe (kläp′pĕ), *Ger.* Key of any wind instrument; a valve.

Klappenflügelhorn (kläp′p'n-flü′g'l-hōrn), *Ger.* The keyed bugle.

ä *arm*, ă *add*, ā *ale*, ĕ *end*, ē *eve*, ĭ *ill*, ī *isle*, ō *old*, ŏ *odd*, oo *moon*, ŭ *but*, ü *Fr. sound*, kh *Ger. ch.* nb *nasal.*

Klappenhorn (kläp'p'n-hōrn), *Ger.* A keyed horn.
Klapptrompete (kläp-tröm-pä'tĕ), *Ger.* A keyed trumpet.
Klar (klär), *Ger.* Clear, bright.
Klarheit (klär'hīt), *Ger.* Clearness, plainness.
Klarinette (klä'rĭ-nĕt-tĕ), *Ger.* A clarinet.
Klärlich (klär'lĭkh), *Ger.* Clearly, distinctly.
Klassisch (kläs'sĭsh), *Ger.* Classical, of high rank. Approved.
Klausel (klou'zel), *Ger.* A close; a regular section of a movement.
Klavier (klä-fēr'), *Ger.* Pianoforte; harpsichord. See *Clavier*.
Klavierauszug (klä-fēr'ows-tzoog), *Ger.* Edition for pianoforte. An arrangement of a score for pianoforte.
Klaviersonaten (klä-fēr'sō-nä-tĕn), *Ger.* Pianoforte sonata.
Klavierspieler (klä-fēr-spē'ler), *Ger.* Pianoforte-player.
Klein (klīn), *Ger.* Minor, speaking of intervals.
Kleinbass (klīn'bäss),
Kleinbassgeige (klīn'bäss-gī-gĕ), *Ger.* } Violoncello.
Kleinlaut (klīn'lout), *Ger.* Small or low in tone or voice.
Klingbar (klīng'bär), *Ger.* Resonant, sonorous.
Klingel (klīng'ĕl), *Ger.* A bell.
Klingeln (klīng-ĕln), *Ger.* To ring or sound a small bell; to jingle.
Klingen (klīng'ĕn),
Klingend (klīng'ĕnd), *Ger.* } Sonorous, resonant, ringing.
Klinggedicht (klīng'gĕ-dīkht), *Ger.* Sonnet.
Klingklang (klīng'kläng), *Ger.* Tinkling, bad music.
Klingspiel (klīng'spēl), *Ger.* The sound or noise of instruments.
Klutter (kloot'tĕr), *Ger.* A bird-call.
Knabenstimme (knä'bĕn-stĭm'mĕ), *Ger.* A boy's voice, counter tenor.
Knee-stop.
Knell. The tolling of a bell at a death or funeral.
Kniegeige (knē'gī-ghĕ), *Ger.* Viol da gamba, violoncello.
Knieröhre (knē'rö-rĕ), *Ger.* A pipe, or tube, bent like a knee.
Kollectivauszug (kŏl'lĕk-tēf'ows-tzoog), *Ger.* A collected selection of an author's works.
Kollo (kŏl-lō). *Jap.* A Japanese instrument, somewhat resembling a harp.
Kombinationspedale (kŏm'-bī-nä-tsī-ōns'-pĕ-dä'lĕ), *Ger.* Combination pedal. A pedal controlling a combination of organ-stops.
Kombinationstöne (kŏm'bĭ-nä-tsī-ōns'tö-nĕ), *Ger.* Combination tones. Resultant tones formed by the differences of two sounding tones.

Komiker (kō'mĭ-kĕr), *Ger.* A writer of burlettas; also a comic performer.
Komisch (kō'mĭsh), *Ger.* Comical.
Komma (kŏm'mä), *Ger.* Comma; a musical section or division. An interval equal to about an eighth of a diatonic step.
Komödie (kŏ-mö'dĭ-ĕ), *Ger.* Comedy, play.
Komponiren (kŏm-pō-nē'r'n), *Ger.* To compose.
Komponist (kŏm'pō-nĭst), *Ger.* A composer.
Komposition (kŏm'pō-zĭt-sĭ-ōn), *Ger.* A composition.
Kompositionslehre (kŏm'pō-zĭt-sĭ-ōns'lä-rĕ), *Ger.* The art of composition. A textbook in musical composition.
Konservatorium (kōn-sär-vä-tō'rĭ-oom). *Ger.* A conservatory; a school of the art of music.
Koons. A Persian drum made of brass, two feet in circumference.
Kopfstimme (kŏpf'stĭm-mĕ), *Ger.* Falsetto, head voice.
Koppel (kŏp'p'l), *Ger.* Coupler; coupling-stop in an organ.
Kor (kōr), *Ger.*
Köre (kö'rĕ), *Ger. pl.* } Choir, chorus. See *Chor*.
Koryphœus (kō-rĭ-fē'ŭs), *Gr.* Chief, or leader, of the dancers.
Kos (kōz), *Hun.* A Hungarian dance.
Kosake (kō-sä'kĕ). A national dance of the Cossacks.
Kraft (kräft), *Ger.* Power, strength, energy.
Kräftig (kräf'tĭgh),
Kräftiglich (kräf'tĭgh-lĭkh), *Ger.* } Power ful, vigorous, full of energy.
Kräftig und kurz (kräf'tĭgh oond koorts), *Ger.* Loud and detached.
Krakoviak (krä-kō-vĭ-äk),
Krakovienne (krä-kō-vĭ-ĕn), *Fr.* } The cracovienne, a Polish dance in 2-4 time, with strongly marked rhythm and much syncopated.
Krebsgängig (krĕbs'gän-gĭgh), *Ger.* Crab-going; inverse imitation; backwards.
Kreischend (krī'shĕnd), *Ger.* Shrieking, screaming.
Kreisfuge (krīs'foo-ghĕ), *Ger.* Circulating fugue; a canon.
Kreisleriana (krīs'lä-rĭ-ä-nä), *Ger.* Like Kreisler. A series of eight piano pieces of Schumann, named after an eccentric character called Kreisler, in one of Hoffmann's novels.
Kreistanz (krīs'tänts), *Ger.* Dance in a circle.
Kreuz (kroits), *Ger.* A sharp.
Kreuz-doppeltes (kroits-dŏp'pĕl-tĕs), *Ger.* A double sharp, × or ##.
Kriegerisch (krē'ghĕr-ĭsh), *Ger.* Warlike, martial.
Kriegsgesang (krēgs'ghĕ-säng'),
Kriegslied (krēgs'lēd), *Ger.* }
A war-song, a soldier's song.
Kriegsspieler (krēgs'spē'lĕr), *Ger.* A musician of a regiment.

ärm, ä add, ā ale, ĕ end, ē eve, ĭ ill, ī isle, ŏ odd, ō old, oo noon, ŭ but, ü *Fr.* sound, kh *Ger. ch*, nh nasal.

Krome. See *Croma*.
Krumm (kroom), *Ger.* Crooked, curved, bent.
Krummbogen (kroom'bō-g'n), *Ger.* A crook for changing the pitch of horns. Inserted, it lengthens the tube, thereby lowering the pitch.
Krummhorn (kroom'hŏrn), *Ger.* Crooked horn. The name of a portable wind instrument, formerly much in use, resembling a small cornet. Organ-builders corrupt this word into cremona, and apply it to one of their organ-stops.
Krustische Instrumente (kroos'tĭ-shĕ ĭn-stroo-mĕn'tĕ), *Ger.* Instruments of percussion, as the drum, cymbals, etc.
Kuhhorn (koo'hōrn), *Ger.* Cow-horn, Swiss horn, Alpine horn.
Kühn (kün), *Ger.* Short.
Kuhreigen (koo'rī-gh'n), *Ger.* Ranz des vaches. A Swiss melody.
Kunst (koonst), *Ger.* Art, skill.
Kunstfuge (koonst'foo-ghĕ), *Ger.* Art fugue. A musically composed and artistically developed fugue (distinguished from an exercise fugue).
Künstler (künst'l'r), *Ger.* Artist.

Kunstpfeifer (koonst'pfī-fĕr), *Ger.* Street musician.
Kunstwerk der Zukunft (koonst'värk dĕr tsoo'koonft), *Ger.* Art work of the future. A term given by Richard Wagner to his peculiar theory of the music of the future; musical composition.
Kuppel (koop'p'l), *Ger.* See *Koppel*.
Kurz (koorts), *Ger.* Short, detached, staccato.
Kürzen (kür'tsĕn), *Ger.* To abridge.
Kurzer Mordent (koorts'ĕr mŏr-dĕnt'), *Ger.* Short mordent.
Kurzer Singesatz (koort'sĕr sĭn'gĕ-säts), *Ger.* Cavatina.
Kurz und rein (koorts'oond rīn), *Ger.* Distinct and clear.
Kürzung (kür'tsoong), *Ger.* Shortening, abbreviation.
Kürzungszeichen (kür'tsoongs-tsī'kh'n), *Ger.* Sign of abbreviation.
Kussir (küs-sĕr), *Fr.* A Turkish musical instrument.
Kyrie eleison (kē'rī-ā ā-lī'zŏn), *Gr.* "Lord, have mercy upon us." The first movement in a Mass.
Kyrielle (kē-rē-ĕl), *Fr.* Litany.

L. Left hand. Notes to be played with the left hand or foot are sometimes written with an L over them.
La. (1) The name of the sixth sol-fa tone of the scale. (2) Applied to A uniformly in French and Italian sol-faing.
La (lä), *It.* } The.
La (lä), *Fr.* }
La bémol (lä bā-mŏl), *Fr.* The note A♭.
La bémol majeur (lä bā-mŏl mä-zhŭr), *Fr.* The key of A♭ major.
La bémol mineur (lä bā-mŏl mē-nŭr), *Fr.* The key of A♭ minor.
Labial. Organ-pipes with lips; called, also, flue pipes.
Labialstimmen (lä-bĭ-äl'stĭm'm'n), *Ger.* Stops belonging to the fluework, not reed-stops.
Labium (lä'bĭ-oom), *Lat.* The lip of an organ-pipe.
La chasse (lä shäss), *Fr.* In the hunting style.
Lacrimando (lä-crī-män'dŏ), *It.* } Sadly; in
Lacrimoso (lä-crī-mŏ'zŏ), *It.* } a mournful, pathetic style.
Lacrimosa (läk'rī-mŏ'zü), *Lat.* "Weeping stands." Part of the Stabat Mater.
Lade (lä'dĕ), *Ger.* Windchest in an organ.

La diese (lä dī-ās'), *Fr.* The note A♯.
Lage (lä'ghĕ), *Ger.* Lay. Position. (1) Of a chord. (2) Of the hand in the shifts of the violin.
Lagnoso (län-yō'zō), *It.* Plaintive, doleful.
Lagrimando (lä-grĭ-män'dŏ), *It.* } Weeping,
Lagrimoso (lä-grĭ-mŏ'zō), *It.* } tearful, in a sad and mournful style.
Lai (lä), *Fr.* Lay, ditty; short, plaintive song.
La maggiore (lä mäd-zhō'rä), *It.* La major; the key of A major.
La majeur (lä mä-zhŭr), *Fr.* The key of A major.
L'ame (l'äm), *Fr.* Soundpost of a violin, viola, etc.
Lament. An old name for harp music of the pathetic kind; applied, also, to the pathetic tunes of the Scotch.
Lamentabile ('ä-mĕn-tä'bĭ-lĕ), *It.* Lamentable, mournful.
Lamentabilmente (lä-mĕn-tä-bĭl-mĕn'tĕ), *It.* Lamentably, mournfully.
Lamentando (lä-mĕn-tän'dŏ), *It.* Lamenting, mourning.
Lamentevole (lä-mĕn-tā'vō-lĕ), *It.* Lamentable, mournful, plaintive.

ä *arm*, ă *add*, ā *ale*, ĕ *end*, ē *eve*, ĭ *ill*, ī *isle*, ō *old*, ŏ *odd*, oo *moon*, ŭ *but*, ü *Fr. sound*, kh *Ger. ch*, nh *nasal*.

Lamentoso (lä-měn-tō'zō), *It.* Lamentable, mournful.

La mineur (lä mī-nūr), *Fr.* The key of A minor.

La minore (lä mē-nō'rě), *It.* La minor; the key of A minor.

Lampons (länh-pônh), *Fr.* Drinking-songs.

Länderer (län'dĕ-rĕr), *Ger.*
Ländler (länd'lĕr), *Ger.* } A country dance or air in a rustic and popular style, in 3-8 or 3-4 time.

Länderisch (län'děr-ĭsh), *Ger.* In the manner or measure of a country dance.

Ländlich (länd'lĭkh), *Ger.* Rural.

Landlied (länd'lēd), *Ger.* Rural song, rustic song.

Landu (län-doo'), *Por.* A Portuguese dance in 2-4 or 2-2 time.

Landums (län-dooms), *Por.* A class of Portuguese music, of a sentimental, melancholy nature.

Lang (läng), *Ger.* Long.

Langsam (läng'säm), *Ger.* Slowly; equivalent to largo.

Langsamer (läng'säm-ĕr), *Ger.* Slower.

Language.
Languid. } In an organ-flute pipe this is the flat piece of metal or wood placed horizontally just inside the mouth.

Languemente (län-gwĕ-měn'tě), *It.* Languishingly.

Languendo (län-gwěn'dō), *It.*
Languente (län-gwěn'tě), *It.* } Languishing, feeble; with languor.
Languido (län-gwē-dō), *It.*

Languettes (län-gätt'), *Fr.* The brass tongues belonging to the reed pipes in an organ.

Largamente (lär-gä-měn'tě), *It.* } Largely,
Largamento (lär-gä-měn'tō), *It.* } fully; in a full, free, broad style of performance.

Large. The longest note formerly in use in ancient music. It is equal to eight semibreves or four breves.

Largement (lärzh-mänh), *Fr.* Full, free in style. See *Largamente.*

Larghetto (lär-gět'tō), *It.* A word specifying a time not quite so slow as that denoted by largo, of which word it is the diminutive.

Larghezza (lär-gět'tsä), *It.* Breadth, largeness, freedom.

Larghissimo (lär-ghěs'sĭ-mō), *It.* Extremely slow; the superlative of largo.

Largo (lär'gō), *It.* A slow and solemn degree of movement.

Largo andante (lär'gō än-dän'tě), *It.* Slow, distinct, exact.

Largo assai (lär'gō äs-sä'ē), *It.* } Very
Largo di molto (lär'gō dē mōl'tō), *It.* } slow.

Largo ma non troppo (lär'gō mä nōn trōp'pō), *It.* Slow, but not too much so.

Largo un poco (lär'gō oon pō-ko), *It.* Rather slow.

Larigot (lär'ĭ-gōt), *Fr.* Shepherd's flute or pipe; an organ-stop tuned an octave above the twelfth; the former named the flageolet.

Laringe (lä-rěn'ghě), *It.* Larynx.

Larmoyant (lär-mwä-yänh), *Fr.* Weeping, with a tearful expression.

Larynx. The upper part of the trachea. It is composed of five annular cartilages, placed above one another, and united by elastic ligaments by which it is so dilated and contracted as to be capable of varying the tones of the voice.

Last shift. On a violin, the shift on the twentieth line, or E.

Laud. To praise with words alone, or with words and music.

Lauda (lä'oo-dä). *It.* Laud; praise; hymn of praise. One of the canonical hours, immediately following matins.

Laudamus te (lou-dä'moos tā), *Lat.* "We praise Thee." Part of the Gloria.

Laudes (lou-děs), *Lat.* } Canticles, or hymns
Laudi (lä'oo-dī), *It. pl.* } of praise, that follow the early Mass.

Laudi spirituali (lou-dē spē-rĭ-too-ä'lē), *Lat.* Sacred songs and dialogues sung by the priests in the oratory.

Lauf (louf), *Ger.* That part of a violin, etc., into which the pegs are inserted; also a rapid succession of notes; a trill.

Läufe (loi'fě), *Ger. pl.* } Rapid divisions of
Läufer (loi'fĕr), *Ger.* } notes; a flight, or run, of rapid notes; a roulade, a trill, or shake.

Launenstück (lou'něn-stük), *Ger.* A voluntary.

Launig (lou'nĭg), *Ger.* Humorous.

Laut (lout), *Ger.* Loud; also sound.

Laute (lou'tě), *Ger.* The lute.

Läuten (loi't'n), *Ger.* To ring, to toll, to sound.

Lautenist (lou't'n-ĭst'), *Ger.* Lute-player, lutanist.

Lautenmacher (lou-t'n-mä'khĕr), *Ger.* Lutemaker.

Lautenschläger (lou-t'n-shlä'ghĕr), *Ger.* }
Lautenspieler (lou-t'n-spē'lĕr), *Ger.* } Lute-player, lutanist.

Lautlos (lout'lōs), *Ger.* Soundless, mute.

La voce (lä vō-tshě), *It.* The voice.

Lay. A song; a species of narrative poetry among the ancient minstrels.

Lay clerk. A vocal officiate in a cathedral, who takes part in the services and anthems, but is not of the priesthood.

Le (lŭh), *Fr.* } The.
Le (lā), *It. pl.* }

Leader. The first, or principal, violin in an orchestra; a director of a choir.

Leading note. The major seventh of any scale; the semitone below the keynote; the major third of the dominant.

Leaning note. See *Appoggiatura.*

ä *arm*, ă *add*, ā *ale*, ĕ *end*, ē *eve*, ĭ *ill*, ī *isle*, ō *old*, ŏ *odd*, oo *moon*, ŭ *but*, ü *Fr. sound*, kh *Ger. ch*, nh *nasal*.

Leaps. A distance composed of several intermediate intervals.
Leben (lā'b'n), *Ger.* Life, vivacity.
Lebendig (lā'bĕn-dĭgh), *Ger.* Lively.
Lebhaft (lāb'hāft), *Ger.* Lively, vivacious, quick.
Lebhaftigkeit (lāb'hāf-tĭgh-kīt), *Ger.* Liveliness, vivacity.
Leçon (lā-sŏnh), *Fr.* A lesson, an exercise.
Ledger lines. } The short extra, or addition-
Leger lines. } al, lines drawn above or below the staff, for the reception of such notes as are too high or too low to be placed on or within the staff.
Left beat. A movement to the left in beating time.
Legabile (lĕ-gä'bĭ-lĕ), *It.* } See *Legato.*
Legando (lĕ-gän'dŏ),
Legare (lĕ-gä'rĕ), *It.* To slur, or bind.
Legare le note (lĕ-gä'rĕ lĕ nō'tĕ), *It.* To join the notes closely; to play legato.
Legatissimo (lĕ-gä-tēs'sĭ-mō), *It.* Exceedingly smooth and connected.
Legato (lĕ-gä'tō), *It.* In a close, smooth, graceful manner; the opposite to staccato. It is often indicated by a sign called a slur, thus, ⌢.
Legato assai (lĕ-gä'tō äs-sä'ĕ), *It.* Very close and connected.
Legato touch. A touch which prolongs the tone until it exactly connects with the next following. It is indicated by the word legato, or by a curved line, ⌢.
Legatura (lĕ-gä-too'rä), *It.* A slur, a ligature.
Legatura di voce (lĕ-gä-too'rä dē vo'tshĕ), *It.* Connection of several tones sung in one breath.
Legende (lā-zhänhd), *Fr.* } A legend; an
Legende (lā-ghĕn-dĕ) *Ger.* } interesting story.
Léger (lā-zhā), *Fr.* Light, nimble.
Légèrement (lā-zhār-mänh), *Fr.* Lightly, nimbly, gaily.
Léger et animé (lā-zhār ĕt än-ĭ-mā), *Fr.* Light and animated.
Légereté (lā-shā'rĕ-tā), *Fr.* Lightness, agility.
Leggenda (lĕd-jĕn'dä), *It.* A legend, a tale.
Leggeramente (led-jĕr-ä-mĕn'tĕ), *It.* Lightly, easily.
Leggeranza (lĕd-jĕr-än'tsä), *It.* } Lightness
Leggerezza (lĕd-jĕr-ĕt'tsä), } and agility.
Leggerissimamente (lĕd-jĕr-ēs-sĭ-mä-mĕn'tĕ), *It.* Very light and sprightly.
Leggerissimo (lĕd-jĕr-ēs' sĭ-mō), *It.* Very light and sprightly.
Leggermente (lĕd-jĕr-mĕn'tĕ), *It.* A light and easy movement.
Leggiadra (lĕd-jĭ-ä'drä), *It.* Graceful, elegant.
Leggiadramente (lĕd-jĭ-ä-drä-mĕn'tĕ), *It.* Gracefully, elegantly.

Leggiardo (lĕd-jĭ-är'dō), *It.* Lightly, delicately.
Leggieramente (lĕd-jĭ-ä-rä-mĕn'tĕ), }
Leggiere (lĕd-jĭ-ä'rĕ), *It.* } Easi-
Leggieremente (lĕd-jĭ-ĕr-mĕn'tĕ), } ly, lightly, delicately.
Leggierezza (lĕd-jĭ-ĕ-rĕt'tsä), *It.* Lightness, delicacy; in a light, elastic style.
Leggiero (lĕd-jĭ-ā'ro), *It.* Light, swift, delicate.
Legno (lān' yō), *It.* Wood. See *Col legno.*
Lehrer (lā'rĕr), *Ger.* Teacher, master.
Lehrerin (lā'rĕr-ĭn), *Ger.* Instructress, mistress.
Leich (līkh), *Ger.* A lay.
Leichenmusik (lī'kh'n-moo-zīk'), *Ger.* Funeral-music.
Leichenton (lī'kh'n-tōn'), *Ger.* A lugubrious sound.
Leicht (līkht), *Ger.* Light, easy, facile.
Leichtheit (līkht'hīt), } Lightness,
Leichtigkeit (līkh'tĭg-kīt), *Ger.* } facility.
Leichtfertig (līkht'fĕr-tĭg), *Ger.* Lightly, carelessly.
Leidenschaft (lī'd'n-shäft), *Ger.* Passion.
Leidenschaftlich (lī'd'n-shäft līkh), *Ger.* Impassioned, passionate.
Leier (lī-ĕr), *Ger.* A lyre, a hurdygurdy.
Leiermädchen (lī'ĕr-mäd'kh'n), *Ger.* A girl who plays on a hurdygurdy.
Leiermann (lī'ĕr-män), *Ger.* A player on a hurdygurdy.
Leierorgel (lī'ĕr-ŏr'g'l), *Ger.* Hand organ, barrel organ.
Leierspieler (lī'ĕr-spē'lĕr), *Ger.* One who plays on a lyre.
Leine (lī'nĕ), *Ger.* A line of the staff.
Leise (lī'zĕ), *Ger.* Low, soft, gentle.
Leitaccord (līt'ak-kōrd), *Ger.* A chord, or harmony, leading instinctively to another, as the chord of the dominant leading to the tonic.
Leiter (lī'tĕr), *Ger.* Leader; also the scale of any key.
Leitereigen (lī'tĕr-ī'gĕn), *Ger.* Such tones as belong to the scale of any key, the notes forming the scale. Peculiar to the scale.
Leiterfremd (lī'tĕr-frĕmd), *Ger.* Accidental sharps or flats which do not belong to the key. Tones not belonging to the key.
Leitmotiv (līt'mō-tēf'), *Ger.* Leading motive. A motive which is much used in the course of a composition as a partial means of musical identification, as the "Swan" and "Grail" motives in "Lohengrin," the "Faith" motive in "Parsifal," etc. Von Weber was one of the first dramatic composers to employ this device, the "Zamiel" motive in "Der Freischütz."
Leitton (līt'tōn), *Ger.* The leading tone, the leading note.

ä *arm*, ă *add*, ā *ale*, ĕ *end*, ē *eve*, ĭ *ill*, ī *isle*, ō *old*, ŏ *odd*, oo *moon*, ŭ *but*, ü *Fr. sound*, kh *Ger. ch.* nh *nasal*.

Lene. An old term applied to a note sustained in one of the harmonic parts of a composition whilst the other parts are in motion.

Leno (lā'nō), *I'.* Weak, feeble, faint.

Lent (länh), *Fr.* Slow.

Lentamente (lĕn-tä-mĕn'tĕ), *It.* Slowly.

Lentando (lĕn-tän'dō), *It.* With increased slowness.

Lentement (länht'-mänh). *Fr.* } Slowly, leis-
Lentemente (lĕn'tĕ-mĕn'tĕ). *It.* } urely.

Lentement très (länht-mänh trā), *Fr.* Very slow.

Lenteur (länh-tûr), *Fr.* Slowness, delay.

Lenteur, avec (länh-tûr ä-vĕk), *Fr.* } With
Lentezza, con (lĕn-tĕt'tsä kōn), *It.* } slowness and delay.

Lentissimamente (lĕn-tĕs'sĭ-mä-mĕn'tĕ), *It.* }
Lentissimo (lĕn-tĕs'sĭ-mō), Extremely slow.

Lento (lĕn'tō), *It.* Slow.

Lento assai (lĕn'tō äs-sä'ī),
Lento di molto (lĕn'tō dē mōl'tō), *It.* } Very
Lento lento (lĕn'tō lĕn'tō), slowly.

Leonine verses. So called from Leo, the inventor. They are verses the end of which rhyme with the middle.

Lesser. Formerly used in the same sense as minor; smaller than the major.

Lesser barbiton. A name formerly given to the kit, or small violin, used by dancing-masters.

Lesser comma. The difference between the comma and the enharmonic dieses; the diachisma.

Lesser lay. One of the two classes among the ancients, comprising sixteen or twenty verses.

Lesson. Formerly applied to exercises or pieces consisting of two or three movements for the harpsichord or pianoforte.

Lestezza (lĕs-tĕt'tsä), *It.* Agility, quickness.

Lestissimamente (lĕs-tĕs-sĭ-mä-mĕn'tĕ), *It.* Very quickly.

Lestissimo (ĕs-tĕs'sĭ-mō), *It.* Very quick

Lesto (lĕs'tō), *It.* Lively, nimble, quick.

Letterale (lĕt-tĕ-rä'lĕ), } Lit-
Letteralmente (lĕt-tĕr-äl-mĕn'tĕ), *It.* } erally, exactly as written.

Leuto (lä-oo'tō), *It.* A lute.

Levè (lĕ-vä), *Fr.* The upstroke of the baton.

Levet. A blast of a trumpet; probably that by which soldiers are called in the morning. (Obsolete.)

Levezza (lĕ-vĕt'tsä), *It.* Lightness.

Levier pneumatique (lĕv-ĭ-ā noo-mä-tĕk'), *Fr.* The pneumatic lever; a series of small bellows, or levers, placed on the windchest of an organ, containing air at a high pressure; when a key is pressed it admits wind to the bellows of the pneumatic lever; when this inflates it opens the pallet, admitting wind to the pipes. By means of this the touch of a large organ may be made very light. The pneumatic lever was invented by S. Barker, about 1825. Modern organs have small pneumatic bellows for every valve; they are operated by electricity. The touch is very light and much more prompt.

Lexicon. A dictionary of terms, or information.

Lezzioni (lĕt-tsĭ-ō'nĕ), *It. pl.* Lessons.

L. H. Initials indicating the use of the left hand in pianoforte music.

Liaison (lē-ä-zōnh), *Fr.* Smoothness of connection; also, a bind or tie.

Liaison de chant (lē-ä-zōnh dŭh shänht), *Fr.* The sostenuto style of singing.

Liberamente (lē-bĕ-rä-mĕn'tĕ), *It.* } Freely,
Librement (lēbr-mänh), *Fr.* } easily, plainly.

Libero (lē'bĕ-rō), *It.* Free, unrestrained.

Libitum (lĭb'ĭ-toom), *Lat.* Pleasure, will. *Ad libitum*, at pleasure. Applied to rate of movement or to a choice of version.

Libretto (lē-brĕt'tō), *It.* The text of an opera or other extended piece of music.

License. A deviation for the time being from the received rules which form the established system of harmony.

Licenza poetica (lē-tshĕn-tsä pō-ā'tĭ-kä), *It.* Poetic license; alterations, or deviations, from common rules.

Liceo (lē-tshä'ō), *It.* Lyceum; an academy; a theater.

Lié (lĭ-ā'), *Fr.* Smoothly; the same as legato.

Liebeslied (lē'bĕs-lēd), *Ger.* Love-song.

Liebhaber (lēb'hä-bĕr), *Ger.* Amateur; a lover of music.

Lieblich (lēb'lĭkh), *Ger.* Lovely, charming.

Lieblichgedacht (lēb'lĭkh-ghĕ-däkht'), *Ger.* A stopped-diapason organ-register of sweet tone.

Lié coulant (lĭ-ā koo-länh), *Fr.* Slurred, flowing.

Lied (lēd), *Ger.* A song, a ballad, a lay. Applicable to any kind of song, but primarily to the German song, in which a close correspondence is sought between the feeling of the poetry and that of the music. *Lieder* are of two varieties: *Strophic*, in which the same music serves for all the stanzas in turn; and *durchcomponirt* (composed all through), in which every stanza has its own music.

Liedchen (lēd'kh'n), *Ger.* A short song or melody.

Lieder (lē'dĕr), *Ger.* Songs.

Liederbuch (lē'dĕr-bookh), *Ger.* A song-book, a hymn-book.

Liederbund (lē'dĕr-boond), *Ger.* A society of song-singers.

Liedercyclus (lē'dĕr-tsē-kloos'), *Ger.* A cycle of songs, as the "Poet's Love" of Schumann, the "Winter Journey" of Schubert.

Liederdichter (lē'dĕr-dĭkh'tĕr), *Ger.* A lyrical poet, a song-writer.

Liederform (lē'dĕr-fōrm), *Ger.* The form, or subject, of a song.

Liederkranz (lē'dĕr-kränts), *Ger.* Glee club.

Liederkreis (lē'dĕr-krīs), *Ger.* A cycle, or wreath, of songs.

Lieder ohne Worte (lē'dĕr ō'nĕ wōr'tĕ), *Ger.* Songs without words.

Liedersammlung (lē'dĕr-säm'loong), *Ger.* Collection of songs.

Liedersänger (lē'dĕr-säng'ĕr), *Ger.* A song-singer, a ballad-singer.

Liederspiel (lē'dĕr-spēl), *Ger.* An operetta, consisting of dialogue and music of a light, lively character.

Liedersprache (lē'dĕr-sprä'khĕ), *Ger.* Words or language adapted to songs.

Liedertafel (lē'dĕr-tä'f'l), *Ger.* Song-table; German glee club, generally consisting of male voices alone.

Liedertäfler (lē'dĕr-tä'flĕr), *Ger.* Glee-singers.

Liedertanz (lē'dĕr-tänts), *Ger.* A dance intermingled with songs.

Lied ohne Worte (lēd ō'nĕ wōr'tĕ), *Ger.* See *Lieder ohne Worte.*

Lier (lēr), *Dut.* A lyre.

Ligare (lē-gä'rĕ), *It.* To bind, to tie, to join together.

Ligato (lē-gä'tō), *It.* See *Legato.*

Ligatur (lĭ-gä-toor'), *Ger.* }
Ligatura (lĭ-gä-too'rä), *It.* } (1) In the old mensurable music a succession
Ligature. } of two or more notes sung to one syllable. As in those days the slur was not in use, the notes were either brought into close proximity or joined together in various ways. (2) In modern music a succession of notes sung to one syllable or in one breath; and also a succession of notes played with one stroke of the bow or in one breath. (3) A syncopation, a note on the unaccented part of a bar tied to one of the same pitch on the following accented part. A dissonance with its preparation. A dissonance is said to be prepared when the dissonant note appeared in the preceding chord as a consonance.

Light. A general term applied to any thin, airy composition; also to the keys of any instrument when they make little resistance to the pressure of the fingers. Such an instrument is said to have a light touch.

Ligne (lānh), *Fr.* A line of the staff.

Lignes additionnelles (lānhs äd-dē-sĭ-ōn-nāl), *Fr.* Leger lines.

Ligneum psalterium (lĭg'nĕ-oom säl-tä'rĭ-oom), *Lat.* The wooden dulcimer, called in Germany the straw fiddle.

Lilt (lĭlt), *Sco.* To sing or play merrily.

Limma (lĭm'mä), *Gr.* An interval used in the ancient Greek music, less by a comma than a major semitone.

Linea (lē-nē'ä), *It.* A line of the staff.

Linea riga (lē'nē-ä rē'gä), *It.* The lines of the staff.

Lines. That portion of the staff on and between which the notes are placed. At their first invention the spaces between them were not used.

Lines, added. Leger lines; lines added above and below the staff.

Lines, ledger. } Lines above or below the
Lines, leger. } staff for the reception of such notes as are too high or too low to be placed upon or within it.

Lines, waving. A line which when placed perpendicularly upon the staff indicates that the notes of the chord are to be played successively one after another. A waving horizontal line shows that the effect of the 8va sign is to be continued as far as the line extends.

Lingua (lĭn'gwä), *It.* The tongue in organ-stop reeds.

Lingual. Pertaining to the tongue; a letter or sound pronounced chiefly by the tongue.

Linie (lē'nĭ-ĕ), *Ger.* A line of the staff.

Linien (lē'nĭ-ĕn), *Ger.* Lines of the staff.

Liniensystem (lē'nĭ-ĕn-sĭs-tām'), *Ger.* A scale; the lines of the staff.

Liniensystem (lē'nĭ-ĕn-sĭs-tām'), *Ger.* The line-system; the staff.

Lining. A term applied to a practice of reading one or two lines of a hymn before singing them, alternating reading and singing.

Link (lĭnk), }
Links (lĭnks), *Ger.* } Left.

Linke Hand (lĭn'kĕ händ), *Ger.* The left hand.

Linos (lē'nŏs), *Gr.* A rustic air; also a dirge.

Liquid. An epithet applied to the smooth succession of the sweet and mellow sounds of any voice or wind instrument, also to the tones themselves, separately considered.

Lira (lē'rä), *It.* A lyre.

Lira da braccio (lē'rä dä brät'tshĭ-ō), *It.* An obsolete bow instrument of the size and shape of the tenor viol, with seven strings, five above and two beside the fingerboard.

Lira da gamba (lē'rä dä gäm'bä), *It.* An instrument similar to the lira da braccio, but held between the knees, and with twelve or sixteen strings.

Lira da gamba, *It.*, also called **Lirone perfetto,** and **Arciviola di lira,** *It.* An obsolete instrument in shape like the lira da braccio, but larger. It was played like the violoncello, and had fourteen or sixteen strings, two of which lay beside the fingerboard.

Lira doppia (lē'rä dŏp'pī-ä), *It.* Double lyre.

Lira grande (lē'rä grän'dĕ), *It.* The viol di gamba, a viol with six strings, formerly much used in Germany.

Lira pagana (lē'rä pä-ghä'nä),
Lira rustica (lē'rä roos-tē'kä), *It.* } A hurdy-gurdy.
Lira tedesca (lē'rä tā-děs'kä),

Lire (lēr), *Fr.* To read.

Lire la musique (lēr lä mü-zēk), *Fr.* To read music.

Liressa (lē-rĕs'sä), *It.* A bad lyre, or harp.

Lirica (lē'rĭ-kä), *It.* } Lyric, lyric poetry; poetry adapted for music.
Lirico (lē'rĭ-kō),

Lirone (lē-rō'nĕ), *It.* A large lyre, or harp.

Liscio (lē'shĭ-ō), *It.* Simple, unadorned, smooth.

Lispelnd (lĭs'pĕlnd), *Ger.* Lisping, whispering.

L'istesso (lĕs-tĕs'sō), *It.* The same.

L'istesso movimento (lĕs-tĕs'sō mō-vĭ-mĕn'-tō),
L'istesso tempo (lĕs-tĕs'sō tĕm'pō), } *It.*
In the same time as the previous movement.

Litania (lĭ-tä'nĭ-a), *Lat.*
Litanie (lĭ-tä-nē), *Fr.* } A litany.
Litanei (lĭ-tä nī'), *Ger.*

Litany. A solemn form of supplication used in public worship.

Little sharp-sixth. A name given by French theorists to the second inversion of the dominant seventh formed on the second degree of the scale, and consisting of a bass note with its minor third, perfect fourth, and major sixth.

Liturgy. The ritual for public worship in those churches which use written forms.

Lituus (lē'too-oos), *Lat.* An instrument of martial music; a kind of trumpet making a shrill sound.

Liuto (lē-oo'tō), *It.* A lute.

Livre (lēvr), *Fr.* A book.

Livret (lēv-rā'), *Fr.* A libretto.

Lo (lō), *It.* The. (Masculine form.)

Lobgesang (lōb'ghĕ-zäng),
Loblied (lōb'lēd), } *Ger.* A hymn or song of praise.

Loco (lō'kō), *It.* Place; a word used in opposition to 8va alta, signifying that the notes over which it is placed are not to be played an octave higher, but just as they are written.

Locrense (lō-krĕn'se), *Gr.* One of the ancient tones or modes.

Locrian (lō'krĭ-än), *Gr.* } The Hyperdorian mode of the ancient Greeks.
Locrico (lō'krĭ-kō),

Logierian system. A system of musical instruction, introduced by John Bernard Logier, which, with instruction on the piano-forte, combines simultaneous performance in classes, and also the study of harmony, modulation, etc. In connection with this system Logier invented and employed the chiroplast.

Lombarda (lŏm-bär'dä), *It.* A species of dance used in Lombardy.

Long. A note formerly in use, equal to four semibreves, or half the length of the large.

Longa (lŏn'gä), *Lat.* A long.

Long appoggiatura. An appoggiatura consisting of a single note forming a part of the melody. It borrows half the length of the next note, and is accented.

Long double. An old character equal in duration to four breves.

Long drum. The large drum used in military bands, carried horizontally before the performer, and struck at both ends.

Long meter. A stanza of four lines in Iambic measure, each line containing eight syllables.

Long mordent. A mordent formed of four notes.

Written. Played.

Long particular meter. A stanza of six lines in Iambic measure, each line containing eight syllables.

Long roll. A drumbeat calling the soldiers to arms.

Long spiel. An ancient Icelandic instrument, long and narrow, and played upon with a bow.

Longue pause (lŏnh pōz), *Fr.* Make a long rest, or pause.

Lontano (lŏn-tä'nō), *It.* Distant, remote, a great way off.

Lontano, da (lŏn-tä'nō dä), *It.* At a distance.

Lorgnette (lŏrn-yĕt'), *Fr.* An opera-glass.

Loure (loor), *Fr.* A dance of slow time and dignified character. It has sometimes three and sometimes four crotchets in a bar.

Lourre (loo-rā'), *Fr.* Smoothly, connectedly. The same meaning as legato.

Louvre (loovr), *Fr.* A name applied to a French air, called also "L'Aimable Vainqueur," for which Louis XIV. had a remarkable predilection. This air has since formed a well-known dance.

Love-song. A song the words and melody of which are expressive of love.

Lugubre (loo-goo'brĕ), *It.* Lugubrious, sad, mournful.

Luinig. A short, plaintive song much used in the Hebrides and on the western coasts of Scotland. It is generally sung by the women at their work and diversions.

Lullaby. A song to quiet infants; a soft, gentle song.

Lundu (loon'doo). *Por.* A Portuguese dance in 2-4 or 2-2 time.

Lunga pausa (loon'gä pä′oo-zä), *It.* A long pause, or rest.
Luogo (loo-ō′gō), *It.* See *Loco*.
Lusing. An abbreviation of lusingato.
Lusingando (loo-zēn-gän′dō), ⎫ Soothing,
Lusingante (loo-zēn-gän′tĕ), ⎬ coaxing;
Lusingato (loo-zēn-gä′tō), *It.* ⎨ persua-
Lusinghevole (loo-zēn-gā′vō-lĕ), ⎭ sively,
insinuatingly; in a playful, persuasive style.
Lusinghevolmente (loo-zēn-gā-vŏl-měn′tĕ), *It.* Soothingly, persuasively.
Lusinghiere (loo-zēn-ghĭ-ā′rĕ), ⎫ Flatter-
Lusinghiero (loo-zĭu-ghĭ-ā′rō), *It.* ⎬ ing,
fawning, coaxing.
Lustig (loos′tĭg), *Ger.* Merrily, cheerfully, gaily.
Lustlied (loost-lēd), *Ger.* A gay, merry song.
Lut (loot), *Fr.* A lute.
Lutanist. A performer upon the lute.
Lute. A very ancient stringed instrument, formerly much used, and containing at first only five rows of strings, but to which six or more were afterward added. The lute consists of four parts, viz., the table; the body, which has nine or ten sides, and is pear-shaped; the neck, which has as many frets, or divisions; and the head, or cross, in which the pins for tuning it are inserted. In playing this instrument the performer strikes the strings with the fingers of the right hand, and regulates the sounds with those of the left, as in playing the guitar. The mandolin is a small lute.
Lute, arch. A stringed instrument resembling the theorbo, by some considered synonymous with it.
Lutenist. ⎫ A performer on the lute.
Luter. ⎭
Luth (loot), *Fr.* A lute.
Luthier (lü-tĭ-ā), *Fr.* Formerly a maker of lutes; at present a maker of stringed instruments of all kinds.
Lutina. A small lute, or mandolin.
Lutist. A player on the lute.
Luttuosamente (loot-too-ō-zä-měn′tĕ), *It.* Sadly, sorrowfully.
Luttuoso (loot-too-ō′zō), *It.* Sorrowful, mournful.
Lydian. See *Greek modes*.

Lydian chant. A chant of a sorrowful, melancholy style.
Lyra (lē′rä), *It.* ⎫ The lyre.
Lyra (lĭr′ä), *Ger.* ⎭
Lyra barbarina (lē′rä bär-bä-rē′nä), *It.* An old instrument, resembling in shape the Spanish guitar, having three double niches, but played with a bow.
Lyra doppia (lē′rä dŏp′pĭ-ä), *It.* Double lyre, not at present used, but supposed to have been a kind of viol da gamba.
Lyra hexachordis (lĭr′ä hĕx′ä-kŏr′dĭs), *Gr.* A lyre with six strings.
Lyra mendicorum (lĭr′ä měn-dĭ-kō′room), *Lat.* A hurdygurdy.
Lyrasänger (lĭr′ä-säng′ěr), ⎫ A performer
Lyraspieler (lĭr′ä-spē′lěr), *Ger.* ⎬ on the lyre.
Lyra-viol. An old instrument of the lyre or harp species; it had six strings and seven frets.
Lyre. One of the most ancient of stringed instruments, said to have been invented by Mercury about the year 2000 A. M., and formed of a tortoise shell; a species of harp. The Greek kithara was an improved lyre. The lyre had originally three or four strings; later, seven. The most advanced form of lyre, perhaps, was the magadis, which is reputed to have had twenty strings.
Lyric. ⎫ These words—which, in the first
Lyrical. ⎭ place, signify "pertaining to the lyre," then, also, "fitted to be sung to the lyre," and, lastly, "appropriate to song"—are especially applied to poetry and music which express individual emotions. The lyrical in poetry and music has been described as the perfect and most euphonious expression, as the ideal representation, or objectivation, of subjective feelings. The words lyric and lyrical are used in distinction from epic (narrative) and dramatic. A lyric drama is a synonym for opera; the lyric stage, for operatic stage. An opera is called lyric when the lyric element predominates over the heroic—sentiment over action.
Lyric comedy. A comedy in which vocal music forms a principal part; comic opera.
Lyric drama. Opera; acting accompanied by singing.
Lyric tragedy. Tragic opera.
Lyriker (lĭr′ĭ-kěr), ⎫ Lyric, lyrical.
Lyrisch (lĭr′ĭsh), *Ger.* ⎭

ä *arm*, ă *add*, ā *ale*, ĕ *end*, ē *eve*, ĭ *ill*, ī *isle*, ō *old*, ŏ *odd*, oo *moon*, ŭ *but*, ü *Fr. sound*, kh *Ger. ch*. nh *nasal*.

(149)

M

M. This letter is used as an abbreviation of Mezzo, also of various other words, as Metronome, Mano, Main, and also in connection with other letters, as M. F. for Mezzo Forte; M. P., Mezzo Piano; M. V., Mezzo Voce; etc.

M. M. Abbreviation for Maelzel's Metronome.

Ma (mä), *It.* But: as: *Allegro ma non troppo*, quick, but not too much so.

Machalath (mä-kä-läth), *Heb.* A musical term employed in the titles to Psalms liii, and lxxxviii, and supposed by some to mean an instrument with holes (perhaps a flute), but by others to indicate well-known tunes to which these psalms were to be chanted.

Machicot (mä-shē'kō), *Fr.* A chorister, a bad singer.

Machol (mä-kōl), *Heb.* Instruments used by the Hebrews. This name is supposed to have been given to two instruments, one of the string and the other of the pulsatile species.

Madriale (mä-drĭ-ä'lĕ), *It.* A madrigal; the name formerly given by the Italians to the intermezzi, or pieces performed between the acts of a play or an opera.

Madrialetto (mä-drĭ-ä-lĕt'tō), a short madrigal.

Madrigal (măd'rĭ-găl). This word of uncertain derivation (*mandra*, flock?) has two significations: (1) A short lyrical poem of no fixed form. A pastoral or amorous song. (2) A vocal composition mostly in four or five parts, often also in six or three parts, more rarely in seven, and still less rarely in two parts. It had its origin in Italy, where it came into vogue in the sixteenth century, flourishing in this and the following century. Next to Italy the madrigal was most successfully cultivated in England. Thomas Morley, one of the most famous madrigalists, tells us (in 1597) that it was, next to the motet, the most "artificial" kind of music, but at the same time one of the most delightful to men of understanding. And he demanded from its composers not only "points" and all sorts of contrapuntal devices, but also "an amorous humor" and an inexhaustible variety of sentiment.

Madrigal, accompanied. A madrigal in which the voices are sustained by a pianoforte or organ.

Madrigale (mä-drĭ-gä'lĕ), *It.* A madrigal.

Madrigalesco (mä-drĭ-gä-lä'sko), *It.* Of, or belonging to, a madrigal.

Mæsa. A mass.

Maesta (mä-ĕs-tä').
Maestade (mä-ĕs-tä'dĕ), *It.*
Maestate (mä-ĕs-tä'tĕ),
} Majesty, dignity, grandeur.

Maestevole (mä-ĕs-tä'vō-lĕ), *It.* Majestic, majestical.

Maestevolmente (mä-ĕs-tĕ-vōl-mĕn'tĕ),
Maestosamente (mä-ĕs-tō-zä-mĕn'tĕ),
} *It.* Majestically, nobly.

Maestoso (mä-ĕs-tō'zo), *It.* Majestic, stately, dignified.

Maestra (mä-ĕs-trä), *It.* An artiste, female performer.

Maestria (mä'ĕs-trē'ä), *It.* Mastery, skill, art, ability.

Maestro (mä'äs'trō), *It.* Master, composer, an experienced, skillful artist.

Maestro al cembele (mä-äs'tro äl tshŏm-bä'lĕ), A skillful pianist, a master of the instrument.

Maestro del coro (mä-äs'trō dĕl kōr'rō), *It.* Master of the choir or chorus.

Maestro di camera (mä-äs'trō dĕ kä'mĕ-rä), *It.* Leader, or conductor, of chamber music.

Maestro di canto (mä-äs'trō dĕ kän'tō), *It.* A singing-master.

Maestro di cappella (mä-äs'trō dĕ käp-pĕl'lä), *It.* Chapelmaster; composer; director of the musical performances in a church or chapel.

Magadis (mä-gä'dĭs), *Gr.* The name of an ancient Greek instrument of the lyre kind. It is said to have had twenty strings, and many think it had a bridge, dividing the strings into two equal parts, thus enabling the player to use octaves at will. All this is rather uncertain.

Magadizing. A term in the ancient Greek music, signifying a vocal performance in octaves, when men and women, or men and boys, joined in the same air.

Magas (mä'gäs), *Gr.* The bridge of stringed instruments.

Maggiolata (mäd-jĭ-ō-lä'tä), *It.* A hymn or song in praise of the month of May.

Maggiore (mäd-jĭ-ō'rĕ), *It.* Greater, in respect to scales and intervals; major; the major key.

Magnificat (măg-nĭf'ĭ-kăt), *Lat.* A part of the Vespers, or evening service, of the Roman Catholic Church.

Main (mănh), *Fr.* The hand.

Main droite (mănn drwăt), *Fr.* Right hand.

Main gauche (mănh gōsh), *Fr.* The left hand.

ä *arm*, ă *add*, â *ale*, ĕ *end*, ē *e͞e*, ĭ *ill*, ī *isle*, ō *old*, ŏ *odd*, oo *moon*, ŭ *but*, ü *Fr. sound*, kh *Ger. ch*, nh *nasal*

Maitre (mĕtr), *Fr.* A master, a director.
Maitre de chapelle (mĕtr dŭh shä-pĕll), *Fr.* Chapelmaster; director of the choir.
Maitre de musique (mĕtr dŭh mü-zēk), *Fr.* Musical director.
Majesta (mä'yĕz-tä), *It.* } Majesty, dignity.
Majesté (mä-zhĕs-tä), *Fr.* }
Majestueux (mä-zhĕs-tü-ŭh), *Fr.* Majestic.
Majeur (mä-zhŭr), *Fr.* Major; major key.
Major. Greater, in respect to intervals, scales, etc.
Major diatonic scale. That scale in which the semitones fall between the third and fourth and seventh and eighth tones, both in ascending and descending.
Major seventh. An interval consisting of five tones and a semitone.
Major sixth. A sixth composed of four tones and a semitone.
Major third. An interval containing two whole tones or steps.
Major tonic. A major scale.
Major triad. A union of any sound with its major third and perfect fifth.
Malagueña (mä-lä-gwoo-än'yä), *Sp.* A fandango.
Malanconia (mä-län-kō,nē'ä), *It.* } Melancholy, sadness.
Malanconico (mä-län-kō'nī-kō), *It.* }
Malincolico (mä-lĭn-kō'lī-kō), *It.* } Melancholy.
Malinconico (mä-lĭu-kō-nē'ä), *It.* }
Malinconicamente (mä-lĭn-kō-nī-kä-mĕn'tĕ), *It.* In a melancholy style.
Malinconico (mä-lĭn-kō'nī-kō),
Malinconioso (mä-lĭn-kō-nī-ō'zō), *It.* } In a melancholy.
Malinconoso (mä-lĭn-kō-nō'zō), } choly style.
Mama (mä-mä), *It.* In drum music a term indicating the right hand.
Manager. One who undertakes the labor of getting up concerts and concer' tours.
Manca (män'kä), *It.* The left.
Mancando (män-kän'dō), *It.* Decreasing, dying away.
Manche (mänh-sh), *Fr.* The neck of a violin or other instrument.
Mandola (män-dō'lä), *It.* A mandoline, or cithern, of the size of a large lute.
Mandoline. An Italian fretted guitar, so called from its almond, or pear, shape. There are several varieties. The Neapolitan, considered the most perfect, has four strings tuned like the violin, G, D, A, E. The Milanese, next in favor, has five double strings, tuned G, C, A, D, E. A plectrum is used by the right hand, and the left is employed in stopping the strings.
Mandolino (män-dō-lē'nō), *It.* A mandolin.
Mandora. } A small kind of lute, or guitar,
Mandore. } with frets and seven gut strings, three of which are duplicates.

Manico (mä'nī-kō), *It.* The neck of the violin, guitar, etc.
Manichord. } Originally an instrument
Manichordon. } with but one string; subsequently a stringed instrument resembling a spinet, or harpsichord.
Manichordiendraht (mä-nī-kōr'dī-ĕn-dräht), *Ger.* Wire for the manichord or clavichord.
Maniera (mä-nī-ā'rä), *It.* } Manner, style.
Maniere (män-ī-är'), *Fr.* }
Maniera affettata (mä-nī-ā'rä äf-fĕt-tä'tä), *It.* An affected style, or delivery.
Maniera languida (mä-nī-ä'rä län'gwī-dä), *It.* A languid, sleepy style.
Manieren (mä-nē'r'n), *Ger. pl.* Graces, embellishments, ornaments.
Männerchor (män'nĕr-kōr), *Ger.* A choir of male voices.
Mannerism. Adherence to the same manner; the constant use of an ever-recurring set of phases; adherence to the same style without freedom or variety.
Männliche Stimme (män'lĭkh-ĕ stĭm'mĕ), *Ger.* A manly voice.
Mano (mä'nō), *It.* The hand.
Mano destra (mä'nō däs'trä), } The
Mano diritta (mä'nō dī-rēt'tä), *It.* } right
Mano dritta (mä'nō drēt'tä), } hand.
Mano sinistra (mä'Lō sĭ-nēs'trä), *It.* The left hand.
Manual. The keyboard for the hands.
Manual (mä-noo-äl'), *Ger.* }
Manuale (mä-noo ä'lĕ), *Lat.* } Manual.
Manuale (mä-noo-ä'lĕ), *It.* }
Manualiter (mä-noo-ä'lī-tĕr), *Ger.* Manually; that is, with the hands alone, without pedals. Organ music.
Manualkoppel (mä-noo-äl-kōp'p'l), *Ger.* A coupler, by means of which a key, or a set of keys, is connected with another set.
Manualmente (mä-noo-äl-mĕn'tĕ), *It.* Manually.
Manualuntersatz (mä-noo-äl'oon'tĕr-sätz), *Ger.* An organ-stop of 32-feet tone, with stopped pipes: the subbourdon.
Manubrio (mä-noo'brī-ō), *It.* The handle, or knob, by which a stop is drawn in an organ.
Marcando (mär-kän'dō), *It.* } Marked, ac-
Marcato (mär-kä'tō), } cented, well pronounced.
Marcatissimo (mär-kä-tēs'sī-mō), *It.* Very strongly marked.
Marcato la melodia (mär-kä-tō lä mĕ-lō'dī-ä), *It.* The melody in a marked style.
March. A musical composition intended to accompany marching, more especially of soldiers. There are two kinds of marches—the quick march, or quickstep, and the slow, or processional, march. Slow marches may be divided into festal and funeral marches. These two last-named species are much more solemn and dignified in

ä *arm*, ă *add*, ä *ale*, ĕ *end*, ē *eve*, ĭ *ill*, ī *isle*, ō *old*, ŏ *odd*, oo *moon*, ŭ *but*, ü *Fr sound*, kh *Ger. ch*, nh *nasal.*

(151)

their movement than the quick marches, but all of them are mostly in 4-4 time. Quick marches consist oftenest of two halves, each of two parts, and each part of eight, twelve, or sixteen bars. The second half is called the trio. For the most part, processional marches have, likewise, this symmetrical rhythmical arrangement of the dance form, but they are not strictly bound to it as quick marches are. Although 4-4 time is the usual march-measure, marches in 2-4, 6-8, and even 3-4, are to be met with.

March, dead. A funeral-march.

Marche (märsh), *Fr.* A march; in harmony, a symmetrical sequence of chords.

Marche harmonique (märsh här-mō-nĕk'), *Fr.* Harmonic progression.

Marcia (mär'tshǐ ä), *It.* A march.

Marcia con moto (mär'tshǐ-ä kōn mō'tō), *It.* A spirited martial movement.

Marcia funebre (mär-tshǐ-ä foo-nā'brĕ), *It.* Funeral-march.

Marciale (mär-tshǐ-ä'lĕ), *It.* See *Marziale*.

Marciata (mär-tshǐ-ä'tä), *It.* A march.

Marked. Accented.

Mark, harmonic. A sign (O) used in music for the violin, violoncello, and harp, to indicate that the notes over which it is placed are to be produced on such parts of the open strings as will give the harmonic sounds.

Markiren (mär-kē'rn), *Ger.* } To mark, to
Marquer (mär-kā), *Fr.* } emphasize.

Markirt (mär-kērt'), *Ger.* Well marked.

Marquez un peu la mélodie (mär-kā ŭnh pŭh lä mā'lō-dē), *Fr.* The melody to be slightly marked, or accented.

Marsch (märsh), *Ger.* A march.

Marschartig (märsh'är-tĭg), *Ger.* In the style of a march.

Märsche (mär'shĕ), *Ger. pl.* Marches.

Marseillaise (mär-säl-yäz), *Fr.* The Marseilles hymn; a French national air.

Martelé (mär-tĕl-lā'), *Fr.* } Hammer-
Martellando (mär tĕl-län'dō), *It.* } ing, strongly marking the notes, as if hammered.

Martellare (mär-tĕl-lä'rĕ), *It.* To hammer, to strike the notes forcibly, like a hammer.

Martellato (mär-tĕl-lä'tō), *It.* Hammered, strongly marked.

Marziale (mär-tsī-ä'lĕ), *It.* Martial, in the style of a march.

Mascharada (mä-skä-rä'dä), *It.* } Music com-
Mascherata (mä-skĕ-rä'tä), } posed for grotesque characters; masquerade music.

Maschera (mä'-kĕ-rä), *It.* A mask.

Mask. } A species of musical
Maske (mäs'kĕ), *Ger.* } drama, or operetta, in-
Masque (mäsk), *Fr.* } cluding singing and dancing, performed by characters in masks; also a utensil used by the ancient Roman actors and singers for the purpose of augmenting the power of the voice.

Mass. A vocal composition, performed during the celebration of high Mass, in the Roman Catholic Church, and generally accompanied by instruments. It consists of five principal movements, the Kyrie, Gloria, Credo, Sanctus, and Agnus Dei.

Mass (mäss), *Ger.* Measure, time.

Mass, high. The Mass celebrated in the Catholic churches by the singing of the choristers; distinguished from the low Mass, in which prayers are read without singing.

Mässig (mäs'sĭg), *Ger.* Moderate, moderately.

Mässig geschwind (mäs'sĭg ghĕ-shwĭnd'), *Ger.* moderately playful.

Mässig langsam (mäs'sĭg läng'säm), *Ger.* Moderately slow.

Mässig schnell (mäs'sĭg shnĕll), *Ger.* Moderately fast and animated.

Massima (mäs'sĭ-mä), *It.* A semibreve.

Massimo (mäs'sĭ-mō), *It.* Augmented, as regards intervals.

Mastersingers. A class of poets who flourished in Germany during the fifteenth and part of the sixteenth centuries and formed a close guild, with many traditional rules for poetic and musical composition.

Masure (mä-zoo'rĕ), } A lively Polish
Masureck (mä-zoo'rĕk), *Ger.* } dance, in 3-8
Masurek (mä-zoo'rĕk), } or 3-4 time,
Masurka (mä-zoor'kä), } quicker than the polonaise, and has an emphasis on one of the unaccented parts of the bar; the mazurka.

Matalan. A small Indian flute, used to accompany the Bayadere dances.

Matassins (mä-täs-sĕn'), *Fr.* A matachin dance; the dancers.

Matelotte (mä'tĕ-lŏt), *Fr.* A French sailor's dance in 3-4 time.

Matinare (mä-tī-nä'rĕ), *It.* To sing matins.

Matinata (mä-tī-nä'tä), *It.* A song for the morning; a serenade.

Matinée (mä-tī-nā), *Fr.* An entertainment given in the early part of the day.

Matinée musicale (mä-tī-nā mü-zĭ-käl'). A musical performance given in the daytime.

Matins. The name of the first morning service in the Roman Catholic Church.

Maultrommel (maul'trŏm-mĕl), *Ger.* A jew's-harp.

Maxima (mäx'ĭ-mä), *Lat.* The name of the longest note used in the fourteenth and fifteenth centuries. See *Large*.

Mazourk (mä-tsoork'), } A lively Pol-
Mazourka (mä-tsoor'kä), } ish dance
Mazur (mä'tsoor'), *Ger.* } of a sen-
Mazurca (mä-tsoor'kä), } timental
Mazurka (mä-tsoor'kä), } character,
Mazurke (mä-tsoor'ke), } in 3-8, or
3-4 time, of a peculiar rhythmic construc-

tion, quicker than the polonaise or polacca. See *Mazurka*.

M. D. The initials of Main Droite, the right hand.

Mean. A term formerly applied to the tenor, or medium, part in compositions for several parts, male and female.

Mean clef. Tenor clef.

Measure. That division of time by which the air and movement of music are regulated; the space between two bar lines on the staff. A rhythmic division, consisting of a certain number of pulses. From this feature measures are classified as two-pulse, three-pulse, four-pulse, six-pulse, nine-pulse, and twelve-pulse. The last three classes are called compound, consisting of two units in which each unit consists of a triplet, or group of three. Hence compound duple measure (six pulses), compound triple (nine), and compound quadruple (twelve). All measures consist of either twos or threes. The main accent always falls upon the first unit, and the bar is intended to show the place of the strong pulse. Considered with reference to the manner in which they are written, measures are described as 2-2, 2-4, 2-8, etc., in which the unit is represented by a half-note, a quarter, or eighth, 3-2, 3-4, 3-8, etc., and so on, of all other forms. The selection of a note-form to represent the unit is purely a matter of taste with the composer, and in no way affects the musical effect. The name measure is often applied to the representation of it, commonly described as "the space between two bars." This is incorrect. A measure is a certain rhythmical division, extending from a strong pulse to the next, or from any pulse to the corresponding place in the next group. The term "bar" is often improperly applied to measure. The bar is simply the line indicating the place of the strong pulse.

Measure, passy. An old, stately kind of dance; a cinque pas.

Mecanisme (měch-än-ĭsm), *Fr*. The mechanical part of playing; the technic.

Mechanically. A word applied to spiritless styles of performance.

Medesimo (mĕ-dā'zĭ-mō), *It.*
Medesmo (mĕ-dĕs'mō), } The same.

Medesmo moto (mĕ-dĕs'mō mō'tō), *It.*
Medesmo tempo (mĕ-dĕs'mō tĕm'pō), } In the same time, or movement, as before.

Mediant (mā'dĭ-ănt), *Lat.* } The third note
Médiante (mā-dĭ-änht'), *Fr.* } of the scale; the middle note between the tonic and the dominant.

Meditatio (mĕ-dĭ-tä'tsĭ-ō), *Lat.* A word formerly used to signify the middle of a chant, or the sound which terminates the first part of the verse in the Psalms.

Medley. A mixture; an assemblage of detached parts or passages of well-known songs or pieces so arranged that the end of one connects with the beginning of another.

Meertrompete (mār'trŏm-pā'tĕ), *Ger.* } Sea
Meerhorn (mār'hōrn), *Ger.* } trumpet.

Mehr (mār), *Ger.* More.

Mehrfach (mār'fākh), *Ger.* Manifold. Applied to an interval, a canon, or a compound organ-stop.

Mehrstimmig (mār-stĭm'mĭg), *Ger.* For several voices.

Meister (mīs'tĕr), *Ger.* Master, teacher.

Meisterfuge (mīs'tĕr-foo'ge), *Ger.* A master fugue, illustrating the utmost art in this variety of composition.

Meistergesang (mīs'tĕr-gŏ-zäng'), *Ger.* Master's song, minstrel's song.

Meistersänger (mīs'tĕr-säng'ĕr), *Ger.* Mastersinger, minstrel.

Meisterstück (mīs'tĕr-stük), *Ger.* Masterpiece.

Mélancolie (mā'län-kō-lē), *Fr.* Melancholy, in a mournful style.

Mélange (mā-länzh), *Fr.* A medley; a composition founded upon several popular airs.

Melisma (mĕ-lĭs'mā), *Gr.* A vocal grace or embellishment; several notes sung to one syllable.

Mellifluous (mĕl-lĭf'loo-ous). Smoothly flowing, very melodious.

Mellow. Soft, melodious.

Melode (mā-lō'dĕ), *It.* Melody, tune.

Melodeon. A reed instrument having a keyboard like the pianoforte. It is supplied with wind by a bellows worked with the feet of the performer, and had originally a pressure bellows, but later a suction bellows.

Melodeon, double-reed. A melodeon with two sets of reeds.

Melodic (mĕ-lŏd'ĭk). Relating to melody.

Melodica. An instrument invented by Stein, at Augsburg, similar to the pianoforte.

Melodic language. The language of melody or song, ideas expressed by a melodious combination of sounds.

Melodico (mĕ-lŏ'dĭk-ō). *It.* Melodious, tuneful.

Melodicon. An instrument invented by Riffel, in Copenhagen, the tones of which are produced from bent metal bars.

Melodics (mĕ-lŏd'ĭks). That part of musical theory treating of melody.

Melodic step. The movement of a voice, or part, from one tone to the following one.

Melodie (mā-lō dē'ä), *It.* Melody, tune.

Mélodie (mā-lō-dē), *Fr.* Melody, tune.

Mélodie bien sentie (mā'lō-dē bĭ-ănh sänh-tē), *Fr.* The melody to be well expressed or accented.

ā arm, ă add, ā ale, ĕ end, ē eve, ĭ ill, ī isle, ŏ old, ŏ odd, oo moon, ŭ but, ü *Fr.* sound, kh *Ger.* ch, nh nasal.

(153)

Mélodieuse (mā-lō-dī-üz), *Fr.* Melodious, smooth.
Mélodieusement (mā-lō-dī-üs-mänh), *Fr.* }
Melodiosamente (mĕ-lō-dī-ō-zä-mĕn'tĕ), *It.* } Melodiously, sweetly.
Mélodieux (mā-lō-dī-üz), *Fr.* } Melodious,
Melodik (mĕ-lō'dĭk), *Ger.* } tuneful.
Melodiosissimo (mĕ-lō-dĭ-ō-sēs'sĭ-mō), *It.* Extremely melodious.
Melodioso (mĕ-lō-dĭ-ō'zō), *It.* } Melodious, mu-
Melodisch (mĕ-lō'dĭsh), *Ger.* } sical, tuneful.
Melodious. Having melody, musical; a term applied to a succession of pleasing sounds. The pleasing quality of melody seems to depend upon rhythmic symmetries, fortunate melodic symmetries, and a happy choice of scale tones upon which emphasis falls.
Melodist. A composer, or singer, of melodies.
Melodista (mä-lō-dĕs'tä), *It.* }
Melodiste (mä-lō-dĕst'), *Fr.* } Melodist.
Melodistic (mĕ-lō-dĭs'tĭk), *Ger.* The rules or science of melody.
Melodium (mĕ-lō'dĭ-oom), *Fr.* A reed instrument of the harmonium class.
Melodize. To make melodious; to form a succession of sounds which shall produce an agreeable effect.
Melodram (mĕ-lō-dräm'), *Ger.* } Melodra-
Melodrame (mĕ-lō-dräm'), *Fr.* } ma. (1) The
Melodramma (mĕ-lō-dräm'mä), *It.* } original meaning of the word was synonymous with "opera." (2) The name has been further applied to a spoken drama accompanied with instrumental music. Ballads and parts of operas and other vocal works have also been sometimes treated melodramatically. (3) A third meaning is that of a play (mostly of a romantic and sensational nature) with incidental and now and then accompanying vocal and instrumental music.
Melodrammatico (mĕ-lō-dräm-mä'tĭ-kō), *It.* Melodramatic.
Melody. A tune; a succession of tones so ordered in rhythm and key as to express a musical idea.
Melody, chromatic. A melody consisting of a series of tones moving by chromatic intervals.
Melody, diatonic. A melody whose tones move by diatonic intervals.
Melody, leading. The principal part of a composition containing several parts.
Melograph. A piano invented in 1827, connected with which was machinery which recorded in notes whatever was improvised on the piano. The invention was not a complete success.
Melologue. A combination of recitative and music.
Meloman (mä'lō-män), *Gr.* } A passionate
Mélomane (mä'lō-män), *Fr.* } lover of music.
Melomanie (mä-lō-mä-nē), *Fr.* } Excessive
Melomany (mĕ-lōm'ä-ny), } love of music; music mania.

Melopea (mä-lō-pā'h), *It.* } The art of form
Mélopée (mä-lō-pā), *Fr.* } ing melody.
Melophare. A lantern, inside of which music paper, previously soaked in oil, is placed, so that the notes can be read when a light is placed inside; used for serenades at night.
Melopiano (mĕ-lō-pĭ ä'nō). A stringed instrument invented in 1870, combining tones resembling those of the pianoforte and organ.
Meloplaste (mĕl'ō-pläst). An instrument for teaching vocal music from a staff without either clefs or notes.
Melopœa (mĕ-lō-pē'ä), *Gr.* A term in ancient music signifying the art, or rules, of composition in melody; melody.
Melopomenos (mĕl-ō-pŏm'ĕ-nōs), *Gr.* Vocal melody.
Melos (mä'lōs), *Gr.* Tune, song, melody. As used by Wagner, melos includes not simply the melody alone, as such, but also the entire implied harmony, in short, the complete musical idea. Melos was a melodiousness which did not necessarily complete itself into melodies. In other words, *Arioso*
Même (mäm), *Fr.* The same.
Même mouvement (mäm moov-mänh), *Fr.* In the same movement.
Men (män), *It.* Less; an abbreviation of Meno.
Men allegro (mĕn äl-lä'grō), *It.* Less quick.
Menéstrels (mĕ-nās-trĕl), *Fr.* Minstrels.
Menétrier (mĕ-nä-trĭ-ā'), *Fr.* A minstrel, a rustic musician.
Meno (mä'nō), *It.* Less.
Meno allegro (mä'nō äl-lä'grō),' *It.* Less quick.
Meno forte (mä'nō fōr'tĕ), *It.* Less loud.
Meno mosso (mä'nō mōs'sō), *It.* Less movement, slower.
Meno piano (mä'nō pē-ä'nō), *It.* Not so softly.
Meno presto (mä'nō prĕs'tō), *It.* Less rapid.
Meno vivo (mä'nō vē'vō), *It.* Not so fast.
Menschenstimme (mĕn'sh'n - stĭm' n.ĕ), *Ger.* Human voice.
Mensur (mĕn-soor'),*Ger.* Measure, applied to time, tune, measurement of intervals; also the diameter, or scale, of organ pipes.
Menuet (mä-noo-ĕ), *Fr.* } A minuet, a
Menuetto (mä-noo-ĕt'tō), *It.* } slow dance in 3-4 time.
Men vivo (mĕn vē'vō), *It.* Less spirit.
Mesaulion (mĕ-saw'lĭ-ōn), *Gr.* Symphonies or ritornelli.
Mescal (mĕs-käl), *Tur.* A Turkish instrument, composed of twenty-three cane pipes of unequal length, each of which gives three different sounds, from the manner of blowing it.
Mescolanza (mĕs-kō-län'tsä), *It.* A medley, a mixture of discordant sounds, bad harmony.

ä *arm*, ä *add*, ā *ale*, ĕ *end*, ē *eve*, ĭ *ill*, ī *isle*, ŏ *old*, ō *odd*, oo *moon*, ŭ *but*, ü *Fr. sound*, kh *Ger. ch*, nh *nasal*.

(154)

Mese (mā'sĕ), *Gr.* A term applied by the ancient Greeks to the sound that completed the second tetrachord, and which was the center of their whole system. It was also the name given to the central string of the lyre, from which all the others were tuned.

Messa (mĕs'sä), *It.* A mass.

Messa di voce (mĕs'sä dī vō'tshĕ), *It.* The gradual swelling and diminishing of the voice.

Messe (măss), *Fr.* } A mass.
Messe (mĕs'sĕ), *Ger.* }

Messe brevi (mĕs'sĕ brā'vī), *It.* A short mass.

Mesto (mĕs'tō), *It.* Sad, mournful, melancholy.

Mestoso (mĕs-tō'zō), *It.* Sadly, mournfully.

Mesure (mā-zür'), *Fr.* The bar, or measure; the species of time.

Mesure à deux temps (mā-zür' ä dŭh tänh), *Fr.* Common time of two beats in a measure.

Mesure à trois temps (mā-zür' ä trwä tänh), *Fr.* Triple time of three beats in a measure.

Mesure demi (mā-zür' dĕ-mē'), *Fr.* Half measure.

Met. An abbreviation of Metronome.

Metal (mĕ-täl'), *Sp.* Strength, compass of the voice.

Metallico (mĕ-täl'lī kō), *It.* } Metallic, clear in
Metallo (mĕ täl'lō), } tone, *bel metallo di voce* means a voice clear, full, and brilliant.

Meter. See *Metre*.

Method. A course of instruction; classification; system.

Méthode (mā-tōd), *Fr.* } A method, system,
Metodo (mā'ō-dō), *It.* } style; a treatise, or book of instruction.

Metre. Measure; verse; arrangement of poetical feet, or of long and short syllables in verse.

Metre, common. A stanza of four lines in iambic measure, the syllables of each being in number and order as follows: 8, 6, 8, 6

Metre, common hallelujah. A stanza of six lines in iambic measure, the syllables in each being in number and order as follows; 8, 8, 6, 8, 8, 6.

Metre, eights. A stanza of four lines in anapestic measure, each line containing eight syllables, and marked thus: 8s.

Metre, eights and sevens. Consists of four lines in trochaic measure, designated thus; 8s and 7s; the syllables as follows: 8, 7, 8, 7.

Metre, eights, sevens, and four. A meter designated thus: 8s, 7s, and 4s, containing six lines in trochaic measure, the syllables being in number and order as follows: 8, 7, 8, 7, 4, 7.

Metre, elevens. Designated thus, 11s, and consisting of a stanza of four lines in anapestic measure, each line containing eleven syllables.

Metre, hallelujah. A stanza of six lines in iambic measure, the syllables of each being in number and order as follows: 6, 6, 6, 6, 8, 8.

Metre, long. Four lines in iambic measure, each line containing eight syllables.

Metre, long particular. Six lines in iambic measure, each line containing eight syllables.

Metre, sevens. Consists of four lines in trochaic measure, each line containing seven syllables.

Metre, short. Consists of four lines in iambic measure, the syllables in number and order as follows: 6, 6, 8, 6.

Metre, short particular. Consists of six lines in iambic measure, the syllables in number and order as follows; 6, 6, 8, 6, 6, 8.

Metre, tens and elevens. A meter designated thus, 10s and 11s, consisting of a stanza of four lines in anapestic measure, the syllables in number and order thus: 10, 10, 11, 11; or of six lines in iambic measure, as follows: 10, 10, 10, 10, 11, 11.

Metre, twelves. A metre designated thus, 12s, consisting of a stanza of four lines in anapestic measure, each line containing twelve syllables.

Metrical. Pertaining to measure, or due arrangement and combination of long and short syllables.

Metrically. In a metrical manner; according to poetic measure.

Metrik (mĕt'rīk), *Ger.* Metrical art.

Metrisch (mĕt'rish), *Ger.* Metrical.

Metro (mā'trō), *It.* } Meter, verse.
Metro (mā-tro), *Sp.* }

Metrometer (mĕ-trō-mĕ'tĕr), *Ger.* } A metrometer.
Metrometro (mā-trō'mĕ-trō), *It.* } nome.

Metronom (mĕ-trō-nōm'), *Ger.* } A machine
Metronome (mĕ'trō-nō'mĕ), *Gr.* } invented by John Maelzel, for measuring the time, or duration, of notes by means of a graduated scale and pendulum, which may be shortened or lengthened at pleasure. When indicated by composers, two characters are given—a note-form and a numeral. The latter shows the place where the pendulum should be set; the former the kind of note which should equal each beat of the pendulum. Sometimes a sign of equality is placed between the note and the numeral. Occasionally the initials M. M. are also used. The latter mean "Maelzel's Metronome." ♩ = 60, ♩ = 60, etc.

Metronome, bell. A metronome with the addition of a small bell which strikes at the commencement of each measure.

Metronome, pocket. A metronome of the size and form of a watch, on one side of which is marked the number of vibrations, and on the other the principal Italian musical terms.

ä *arm*, à *add*, ā *ale*, ĕ *end*, ē *eve*, ĭ *ill*, ī *isle*, ŏ *old*, ō *odd*, oo *moon*, ŭ *but*, ü *Fr. sound*, kh *Ger. ch.* nh *nasal*.

(155)

Mette (mĕt'tĕ), *Ger.* Matins.

Mettere in musica (mĕt'tĕ-rĕ īn moo-zī-kä'), *It.* To set to music.

Mettre d'accord (mātr dăk-kôr), *Fr.* To tune

Mettre en musique (mātr änh mü-zēk). *Fr.* To set to music.

Mettre en repetition (mātr änh rā-pĕ-tē'sĭ-ŏnh, *Fr.* To put in rehearsal.

Metzilloth, Metzilltheim, *Heb.* } Cymbals; otherwise rendered " bells of the horses," which is also correct.

Mez. An abbreviation of Mezzo.

Mez. F. An abbreviation of Mezzo Forte

Mez. Pia. An abbreviation of Mezzo Piano.

Mezza (mĕt'tsä), **Mezzo** (mĕt'tsŏ), *It.* } Medium, in the middle, half.

Mezza bravura (mĕt'tsä brä-voo'rä), *It.* A moderately difficult song.

Mezza forza (mĕt'tsä fŏr'tsä). Moderately loud.

Mezza manica (mĕt'tsä mä'nĭ-kä), *It.* The half-shift, in playing the violin, etc.

Mezzana (mĕt-tsä'nä), *It.* The middle string of a lute.

Mezza orchestra (mĕt'tsä ŏr-kĕs-trä), *It.* Half the orchestra.

Mezza voce (mĕt'tsä vŏ'tshĕ), *It.* Half the power of the voice; with moderate strength of tone.

Mezzo forte (mĕt'tsŏ fŏr'tĕ), *It.* Moderately loud.

Mezzo forte piano (mĕt'tsŏ fŏr'tĕ pē-ä'nŏ), *It.* Rather loud than soft.

Mezzo piano (mĕt'tsŏ pē-ä'nŏ), *It.* Rather soft.

Mezzo soprano (mĕt'tsŏ sŏ-prä'nŏ), *It.* A female voice of lower pitch than the soprano, or treble, but higher than the contralto. The general compass is from A under the lines to A above them.

Mezzo soprano clef. The C clef when placed on the second line of the staff, occurring in old church music or madrigals. The treble, or soprano, clef now supplies its place.

Mezzo staccato (mĕt'tsŏ stäk-kä'tŏ), *It.* A little detached.

Mezzo tenore (mĕt'tsŏ tĕ-nŏ'rĕ), *It.* A half tenor voice, nearly the same as a baritone.

Mezzo tuono (mĕt'tsŏ too-ŏ'nŏ), *It.* A semitone, a half tone.

Mezzo voce (mĕt'tsŏ vŏ'tshĕ), *It.* In a subdued voice.

M. F. The initials of Mezzo Forte.

M. G. The initials of Main Gauche.

Mi (mē), *It.* A syllable used in solfaing to designate E, or the third note of the major scale.

Mi bémol (mē bā'mŏl), *Fr.* The note E-flat.

Mi bémol majeur (mē bā'mŏl mä-zhŭr), *Fr.* The key of E♭ major.

Mi bémol mineur (mē bā'mŏl mī-nŭr), *Fr.* The key of E♭ minor.

Mi contra fa (mē kŏn'trä fä), *Lat.* An expression used by old theorists, meaning a false relation, especially the skip from *fow* of the scale to *seven*.

Microfono (mŏ-krŏ-fŏ'nŏ), *Sp.* } An instru-
Microphone (mī'krŏ-fŏn). } ment for the augmentation of small sounds; a microacoustic.

Middle C. That C which is between the bass and treble staves.

Middle voices. Tenor and alto voices.

Mi diese (mē dī äz'), *Fr.* The note E♯.

Mignon (mēn-yŏnh), *Fr.* Favorite.

Militairement (mĭl-ĭ-târ-mänh), *Fr.* } Milita-
Militare (mē-lī-tä'rĕ), *It.* } ry; in
Militarmente (mē-lī-tär-mĕn'tĕ), *It.* } a warlike, martial style.

Military music. Music intended for military bands; marches, quicksteps, etc.

Milote (mē-lŏ'tĕ), *Sp.* An Indian dance.

Mi majeur (mē mä-zhŭr), *Fr.* The key of E major.

Mimes (mē'mĕs). A kind of vocal, mimic actors, formerly very numerous in Europe.

Mi mineur (mē mī-nŭr'), *Fr.* The key of E minor.

Minaccevolmente (mē-nät-tshĕ-vŏl-mĕn'tĕ), *It.* In a threatening, menacing manner.

Minacciando (mē-nät-tshī-än'dŏ), } *It.*
Minaccievole (mē-nät-tsī-ä'vŏ-lĕ), }
Threatening, menacing.

Minacciosamente (mē-nät-tshī-ŏ'zä-mĕn te), *It.* Threatening, menacing, in a menacing manner.

Minaccioso (mē-nät-tshī-ŏ'zĕ), *It.* Threatening, menacing, in a menacing manner.

Minagnghinim (mī nängd'ghī-nīm), *Heb.* A pulsatile instrument used by the Hebrews, consisting of a square table of wood furnished with a handle; over this table was stretched an iron chain and a hempen chord which passed through balls of wood or brass, and striking against the table when the instrument was in motion, produced a clear, ringing sound.

Minder (mĭn'dĕr), *Ger.* Minor, less, not so much.

Mineur (mī-nŭr'), *Fr.* Minor.

Minim. A half-note; a note equal to one half of a semibreve.

Minima (mē'nī-mä), *It.* }
Minime (mĭn-ēm'), *Fr.* } A minim.

Minim rest. A mark of silence equal in duration to a minim, made thus, —.

Minnedichter mĭn'nĕ-dĭkh'tĕr), } Min-
Minnesänger (mĭn'nĕ-säng-ĕr), *Ger.* } strels
Minnesinger (mĭn'nĕ-sĭng-ĕr), } of the twelfth and thirteenth centuries, who wan-

---

ä *arm*, ă *add*, ā *ale*, ĕ *end*, ē *eve*, ĭ *ill*, ī *isle*, ŏ *old*, ō *odd*, oo *moon*, ŭ *but*, ü *Fr. sound*, kh *Ger. ch*, nh *nasal*.

(156)

dered from place to place, singing a great variety of songs and melodies.

Minor. Less, smaller, in speaking of intervals, etc.

Minor canons. Those clergymen of a cathedral or chapel who occasionally assist at the performance of the service and anthem.

Minor diatonic scale. There are two kinds: one where the semitones fall between the second and third and seventh and eighth, both in ascending and descending; in the other the semitone falls between the second and third and seventh and eighth ascending, and descending, between the fifth and sixth and second and third. The former is the harmonic, the latter the melodic form.

Minore (mē-nō'rĕ), *It.* Minor.

Minor key. } One of the modern modes,
Minor mode. } or scales, in which the third note is a minor third from the tonic.

Minor second. The smallest interval in practicable use, a half-step.

Minor seventh. An interval consisting of four tones and two semitones.

Minor sixth. An interval composed of three tones and two semitones.

Minor tactus. Among the ancients, the act of beating time; consisting of a semitone in a bar.

Minor third. A diatonic interval containing three semitones.

Minor threefold chord. A minor triad.

Minor triad. A union of any tone with its minor third and perfect fifth.

Minstrels. Wandering poets or musicians.

Minstrelsy. The art or profession of a minstrel.

Minue (mĕ'noo-ä), *Sp.* A minuet.

Minuet. A dance of French origin in ternary time—usually in 3-4, sometimes in 3-8 time. Its movement and character changed in the course of its career. A courtly stateliness and well-regulated gaiety are its most prominent features. By its introduction, first, into the suite and partita, and afterwards into the sonata, symphony, etc., it has become an artistic form of importance. In the sonata and symphony it generally consists of two minuets, each of two parts, the first minuet being repeated after the second, which is called the trio. The composers in thus treating the minuet artistically have by no means always retained the original nature of the dance; on the contrary, have produced under this name pieces very different in movement and character.

Minuettina (mē - noo - ĕt - tē' nä), *It.* A little minuet.

Minuetto (mē-noo-ĕt'tō), *It.* A minuet.

Miracle-Plays. "The Miracle-Play is distinguished from the Mystery because it connects itself less closely with the Scriptures and the services of the Church, and embodies, for the most part, various apocryphal legends about the saints and the Virgin."

Miserere (mē-sĕ-rā'rĕ), *Lat.* "Have mercy." A psalm of supplication.

Misericordia (mē'sĕ-rĭ-kōr'dĭ-ä), *Lat.* A small movable seat in the choir of a church; a miserere.

Miskin. A little bagpipe.

Missa (mĕs'sä), *Lat.* A mass.

Missa brevis (mĕs'sä brā'vĭs), *Lat.* A short mass.

Missa canonica (mĕs'sä kä-nŏ'nĭ-kä), *Lat.* A canonical mass.

Missal. The massbook.

Missa pro defunctis (mĕs'sä prō dĕ-foonk'tĭs), *Lat.* A requiem; a mass for departed souls.

Missa solennis (mĕs'sä sŏ-lĕn'nĭs), *Lat.* A solemn mass, for high festivals.

Missel (mĕs-s'l), *Fr.* Missal; the massbook.

Misshällig (mĭss'häl'lĭg), *Ger.* Dissonant, discordant.

Misshälligkeit (mĭss'häl-lĭg-kīt), *Ger.* Dissonance, discordance.

Misshellig (mĭss'hĕl-lĭg), *Ger.* See *Misshällig*.

Missklang (mĭss'kläng), *Ger.* Discordant, out of tune. (Not the same as dissonant.)

Missklänge (mĭss'kläng'ĕ), *Ger. pl.* Discordant sounds.

Missklingen (mĭss'klĭng-ĕn), *Ger.* To sound discordant.

Misslaut (mĭss'lout), *Ger.* Unharmonious, discordant sound.

Misslauten (mĭss'lou-t'n), *Ger.* To sound inharmoniously.

Misslautend (mĭss'lou-tĕnd), *Ger.* Dissonant, discordant.

Missstimmen (mĭss'stĭm-m'n), *Ger.* To put out of tune.

Misteriosamente (mĕs-tĕ-rĭ-ō-zä-mĕn'tĕ), } *It.*
Misterioso (mĕs-tĕ-rĭ-ō'zō),
Mysteriously, in a mysterious manner.

Mistero, con (mĕs-tā'rō), *It.* With an air of mystery.

Misto (mĕs-tō), *Gr.* Mixed; a term given by the ancients to some of their modes.

Misura (mē - soo'rä), *It.* A bar, a measure; time.

Misurato (mē - soo - rä'tō), *It.* Measured; in strict, measured time.

Mit (mĭt), *Ger.* With, by.

Mit abwechselnden Manualen (mĭt äb'vĕkh-sĕln-dĕn mä - noo - ä'l'n), *Ger.* Alternately, from the choir to the great organ.

Mit ganz schwachen Registern (mĭt gänts shvä'kh'n rĕ-ghĭs'tĕrn), *Ger.* With very soft stops.

Mit Gefühl (mĭt ghĕ-fül'), *Ger.* With feeling and sentiment.

ä *arm*, ă *add*, ā *ale*, ĕ *end*, ē *eve*, ĭ *ill*, ī *isle*, ŏ *old*, ō *odd*, oo *moon*, ŭ *but*, ü *Fr. sound*, kh *Ger. ch*, nh *nasal*.

Mit Keckheit (mĭt kĕk'hīt), *Ger.* With vigor and boldness; in the bravura, or dashing, style.

Mitklang (mĭt'kläng), *Ger.* Resonance.

Mitlaut (mĭt'lout), *Ger.* } Concord, consonance.
Mitlauter (mĭt'lou-tĕr),

Mitlauten (mĭt'lou-t'n), *Ger.* To sound at the same time, or in common with.

Mitleidsvoll (mĭt'līds-fŏl), *Ger.* Compassionate.

Mit sanften Stimmen (mĭt sänf't'n stĭm'm'n), *Ger.* With soft stops.

Mit starken Stimmen (mĭt stär'k'n stĭm'm'n), *Ger.* With loud stops.

Mittel=C (mĭt'tĕl-tsä), *Ger.* Middle C. See *Diagram of Clefs*.

Mittelcadenz (mĭt't'l-kä-dĕnts'), *Ger.* A half, or imperfect, cadence.

Mittellaut (mĭt'tĕl-lout), *Ger.* Middle sound.

Mittelmässig (mĭt't'l-mäs'sĭg), *Ger.* Middling.

Mittelstimme (mĭt't'l-stĭm'mĕ), *Ger.* The mean or middle voice, or part; the tenor.

Mit voller Orgel (mĭt fŏl'lĕr ŏr'g'l), *Ger.* With full organ.

Mixolydian. (1) In the ancient Greek system the name of one of the octave species b c d c͡f g a b, also called Hyperdorian, and of one of the transposition scales. (2) In the old ecclesiastical system it is the name of the seventh (the fourth authentic) mode, or tone (g a b͡c d͡e f͡ g).

Mixture. An organ-stop consisting of several ranks of pipes—from two to five pipes sounding different harmonic notes corresponding to each key. Modern mixtures contain only octaves and fifths, the latter voiced softly and in flute quality. They impart brightness to the full organ tone, but are not so indispensable as before organ-voicing had become so advanced. Formerly it was very difficult to secure the harmonic overtones from the fundamental pipes. The tone was therefore dull and heavy. Mixtures were invented to remedy this. The old mixtures, called also furniture, cymbal, etc., contained thirds, which, when played in chords, produced a hideous snarling.

Mode. Species of scale. In the modern system of music there are only two modes, the major and minor; in the ancient Greek and the mediæval ecclesiastical system there was a much greater number.

Mode, major. That in which the third from the keynote is major.

Mode, minor. That which in the third degree from the tonic forms the interval of a minor third.

Moderamento (mō-dĕ-rä-mĕn'tō), *It.* }
Moderato (mō-dĕ-rä'tō),
Moderately; in moderate time.

Moderatissimo (mō-dĕ-rä-tēs'sĭ-mō), *It.* In very moderate time.

Moderato assai con molto sentimento (mō-dĕ-rä'tō äs-sä'ē kōn mōl'tō sĕn-tĭ-mĕn'tō), *It.* A very moderate degree of quickness with much expression.

Moderazione (mō-dĕ-rä-tsĭ-ō'nĕ), *It.* Moderation.

Modere (mo-där'), *Fr.* Moderate.

Modern. Not in the ancient style.

Moderna, alla (mō-där'nä äl'lä), *It.* In the modern style.

Modestamente (mō-dĕs-tä-mĕn'tĕ), *It.* }
Modesto (mō-dĕs'tō),
Modestly, quietly, moderately.

Modificazioni (mō-dĕ-fĭ-kä-tsĭ-ō'nĕ), *It. pl.* Modifications, light and shade of intonation, slight alterations.

Modinha (mō-dēn'ä), *Por.* A short Portuguese song.

Mod. An abbreviation of Moderato.

Modo (mō'dō), *It.* }
Modo (mō'dō), *Sp.* A mode, a scale.

Modo maggiore (mō'dō mäd-jĭ-ō'rĕ), *It.* The major mode.

Mod'to. An abbreviation of Moderato.

Modolare (mō-dō-lä'rĕ), *It.* } To modulate;
Modulare (mō-doo-lä'rĕ), to accommodate the voice or instrument to a certain intonation.

Modulante (mō-doo-län'tĕ), *It.* Modulating.

Modulate. To move from one key to another in a manner agreeable to the ear.

Modulate, Modulation. The primary meaning of "to modulate" is "to form after a certain mode, to measure off properly." In music it originally meant "to measure rhythmically," then, also, "to measure melodically"—melodic measurement being synonymous with "inflection." In modern technical terminology "to modulate" signifies "to change the key;" "modulation," "a change of key." Modern usage differs much from that current with Bach and his contemporaries. According to modern ideas, any chord may follow any other whenever it can be introduced smoothly or with suitable musical effect. Such a chord may be apparently foreign to the key of the first chord, but it is not now regarded as constituting a modulation unless the ear is unsettled from the original tonic, which is by no means universally the case. Hence the idea of key has been materially enlarged, so as to include all possible chords which can be led into smoothly from any chord in the key. A modulation is said to be abrupt when the new key comes suddenly, as when from the key of C we suddenly go to the key of A♭ and remain there. As opposed to the usual modulation by a succession of fifths, as practiced in the time of Bach. Bach, however, uses almost all chords which have been used since.

ä *arm*, ă *add*, â *ale*, ĕ *end*, ē *eve*, ĭ *ill*, ī *isle*, ō *old*, ŏ *odd*, oo *moon*, ŭ *but*, ü *Fr. sound*, kh *Ger.* ch, nh *nasal*.

Modulation, abrupt. Sudden modulation into keys which are not closely related to the original key.

Modulation, deceptive. Any modulation by which the ear is deceived and led to an unexpected harmony.

Modulation, enharmonic. A modulation effected by altering the notation of one or more intervals belonging to some characteristic chord, and thus changing the key and the harmony from that into which it would naturally have resolved. The chords which admit of these alterations are, first, the diminished seventh and its inversions; secondly, the dominant seventh not inverted, and the chord of the superfluous sixth and perfect fifth.

Modulation, passing. } A form of modulation which leaves a
Modulation, transient. } key nearly as soon as entered upon.

Modulatore (mō-doo-lä-tō'rĕ), *It.* Singer, tuner.

Modulazione (mō-doo-lä-tsǐ-ō'nĕ), *It.* Modulation.

Moduliren (mō-doo-lē'r'n), *Ger.* To modulate.

Modus (mō'doos), *Lat.* A key, mode, scale.

Mohinda. A short Portuguese love-song.

Mohrentanz (mō'-rĕn-tänts), *Ger.* Morisco, morris dance.

Moins (mwä), *Fr.* Less.

Moll (mōll), *Ger.* Minor.

Molla (mōl'lä), *It.* A key of the flute, etc., for raising or lowering a note.

Molle (mōl), *Fr.* Soft, mellow, delicate.

Mollemente (mōl-lĕ-mĕn'tĕ), *It.* Softly, gently, delicately.

Mollis (mōl'lĭs), *Lat.* Soft.

Molltonart (mōll'tōn'ärt), *Ger.* Minor key, or scale.

Moltisonante (mōl-tē-zō-nän'tĕ), *It.* Resounding, very sonorous.

Molto (mōl'tō), *It.* Much, very much, extremely, a great deal.

Molto adagio (mōl'tō ä-dä'jĭ-ō), *It.* Extremely slow.

Molto allegro (mōl'tō al-lā'grō), *It.* Very quick.

Molto carattere, con (mōl'tō kä-rät-tĕ-rĕ, kōn), *It.* With character and emphasis.

Molto mosso (mōl'tō mōs'sō), *It.* Much movement, much motion.

Molto slargando (mōl'tō slär-gän'dō), *It.* Much extended; much slower.

Molto sostenuto (mōl'tō sōs-tĕ-noo'tō), *It.* Very sustained; very legato.

Molto staccato con grazia (mōl'tō stäk-kä'tō kōn grä'tsǐ-ä), *It.* In staccato style, and with grace.

Molto vibrato (mōl'tō vǐ-brä'tō), *It.* Very violent or rapid.

Molto vivace (mōl'tō vǐ-vä'tshĕ), *It.* Very lively.

Monacordo (mō-nä-kōr'dō), *It.* } (1) An in-
Monochord (mōn-ō-kōrd). } strument formerly used for the measurement of intervals. It had one string and a movable bridge. (2) Also a name of the tromba marina, or trumscheit. (3) A clavichord.

Monaulos (mōn'on-lōs), *Gr.* An ancient flute, played through the mouthpiece at the end like the flageolet.

Monferina (mōn-fĕ-rē'nä), *It.* A lively Italian dance in 6-8 time.

Monochord pedal. The one-stringed pedal.

Monocorde (mōn-ō-kōrd'). *Fr.* } On one string
Monocordo (mō-nō-kōr'dō), *It.* } only. See also *Monochord*.

Monodia (mō-nō-dē'ä), *It.* } A composition
Monodie (mōn-ō-dē), *Fr.* } for a single voice.
Monody (mōn-ō-dy). } The term originally applied to church solos. Also a composition with a single idea.

Monodic. For one voice, a solo.

Monodist. One who writes a monody.

Monodram (mō-nō-dräm'), *Ger.* } A musical
Monodrama (mō-nō-drä'mä), *It.* } drama, in which only one actor appears; a monodrama.

Monodrame (mōn-ō-dräm), *Fr.* A drama performed by a single individual.

Monologue. A soliloquy; a poem, song, or scene written and composed for a single performer.

Monophonic (mōn-ō-fō'nĭk), *Gr.* In one part only.

Monotone. Uniformity of sound; one and the same sound.

Monotonia (mō-nō-tō'nǐ-ä), *Sp.* } Monotony;
Monotonie (mōn-ō-tō-nē), *Fr.* } sameness of
Monotonie (mō'nō-tō-nē'), *Ger.* } sound.

Monotonous (mō-nŏt'ō-nŭs). An epithet applied to any instrument which produces but one tone or note; as the drum, tambourine, etc.

Monotony. A wearisome uniformity of sound; a continued repetition of the same tone or notes.

Montant (mōnh-tänh), *Fr.* Ascending.

Monter (mōn-tĕh), *Fr.* (1) To put strings on an instrument; to tune them. (2) To put the parts of a wind instrument together. (3) To ascend.

Montré (mōnh-trä'), *Fr.* Mounted; in front; a term applied to the organ-pipes which are placed in front of the case; commonly a diapason.

Montré d'orgue (mōnh-trä d'ōrg), *Fr.* The range of pipes in the front of an organ.

Moorish drum. A tambourine.

Moralités (*Fr.*), **Moralities.** Allegorical plays popular in the middle ages. The object of these plays was to point a moral, and among

Morbidezza, con (mŏr-bĭ-dĕt'sä kōn), *It.* With excessive delicacy.

Morceau (mŏr-sō'), *Fr.* A choice and select musical piece, or composition; a fine phrase or passage.

Morceau d'ensemble (mŏr-sō' d'äuh-sänhbl), *Fr.* A piece harmonized for several voices.

Mordante (mŏr-dän'tĕ), *It.* See *Mordente*.

Mordente (mŏr-dĕn'tĕ), *It.* Transient shake, or beat; an embellishment formed by two or more notes, preceding the principal note.

Mordente, long. The short mordente repeated.

Mordente, short. An embellishment consisting of the note over which Written. Played. the sign is placed and the note below it, thus: A similar sign without the vertical stroke indicates the Prall-trill, which is a precisely similar embellishment, employing the note above. The accent falls upon the first tones.

Morendo (mō-rĕn'dō), *It.* } Dying away; ex-
Moriente (mō-rĭ-ĕn'tĕ), *It.* } piring; gradually diminishing the tone and the time.

Moresca (mō-rĕs'kä), *It.* } Moorish; morris
Moresque (mō-rĕsk'), *It.* } dance, in which bells are jingled at the ankles and swords clashed.

Morgengesang (mŏr'g'n-ghĕ-zäng'), *Ger.* }
Morgenlied (mŏr'g'n-lēd), *Ger.* }
Morning song or hymn.

Morgenständchen (mŏr'g'n-ständ'kh'n), *Ger.* Morning serenade.

Morisco (mō-rĕs'kō), *It.* In the Moorish style. See *Moresca*.

Morisk (mō-rĭsk). The morris dance.

Mormoramento (mŏr-mō-rä-mĕn'tō), *It.* A murmur, warbling, buzzing, purling.

Mormorando (mŏr-mō-rän'dō), } With a
Mormorevole (mŏr-mō-rä'vō-lĕ), *It.* } gentle,
Mormoroso (mŏr-mō-rō'zō), } murmuring sound.

Morrice dance. } A peculiar kind of dance
Morris dance. } practiced in the middle
Morriske dance. } ages. It is supposed to have been introduced into England by Edward III. In the morris dance bells were fastened to the feet of the performer.

Mort. A tune sounded at the death of game.

Mosso (mŏs'sō), *It.* Moved, movement, motion.

Mosso, molto (mŏs'sō mŏl'tō), *It.* Quick, with much motion.

Mostra (mŏs'trä), *It.* A direct (∿), which, when placed on a line, indicates the first note upon the next page.

Mot (mō), *Fr.* Literally, a word; a note or brief strain on a bugle.

Motet. } A vocal composition in several
Motett. } parts, generally without instrumental accompaniment, set to a sacred text, usually words taken from the Bible. Obligato instrumental accompaniments, which came into vogue in the seventeenth century, but are to be met with before and after that time, have to be regarded as exceptional. The motet is one of the oldest forms of mensurable music, and has, of course, undergone many changes. Protestant Germany cultivated it zealously, developing it according to her own taste and mental bias. In earlier times it was the sacred counterpart of the secular madrigal (*q. v.*).

Motette (mō-tĕt'), *Ger.* }
Motet (mō-tā'), *Fr.* } A motet.
Motetto (mō-tĕt'tō), *It.* }

Motetten (mō tĕt-t'n), *Ger.* } Motets.
Motetti (mō-tĕt'tē), *It.* }

Motetto per voci sole (mō-tĕt'tō pär vō'tshĕ sō-lä'), *It.* A motet for voices without accompaniment; a motet each part of which is for a single voice.

Motetus (mō-tĕt'oos), *Lat.* A motet.

Motif (mō-tēf'), *Fr.* Motive, theme, subject.

Motion. (1) The melodic progression of a part considered by itself. It may be either conjunct or disjunct—that is, the progression may be by degrees or by skips. (2) The melodic progression of two or more parts considered in their relation to each other. There are three kinds of motion: (*a*) Similar motion, when two parts ascend and descend together. (*b*) Contrary motion, when the one ascends and the other descends. (*c*) Oblique motion, when one part remains stationary while the other ascends or descends. The simultaneous combination of these three kinds of progression is called "mixed motion." (3) Also used of rhythmic motion, as pulse motion, meaning that the prevailing tone length is that of the measure pulse, half-pulse motion, where the prevailing motion is of half-pulse, etc. Also "eighth-note motion," meaning that the prevailing entrances of tones in a single voice, or of tones in different voices, fall at the uniform period of an eighth-note.

Motive. The characteristic and predominant passage of an air; the theme, or subject, of a composition.

Motivo (mō-tē'vō), *It.* Motive; the theme, or subject, of a musical composition.

Moto (mō'tō), *It.* Motion, movement; *con moto*, with motion, rather quick.

Moto accelerato (mō'tō ät-tshä-lĕ-rä'tō), *It.* Accelerated motion.

Moto contrario (mō'tō kŏn-trä'rĭ-ō), *It.* Contrary motion.

Moto obliquo (mō'tō ōb-lē'kwō), *It.* Oblique motion.

Moto precedente (mō'tō prä-tshĭ-dĕn'tĕ), *It.* The same time as the preceding movement.

Moto primo (mō'tō prē'mō), *It.* The same time as the first.

Moto retto (mō'tō rĕt'tō), *It.* Direct, or similar, motion.
Motteggiando (mŏt-tĕd-jī-än'dō), *It.* Jeeringly, mockingly, jocosely.
Mottetto (mŏt-tĕt'tō), *It.* A motet.
Motus (mō'toos), *Lat.* Motion, movement.
Motus contrarius (mo'toos kŏn-trä'rĭ-oos), *Lat.* Contrary motion.
Motus obliquus (mō'toos ŏb-lē'kwoo-oos), *Lat.* Oblique motion.
Motus rectus (mō'toos rĕk'toos), *Lat.* Direct, or similar, motion.
Mouthpiece. That part of a trumpet, horn, etc., which is applied to the lips.
Mouvement (moov-mänh), *Fr.* } Motion,
Movimento (mō-vī-mĕn'tō), *It.* } movement, impulse; the time of a piece.
Mouvement de l'archet (moov-mänh dŭh l'är-shā), *Fr.* Bowing, the movement of the bow.
Movement. Manner of going; as, polka movement, march movement, etc. The name given to any portion of a composition comprehended under the same measure or time; a composition consists of as many movements as there are positive changes in measure and tempo.
Movimento contrario (mō-vī-mĕn'tō kŏn-trä'rĭ-ō), *It.* Contrary movement.
M. P. The initials of Mezzo Piano.
M. S. The initials of Mano Sinestra.
Mu. A syllable applied to the fourth note of the Hebrew scale in solfaing.
Nuance (mü-änhs'), *Fr.* A change, or variation, of notes; a nuance.
Muet (mü-ā'), *Fr.* Mute.
Mund (moond), *Ger.* The mouth.
Mundharmonica (moond-här-mō'nĭ-kä), *Ger.* The jew's-harp; or, a mouth harmonica.
Mundstück (moond'stük), *Ger.* Reed, mouthpiece.
Münster (mün'stĕr), *Ger.* Minster, cathedral.
Munter (moon'tĕr), *Ger.* Lively, sprightly.
Munterkeit (moon'tĕr-kīt), *Ger.* Liveliness, briskness, vivacity.
Murmeln (moor'mĕlu), *Ger.* To murmur.
Murmelnd (moor'mĕlnd), *Ger.* Murmuring.
Murmur. A low, indistinct sound.
Mus. Bac. An abbreviation of Bachelor of Music. (Little used.)
Mus. Doc. An abbreviation of Doctor of Music.
Muse. Name originally given to the muzzle, or tube, of the bagpipe. One of the nine fabled goddesses presiding over art, literature, or music.
Musetta (moo-zĕt-tä), *It.* } (1) A small, imperfect instrument
Musette (mü-sĕt'), *Fr.* } of the oboe kind. (2) A French bagpipe. (3) A pastoral air in imitation of the music of the latter instrument, with a drone bass, in 6-8, 3-4, and also in 2-4 and 4-4 time. Such airs have also been used as dance tunes.
Music. The science of harmonical sounds, which treats of the principles of harmony, or the properties, dependencies, and relations of sounds to each other.
Musica (moo'zĭ-kä), *It.* Music.
Musica antiqua (moo'sĭ-kä än-tĭ-kwä), *Lat.* Ancient music.
Musica da camera (moo'zĭ-kä dä kä'mĕ-rä), *It.* Music for the chamber.
Musica da chiesa (moo'zĭ-kä dä kē-ā'zä), *It.* Church music.
Musica da teatro (moo'zĭ-kä dä tā-ä'trō), *It.* Dramatic music.
Musicale (moo'zĭ-kä-lĕ), *It.* Musical, belonging to music.
Musical brachygraphy. The art of writing musical notation in an abbreviated style by means of signs, characters, etc.
Musical clocks. Clocks containing an arrangement similar to a barrel organ, moved by weights and springs and producing various tunes.
Musical convention. A gathering of choristers and teachers for the study and practice of music.
Musical design. The invention and conduct of the subject; the disposition of every part; the general order of the whole; counterpoint.
Musical director. A conductor; one who has charge of public musical performances.
Musical drama. Opera, lyric drama.
Musical ear. The ability of determining by the sense of hearing the finest gradation of sound.
Musicalement (mü-zĭ-käl-mänh), *Fr.* }
Musicalmente (moo-zĭ-käl-mĕn'tĕ), *It.* } Musically, harmoniously.
Musical glasses. Drinking-glasses so tuned in regard to each other that a wet finger being passed round their brims they produce the notes of the diatonic scale, and are capable of giving the successive sounds of regular tunes or melodies.
Musical grammar. The rules of musical composition.
Musically. In a musical, melodious manner.
Musical nomenclature. The vocabulary of names and technical terms in music.
Musical pantomime. A dramatic performance, the ideas and sentiments of which are expressed by music and gestures.
Musical science. The theory of music, in contradistinction from the practice, which is an art; the general principles and laws of combining tones for art purposes. It includes harmony, counterpoint, canon and fugue, form, orchestration, etc.
Musical soirée. An evening musical entertainment, public or private.

ă arm, ä add, ā ale, ĕ end, ē eve, ĭ ill, ī isle, ō old, ŏ odd, oo moon, ŭ but, ü *Fr.* sound, kh *Ger. ch*, nh *nasal.*

Musical terms. Words or phrases appended to passages of music, indicating the manner in which they should be performed.

Musica plana (moo'sĭ-kä plä'nä), *Lat.* Plain chant or song. The traditional tunes for intoning the various offices of the church.

Music, enharmonic. Music that proceeds by intervals smaller than the diatonic and chromatic, or music which progresses from one key to another by means of enharmonic changes, as when, e. g., the chord of C♯ is followed by that of A♭, the former being enharmonically changed into the chord of D♭.

Music, field. Martial music.

Music, Gregorian. Those chants and melodies introduced into the Roman Catholic service by St. Gregory in the sixth century.

Music, hunting. Music suited to the chase.

Musician. One who understands the science of music, or who sings, or performs on some instrument according to the rules of art.

Musicien (mü-zĕ-sĭ-änh), *Fr.* Musician.

Musico (moo'zĭ-kō), *It.* A musician; a professor or practitioner of music. The name was also applied to those male vocalists who formerly sang soprano parts.

Music of the future. A term applied to the music of Richard Wagner and others of his school.

Music-recorder. An instrument to be attached to a pianoforte for the purpose of recording upon paper the notes that are played.

Music-timekeeper. An English instrument designed to enable a performer to keep time in any measure in which a piece of music is written.

Music-trademark. A mark adopted by the United States Board of Music Trade, being a star enclosing figures denoting the retail price of the work upon which it is printed, the figures representing the number of dimes at which it is sold.

Musicus (moo'zĭ-koos), *Ger.* A musician.

Musiker (moo'zĭ-kĕr), *Ger.* A musician.

Musikfest (moo-sĭk'fĕst), *Ger.* A musical festival.

Musiklehrer (moo-zĭk-lä'rĕr), *Ger.* Teacher of music.

Musikprobe (moo-zĭk-prō'bĕ), *Ger.* A musical rehearsal.

Musikverein (moo-zĭk'fĕ-rīn'), *Ger.* A musical society.

Musikzeitung (moo-zĭk-tsī'toong), *Ger.* A musical paper,

Musique (mü-zēk), *Fr.* Music.

Musique d'eglise (mü-zēk dā-glēz), *Fr.* Church music.

Muta (moo'tä), *It.* Change; in horn and trumpet music it means to change the crooks; in drum parts it means that the tuning of the drum is to be altered.

Mutation. Change, transition; the transformation of the voice occurring at the age of puberty.

Mutation (mü-tä-sĭ-ōnh), *Fr.* } Mutation.
Mutazione (moo-tä-tsĭ-ō'nĕ), *It.* }

Mutation, or filling-up stops, are those which do not give a sound corresponding to the key pressed down—such as the quint, tierce, twelfth, etc.

Mute. A small instrument of brass, ivory, or wood, sometimes placed on the bridge of a violin, viola, or violoncello, to diminish the tone of the instrument by damping or checking its vibrations. Also a round piece of wood with apertures, placed in the bell of wind instruments in order to reduce the volume of tone.

Muthig (moo'tĭg), *Ger.* Courageous, spirited.

Muthwillig (moot'vĭl-lĭg), *Ger.* Mischievous, lively.

Mutiren (moo-tĕ'r'n), *Ger.* To change the voice from soprano to tenor, baritone, or bass.

Mystères (mĭs-tār), *Fr.*   } A kind of re-
Mysterien (mē-stä'rē'u), *Ger.* } ligious dra-
Mysteries.   } ma; rude theatrical representations of sacred history in vogue during the middle ages, and deriving their name from the mysteries of the Christian faith of which they treat. The scope of their subjects extends from the Creation to the Last Judgment, comprehending "the whole scheme of man's fall and redemption." The Passion-Plays still performed at Ammergau and some other places are survivals of the old Mysteries.

Nabla (nä-blä), *Heb.* The nebel, a ten-stringed instrument of the ancient Hebrews; the harp of the Jews, sometimes written Nebel Nasar.

Nacaire (nä-kär), *Fr.*   } A brass drum
Nacara (nä'kä-rä), *It.*   } with a loud, metal-
Nacarre (nä'kä-rē), *It. pl.* } lic tone, formerly much used in France and Italy.

Nacchera (näk'kĕ-rä), *It.* Kettledrums.

Nachahmung (näkh-ä'moong), *Ger.* Imitation. The more or less exact repetition of a motive, phrase, or passage at the same or a different pitch, in a different voice.

Nach Belieben (näkh bā-lē'b'n), *Ger.* At pleasure. The same as Ad libitum.

Nachdruck (näkh'drook), *Ger.* Emphasis, accent.
Nachdrücklich (näkh'drük-lĭkh), *Ger.*
Nachdrucksvoll (näkh'drooks-fōl), } Energetic, emphatic, forcible.
Nachhall (näkh'häll), *Ger.* Reverberation, echo.
Nachklang (näkh'kläng), *Ger.* Resonance, echo.
Nachklingen (näkh'klĭng-ĕn), *Ger.* } To ring,
Nachschallen (näkh'shäl-l'n), } to echo, to resound.
Nachlassend (näkh-läs'sĕnd),*Ger.* Slackening in time.
Nachlässig (näkh-läs'sĭgh), *Ger.* Slackening, meaning somewhat carelessly; letting up.
Nachschlag (näkh'shläg),*Ger.* Additional, or afternote.
Nachspiel (näkh'spēl),*Ger.* Afterplay; a postlude, or concluding piece.
Nächstverwandte Töne (näkhst'fĕr-wänd'tĕ tö'nĕ), *Ger.* The nearest relative keys.
Nachthorn (näkht'hŏrn),*Ger.* Nighthorn; an organ-stop of 8-feet tone, nearly identical with the quintation, but of larger scale and more hornlike tone.
Nachtschläger (näkht'shlä'gĕr), *Ger.* }
Nachtigall (näkht'ĭ-gäll), Nightingale.
Nachtständchen (näkht'ständ-kh'n), *Ger.* A serenade.
Nachtstück (näkht'stŭck),*Ger.* A serenade, a nocturne.
Nach und nach (näkh oond näkh), *Ger.* By little and little, by degrees.
Nafie (nä-fē). A Persian trumpet.
Nafiri (nä-fē-rē). An Indian trumpet.
Nagarah (nä-gä'rä), *Per.* The kettledrum of the Persians.
Nagelgeige (*Ger.*), **Nailfiddle.** The tones of this instrument are produced from a series of nails by friction, generally by means of a bow.
Naïf (nä-ēf), *Fr.* }
Naïv (nä-ēf'), *Ger.* } Simple, artless, natural.
Naïve (nä-ēv), *Fr.* }
Naïvement (nä-ēv'mänh), *Fr.* Simple, naturally.
Naked. A term significantly applied by modern theorists to fourths, fifths, and other chords when unaccompanied.
Nakokus (nä-kō'kŭs). The name of an instrument much used by the Egyptians in their Coptic churches, and in their religious processions, consisting of two brass plates suspended by strings and struck together by way of beating time. Corresponding to the sistrum and to the bell struck during the sacrifice of the Mass to notify distant auditors of an especially solemn moment.
Nänien (nä-nĭ-ĕn), *Ger.* A dirge, an elegy.
Narrante (när-rän'tĕ), *It.* In a narrative style.

Narrator. A name formerly given to the chief performer in an oratorio.
Narrentanz (när'r'n-tänts), *Ger.* A foolish dance; a fool's dance.
Nasal tone. That reedy, unpleasant tone produced by the voice when it issues in too great a degree through the nostrils.
Nasard. }
Nasat. } An old name for an organ-stop,
Nassat. } tuned a twelfth above the diapasons.
Nazard. }
Nasardo (nä-zär'dō), *Sp.* One of the registers of an organ.
Nason. A very quiet and sweet-toned flute-stop, of 4-feet scale, sometimes found in old organs.
Nationallied (nä-tsĭ-ō-näl'lēd), *Ger.* National song.
National music. } Music identified with the
National song. } history of a nation, or the manners and customs of its people, either by means of the sentiment it expresses or by long use.
Natural. A character marked ♮, used to contradict a sharp or flat.
Naturale (nä-too-rä'lĕ), *It.* Natural, easy, free.
Natural harmonic series. Harmonics; partial tones.
Natural harmony. The harmony of the triad, or common chord.
Naturali suoni (nä too-rä'lē soo-ō'nī), *It.* Sounds within the compass of the human voice; natural sounds.
Natural keys. Those which have no sharp or flat at the signature, as C major and A minor.
Naturalmente (nä-too-räl-mĕn'tĕ), *It.* Naturally.
Natural modulation. That which is confined to the key of the piece and its relatives.
Naturhorn (nä-toor'horn), *Ger.* The natural horn, the horn without valves.
Natürliche Intervalle (nä-tūr'lĭkh-ĕ ĭn-tĕr-väl'lĕ), *Ger.* Natural intervals, intervals proper to the key, not such as are altered by sharps or flats; more especially are so named those belonging to the C major scale, without any sharps or flats at all.
Naturtöne (nä-toor'tö-nĕ), *Ger.* Natural, or open, notes; the natural harmonic series, the notes which, for instance, on the horn, can be produced without stopping, or any mechanical means.
Naturtrompete (nä-toor'trom-pä-tĕ), *Ger.* A natural trumpet, one without valves.
Naublum (naw-bloom), *Heb:* See *Nabla*.
Nautical songs. Songs relating to the sea
Nay (nä), *Tur.* A Turkish flute; the nei.
Neapolitan sixth. A chord composed of a minor third and minor sixth, and occurring on the subdominant, or fourth degree

ä *arm*, ă *add*, ā *ale*, ĕ *end*, ē *eve*, ĭ *ill*, ī *isle*, ō *old*, ŏ *odd*, oo *moon*, ŭ *but*, ü *Fr. sound*, kh *Ger. ch*, nh *nasal*.

(163)

of the scale. In the key of C (major or minor) this chord is really the same as the first inversion of the triad of D♭.

Nebel (nā-běl),
Nebel nassor (nā-běl näs sōr), *Heb.* } The name given by the ancient Jews to their ten-stringed harp, supposed to have been triangular in form and used in religious worship.

Neben (nā'b'n), *Ger.* Accessory. (Much used in compounds.)

Nebennote (nā'b'n-nō'tĕ), *Ger.* Auxiliary note.

Nebenregister (nā'b'n-rĕ-ghĭs'tĕr),
Nebenzüge (nā'b'n-tsü'gĕ), *Ger.* } Secondary or accessory stops in an organ, such as couplers, tremulant, bells, etc.

Nebenstimmen (nā'b'n-stĭm'mĕn), *Ger.* Accessory voices. Applied to subordinate voices in contrapuntal work, and to organ-stops unavailable for solo or foundation purposes, such as the twelfth, mixtures, etc.

Necessario (nā-tshĕs-sä'rĭ-ó), *It.* A term indicating that the passage referred to must not be omitted.

Nechiloth (něk'ĭ-lōht), *Heb.* A wind instrument of the Hebrews, formed of a double set of pipes.

Neck. That part of a violin, guitar, or similar instrument, extending from the head to the body, and on which the fingerboard is fixed.

Neghinoth (nĕ'ghi-nōth),
Neginoth (nĕ'gĭ-nōth), *Heb.* } A word fixed at the head of certain of the psalms, and supposed to announce the particular tune to which they were to be sung, answering to the modern giving out. Neginoth was also the name given to ancient stringed instruments.

Negligente (něl-yĕ-jěn'tĕ), *It.* Negligent; unconstrained.

Negligentemente (něl-yĭ-jěn-tĕ-měn'tĕ), *It.* Negligently.

Negligenza (něl-yĭ-jěn'tsä), *It.* Negligence, carelessness.

Negli (něl'yĭ), *It. pl.* } In the; at the.
Nei (nā'ĭ),

Nei (nā'ĕ), *Tur.* A fashionable musical instrument of the Turks, being a flute made of cane.

Nekeb (nā'kĕb), *Heb.* A wind instrument of the ancient Hebrews, formed of a single tube.

Nel (něl), *It.*
Nella (něl'lä), *It.*
Nelle (něl'lĕ), *It. pl.* } In the; at the.
Nello (něl'lō), *It.*
Nell' (něl), *It.*

Nel battere (něl bät-tä'rĕ), *It.* In the downbeat of the measure.

Nel tempo (něl těm'pō), *It.* In time, in the previous time.

Nete (nā'tĕ), *Gr.* The last, or most acute, string of the lyre; the name given by the ancient Greeks to the fourth, or most acute, chord of each of the three tetrachords which followed the first two or deepest two.

Nete diezeugmenon (nā-tĕ dē-zoog'mĕ-nŏn), *Gr.* The final, or highest, sound of the fourth tetrachord, and the first, or gravest, of the fifth.

Nete hyperbolæon (nā-tĕ hē'pĕr-bō'lē-ŏn), *Gr.* The last sound of the hyperbolæon, or highest tetrachord, and of the great system, or diagram, of the Greeks.

Nete synemmenon (nā-tĕ sĭ-něm'mĕ-nŏn), *Gr.* The fourth, or most acute, sound of the third tetrachord, when conjoint with the second.

Net (nā), *Fr.*
Nett (nĕt), *Ger.*
Nettamente (nět-tä-měn'tĕ), *It.*
Nette (nāt), *Fr.*
} Neatly, clearly, plainly.

Nettete (nāt-tā), *Fr.*
Nettheit (nět'hĭt), *Ger.*
Nettigkeit (nět-tĭg-kĭt), *Ger.*
} Neatness, clearness, plainness.

Netto (nět'tō), *It.* Neat, clear; quick, nimble.

Neu (noi), *Ger.* New.

Neumes (nūms). (1) An early system of notation by means of points, commas, hooks, etc. By and by one, two, and more lines were introduced to remedy the vagueness of the signs, and finally our present notation developed out of it. (2) Melodic phrases at the close of a verse, most frequently found on the last syllable of Alleluia.

Neun (noin), *Ger.* Nine.

Neunachtel Takt (noin-äkh't'l täkt), *Ger.* Measure in nine-eighth time.

Neunte (noin'tĕ), *Ger.* A ninth.

Neunzehnte (noin'tsĕn-tĕ), *Ger.* Nineteenth.

Neuvième (nüh-vĭ-äm'), *Fr.* The interval of a ninth.

Nicht (nĭkht), *Ger.* Not.

Nieder (nē'd'r), *Ger.* Down; used in composition with other words.

Niederschlag (nē'dĕr-shläg), *Ger.* The downbeat, or accented part of the bar.

Niederstrich (nē'dĕr-strĭkh), *Ger.* The down bow.

Niedrig (nē'drĭg), *Ger.* Low, or deep, in voice.

Nina (nē'nä), *It.* A lullaby.

Nine-eighth measure. A measure containing nine eighth-notes, or their equivalent, marked 9-8.

Nineteenth. An interval comprising two octaves and a fifth; also an organ-stop, tuned a nineteenth above the diapason. See *Larigot.*

Ninth. An interval consisting of an octave and a second.

Nobile (nō'bĭ-lĕ), *It.* Noble, grand, impressive.

ä *arm,* å *add,* ā *ale,* ë *end,* ē *eve,* ĭ *ill,* ī *isle,* ŏ *old,* ŏ *odd,* oo *moon,* ŭ *but,* ü *Fr. sound,* kh *Ger. ch,* uh *nasal.*

Nobilita, con (nō-bē′lĭ-tä kōn), *It.* With nobility; dignified.
Nobilmente (nō-bĭl-mĕn′tĕ), *It.* } Nobly,
Noblement (nō-bl-mänh), *Fr.* } grandly.
Nobilmente et animato (nō-bĭl-mĕn′tĕ ĕd ä-nĭ-mä′tō), *It.* With grandeur and spirit.
Noch (nōkh), *Ger.* Still, yet.
Noch schneller (nōkh shnĕl′lĕr), *Ger.* Still quicker.
Nocturn. } A composition of a light and elegant character suitable for evening recreation; also a piece resembling a serenade to be played at night in the open air.
Nocturne. }
Nocturne (nŏk-türn), *Fr.* } A nocturne.
Nocturno (nŏk-toor′nō), *It.* }
Nodal points. } In music the fixed points of a sonorous chord, at which it divides itself when it vibrates by aliquot parts and produces the harmonic sounds; as the strings of the œolian harp.
Nodes }
Noel (nō-ĕl), *Fr.* A Christmas carol or hymn
Noire (nwär), *Fr.* Black note; a crotchet.
Noire pointée (nwär pwänh-tä), *Fr.* A dotted crotchet.
Nomenclature, musical. A vocabulary of names and technical terms employed in music.
Nomes (nō′mĕs), *Gr.* Certain airs in the ancient music sung to Cybele, the mother of the gods, to Bacchus, to Pan, and other divinities. The name nome was also given to every air the composition of which was regulated by certain determined and inviolable rules.
Non (nōn), *It.* Not, no.
Nona (nō′uä), *It.* The interval of a ninth.
Nona chord. The dominant chord with a third added to it.
Nonetto (nō-nĕt′tō), *It.* A composition for nine voices or instruments.
Non tanto (nōn tän′tō), *It.* Not so much, not too much.
Non troppo (nōn trŏp′pō), *It.* Not too much, moderately.
Non troppo allegro (nōn trŏp′pō äl-lā′grō), *It.* }
Non troppo presto (nōn trŏp′pō prĕs′tō), *It.* } Not too quick.
Nonuplet. A group of nine notes of equal length.
Normal (nōr-mäl′), *Ger.* Normal, proper.
Normalton (nōr-mäl′tōn), *Ger.* The normal tone, the tone A, the sound to which instruments are tuned in an orchestra.
Normaltonleiter (nōr-mäl-tōn′lī-tĕr), *Ger.* The natural scale, the scale of C, the open key.
Nota (nō′tä), *It.* } A note.
Nota (nō′tä), *Lat.* }
Nota buona (nō′tä boo-ō′nä), *It.* A strong, or accented, note.

Nota cambiata (nō′tä käm-bĭ-ä′tä), *It.* A changed, or irregularly transient, note; a passing note.
Nota caratteristica (nō′tä kä-rät-tĕ-rĕs′tĭ-kä), *It.* A characteristic, or leading, note.
Nota cattiva (nō′tä kät-tē′vä), *It.* A weak, or unaccented, note.
Nota contra notam (nō′tä kōn′trä nō′täm), *It.* Note against note. See *Counterpoint*.
Nota coronata (nō′tä kō-rō-nä′tä), *It.* A note marked with a hold.
Nota d' abbellimento (nō′tä d′äb-bĕl-lĭ-mĕn′-tō), *It.* A note of embellishment, an ornamental note.
Nota di passaggio (nō′tä dē päs-säd′jĭ-ō), *It.* A passing note, a note of regular transition.
Nota di piacere (nō′tä dē pē-ä-tshā′rĕ), *It.* An optional grace note, an ad libitum embellishment.
Nota sensibile (nō′tä sĕn-sē′bĭ-lĕ), *It.* }
Nota sensibilis (nō′tä sĕn-sē′bĭ-lĭs), *Lat.* }
The sensible, or leading, note of the scale.
Nota signata (nō′tä sĭg-nä′tä), *Lat.* A note marked with a sign.
Nota sostenuta (nō′tä sōs-tĕ-noo′tä), *It.* A sustained note.
Notation. The art of representing by notes, characters, etc., all the different musical sounds.
Notation, numerical. A system of notation first introduced by Rousseau, in which the first eight of the numerals are used for designating scale tones, and points, ciphers, etc., for such characters as represent pauses, time, etc.
Notazione musicale (nō-tä-tsĭ-ō′nĕ moo-zĭ-kä′lĕ), *It.* Musical notation.
Note. A character indicating musical utterance. By its formation it indicates the duration of a tone, and by its situation upon the staff its proper pitch.
Note, connecting. A note held in common by two chords.
Note d'agrement (nōt d′ä-grā-mänh), *Fr.* An ornamental note.
Note de passage (nōt düh päs-säzh), *Fr.* A passing note; a note of regular transition.
Note diesée (nōt dĭ-ā-zā), *Fr.* Note marked with a sharp.
Note, double. The ancient breve.
Note, double-dotted. A note whose length is increased three fourths of its original value by the dots placed after it.
Note, double-stemmed. A note having two stems, one upward and the other downward, showing that it belongs to two different voices. In pianoforte music a double-stemmed note generally belongs to the melody in its longer signification, and to the accompaniment in its shorter signification. In the bass, half-notes with two stems often occur, in which case

ä *arm*, ă *add*, â *ale*, ĕ *end*, ē *eve*, ĭ *ill*, ī *isle*, ŏ *old*, ō *odd*, oo *moon*, ŭ *but*, ü *Fr. sound*, kh *Ger. ch.* nh *nasal*.

the upper stem belongs to a quarter-note, supposed to be concealed behind the half-note, and belonging to the voice having the chords above. Such a note is held its longer value, but the chord or other notes belonging to the quarter-note stem enter after one beat.

Noten (nō'tʼn), *Ger. pl.* Notes. Used in composition with other words.
Notenblatt (nō'tʼn-blät), *Ger.* A sheet of music.
Notenbuch (nō'tʼn-bookh), *Ger.* Music-book, notebook.
Notenschrift (nō'tʼn-shrĭft), *Ger.* Musical manuscript.
Notensystem (nō'tʼn-sĭs-täm'), *Ger.* The staff.
Note of modulation. A note which introduces a new key, usually applied to the leading note or sharp seventh.
Note, open. A note produced on the strings of a violin, guitar, etc., when not pressed by the finger.
Note, pedal. A note held by the pedal while the harmony forming the remaining parts is allowed to proceed.
Note, quarter. A crotchet.
Noter (nō-tā), *Fr.* To write out a tune or air.
Note, reciting. The note in a chord upon which the voice dwells until it comes to a cadence.
Note scolte (nō'tĕ skŏl'tĕ), *It.* Staccato note.
Notes coulees (nŏt koo-lā), *Fr.* Slurred notes.
Notes de gout (nŏt dŭh goo), *Fr.* Notes of embellishment.
Note, sensible (nŏt sänh-sēbl), *Fr.* The leading note of the scale; the seventh of the scale.
Note, sixteenth. A semiquaver.
Note, sixty-fourth. A hemidemisemiquaver.
Notes liees (nŏt lē-ā), *Fr.* Tied notes.
Notes syncopees (nŏt sēn-kō-pā), *Fr.* Syncopated notes.
Note, thirty-second. A demisemiquaver,
Note, triple-dotted. A note whose value is increased seven eighths by three dots after it.
Note, whole. A semibreve,
Notturni (nŏt-toor'nĭ), *It.* Nocturnes.
Notturno (nŏt-toor'nō), *It.* A nocturne; a light, elegant composition suitable for an evening performance; a serenade.
Nourrir le son (noo-rēr lŭh sōnh), *Fr.* To commence, or attack, a note in singing, forcibly, and sustain it.
Nourrissons (noor-rĕs-sōnh), *Fr.* Bards, poets.
Nouvelle methode (noo-vâl' mā-tŏd), *Fr.* A new method.
Nova (nō'vä), *It.* A species of small flute or pipe.
Novemole. A group of nine notes, to be performed in the same time as six of equal value.
Novice (nŏv-ĭs). A beginner; one unskilled.
Nuances (nü-änh-sʼ), *Fr. pl.* Lights and shades of expression, variety of intonation. A system of notation.
Numerical notation. A system of notation first introduced by Rousseau, in which numerals were substituted as names of scale tones, 1, 2, 3, etc. The numerals were written upon a line for the standard octave, above the line for the octave above, and below the line for the octave below. A similar notation had a local currency in Massachusetts about 1851; it was called Day & Beal's "One-Line System." The measure was represented in nearly the usual manner. In France a similar system is in use among the Orpheonists. It was invented or improved by M. Paris, the inventor of the "time-names."
Nuovo (noo-ō'vō), *It.* New; *di nuovo*, newly, again.
Nuptial - songs. Wedding-songs, marriage-songs.
Nut. The small bridge at the upper end of the fingerboard of a guitar, over which the strings pass to the pegs or screws.

O, *It.* Or. *Violino o flauto*, violin or flute.
O (ō) before a consonant, *It.* } Or, as, either.
Od (ŏd) before a vowel,
Obbligato (ŏb-blĭ gä'tō), *It.* } Indispensable, necessary;
Obbligati (ŏb-blĭ-gä'tē), *It. pl.* a part or parts
Obligé (ŏb-lĭ-zhä'), *Fr.* which can not
Obligat (ŏb-lĭ-gät'), *Ger.* be omitted, being indispensably necessary to the idea. Generally speaking, every independent part is obbligato. The expression "organ obbligato," for instance, indicates that the organ is not simply a reinforcement of the other parts, but has something of its own to say. The obbligato instrumental part frequently to be met with in the arias of older operas, oratorios, etc., vied, concerted, with the vocal part. Titles

such as these were very common: *Aria con violino obbligato*, or *flauto obbligato*.

Ober (ō'bĕr), *Ger.* Upper, higher.

Obermanual (ō'bĕr-mä-noo-äl'), *Ger.* The upper manual.

Oberstimme (ō'bĕr-stĭm'mĕ), *Ger.* Treble, upper voice part.

Obertasten (ō'bĕr-täs't'n), *Ger.* The black keys.

Obertheil (ō'bĕr-tīl'), *Ger.* The upper part.

Oberwerk (ō'bĕr-wärk), *Ger.* Upper work, highest row of keys.

Oblique motion. A relative motion of two voices in which one moves while the other remains stationary.

Obliquo (ōb-lē'kwō), *It.* Oblique.

Oboe (ō'bō-ĕ), *Ger.* } A hautboy; also the
Oboe (ō-bō-ā'), *It.* } name of an organ-stop. (1) A wood wind instrument with a mouthpiece consisting of a double reed. Its extreme compass extends from b♭ or b♯ to f'''. Music for the oboe is written in the G clef, and written as it sounds. This is the oboe of our orchestras. In military bands are also sometimes to be met with oboes in B♭ and a soprano oboe in E♭, which are, of course, transposing instruments. (2) There are, likewise, organ-stops of the name of oboe, of 8-feet and more rarely of 4-feet pitch. (3) For other kinds of oboe, oboes now obsolete, see the following articles:

Oboe basso (ō-bō-ā' bäs'sō), *It.* This obsolete instrument stood a minor third lower than the ordinary oboe.

Oboe da caccia (ō-bō-ā' dä kät'tshĭ-ä), *It.* A larger species of oboe, with the music written in the alto clef. Its natural key was F or E♭.

Oboe d'amore (ō-bō-ā' d'ä-mō'rĕ), *It.* } A spe-
Oboe lungo (ō-bō-ā' loon'gō), *It.* } cies of oboe, longer than the ordinary oboe, with a thinner bore and lower pitch.

Oboi (ō-bō-ē'), *It.* Hautboys.

Oboist. A performer on the oboe or hautboy.

Oboista (ō-bō-ēs'tä), *It.* An oboist.

Octachord. An instrument or system comprising eight sounds or seven degrees.

Octaphonic. Composed of eight voices.

Octava alta (ōk-tä'vä äl'tä), *It.* Play the passage an octave higher.

Octava grave (ōk-tä'vä grä'vä), *Sp.* Octave below.

Octave. The interval from any tone to the eighth above or below in the same scale. The octave above any tone is produced by exactly twice as rapid a vibration frequency, and the octave below by exactly half as many vibrations. The most fundamental principle in harmony is that octaves are equivalent and may be interchanged in any chord without changing its harmonic character.

Octave clarion. A two-feet reed-stop in an organ.

Octave flute. A small flute an octave higher than the German or ordinary flute; a piccolo.

Octave hautboy. A 4-feet organ reed-stop; the pipes are of the hautboy species.

Octave, large. The third octave, indicated in the German tablature by capital letters.

Octave, large, once-marked. The second octave, indicated by capital letters having a single line below.

Octave, large, twice-marked. The first octave, indicated by capital letters having two lines below them.

Octaves, consecutive. Two parts moving in unison or octaves with each other.

Octaves, covered. Certain apparent consecutive octaves which occur in harmony, in passing by similar motion to a perfect concord.

Octave, small. The fourth octave, so called because indicated by small letters in the German tablature.

Octave, small, five-times marked. The ninth octave, represented by small letters with five lines above them.

Octave, small, four-times marked. The eighth octave, represented by small letters with four lines above them.

Octave, small, once-marked. The fifth octave, indicated by small letters with one line above them.

Octave, small, six-times marked. The tenth octave, indicated by small letters with six lines above them.

Octave, small, thrice-marked. The seventh octave, indicated by small letters with three lines above them.

Octave, small, twice-marked. The sixth octave, indicated by small letters with two lines above them.

Octaves, short. Those lower octaves of an organ the extreme keys of which, on account of the omission of some of the intermediate notes, lie nearer to each other than those of the full octave.

Octave staff. A system of notation introduced by a Mr. Adams, of New Jersey, which consists of three groups of lines combined, comprising three octaves of ordinary vocal music, dispensing with flats and sharps, and giving to each tone its own position.

Octave stop. An organ-stop of four-feet pitch, hence an octave above the diapason; the position of fingers for stopping the interval of an octave upon the fingerboard; a mechanical stop in reed-organs, coupling the keys an octave above, or borrowing within the instrument in such a manner that octaves result.

Octavflötchen (ōk-täf'flöt'kh'n), *Ger.* An octave flute; a flageolet.

Octavflöte (ōk-täf'flö'tĕ), *Ger.* Octave flute, flageolet; also an organ-stop of four-feet scale.

Octaviötlein (ŏk-täf'flöt'lĭn), *Ger.* An octave flute.

Octavfolgen (ŏk-täf-fŏl'ghĕn), *Ger.* Octave-succession; parallel motion by octaves.

Octavin (ŏk-tä-vänh), *Fr.* An organ-stop of two-feet scale.

Octavine (ŏk-tä-vēn'), *Fr.* The small spinet.

Octet. } A composition for eight parts, or
Octett. } for eight voices.

Octetto (ŏk-tĕt'tō), *It.* An octet.

Octo=bass. A monster double bass, invented by M. Vuillaume, of Paris. It is of colossal size, about twelve feet high. Stopping is effected by means of keys and pedals. The tone is full and strong without roughness.

Octochord (ŏk'tō-kŏrd), *Lat.* An instrument like a lute, with eight strings.

Octoplet. A group of eight notes of equal value, played in the time of nine or some other natural rhythmic group.

Octuor (ŏk-twŏr), *Fr.* A piece in eight parts, or for eight voices or instruments.

Ode. A Greek word, signifying an air or song; a lyrical composition of greater length and variety than a song, resembling the cantata.

Odelet. A short ode.

Odeon (ō'dă-ŏn), *Ger.* } A building for odes.
Odeum (ō-dā-oom), *Lat.* } A public building for musical purposes.

Oder (ō'dĕr), *Ger.* Or, or else; *für ein oder zwei Claviere*, for one or two manuals.

Œuvre (üvr), *Fr.* Work, composition, piece—a term used in numbering a composer's published works in the order of their publication.

Œuvre premier (üvr prĕ-mĭ-ā'), *Fr.* The first work.

Offen (ŏf'f'n), *Ger.* Open. Applied to organ-pipes. Also used in composition.

Offenbar (ŏf'f'n-bär), *Ger.* Open to view, unconcealed.

Offenflöte (ŏf'f'n-flö'tĕ), *Ger.* An open-flute organ-stop. See also *Clarabella*.

Offertoire (ŏf'fĕr-twär), *Fr.* } A hymn,
Offertorio (ŏf'fĕr-tō'rĭ-ō), *It.* } prayer,
Offertorium (ŏf'fĕr-tō'rĭ-oom), *Lat.* } anthem,
Offertory (ŏf'fĕr-tō-ry). } or instrumental piece sung or played during the collection of the offertory.

Offertorio (ŏf'fĕr-tō'rĭ-ō), *Sp.* Offertory.

Oficleida (ō-fĭ-klā-ĭ-dä), *It.* } The ophicleide;
Oficleide (ō-fĭ-klā-ĭ-dĕ), *It.* } a French bass horn.

Ohne (ō'nĕ), *Ger.* Without.

Ohne Pedale (ō'nĕ pĕ-dā'lĕ), *Ger.* Without the pedals.

Oktave (ŏk-tä'fĕ), *Ger.* Octave, eighth.

Ole (ō'lĕ), *Sp.* (El ole.) Spanish dance with castanets, in slow 3-4 measure.

Olio. A miscellaneous collection of musical pieces.

Olivettes (ō-lĭ-vĕt'), *Fr.* The dances of the peasants in the Provence after the olives are gathered.

Omnes (ŏm'nĕs), *Lat.* } All. See *Tutti*.
Omnia (ŏm'nĭ-ä), *Lat.* }

Omnitonique (ŏm-nĭ-tŏn-ēk'), *Fr.* Having all the tones. Capable of the whole chromatic scale.

Once=marked octave. The name given in Germany to the notes between inclusive; these notes are expressed by small letters with one short stroke.

Ondeggiamento (ŏn-dăd-jĭ-ä-mĕn'tō), *It.* Waving; an undulating or tremulous motion of the sound; also a close shake on the violin.

Ondeggiante (ŏn-dăd-jĭ än'tĕ), *It.* Waving, undulating, trembling.

Ondulé (ŏnh-dü-lā'), *Fr.* Waving, trembling.

Onduliren (ŏn-doo-lē'r'n), *Ger.* A tremulous tone in singing or in playing the violin, etc.

Ongarese (ŏn-gä-rā'zĕ), *It.* } Hungarian.
Ongherese (ŏn-ghĕ rā'zĕ), *It.* }

Onzieme (ŏnh-zhĭ-ăm), *Fr.* Eleventh.

Op. Abbreviation of Opus, work.

Open diapason. An organ-stop, generally made of metal, and thus called because the pipes are open at the top. It commands the whole scale, and is the most important stop of the instrument.

Open harmony. Chord-positions in which the upper three voices generally or uniformly exceed the compass of an octave.

Open note. A half-note, a whole note.

Open pipes. Organ-pipes with open ends, instead of being closed with a stopper or chimney. All the free voices in an organ are produced by open pipes. All the voices produced by stopped pipes are somewhat veiled in character, or flute-like.

Open tone. A tone produced by an open string, or by a wind instrument without using the valve or keys. A tone open and free in quality.

Oper (ō'pĕr), *Ger.* } A drama set to music.
Opera (ō-pĕ-rä), *It.* } According to the best modern practice the opera consists of almost every variety of music, not alone songs, duets, trios, and other concerted pieces, choruses, elaborate finales, and richly instrumented orchestral accompaniment, but also melodramatic music, which accompanies the action, even in those moments when there is no singing in progress.

Preludes and interludes are elaborate orchestral pieces, often reaching symphonic proportions.

Opera music has for its problem to interpret the drama and to intensify its impression, and in order to accomplish this it is at liberty to employ the complete resources

---

ä *arm*, ă *add*, ā *ale*, ĕ *end*, ē *eve*, ĭ *ill*, ī *isle*, ō *old*, ŏ *odd*, oo *moon*, ŭ *but*, ü *Fr. sound*, kh *Ger. ch*, nh *nasal*.

of the art, almost to an unrestricted degree. When there is a dramatic action progressing before the eyes of the spectator, many strange musical combinations become intelligible which without such explanation would seem far-fetched or impossible. Hence opera has had great influence upon the progress of music as an art.

Opera is divided into schools according to the emphasis placed upon the different elements composing it. French opera, for instance, places the text in the foremost place, and the dramatic movement next; hence it does not permit itself the arias and long musical pieces of the Italians, or of the Germans. German opera places the drama first, and the music second, not only as an accompaniment, but still more as a musical interpreter of the inner spirit of the progressing actions, and of the drama as a whole. Italian opera places the voice and the art of singing first, and the drama second. Hence this school has produced the great bulk of arias which are available for concert performances, apart from the dramatic action. Most of the German arias existing are available for separate performance, having been composed after Italian principles.

Opera was first invented about the year 1600, as a sort of revival of the classic Greek drama. Its greatest works have been composed within the present century, or immediately before it (1790 to 1895).

Opera buffa (ŏ'pĕ-rä boof'fä), *It.* An opera upon a comic or farcical subject, in which music is treated lightly and for the purpose of pleasing. The farce is the main thing. Occasionally high-class opera is distinctly burlesqued, giving rise to buffa arias; the absurdity may be musical or may turn upon the text.

Opera buffe (ŏ'pĕ-rä boof-fĕ), *It.* Comic opera.

Opera, comic. An opera interspersed with light songs, amusing incidents, dances, etc.

Opera di camera (ŏ'pĕ-rä dē kä'mŏ-rä), *It.* A short opera to be performed in a room.

Opera, grand. An opera consisting of a deep and intricate plot and a great variety of incidental events.

Opéra héroïque (ō-pä-rä hā-rō-ēk'), *Fr.* An heroic opera.

Opera-libretto. The text of an opera; a small book containing the words of an opera.

Opéra lyrique (ō-pä-rä leer-eek'), *Fr.* A lyric opera; an opera in which the songs are lyrical rather than dramatic; *i. e.*, do not lend themselves to the progress of the action, but are simply pleasing and, perhaps, expressive pieces of music.

Opera seria (ŏ'pĕ-rä sā'rĭ-ä), *It.* } A serious, or
Opéra sérieux (ō-pä-rä sā-rĭ-ŭh), *Fr.* } tragic, opera.

Operatic. In the style of an opera.

Operetta (ō-pĕ-rĕt'tä), *It.* A small opera, of light and pleasing character. It may be simply comedy, or it may even degenerate into farce.

Operndichter (ō'pärn-dĭkh'tĕr), *Ger.* An operatic poet; writer of operatic librettos.

Ophicleide (ŏf'ĭ-klīd). A large bass wind instrument of brass, of modern invention, sometimes used in large orchestras, but chiefly in military music. It has a compass of three octaves, and the tone is loud and of deep pitch.

Ophicleide stop. The most powerful manual reed-stop known in an organ, of 8- or 4-feet scale, and is usually placed upon a separate soundboard, with a great pressure of wind.

Ophicleidist. A performer on the ophicleide.

Opus (ō'poos), *Lat.* } Work, composition; as,
Opus (ō'poos), *Ger.* } Op. 1, the first work, or publication, of a composer.

Opusculum (ō-poos'koo-loom), *Lat.* A short, or little, work.

Opus posthumum (ō'poos pŏst-hoo'moom), *Lat.* A posthumous work, published after the death of a composer.

Orage (ō-räzh'), *Fr.* A storm; a composition imitating a storm.

Oratoire (ōr-ä-twär'), *Fr.* Oratorio.

Oratorio. A musical work upon a Biblical subject, consisting of solos, choruses, orchestral accompaniment, and containing an implied action or story. Oratorio is part of the great "stilo rappresentativo" in music, the art of representing something by means of music, or accompanied by music. Originally the same as an opera with religious intention, and adapted for use as part of a festival church service, it has digressed into something much more elaborate. The great oratorios aim at the noble, the heroic, and the sublime in dramatic and historical conception no less than in musical execution. Hence it is in this department that music has found itself unfettered by the necessity for pleasing or of adapting itself to moderate conditions. The ideal has been sought, regardless of lesser considerations, hence such works as those of Handel, Bach, and many by later writers.

Oratorio (ō-rä-tō'rĭ-ō), *It.* }
Oratorium (ō'rä-tō'rĭ-oom), *Lat.* } Oratorio.
Oratorium (ō'rä-tō'rĭ-oom), *Ger.* }

Orchestra (or'kĕs-trä). A full company of instruments and players. A modern symphony orchestra consists of about 80 to 100 players, in the following proportions: Violins, 40; violas, 'cellos, and basses, 30; oboes, flutes, clarinets, and bassoons, 11; horns, trumpets, and trombones, 9; tympani and percussion, 4; total, 94. If further enlargement is desired, the strings are strengthened. In modern practice the orchestra is handled in groups, forming a string orchestra, the wood wind and the brass. These groups often contrast with each other throughout a work, playing all to-

---

ä *arm*, ă *add*, ā *ale*, ĕ *end*, ē *ere*, ĭ *ill*, ī *isle*, ō *old*, ŏ *odd*, oo *moon*, ŭ *but*, ü *Fr. sound*, kh *Ger. ch*, nh *nasal*.

gether in the most intense portions only. (2) Also the place in which the players sit to play, or the part of the auditorium nearest the place of the players.

Orchester (ŏr'kĕs-tĕr), *Ger.* ⎫
Orchestra (ŏr-kăs'trä), *It.* ⎬ The orchestra.
Orchestre (ŏr-kĕstr), *Fr.* ⎭

Orchesterverein (ŏr-kĕs'tĕr-vĕr-rīn'), *Ger.* An orchestral society; instrumental association.

Orchestration. The art of writing or arranging music for an orchestra. The greatest writers upon this subject are Berlioz and F. A. Gevaert. The greatest masters of the art itself have been Berlioz, Beethoven, Mozart, Weber, and Wagner. There are now many modern masters who excel in the art of orchestral coloring.

Orchestrer (ŏr-kĕs-trā'), *Fr.* To score.

Orchestrina (ŏr-kĕs-trē'nä). ⎫ An instrument
Orchestrion (ŏr-kĕs'trĭ-ŏn). ⎬ composed of pipes and other sounding apparatuses, played automatically (by means of a barrel) for the imitation of orchestral effects. Many of these instruments are of great size, and produce extraordinarily fine effects.

Ordinario (ŏr-dĭ-nä'rĭ-ō), *It.* Ordinary, usual, common; *a tempo ordinario*, in the usual time.

Orecchia (ō-rā'kĭ-ä), ⎫ *It.* ⎬ The ear.
Orecchio (ō-rā'kĭ-ō), ⎭

Orecchia musicale (ō-rā'kĭ-ä moo-zĭ-kä'lĕ), *It.* A musical ear.

Orecchiante (ō-rā'kĭ-än-tĕ), *It.* Singing by ear.

Organ. A keyboard instrument in which sound is produced by means of pipes which are blown on the principle of whistles, by means of compressed air which comes from the windchests and bellows, along windtrunks, and is admitted to the pipes by the opening of a pallet, or valve, actuated by the player's finger upon a key.

An organ may have from one to five keyboards, and from one to twenty stops (or sets of pipes) to each keyboard. The keyboards played by the hands are called manuals; those which the feet play are called pedales. The latter are used for the very low bass tones only.

A stop is a set of pipes voiced all alike, one pipe to each key of the keyboard to which the stop appertains.

The usual number of pipes in a stop is sixty-one, but mixtures have from three to five times as many, and a corresponding multiplication of sounds.

The stops are classified as diapason, flute, string, and reed. The former furnish the foundation, the others are for specialties of tone.

Pipes are of wood or metal, the latter a special alloy of lead and tin, the tin in good examples reaching fifty percent, or more.

In former times each key pulled down a long pallet, or valve, and when several keyboards were coupled, the touch was extremely heavy. In modern organs the action is pneumatic or electric. In the latter case the parts of the organ can be distributed in any convenient place without impairing the organist's control over them; but when a pipe stands too far away so much time is lost in the sound coming that blurring is often produced.

When there are four manuals, the most important is called the great, the next the swell, the choir, and the solo. At present nearly or quite all the manual stops are made louder or softer by means of swells, and there is no settled order of placing the manuals, except that the choir organ is generally lowest, the great next, the swell next, and the solo uppermost.

The wind pressure often varies in different parts of the same organ from what is called "three-inch" to "five-inch" or "six-inch"—the dimensions having reference to a column of water which the pressure will balance. About three-and-a-half-inch wind is normal for small halls; solo stops take the higher pressures.

Owing to the modern improvements in the organ it is now capable of much expression, and in point of sustained power and massiveness of tone it is as often called the "king of instruments." Great improvements have been made in the art of voicing, whereby modern organs reproduce orchestral effects with considerable oraissemblance.

Organ, barrel. A hand organ.

Organ, bellows. A machine for supplying the pipes of an organ with wind.

Organ-blower. One who works the bellows of an organ.

Organ, buffet. A very small organ.

Organe (ŏr-gän), *Fr.* An organ.

Organ, enharmonic. ⎫ An instrument of
Organ, euharmonic. ⎬ American origin, containing three or four times the usual number of distinct sounds within the compass of an octave, furnishing the precise intervals for every key, the tones comprising the scale of each key being produced by pressing a pedal corresponding to its keynote.

Organetto (ŏr-gä-nĕt'tō), *It.* A small organ.

Organ, hand. A common wind instrument carried about the street, consisting of a cylinder, turned by hand, the revolution of which, causing the machinery to act upon the keys, produces a number of well-known airs and tunes.

Organ, harmonium. A reed instrument, the reeds of which are voiced to imitate organ-stops.

Organique (ŏr-gän-ēk), *Fr.* Relating to the organ.

Orgelmusik (ŏr'gh'l-moo-zīk'), *Ger.* Organ music.

Organist. A player on the organ.

Organista (ŏr-gä-nĕs'tä), *It.* ⎫ An organist.
Organista (ŏr-gä-nĕs'tä), *Sp.* ⎭

Organistrum (ŏr-gä-nĭs'troom), *Lat.* An ancient instrument of the hurdygurdy variety, in which strings were actuated by wheel, and the tones controlled by keys acting upon the keyboard. In use about 1100 A. D.
Organi vocali (ŏr-gä'nē vō-kä'lē), *It. pl.* The vocal organs.
Organ-loft. That part of the gallery of a church where the organ is placed.
Organo (ŏr-gä'nō), *It.* An organ.
Organo pieno (ŏr-gä'nō pē-ā'nō), *It.* } The
Organo pleno (ŏr-gä'nō plā'nō), *Lat.* } full organ with all the stops drawn.
Organo portatile (ŏr-gä'nō pŏr-tä'tĭ-lĕ), *It.* A portable organ.
Organo simplex (ŏr-gä'nō sĭm'plĕx), *Lat.* A term occurring frequently in the writings of the musical monks, and seems to mean the unisonous accompaniment of a single voice in the versicles of the service.
Organ point. A long pedal note, or stationary bass, upon which is formed a series of chords, or harmonic progressions.
Organ tone. A tone that commences, continues, and closes with a uniform degree of power.
Organum. A word used in various senses by the ancient composers. Sometimes it meant the organ itself; at other times it meant that kind of choral accompaniment which comprehended the whole harmony then known, also a brazen vessel forming a principal part of the hydraulic organ.
Orgel (ŏr'ghĕl), *Ger.* An organ.
Orgelbälge (ŏr'ghĕl-bäl'ghĕ), *Ger.* Organ-bellows.
Orgelbank (ŏr'ghĕl-bänk), *Ger.* Organist's seat.
Orgelbauer (ŏr'ghĕl-bou'ĕr), *Ger.* Organ-builder.
Orgelbühne (ŏr'ghĕl-bü'nĕ), *Ger.*} Organ-loft.
Orgelchor (ŏr'ghĕl-kŏr), *Ger.*}
Orgelgehäuse (ŏr'ghĕl-ghĕ-hoy'zĕ), *Ger.* Organ-case.
Orgelkasten (ŏr'ghĕl-käs't'n), *Ger.* A cabinet organ; organ-case.
Orgelklang (ŏr'ghĕl-kläng), *Ger.* Sound or tone of an organ.
Orgelkunst (ŏr'ghĕl-koonst), *Ger.* The art of organ-playing; art of constructing an organ.
Orgeln (ŏr'gĕln), *Ger.* To play on the organ.
Orgelpfeife (ŏr'ghĕl-pfī'fĕ), *Ger.* Organ-pipe.
Orgelplatz (ŏr'ghĕl-pläts), *Ger.* Organ-loft.
Orgelpunkt (ŏr'ghĕl-poonkt'), *Ger.* Organ point; pedal point.
Orgelregister (ŏr'ghĕl-rĕ-ghĭs't'r), *Ger.* Organ-stop.
Orgelschule (ŏr'gĕl-shoo'lĕ), *Ger.* School or method for the organ.
Orgelspiel (ŏr'ghĕl-spēl), *Ger.* Playing on an organ; piece played on an organ.

Orgelspieler (ŏr'ghĕl-spē'lĕr), *Ger.* An organ-player.
Orgelstein (ŏr'ghĕl-stīn), *Ger.* Pan's pipes.
Orgelstimmen (ŏr'ghĕl-stĭm'mĕn), *Ger.* Row of pipes in an organ.
Orgelstücke (ŏr'ghĕl-stü'kĕ), *Ger.* Organ pieces.
Orgeltreter (ŏr'ghĕl-trā'tĕr), *Ger.* Organ-treader, bellows-tender, or bellows-blower.
Orgelvirtuose (ŏr'ghĕl-vĭr-too-ō'zĕ), *Ger.* An accomplished organ-player.
Orgelzug (ŏr'ghĕl-tsoog'), *Ger.* Organ-stop, or row of pipes.
Orgue (ŏrg), *Fr.* An organ.
Orgue de salon (ŏrg dŭh sä-lônh), *Fr.* } The
Orgue expressif (ŏrg ĕgz-prä-sēf), *Fr.* } harmonium.
Orgue hydraulique (ŏrg hī-drō-lĕk), *Fr.* Hydraulic organ; water organ.
Orgue plein (ŏrg plănh), *Fr.* Full organ; all the stops drawn.
Orgue portatif (ŏrg pŏr-tä-tēf),
Orgue portatif de barbarie (ŏrg pŏr-tä-tēf dŭh bär-bä-rē), } *Fr.*
A portable organ, a barrel organ, a street organ.
Orgue positif (ŏrg pō-zĭ-tēf), *Fr.* The choir organ in a large organ; also a small fixed organ, thus named in opposition to a portative organ.
Orgues de barbarie (ŏrg dŭh bär-bä-rē), *Fr.* Barbarian organs—an epithet applied by the French to street organs.
Original key. The key in which a composition is written.
Ornamental notes. Appoggiaturas, grace notes; all notes not forming an essential part of the harmony, but introduced as embellishments.
Ornamenti (ŏr-nä-mĕn'tē), *It. pl.* Ornaments, graces, embellishments, as the appoggiatura, turn, shake, etc.
Ornatamente (ŏr-nä-tä-mĕn'tĕ), *It.* } Ornamented,
Ornato (ŏr-nä'tō), *It.* } adorned, embellished.
Ornate (ŏr-nāt'). A style of music, or musical execution, highly ornamental.
Ornements (ŏrn-mänh), *Fr.* Graces, embellishments.
Orotund. A mode of intonation directly from the larynx, which has a fullness, clearness, smoothness, and ringing quality which form the highest perfection of the human voice.
Orphéon (ŏr-fā'ônh), *Fr.* } Species of musical
Orphéoron (ŏr-fā'ō-rŏnh), *Fr.* } instruments, of which nothing is now known.
Orpheus (ŏr'fĕ-ŭs). A poet in Greek mythology, said to have the power of moving inanimate bodies by the music of his lyre. The myth of Orpheus relates that by the

power of his music he visited the lower world and brought back to life his departed Eurydice.

Osservanza (ŏs-sĕr-văn'tsä), *It.* Observation, attention, strictness in keeping time.

Osia (ō-zē'ä), *It.*
Ossia (ŏs-sē'ä), } Or, otherwise, or else.

Ossia piu facile (ŏs-sē'ä pē-oo fä'tshĭ-lĕ), *It.* Or else in this more easy manner.

Ostinato (ŏs-tĭ-nä'tō), *It.* Obstinate, continuous, unceasing; adhering to some peculiar melodial figure, or group of notes.

Ottava (ŏt-tä'vä), *It.* An octave, an eighth.

Ottava alta (ŏt-tä'vä äl'tä), *It.* The octave above; an octave higher; marked thus, 8va.

Ottava bassa (ŏt-tä'vä bäs'sä), *It.* The octave below; marked thus, 8va bassa.

Ottava supra (ōt-tä'vä soo'prä), *It.* The octave above.

Ottavina (ŏt-tä-vē'nä), *It.* The higher octave.

Ottavino (ŏt-tä-vē'nō), *It.* The flauto piccolo, or small octave flute.

Ottemole. A group of eight notes, marked with the figure 8.

Ottetto (ōt-tĕt'tō), *It.* A composition in eight parts, or for eight voices or instruments.

Ou (oo), *Fr.* Or.

Ougab (oo-gäb), *Heb.* An ancient instrument formed of reeds of unequal lengths bound together.

Ouie (oo-ē), *Fr.* The hearing; *l'ouie d'un instrument*, the soundhole of an instrument.

Outer voices. The highest and lowest voices.

Out of tune. Want of tune; discord.

Ouvert (oo-vär), *Fr.* Open.

Overture (oo-vâr-tūr), *Fr.*
Overtura (ō-vĕr-too'rä), *It.*
Ouvertüre (ō-fĕr-tü'rĕ), *Ger.*
Overture.
} An introductory symphony to an oratorio, opera, etc., generally consisting of three or four different movements; also an independent piece for a full band or orchestra, in which case it is called a concert overture and resembles a sonata-piece with introduction.

Overtura di ballo (ō-vĕr-too'rä dē bäl'lō), *It.* An overture composed upon or introducing dance melodies.

Overstrung pianoforte. Where the strings of at least two of the lowest octaves are raised, running diagonally in respect to the other strings above them.

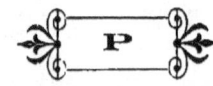

P. Abbreviation for Piano; also for Poco. Thus, p. a p., poco a poco. Also abbreviation for Parte, as, colla p., colla parte.

Padiglione (pä-dĕl-yĭ-ō'nĕ), *It.* The bell of wind instruments.

Padovano, Padavane, *or* **Paduane** (pä-do-vä'nō), *It.* Paduan. An Italian dance in ternary rhythm. Sometimes considered to be the same as Pavan, which, however, is by no means certain.

Paisana (pä-ĭ-zä'nä), *Sp.* A Spanish country dance.

Palco (päl'kō), *It.* The stage of a theater.

Pallet. A spring valve in the windchest of an organ covering a channel leading to a pipe or pipes.

Palmadilla (päl-mä-dĕl'yä), *Sp.* A Spanish dance.

Pan. One of the deities in Grecian mythology, so called because he exhilarated the minds of all the gods with the music of his pipe which he invented, and with the cithern, which he played skillfully as soon as he was born.

Panathenæ (pä'nä-thā'nē), *Gr.* An Athenian festival at which contests in singing and playing on the flute and cithera were held.

Pandean pipes.
Pan's pipes. } One of the most ancient and simple of musical instruments; it was made of reeds or tubes of different lengths, fastened together and tuned to each other, stopped at the bottom and blown into by the mouth at the top.

Pandoran (pän-dō'rän), *Gr.*
Pandora (pän-dō'rä), *It.*
Pandore (pän-dō'rĕ), *Ger.*
Pandura (pän-doo'rä), *It.*
Pandure (pänh'dür), *Fr.*
} An ancient stringed instrument resembling a lute, a bandore. See *Bandora*.

Panflöte (pän-flö'tĕ), *Ger.* Pandean pipes.

Panharmonicon. An automatic instrument invented by Maelzel, which produced the sounds of a variety of instruments A kind of orchestrion.

Pantaleone (pän'tä-lĕ ō'nĕ). An instrument invented by Pantaleon Hebenstreit, and much celebrated in the beginning of the eighteenth century. It was more than nine feet long, nearly four feet wide, and had one hundred and eighty-six strings of gut, which were played on with two small sticks like the dulcimer.

Pantalon (pänh-tä-lōnh), *Fr.* One of the movements of the quadrille.

Pantomime. An entertainment in which not a word is spoken or sung, but the sentiments are expressed by mimicry and gesticulation accompanied by instrumental music.

Pantomimist. One who acts in a pantomime.

Papagenoflöte (pä-pä-ghä'nō-flō'tĕ), *Ger.* Pan's Pipe, mouth organ.

Parallelbewegung (pä-rä-lĕl-bĕ-wä'goong), *Ger.* Parallel motion. On consecutives.

Parallel intervals. Intervals passing in two parallel parts in the same direction; consecutive intervals.

Parallel keys. The major and its relative minor.

Parallel motion. The motion of two voices in the same direction in equal intervals, whereby the same distance is maintained continually. All forms of parallel motion are weak contrapuntally, except parallel octaves when used for strengthening a melody. In this sense they are in constant use in all large compositions. Parallel thirds and sixths are weak because when this motion is maintained for more than three steps in succession, the second voice becomes the mere satellite of the first. Parallel fifths are invariably wrong when audible. They imply a faulty progression of fundamental harmonics.

Paralleltonarten (pä-rä-lĕl-tōn-är-t'n), *Ger.* Parallel keys. Related keys. Keys having many tones in common.

Paraphrase. An explanation of some text or passage in a more clear and ample manner than is expressed in the words of the author. A free transcription of an air or passage for some instrument other than that for which it was originally composed.

Parfait (pär-fä'), *Fr.* Perfect, as to intervals, etc.

Parlando (pär-län'dō), *It.* } Accented; in a
Parlante (pär-län'tĕ) } declamatory style; in a recitative or speaking style.

Parnassus. A mountain in Greece, celebrated in mythology as sacred to Apollo and the Muses, and famous, also, for the Castilian Spring and the temple of Apollo.

Parody. Music or words slightly altered and adapted to some new purpose.

Part. The music for each separate voice or instrument.

Parte (pär'tĕ), *It.* A part or portion of a composition; a part or rôle in an opera.

Parte cantante (pär'tĕ cän-tän'tĕ), *It.* The singing or vocal part; the principal vocal part having the melody.

Parterre (pär-tärr'), *Fr.* The pit of a theater.

Partial turn. A turn consisting of the chief note and three small notes, the leading note of which may be either a large or small second above the principal.

Parti di ripieno (pär'tĕ dē rē-pī-ā'nō), *It.* Parts not obligato; supplementary parts.

Partie (pär-tē), *Fr.* See *Parte*.

Parties de remplissage (pär-tē duh ränh-plĕ-säzh), *Fr.* Parts which fill up the middle harmony between the bass and upper part.

Partimento (pär-tĭ-mĕn'tō), *It.* An exercise, figured bass.

Partita (pär-tē'tä), *It.* An old term synonymous with variation.

Partition (pär-tē-sĭ-ōnh), *Fr.* } A score, a full
Partitur (pär-tĭ-toor), *Ger.* } score, or en-
Partitura (pär-tĭ-too'rä), *It.* } tire draft of
Partizione (pär-tē-tsĭ-ō'nĕ), *It.* } a composition for voices or instruments, or both.

Partito (pär-tē'tō), *It.* Scored, divided into parts.

Partiturspiel (pär-tĭ-toor'spēl, *Ger.* Playing from the score.

Partsongs. Songs for voices in parts, introduced in Germany in the present century.

Pas (pä), *Fr.* A step, a dance.

Paspie (päs'pĭ-ā, *Sp.* A kind of dance.

Paspy. See *Passepied*.

Pas redoublé (pä rĕ-doo-blā), *Fr.* A quickstep; an increased, redoubled step.

Passacaglio (päs-sä-käl'yĭ ō), *It.* } A species
Passacaille (päs-sä-käl), *Fr.* } of chacone, a slow dance with divisions on a ground bass in 3-4 time and always in a minor key.

Passage. Any phrase or short portion of an air, or other composition. Every member of a strain or movement is a passage.

Passaggio (päs-säd'jĭ-ō), *It.* A passage or series of notes.

Passamezzo (päs-sä-mĕt'sō), *It.* An old slow dance, little differing from the action of walking.

Passepied (päss-pĭ'ā), *Fr.* A sort of jig; lively old French dance in 3-4, 3-8, or 6-8 time; a kind of quick minuet, with three or more strains or reprises, the first consisting of eight bars.

Pas seul (pä sŭl), *Fr.* A dance by one performer.

Passing modulation. A transient modulation.

Passing tones. Dissonances introduced upon the weak part of the beat, leading across from one consonant tone to another, by conjunct movement, or stepwise, and not by skips.

Passionata (päs-sĭ-ō-nä'tä),
Passionatamente (päs-sĭ-ō-nä-tä-mĕn'tĕ), } *It.*
Passionate (päs-sĭ-ō-nä'tĕ),
Passionato (pä-sĭ-ō-nä'tō),
Passionate, impassioned, with fervor and pathos.

Passione, (päs-sĭ-ō'nĕ), *It.* Passion, feeling.

Passion music. Music composed for describing the Passion of our Lord. Used in Holy Week.

Passionsmusik, (päs-sĭ-ōns-moo-zēk'), *Ger.* Passion music.

Pasticio (päs-tēt'tshĭ-ō), *It.* } A medley, an
Pastiche (päs'tēsh) *Fr.* } opera made up

ä *arm*, ă *add*, ā *ale*, ĕ *end*, ē *eve*, ĭ *ill*, ī *isle*, ō *old*, ŏ *odd*, oo *moon*, ŭ *but*, ü *Fr. sound*, kh *Ger. ck*, nh *nasal*.

(173)

of songs, etc., by various composers; the poetry being written to the music, instead of the music to the poetry.

Pastoral. A musical drama, the personages and scenery of which are chiefly rural. A pastoral is also any lyrical production, the subject of which is taken from rural life; and the Italians give the same name to an instrumental composition written in the pastoral style.

Pastòrale (päs-tō-rä'lĕ), *It.* }
Pastorelle (päs-tō'rĕl). *Fr.* } belonging to a shepherd; a soft movement in a pastoral and rural style.

Pastoral flute. Shepherd's flute.

Pastourelle (päs-too-rĕll'), *Fr.* One of the movements of a quadrille.

Patetica (pä-tä'tĭ-kä), *It.* Pathetic.

Pateticamente (pä-tä'tĭ-kä-mĕn'tĕ), *It.* Pathetically.

Patetico (pä-tä'tĭ-kō), *It.*
Pathétique (pä-tā-tēk), *Fr.* } Pathetic.
Pathetisch (pä-tā'tĭsh), *Ger.*

Pathetic. Applied to music when it excites emotions of sorrow, pity, sympathy, etc.

Patimento (pä-tĭ-mĕn'tō), *It.* Affliction, grief, suffering.

Patriotic. Songs having for their theme love of country.

Pauker (pou'kĕr), *Ger.* Kettledrummer.

Pausa (pä-oo'zä), *It.* }
Pausa (pou'zä), *Lat.* } A pause.

Pause (pou'zĕ), *Ger.* A rest.

Pause. A character (⌒) which lengthens the duration of a note, or rest, over which it is placed, beyond its natural value, or at the pleasure of the performer. When placed over a double bar it shows the termination of the movement or piece.

Pause demi (pŏz dĕ-mē'), *Fr.* A minim rest.

Pavan, *Eng.* }
Pavana (pä-vä'nä), *It.* } A grave, stately
Pavane (pä-vänh'), *Fr.* } dance, which took its name from *pavo*, a peacock. It was danced by princes in their mantles, and ladies in gowns with long trains whose motions resembled those of a peacock's tail. It was in 3-4 time and generally in three strains, each of which was repeated.

Paventato (pä-vĕn-tä'tō), *It.* } Fearful, tim-
Paventoso (pä-vĕn-tō'zō), *It.* } orous, with anxiety and embarrassment.

Pavillion (pä-vē-yŏnh), *Fr.* The bole of a horn or other wind instrument.

Pavillion chinois (pä-vē-yŏnh she-nwa), An instrument consisting of an upright pole with numerous little bells, which impart brilliancy to lively pieces and pompous military marches.

Peal. A set of bells tuned to each other; the changes rung upon a set of bells.

Pean. A pæan; a song of praise.

Ped. An abbreviation of Pedal.

Pedal. A lever operated by the foot. Organ-pedals are keys corresponding to those of the key-manual, which command the low basses. The general compass of an organ-pedalier is two octaves and a half, from CCC to F. The pedals are played by both feet, using heel and toe as convenient. The use of the toe is indicated by the mark V, over the note for the right foot, or under it for the left. The heel is indicated in the same manner by the sign O.

The organ has also other pedals called "composition pedals," which command certain combinations of stops. There are, moreover, what are called "swell-pedals," which operate the swell-blinds, and shut in or liberate the sound. Swell-pedals are simply plain levers, which may be fixed by a racket at any position desired, or, more commonly, "balanced," operated by the heel and toe, and remaining at any point desired.

The pianoforte has two or three pedals. That upon the right is called the damper-pedal, and its office is to raise the dampers from the keys, either for permitting tones to continue after the fingers have left the keys or for promoting sympathetic resonance. The use of the damper-pedal is indicated by the character Ped., and its cessation by the mark ✳ or ⊕. The damper-pedal is used very many times where no marks appear. It is permissible everywhere, subject to the following restrictions: 1, that no blurring of melody or harmony (intermingling of dissimilar harmonic elements) is made by its use; 2, that the indicated phrasing is not covered up by it.

The pedal at the extreme left is called the "soft pedal." On grand pianos it shifts the action so that the hammers strike upon only two of the three strings of the unison. In the upright it brings the hammers nearer the strings. Its use is indicated by the words *Una corda*, or *Verschiebung*, and its discontinuance by the words "tre corde." The soft pedal is permissible whenever it is desired to diminish the volume of sound.

When there is a third pedal (between the two others) it is generally a tone-sustaining pedal, whose office it is to sustain a tone taken while it is in use, whereas the damper-pedal operates all the dampers together. The tone-sustaining pedal is in effect a damper-pedal which operates upon only the single tone or chord which may be held at the moment when the pedal is pressed. These will be sustained as long as the pedal is held, while all that may be taken during its use will be unaffected. This device is more and more important as the vibration of the pianoforte becomes longer.

The harp is furnished with eight pedals, of which the middle one opens or closes the little panel in the sounding case, and corresponds to the piano soft and loud pedal. The seven pedals along the sides are named for the notes which they severally affect, A, B, etc. The harp is set in the key of C♭. When a pedal is depressed to its first notch, it revolves a disk which shortens the strings of the same name throughout the instrument, raising the pitch a half-step; when depressed to the second notch it raises the pitch a whole step. Hence, when the A pedal is depressed one notch it makes all the A-flats A-natural; and when to its second notch it makes them A-sharp. In this way the instrument is adjusted to any desired signature, and accidentals are introduced in this way in the course of a piece. The pedals here described are what are called "double-acting," and were invented by Sebastian Erard, about 1823.

The reed organ and the harmonium have two pedals, which are employed in operating the bellows.

Pedalclaves (pĕ-däl'klä'fĕs),
Pedalclaviatűr (pĕ-däl'klä'vĭ-ä-toor'), *Ger.*
The pedal keyboard in an organ.

Pedale, doppelte (pĕ-dä'lĕ dŏp'pĕl-tĕ), *Ger.*
Pedale doppio (rĕ-dä'lĕ dŏp'pĭ-o), *It.*
Double pedals, in organ-playing; playing the pedals with both feet at once.

Pedale d'organo (pĕ-dä'lĕ d'ŏr'gä-nō), *It.* The pedals of an organ.

Pédales (pĕ'däl), *Fr. pl.* The pedals.

Pédales de combinaison, *Fr.* Combination pedals.

Pedalflügel (pe-däl'flü'g'l), *Ger.* A grand piano with a pedal keyboard.

Pedalharfe (pĕ-däl'här'fĕ), *Ger.*)
Pedalharp. A harp with pedals, to produce the semitones.

Pedaliera (pĕ-dä-lĭ-ä'rä), *It.* The pedal keys of an organ.

Pedal keys. That set of keys belonging to an organ, or similar instrument, which is played by the feet.

Pedal note. A note held by the pedal, or the bass voice, while the harmony formed by the other parts proceeds independently.

Pedal Point. A harmonic phrase, consisting of a single tone prolonged, while the remaining voices proceed with chords many of which are dissonant with the prolonged tone. The opening and closing chords must be those of the prolonged tone. Pedal point derives its name from the pedal of the organ, which originally held the prolonged tone. Pedal points are sometimes made with a soprano tone, but not so often.

Pentachord. An instrument with five strings, a scale or system of five diatonic sounds.

Pentatonic scale. A scale of five notes, sometimes called the Scotch scale, and similar to the modern diatonic major scale, with the fourth and seventh degrees omitted—do, re, mi, sol, la, do; or, in minor, la, do, re, mi, sol, la. In use the seventh degree is sometimes introduced as a passing tone just at the close. This is probably a modern innovation.

Penultimate (pĕ-nŭl'tĭ-māt). The last syllable but one.

Per (pär), *It.* For, by, through, in.

Percussion.) Striking, applied to instruments, notes, or chords; or the touch on the pianoforte. A general name for all instruments that are struck, as a gong, drum, bell, tabor, etc.
Percussione (pĕr-koos-sĭ-ō'nĕ), *It.*

Perdendo (pĕr-dĕn'dō). *It.*) Gradually decreasing the tone and the time; dying away, becoming extinct.
Perdendosi (pĕr-dĕn-dō'zĭ).

Perfect. A term applied to certain intervals and chords.

Perfect cadence. Dominant harmony followed by that of the tonic; a close upon the keynote preceded by the dominant.

Perfect close. A perfect cadence.

Perfect concords.) These are the unison, the perfect fourth, perfect fifth, and the octave.
Perfect consonances.

Perfect fifth. An interval equal to three whole tones and one semitone.

Perfect fourth. An interval equal to two whole tones and one semitone.

Perfect octave. An interval equal to five whole tones and two semitones.

Perfetto (pĕr-fĕt'to, *It.* Perfect, complete.

Perigourdine (pĕr-ĭ-goor-dĕn). A French dance in 3-8 time.

Period) A complete musical sentence.
Période (pä-rĭ-ŏd'. *Fr.*
Periode (pĕ-rĭ-ō'dĕ), *It.*

A period. The simple period consists of eight measures, disposed in two sections of similar extent and rhythmic construction; each section is a so composed of two phrases, and each phrase of two motives. Hence the following scheme:

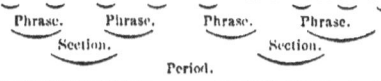

Motive. Motive. Motive. Motive. Motive. Motive. Motive. Motive.
Phrase. Phrase. Phrase. Phrase.
Section. Section.
Period.

The two sections of the period stand towards each other in the relation of subject and predicate, or, as formerly called, Protasis (awakening expectation), and Apodasis (answering expectation). In simple lyric periods the two phrases of the section often bear a similar relation to each other, the first phrase awakening expectation and the second partially answering it; the third phrase repeats the first, and the fourth completes the answer. Hence the scheme of a lyric period, of which examples are numerous, as for instance, in the first eight or sixteen measures of almost any Beethoven slow movement.

Subject. Partial Answer. Subject. Complete Answer.
Phrase A. Phrase B. Phrase C (A). Phrase D (B modified).

Certain theorists apply the names Phrase and Section in reversed order to this, calling the smaller member a section, and the half-period a phrase. This usage is not so well sanctioned, and is not so consonant with best German usage.

Periods are shortened by cutting short a measure in the last phrase, or lengthened by repeating the cadence, with or without modification.

A complex period is one in which one or more sections are repeated. See "Primer of Musical Form." (W. S. B. M.)

A dependent period is one which depends upon something else to complete the sense. This may have been already advanced in a previous period, in which case the dependent period will begin upon some chord other than its own tonic — generally its dominant; it will finally end with a complete cadence upon the tonic. More properly, however, the dependence is shown by an imperfect cadence upon the dominant instead of the tonic, in which case another period has the task of fully completing it by presenting its leading idea and fully answering it upon its own tonic. Any period which ends upon some other than its own tonic chord is dependent.

Période musicale (pā-rĭ-ōd mü-zē-käl), *Fr.* A musical period.

Periodenbau (pĕ-rĭ-ō'd'n-bou'), *Ger.* Composition; the construction of musical periods.

Perlé (pĕr-lā', *Fr.* Pearled, brilliant; *cadence perlee*, brilliant cadence.

Perpetual fugue. A canon so constructed that its termination leads to its beginning, and hence may be perpetually repeated.

Perpetuo (pĕr-pä'too-ō), *It.* Perpetual.

Perpetuum mobile (pĕr-pä'too-oom mō'bĭ-lĕ), *Lat.* Perpetual motion. A name applied to certain compositions which go rapidly and without opportunity of pause.

Per recte et retro (pĕr rĕk'tĕ ĕt rā'trō), *Lat.* Forward, then backward; the melody or subject reversed, note for note.

Pesante (pĕ-zän'tĕ), *It.* Heavy, ponderous; with importance and weight, impressively.

Pesantemente (pĕ-zän-tĕ-mĕn'tĕ), *It.* Heavily, forcibly, impressively.

Petit (pĕ-tē'), *Fr.* Little, small.

Petit chœur (pĕ-tē'kür), *Fr.* Little choir; a sacred composition in three parts.

Petites flutes (pĕ-tēt' flüt), *Fr.* The small flutes; the octave or piccolo flutes.

Petto (pĕt'tō), *It.* The chest, the breast; *voce di petto*, the chest voice.

Peu (pŭh), *Fr.* Little, a little.

Peu à peu (pŭh ä pŭh), *Fr.* Little by little, by degrees.

Pezze (pĕt'sĕ), *It. pl.* Fragments, scraps; select, detached pieces.

Pezzi concertanti (pĕt'sĭ kŏn-tshĕr-tän'tĕ), *It. pl.* Concertante pieces, in which each instrument has occasional solos.

Pezzi di bravura (pĕt'sĭ dĕ brä-voo'rä), *It.* Compositions for the display of dexterity or rapid execution.

Pezzo (pĕt'sō), *It.* A fragment; a detached piece of music.

Pf. Abbreviation of Poco forte; a little louder.

Pfeife (pfī'fĕ), *Ger.* Pipe, fife, flute.

Pfeifen (pfī'f'n), *Ger.* To play on a fife or flute.

Pfeifendeckel (pfī'f'n-dĕk'ĕl), *Ger.* The stopper, or covering, of an organ-pipe.

Pfeifer (pfī'fĕr), *Ger.* A fifer, a piper.

Phantasie (fän-tä-zē), *Ger.* See *Fantasia*.

Phantasiebilder (fän-tä-sē'bĭl'd'r), *Ger.* Fancy pictures.

Phantasiestücke (fän-tä-sē'stü'ke), *Ger.* Fancy pieces. Name applied by Schumann to his Opus 12.

Phantasiren (fän-tä-zē'r'n), *Ger.* Improvising.

Phantasirte (fän-tä-zĭr'tĕ), *Ger.* Improvised.

Phantasy. The fancy, the imagination.

Philharmonic (fĭl-här-mŏn'ĭk), *Gr.* Music-loving.

Phisharmonica (fĭs-här-mŏn'ĭ-kä). A kind of octagonal accordeon.

Phone (fō'nĕ), *Gr.* The voice; a sound, or tone.

Phonetic. Vocal, representing sounds.

Phonetics. } The doctrine, or science, of
Phonics. } sounds, especially those of the human voice.

Phonometer. An instrument for measuring the vibrations of sounds.

Phorminx (fŏr'mĭnx), *Ger.* A stringed instrument of remote antiquity, resembling the lyre.

Photinx (fō'tĭnx), *Gr.* Name given by the ancients to their crooked flute.

Phrase. A short musical sentence; a musical thought, or idea.

Phrase, extended. } Any variation of a melody by which three measures are used instead of two.
Phrase, irregular. }

Phrasing. The art of musical delivery in such a way as to bring out the idea. Hence to connect the tones within the phrase, and to define the boundaries of the phrases. Also to form the phrase properly, as to its increasing or diminishing intensity. Hence the art of singing or playing with expression.

Physharmonica (fĭs-här-mŏn'ĭ-kä), *Ger.* An instrument, the tone of which resembles that of the reed-pipes in an organ, and is produced by the vibration of thin metal tongues, of a similar construction to those of the harmonium; the name is also applied to a stop in the organ with free reeds, and with tubes of half the usual length.

ă *arm*, ă *add*, ā *ale*, ĕ *end*, ē *eve*, ĭ *ill*, ī *isle*, ō *old*, ŏ *odd*, oo *moon*, ŭ *but*, ü *Fr. sound*, kh *Ger. ch*, nh *nasal*.

Piacere (pē-ä-tshä'rĕ), *It.* Pleasure, inclination, fancy ; *a piacere*, at pleasure.
Piacevole (pē-ä-tshä'vō-lĕ), *It.* Pleasing, graceful, agreeable.
Piacevolezza (pē-ä-tshĕ-vō-lĕt'zä), *It.* Gracefulness, sweetness.
Piacevolmente (pē-ä-tshĕ-vōl-mĕn'tĕ), *It.* Gracefully, delicately.
Piacimento (pē-ä-tshī-mĕn'tō), *It.* See *Piacere*.
Piagendo (pē-ä-gĕn'dō), *It.* Plaintively, sorrowfully.
Piagnevole (pē-äu-yä'vō-lĕ), *It.* Mournful, doleful, lamentable.
Pianamente (pē-ä-nä-mĕn'tĕ), *It.* Softly, gently, quietly.
Pianettó (pē-ä-nĕt'tō), *It.* Very low, very soft.
Piangevole (pē-än-gä'vō-lĕ), *It.* Lamentable, doleful.
Piangevolmente (pē-än-gä-vōl-mĕn'tĕ), *It.* Lamentably, dolefully.
Pianino (pē-ä-nē'nō), *It.* An upright pianoforte.
Pianissimo (pē-ä-nēs'sī-mō), *It.* Extremely soft.
Pianissimo quanto possibile (pē-ä-nēs'sī-mō kwän-tō pōs-sē-bī-lĕ), *It.* As soft as possible.
Pianist. An amateur or professional player on the pianoforte.
Pianiste (pē-än-ēst'), *Fr.* Pianist.
Piano (pē-ä'nō), *It.* Soft, gentle.
Piano à queue (pē-ä'nō ä küh), *Fr.* A grand pianoforte.
Piano assai (pē-ä'nō äs-sä'ī), *It.* As soft as possible.
Piano carré (pē-ä'nō kär-rā), *Fr.* A square pianoforte.
Piano droit (pē-ä'nō drwä), *Fr.* An upright pianoforte.
Pianoforte. An instrument made in various shapes, such as square (table-shaped), upright (cabinet-shaped), and grand ("wing-shaped ;" hence German *Flugel*). The pianoforte consists essentially of a sounding-board of thin fir wood, supported by a frame and ribs. Across this board are certain bridges, over which the wire strings are drawn and made fast to hitchpins at the right and tuning-pins at the left, or in the wrestplank. The frame which supports the tension of the strings was formerly of wood, but in 1825 an American, Alpheus Babcock, of Boston, invented an iron plate, which strengthened the wooden frame, and in process of time has itself been strengthened until it carries the entire tension of the strings. The wrestplank, in which the tuning-pins turn, rests upon a shoulder, or arch, of the iron frame.

The pianoforte was the successor of the clavier and harpsichord, and differed essentially from them in the manner in which the strings are made to sound. In the clavier it was by a brass tangent which pushed the wire; in the harpsichord it was by means of a quill plectrum, which plucked the wire, and upon the pianoforte it is by means of a hammer, which, being actuated by the motion of the key, drives against the string and rebounds instantly, so that the string is left as free as the string of a dulcimer struck by a hammer in the hand. The escapement mechanism invented by Christofori was the foundation of all that have been made since. The main parts of the present action were invented by Sebastian Erard, of Paris, early in the first quarter of the present century, but many improvements have been made since. All the early hammers were covered with leather, which soon became hard, causing the tone to become twangy. The discovery of a method of felting hammer-coverings, and of putting them upon the hammers by machinery, was discovered about 1855, and was first practiced by the firm of Nunns & Clarke, of New York. Overstringing was first successfully accomplished by Steinway & Sons, of New York, in 1855. Many important improvements had previously been made by Jonas Chickering between 1830 and 1850.

The tone of the pianoforte apparently depends upon three elements conjointly : The sounding-board and its treatment, the scale (the relative length of strings, their weight, and the point where the hammer strikes them), and the hammers. The durability depends upon general solidity of construction, the use of approved material, and scientific adjustment of the instrument in all its parts to sustain the great tension, which in large concert grands now amounts to above eighteen tons. The greatest difficulty is the sounding-board. In the nature of the case this has to be of thin wood, yet the strings must pull across the bridges with great power, pressing down against the board, in order that the vibration may be more abundant and the whole of it come into the sounding-board, where it is reinforced by the natural resonance of the wood and so transferred to the atmosphere. The board is put in "crowning," as it is called, or convex, and the tendency of the strings, combined with the progressive desiccation of the wood, is to crush out this convexity, which, being done, the tone becomes flabby.

The American pianofortes are generally recognized as larger, more sonorous, and in several respects better than most foreign ones; and our leading houses are generally regarded as leading all the world. Particularly is this true because of the large number of important improvements in the instrument made by the leading makers, in which they have been generally followed by all other good makers, American as well as foreign. In America there is a great development of the industry of making pianofortes of moderate price, in which respect, combining fair tonal qualities with showy appearance and durability, American makers lead the world. These lower-priced in-

ä arm, ă add, ā ale ĕ end, ē eve, ĭ ill, ī isle, ŏ old, ŏ odd, oo moon, ŭ but, ü Fr. sound, kh Ger. ch. nh nasal.

struments generally make a fair imitation of the qualities of the best, and the makers have shown great progressiveness in finding ways of doing this within the limitation of expense. The best pianoforte depends for its success, after the maker has secured a good scale, and the requisite solidity, upon the sounding-board and its treatment, and upon the hammers. These two elements are matters of individual adjustment by highly skilled labor, of artistic instinct, and even then the final result is somewhat uncertain, exactly as in making violins, or any other apparatus in which results are obtained by a skilled adjustment of parts cooperating with individualities of material. This being the case, it is not likely that the gap between the pleasing pianofortes of commercial grade, and the exceptional tonal qualities of the very best, can ever be very much narrowed.

The pianoforte owes its popularity to its success in representing all properties of music. Melody, harmony, expression, and some degree of singing quality and tone-color are placed by it at the disposal of the player, and upon it he is able to give an intelligible account of by far a larger variety of music, both high and low, than upon any other musical instrument.

Down to about 1872 the square pianoforte was the form mainly current in America. The first American grand pianoforte was made by Jonas Chickering in 1828. About 1870 improvements in the upright resulted in perfecting this form, whereby, combined with solidity, the tonal capacity very nearly approached that of the grand, and this form therefore came more and more to the head, so that at the present time there are no square pianos made, except to special order. The advantage which the grand piano possesses over the upright is in having a larger sounding-board, greater solidity, and consequently a larger and more sympathetic tone. The action also has one additional lever between the finger and the hammer, whereby the touch is magnified and a smaller effort of the player effects a perceptible modification of the tone. The manufacture and sale of grand pianofortes has enormously increased in recent years.

Pian-pianissimo (pē-än′pē-ä-nēs′sĭ-mō), *It.* Exceedingly soft and gentle.

Pian-piano (pē-än̥-pē-ä′nō), *It.* Very softly, with a low voice. See *Piano-piano.*

Pianoforte action. The mechanism of a pianoforte.

Pianoforte hammer. That part of the mechanism of a pianoforte which strikes the wires.

Pianoforte score. The score, or music, of an orchestral or choral work, arranged condensed upon two staves convenient for performance upon the pianoforte. The pianoforte arrangement of an orchestral work contains as much of the music as the arranger believes practicable for the player. The pianoforte score of a choral work includes the vocal parts upon their own staves and the orchestral parts condensed upon two staves, as in the arrangements from orchestral works. Hence, for purposes of study, except where it is a question of tone-color and the art of instrumentation, the pianoforte score offers all necessary advantages.

Piano mezzo (pē-ä′nō mĕt′zō), *It.* Moderately soft.

Piano-piano (pē-ä′nō-pē-ä′no), *It.* Very soft.

Piano sempre staccato e marcato il basso (pē-ä′nō sĕm-prĕ stäk-kä′tō mär-kä′tō ĕl bäs′sō,. *It.* Soft, with the bass always well marked and detached.

Piano solo. For the pianoforte only.

Piano-violino (pē-ä′nō vē-ō-lē′nō), *It.* A curious instrument, invented in 1837. It was a common piano, containing a violin arrangement inside of it, which was set in motion by a pedal. When this instrument was played upon it gave the sound of both violin and piano.

Piatti (pē-ät′tē), *It. pl.* Cymbals.

Pib (pēb), *Wel.* A pipe, a fife.

Pibcorn, *or*, **hornpipe.** The name given by the Welsh to a wind instrument consisting of a wooden pipe with holes at the sides and a horn at each end, the one to collect the wind blown into it by the mouth, and the other to carry off the sounds as modulated by the performer.

Pibroch (pē′brŏh). A wild, irregular species of music, peculiar to the Highlands of Scotland, performed on the bagpipe.

Picchiettato (pē-kĭ-ĕt-tä′tō), *It.* Scattered, detached; in violin-playing a staccato made by means of the bow bounding upon the strings; hence not nearly so short as the staccato made by plucking the strings (pizziccato). The picchiettato implies a duration about equal to three quarters of the apparent duration of the note. Picchiettato is indicated by means of a straight mark over the note and a dot under the mark, or a slur over several notes and a dot over each one. The corresponding effect upon the pianoforte might be produced by playing several tones with one finger.

Picciolo (pēt-tshĭ-ō′lō),
Piccolino (pē-kō-lē′nō), *It.* } Small, little.
Piccolo (pē′kō-lō),

Piccolo. A 2-feet organ-stop, of wood pipes, producing a bright and clear tone, in unison with the fifteenth.

Piccolo flute. A small flute.

Piccolo pianoforte. A small upright pianoforte.

Pièce (pĭ-äs′), *Fr.* A composition or piece of music; an opera or drama.

Pieds (pĭ-ā′), *Fr. pl.* The foot; *avec les pieds,* with the feet, in organ-playing.

Piena (pē-ā'nä), *It.* } Full.
Pieno (pē-ā-nō),
Pienamente (pē-ā-nä-mēn'tē), *It.* Fully.
Pieno coro (pē-ā'nō kō'rō), *It.* A full chorus.
Pieno organo (pē-ā'nō ōr-gä'nō), *It.* With the full organ.
Pieta (pē-ā'tä),
Pietosamente (pē-ā-tō-zä-mēn'tē), } *It.*
Pietoso (pē-ā-tō'zō),
Compassionately, tenderly; implying, also, a rather slow and sustained movement.
Pifara (pē-fä'rä), *It.* A fife.
Pifferare (pĭf-fĕ-rä'rĕ), *It.* To play upon the fife; also a piper, such as, in Italy, play pastoral airs in the streets at Christmas. One of the e airs forms the basis of Handel's Pastoral Symphony in the "Messiah."
Pifferina (pĭf-fĕ-rē'nä), *It.* A little fife.
Piffero (pĭf'fĕ-rō), *It.* A fife, or small flute; also an organ-stop of 4 feet.
Pincé (pănh-sā), *Fr.* Pinched; an ornament called a mordent. See *Pizzicato.*
Pincer (pănh-sā), *Fr.* To play upon a musical instrument.
Pinces (pănh-s), *Fr.* A general name for stringed instruments.
Pipe. Any tube formed of a reed, or of metal, or of wood, which, being blown at one end, produces a musical sound. The pipe, which was originally no more than a simple oaten straw, was one of the earliest instruments by which musical sounds were attempted.
Piper. A performer on the pipe. Pipers were formerly one of the class of itinerant musicians, and performed on a variety of wind instruments, as the bagpipe, musette, etc.
Piqué (pĭ-kā'), *Fr.* } To play on the violin,
Piquer (pĭ-kā'), } etc., a series of notes a little staccato, and with a light pressure of the bow to each note.
Piquiren (pē-kē'r'n), *Ger.* Detached; equivalent to picchiettato.
Piston. A kind of valve used in brass instruments to alter the pitch.
Pitch. The acuteness, or gravity, of any particular sound, or the tuning of any instrument.
Pitch, concert. The pitch generally adopted for some one given note, and by which every other note is governed. American concert pitch at the present time (1895) is based upon an A having 431 vibrations.
Pitchpipe. An instrument formerly used to sound the keynote of any vocal composition.
Piu (pē'oo), *It.* More.
Piu allegro (pē'oo äl-lā'grō), *It.* A little quicker, more lively.
Piu che lento (pē'oo kĕ lĕn'to), *It.* Slower than lento.
Piu forte (pē'oo fŏr'tĕ), *It.* Louder.

Piu lento (pē'oo lĕn'to), *It.* More slowly.
Piu mosso (pē'oo mōs'sō), *It.* } More motion,
Piu moto (pē'oo mō'tō), } quicker.
Piu piano (pē'oo pē-ä'nō), *It.* Softer.
Piu piu (pē'oo pē'oo), *It.* Somewhat more.
Piu posto (pē'oo pōs'tō), *It.* Rather, inclined to; it also means quicker.
Piu posto allegro (pē'oo pōs'tō äl-lā'grō), *It.* Rather quicker.
Piu posto lento (pē'oo pōs'tō lĕn'tō), *It.* Rather slower.
Piu presto (pē'oo prĕs'tō), *It.* Quicker, more rapidly.
Piu vivo (pē'oo vē'vō), *It.* More lively, more animated.
Piva (pē'vä), *It.* A pipe, a bagpipe.
Pizzicando (pĭ-tsĭ-kän'dō), *It.* } Pinched;
Pizzicato (pĭ-tsĭ-kä'tō), } meaning that the strings of the violin, violoncello, etc., are not to be played with the bow, but pinched, or snapped, with the fingers, producing a staccato effect.
Placidamente (plä-tshĭ-dä-mĕn'tĕ), *It.* Calmly, placidly, quietly.
Placido (plä-tshē'dō), *It.* Placid, tranquil, calm.
Plagal. Those ancient modes in which the melody was confined within the limits of the dominant and its octave.
Plagal cadence. A cadence in which the final chord on the tonic is preceded by the harmony of the subdominant.
Plagalisch (plä gä'lĭsh), *Ger.* Plagal.
Plain chant (plăn shänh), *Fr.* The plain song.
Plain song. The name given to the old ecclesiastical chant when in its most simple state and without those harmonic appendages with which it has since been enriched. The choral service of the Protestant Episcopal Church is founded upon the Plain Song. All the priest's cantillation at the altar in the Roman Catholic Church is also a part of the Plain Song.
Plainte (plănht), *Fr.* A complaint, a lament.
Plaintif (plănh-tēf), *Fr.* Plaintive, doleful.
Plaisant (plä-zănh), *Fr.* Pleasing.
Plaisanteries (plä-zän-t'rē), *Fr.* Amusing, light compositions.
Planxty. Old harp music of a lively, tuneful kind.
Plaqué (plä-kā'), *Fr.* Struck at once, without any arpeggio or embellishment.
Plectraphone. An ingenious invention which, attached to the piano, produces a very clever imitation of the mandolin.
Plectrum (plĕk'troom), *Lat.* A quill, or piece of ivory or hard wood, used to twitch the strings of the mandolin, lyre, etc.
Plein jeu (plănh zhü), *Fr.* Full organ; the term is also applied to a mixture stop of several ranks of pipes.

ä *arm*, ā *add*, ă *ale*, ĕ *end*, ē *eve*, ĭ *ill*, ī *isle*, ŏ *old*, ō *odd*, oo *moon*, ŭ *but*, ü *Fr. sound*, kh *Ger. ch*, nh *nasal.*

Plein jeu harmonique (plănh zhŭ här-môuh-ĕk'), *Fr.* A mixture stop in an organ.

Pleno organo (plā'nō ŏr-gä'uō), *Lat.* Full organ.

Plettro (plĕt'trō), *It.* A bow, a fiddlestick; also a plectrum.

Plus (plü), *Fr.* More.

Plus animé (plü sĭ-nĭ-mā), *Fr.* With more animation.

Plus lentement (plü länht-mäuh), *Fr.* Slower, more slowly.

Pneumatic (nū-măt'ĭk). Relating to the air or wind; a term applied to all wind instruments collectively.

Pneumatic action. } Mechanism intended to
Pneumatic lever. } lighten the touch, etc., in large organs. The pneumatic lever consisted of a bellows about three inches by fourteen, which became inflated whenever the corresponding organ-key was depressed. Inasmuch as only a small valve was needed to inflate such a bellows, the touch was very light. The bellows opened the pallet, admitting wind to the corresponding pipes. The saving in elasticity and lightness of touch was very important in large organs, where, without some such appliance, a weight of several pounds is sometimes necessary to operate a key. There was a certain loss of time and of precise attack, wh'ch was reduced to a minimum by increasing the pressure of the wind operating the pneumatic lever. It was invented by one Barker in 1837, and greatly improved by Ira Bassett in 1888. The pneumatic lever is now displaced by a pneumatic action, which accomplishes the same result much better by means of a small pneumatic under every pipe. These are now operated by electricity.

Pneumatic organ. An organ moved by wind, so named by the ancients to distinguish it from the hydraulic organ, moved by water.

Pochessimo (pŏ-kĕs'sĭ-mō), *It.* A very little, as little as possible.

Pochette (pō-shĕt), *Fr.* A kit, a small violin used by dancing-masters.

Pochettino (pō-kĕt-tē'nō), } A little; as,
Pochetto (pō-kĕt'tō), *It.* } retard un po-
Pochino (pō-kē'nō), } chettros, a little slower.

Poco (pō'kō), *It.* Little.

Poco adagio (pō'kō ä-dä'jĭ-ō), *It.* A little slower.

Poco allegro (pō'kō äl-lā'grō), *It.* A little faster.

Poco animato (pō'kō ä-nĭ-mä'tō), *It.* A little more animated.

Poco a poco (pō'kō ä pō'kō), *It.* By degrees, little by little.

Poco a poco crescendo (pō'kō a pō'kō krĕ-shĕn'dō), *It.* Gradually louder and louder.

Poco a poco diminuendo (pō'kō ä pō'kō dē-mē-noo-ĕn'dō), *It.* Gradually diminishing.

Poco a poco, piu di fuoco (pō'kō ä pō'kō pē-oo dē foo-ō'kō), *It.* With gradually increasing fire and animation.

Poco a poco piu lento (pō'kō ä pō'kō pē'oo lĕn'tō), *It.* Gradually slower and slower.

Poco a poco, piu moto (pō'kō ä pō'kō pē'oo mō'tō), *It.* Gradually increasing the time.

Poco a poco rallentando (pō'kō ä pō'kō räl-lĕn-tän'dō), *It.* Gradually diminishing.

Poco forte (pō'kō fōr'tĕ), *It.* Moderately loud, a little loud.

Poco largo (pō'kō lär'gō), } Moderately
Poco lento (pō'kō lĕn'tō), *It.* } slow.

Poco meno (pō'kō mā'nō), *It.* A little less, somewhat less.

Poco piano (pō'kō pē-ä'nō), *It.* Somewhat soft.

Poco piu (pō'kō pē'oo), *It.* A little more, somewhat more.

Poco piu allegro (pō'kō pē'oo äl-lā'grō), *It.* A little quicker.

Poco piu che allegretto (pō'kō pē'oo kē äl-lĕ-grĕt'tō), *It.* A little quicker than allegretto.

Poco piu che andante (pō'kō pē'oo kē än-dän'tĕ), *It.* A little slower than andante.

Poco piu forte (pō'kō pē-oo fōr'tĕ), *It.* A little louder.

Poco piu largo (pō'kō pē'oo lär'gō), } A lit-
Poco piu lento (pō'kō pē'oo lĕn'tō), *It.* } tle slower.

Poco piu mosso (pō'kō pē'oo mōs'sō), *It.* A little faster.

Poco piu piano (pō'kō pē'oo pē-ä'nō), *It.* A little softer.

Poco presto (pō'kō prĕs'tō), *It.* Rather quick.

Poco presto accelerando (pō'kō prĕs'tō ät-tshĕl-ĕ-rän'dō), *It.* Gradually accelerate the time.

Poetic. A term sometimes applied to descriptive music, indicating an underlying poetic conception.

Poetique (pō-ĕ-tĕk), *Fr.* Poetic.

Poggiato (pŏd-jĭ-ä'tō), *It.* Dwelt upon, leaned upon.

Poi (pō'ē), *It.* Then, after, afterwards; *piano poi forte*, soft, then loud.

Poi a poi (pō'ē ä pō'ē), *It.* By degrees.

Point (pwänh), *Fr.* A dot.

Point d'arrêt (pwänh där-rā), *Fr.* Point of arrest; a hold over a rest, which it prolongs indefinitely.

Point de repos (pwänh düh rē-pō'), *Fr.* A pause.

Point d'orgue (pwänh dōrg), *Fr.* Organ point.

Pointée (pwänh-tā), *Fr.* Dotted; *blanche pointée*, a dotted minim.

Point final (pwänh fĭ näl'), *Fr.* A final, or concluding, cadence.

Point of repose. A pause, a cadence.

Point, organ. A long, or stationary, bass note, upon which various passages of melody and harmony are introduced.

ä *arm*, ă *add*, ā *ale*, ĕ *end*, ē *eve*, ' *ill*, ī *isle*, ō *old*, ŏ *odd*, oo *moon*, ŭ *but*, ü *Fr. sound*, kh *Ger. ch*, nh *nasal*.

Poi segue (pō'ĕ sā'gwĕ),
Poi seguente (pō'ĕ sā-gwĕn'tĕ), *It.* } Then follows, here follows.

Poi segue il rondo (pō'ĕ sā'gwĕ ĕl rōn'dō), *It.* After this the rondo.

Polacca (pō-lăk'kä), *It.* A polonaise, or in the style of a polonaise.

Polka. A lively Bohemian or Polish dance, in 2-4 time, the first three quavers in each bar being accented, and the fourth quaver unaccented.

Polka mazurka (pōl'kä mä-zūr-kä). A dance in triple time, played slow, and having its accent on the last part of the measure.

Polka redowa (pōl'kä rĕd'ō ä). A dance tune in triple time, played faster than the polka mazurka, and having its accent on the first part of the measure.

Polonaise (pōl-ō-nāz'). A chivalrous Polish dance in 3-4 measure, having, however, a movement of six eighths (in rhythm of twos) with an extra accent upon the fifth. The second eighth-note is generally divided into two sixteenths. The rhythm of the polonaise should be strictly observed.

Polska (pōls'kä), *Sw.* A Swedish dance in 3-4 measure.

Polymorphous (pŏl-ĭ-mōr'foos), *Gr.* Of many forms, a term generally used in reference to canons.

Polyphonia (pōl-ĭ-fō'nĭ-ä), *Gr.* A combination of many sounds; a composition for many voices.

Polyphonic (pŏl ĭ-fŏn-ĭk).
Polyphonous (pō-lĭf'ō-nŭs), } Full-voiced, for many voices.

Polyphony (pō-lĭf'ō-ny).

Pommer (pŏm'm'r), *Ger.* An obsolete family of instruments of the oboe kind. See *Bombardon*.

Pompös (pŏm-pōs'), *Ger.* Pompous, majestic.

Pomposamente (pŏm-pō-zä-mĕn'tĕ), *It.* Pompously, stately.

Pomposo (pŏm-pō'zō), *It.* Pompous, stately, grand.

Ponderoso (nŏn-dĕ-rō'zō), *It.* Ponderously, massively, heavily.

Ponticello (pŏn-tĭ-tshĕl'lō), *It.* The bridge of the violin, guitar, etc.

Pont-neuf (pŏnh-nŭf), *Fr.* A street ballad, a vulgar song.

Portamento (pŏr-tä-mĕn'tō), *It.* A term applied by the Italians to the manner or habit of sustaining and conducting the voice. A singer who is easy and yet firm and steady in the execution of passages and phrases is said to have a good portamento. It is also used to connect two notes separated by an interval, by gliding the voice from one to the other, and by this means anticipating the latter in regard to intonation.

Portamento di voce (pŏr-tä-mĕn'tō dē vō'tshĕ), *It.* Carrying the voice; the blending of one tone into another.

Portando la voce (pŏr-tän'dō lä vō'tshĕ). Carrying the voice, holding it firmly on the notes.

Portative. A portable organ.

Portato (pŏr-tä'tō), *It.* Noulegato.

Porte de voix (pŏrt dŭh vwä), *Fr.* Portamento. Also an appoggiatura, or beat.

Portée (pŏr-tā), *Fr.* The staff.

Porter la voix (pŏr-tā lä vwä), *Fr.* To carry the voice.

Posato (pō-zä'tō), *It.* Quietly, steadily.

Posaune (pō-zou'nĕ), *Ger.* A trumpet; also a trombone, a sackbut; also an organ-stop. See *Trombone*.

Posaunenzug (pō-zou'nĕn-tsoog'), *Ger.* A sackbut.

Positif (pō-zĭ-tēf'), *Fr.* } The choir organ,
Positiv (pō-sĭ-tĭf'), *Ger.* } or lowest row of keys with soft-toned stops in a large organ; also a small fixed organ, thus named in opposition to a portative organ, especially when the pipes of the choir organ are brought forward and placed behind the organist, when they are called the *Rückpositif*.

Position. A shift on the violin, tenor, or violoncello; the arrangement or order of the several members of a chord.

Position. (1) With reference to chords, which are said to be in fundamental position when they are not inverted, and in open position when the upper three voices exceed the compass of an octave, but otherwise in close position. (2) With reference to the position of the hand upon the fingerboard of stringed instruments, the first position being that nearest the nut; then progressively moving one note toward the bridge the second, the third, and the other positions.

Possibile (pōs-sē'bĭ-lĕ), *It.* Possible; *il piu forte possibile*, as loud as possible.

Posthorn (pŏst'hŏrn), *Ger.* A species of bugle.

Posthume (pos-tum), *Fr.* Posthumous; published after the death of the author.

Postlude (pŏst'loo-dĕ),
Postludium (pŏst-loo'dĭ-oom), *Lat.* } Afterpiece, concluding voluntary.

Potenza (pō-tĕn'tsä), *It.* A name applied by the ancients to the notes and signs of music; any sound produced by an instrument.

Potpourri (pō'poor-rē). A medley; a capriccio or fantasia in which favorite airs and fragments of musical pieces are strung together and contrasted.

Pouce (nooss), *Fr.* The thumb; a term used in guitar music, indicating that the thumb of the right hand must be passed lightly over all the strings.

Poule (pool), *Fr.* One of the movements of a quadrille.

Pour (poor), *Fr.* For.

ä *arm*, ă *add*, ā *ale*, ĕ *end*, ē *eve*, ĭ *ill*, ī *isle*, ō *old*, ŏ *odd*, oo *moon*, ŭ *but*, ü *Fr. sound*, kh *Ger. ch*, nh *nasal*.

(181)

Pour faire passer dessous le pouce (poor fär päs-sä dĕs-soo lŭh poos), *Fr.* To pass the thumb under the fingers.

Pour finir (poor fĭ-nēr'), *Fr.* To finish; indicating a chord or bar which is to terminate the piece.

Pour la première fois (poor lä prä-mēr' fwä), *Fr.* For the first time, meaning that on the repetition of the strain this passage is to be omitted.

Pour reprendre au commencement (poor rŏ-prändr ō kŏm-mänhs-mänh), *Fr.* To go back to the beginning.

Poussé (poos-sä), *Fr.* Pushed; meaning the upbow.

P. P. Abbreviation of Pianissimo.

Prächtig (präkh'tĭgh), *Ger.* In a splendid, pompous, magnificent manner.

Präcis (prä-tsēs'), *Ger.* Precise, exact.

Practice. The studious repetition of a passage in order to master it. Inasmuch as practice has the design of forming a secondary automatism in performing the passage, it is necessary that the repetitions should invariably be without error, and the motions should be taken most of the time slowly, in order that they may be perfectly performed. Only a very small proportion of the practice should be as rapid as the passage is intended to go.

Præcentor (prä-tsĕn'tŏr), *Lat.* Precentor, leader of the choir.

Pralltrill (präl'trĭl), *Ger.* A variety of mordent made with the note written and the next above in the same scale, except where otherwise directed by an accidental over the sign. Examples:

Präludien (prä-loo'dĭ-ĕn), *Ger.* Preludes.

Präludieren (prä-loo-dē'r'n), *Ger.* To prelude, to play a prelude.

Präludium (prä-loo'dĭ-oom), *Ger.* A prelude, an introduction.

Precentor. The appellation given formerly to the master of the choir.

Precipitamente (prä-tshē-pĭ-tä-mĕn'tĕ), } *It.*
Precipitato (prä-tshē-pĭ-tä'tō),
In a precipitate manner, hurriedly.

Precipitando (prä-tshē-pĭ-tän'do), *It.* Hurrying.

Precipitazione (prä-tshē-pĭ-tä-tsĭ-ō'nĕ), *It.* Precipitation, haste, hurry.

Précipité (prä-sē-pĭ-tä), *Fr.* Hurried, accelerated.

Precipitoso (prä-tshē-pĭ-tō'zō), *It.* Hurrying, precipitous.

Precisione (prä-tshē-zĭ-ō'nĕ), *It.* Precision, exactness.

Preciso (prä-tshē'zō), *It.* Precise, exact, exactly.

Preghiera (prä-ghĭ-ā'rä), *It.* Prayer, supplication.

Prelude. A short introductory composition, or extempore performance, to prepare the ear for the succeeding movements.

Preludio (prä-loo'dĭ-ō), *It.* } A prelude, or introduction.
Preludium (prä-loo'dĭ-oom), *Lat.*

Premier (prĕm-ĭ-ā), *Fr.* } First.
Première (prä-mēr'),

Première dessus (prä-mēr' dĕs-sü), *Fr.* First treble, first soprano.

Première fois (prä-mēr' fwä), *Fr.* First time.

Première partie (prä-mēr' pär-tē), *Fr.* First part.

Preparation. That disposition of the harmony by which discords are lawfully introduced. A discord is said to be prepared when the discordant note is heard as a consonance in the preceding chord and in the same part.

Preparative notes. Appoggiaturas, or leaning notes.

Preparazione (prä-pä-rä-tsĭ-ō'nĕ), *It.* Preparation.

Prepared discord. That discord the discordant notes of which have been heard in a concord.

Prepared shake. A shake preceded by two or more introductory notes. Prepared shake, or trill.

Prés de la table (prä düb lä täbl), *Fr.* Near the soundboard.

Pressante (prĕs-sänht'), *Fr.* Pressing on, hurrying.

Pressure tone. A sudden crescendo; ex.:

Prestamente (prĕs-tä mĕn'tĕ), *It.* Hurriedly, rapidly.

Prestant (prĕs-tänh), *Fr.* The open diapason stop in an organ, of either 32-, 16-, 8-, or 4-feet scale. See *Prästanten*.

Prestezza (prĕs-tĕt'sä), *It.* Quickness, rapidity.

Prestissimamente (prĕs-tĕs-sĭ-mä-mĕn'tĕ), } *It.*
Prestissimo (prĕs-tĕs'sĭ-mō),
Very quickly, as fast as possible.

Presto (prĕs'tō), *It.* Quickly, rapidly.

Presto assai (prĕs'tō äs'säī), *It.* Very quick; with the utmost rapidity.

Presto ma non troppo (prĕs'tō mä nōn trōp'pō), *It.* Quick, but not too much so.

Prière (prē-ār), *Fr.* A prayer, supplication.

Prima (prē'mä), *It.* First, chief, principal.

Prima buffa (prē'mä boof-fä), *It.* The principal female singer in a comic opera.

ä *arm*, ă *add*, ā *ale*, ĕ *end*, ē *eve*, ĭ *ill*, ī *isle*, ō *old*, ŏ *odd*, oo *moon*, ŭ *but*, ü *Fr. sound*, kh *Ger. ch*, nh *nasal.*

Prima donna (prē'mä dŏn'nä), *It.* Principal female singer in a serious opera.

Prima donna assoluta (prē'mä dŏn'nä äs-sō-loo'tä), *It.* First female singer in an operatic establishment; the only one who can claim that title.

Prima parte (prē'mä pär'tĕ), *It.* First part.

Prima parte repetita (prē'mä pär'tĕ ra-pĕ-tē'-tä), *It.* Repeat the first part.

Primary chord. The common chord; the first chord.

Prima vista (prē'mä vēs'tä), *It.* At first sight.

Prima volta (prē'mä vŏl'tä), *It.* The first time.

Prime (prē'mĕ), *Ger.* First note, or tone of a scale.

Prime donne (prē'mĕ ŏn'nĕ), *It.* The plural of prima donna.

Primes. Two notes placed on the same degree of the staff, and having the same pitch of sound.

Primo (prē'mō), *It.* Principal, first.

Primo buffo (prē'mō boof'fō), *It.* First male singer in a comic opera.

Primo musico (prē'mō moo'zĭ-kō), *It.* Principal male singer.

Primo tempo (prē'mō tĕm'pō), *It.* The first, or original, time.

Primo tenore (prē'mō tĕ-nō'rĕ), *It.* } The first
Primo uomo (prē'mō oo-ō'mō), *It.* } tenor singer.

Primo violino (prē'mō vē-ō-lē'nō), *It.* The first violin.

Primtöne (prĭm-tö'nĕ), *Ger. pl.* Fundamental tones, or notes.

Principal, or octave. An important organ-stop, tuned an octave above the diapasons, and therefore of four-feet pitch on the manual, and eight-feet on the pedals. In German organs the term Principal is also applied to all the open diapasons of 32, 16, 8, and 4 feet.

Principal bass. An organ-stop of the open-diapason species on the pedals.

Principal close. The usual cadence in the principal key, so called because generally occurring at the close of a piece.

Principale (prēn'tshĭ-pä-lĕ), *It.* Principal, chief; *violino principale*, the principal violin.

Principalmente (prēn-tshĭ-päl-mĕn'tĕ), *It.* Principally, chiefly.

Principal voices. The highest and lowest; the soprano and bass.

Pringeige (prĭn'ghī-ghĕ), *Ger.* The first violin.

Probe (prō'bĕ), *Gr.* Proof, trial, rehearsal.

Professeur de chant (prō-fĕs-sŭr dŭh shänh), *Fr.* A professor of vocal music; a singing-master.

Professeur de musique (prō-fĕs-sŭr dŭh mü-zĕk'), *Fr.* }
Professore di musica (prō-fĕs-sō'rĕ dē moo'zĭ-kä), *It.* }
Professor of music. In the universities the professor of music enjoys academical rank, confers musical degrees, lectures on harmonic science, etc.

Programme (prō-grăm'mĕ), *It.* A programme.

Programme. An order of exercises for musical or other entertainments.

Programme music. Music designed to represent a specified series of incidents. Among the first to apply this principle were the Abbé Vogler, Weber, and Berlioz. The latter afforded brilliant examples.

Progression. A succession of triads, or perfect chords, which are confined to the tonic.

Progressione (prō-grĕs-sĭ-ō'nĕ), *It.* Progression.

Progressive. Advancing by degrees.

Prolatio (prō-lä'tsĭ-ō), *Lat.* Adding a dot, to increase, or lengthen, the value of a note.

Prolazione (prō-lä tsĭ-ō'nĕ), *It.* Prolation.

Prolonged shake. A shake which can be opened or closed at pleasure.

Prolongement (prō-lŏn-zhä-mänh), *Fr.* The prolongation; part of the action of the piano, retaining the hammer away from its rest.

Promenade concert. A vocal or instrumental concert during which the hearers are at liberty to promenade the hall instead of being seated.

Promptement (prŏnht-mänh), *Fr.* } Readily,
Prontamente (prŏn-tä-mĕn'tĕ), *It.* } quickly, promptly.

Pronto (prŏn'tō), *It.* Ready, quick.

Pronunziare (prō-noon-tsĭ-ä'rĕ), *It.* To pronounce; to enunciate.

Pronunziato (prō-noon-tsĭ-ä'tō), *It.* Pronounced.

Proportio (prō-pŏr'tsĭ ō), *Lat.* Proportion: applied to intervals with reference to their relative dimensions and to notes with reference to their relative duration.

Proposta (prō-pŏs'tä), *It.* Subject, or theme, of a fugue.

Proscenio (prōs-shä'nĭ-ō), *It.* } Proscenium.
Proscenio (prōs-thä'nĭ-ō), *Sp.* }

Proscenium (prōs-sēn'ĭ-ŭm). The front part of the stage, where the curtain separates the stage from the audience.

Proslambanomenos (prŏs-läm-bä-nŏm'ĕ-nŏs), *Gr.* The lowest note in the Greek system, equivalent to A on the first space in the bass of the modern.

Prosodia (prō-sō'dĭ-ä), *Gr.* A sacred song, or hymn, sung by the ancients in honor of the gods.

Prosody. That part of the laws of language dealing with quantity (or the time of syllables) and accent (the relative emphasis of syllables).

ā *arm*, ă *add*, ā *ale*, ĕ *end*, ē *eve*, ĭ *ill*, ī *isle*, ō *old*, ŏ *odd*, oo *moon*, ŭ *but*, ü *Fr.sound*, kh *Ger. ch*, nh *nasal*.

(183)

Protasis (prō'tā-sĭs), *Gr.* That part of a sentence which awakens expectation, to be answered later by the podasis. The subject.

Prova (prō'vä), *It.* Proof, trial, rehearsal.

Prova generale (prō'vä jĕn-ĕ-rä'lĕ), *It.* The last rehearsal previous to a public performance.

Psalm. A sacred song or hymn.

Psalmbuch (psälm'bookh), *Ger.* A psalter; a book of psalms.

Psalmen (psäl'mĕn), *Ger.* To sing, to chant psalms.

Psalmgesang (psälm'gĕ-säng'), *Ger.* Psalmody.

Psalmist. A composer, writer, or singer, of psalms or sacred songs.

Psalmlied (psälm'lēd), *Ger.* Psalm, sacred song or hymn.

Psalmodie (psäl'mō-dē), *Fr.* Psalmody.

Psalmody. The practice or art of singing psalms; a collection of music designed for church service.

Psalter. The Book of Psalms.

Psalter (psäl'tĕr), *Ger.* Psaltery.

Psalterion (psäl-tä-rĭ-ŏnh), *Fr.* } A stringed
Psalterium (psäl-tä'rĭ-oom), *Lat.* } instrument
Psaltery. } much used by the Hebrews, supposed to be a species of lyre, harp, or dulcimer.

Psaume (psōm), *Fr.* A psalm.

Pseautier (psō-tĭ-ä), *Fr.* A psalter, or book of psalms.

Pulcha (pool'kä), *Russ.* A Russian dance, the original of the polka.

Pulsatile (pŭl'sa-tĕl'). Striking; instruments of percussion, as the drum, tambourine, etc.

Punctum contra punctum (poonk'toom kŏn'trä poonk'toom), *Lat.* Point against point. See *Counterpoint*.

Punctus (poonk'toos), *Lat.* A dot, a point.

Punkt (poonkt), *Ger.* A dot.

Punkte (poonk'tĕ), *Ger.* Dots.

Punktirte Noten (poonk-tīr'tĕ nō't'n), *Ger.* Dotted notes.

Punta (poon'tä), } *It.* } The point, the top; also
Punto (poon'tō), } a thrust, or push.

Punta d' arco (poon'tä där'kō), } *It.*
Punta del' arco (poon'tä dĕl är'kō), } The point or tip of the bow.

Puntato (poon-tä'tō), *It.* Pointed, detached, marked.

Punto d' accressimento (poon'tō däk-krĕs-sĭ-mĕn'tō), *It.* The point of augmentation.

Punto di divisione (poon'tō dē dē-vē-sĭ-ō'nĕ), *It.* Point of division.

Punto d' organo (poon'tō dōr-gä'nō), *It.* Organ point.

Punto per punto (poon'tō pĕr poon'tō), *It.* Note for note.

Pupitre (pü-pētr), *Fr.* A music-desk.

Pyramidon (pī-räm'ĭ-dŏn), *Gr.* An organ-stop of 16- or 32-feet tone, on the pedals, invented by the Rev. F. A. G. Ouseley. The pipes are four times larger at the top than at the mouth, and the tone of remarkable gravity, resembling that of a stopped pipe in quality.

Pyrrhics (pĭr'hĭks). A metrical foot, consisting of two short syllables. ⏑ ⏑

Pythagorian lyre. An instrument said to have been invented by Pythagoras.

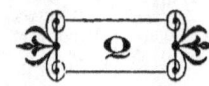

Quadrat (kwä-drät'), *Ger.* A square. The mark called a natural, ♮.

Quadratmusik (kwäd rät'moo-zēk'), *Ger.* A name sometimes applied to the old mensurable music written in square notes.

Quadricinium (kwä-drĭ-tsē'nĭ-oom), *Lat.* }
Quadripartite (käd-rĭ-pär-tēt'), *Fr.* }
A quartet, a composition in four parts.

Quadriglio (kwä-drēl'yĭ-ō), *It.* Quadrille.

Quadrille (kä-drēl'), *Fr.* A French dance, or set of five consecutive dance movements, called La Pantalon, La Poule, L'Été, La Treuise (or La Pastourelle) and La Finale. The movements are in 6-8 or 2-4 measure.

Quadro (kwä'drō), *It.* The mark called a natural, ♮.

Quadruple. Fourfold.

Quadruple counterpoint. Counterpoint in four parts, all of which may be inverted, and each of them taken as a bass, middle, or high part.

Quadruple croche (käd-rŭpl krōsh), *Fr.* }
Quadruple quaver. }
Four-hooked; a half-demisemiquaver, or semidemisemiquaver.

Quadruplo (kwä'droo-plō), *It.* In four parts.

Quantity, The relative duration of notes or syllables.

Quarta (kwär'tä), } *It.* } A fourth; also the
Quarto (kwär'tō), } fourth voice, or instrumental part.

Quart de soupir (kär düh soo-pēr), *Fr.* A semiquaver rest.

Quarte (kärt), *Fr.* } A fourth.
Quarte (kwär′tĕ), *Ger.*

Quarter-note. A black note with a stem. Its duration is equal to one quarter of a whole note.

Quarter-rest. A pause equal in duration to a quarter-note.

Quarter tone. A small interval, approximately equal to one quarter of a diatonic second. Several intervals of this character arise enharmonically, when it is attempted to carry out musical pitches into remote keys according to the mathematical exactness of pure harmonic intervals. Approximately the interval between C♯ and D♭ is a quarter-step; in some cases, but not in all, according to the manner in which the several pitches are arrived at.

Quartes (kärt), *Fr.* Fourths.

Quartet } A composition
Quartett (kwär-tĕtt), *Ger.* for four voices
Quartetto (kwär-tĕt′tō), *It.* or instruments.

Quartet, stringed. A quartet, or composition, arranged for four stringed instruments, consisting of first and second violins, viola, and violoncello.

Quartettino (kwär-tĕt-tē′nō), *It.* A short quartet.

Quartet, wood. A quartet consisting of the flute, oboe, clarinet, and bassoon.

Quartfagott (kwärt′fä-gŏt′), *Ger.* } An old
Quart-fagotto (kwärt fä-gŏt′tō), *It.* sort of bassoon, formerly used as a tenor to the hautboy; called, also, *Dulcino* and *Dulzain*.

Quartflöte (kwärt′flö′tĕ), *Ger.* A flute sounding a fourth above.

Quartgeige (kwärt′ghī-ghĕ), *Ger.* A small violin, a fourth above the usual violin. Piccolo violin.

Quarto (kwär′tō), *It.* The fourth; the quarter-note.

Quartsextaccord (kwärt′sĕxt-äk-kŏrd′), *Ger.* Chord of the sixth and fourth; second inversion of the triad.

Quasi (kwä′zē), *It.* In the manner of, in the style of.

Quasi allegretto (kwä′zē äl-lĕ-grĕt′tō), *It.* Like an allegretto.

Quasi andante (kwä′zē än-dän′tĕ), *It.* In the style of an andante.

Quasi presto (kwä-zī prĕs′tō), *It.* Like a presto.

Quasi recitativo (kwä′zī rā-tshī-tä-tē′vō), *It.* Resembling a recitative.

Quasi una fantasia (kwä′zī oo′nä fän-tä′zī-ä), *It.* As if it were a fantasia.

Quatrain. A stanza of four lines rhyming alternately.

Quatre (kätr), *Fr.* } Four; *a quatre mains*,
Quattro (kwät′trō), *It.* or, *a quattro mani*, for four hands; a pianoforte duet.

Quattricoma (kwät′trī-kō′mä), *It.* A demisemiquaver.

Quatuor (kwä′too-ōr), *Lat.* A quartet.

Quaver. A note equal to half a crotchet.

Quaver-rest. A mark of silence equal in value to an eighth-note.

Querflöte (kwär′flö′tĕ), *Ger.* German flute. See *Flauto traverso*.

Querpfeife (kwär′pfī′fĕ), *Ger.* A fife.

Querstand (kwär′ständ), *Ger.* False relation; in harmony. A chromatic tone not prepared in the same voice. See *False relation*.

Querstriche (kwär′strī′khĕ), *Ger.* Ledger lines.

Questa (kwäs′tä), *It.* } This, or that.
Questo (kwäs′tō), *It.*

Queue (kŭh), *Fr.* The tail, or stem, of a note; also the tailpiece of a violin, etc.

Quickstep. A lively march, generally in 2-4 time.

Quieto (kwē-ā′tō), *It.* Quiet, calm, serene.

Quills. The plectrums, or instruments formerly used instead of the fingers in playing upon the harp, guitar, etc.

Quinque (kwĭn′kwĕ), *Lat.* Five.

Quint (kwĭnt), *Lat.* } A fifth; also the name
Quinta (kwēn′tä), *It.* of an organ-stop
Quinte (känht), *Fr.* sounding a fifth, or
Quinte (kwĭn′tĕ), *Ger.* twelfth, above the foundation stops. The E string of the violin.

Quintadena. An organ-stop of wood, voiced between a stopped diapason and a gamba.

Quintaton (kwĭn′tä-tōn′), *Ger.* A manual organ-stop of 8-feet tone; a stopped diapason of rather small scale producing the twelfth, as well as the ground tone; it also occurs as a pedal-stop of 2- and 16-feet tone.

Quintbass. An organ pedal-stop. See *Quint*.

Quintenzirkel (kwĭn′tĕn-tsīr′k'l), *Ger.* Circle of fifths, beginning with any tone and returning through a succession of fifths and octaves to the same tone, or one enharmonic with it. The Quintenzirkel beginning with C returns to B♯ after twelve fifths.

Quintet. A composition for five voices or instruments.

Quintetto (kwēn-tĕt′tō), *It.* } A quintet.
Quintétte (känh-tĕt), *Fr.*

Quint-fagott (kwĕnt′ fä-gŏt′), *Ger.* The small bassoon or fagottina, sounding a fifth higher than the common bassoon.

Quintgedackt (kwĭnt′ghĕ-däkt′), *Ger.* An organ-stop of the stopped-diapason species, sounding the fifth above.

Quintoire (känh-twär), *Fr.* An old French term applied to a species of descant consisting chiefly of fifths.

Quintole (kwĭn′tō-lĕ), *Lat.* A group of five notes, having the same value as four of the same species.

Quintuple. A species of time now seldom used, containing five parts in a bar.

Quire. A choir, a body of singers; that part of a church where the choristers sit. See *Choir*.

ă arm, ă add, ā ale, ĕ end, ē eve, ĭ ill, ī isle, ō old, ŏ odd, oo moon, ŭ but, ü *Fr.* sound, kh *Ger. ch*, nh *nasal*.

(185)

Qui tollis (kwī tŏl'lĭs), *Lat.* "Thou who takest away the sins of the world." A part of the Gloria.

Quodlibet (kwŏd'lĭ-bĕt), *Lat.* A medley of airs, etc., out of different works, or by various composers; a musical potpourri.

Quoniam Tu solus (quō'nĭ-ăm too sō'loos), *Lat.* "Thou only art holy." Part of the Gloria.

R, *or*, **R. H.** Indicates the right hand in pianoforte-playing.
Rabani (rä-bä'nē), } A species of tambourine used by the negroes.
Rabbana (rä-bä'nä). }
Rabbia (räb'bĭ-ä), *It.* Rage, fury, madness.
Raccourcir (rä-coor-sēr), *Fr.* To abridge.
Rackett, *or*, **Rankett** (räk'kĕt), *Ger.* (1) A family of wood wind instruments, long ago obsolete. (2) Obsolete names for organ-stops, generally reed-pipes of 8- or 16-feet pitch.
Rackettfagott (räk'kĕt-fä-gŏt'), *Ger.* A kind of bassoon, now obsolete. It belonged to the bombarde family.
Racler (räk-lā), *Fr.* To scrape. Said of a poor player.
Racleur (rä-klŭr), *Fr.* A poor player.
Raddolcendo (räd-dŏl-tshĕn'dō), *It.* } With increasing softness; becoming softer by degrees.
Raddolcente (räd-dŏl-tshen'tĕ), }
Raddoppiamento (räd-dŏp-pĭ-ä-mĕn'tō), *It.* Augmentation; reduplication; the doubling of an interval.
Raddoppiato (räd-dŏp-pĭ-ä'tō), *It.* Doubled, increased, augmented.
Radical bass. The fundamental bass; the roots of the various chords.
Raggione (räd-jĭ-ō'nĕ), *It.* Ratio; proportion.
Ragoke. A small Russian horn.
Rallentamento (räl-lĕn-tä-mĕn'tō),
Rallentando (räl-lĕn-tän'dō), *It.* }
Rallentato (räl-lĕn-tä'tō),
The time gradually slower, and the sound gradually softer.
Rallentando assai (räl-lĕn-tän'dō äs-sä'ī), *It.* A great slackening of the time.
Ranz des vaches (ränh dĕ väsh), *Fr.* Pastoral airs played by the Swiss herdsmen, to assemble their cattle together for the return home.
Rapidamente (rä-pē-dä-mĕn'tĕ), *It.* Rapidly.
Rapidamente e brillante (rä-pē-dä-mĕn'tĕ ā brĭl-län'tĕ), *It.* Rapidly and brilliantly.
Rapidita (rä-pē-dĭ-tä'), *It.* Rapidity.
Rapido (rä'pĭ-dō), *It.* Rapid.
Rapsodie (räp-sō-dē'), *Fr.* } A capriccio, a fragmentary piece, a wild, unconnected composition.
Rapsody (răp'sō-dy), *Eng.* }

Rasch (räsh), *Ger.* Swift, spirited.
Rasegesang (rä'zĕ-ghĕ-zäng'), *Ger.* } A wild song, a dithyrambic.
Raselled (rä'zĕ-lĕd'), }
Räthselcanon (räth's'l-kä-nōn), *Ger.* Enigmatic canon. A canon written upon a single line, without marks to indicate where the following voices should enter.
Rattenendo (rät-tĕ-nĕn'dō), *It.* } Holding back, restraining the time.
Rattenuto (rät-tĕ-noo'tō), }
Rattezza (rät-tĕt'sä), *It.* Swiftness, rapidity.
Raucedine (rä-oo-tshĕ-dē'nĕ), *It.* Hoarseness.
Rauco (rä-oo-kō), *It.* Hoarse, harsh.
Rauh (rou), *Ger.* } Rough.
Rauque (rōk), *Fr.* }
Rauscher (row'sher), *Ger.* A passage in which every two tones are several times repeated.
Rauschflöte (roush'flō'tĕ), *Ger.* A mixture stop of two ranks of pipes, sounding the twelfth and fifteenth.
Rauschpfeife (roush'pfī-fĕ), *Ger.* } Rustling fifth; a mixture-stop in German organs, the twelfth and fifteenth on one slide.
Rauschquint (roush'quĭnt), }
Ravanastron. A very simple form of bow instrument, common in the East.
Ravvivando (räv-vĭ-vän'dō), *It.* Reviving, quickening, accelerating.
Ravvivando il tempo (räv-vĭ-vän'dō ĭl tĕm'pō), *It.* Accelerating the time.
Re (rā). A syllable applied in solfaing to the second degree of the major scale, or in France and Italy to the note D, irrespective of key place.
Reading music. The art of recognizing and feeling musical effects from the written notation.
Rebec. } A Moorish word signifying an instrument with two strings played with a bow. The Moors brought the rebec into Spain, whence it passed into Italy, and after the addition of a third string obtained the name of rebecca, whence the old English rebec, or fiddle with three strings.
Rebecca. }
Rebecchino (rā-bĕk-kē'nō), *It.* Small rebec guitar.
Re bémol (rĕ bā-mŏl), *Fr.* The note D♭.
Re bémol majeur (rĕ bā-mŏl mä-zhŭr), *Fr.* The key of D♭ major.

Rebab.
Rebeb. } A rebec.

Recension (rā-tsänh-sĭ-ŏnb), *Fr.* An analytical criticism. Also used of careful or analytical editing.

Recheat. An old term for a series of notes which huntsmen sound on a horn to recall the dogs from a false scent.

Recherché (rĕ-shĕr-shā), *Fr.* Rare, affected, formal.

Recht (rĕkht), *Ger.* Right.

Rechte Hand (rĕkh'tĕ händ), *Ger.* Right hand.

Recit (rā-sēt), *Fr.* Recitative.

Recitado (rā-tsǐ-tä'dō), *Sp.* Recitative.

Recital. A recital of choice music by a solo artist. Distinguished from concert by being exclusively musical, the idea of display not entering into the concept.

Recitando (rā-tshǐ-tän'dō), *It.* } Declamatory,
Recitante (rā-tshǐ-tän'tĕ), } in the style of a recitative.

Recitatif (rĕ-sǐ-tä-tēf'), *Fr.* }
Recitativ (rĕ-tsǐ-tä-tĭf'), *Ger.* } Recitative.
Recitativo (rĕ-tshǐ-tä-tē'vō), *It.* }

Recitative (rĕ-sǐ-tä-tĕv'). A musical form in which a text is recited to musical cadence. Recitative ranges all the way in musical quality, from the *recitativo secco* (dry recitative), in which, aided simply by a chord now and then for insuring the intonation, the musical cadence seeks merely to deliver the text effectively, up to a *recitativo accompagnato stromentato* (accompanied and instrumented recitative), in which the musical phrases have perceptible melodic quality, while the instrumentation colors and intensifies the dramatic effect. The latter variety approaches very nearly to arioso, and shades into it by imperceptible degrees. To mention a familiar example, the four recitatives in Handel's " Messiah," narrating the appearance of the angels to the shepherds, afford two examples of recitativo secco, and two of recitativo accompagnato. In operatic recitative the instrumental accompaniment often plays an important part; even where the vocal phrases themselves are not highly accompanied, the instrumental interlude often takes on a highly dramatic coloring. All the old operas of Mozart's time, and before, have a great deal of recitativo secco, which is generally accompanied by the 'cello only. In the latter works of Wagner there is little or no recitative of this character, but an accompanied recitative, or more properly arioso, takes its place. In the first operas (Peri's " Eurydice ") a similar usage prevailed, but with the difference that in Peri's mere verbal delivery is the end sought in the musical cadence, whereas in Wagner the accompaniment rises to symphonic elaboration in the effort to interpret the feeling of the text, and the whole form is intensely musical as well as dramatic in the best sense.

Recitative accompanied. A recitative is said to be accompanied when, besides the bass, there are parts for other instruments, as violins, flutes, hautboys, etc.

Recitativo instromentato (rĕ-tshǐ-tä-tē'vō in-strō-mĕn-tä'tō), *It.* Accompanied recitative.

Recitativo parlante (rĕ-tshǐ-tä-tē'vō pär-län'tĕ), } *It.*
Recitativo secco (rĕ-tshǐ-tä-tē'vō sĕk'kō), } Unaccompanied recitative; also, when accompanied only by the violoncello and double bass, or the pianoforte or organ.

Recitativo stromentato (rĕ tshǐ-tä-tē'vō strō-mĕn-ta-tō). Recitative accompanied by the orchestra. See *Recitativo instromentato*.

Rezitativzug (rĕ-tsǐ-tä-tēf'tsoog), *Ger.* Recitative stop.

Recitazione (rĕ- tshǐ- tä- tsǐ- ō'nĕ), *It.* Recitation.

Réciter (rā-sǐ-tā'), *Fr.* To recite.

Reciting note. The note in a chant upon which the voice dwells until it comes to a cadence.

Recorder. An old wind instrument of the flageolet kind, but of smaller bore and shriller tone. Mentioned in Shakesp. are.

Recreation. A composition of attractive style, designed to relieve the tediousness of practice; an amusement.

Récréations musicales (rĕk-rā-ā'sǐ-ōnh mu-zǐ-käl'), *Fr.* Musical recreations.

Recte (rĕk'tĕ), *Lat.* Right, straight, forward.

Recte et retro (rĕk'tĕ ĕt rā'trō), *Lat.* Forward, then backward; the subject, or melody, reversed, note for note.

Reddita (rĕd-dē'tä), } *It.* } Return to the sub-
Redita (rĕ-dē'tä), } ject; repetition of a melody.

Rédièse (rā-dǐ-ās), *Fr.* } Re sharp. D♯.
Rediesis (rā-dē-ā'sēs), *It.* }

Redondilla (rĕ-dōn-dēl'yä), *Sp.* A roundelay, a stanza of four lines of eight syllables each.

Redowa (rĕ'dō-wä), } A Bohemian
Redowak (rĕ'dō-wäk) } dance, in 2-4 and
Redowazka (rĕ'dō-wäts-kä), } 3-4 time alternately. Modern redowas confine themselves to 3-4 measure.

Redublicato (rĕ-doob-lǐ-kä'tō), *It.* Redoubled.

Reduciren (rĕ'doo-tsǐr'ĕn), *Ger.* To reduce, or arrange, a full instrumental score, for a smaller band, or for the pianoforte or organ.

Reed. The flat piece of cane placed on the beak, or mouthpiece, of the clarinet and bassethorn; this is called a single reed. The double reed is the mouthpiece of the hautboy, English horn and bassoon, formed of two pieces of cane joined together. Organs and reed organs have metal reeds of different forms, called " free " and " impinging," or striking, reeds. The free reed consists of a small socket of brass and a vibrating tongue, one end of which swings entirely through the socket at each vibration. In

ä *arm*, ă *add*, â *ale*, ĕ *end*, é *eve*, ĭ *ill*, ī *isle*, ŏ *old*, ō *odd*, oo *moon*, ŭ *but*, ü *Fr. sound*, kh *Ger. ch*, nh *nasal.*

(187)

reed-organs the reed obtains large resonance from the wooden reed-board, which acts as sounding-board. The organ-reed obtains its resonance from the pipe which it causes to vibrate. And the voice is determined in part by the shape and size of this pipe. The impinging, or striking, reed is used only in the organ (for trumpet, oboe, and cornopeon-stops). Its tongue strikes against the opening into the pipe, which it completely covers, instead of playing through it, as in the free reed. Its tone is, therefore, very much more metallic and snarly. Organ-reeds of both varieties are tuned by a sliding wire, which shortens or lengthens the vibrating portion of the tongue, in order to adjust the intonation of the reed to that of the other parts of the instrument. Free reeds are much more apt to be out of tune than impinging reeds, but their tone when in tune is much better. The reeds in reed-organs are permanent, and do not get out of tune except through weakening of the metal tongue, which happens after much use, or through the development of flaws in the metal. In brass instruments, of the horn and trumpet class the lips of the player perform the function of a reed. The human voice is also a reed instrument.

Reed instruments. Instruments whose sounds are produced by the action of air upon reeds formed of metal or wood.

Reed pipe. A pipe formed of reed, used singly or in numbers, as the pipes of Pan, in ancient times, or in connection with other kinds of pipes, as in the organ.

Reed-stops. Organ-stops in which the sound is made by reeds.

Reel. A lively Scotch dance. Originally the term Rhay, or Reel, was applied to a very ancient English dance, called the Hay. The reel is generally in 4-4 measure, but sometimes in 6-8. See *Rhay*.

Refrain. The burden of a song; a ritornel; a repeat.

Regal. A portable organ, used in former times in religious processions.

Regel (rā'g'l), *Ger.* Rule.

Regens chori (rä'gĕns kō'rĭ), *Lat.* The choir-master in German churches.

Regimental band. A company of musicians attached to a regiment; a military band.

Regina cœli (rā-gē'nä tsā'lĭ), *Lat.* Queen of Heaven; a hymn to the Virgin.

Register. The stops, or rows of pipes, in an organ; also applied to the high, low, or middle parts, or divisions, of the voice; also the compass of a voice or instrument.

Registering. The management of the stops in an organ.

Registerstimme (rĕ-ghĭs'tĕr-stĭm'mĕ), *Ger.* Speaking-stops of an organ, as distinguished from mechanical stops (couplers, etc.).

Registre (rĕg-ĕstr'), *Fr.*
Registro (rĕ-jĕs'trō), *It.* } Register, draw-stop.

Registrirung (rā-ghĭs-trē'roong), *Ger.* The art of registration.

Rehearsal (rĕ-hĕr'săl). A trial, or practice, previous to a public performance.

Reihen (rī'ĕn), *Ger.* Song, dance.

Reihentanz (rī'ĕn-tänts'), *Ger.* Circular dance.

Rein (rīn), *Ger.* Pure, clear, perfect; *kurz und rein*, distinct and clear.

Reine Stimme (rī'nĕ stĭm'mĕ), *Ger.* Clear voice.

Reiselied (rī'zĕ-lēd'), *Ger.* A traveling song; a pilgrim's hymn, or song.

Related. A term applied to those chords, modes, or keys, which, by reason of their affinity and close relation, admit of an easy and natural transition from one to the other.

Relation. That connection which any two sounds have with one another in respect of the interval which they form.

Relation of keys. Affinity of keys, arising from the identity of one or more chords appertaining to both. The relationship becomes closer and closer according to the number of such coincidences. According to modern usage all keys are related, and there is scarcely any chord which might not, in some way, follow any other. It is obvious, however, that entire keys are related in proportion to the number of chords they have in common. For it is a very different thing to introduce a single strange chord (which may be taken as belonging to the chromatic key) and to bodily go into the entire foreign key to which such a chord ostensibly belongs. See *Modulation*.

Relatio non harmonica (rĕ-lä'tsĭ-ō nōn här-mō'nĭ-kä), *Lat.* False relation.

Relative keys. Keys which only differ by one sharp, or flat, or which have the same signatures.

Religiosamente (rĕ-lē-jĭ-ō-zä-mĕn'tĕ), *It.*
Religioso (rĕ-lē-jĭ-ō'zō), Religiously, solemnly, in a devout manner.

Re majeur (rä mä-zhŭr), *Fr.* D major.

Re mineur (rä mē-nŭr), *Fr.* D minor.

Remote keys. Those keys whose scales have few tones in common, as the key of C and the key of D♭.

Remplissage (ränh-plī-säzh), *Fr.* Filling up; the middle parts; also a term applied to the decorative flourishes introduced in concertos and bravura airs.

Rentrée (ränh-trā'), *Fr.* Return; reentry of the subject or theme.

Renversement (ränh-vĕrs-mänh), *Fr.* An inversion.

Renverser (ränh-vĕr-sā), *Fr.* To invert.

Renvoi (ränh-vwä), *Fr.* A repeat; the mark of repetition.

Repeat 8va. Repeat an octave higher.

ä *arm*, ă *add*, ā *ale*, ĕ *end*, ē *eve*, ĭ *ill*, ī *isle*, ō *old*, ŏ *odd*, oo *moon*, ŭ *but*, ü *Fr. sound*, kh *Ger. ch*, nh *nasal*.

Repeat. Two or more dots to the left or right of a double bar, indicating that certain measures or passages on the same side of the bar are to be sung or played twice. *Sign of Repetition.*

Repercussio (rĕ-pĕr-koos'sĭ-ō), *Lat.* The answer, in a fugue.

Repercussion. A frequent repetition of the same sound. A technical term in fugue, to denote the reappearance of the subject.

Repertoire (rā-pĕr-twär), *Fr.* Repertory. The entire list of works ready for performance, or practicable after certain preparation.

Répertoire de l'opéra (rā-pĕr-twär dŭh lō-pā'-rä), *Fr.* A collection of pieces from an opera.

Repetent (rĕ-pĕ-těnt'), *Ger.* A teacher who conducts the rehearsals.

Repetimento (rĕ-pĕ-tĭ-měn'tō), *It.* } Repeti-
Repetizione (rĕ-pĕ-tĭ-tsĭ-ō'ně), tion.

Répétition (rā-pā-tĕ-sĭ-ŏnh), *Fr.* Rehearsal; repetition.

Repetitore (rĕ-pĕ-tĭ-tō'rĕ), *It.* The director of a rehearsal.

Replica (rä' plĭ-kä), *It.* Reply, repetition. See also *Repercussio.*

Replicato (rĕ-plĭ-kä'tō), *It.* Repeated.

Replique (rä-plĕk), *Fr.* (1) Octave. (2) Answer (in fugue). (3) Interval arising from inversion. (4) Small notes inserted in a part to guide the performer.

Reply. The answer, in fugue.

Réponse (rā-pŏnhs), *Fr.* The answer, in a fugue. The subject very slightly modified so as to lead back to the tonic.

Repos (rā-pō), *Fr.* A pause.

Reprise (rā'prēz), *Fr.* The burden of a song; a repetition, or return, to some previous part; in old music, when a strain was repeated, it was called a reprise.

Requiem (rā'kwĭ-ĕm), *Lat.* A mass, or musical service, for the dead.

Resin. Rosin.

Resolutio (rĕz-ō-loo'tsĭ-ō), *Lat.* Resolution.

Resolution. The solution of a dissonance. All dissonances are temporary substitutions in place of consonant tones, and the resolution generally consists of the progression of the dissonant tone one step to the consonant tone which it displaced. See *Dissonance.*

Resoluzione (rĕs-ō-loo-tsĭ ō'nĕ), *It.* Resolution, decision, firmness; also the progression from a discord to a concord.

Resonance. The answering of one sound to another. Every sounding body resonates or answers to all tones which it contains itself. A room resonates or echoes to such tones as are part of its natural tone. Every pianostring, when the dampers are raised, resonates or answers every other string which produces its own tone or one of its partials. The human head resonates according to the clearness of the cavities and the direction of the tone formed in the throat. An echo is not a resonance. An echo is merely a reflection of sound-waves, and not an answer with waves newly created.

Resonanzboden (rĕ-sō-nänts'bō'd'n), *Ger.* Resonance bodies. The sounding-board of a pianoforte, etc.

Response. Response, or answer, of the choir. The name of a kind of anthem sung in the Roman Catholic Church after the morning lesson. In a fugue the response is the repetition of the given subject by another part

Responsivo (rĕ spŏn-sē'vō), *It.* Responsively.

Responsorien (rĕ-spŏn-sö'rĭ-ĕn),
Responsorium (rĕ-spŏn-sö'rĭ-oom), *Lat.* }
Responsum (rĕ-spŏn'soom),
See *Response.*

Resserrement (rĕs-sär'mänh), *Fr.* See *Stretto.*

Rest. Rhythmic silence. Characters indicating rhythmic silence. During rest the rhythm goes right on, and this circumstance distinguishes musical rest from mere cessation. Rests correspond in denomination and value to all the different forms of note.

Whole Half Quarter 8th 16th 32d 64th

Rests may be augmented by dots and double dots, exactly the same as notes.

Restrictio (rĕ-strĭk'tĭ-ō), *Lat.* The stretto in a fugue.

Resultant tones. Tones formed by the coincidences of vibrations when two tones are sounding together. These tones were first discovered by the violinist Tartini, who used them as a guide to correct intonation in double stopping far up the fingerboard. They may easily be observed upon the reed organ by taking a single set of reeds and prolonging E and G (4th and 5th spaces of the treble staff) forte. A low humming will presently be heard, which, upon comparison, will be found to be middle C. Upon changing to D and F, one degree lower, the humming will change to B♭.

Resurrexit (rā-sŭr-rĕx'ĭt), *Lat.* "And rose again." Part of the Credo of the Mass.

Retard. To gradually slacken the movement. A retard denotes the dying away of the impulse immediately producing the strain, and is generally preparatory to a new strain following, or else preparatory to the final close. A retard is gradual and cumulative in character, slackening the movement very gradually, and completing the slackening upon the note preceding the resumption of the new idea, if there be one. The common mistake is to retard too suddenly, and too soon. As a rule every retard in music is prepared by an *accelerando* a little time previously, in approaching the climax after which the retard generally comes.

ä *arm*, ă *add*, ā *ale*, ĕ *end*, ē *eve*, ĭ *ill*, ī *isle*, ō *old*, ŏ *odd*, oo *moon*, ŭ *but*, ü *Fr. sound*, kh *Ger. ch*, nh *nasal*

(189)

Retardando (rĕ-tär-dän'dō), *It.* A retarding of the movement.

Retardation. Slackening, or retarding the time; also a suspension, in harmony, prolonging some note of a previous chord into the succeeding one.

Retraite (rĕ-trät), *Fr.* Retreat; tattoo, in military music.

Retro (rĕ-trō'), *Lat.* Backward, the melody reversed, note for note.

Retrograde (rĕ'trō-grăd'). Going backward.

Retrograde. An imitation repeating the subject note for note, backwards, beginning with the last note.

Retrogrado (rā-trō-grä'dō), *It.* Retrograde, going backward.

Retto (rĕt'tō), *It.* Right, straight, direct.

Réveille (rĕ-vā'yĕ), *Fr.* Awaking, a military morning signal; also horn music played early in the morning to awake the hunter.

Reversed. An imitation repeating a melodic motion in opposite direction, answering upward progressions with downwards, and the like. The union of retrograde and reversed imitation gives an imitation in which the subject is repeated note for note backwards, and in opposite direction of up and down. These are merely mechanical devices for securing something apparently new in the working out of a fugue or thematic group.

Reversed motion. Imitation by contrary motion, in which the ascending intervals are changed into descending and *vice versa*.

Revoice. To repair an organ-pipe so as to restore its proper quality of tone.

R. H. In pianoforte music used to indicate the right hand.

Rhapsodie (răp-sō-dē'), *Ger.* } See *Rapsodie*.
Rhapsody.

Rhapsodists. Greek minstrels, of the time of Homer and later.

Rhythm. } Measured movement in time. All
Rhythmus (rĭt'moos), *Ger.* music begins by selecting a certain key, or group of chords, within which, or in relation to which, all the melodic and harmonic movements take place. In like manner it also selects a certain rate of pulsation and a certain measure, within which, or in relation to which, all the rhythm of the piece takes place. Hence, in general, the rhythm of a piece of music is the time motion against the background of pulsation and measure. A rhythm is said to be completed when it reaches a symmetrical grouping and closes with an accent. This is also sometimes called a rhythmus. In orchestral works, and in elaborate pianoforte works, several rhythms are going on at the same time. This appears in simple pieces, where there is a rhythm of the melody as such, a rhythm of the accompaniment, and a rhythm of the two together.

Rhythme (rĭthm), *Fr.* Rhythm.

Rhythmical. Conformable to rhythm.

Rhythmically. In a rhythmical manner.

Rhythmique (rĭth-mēk'), *Fr.* } Rhythmical.
Rhythmisch (rĭv'mlsh), *Ger.*

Ribattere (rē-bät'tĕ-rĕ), *It.* To reverberate.

Ribattuta (rē-bät-too'tä), *It.* A beat, a passing note.

Ricercare (rē-tshĕr-kä'rĕ), } Sought
Ricercari (rē-tshĕr-kä'rē), *pl.* *It.* { after; this
Ricercata (rē-tshĕr-kä'tä), { term is ap-
Ricercato (rē-tshĕr-kä'tō), } plied to every kind of composition wherein researches of musical design are employed. It is suitable to certain figures replete with contrapuntal artifices, also to madrigals, and the term was formerly applied to solfeggi, and also to instrumental exercises when of considerable difficulty.

Ricordanza (rē-kŏr-dän'tsä), *It.* Remembrance, recollection.

Riddone (rĕd-dō'nĕ), *It.* A roundelay; a village dance.

Rideau d'entr'acte (rē-dō d'änh-tr'äkt), *Fr.* Drop scene.

Ridevolmente (rē-dĕ-vŏl-mĕn'tĕ), *It.* Ludicrously, pleasantly.

Ridicolosamente (rē-dĭ-kō-lō-zä-mĕn'tĕ), *It.* Ridiculously.

Ridotto (rē-dŏt'tō), *It.* Reduced; arranged or adapted from a full score; also an entertainment consisting of singing and dancing; a species of opera.

Riesenharfe (rē'z'n-här'fĕ), *Ger.* Æolian harp.

Rifiormenti (rē-fē-ōr-mĕn'tĕ), *It. pl.* Ornaments, embellishments.

Rigadoon. A lively old French or Provencal dance in triple time.

Rigodon (rē-gō-dōnh), *Fr.* A rigadoon.

Rigoletto (rē-gō-lĕt'tō), *It.* A round dance.

Rigoll. An old instrument consisting of several sticks placed by the side of each other, but separated by beads. It was played by being struck with a ball at the end of a stick.

Rigore (rē-gō'rĕ), *It.* Rigor, strictness; *al rigore di tempo*, with strictness as to time.

Rigoroso (rē-gō-rō'zō), *It.* Rigorous, exact, strict.

Rilasciando (rē-lä-shĭ-än'dō), *It.* Relaxing the time, giving way a little.

Rinforzando (rĕn-fōr-tsän'dō), } Strength-
Rinforzare (rĕn-fōr-tsä'rĕ), *It.* { ened, re-
Rinforzato (rĕn-fōr-tsä'tō), { inforced;
Rinforzo (rĕn-fōr'tsō), } a repeated reinforcement of tone or expression; indicating that several notes are to be played with energy and emphasis.

Ripetitura (rē-pĕ-tē-too'rä), *It.* } Repeti-
Ripetizione (rē-pĕ-tē-tsĭ-ō'nĕ), { tion; the burden of a song; a refrain.

Ripieni (rē-pĕ-ā'nē), *pl.* *It.* } The tutti, or
Ripieno (rē-pĕ-ā'nō), { full, parts which

fill up and augment the effect of the full chorus of voices and instruments. In a large orchestra all the violins, violas, and basses, except the principals, are sometimes called ripieni.

Ripienist. A player of the ripieno, or tutti, parts in an orchestra.

Riposta (rē-pōs'tä), *It.* Repeat.

Ripresa (rē-prä'zä), } Repetition, reiter-
Riprese (rē prä'zē), *It.* } ation.

Risentitamente (rē-sĕn'tĭ-tä-mĕn'tĕ), } *It.*
Risentito (rē-sĕn-tē'tŏ),
Marked, distinct, forcibly, firmly.

Risolutamente (rē-zō-loo-tä-mĕn'tĕ), *It.* Resolutely, boldly.

Risolutissimo (rē zō-loo-tēs'sĭ-mō), *It.* Very resolutely, as boldly as possible.

Risoluto (rē-zō-loo'tō), *It.* Resolved, resolute, bold.

Risoluzione (rē- zō- loo- tsĭ- ō' nē), *It.* Resolution, determination; also the resolution of a discord.

Risonante. Resounding, ringing, sounding.

Risposta (rēs - pōs' tä), *It.* The answer in a fugue.

Rissonanza (rē-sō-näu'tsä), *It.* Resonance.

Ristretto (rē-strĕt'tō), *It.* The stretto, the restriction, or contraction, of the subject, in a fugue.

Risvegliato (rēs-väl-yĭ-ä'tō), *It.* Awakened, reanimated.

Rit. } Abbreviations of Ritardando.
Ritard. }

Ritardando (rē-tär-dän'dŏ), *It.* Retarding, delaying the time gradually.

Ritardato (rē-tär-dä'tō), *It.* Retarded, delayed.

Ritardo (rē-tär'dō), *It.* Retardation, gradual delay; in harmony prolonging some note of a previous chord into the succeeding one.

Ritardo un pochettino (rē - tär' dō oon pō-kĕt-tē'nō), *It.* Slacken the time a little.

Riten. An abbreviation of Ritenuto.

Ritenendo (rē-tĕ-nĕn'dō), } Detaining,
Ritenente (rē-tĕ-nĕn'tĕ), *It.* } holding back the time.

Ritenuto (rē-tĕ-nĕn'tō), } Detained, slower,
Ritenuto (rē-tĕ-noo'tō), *It.* } kept back; the effect differs from ritardando, by being done at once, while the other is effected by degrees.

Ritmo (rēt'mō), *It.* Rhythm, cadence, measure.

Ritmo a tre battute (rēt'mō ä trā bät-too'tĕ), *It.* Rhythm in three beats.

Ritornel (rē-tŏr-nĕl', *It.* } The burden of
Ritornello (rē-tŏr-nĕl'lō), *It.* } a song; also a
Ritournelle (rē-toor-nĕl'), *Fr.* } short symphony or introduction to an air, and the symphony which follows an air: it is also applied to tutti parts introductory to, and between, or after, the solo passages in a concerto.

Ritual. The directions and text of formal services, such as those of the church, secret societies, etc.

Riverso (rē-vĕr'sō), } See Rovescio.
Riverscio (rē-vĕr-shĭ'ō), *It.* }

Rivolgimento (rē-vōl-yĭ-mĕn'tō), *It.* Inversion of the parts, in double counterpoint.

Rivoltato (rē-vōl-tä'tō), } Inverted, in coun-
Rivolto (rē-vōl'tō), *It.* } terpoint.

Roccoco (rō-kō'kō). } Old-fashioned, odd.
Rococo (rō-kō'kō). }

Roehrquint (rör'quĭnt), *Ger.* } Reed - fifth;
Rohrquint (rör'quĭnt), *Ger.* } an organ-stop, sounding the fifth above the diapasons.

Rohr (rör), *Ger.* Reed, pipe.

Röhre (rö'rĕ), *Ger. pl.* Reeds.

Rohrflöte (rör'flö'tĕ), *Ger.* Reed flute, a stopped diapason in an organ.

Rohrwerk (rör'wĕrk), *Ger.* Reed-work; the reed-stops in an organ.

Role (rōll), *Fr.* A part or character performed by an actor in a play or opera.

Rolling. A term applied to that rapid pulsation of the drum by which the sounds so closely succeed each other as to beat upon the ear with a rumbling continuity of effect.

Roll, long. A prolonged roll of drums signalizing an attack by the enemy, and for the troops to place themselves in line of battle.

Rollo (rōl'lō), *It.* The roll on the drum and tambourine.

Romance (rō-mäns). *Fr.* } Formerly the
Romanza (rō-män'tsä), *It.* } name given to
Romanze (rō-män'tsĕ), *Ger.* } the long lyric tales sung by the minstrels; now a term applied to an irregular, though delicate and refined composition in lyric style.

Romanesca (rō-mä-nĕs'kä), *It.* } A favorite
Romanesque (rō-män-ĕsk), *Fr.* } Roman or Italian dance of the sixteenth century, resembling the galliard.

Romantic. Interesting, strange, exciting. In poetry applied to the movement beginning near the close of the eighteenth century, Goethe and Schiller being the leading exponents. In music to a similar tendency to make thought free and truly responsive to the inner life. Hence in music the works of Chopin, Schumann, and others, which were measurably free from classical restrictions and carried out their ideas in any direction the fancy took them; whereas Bach and the composers before him were constantly hampered by the ideal of treating a selected musical idea in a certain manner, which in the hands of common composers became merely pedantic and learned. According to some philosophers the essence of the romantic spirit differs from the classic in this: That, whereas the ideal of classical art was to represent the eternal and ideal, the idea of the romantic is that everything which the individual experiences is of interest to the whole race. Hence a vastly greater latitude of styles and forms.

ä *arm*, ā *add*, ă *ale*, ĕ *end*, ē *eve*, ĭ *ill*, ī *isle*, ō *old*, ŏ *odd*, oo *moon*, ū *but*, ü *Fr. sound*, kh *Ger. ch*, nh *nasal*.

Romantique (rō-mänh-tĕk'), *Fr.* \
Romanzesco (rō-mänh-tsĕs'kō), *It.* } Romantic song, or ballad, common in the fourteenth century, and so called on account of form, by which it constantly returned to the first verse, and thus went round.

Ronde (rŏnd), *Fr.* A semibreve.

Rondeau (rŏnh'dō), *Fr.* } \
Rondo (rŏn'dō), *It.* } A composition, vocal or instrumental, generally consisting of three strains, the first of which terminates in a cadence on the tonic and is repeated several times during the movement.

Rondeau mignon (rŏnh-dō' mē-yŏnh), *Fr.* A favorite rondo.

Rondiletta (rŏn-dĭ-lĕt'tä), \
Rondinetto (rŏn-dĭ-nĕt'tō), *It.* { A short and easy rondo. \
Rondino (rŏn-dē'nō), \
Rondoletto (rŏn-dō-lĕt'tō),

Rondo form. In the style of a rondo.

Root. The fundamental note of any chord.

Rosalie (rō-sa'lĭ-ĕ), *Ger.* A derisive name sometimes applied to cheaply constructed musical passages, consisting of sequences and common harmonies.

Rostral (rŏs-träl'), *Ger.* A music-pen.

Rota (rō'tä), *It.* A wheel; applied to a canon, or a round.

Rote. Name formerly applied to the hurdy-gurdy.

Rote, singing by. The act of singing, not from a knowledge of music, but from listening to the singing of others.

Rotondo (rō-tŏn'dō), *It.* Round, full.

Rotte (rŏt'tĕ), *It.* Broken, interrupted.

Roulade (roo-läd), *Fr.* A florid vocal passage; a division, or rapid series of notes, using only one syllable.

Roulement (rool-mänh), *Fr.* A roll, or shake, upon the drum or tambourine; prolonged reiterations of one note, upon the guitar, etc.

Round. A species of canon in the unison or octave; also a vocal composition in three or more parts, all written in the same clef, the performers singing each part in succession. They are called rounds because the performers follow one another in a circulatory motion.

Roundel. } From the French word roundelet; a species of antique rustic \
Roundelay. }

Roverscio (rō-vär'shĭ-ō), *It.* } See *Roescio*. \
Rovesio (rō-vä-sĭ-ō),

Rovesciamento (rō-vä-shĭ-ä-mĕn'tō), } *It.* \
Rovescio (rō-vä'shĭ-ō), }
Reverse motion, the subject backward, in double counterpoint.

Rubato (roo-bä'tō), *It.* Robbed, stolen; taking a portion of the duration from one note, and giving it to another. See *Tempo rubato*.

Rückgang (rĕk'gäng), *Ger.* Going back. The part of the sonata preceding the return of the principal.

Rückung (rĕk'oong), *Ger.* Syncopation.

Rudiments. The first elements, or principles, of music.

Ruhepunct (roo'hĕ-poonkt'), *Ger.* } Pause, \
Ruhepunkt (roo'hĕ-poonkt), } point of rest or repose; a cadence.

Ruhestelle (roo'hĕ-stĕl'lĕ), *Ger.* } A pause, \
Ruhezeichen (roo'hĕ-tsī'kh'n), } a rest.

Ruhig (roo'hĭg), *Ger.* Calm, quiet, tranquil.

Rule of the octave. The art of accompanying the scale, either ascending or descending, when taken in the bass, with the proper chords for harmony.

Rullando (rool-län'dō), *It.* } Rolling on the \
Rullante (rool-län'tĕ), } drum or tambourine.

Run. A rapid flight of notes introduced as an embellishment; a roulade.

Rundgedicht (roond'gĕ-dĭkht'), *Ger.* } Rondeau, \
Rundgesang (roond'gĕ-zäng'), } roundelay, a convivial song.

Running passages. Divisions; series of notes appropriated to a single syllable.

Russe (rüss), *Fr.* Russian; *à la Russe*, in the Russian style.

Russian bassoon. A deep-toned instrument of the serpent species, sometimes used in military bands.

Rustico (roos'tĭ-kō), *It.* Rural, rustic.

Rutscher (root'shĕr), *Ger.* The dance called a galopade.

ä *arm*, à *add*, ä *ale*, ē *end*, ĕ *eve*, ī *ill*, ĭ *isle*, ō *old*, ŏ *odd*, oo *moon*, ū *but*, ü *Fr. sound*, kh *Ger. ch*, nh *nasal*.

S. Abbreviation of Segno or Sinistra.

Saccade (săk-kăd′), *Fr.* A firm pressure of the violin-bow against the strings, enabling the player to produce two, three, or four notes at one stroke.

Sackbut. An old bass wind instrument, resembling a trombone. The sackbut of the Bible was a stringed instrument.

Sackpfeife (săk′pfī′fĕ), *Ger.* A bagpipe. See *Cornamusa*.

Sacred music. Music composed for public religious worship or private devotion; oratorios, psalmody, etc.

Saengerfest (săng′ĕr-fĕst′), *Ger.* A festival of singers.

Saison (sā′sŏnh), *Fr.* The musical season.

Saite (sī′tĕ), *Ger.* A string of a musical instrument.

Saiteninstrument (sī′t′n-ĭn-stroo-mĕnt′), *Ger.* A stringed instrument.

Saitenklang (sī′t′n-kläng′), *Ger.* The sound, or vibration, of a string.

Saitenspieler (sī′t′n-spē′lĕr), *Ger.* Player on a stringed instrument.

Saitenton (sī′t′n-tōn′), *Ger.* The tone of a stringed instrument.

Saitig (sī′tĭg), *Ger.* Stringed.

Salcional (săl-sĭ-ō-näl′),
Salicet (să-lĭ-sā′), *Fr.* } An eight- or sixteen-feet organ-stop of small scale and stringy tone.
Salicional (să-lē-sĭ ō-näl′),

Salle de concert (săll dŭh kŏnh-sărt′), *Fr.* A concert-room.

Salle de musique (săll dŭh mü-zĕk′), *Fr.* A music-room.

Salm (sălm), *Ger.*
Salmo (săl-mō), *It.* } A psalm.

Salonmusik (sä′lōu-moo-zĕk′), *Ger.* Salon music; music for the drawing-room; hence music of a pleasing and not profound character.

Salpinx. The ancient Greek trumpet.

Saltando (săl-tän′dō), *It.* Leaping, proceeding by skips or jumps.

Saltarello (säl-tä-rĕl′lō), *It.* A Roman or Italian very quick dance, deriving its name from the introduction of leaping skips, in 2-4, 6-8, or 6-4 measure.

Salteretto (säl-tĕ-rĕt′tō), *It.* A musical figure in 6-8 time, the first and fourth quavers being dotted; very usual in movements alla Siciliana.

Saltero (säl-tā′rō), *It.* Psaltery, instrument with ten strings.

Salto (säl′tō). *It.* A leap, or skip, from one note to a distant one; also a dance.

Salve regina (säl′vĕ rä-gē′nä), *Lat.* "Hail, Queen;" a hymn to the Virgin Mary.

Sambuca (säm-boo′kä), *It.* An ancient stringed instrument used by the Greeks, the peculiar structure of which is unknown.

Sammlung (säm′loong), *Ger.* A collection of airs, etc.

Sampogna (säm-pōn′yä), *It.* A species of pipe. See *Zampogna*.

Sampunia. A pneumatic instrument used by the ancient Hebrews, resembling the modern bagpipe.

Sanctus (sănk′toos), *Lat.* "Holy;" the fourth movement of the Mass.

Sanft (sănft), *Ger.* Soft, mild, smooth; *mit sanften Stimmen*, with soft stops.

Sanftgedackt (sănft′ghĕ-däkt), *Ger.* A soft-toned stopped pipe.

Sanftheit (sănft′hīt), *Ger.* Softness, smoothness, gentleness.

Sänftig (sănf-tĭg), *Ger.* Soft, gentle.

Sanftmuth (sănft′moot),
Sanftmüthigkeit (sănft′mü-tĭg-kīt), } *Ger.* Softness, gentleness.

Sanftmüthig (sănft′ mü - tĭg), *Ger.* Softly, gently.

Sang (săng), *Ger.* Song.

Sänger (săng′ĕr), *Ger.* A singer.

Sängerbund (săng′ĕr-boond′), *Ger.* A league, or brotherhood, of singers; a convention of singing societies.

Sängerverein (săng′ĕr-fĕr-rīn′), *Ger.* Singers' union.

Sans (sănh), *Fr.* Without.

Sans frappé (sănh frăp-pā′), *Fr.* Without striking; play the notes without striking them hard or forcibly.

Sans pédales (sănh pā-däl), *Fr.* Without the pedals.

Santur (săn-toor), *Tur.* A Turkish stringed instrument; the psaltery.

Saquebute (săk-büt), *Fr.* The sackbut.

Saraband (săr-ä-bănd′, *Eng.*
Sarabanda (sär-ä-bän′dä), *It.*
Sarabande (săr-ä-bănd), *Fr.*
Sarabande (sär-ä-bän′dĕ), *Ger.* } A dance said to be originally derived from the Saracens, and danced with castanets; it is in slow 3-4 or 3-2 time, and characterized by the second note of the measure being prolonged through the second and third beats, which gives gravity and majesty to the movement.

Sarrusophones (sär′roos-ō-fōnes). A family of reed brass instruments, with reed mouthpieces. They are made in eight sizes.

Sattel (sät′t'l), *Ger.* The nut of the fingerboard of the violin, etc.

Satz (säts), *Ger.* Musical passage, composition, theme. Applied to pieces of all dimensions, from a single phrase to a complete sonata or rondo movement. A single piece.

Saut (sō), *Fr.* See *Salto.*

Sautereau (sō-tĕ-rō), *Fr.* The jack of the spinet.

Sawtry. A term used in olden times for psaltery.

Sax-horn. A brass instrument introduced by M. Sax, with a wide mouthpiece and three, four, or five cylinders, and much used in military bands; the tone is round, pure, and full.

Saxophones. A family of brass wind instruments invented by M. Sax. The body of these instruments is a parabolic cone of brass, provided with a set of keys; their tones are soft and penetrating in the higher part, and full and rich in the lower part of their compass. The saxophones are six in number, the high, the soprano, the alto, the tenor, the baritone, and the bass; they are played with a single reed and a clarinet mouthpiece.

Saxotromba. A brass instrument introduced by M. Sax, with a wide mouthpiece and three, four, or five cylinders; the tone is of a shrill character, partaking of the quality both of the trumpet and the bugle.

Sax-tuba. A brass instrument introduced by M. Sax, with a wide mouthpiece and three cylinders; the tone is very sonorous and deep.

Sbalzo (sbäl′tsō), *It.* Skip, or leap, in melody.

Sbarra doppia (sbär′rä dōp′pī-ä), *It.* A double bar.

Scagnello (skän-yäl′lō), *It.* The bridge of the violin, etc.

Scala (skä′lä), *It.* A scale, or gamut.

Scala cromatica (skä′lä krō-mä′tī-kä), *It.* The chromatic scale.

Scald. A Scandinavian poet-musician.

Scale. From the Latin word *scala.* The denomination first given to the arrangement made by Guido of the six syllables ut, re, mi, fa, sol, la: also called the gamut. The tones of a key arranged in regular order according to pitch. The tone compass of any instrument. The general dimensions or proportions of an instrument or a set of instruments.

Scale, chromatic. A scale proceeding by half-steps, as when every key of the piano is touched in succession.

Scale, diatonic major. A scale composed of the tones of the major mode, having half-steps between three and four and seven and eight.

Scale, enharmonic. A scale proceeding by intervals less than the diatonic and chromatic.

Scale, German. A scale of the natural notes formed of A, H, C, D, E, F, G, the B being reserved to express B♭.

Scale, Guido's. The syllables ut, re, mi, fa, sol, la, used by Guido d'Arezzo, called also the Aretinian scale; the syllable si was introduced afterward.

Scale, minor diatonic. The scale of the minor mode, having a minor third and sixth, the other degrees being the same as in the major of the same tonic.

Scale, natural. The scale of C, called natural because it does not require the aid of flats or sharps.

Scale of A major. A, B, C♯, D, E, F♯, G♯, A. Three sharps.

Scale of A♭ major. A♭, B♭, C, D♭, E♭, F, G, A♭. Four flats.

Scale of A minor. A, B, C, D, E, F, G♯, A. Natural.

Scale of A♭ minor. A♭, B♭, C♭, D♭, B♭, F♭, G♭, A♭. Seven flats.

Scale of B major. B, C♯, D♯, E, F♯, G♯, A♯, B. Five sharps.

Scale of B minor. B, C♯, D, E, F♯, G, A♯, B. Two sharps.

Scale of C major. C, D, E, F, G, A, B, C. Natural.

Scale of C minor. C, D, E♭, F, G, A♭, B♭, C. Three flats.

Scale of C major. C, D, E, F, G, A, B, C. Natural.

Scale of C♯ minor. C♯, D♯, E, F♯, G♯, A, B♯, C♯. Four sharps.

Scale of D major. D, E, F♯, G, A, B, C♯, D. Two sharps.

Scale of D minor. D, E, F, G, A, B♭, C♯, D. Two sharps.

Scale of D♭ major. D♭, E♭, F, G♭, A♭, B♭, C, D♭. Signature five flats.

Scale of E♭ major. E♭, F, G, A♭, B♭, C, D, E♭. Three flats.

Scale of E♭ minor. E♭, F, G♭, A♭, B♭, C♭, D♭, E♭. Six flats.

Scale of E major. E, F♯, G♯, A, B, C♯, D♯, E. Four sharps.

Scale of E minor. E, F♯, G, A, B, C♯, D♯, E. One sharp.

Scale of F major. F, G, A, B♭, C, D, E, F. One flat.

Scale of F minor. F, G, A♭, B♭, C, D♭, E♭, F. For four flats.

Scale of F♯ major. F♯, G♯, A♯, B, C♯, D♯, E, F♯. Six sharps.

Scale of F♯ minor. F♯, G♯, A, B, C♯, D, E♯, F♯. Three sharps.

Scale of G major. G, A, B, C, D, E, F♯, G. One sharp.

Scale of G minor. G, A, B♭, C, D, E♭, F♯, G. Two flats.

Scale of G♯ minor. G♯, A♯, B, C♯, D♯, E, F×, G.

Scemando (shĕ-mäṅ'dō), *It.* Diminishing, decreasing in force.

Scena (shä'nä), *It.* A scene, or portion, of an opera or play.

Scenario (shĕ-nä'rĭ-ō), *It.* Actor's guide-book; a programme; scenes, decorations.

Scere. Part of an act, portion of an opera; an act generally comprises several scenes.

Scenic music. Music adapted to dramatic performances.

Schäferlied (shä'fĕr-lēd), *Ger.* Pastoral song, shepherd's song.

Schäferpfeife (shä'fĕr-pfī'fĕ), *Ger.* Shepherd's pipe.

Schäfertänze (shä'fĕr-tän'tsĕ), *Ger. pl.* Shepherd dances.

Schalkhaft (shälk'häft), *Ger.* Playful, roguish.

Schall (shäll), *Ger.* Sound.

Schallbecken (shäll-bĕk'ken), *Ger.* Cymbal.

Schallloch (shäll'lökh), *Ger.* Sound-hole.

Schallrohr (shäll'ror), *Ger.* Speaking-trumpet.

Schallstück (shäll'stük), *Ger.* The bell of a trumpet, bugle, horn, etc.

Schalltrichter (shäll'trĭkh-tĕr), *Ger.* The bell of wind instruments.

Schalmay (shäll-mī'), **Schalmei** (shäll-mī'), *Ger.* } A shawm; also an 8-feet reed organ-stop; the tone resembles that of the cremona, or clarinet.

Scharf (shärf), *Ger.* Sharp, acute; a shrill mixture stop, of several ranks of pipes.

Schauspiel (shou'spēl), *Ger.* Drama, dramatic piece.

Schauspieler (shou-spē'lĕr), *Ger.* Actor, player.

Schelle (shĕl'lĕ), *Ger.* A bell; a jingle.

Schellenbaum (shĕl'lĕn-bowm), *Ger.* "Jingle-tree." The high stand of bells sometimes used in orchestral and band music for oriental coloring.

Scherz (shärts), *Ger.* } Play, sport, jest. A **Scherzo** (skĕr'tsō), *It.* } name given to a great variety of instrumental compositions, and indicative of their character rather than their form. Scherzi occur as single pieces, as items of sets of pieces (partite, etc.), and as movements of larger compositions. The scherzo was introduced into the sonata towards the end of the last century, and soon after also into the symphony and other kindred forms, where it frequently takes the place of the minuet. Its form in the sonata, etc., was at first that of the minuet (a first division of two parts; a second division, or trio, of two parts, and a repetition of the first division); afterwards this form was developed and treated with greater freedom. This developed minuet-form is the most common form of the scherzo; but there are scherzi with two trios, scherzi in form resembling that of the first movement of a sonata, and scherzi irregularly and fantastically constructed. Triple measure is oftenest to be met with, more especially 3-4 measure, but also 2-4 time occurs.

Scherzando (skĕr-tsän'dō), *It.* } Playful, **Scherzante** (skĕr-tsän'tĕ), *It.* } lively, **Scherzevole** (skĕr-tsā'vō-lĕ), *It.* } sportive, **Scherzhaft** (shärtshäft), *Ger.* } merry.

Scherzoso (skĕr-tsō'so, *It.* Merry, playful, jocose.

Scherzozamente (skĕr-tsō-sä-měn'tĕ), *It.* Merrily, playfully, sportively.

Schiettamente (skĕ-ĕt-tä-měn'tĕ), *It.* Simply, unadorned.

Schietto (skĕ-ĕt'tō), *It.* Simple, plain, neat.

Schisma (skĭsmä), *Gr.* A very minute difference between the sound of intervals. In ancient music, a small interval equal to the half of a comma, or the eighteenth part of a tone.

Schlachtgesang (shläkht'ghĕ-säng), } *Ger.* **Schlachtlied** (shläkht'lēd), } War song, battle-song.

Schlag (shläg), *Ger.* Stroke, blow; a beat, as regards time.

Schlagen (shlägh'n), *Ger.* To strike, to beat; to warble or trill.

Schlagfeder (shlägh'fä-d'r), *Ger.* A plectrum.

Schlaginstrumente (shlägh'ĭn-stroo-měn'tĕ), *Ger. pl.* Instruments of percussion. Formerly key-board instruments also.

Schlecht (shlĕkht), *Ger.* Faulty.

Schlechtertacttheile (shlĕkh-tĕr-täkt'thī-lĕ), *Ger.* The unaccented parts of the measure.

Schleifbogen (shlīf'bō'gh'n), *Ger.* A slur.

Schleifen (shlī'f'n), *Ger.* To slide, to glide.

Schleifer (shlī'fĕr), *Ger.* Slurred note, gliding note.

Schleifezeichen (shlī'fĕ-tsī'īkh'n), *Ger.* A slur, a mark of the legato style.

Schleppend (shlĕp'pĕnd), *Ger.* Dragging, drawling.

Schluss (shlooss), *Ger.* The end, conclusion.

Schlüssel (shlüs's'l), *Ger.* A clef.

Schlussfall (shlooss'fäll), *Ger.* A cadence.

Schlusssatz (shlooss'säts), *Ger.* A closing passage.

Schlusszeichen (shlooss-tsī'kh'n), *Ger.* A pause.

Schmeichelnd (shmī-khĕlnd), *Ger.* Coaxingly, caressingly.

Schmerz (shmärts), *Ger.* Grief, sorrow.

Schmerzhaft (shmärts'häft), *Ger.* Dolorous, sorrowful.

Schnabel (shnä'b'l), *Ger.* A beak; a mouth-piece, as of the clarinet.

ă *arm,* ă *add,* ā *ale,* ĕ *end,* ē *eve,* ĭ *ill,* ī *isle,* ŏ *old,* ō *odd,* oo *moon,* ŭ *but,* ü *Fr. sound,* kh *Ger. ch,* nh *nasal.*

(195)

Schnabelflöte (shnä′b'l-flö′tĕ), *Ger.* A beak-flute, *i. e.*, flageolet.

Schnarrpfeifen (shnärr′pfi-f'n), *Ger.* } Reed-
Schnarrwerk (shnärr′wärk), pipes, reedwork, or stops, in an organ.

Schnecke (shnĕk′kĕ), *Ger.* A snail; the scroll at the top of a violin.

Schnell (shnĕll), *Ger.* Quickly, rapidly; *etwas bewegter schnell*, a little quicker.

Schnelle (shnĕl′lĕ), *Ger.* } Quickness,
Schnelligkeit (shnĕl′lig-kit), *Ger.* swiftness, rapidity.

Schneller (shnel′lĕr), *Ger.* Quicker, faster. Also a quick and short trill.

Schnellwalzer (shnĕll′wäl′tsĕr), *Ger.* Quick waltzes.

Schollrohr (shöll′rör), *Ger.* Trumpets, bugles, brass wind instruments.

Schottisch (shŏt′tĭsh), *Ger.* A modern dance, rather slow, in 2-4 time.

Schräge Bewegung (schrä′ghĕ bā-wä′ ghoong), *Ger.* Oblique motion.

Schreibart (shrīb′ärt), *Ger.* Style, manner of composing.

Schreiber (shrī′bĕr), *Ger.* A music-copyist.

Schreiend (shrī′ĕnd), *Ger.* Acute, shrill, screaming.

Schreiwerk (shrī′wärk), *Ger.* Shrill work; acute or mixture stops.

Schrittmässig (shrĭt′mäs′sĭg), *Ger.* Slow time, andante.

Schuiftromppet (shwĭf′ tröm-pĕt), *Dut.* A sackbut.

Schule (shoo′lĕ), *Ger.* A school, or method, for learning any instrument; also a peculiar style of composition, the manner, or method, of an eminent composer, teacher, or performer.

Schulgerecht (shool′ghĕ-rĕkht′), *Ger.* Regular, in due form; written correctly, in accordance with the rules and principles of musical art. Used derogatorily, as denying higher qualities.

Schultergeige (shool′t'r-ghī′ghĕ), *Ger.* Shoulder violin, as distinguished from "nce viol," 'cello.

Schusterfleck (shoos′tĕr-flĕk′), *Ger.* See *Rosalia*.

Schwach (shwäkh), *Ger.* Piano, soft, weak.

Schwächer (shwä′khĕr), *Ger.* Fainter, softer, more piano.

Schwache Stimme (shwäkh′ĕ stĭm′mĕ), *Ger.* A weak voice.

Schwärmer (schwär′m'r), *Ger.* A passage in which each pair of tones are several times repeated.

Schwebung (shwĕ-boong), *Ger.* Waving; a lighter species of tremulant, for the more delicate stops, such as the vox humana, etc.

Schweige (shwī′ghĕ), *Ger.* A rest.

Schweizerflöte (shwī′tsĕr-flötĕ), } *Ger.*
Schweizerpfeife (shwī-tsĕr-pfī′fĕ),
Swiss flute, or pipe.

Schwellen (shwĕl′l'n), *Ger.* To swell, to increase in loudness.

Schwer (shwär), *Ger.* Heavily, ponderously.

Schwermüthig (shwär-mü′tĭg), *Ger.* In a pensive, melancholy style.

Schwiegel (shwē′g'l), *Ger.* An organ-stop of the flute species, of metal, pointed at the top.

Schwindend (shwĭn′d'nd), *Ger.* Dying away.

Schwingung (shwĭng′oong), *Ger.* Vibration of a string, etc.

Scialumo (sē-ä-lü′mō), *Fr.* A word employed in clarionet music, signifying that the notes are to be played an octave lower than written.

Scioltamente (shē-ōl-tä-mĕn′tĕ), *It.* With freedom, agility; easily, the notes being rather detached than legato.

Scioltezza (shē-ōl-tĕt′sä), *It.* Freedom, ease, lightness.

Sciolto (shē-ōl′tō), *It.* Free, light. See *Scioltamente*.

Scolia (skō′lĭ-ä), *Gr.* Among the ancients songs in general, but more especially those of a festive kind.

Scordatura (skōr-dä-too′rä), *It.* Tuning a violin differently, for the more easily performing certain peculiar passages.

Score. An arrangement of the vocal and instrumental parts of a composition in equal lines, with bars drawn across the entire number (whence the name "score") in such a way as to present the whole detail to the eye at once. A piano score of a vocal work contains all the voice parts, each on its own staff, and the pianoforte accompaniment. The copy of an opera for piano solo is not a score, but an arrangement, since the vocal parts are not shown. The only kind of copy to which the term score applies without limitation is the full orchestra score, which also contains all the vocal parts. This is the score, or German Partitur. Composers generally write first a piano score, indicating the leading instruments for each motive as it occurs. From this the full score is afterwards developed, and in carrying out the instruments complete much detail is often added, leading later to a new piano score, in which the salient parts of this detail are included. The term score does not properly apply to the printed copy of a pianoforte composition. But a "score" of a trio, quartette, or even a composition for two pianos, whenever the copy contains all the parts, is correct.

Scorrendo (skōr-rĕn′dō), *It.* Gliding from one sound into another.

Scotch scale. The pentatonic scale, consisting of the tones do, re, mi, sol, la, do. Many Scotch melodies are mainly confined to this selection of tones in key, whence the term Scotch.

ä *arm*, ă *add*, ā *ale*, ĕ *end*, ē *eve*, ĭ *ill*, ī *isle*, ŏ *old*, ŏ *odd*, oo *moon*, ŭ *but*, ü *Fr. sound*, kh *Ger. ch.* nh *nasal*.

Scotch snap. A peculiarity in Scotch tunes, and those written in imitation of the Scotch character. It is the lengthening of the time of a second note at the expense of the one before it, placing a semiquaver before a dotted quaver. It gives emphasis and spirit to dance tunes, and, when well applied, has a lively effect.

Scozzese (skŏt-sā'zĕ), *It.* In the Scotch style.

Scuola (skoo-ō'lä), *It.* A school; a course of study.

Sdegnante (sdän-yün'tĕ), *It.* Angry, passionate.

Sdegno (sdăn'yō), *It.* Anger, wrath, passion.

Sdegnosamente (sdän-yō-zä mĕn'tĕ), *It.* Scornfully, disdainfully.

Sdrucciolamento (sdroot-tshī-ō lä-mĕn'tō),
Sdrucciolato (sdroot-tshī-ō-lä'tō), } *It.*
Sliding the fingers along the strings or the keys of an instrument

Se (sā), *It.* If, in case, provided, as, so, etc.

Se bisogna (sā bē-sōn'yä), *It.* If necessary, if required.

Sec (sĕk), *Fr.* } Dry, unornamented, cold-
Secco (sĕk'kō), *It.* } ly; the note, or chord, to be struck plainly, without ornament or arpeggio.

Seccarara (sĕk-kä-rä'rä), *It.* A Neapolitan dance.

Sechs (sĕkhs), *Ger.* Six.

Sechsachteltakt (sĕkhs-äkh't'l-täkt), *Ger.* Measure in 6-8 time.

Sechssaitig (sĕkhs-sī'tĭg), *Ger.* Instrument with six strings.

Sechstel (sĕkhs'tĕl), *Ger.* A sixth.

Sechstheilig (sĕkhs-tī'lĭg), *Ger.* In six parts.

Sechzehnfüssig (sĕkh'tsän-füs'sĭg), *Ger.* Sixteen feet, applied to organ-pipes, or pitch, a 16-feet tone being an octave below the normal pitch.

Sechzehnte (sĕkh'tsän-tĕ), *Ger.* Sixteenth.

Sechzehntel (sĕkh'tsän-tĕl), *Ger.* Semiquaver.

Sechzehntelpause (sĕkh-tsän'-tĕl-pou'zĕ), *Ger.* A semiquaver rest.

Second. The interval between any tone of the scale and the next above, or below. It derives its name from the fact that in reckoning intervals both tones are counted as well as all that lie between. Seconds are always represented upon adjacent degrees of the staff. But the representation is determined by nature of the interval and not the interval by the form of the representation.
A minor second is equal to one half-step; a major second to two half-steps; an augmented second to three half-steps, being equal to a minor third, from which, however, it easily distinguishes itself by the manner in which it is used.

Seconda (sā-kŏn'dä), *It.* Second, a second.

Seconda donna (sā-kŏn'dä dŏn'nä), *It.* Second female singer.

Seconda volta (sā-kŏn'dä vŏl'tä), *It.* The second time.

Seconda volta molto crescendo (sĕ-kŏn'dä vŏl'tä mŏl'tŏ krĕ-shĕn'dō), *It.* Much louder the second time.

Seconde (sā-kŏnhd), *Fr.* Second.

Seconde fois (sā-kŏnhd fwä), *Fr.* Second time.

Secondo (sā-kŏn'dō), *It.* Second, a second.

Second soprano. The low soprano.

Second subject. The counter subject of a fugue when it remains unchanged in all the parts.

Second tenor. Low tenor.

Second treble. Low treble.

Sectio canonis (sĕk-tsī'ō kä-nō'nĭs), *Lat.* The section of the canon. The mathematical division of a string for determining the exact nature of intervals. This operation was performed by the Alexandrian mathematicians (Claudius Ptolemy, etc., about 200 A.D.) upon a monochord. See "Hawkins' History of Music."

Section. A musical form consisting of two phrases, the section being half of a simple period. The name section is applied by a few theorists to what is more properly called a phrase, and conversely the two-phrase form is by them called a phrase. See *Period*.

Secular music. Music which is composed for the theater or chamber; an expression used in opposition to sacred music, which is for the church, or worship.

Secunde (sĕ-koon'dĕ), *Ger.* Second.

Secundum artem (sĕ-koon'doom är'tĕm), *Lat.* According to art or professional rule; with skill and accuracy.

Sedesima (sā-dä'sĭ-mä), *It.* Sixteenth. Applied to intervals, and to an organ-stop.

Seelenamt (sā'l'n-ämt),
Seelenmesse (sā'l'n mĕs'ĕ), } *Ger.* Requiem, or mass for departed souls.

Seer. The ancient name for a bard or rhapsodist.

Segno (sān'yō), *It.* A sign, 𝄋; *al segno*, return to the sign; *dal segno*, repeat from the sign.

Segue (sā'gwĕ),
Seguito (sā-gwē'tō), } *It.* Follows, now follows, as follows; it also means, go on; in a similar, or like, manner, showing that a passage is to be played like that which precedes it.

Segue coro (sā-gwĕ kō'rō), } *It.* The
Segue il coro (sā-gwĕ ĕl kō'rō), } chorus follows, go on to the chorus.

Segue il duetto (sā-gwĕ ĕl doo-ĕt'tō), *It.* The duet follows.

Segue il menuetto (sā-gwĕ ĕl mĕ-noo-ĕt'tō), *It.* The minuet follows.

Segue la finale (sā-gwĕ lä fē-nä'lĕ), *It.* The finale now follows.

ā *arm*, ă *add*, ā *ale*, ĕ *end*, ē *eve*, ĭ *ill*, ī *isle*, ō *old*, ŏ *odd*, oo *moon*, ŭ *but*, ü *Fr. sound*, kh *Ger. ch*, nh *nasal*.

Seguendo (sĕ-gwĕn'dŏ), *It.* } Following, next.
Seguente (sĕ-gwĕn'tĕ),

Seguenza (sä-gwĕn'tsä), *It.* A sequence.

Segue senza interruzione (sĕ-gwĕ sĕn'tsä ĕn'-tĕr-roo-tsĭ-ŏ'nĕ), *It.* Go on without stopping.

Segue subito senza cambiare il tempo (sä-gwĕ s o'bĭ-tŏ sĕn'tsä käm-bĭ-ä'rĕ), *It.* Proceed directly, and without changing the time.

Seguidilla (sä-gwĕ-dĕl'yä), *Sp.* A favorite Spanish dance in 3-4 time.

Seguito (sĕ-gwĕ'tŏ), *It.* Followed, imitated.

Sehnsucht (sān'sookht), *Ger.* Desire, longing; ardor, fervor.

Sehnsüchtig (sān'sükh-tĭg), *Ger.* Longingly.

Sehr (sār), *Ger.* Very, much, extremely.

Sehr lebhaft (sār lĕb'häft), *Ger.* Very lively; extremely animated and vivacious.

Sei (sā'ī), *It.* Six.

Seitenbewegung (sī't'n-bĕ-wĕ'goong), *Ger.* Oblique motion.

Seitensatz (sī't'n-sätz), *Ger.* Sidepiece. An episode, or second subject, in an overture, sonata, or symphony.

Sekunde (sĕ-koon'dĕ), *Ger.* Second.

Selah (sā-lä), *Heb.* A term anciently used to indicate the interlude, in which the priests should blow the trumpets, to carry up the sentiments expressed for a memorial before God.

Semi (sĕm'-Ĭ), *Lat.* Half.

Semibescroma, *It.* A sixty-fourth note.

Semibreve (sĕm'Ĭ-brĕv), *Eng.*
Semibreve (sĕm-Ĭ-brā'vĕ), *It.*
Semibrevis (sĕm-Ĭ-brā'vĭs), *Lat.*
Half a breve; the longest note now in general use.

Semibreve rest. A rest equal in duration to a semibreve.

Semichorus. A chorus to be sung by half or only a few of the voices.

Semicroma (sĕm-Ĭ-krŏ'mä), *It.* A semiquaver.

Semidemisemiquaver. A half demisemiquaver; sixty-four of them being equal to a semibreve.

Semidemisemiquaver rest. A rest equal in duration to a semidemisemiquaver.

Semi-fusa (sĕm-Ĭ-foo'sä), *Lat.* A semiquaver.

Seminar (sĕm'Ĭ-nŭr), *Ger.* A school for teachers.

Semiographie (sĕm'Ĭ-ŏ-grä'fē), *Gr.* } The art
Semieographie (sĕm'Ĭ-ŏ-grä'fē), of notation, or writing music in notes.

Semipausa (sĕ'mĭ-pow-zä), *Lat.* A half-rest.

Semiquaver. A note equal to half a quaver; a sixteenth note.

Semiquaver rest. A rest equal in duration to a semiquaver.

Semitone (sĕm'Ĭ-tōn), *Eng.* } A half-
Semitonium (sĕ'mĭ-tŏ'nĭ-oom), *Lat.* } tone. Improperly used for half step.

Semitonium modi (sĕ-mĭ-tŏ'nĭ-oom mō'dĭl), *Lat.* The leading note, or major seventh.

Semituono (sĕ-mĭ-too-ŏ'nŏ), *It.* A semitone.

Semplice (sĕm'plĭ-tshĕ), *It.* Simple, pure, plain.

Semplicemente (sĕm-plĭ-tshĕ-mĕn'tĕ), *It.* Simply, plainly, without ornament.

Semplicissimo (sĕm-plĭ-tshēs'sĭ-mŏ), *It.* With the utmost simplicity.

Semplicita (sĕm-plē'tshĭ-tä), *It.* Simplicity, plainness.

Sempre (sĕm'prĕ), *It.* Always, evermore, continually.

Sempre forte (sĕm'prĕ fōr'tĕ), *It.* Always loud.

Sempre legato (sĕm'prĕ lĕ-gä'tŏ), *It.* Always smooth.

Sempre piano (sĕm'prĕ pē-ä'nŏ), *It.* Always soft.

Sempre piu affrettando il tempo (sĕm'prĕ pē'oo äf-frĕt-tän'dŏ ĕl tĕm'pŏ), *It.* Continually increasing the time.

Sempre piu forte (sĕm'prĕ pē'oo fōr'tĕ), *It.* Continually increasing in power.

Sempre piu presto (sĕm'prĕ pē'oo prĕs'tŏ), *It.* Continually quicker.

Sempre ritardando (sĕm'prĕ rĕ-tär-dän'dŏ), *It.* Always slower; slower and slower.

Sempre staccato (sĕm'prĕ stäk-kä'tŏ), *It.* Always detached; staccato throughout.

Sensibile (sĕn-sē'bĭ-lĕ), *It.* Sensible, expressive, with feeling.

Sensibilita (sĕn-sĭ-bē'lĭ-tä), *It.* Sensibility, expression, feeling.

Sensibilmente (sĕn-sĭ-bĭl-mĕn'tĕ), *It.* Sensibly, expressively, in a feeling manner.

Sensible (sän-sēbl'), *Fr.* The leading note, or major seventh, of the scale.

Sentences. Certain interlude strains sometimes introduced into the service of the established Church, especially of particular chapels; short anthems.

Sentimento (sĕn-tĭ-mĕn'tŏ), *It.* Feeling, sentiment, delicate expression.

Senza (sĕn-tsä), *It.* Without.

Senza accompagnamento (sĕn-tsä äk-kŏm-pän-yä-mĕn'tŏ), *It.* Without accompaniment.

Senza battuta (sĕn'tsä bät-too'tä), *It.* At the pleasure of the performer, as regards the beat or time.

Senza fiori (sĕn-tsä fē-ŏ'rĭ), } *It.*
Senza ornamenti (sĕn-tsä ŏr-nä-mĕn'tĕ), Without ornaments, without embellishments.

Senza interruzione (sĕn-tsä ĭn-tĕr-roo-tsĭ-ŏ'nĕ), *It.* Without interruption.

Senza oboe (sĕn'tsä ŏ'bŏ-ā), *It.* Without the hautboy.

ä *arm*, ă *add*, ā *ale*, ĕ *end*, ē *eve*, ĭ *ill*, ī *isle*, ŏ *old*, ŏ *odd*, oo *moon*, ŭ *but*, ü *Fr. sound*, kh *Ger. ch*, nh *nasal*

(193)

Senza organo (sĕn'tsä ôr-gä'nō), *It.* Without the organ.
Senza pedale (sĕn'tsä pō-dä'lĕ), *It.* Without the pedals.
Senza piano (sĕn'tsä pē-ä'nō), *It.* Without the piano.
Senza repetizione (sĕn'tsä rä-pŏ-tē-tsĭ-ō'- nō), *It.*
Senza replica (sĕn'tsä rä'plĭ-kä), Without repetition.
Senza rigore (sĕn'tsä rē-gō'rĕ), *It.* Without regard to exact time.
Senza sordini (sĕn'tsä sōr-dē'nĭ), *It. pl.* Without the dampers, in pianoforte-playing, meaning that the dampers are to be raised from the strings.
Senza sordino (sĕn'tsä sōr-dē'nō), *It.* Without the mute, in violin-playing, etc.
Senza stromenti (sĕn'tsä strō-mĕn'tĭ), *It. pl.* Without instruments.
Senza tempo (sĕn'tsä tĕm'pō), *It.* Without regard to the time; in no definite time.
Se piace (sä pē-ä'tshĕ), *It.* At will, at pleasure.
Septet (sĕp-tĕt'), *Eng.*
Septetto (sĕp-tĕt'tō), *It.* A composition for seven voices or instruments.
Septieme (sĕt-ĭ-ām'), *Fr.*
Septime (sĕp-tē'mĕ), *Ger.* The interval of a seventh.
Septimenaccord (sĕp-tĭ-mĕn-äk-kŏrd), *Ger.* The chord of the seventh, comprising the root, the third, fifth, and seventh.
Septimole (sĕp'tĭ-mō'lĕ), *Lat.*
Septiole (sĕp'tĭ-ō'lĕ), A group of seven notes, having the value and to be played in the time of four of the same species.
Septole (sĕn-tō'lĕ), *Lat.* A group of seven notes in the time of six or eight.
Septuor (sĕp-too-ōr), *Fr.* A composition for seven voices or instruments.
Septuplet (sĕp-too-plĕt), A group of seven equal notes in the time of six or eight of the same name.
Sequence (sē-kwĕns), *Eng.*
Sequence (sä-känhss), *Fr.*
Sequenz (sĕ kwĕnts'), *Ger.*
Sequenza (sĕ-kwĕn'tsä), *It.* A series, or progression, of similar chords, or intervals, in succession.
Seraphine (sĕr'ä-fēn). A species of harmonium.
Sérénade (sä-rĕ-näd'). *Fr.*
Serenata (sä-rĕ-nä'tä), *It.* Night music; an evening concert in the open air and under the window of the person to be entertained. Also a musical composition on an amorous subject. Also any light, pleasing instrumental composition comprising several movements.
Sereno (sĕ-rä'nō), *It.* Serene, calm, tranquil, cheerful.
Seria (sä'rĭ-ä),
Serioso (sĕ-rĭ-ō'zō), *It.* Serious, grave; in a serious, sedate style.
Sérieusement (sä-rĭ-ŭs-mänh), *Fr.* Seriously, gravely.

Serinette (sĕr-ĭ-nĕt), *Fr.* A bird organ.
Seringhi (sĕ-rēn'ghē), *Hin.* A Hindoo instrument of the violin class.
Serio (sä'rĭ-ō), *It.* Serious, grave.
Serio-comic. A song combining the grave with the ludicrous or humorous.
Serpent (sĕr-pĕnt), *Eng.*
Serpente (sĕr-pĕn'tĕ), *It.*
Serpentono (sĕr-pĕn-tō'nō), *It.* A bass wind instrument, of deep, coarse tone, resembling a serpent in form. It is chiefly used in military bands, though nearly superseded by the ophicleide; the name is sometimes given to a reed-stop in an organ.
Service. A musical composition adapted to the services of religious worship. Those for Anglican use are generally known by the name of the composer and the leading key, as, " Burnley, in A," " Stainer, in F," etc.
Service-book. A missal ; a book containing the musical service of the church.
Service, choral. The Anglican service intoned, instead of spoken.
Sesqui (sĕs'kwĭ), *Lat.* A Latin particle, signifying a whole and a half, and which, when joined with *altera, terza, quarta*, etc., expresses a kind of ratio.
Sesquialtera (sĕs'kwĭ-äl'tĕ-rä), *Lat.* The name given by the ancients to that ratio which includes one and a half to one. An organ-stop, comprising two or more ranks of pipes, of acute pitch.
Sesta (sĕs'tä), *It.*
Sesto (sĕs'tō), The interval of a sixth. See, also, *Sexte.*
Sestet (sĕs-tĕt'), *Eng.*
Sestetto (sĕs-tĕt'tō), *It.* A composition for six voices or instruments.
Sestina (sĕs-tē'nä),
Sestola (sĕs-tō'lä), *It.* A sextole.
Sette (sĕt'tĕ), *It.* Seven.
Settima (sĕt'tĭ-mä),
Settimo (sĕt'tĭ-mō), *It.* The interval of a seventh.
Settima maggiore (sĕt'tĭ-mä mäd-jĭ-ō'rĕ), *It.* Major seventh.
Settima minore (sĕt'tĭ-mä mē-nō'rĕ), *It.* Minor seventh.
Settimola (sĕt-tĭ-mō'lä), *It.* A septimole.
Set to music. An expression applied to any language to which music is adapted. Such a composition is said to be set to music.
Setzart (sĕts'ärt), *Ger.* Style, or manner, of composition.
Setzkunst (sĕts'koonst), *Ger.* The art of musical composition.
Sevens and eights metre. A metre consisting of a stanza of eight lines, in trochaic measure, and designated thus, 7s and 8s.
Sevens and fives metre. Consists of a stanza of four lines, in trochaic measure, and designated, 7s and 5s.
Sevens and sixes metre. A meter designated thus, 7s and 6s, consisting of a stanza of eight lines in trochaic and iambic measure.

ä *arm*, ă *add*, ā *ale*, ĕ *end*, ē *eve*, I *ill*, ī *isle*, ŏ *old*, ō *odd*, oo *moon*, ŭ *but*, ü *Fr. sound*, kh *Ger. ch.* nh *nasal.*

(199)

Sevens, eights, and sevens meter. A meter designated thus, 7s, 8s, and 7s, consisting of a stanza of eight lines in iambic measure, with number of syllables corresponding to the designation.

Sevens metre. A stanza of four lines in trochaic measure, each line containing seven syllables.

Sevens, sixes, and eights metre. A metre designated thus, 7s, 6s, and 8s, consisting of eight lines in trochaic and iambic measure.

Seventh. An interval between any tone of the scale and the next but five above or below. There are three kinds of seventh: The major, equal to eleven half-steps, occurs between the tonic and the seventh degree of the major scale, and nowhere else. The minor, equal to ten half-steps, occurs between re and do, mi and re, sol and fa, la and sol, si and la. The diminished, equal to nine half-steps, occurs between si and fa and nowhere else.

Severamente (sĕ-vĕr-ä-mĕn'tĕ), *It.* Severely, strictly, rigorously.

Severita (sĕ-vĕ-rī-tä'), *It.* Severity, strictness.

Sexta (sĕx'tä), *Lat.* Sixth.

Sexte (sĕx'tĕ), *Ger.* A sixth; also the name of an organ-stop with two ranks of pipes, sounding the interval of a major sixth, a twelfth, and tierce on one slide.

Sextet. A composition for six voice parts, or instruments. More commonly used in instrumental music to designate a chamber composition (sonata form) for six instruments.

Sextetto. See *Sestetto*.

Sextuor (sĕx'twŏr), *Fr.* A sextet.

Sextole (sĕx'tō-lĕ), } *Lat.* } A group of six
Sextuplet (sĕx'too-plĕt), notes, having the value, and to be played in the time, of four.

Sextuple measure. The name formerly given to measures of two parts, composed of six equal notes, three for each part. This is more generally called, now, compound double measure.

Sf., or **Sfz.** Abbreviation of Sforzando.

Sfogato (sfō-gä'tō), *It.* A very high soprano.

Sforza (sfŏr'zä), *It.* Forced, with force and energy.

Sforzando (sfŏr-tsän'dō), } *It.* } Forced: one
Sforzato (sfŏr-tsä'tō), particular chord, or note, is to be played with force and emphasis.

Sforzare la voce (sfŏr-tsä'rĕ lä vō'tshĕ), *It.* To overstrain the voice.

Sforzatamente (sfŏr-tsä-tä-mĕn'tĕ), *It.* Impetuously, energetically.

Sfuggito (sfood-jē'tō), *It.* Avoided, shunned, rambling. See *Cadenza sfuggita*.

Sgallinacciare (sgäl-lī-nä-tshi-ä'rĕ), *It.* To crow; a bad method of singing.

Shake. An ornament produced by the rapid alternation of two successive notes, comprehending an interval not greater than a whole step, nor less than a half step.
Written. Played.
Plain shake, or trill.

Shake, double. Two simultaneous shakes on notes which are either sixths or thirds to each other.
Double shake.

Shake, passing. A short trill used in flowing passages of quavers or semiquavers, without breaking the time, or interfering with the natural course of the melody.

Shake, prepared. A shake preceded by two or more introductory notes.

Sharp. A character (#) indicating an elevation of a half-step. Applied to a staff degree. Sharps are either in signature or accidental. Accidental sharps affect the staff degree through the measure in which they occur; signature sharps affect the degree and all its octaves on the same staff throughout the line.

Sharp, double. A double sharp is equivalent to two sharps, implying an elevation of two half-steps. Always applied as accidental, and only to a degree which has already been once sharped.

Shawm. A wind instrument of the ancient Hebrews, supposed to be of the reed or hautboy species.

Sheminith (shĕm-I-nĭth), *Heb.* A stringed instrument. It was also sometimes used to denote a species of music, and also a particular part of a composition.

Shepherd's flute. A pastoral flute, shorter than the transverse flute, and blown through a lippiece at the extremity.

Shift. A change of position of the left hand, in playing the violin, etc., whereby the second finger is placed successively one degree farther down the fingerboard until the very high notes are reached.

Shiginoth (shē'ghī-nŏth), *Heb.* According to variable tunes.

Shofar (shō'fär), *Heb.* A trumpet, or bent horn, so called because it gave a brilliant, clear, ringing sound.

Short appoggiatura. A grace note. A small note with a stroke through the stem, played very quickly before its principal note. See *Melodic Embellishments* in introduction.

Short hallelujah metre. A stanza of six lines in iambic measure.

Short metre. A stanza of four lines in iambic measure.

Short mordent. A mordent consisting of two notes, viz.: that having the sign over it, and that below or above it, before the principal note.

Short octaves. A term applied to the lower notes in old organs, where some of the notes were omitted.

Short particular metre. A stanza of six lines in iambic measure.

Short shake. An embellishment formed by two or more notes preceding the principal note.

Shrill. An epithet applied to those acute sounds which form the upper part of the scale of soprano voices and treble instruments.

Si (sē), *Fr.* Applied in solfaing to the note B.

Si bémol (sē bā-mōl), *Fr.* } The note B♭.
Si bemolle (sē bā-mōl'lě), *It.*

Si bemol majeur (sē bā-mōl mä-zhŭr), *Fr.* The key of B♭ major.

Si bemol mineur (sē bā-mōl mē-nŭr'), *Fr.* The key of B♭ minor.

Sibilus (sē'bĭ-loos), *Lat.* A little flute, or flageolet, used to teach birds to sing.

Siciliana (sē-tshē-lĭ-ä'nä), *It.* } A dance of
Siciliano (sē-tshē-lĭ-ä'nō), the Sicilian peasants, a graceful movement of a slow, soothing, pastoral character, in 6-8 or 12-8 time.

Side drum. The common military drum, so called from its hanging at the side of the drummer when played upon. Called also snare drum, from two strings of catgut called snares, stretched across the lower head in order to check reverberation. This instrument, whose military use is very old, dates as orchestral instrument only from the time of Rossini, who first introduced it in the overture to "La Gazza Laddra."

Si diese (sē dī-āz), *Fr.* The note B♯.

Sieben (sē'b'n), *Ger.* Seven.

Siebenklang (sē'b'n-kläng'), *Ger.* Heptachord, a scale of seven notes.

Siebente (sē'běn-tě), *Ger.* Seventh.

Siebenzehnte (sē'b'n-tsēn-tě), *Ger.* Seventeenth.

Siegesgesang (sē'ghěs-ghě-säng'), } *Ger.*
Siegeslied (sē'ghěs-lēd'),
A triumphal song.

Siegesmarsch (sē'ghěs-märsh'), *Ger.* A triumphal march.

Siffflöte (sĭff'flō'tě), *Ger.* An organ-stop of 2- or 1-foot scale, of the Hohlflute species.

Siffler (sĭf-flā), *Fr.* To make a hissing noise.

Sifflet (sĭf-flā), *Fr.* A catcall, a squeaking instrument used in playhouses to condemn a performance.

Signalhorn (sĭg-näl'horn), *Ger.* A bugle.

Signatur (sĭg'nä-toor'), *Ger.* } Name given to
Signature. the sharps or flats placed at the beginning of a piece, and at the commencement of each staff, to indicate the key in which it is written. The signature adjusts the staff to the demands of the key in which the piece is written, except in the case of the minor mode, which is always written with the signature of the relative major, and a regular accidental, a sign of the elevation (a sharp or natural), upon the seventh degree. The sharps or flats of the signature affect not only the lines and spaces upon which they are placed, but all octaves above or below upon the same staff.

Signature, time. Figures, in the form of a fraction, placed at the beginning of a piece to indicate the time. The upper of the two figures tells the number of pulses in a measure, and the lower the kind of note which represents one pulse, and accordingly is taken for the time unit of the piece, all other notes being valued in relation to it.

Signe (sēn), *Fr.* The sign :S:. See *Segno*.

Signes accidentels (sēn āk-sĭ-dänh't'l), *Fr.* Accidental sharps, flats, or naturals.

Signes de silences (sēn dē sĭ-länhs'), *Fr.* Rests.

Signs of abbreviation. Strokes, waving lines, dots, and figures, employed to denote a repetition of notes, continuation of rests, etc.

Siguidilla (sē-gwē-dēl'yä), *Sp.* See *Seguidilla*.

Silence (sē-länhs), *Fr.* } A rest.
Silenzio (sē-lěn'tsī-ō), *It.*

Si leva il sordino (sē lā'vä ēl sōr-dē'nō), *It.* Take off the mute.

Si levano i sordino (sē lě-vä'nō ē sōr-dē'nō), *It.* Raise the dampers.

Silver trumpet. The chatsoteroth of the ancient Hebrews, straight, a cubit long, with a bell-shaped mouth.

Si maggiore (sē mäd-jōr'ē), *It.* B major.

Si majeur (sē mä-zhŭr), *Fr.* The key of B major.

Simile (sē'mĭ-lē), *It.* Similarly; in like manner.

Si mineur (sē mĭ-nŭr'), *Fr.* The key of B minor.

Si minore (sē mĭ-nō'rē), *It.* B minor.

Simplified. Rendered free from difficult passages.

Sin', *It.* As far as. See *Sino*.

Sin' al fine (sēn äl fē'nē), *It.* To the end, as far as the end.

Sin' al segno (sīn äl sān'yō), *It.* As far as the sign.

Si naturrel (sē nät-oo-rěl), *Fr.* B.

Sincopa (sĭn'kō-pä), } *It.* See *Syncopato*.
Sincope (sĭn'kō-pě),

Sinfonia (sĭn-fō'nĭ-ä), *It.* } An orchestral
Sinfonie (sänh-fō-nē'), *Fr.* composition in many parts; a symphony.

Sinfonia a pittorica (sĭn-fō-nē′ä ä pēt-tō′rĭ-kä), *It.* A symphony descriptive of scenes and events.

Sinfonia concertante (sĭn-fō-nē′ä kŏn-tsher-tän′tĕ),
Sinfonia concertata (sĭn-fō-nē′ä kŏn-tsher-tä′tä),
Sinfonia concertate (sĭn-fō-nē′ä kŏn-tsher-tä′tĕ), } *It.*
A concerto for many instruments; a concerto symphony.

Sinfonia da camera (sĭn-fō-nē′ä dä kä′mĕ-rä), *It.* Symphonies composed for chamber use, as quartets, trios, etc.

Sinfonia eroica (sĭn-fō-nē′ä ā-rō′ĭ-kä), *It.* A symphony in the heroic style.

Sinfonie (sĭn′fō-nē′), *Ger.* A symphony.

Sing. To perform melody with the voice. The singing voice differs primarily from the speaking voice in two particulars: First, the intonation is at a determinate pitch, and the voice is carried directly from one intonation to another without any break in the continuity of tone except where the idea breaks. Second, the tone quality is of better grade and finer resonance. The act of singing implies an emotional excitation to which speaking would not be adequate. In all very emotional speech the tone assumes certain qualities of singing.

Singakademie (sĭng′ä-kä-dĕ-mē′), *Ger.* Vocal academy.

Singanstalt (sĭng′än-stält′), *Ger.* Singing club.

Singart (sĭng-ärt), *Ger.* Manner, or style, of singing.

Singbar (sĭng′bär), *Ger.* That may be sung, singable.

Singen (sĭng′ĕn), *Ger.* To sing, to chant; singing, chanting.

Singend (sĭng′ĕnd), *Ger.* See *Cantabile.*

Singgedicht (sĭng′ghĕ-dĭkht′), *Ger.* Hymn, poem intended to be sung.

Singhiozzando (sĭn-ghĭ-ōt-sän′dō), *It.* Sobbingly.

Singkunst (sĭng′koonst), *Ger.* The art of singing.

Single-action harp. A harp with pedals, by which each string can be raised one semitone.

Single chant. A simple harmonized melody, extending only to one verse of a psalm, as sung in cathedrals, etc.

Singmährchen (sĭng′mär′kh'n), *Ger.* A ballad.

Singmanieren (sĭng′mä-nē-r'n), *Ger.* Singing embellishments.

Singschauspiel (sĭng′shou-spel), *Ger.* Singing-drama; a drama with songs, etc., interspersed.

Singschule (sĭng′shoo′lĕ), *Ger.* Singing-school; a school, or method, for the voice.

Singschüler (sĭng′shü′lĕr), *Ger.* Singing-pupil.

Singspiel (sĭng′spĕl), *Ger.* An opera, melodrama, a piece interspersed with songs.

Singstimme (sĭng′stĭm′mĕ), *Ger.* Singing-voice; a vocal part.

Singstimmen (sĭng′stĭm′mĕn), *Ger. pl.* The voices; the vocal parts.

Singstück (sĭng′stük), *Ger.* Air, melody.

Singstunde (sĭng-stoon′dĕ), *Ger.* Singing-lesson.

Singtanz (sing-tänts), *Ger.* Dance, accompanied by singing.

Singverein (sĭng′fĕr-rīn′), *Ger.* A choral society.

Singweise (sĭng′wī′sĕ), *Ger.* Melody, tune.

Siniestra (sē-nĭ-äs′trä), *Sp.*
Sinistra (sĭn-ĭs-trä), *Lat.* } The left hand.

Sinistræ (sĭn-ĭs-trä), *Lat.* Left-handed flutes. See *Dextræ.*

Sinistra mano (sĭ-nĭs′trä mä′nō), *It.* The left hand.

Sinkopace. A five-step dance. Cinquepace. A galliard.

Sino (sē′nō),
Sin' (sēn), } *It.* To, as far as, until; *con fuoco sin' al fine,* with spirit to the end.

Sinò al fine pianissimo (sē′nō äl fē′nē pē-ä-nĭs′sĭ-mō), *It.* Pianissimo to the end.

Sino al segno (sē′nō äl sān′yō), *It.* As far as the sign.

Si piace (sē pē-ä-tshĕ), *It.* At pleasure, as you please.

Si raddoppia il tempo (sē räd-dōp′pĭ-ä ĕl tĕm′pō), *It.* Redouble the time; as fast again.

Siren. In ancient mythology a goddess who enticed men into her power by the charms of music and devoured them.

Sirene. An instrument used for ascertaining the velocity of aerial vibration, corresponding to the different pitches of musical sounds.

Siren song. A song of a bewitching, fascinating style.

Sirenengesang (sē-rĕn′ĕn-ghĕ-säng′), *Ger.* Siren-song; a soft, luscious, seductive melody.

Si replica (sē rä′plĭ-kä), *It.* A repeat; to be repeated.

Si replica una volta (sē rä′plĭ-kä oo′nä vōl′tä), *It.* Play the part over again.

Si scriva (sē scrē′vä), *It.* As written, without any alterations or embellishments.

Si segue (sē sā′gwĕ), *It.* Go on.

Sistrum (sĭs′troom), *Lat.* An instrument of percussion of very great antiquity, supposed to have been invented by the Egyptians, and was much used by the priests of Iris and Osiris in sacrifice. It consisted of a rod of iron, bent into an oval or oblong shape, or square at two corners and curved at the others, and furnished with a number of movable rings, so that, when shaken, or struck with another rod of iron, it emitted the sound desired. It answered the same purpose as the bell in the Mass.

Si tace (sē tä′tshĕ), *It.* Be silent.

ä *arm,* ă *add,* ā *ale,* ĕ *end,* ē *eve,* ĭ *ill,* ī *isle,* ō *old,* ŏ *odd,* oo *moon,* ŭ *but,* ü *Fr. sound,* kh *Ger. ch,* nh *nasal.*

Six-eighth measure. A measure having the value of six eighth-notes, marked 6-8.

Sixes and fives metre. A metre consisting of a stanza of eight lines in iambic or trochaic measure, designated thus, 6s & 5s.

Sixes and four. A metre designated thus, 6s & 4, consisting of a stanza of four lines in iambic measure.

Sixes and tens. A metre designated thus, 6s & 10s, consisting of a stanza of six lines in iambic measure.

Sixes metre. A metre designated thus, 6s, consisting of a stanza of eight lines of six syllables each, in iambic measure.

Sixes and sevens and eights metre. A metre designated thus, 6s, 7s, & 8s, consisting of a stanza of eight lines, in iambic measure.

Sixième (sēz-I-âm'), *Fr.* A sixth.

Six pour quatre (sēz poor kätr), *Fr.* A double triplet, or sextuplet; six notes to be played in the time of four.

Sixte (sēkst), *Fr.* A sixth.

Sixteenth note. A semiquaver.

Sixteenth rest. A pause equal in duration to a sixteenth note.

Sixtes (sēkst), *Fr.* Sixths.

Sixth. The interval between any tone of the scale and the next but four above or below. A sixth is represented upon the staff by a line and a space with two lines between. There are three sixths in use: The minor, equal to eight half-steps, as between mi and do; the major, nine half-steps, as between sol and me; and the augmented, of ten half-steps, as between fa and re-sharp. The major and minor sixths are classed as imperfect consonances.

Sixth-chord. The first inversion of the triad.

Sixty-fourth note. A hemidemisemiquaver.

Sixty-fourth rest. A pause equal in point of duration to a sixty-fourth note.

Skalde (skäl'dŏ), *Ger.* A scald; ancient Scandinavian bard.

Skip. A term applied to any transition exceeding that of a whole step.

Skizzen (skĭts'sĕn), *Ger. pl.* Sketches; short pieces.

Slargando (slär-gän'dŏ), *It.* } Extending,
Slargandosi (slär-gän-dŏ'zĭ), *It.* } enlarging, widening; the time to become gradually slower.

Slentando (slĕn-tän'dŏ), *It.* Relaxing the time, becoming gradually slower.

Slide. (1) The movable part of the trombone and slide trumpet, by which the length of the tube can be increased. A slide consists of a tube in the shape of a U, with prolonged shanks wide enough to admit of the insertion of two shanks of the remaining part of the instrument. What on the horn and the ordinary trumpet is affected by crooks and valves can be easily and more perfectly accomplished on the trombone and slide trumpet by the slide. In the case of the B♭ trombone, for instance, the player can change the key of the instrument by drawing the slide more and more out into A, A♭, G, G♭, F, and E. (2) An ornament consisting of two or more quick notes proceeding diatonically to the principal note. (3) A sliding strip of lath, which in the organ cuts off a rank of pipes from their wind.

Slide, tuning. An English instrument producing thirteen semitones and used for pitching the keynote.

Slogan. The war-cry, or gathering-word, of a Highland clan in Scotland.

Slur. A curved line over two or more notes, to show that they must be played smoothly.

Small octave. The name given in Germany to the notes included between C on the second space of the bass staff and the B above, these notes being expressed by small letters, as a, b, c, d, etc.

Smaniante (smä-nĭ-än'tŏ), } Furious, vehe-
Smaniato (smä-nĭ-ä'tŏ), *It.* } ment, frantic;
Smanioso (smä-nĭ ō'zō), } with rage.

Sminuendo (smē-noo-ĕn'-dŏ), } Diminish-
Sminuito (smē-noo-ē'tŏ), *It.* } ing, decreas-
Smorendo (smō rĕn'dŏ), } ing; gradually softer.

Smorfiozo (smŏr-fĭ-ō'zō), *It.* Affected, coquettish, full of grimaces.

Smorz. An abbreviation of Smorzando.

Smorzando (smŏr-tsän'dŏ), *It.* } Extinguish-
Smorzato (smŏr-tsä'tŏ), } ed, put out, gradually dying away.

Snare drum. The side drum.

Soave (sō-ä'vĕ), *It.* A word implying that a movement is to be played in a gentle, soft, and engaging style.

Soavemente (sō-ä-vĕ-měn'tĕ), *It.* Sweetly, agreeably, delicately.

Soggetto (sŏd-jĕt'tŏ), *It.* Subject, theme, motive.

Soggetto di fuga (sŏd-jĕt'tŏ dē foo'gä), *It.* Subject of the fugue.

Soggetto invariato (sŏd-jĕt'tŏ ĭn-vä-rĭ-ä'tŏ), *It.* The invariable subject—a term applied to the subject of counterpoint when it does not change the figure, or situation, of the notes.

Soggetto variato (sŏd-jĕt'tŏ vä-rĭ-ä'tŏ), *It.* Variable subject—a term applied to the subject of a counterpoint when it changes the figure, or situation, of the notes.

Soirée musicale (swä-rā' mü-zĭ-käl'), *Fr.* A musical evening.

Sol (sōl). A syllable applied by the Italians to G, the fifth sound of the diatonic scale or octave of C.

Sola (sō'lä), *It.* Alone. See *Solo*.

Sol bemol (sōl bā'mŏl), *Lat.* The note G♭.

Sol bémol majeur (sōl bā-mōl mä-zhūr'), *Fr.* The key of G♭ major.

Sol bémol mineur (sŏl bā-mŏl mē-nŭr), *Fr.* The key of G♭ minor. (Not in use.)
Sol diese (sŏl dī-āz), *Fr.* The note G♯.
Sol diese mineur (sŏl dī-āz mē-nŭr), *Fr.* The key of G♯ minor.
Solenne (sō-lĕn'nĕ), *It.* Solemn.
Solennemente (sō-lĕn-nĕ-mĕn'tĕ), *It.* Solemnly.
Solfa. To pronounce the names of the notes sung.
Solfaing. Singing the notes of the scale to the monosyllables applied to them by Guido. See *Solmization.*
Solfege (sŏl-fāzh), *Fr.*
Solfeggi (sŏl-fĕd'jī), *It.*
Solfeggio (sŏl-fĕd'jĭ-ō), *It.* } Exercises for the voice according to the rules of solmization.
Solfegglare (sŏl-fĕd-jĭ-ä'rĕ), *It.* To practice solfeggi.
Solfeggiren (sŏl-fĕg-gī'r'n), *Ger.*
Solfier (sŏl-fī-ā), *Fr.* } To solfa.
Soli (sō'lī), *It.* A particular passage played by principals only, one performer to each part.
Solist. The solo-player. Also sometimes called soloist.
Sol majeur (sŏl mä-zhŭr), *Fr.* The key of G major.
Sol mineur (sŏl mē-nŭr), *Fr.* The key of G minor.
Solmisare (sŏl-mī-zä'rĕ), *It.*
Solmisiren (sŏl-mī-sē'rĕn), *Ger.*
Solmizare (sŏl-mī-tsä'rĕ), *It.* } The practice of the scales, applying to the different tones their respective syllables, do, re, mi, fa, sol, la, si. To this kind of vocal exercise the practice of solfeggi is added.
Solmization (sŏl-mī-zā'shŭn), *Eng.* The art of singing by solfa, i. e., by use of the scale syllables. In Italy, France, and Germany, the scale-names do, re, mi, fa, sol, la, si, do are applied to C, D, E, etc., according to the scale of C, no matter what the key may be. In this usage the solfa amounts merely to an arbitrary set of words for preparatory stages of vocal training. But according to the system practiced in America and by the tonic solfaists in England the syllables are applied to the degrees of the scale, do to one, re to two, etc., through the keys. In this usage the syllables become associated with certain relations of tone in key, and are a help to identifying key-relations. They are therefore peculiarly advantageous in the earlier stages of study. There comes a time, however, when the introduction of modulations and arbitrary dissonances renders the solfa rather complicated, and the best musicians are not yet agreed whether, on the whole, some other system might be invented which would afford the help without the disadvantages mentioned.
Solo (sō'lō), *It.*
Solo (sō'lō), *Fr.*
Solo (sō'lō), *Ger.* } A composition for a single voice or instrument.

Solomanie (sō-lō-mä-nē), *Tur.* The Turkish flute, entirely open and without any reed.
Solosänger (so'lō-sän'gĕr), *Ger.* Solo-singer, principal singer.
Solo-soprano (sō'lō sō-prä'nō), *It.* For soprano only.
Solospieler (sō'lō-spē'lĕr), *Ger.* Solo-player.
Somma (sŏm'mä), *It.* Extreme, exceedingly great.
Somma espressione (sŏm-mä ĕs-prĕs-sī-ō'nĕ), *It.* Very great expression.
Son (sŏnh), *Fr*
Son (sŏn), *Sp.* } Sound.
Son aigu (sŏnh ā-gü), *Fr.* A sharp, acute sound.
Sonante (sō-nän'tĕ), *Sp.* Sounding, sonorous.
Sonare (sō-nä'rĕ), *It.* To sound, to have a sound, to ring, to play upon.
Sonare alla mente (sō-nä'rĕ äl'lä mĕn'tĕ), *It.* Formed according to the mind; to play extempore, to improvise.
Sonata (sō-nä'tä), *It.* Something sounded. Hence an instrumental composition. This appears to have been the original meaning of the word. Sonata Form designates what is sometimes called the Principal Form in music, or the ideal form toward which all compositions tend which are neither purely lyric, fugal, nor dance.
The sonata affords one of the most instructive illustrations of development to be found in music. Originally it was derived from dance forms, each movement being a serious enlargement of some popular rhythm, but carried out thematically and contrapuntally, i. e., without lyric episodes. Bach's sonatas for organ, and for violin solos, consist of from three to five movements of this kind, duly contrasted among themselves. The trio organ sonatas are extended in form and beautifully written. All they lack for modern hearing is occasional points of lyric episode. The innovation made by Haydn consisted of adding these points of lyric repose, both as episodes in the allegro movements and as foundation for the slow movements. Mozart added to Haydn's work a still more distinct return to the folksong as the type of the lyrical moments in a sonata. As practiced by these great masters the sonata consisted of three movements or four. First, an allegro, following a certain type of treatment (of which presently); then a slow movement, generally an andante cantabile or an adagio; then a rondo or finale. Beethoven made several innovations upon this order, first by inserting a third movement between the slow movement and the finale. This is a menuet or a scherzo with trio. His further innovations consisted in intensifying the lyric movements and moments, and in making them still more deep and heartfelt.
The sonata-piece (Sonatasatz) is the principal movement in a sonata. The entire sonata-piece divides into three chapters: First, from the beginning to the double bar.

This contains all the original material of the entire movement. There is, first, a principal, or leading, subject, which generally is thematic in character, closes in the dominant, and leads off toward the second by means of passage or modulating periods, derived in part from the material of the principal. Then comes the second, in the dominant of the original key, or in the relative major, if that had been minor. The second is also called by the Germans *Gesanggruppe*, "song-group," in token of its lyric character. After some sixteen or thirty-two measures of this, passage work may or may not intervene, leading to the partial close, which brings around to a cadence upon the dominant of the original key at the double bar, where is always marked a repeat for the entire work up to this part. In some instances, as in Beethoven's Sonata Appassionata, the modulating material after the principal is so much enlarged and so interesting as to become almost an equal factor with the principal, the second, and the close in affording material for the later development. The second chapter of the sonata-piece follows the double bar, and consists of an elaboration (German *Durchführungssatz*, "working-out piece") a free fantasia upon motives already introduced. This, after suitable development, leads into a pedal point upon the dominant of the principal key, leading to the third chapter of the sonata-piece, the repetition, or reprise, in which all the matter of the first chapter comes again, with little modification, except that the principal is sometimes slightly abridged, and the second is now in the principal key of the work, leading to the close in that key.

The sonata-piece is the type of most overtures (all which are not potpourris), and is at the foundation of all works in sonata form, such as sonatas, chamber duos, trios, quartets, etc., concertos and symphonies. Its great advantage for the composer is its liberality of opportunity in thematic and lyric directions combined, thus permitting a composer to give his fancy loose rein, and make new works, at once interesting and beautiful, in whatever style may happen to please him.

The slow movements of sonatas are often largely upon the same lines, except that, owing to the greater time occupied by a slow movement, the forms have to be shorter, and the elaborations are greatly abridged. This is in consequence of the limitation to the persistence of musical impressions. An elaboration becomes intelligible to a hearer only when he remembers the musical material in its unelaborated form, and this will be only a certain very short interval after he has heard it. Moreover, there is better effect in a slow movement in developing a lyric theme, as we find in many symphonies by Beethoven, Brahms, and the other great writers.

The third movement in a sonata of four movements is generally a song form with trio. This is the lightest division of the work. The last movement is either a rondo or a finale. The latter is a sonata-piece, if taken as leading movement. The rondo comes from a different source, and is lighter. See *Rondo*. In several instances Beethoven introduced other kinds of movement in his so-called sonatas. An air and variations are met with as first movement, or as second, and in one instance, two instances, at least, as last movement.

In the Sonata, Opus 110, the last movement is a fugue. Hence the proper definition of a sonata will be a composition in which one or more movements are in the form of a sonata-piece.

Sonata da camera (sō-nä'tä dä kä'mĕ-rä), *It.* A sonata designed for the chamber or parlor.

Sonata di bravura (sō-nä'tä dē brä-voo'rä), *It.* A brave, bold style of sonata.

Sonata di chiesa (sō-nä'tä dē kē-ā'zä), *It.* A church sonata, an organ sonata.

Sonata, grand. A massive and extended sonata, consisting usually of four movements.

Sonate (sō-nä'tĕ), *Ger.* A sonata.

Sonatina (sō-nä-tē'nä), *It.* } A short, easy
Sonatine (sō-nä-tēn), *Fr.* } sonata.

Son doux (sŏnh doo), *Fr.* Soft sound.

Sonetto (sō-nĕt'tŏ), *It.* A sonnet.

Sonevole (sō-nä'vŏ-lĕ), *It.* Sonorous, ringing, sounding.

Song. That which is sung. A melody; a poem set to music for a single voice, or for several voices (partsong). Songs are distinguished as strophic, in which .he same music answers to all the stanzas of the text, and "through-composed," in which each stanza has its own music. Also songs are distinguished as folksongs, which are simple melodies of unpretending musical quality, and art songs, in which the music seeks solely to interpret the text, hampered only by the practicability for the voice and the proper limits of an accompaniment. Of the latter kind Schubert and Schumann wrote some beautiful examples, which stand as models.

Song, bacchanalian. A song which either in sentiment or style relates to scenes of revelry.

Song, boat. A song sung by the rowers; gondolier-song.

Song, erotic. A love-song.

Songform. In the form of a song. A musical form consisting of one, two, three, or at most five, periods making a unity. The principal subjects of all the Beethoven Andante Cantabiles are practically songforms. So are menuets, scherzi, and the individual ideas of most dances.

A second form is often added in a related key. This is called a trio, and is merely an independent and contrasting songform. After this a return is made to the first songform. Of long examples of songform Schumann left the best in the first movements

SON   DICTIONARY OF MUSIC.   SOU

of his Novelettes, in *E*, Opus 21, No. 7, and in B minor, Opus 99.
    The periods in a songform are lyrical in rhythm, if not in essential nature.

Songs without words. Pianoforte pieces of a poetical character, consisting of a melody with an accompaniment.

Sonnet. A short poem of fourteen lines, two stanzas of four verses each, and two of three each, the rhymes being adjusted by a particular rule.

Sono (sō'nō), *It.* A sound.

Sonoramente (sō-nō-rä-měn'tĕ), *It.* Sonorously, harmoniously.

Sonore (sō-nōr'), *Fr.* } Sonorous, harmoni-
Sonoro (sō-nō'rō), *It.* } ous, resonant.

Sonoridad (sō-nō-rĭ-däd), *Sp.* Sonorousness.

Sonorita (sō-nō-rĭ-tä'), *It.* } Harmony, sound,
Sonorité (sō-nō-rĭ-tā'), *Fr.* } sonorousness; having sonority.

Sonorous (sō-nōr'ous). An epithet applied to whatever is capable of yielding sound; full or loud in sound; rich-toned; musical.

Sons harmoniques (sōnhs här-mōnh-ēk'), *Fr. pl.* Harmonic sounds.

Sons pleins (sōnhs plănh), *Fr. pl.* In flute music this means that the notes must be blown with a very full, round tone.

Sonus (sō'noos), *Lat.* Sound, tone.

Sopra, *It.* Above, upon, over, before.

Sopra dominante (sō'prä dō-mĭ-nän'tĕ). The fifth, or upper dominant.

Sopran (sō-prän'), *Ger.* } The treble, the high-
Soprano (sō-prä'nō), *It.* } est kind of female voice; a treble, or soprano, singer.

Soprana chorda (sō-prä'nä kōr'dä), *It.* The E string of a violin.

Soprani (sō-prä'nĭ), *It. pl.* Treble voices.

Sopranist. A male soprano.

Soprano acuto (sō-prä'nō ä-koo-tō), *It.* High soprano.

Soprano clef. The treble or G clef.

Soprano clef. The C clef on the first line of the staff for soprano, instead of using the G clef on the second line for that part.

Soprano clef, mezzo. The C clef when placed on the second line of the staff, formerly used for the second treble voice, and for which the soprano clef is now substituted.

Soprano concertato (sō-prä'nō kōn-tshěr-tä'tō), *It.* The soprano solo part, the part for a solo treble voice in a chorus.

Soprano concertina. A concertina having the compass of a violin.

Soprano mezzo (sō-prä'nō měz'zō), *It.* A species of female voice between soprano and alto.

Soprano naturel (sō-prä'nō nä-too-räl), *It.* A natural soprano. A falsetto.

Soprano, second. Low soprano.

Soprano secundo od alto (sō-prä'nō sä-koon'-dō ōd ül'tō), *It.* The second soprano or alto.

Sopranstimme (sō-prän'stĭm'mĕ), *Ger.* A soprano voice.

Sopra quinta (sō'prä quĭn'tä), *It.* Upper dominant.

Sopra una corda (sō'prä oo'nä kōr'dä), *It.* On one string.

Sorda (sōr'dä), *It.* Muffled, veiled tone.

Sordamente (sōr-dä-měn'tĕ), *It.* Softly, gently; also damped, muffled.

Sordine. A small instrument, or damper, in the mouth of a trumpet, or on the bridge of a violin or violoncello, to make the sound more faint and subdued. A mute.

Sordini (sōr-dē'nĭ), *It. pl.* Mutes in violin-playing and the dampers in pianoforte music. See *Con sordini* and *Senza sordini.*

Sordini levati (sōr-dē'nĭ lĕ-vä'tĕ), *It.* The dampers removed.

Sordino (sōr-dē'nō), *It.* A sordine. A mute.

Sorgfältig (sōrg'fäl-tĭgh), *Ger.* Carefully.

Sorgfältig gebunden (sōrg'fäl-tĭgh ĝĕ-boon'-d'n), *Ger.* Very smoothly.

Sortita (sōr-tē'tä), *It.* The opening air in an operatic part; the entrance aria.

Sospensione (sōs-pĕn-sĭ-ō'nĕ), *It.* A suspension.

Sospirando (sōs-pĭ-rän'dō),   }   Sighing,
Sospirante (sōs-pĭ-rän'tĕ),   *It.* { very sub-
Sospirevole (sōs-pĭ-rä'vō-lĕ),   }   dued, dolce-
Sospiroso (sōs-pĭ-rō'zō),   ful.

Sospiro (sōs-pē'rō), *It.* A crotchet rest.

Sostenendo (sōs-tĕ-něn'dō), } Sustaining
Sostenuto (sōs-tĕ-noo'tō),   *It.* } the tone, keeping the notes down their full duration.

Sostenuto molto (sōs-tĕ-noo'tō mōl'tō), *It.* In a highly sustained manner.

Sotto (sōt'tō), *It.* Under, below.

Sotto voce (sōt-tō vō'tshĕ), *It.* Softly, in a low voice, in an undertone.

Soubrette (soo-brĕtt'), *Fr.* A female singer for a subordinate part in a comic opera.

Soufflerie (soof-flĕ-re), *Fr.* The machinery belonging to the bellows in an organ.

Sound. The impression made upon sense-perception by vibrations of the air, originating in the air itself, or communicated to it by any sounding body. The pitch of the sound depends upon the frequency of the vibrations, which are inaudible when they fall below the rate of from 8 to 32 per second, or when they rise above the rate of about 40,000 per second. The intensity of the sound depends upon the amplitude of the vibration—the impression of intensity being, perhaps, referred back to a theory that greater force is behind the ample vibration.

    Sounds differ in respect to consistency within themselves. Some, as, for instance,

---

ä *arm*, ă *add*, ā *ale*, ĕ *end*, ē *eve*, ĭ *ill*, ī *isle*, ō *old*, ŏ *odd*, oo *moon*, ŭ *but*, ü *Fr. sound*, kh *Ger. ch*, nh *nasal*.

(206)

a blow upon a block of wood, are dull and confused; so, also, a blow upon an iron kettle, or a wooden box. In these cases several rates of vibration are in operation at the same time. Again, when a stretched string vibrates and makes a tone, there are also several rates of vibration in operation at the same time, the string vibrating not only in its full length but also in various aliquot parts, whereby the sounds of several different pitches are produced. In the case of the string all these rates are multiples of the rate of the full string, and the resulting partial tones mutually combine and coalesce, so that the individual elements composing them can not be made out by ordinary ears. Hence what is called a musical tone, the essential element of which is *consistency within itself*, so that the vibrations combine into a harmonious and complete whole. The opposite of tone is noise, which is simply a sound so inconsistent and contradictory in the conflicting rates of vibration composing it that it affords the ear no repose whatever, and therefore it has no musical character. Noises are of limited application in music, the kettledrums, triangles, cymbals, and bass drum being practically less offensive noises. They are employed for the sake of rendering the ensemble more imposing, and their empty character, from a musical standpoint, is glossed over by an imposing amplitude of brilliant tone from the brass and other telling qualities.

The timbre, or color, of tone depends upon the selection and relative importance of the partial tones present in the klang, or tone. This subject is fully investigated in Helmholtz's great work on "Sensations of Tone," ("Tonempfindung.") The difference between the color of tones derived from the violin, flute, cornet, or other instruments, depends wholly upon the nature and relative importance of partial tones composing them. These again are influenced by the nature of the sounding material, brass lending itself to the production of high upper partials, in which the flute is comparatively poor. Of all forms of tone that derived from strings reinforced by wooden sounding-boards is the most satisfactory, excepting the tones of the human voice, which admit of assuming almost any kind of timbre.

All stringed instruments are susceptible to considerable tonal variety, according to the skill with which the vibration is incited. In those of the violin family this is done by skillfully handling the bow. The tone of the harp is very much modified by the manner in which the finger plucks the string; and even in the pianoforte, where mechanism would seem to have been most exact, the tone is largely influenced by the manner in which the keys are attacked. The use of the pedal also influences the quality of the piano tone, the finer shades being impossible without the help of the pedal.

Soundboard. } The thin board over which
Sounding=board. } the strings of the pianoforte and similar instruments are distended. The vibrating table of any wooden instrument.

Soundholes. The *f* holes in the belly of instruments of the violin family; the round hole in the belly of the guitar, etc. They are designed to afford more perfect communication with the outer air.

Soundpost. A small post, or prop, within a violin, nearly under the bridge.

Sound=register. An apparatus invented in Paris in 1858, by means of which sounds are made to record themselves, whether those of musical instruments or of the voice in singing or speaking.

Soupir (soo-per), *Fr.* A crotchet rest.

Sourdeline (soor'dĭ-len), *Fr.* An Italian bag pipe, or musette.

Sourdement (soord'mänh), *Fr.* In a subdued manner.

Sourdine (soor-den), *Fr.* The name of a harmonium-stop. See, also, *Sordino*.

Sous (soo), *Fr.* Under, below.

Sous=chantre (soo shänhtr'), *Fr.* A sub-chanter.

Sous=dominante (soo dō-mĭ-nänht'), *Fr.* The subdominant, or fourth of the scale.

Sous=médiante (soo mä-dĭ-änht), *Fr.* The submediant, or sixth of the scale.

Sous=tonique (soo tŏn-ek'), *Fr.* The seventh of the scale, or subtonic.

Soutenir (soo-tĕ-ner'), *Fr.* To sustain a sound.

Souvenir (soo-vĕ-ner'), *Fr.* Recollection, reminiscence.

Spaces. The intervals between the lines of the staff.

Spagnoletta (spän-yō-lĕt'tä), *It.* A Spanish dance, a species of minuet.

Spagnuola (spän-yoo-ō'lä), *It.* The guitar.

Spalla (späl'lä), *It.* Shoulder. See *Viola da spalla*.

Spanisch (spän-ĭsh), *Ger.* } In the Span-
Spagnolesco (spän-yō-lĕs'kō), *It.* } ish style.

Spassapensiere (späs-sä-pĕn-sĭ-ä'rĕ), *It.* The jew's-harp.

Spasshaft (späss'häft), *Ger.* Sportively, playfully, merrily.

Spasshaftigkeit (späss'häf-tĭg-kīt), *Ger.* Sportiveness, playfulness.

Spatium spä-shĭ-oom), *Lat.* } A space between
Spazio spä'tsĭ-ō), *It.* } the lines where music is written; a distance, an interval.

Spianato (spe-ä-nä'tō), *It.* Smooth, even; legato.

Spiccato (spĕk-kä'tō), *It.* Separated, pointed, distinct, detached; in violin music it means that the notes are to be played with the point of the bow.

Spiel (spēl), *Ger.* Play, performance.

Spielart (spēl′ärt), *Ger.* Manner of playing, style of performance.

Spielen (spē′l'n), *Ger.* To play on an instrument.

Spieler (spē′lĕr), *Ger.* Performer.

Spielmanieren (spēl′mä-nē′r'n), *Ger.* Playmanners. Instrumental ornaments, graces.

Spinet (spĭn′ĕt), *Eng.* } A stringed instrument, formerly much
Spinett (spĭ-uĕt′), *Ger.*
Spinetta (spĭ-nĕt′tä), *It.* } in use, somewhat similar to the harpsichord, and, like that, consisting of a case, sounding-board, keys, jacks, and a bridge. It was evidently derived from the harp, and was originally called the couched harp, though since denominated spinet, from its quills, which resemble thorns, called in Latin *spinæ*. The spinet was a small harpsichord, in square form, whereas the larger instrument had the shape of a grand piano.

Spirito (spē′rĭ-tō), *It.* Spirit, life, energy.

Spiritosamente spē-rĭ-tō-zä-mĕn′tĕ), } *It.*
Spiritoso (spē-rĭ-tō′zo),
Lively, animated, brisk, spirited.

Spirituale (spē-rĭ-too-ä′lĕ), *It.* } Sacred, spir-
Spirituel (spĭr-ē-too-ăl′), *Fr.* } itual.

Spirituoso (spē-rĭ-too-ō′zō), *It.* See *Spiritoso*.

Spissi gravissimi (spĭs′sĭ grä-vĭs′sĭ-mĭ), *Lat.* Hypatoides—the deep, or bass, sounds of the ancient Greek system.

Spissus (spĭs-soos), *Lat.* Thick; full, referring to intervals.

Spitz (spĭtz), *Ger.* Point.

Spitzflöte (spĭtz-flö′tĕ), *Ger.* } Pointed flute;
Spitzflute (spĭtz-floo′tĕ), an organstop of a soft, pleasing tone, the pipes of which are conical and pointed at the top.

Spitzharfe (spĭtz′här-fĕ), *Ger.* Pointed harp. A small harp with two sounding-boards and two rows of strings.

Spitzquinte (spĭtz-kwĭn′tĕ), *Ger.* An organstop with pointed pipes, sounding a fifth above the foundation stops.

Spondee (spŏn-dā), *Lat.* A musical foot consisting of two long notes or syllables,— —

Sprung (sproong), *Ger.* A skip.

Square B. Name formerly given to B-natural on account of its shape.

Square piano. A piano made in square form, the strings and sounding-board lying horizontally, and the keyboard upon one of the long sides of the instrument. Now nearly obsolete, on account of lack of room for the three stringed unisons which nearly all modern pianos contain, and also because in square pianos each action has to be fitted to the instrument to which it belongs, whereas in uprights the parts are interchangeable.

Sta (stä), *It.* This, as it stands; to be played as written.

Stabat mater (stä′bät mä′tĕr), *Lat.* The Mother stood—a hymn on the crucifixion.

Stabile (stä′bĭ-lĕ), *It.* Firm.

Stac. An abbreviation of Staccato.

Staccare (stäk-kä′rĕ), *It.* To detach, to separate each note.

Staccatissimo (stäk-kä-tĭs′sĭ-mō), *It.* Very much detached; as staccato as possible.

Staccato (stäk-kä′tō, *It.* Detached, distinct, separated from each other.

Staccato delicatamente (stäk-kä′tō dĕl-ĭ-kä-tä-mĕn′tĕ), *It.* In staccato style, lightly and delicately.

Staccato marks. Small dots or dashes placed over or under the notes, thus:

No difference is now made in playing the dotted staccato signs and the pointed ones. Formerly it was taught that the dots represented a half staccato.

Staccato touch. A sudden lifting up of the fingers from the keys, giving to the music a light, detached, airy effect. A staccato touch is one which has an attack, but is not followed by a clinging pressure for maintaining the tone. In general staccato tones are made very short, but occasionally the pedal is used in such a way that the tone has a resonance slightly longer than the repose of the finger upon the key. Upon the violin an ordinary staccato is played with the bow, the resulting tones being, therefore, merely somewhat separated from each other, but of the same quality. The extreme staccato is made pizzicato, as it is called, by plucking the strings with the fingers, whereby the tone is extremely short and of limited sonority.

Stadtmusikus (städt′moo′sĭ-koos), } *Ger.*
Stadtpfeifer (städt′pfī′fĕr),
Town musician.

Staff. The five horizontal and parallel lines on and between which the notes are written. The lines and spaces are named as follows:

————————First added line above.
          Space above.
Fifth line ————————
          Fourth space.
Fourth line ————————
          Third space.
Third line ————————
          Second space.
Second line————————
          First space.
First line ————————
          Space below.
————————First added line below.
————————Second added line below.

Staff, bass. The staff marked with the bass clef.

Staff, tenor. The staff marked with the tenor clef.

Staff, treble. The staff marked with the treble clef.

Stagione (stä-jĭ-ō′nĕ), *It.* The season, the musical season.

Stammaccord (stäm'äk-kŏrd), *Ger.* A radical or fundamental chord, from which others are derived.

Stampita (stäm-pē'tä), *It.* An air, a tune, a song.

Ständchen (ständ'khĕn), *Ger.* A serenade.

Standhaftigkeit (ständ'häf-tĭg-kīt'), *Ger.* Firmness, resolution.

Stand, music. A light frame designed for holding sheets or books, for the convenience of performers.

Stanghetta (stän-gŏt'tä), *It.* A bar-line. The fine line drawn across, and perpendicular to, the staff.

Stanza (stän'tsa), *It.* A verse of a song or hymn.

Stark (stärk), *Ger.* Strong, loud, vigorous.

Starke Stimmen (stär'kĕ stĭm-mĕn), *Ger.* Loud stops; *mit starken Stimmen*, with loud stops.

Stave. Name formerly given to the staff.

Steg (stāgh), *Ger.* The bridge of a violin, etc.

Stem. The thin stroke which is drawn from the head of a note.

Stem, double. A stem drawn both upward and downward from a note, indicating that the no.e belongs to two parts, in one of which it has its natural and appropriate length, as shown by its face, while in the other it may be shorter, corresponding to the notes that follow it.

Stentando (stĕn-tän'dō), *It.* Delaying, retarding.

Stentato (stĕn-tä'tō), *It.* Hard, forced, loud.

Stentorian. Extremely loud.

Stentorophonic tube. A speaking trumpet, so called from Stentor. The stentorophonic horn of Alexander the Great is famous; it was so powerful that he could give orders at a distance of one hundred stadia, which is about twenty English miles, so they say.

Step. The larger diatonic interval between two consecutive tones of the major scale. A step is equal to two half-steps.

Step, half. The smallest interval in the tempered scale, eleven of them making an octave. The interval from any piano-key to the next. Half-steps are sometimes, irrationally, called semitones.

Sterbend (stär'bĕnd), *Ger.* Dying away, the same as morendo.

Steso (stā'zō), *It.* Extended, diffused, large.

Stesso (stĕs'sō), *It.* The same; *l'istésso tempo*, in the same time.

Sticcado (stĭk-kä'dō), *It.*
Sticcato (stĭk-kä'tō), *It.* } An instrument consisting of little bars of wood rounded at the top and resting on the edges of a kind of open box. They gradually increase in length and thickness, are tuned to the notes of the diatonic scale, and are struck with a little ball at the end of a stick.

Sticker. A portion of the connection, in an organ, between the keys or pedals and the valve; a short link attached to a key or pedal, and acting on the backfall.

Stile (stē'lĕ), *It.* Style.

Stile a cappella (stē'lĕ ä käp-pĕl'lä), *It.* In the chapel style.

Stile grandioso (stē'lĕ grän-dĭ-ō'zō), *It.* In a grand style of composition, or performance.

Stile rigoroso (stē'lĕ rĭ-gō-rō'zō), *It.* In a rigid, strict style.

Still (stĭll), *Ger.* Calmly, quietly.

Stillgedakt (stĭll-gĕ-däkt'), *Ger.* A stopped diapason, of a quiet tone.

Stilo (stē'lō), *It.* Style, manner of composition or performance.

Stilo alla cappella (stē'lō äl' ä l ä-pĕl'lä), *It.* In the church or chapel style.

Stilo di recitativo (stē'lō dē rä-tshĕ-tä-tē'vō), *It.* In style of recitative.

Stimme (stĭm'mĕ), *Ger.* The voice, sound; also the soundpost in a violin, etc.; also a part in vocal or instrumental music; also an organ-stop or register.

Stimmen (stĭm'm'n), *Ger. pl.* Parts or voices; also organ-stops.

Stimmführung (stĭm'füh-roong), *Ger.* Voice movement.

Stimmgabel (stĭm'gä'b'l), *Ger.* Tuning-fork.

Stimmhammer (stĭm'häm'mĕr), *Ger.* Tuning-key, tuning-hammer.

Stimmhorn (stĭm'hŏrn), *Ger.* Tuning-cone for metal organ-pipes.

Stimmstock (stĭm'stŏk), *Ger.* The soundpost of a violin, etc.

Stimmumfang (stĭm'oom-fäng), *Ger.* Compass of a voice.

Stimmung (stĭm'moong), *Ger.* Tuning, tune, tone.

Stimmweite (stĭm'wī-tĕ), *Ger.* Voice-breadth, compass.

Stinguendo (stĭn-guĕn'dō), *It.* Dying away, becoming extinct.

Stiracchiato (stē-räk-kĭ-ä'tō), *It.* } Stretched,
Stirato (stē-rä'tō), *It.* } forced, retarded. See *Allargando*.

Stonante (stō-nän'tĕ), *It.* Discordant, out of tune.

Stop. A register, or row of pipes, in an organ; on the violin, etc., it means the pressure of the finger upon the string.

Stop, bassoon. A reed stop in an organ, resembling the bassoon in quality of tone.

Stop, claribel. A stop similar to the clarinet stop.

Stop, clarion, *or* **Octave trumpet.** A stop resembling the tone of a trumpet, but an octave higher than the trumpet stop.

Stop, cornet. A stop consisting of five pipes to each note.

Stop, cremona. A reed stop in unison with the diapasons.

Stop, double diapason. An open set of pipes tuned an octave below the diapasons.

Stop, double trumpet. The most powerful reed stop in the organ, the pipes being of the same length as the double diapason, to which it is tuned in unison.

Stop, dulciana A stop of peculiar sweetness of tone, which it chiefly derives from the bodies of its pipes being longer and smaller than those of the pipes of other stops.

Stop, faggotto. The bassoon stop.

Stop, fifteenth. A stop which derives its name from its pitch, or scale, being fifteen notes above that of the diapason.

Stop, flute. An organ-stop, resembling in tone a flute or flageolet.

Stop, hautboy. A reed stop having a tone in imitation of the hautboy.

Stop, larigot, *or* **Octave twelfth.** A stop the scale of which is an octave above the twelfth. It is only used in the full organ.

Stop, mixture, *or* **furniture.** A stop comprising two or more ranks of pipes shriller than those of the sesquialtera, and only calculated to be used together with that and other pipes.

Stop, nazard. Twelfth stop.

Stop, open diapason. A metallic stop which commands the whole scale of the organ, and which is called open, in contradistinction to the stop diapason, the pipes of which are closed at the top.

Stop, organ. A collection of pipes, similar in tone and quality, running through the whole, or a great part, of the compass of the organ; a register.

Stopped. Closed with a stopper. Applied to certain organ-pipes.

Stop, principal. A metallic stop, originally distinguished by that name, because holding, in point of pitch, the middle station between the diapason and the fifteenth, it forms the standard for tuning the other stops. In German organs the principal is the open diapason.

Stop, salicional. A string stop.

Stops, compound. An assemblage of several pipes in an organ, three, four, five, or more to each key, all answering at once to the touch of the performer.

Stops, draw. Stops in an organ placed on each side of the rows of keys in front of the instrument, by moving which the player opens or closes the stops within the organ.

Stop, sesquialtera. A stop resembling the mixture, running through the scale of the instrument, and consisting of three, four, and sometimes five ranks of pipes, tuned in thirds, fifths, and eighths.

Stops, foundation. The diapasons and principal, to which the other stops, be they few or many, are tuned, and which are absolutely required in an organ.

Stops, mutation. In an organ the twelfth, tierce, and their octaves.

Stop, solo. A stop intended for solo use.

Stops, Organ. A stop in an organ is properly a complete set of pipes of uniform tone-quality. There are four varieties of tone, called diapason, string, flute, and reed. The diapasons are metal pipes of large body and clear, solid sound, which in modern organs has rather more string-quality than formerly, because it is found that this quality blends better and pleases the ear. The diapason class includes the open diapasons, principal or octave, the fifteenth, and the mixtures. The pedal diapasons are sometimes made of wood, in order to save expense, but the tone is not so good. The string family of stops have metal pipes, preferably of tin or a large percentage of tin, small diameter, and frequently with a small hole at a certain distance, for promoting the formation of the overtones, upon which the cutting quality of the string tone depends. The names usually given them are Gamba, Keraulophon, Salicional.

The flute stops are of wood, like the stopped diapason, claribel, etc., or of metal voiced like wood, such as the flute harmonique, flauto traverso, etc. The reed stops are sounded by means of a striking or a free reed (which see), and are commonly named oboe, cornopeon, trumpet, vox angelica, voxhumana, etc.

Mixture stops are compound stops, producing octaves of the fundamental, and, generally, one fifth, voiced like a flute. A mixture having three elements is called a three-rank mixture. This is the usual number, but five ranks are not infrequent. The mixture stops are used only in full organ passages, and are intended to reinforce the upper partial tones, which it is not easy to secure from pipes in sufficient volume.

The variety of names of organ-stops is excessive, but necessitated by the number of stops in large modern organs, often reaching to more than one hundred. Hence the stops of any given family are shaded from each other by degrees which are almost imperceptible, except to an expert. However many the stops may be in number, there are only these four varieties of tone.

The name "stop" is sometimes applied to the draw-knobs, by which the stops are brought into connection with the keyboard, or cut off.

Stops, reed. Stops consisting of pipes, upon the end of which are fixed thin, narrow plates of brass, which, being vibrated by the wind from the bellows, produce a reedy brilliancy of tone.

Stop, stopped diapason. A stop the pipes of which are generally made of wood, and its bass, up to middle C, always of wood. They are only half as long as those of the open diapason, and are stopped at the upper end with wooden stoppers, or plugs, which render the tone more soft and mellow than that of the open diapason.

Stop, stopped unison. The stopped diapason stop.

Stop, tierce. A stop tuned a major third higher than the fifteenth, and only employed in the full organ.

Stop, treble forte. A stop applied to a melodeon, or reed organ, by means of which the treble part of the instrument may be increased in power, while the bass remains subdued.

Stop, tremolo. A contrivance by means of which a flue, tremulous effect is given to some of the registers of an organ.

Stop, trumpet. A stop so called because its tone is imitative of a trumpet. In large organs it generally extends through the whole compass.

Stop, twelfth. A metallic stop so denominated from its being tuned twelve notes above the diapason. This stop, on account of its pitch, or tuning, can never be used alone; the open diapason, stopped diapason, principal, and fifteenth, are the best qualified to accommodate it to the ear.

Stop, vox humana. A stop the tone of which resembles the human voice.

Storta (stŏr′tä), *It.* A serpent. See that word.

Stortina (stŏr-tē′nä), *It.* A small serpent.

Str. Abbreviation for Strings.

Straccinato (strä-tshī-nä′tō), *It.* See *Strascinato*.

Stradivari. The name of a very superior make of violin, so called from their makers, Stradivarius (father and son), who made them at Cremona, Italy, about A. D. 1650.

Strain. A portion of music divided off by a double bar.

Strascicando (strä-shī-kän′dō), *It.* Dragging the time, trailing, playing slowly.

Strascinando (strä-shī-nän′dō), *It.* Dragging the time, playing slowly.

Strascinando l'arco (strä-shī-nän′dō lär-kō). Keeping the bow of the violin close to the strings, as in executing the tremolando, so as to slur or bind the notes closely.

Strascinato (strä-shī-nä′tō), *It.* Dragged along, played slowly.

Strascino (strä-shē′nō), *It.* A drag. This grace, or embellishment, is chiefly confined to vocal music, and only used in slow passages. It consists of an unequal and descending motion, and generally includes from eight to twelve notes, and requires to be introduced and executed with great taste and judgment.

Strathspey. A lively Scotch dance, in common time.

Stravagante (strä-vä-gän′tĕ), *It.* Extravagant, odd, fantastic.

Stravaganza (strä-vä-gän′tsä), *It.* Extravagance, eccentricity.

Street organ. Hand organ.

Streich (strīkh), *Ger.* String. Used in composition, as, *Streichinstrumente*, stringed instruments; *Streichquartet*, stringed quartet, etc.

Streng (strĕng), *Ger.* Strict, severe, rigid.

Strenge gebunden (strĕn′ghĕ ghĕ-boon′d'n), *Ger.* Strictly legato, exceedingly smooth.

Streng im Tempo (strĕng ĭm tĕm′pō), *Ger.* Strictly in time.

Strepito (strā′pĭ-tō), *It.* Noise.

Strepitosamente (strā-pĭ-tō-sä-mĕn′tĕ), *It.* With a great noise.

Strepitoso (strā-pĭ-tō′zō), *It.* Noisy, boisterous.

Stretta (strĕt′tä), *It.* A concluding passage, coda, or finale, in an opera, taken in quicker time to enhance the effect.

Stretto (strĕt′tō), *It.* Pressed, close, contracted; formerly used to denote that the movement indicated was to be performed in a quick, concise style. In fugue-writing that part where the subject and answer succeed one another very rapidly.

Strich (strīkh), *Ger.* Stroke, the manner of bowing.

Stricharten (strīkh är-t'n), *Ger.* Different ways of bowing.

Strict canon. A canon in which the imitation is complete, each voice exactly repeating the other.

Strict composition. A composition in which voices alone are employed; that which rigidly adheres to the rules of art.

Strict fugue. Where the fugal form and its laws are rigidly observed.

Strict inversion. The same as simple inversion, but requiring that whole tones should be answered by whole tones, and semitones by semitones.

Strictly inverted imitation. A form of imitation in which half and whole tones must be precisely answered in contrary motion.

Strict style. A style in which a rigid adherence to the rules of art is observed.

Strident (strē-dänh), *Fr.* } Sharp, shrill,
Stridente (strē-dĕn′tĕ), *It.* } acute.
Stridevole (strē-dĕ-vō′lĕ), *It.* }

Striking reed. That kind of reed pipe in an organ in which the tongue strikes against the tube in producing the tone.

String band. A band of stringed instruments only.

Stringed instruments. Instruments whose sounds are produced by striking or drawing strings, or by the friction of a bow drawn across them.

Stringendo (strĕn-gĕn′dō), *It.* Pressing, accelerating the time.

String pendulum. A Weber chronometer.

String quartet. A composition for four instruments of the violin species, as two violins, a viola, and violoncello.

Strings. Wires, or chords, used in musical instruments, which, upon being struck or drawn upon, produce tones; the stringed instruments in a band or orchestra.

Strings, latten. Wires made of a composition consisting of copper and zinc.

Strings, open. The strings of an instrument when not pressed.

Strisciando (strē-shĭ-än'dō), *It.* Gliding, slurring, sliding smoothly from one note to another.

Strofa (strō'fä), **Strofe** (strō'fĕ), *It.* } A strophe, stanza.

Strohfiedel (strō'fē-d'l), *Ger.* Straw fiddles. A xylophone composed of rods of wood, which, when struck by a little mallet, give out musical sounds.

Stroke, diagonal. A transverse heavy stroke, having a dot each side of it, denoting that the previous measure or the previous group of notes in the same measure is to be repeated.

Stroke, double. Two strokes or dashes drawn over or under a semibreve or through the stem of a minim or crotchet, implying that such note must be divided into as many semiquavers as are equivalent to it in duration.

Stroke, single. A stroke or dash drawn over or und r a semibreve, or through the stem of a minim or crotchet, implying that such a note must be divided into as many quavers as are equivalent to it in duration.

Stroke, transverse. A heavy stroke placed above a fundamental note to indicate the intervals of changing notes, and also used for anticipation in an upper part.

Stroke, triple. Three strokes or dashes placed over or under a semibreve, or through the stem of a minim or crotchet, implying that such note must be divided into as many demisemiquavers as are equivalent to it in duration.

Strombazzata (ström-bät-tsä'tä), **Strombettata** (ström-bĕt-tä'tä), *It.* } The sound of a trumpet.

Strombettare (ström-bĕt-tä'rĕ), *It.* To sound or play on the trumpet.

Strombettiere (ström-bĕt-tĭ-ā'rĕ), *It.* A trumpeter.

Stromentato (strŏ-mĕn-tä'tŏ), *It.* Instrumented, scored for an orchestra.

Stromenti (strō-mĕn'tē), *It. pl.* Musical instruments.

Stromenti da flato (strō-mĕn'tē dä fē-ä'tō), **Stromenti di vento** (strō-mĕn'tē dē vĕn'tō), } *It. pl.* Wind instruments.

Stromenti d'arco (strō-mĕn'tē d'är'kō), *It. pl.* Instruments played with the bow.

Stromenti di rinforzo (strō-mĕn'tē dē rīn-fŏr'tsō), *It. pl.* Instruments employed to support or strengthen a performance.

Stromento (strō-mĕn'tō), *It.* An instrument.

Strophe. In the ancient theater, that part of a song or dance around the altar which was performed by turning from the right to the left. It was succeeded by the antistrophe, in a contrary direction. Hence, in ancient lyric poetry, the former of two stanzas was called the strophe, and the latter the antistrophe. The epode, or aftersong, followed after.

Stück (stük), *Ger.* Piece, air, tune, musical entertainment.

Stückchen (stük'khĕn), *Ger.* Little airs or tunes.

Studien (stoo'dĭ-ĕn), *Ger. pl.* Studies.

Studio (stoo'dĭ-ō), *It.* } A study, an exercise intended for the practice of some particular difficulty.

Stufe (stoo'fĕ), *Ger.* Step, degree.

Stufe der Tonleiter (stoo'fĕ dĕr tōn'lī-tĕr), *Ger.* A degree of the scale.

Stufen ((stoo'f'n), *Ger.* Steps or degrees.

Stufenweise (stoo'f'n-wī'sĕ), *Ger.* By degrees.

Stürmisch (stür'mīsh), *Ger.* Impetuously, boisterously, furiously.

Stürze (stür'tse), *Ger.* The bell of wind instruments.

Style. That manner of composition or performance on which the effect chiefly, if not wholly, depends. The distinction "strict" and "free" style is often made. By strict style is meant a manner of composition in which a certain number of voice-parts are carried through in accordance with the principles of this form of composition, which substantially are that only triads and their first inversions are to be used, and that no dissonances are employed, except those proper to strict counterpoint. In free composition, or style, the number of voices may vary from strain to strain, and dissonances are freely introduced. Accompaniments must be obligato, etc.

Stylo (stē'lō), *It.* Style.

Stylo dramatico (stē'lō drä-mä'tĭ-kō), *It.* In dramatic style.

Stylo ecclesiastico (stē'lo ek-klä-zĭ-äs'tĭ-kō), *It.* In church style.

Stylo fantastico (stē'lō fän-täs'tĭ-kō), *It.* An easy, humorous style free from all restraint.

Stylo rappresentativo (stē'lō räp-prä-zĕn-tä-tē'vō), *It.* The name originally applied to music written for opera, meaning that the chief office of the music was to represent the poetry. At first this meant simply the spirit of the declamation; later the "representation" was enlarged to the point where music itself became elaborated in order to give fuller representation to the spirit of the poem and the dramatic situation, no less than of the words merely.

Stylo recitativo (stē'lō rā-tsĭ-tä-tē'vō), *It.* In the style of a recitative.

ä *arm*, å *add*, ā *ale*, ĕ *end*, ē *eve*, ĭ *ill*, ī *isle*, ō *old*, ŏ *odd*, oo *moon*, ŭ *but*, ü *Fr. sound*, kh *Ger. ch*, nh *nasal*.

Su (soo), *It.* Above, upon.

Suabeflute. An organ-stop of pure liquid tone, not so loud as the Waldflute; it was invented by William Hill, of London.

Suave (soo-ä'vĕ, *It.*
Suave (soo-ä'vĕ), *Sp.*
Suave (swäv), *Fr.* } Sweet, mild, agreeable, pleasant.

Suavemente (soo-ä-vĕ-mĕn'tĕ), *Sp.*
Suavemente (soo-ä-vĕ-men'tĕ), *It.*
Suavita (soo-ä-vĭ-tä'), *It.* } Suavity, sweetness, delicacy.

Sub (sŭb), *Lat.* Under, below, beneath.

Subbass (soob'bäss), *Ger.* Underbass; an organ register in the pedals, usually a double-stopped bass of 32- or 16-feet tone, though sometimes open wood-pipes of 16 feet, as at Haarlem; the groundbass.

Subbourdon. An organ-stop of 32-feet tone, with stopped pipes.

Subdominant. The fourth note of any scale or key.

Subitamente (soo-bĭ-tä-mĕn'tĕ), *It.*
Subito (soo'bĭ tŏ), } Suddenly, immediately, at once.

Subject. A melody or theme; a leading text or motivo.

Subject, counter. The counterpoint of the subject, which every voice in a fugue performs after giving out the subject.

Submediant. The sixth tone of the scale.

Suboctave. An organ-coupler producing the octave below.

Subprincipal. Underprincipal; that is, below the pedal diapason pitch; in German organs this is a double open bass stop of 32-feet scale.

Subsemitone. The semitone below the keyboard, the sharp seventh of any key.

Subsemitonium modi (soob-sĕm-ĭ-tō'nĭ-oom mō'dĭ). *Lat.* The leading note.

Subtonic. Under the tonic; the semitone immediately below the tonic.

Succentor (sook-sĕn'tŏr), *Lat.* A subchanter, a deputy of the precentor. A bass singer.

Sudden modulation. Modulation to a distant key, without any intermediate chord to prepare the ear.

Suffocato (soof - fō - kä' tō), *It.* Suffocated. Choked, as if with grief.

Sui (soo'ĭ), *It.* Sul.

Suite (swēt), *Fr.* A series, a succession; *une suite de pièces*, a series of lessons, or pieces.

Suite (swēt), *Fr.* A series, a set; *i. e.*, a series, or set, of pieces (suite de pièces). In the earlier part of the eighteenth century, and anterior to that time, a suite consisted in most cases of dances, to which, however, was often added a prelude as an introductory first piece. Other pieces than dances were also occasionally interspersed—for instance, in some of J. S. Bach's suites we find an air. As to the dances, they were artistically treated, differing from those intended to be danced to, both in form and style, and not unfrequently also in character. Bach's Suites Anglaises are all open with a prelude, but his Suites Françaises are without such an introductory piece. The first of Bach's Suites Anglaises contains the following pieces: (1) Prelude; (2) Allemande; (3) Courante; (4) Sarabande; (5) Bourée; (6) Gigue. Instead of the bourée we find in others of the master's suites a gavotte, or a menuet, or a passepied. The allemande is generally the first of the dances; the order and selection of the other dances were less settled, but the courante and sarabande were very common as the second and third constituents, as was also the gigue as the last. Other dances to be met with in suites are the loure, anglaise, polonaise, pavane, etc. As a rule the pieces are all in the same key. Their number differed. In recent times composers have taken the suite again into favor. But the modern suite is more varied than the old; its constituents comprise not only dances of the past and present, but also characteristic pieces of all sorts, even fugues. It need hardly be added that the moderns do not, like their forefathers, adhere to unity of key.

Suivez (swē-vă), *Fr.* Follow, attend, pursue; the accompaniment must be accommodated to the singer or solo player.

Sujet (sü-zhä), *Fr.* A subject, melody, or theme.

Sul (sol),
Sull' (sool), *It.* } On, upon the.
Sulla (sool'lä),

Sul A. On the A string.

Sul D. On the D string.

Sulla mezza corda (sool'lä mĕt'sä kŏr'dä), *It.* On the middle of the string.

Sulla tastiera (sool-lä täs-tĭ-ā'rä), *It.* Upon the keys, upon the fingerboard.

Sul ponticello (sool pŏn-tĭ-tshĕl'lō), *It.* On or near the bridge.

Sumara. A species of flute having two pipes, common in Turkey; the shorter pipe is used for playing airs, and the longer for a continued bass.

Summational tones. See *Resultant tones.*

Sumpunjah (soom-poon-yäh), *Heb.* The dulcimer of the ancients. It was a wind instrument made of reeds; by the Syrians called samboujah and by the Italians zampogna.

Sumsen (soom's'n), *Ger.* To hum.

Suo loco (soo'ō lō'kō), *It.* In its own or usual place.

Suonantina (soo-ō-nän-tē'nä), *It.* A short, easy sonata.

Suonare (soo-ō-nä'rĕ), *It.* To play upon an instrument.

Suonare le campane (soo-ō-nä'rĕ lĕ käm-pä'nĕ), *It.* To ring the bells.

Suonar sordamente (soo-ō-när' sor-dä-mĕn'tĕ). *It.* To play softly.

ă *arm*, ă *add*, ā *ale*, ĕ *end*, ē *eve*, ĭ *ill*, ī *isle*, ŏ *old*, ŏ *odd*, oo *moon*, ŭ *but*, ü *Fr. sound*, kh *Ger. ch.* nh *nasal.*

Suonata (soo-ō-nä′tä), *It.* A sonata.
Suoni (soo-ō′nī), *It. pl.* Sounds.
Suoni armonichi (soo-ō′nī är-mō′nī-kī), *It. pl.* Harmonic sounds.
Suono armonioso (soo-ō′nō är-mō-nī-ō′zō), *It.* Harmonious sounds.
Superano (soo-pĕr-ä′nō), *Sp.* Soprano.
Superdominant. The note in the scale next above the dominant.
Superfluous intervals. Those which are one semitone more than the perfect, or major, intervals. See *Augmented intervals*.
Superoctave. An organ-stop tuned two octaves, or a fifteenth, above the diapasons; also a coupler producing the octave above.
Supersus (soo-pĕr′soos), *Lat.* Name formerly given to trebles when their station was very high in the scale.
Supertonic. } The note
Supertonique (sü-pĕr-tŏnh-ĕk′), *Fr.* } next above the tonic, or key-note; the second note of the scale.
Supplichevole (soop-plī-kä′vō-lĕ),
Supplichevolmente (soop-plī-kä-vōl-mĕn′tĕ)
It. In a supplicatory manner.
Sur (soor), *It.* } On, upon, over.
Sur (sür), *Fr.* }
Surdeline. The old Italian bagpipe, a large and rather complicated instrument consisting of many pipes and conduits for the conveyance of the wind, with keys for the opening of the holes by the pressure of the fingers, and inflated by means of bellows, which the performer blows with his arm at the same time that he fingers the pipe.
Sur la quatrième corde (sür lä kät-rī-äm kŏrd), *Fr.* On the fourth string.
Sur la seconde corde (sür lä sä-kŏnhd kŏrd), *Fr.* Upon the second string.
Sur una corda (soor oo′nä kŏr′dä), *It.* } Upon
Sur une corde (sür ünh kŏrd), *Fr.* } one string.
Suspended cadence. See *Interrupted Cadence.*
Suspension. The clashing effect of a dissonant tone which having been a consonant tone in one chord is retained, suspended, after the beginning of the next following chord, in which it is dissonant. The dissonance presently subsides, or gives place to the consonant tone (generally one degree below), which it had displaced. This disappearance of the dissonance is called its *resolution.* The appearance of the proposed dissonant tone as one of the regular members of the previous chord is called its *preparation.*
Suspension, double. A suspension retaining two notes, and requiring a double preparation and resolution.
Suspension, single. A suspension retaining but one note, and requiring only a single preparation and resolution.

Suspension, triple. A suspension formed by suspending a dominant or diminished seventh on the tonic, mediant, or dominant, of the key.
Süss (süss), *Ger.* Sweetly.
Süssflöte (süss′flö′tĕ), *Ger.* In organs, the soft flute.
Sussurando (soos-soo-rän′dō), *It.* } Whisper-
Sussurante (soos-soo-rän′tĕ), } ing, murmuring.
Sussuration. A whispering; a soft, murmuring sound.
Sustained. Notes are said to be sustained when their sound is continued through their whole time or length. See *Sostenuto.*
Svegliato (sväl-yī-ä′tō), *It.* Brisk, lively, sprightly.
Svegliatojo (svĕl-yī-ä-tō′yō), *It.* An alarm bell.
Svelto (svĕl′tō), *It.* Free, light, easy.
Swell. A gradual increase of sound.
Swell organ. In organs having three rows of keys, the third, or upper, row controlling a number of pipes enclosed in a box, which may be gradually opened or shut, and thus the tone increased or diminished by degrees.
Swell pedal. That which raises the dampers from the strings or opens the swell-blinds of the organ.
Syllables, Guidonian. The syllables ut, re, mi, fa, sol, la, used by Guido for his system of tetrachords.
Symbal. See *Cymbal.*
Sympathetic strings. Strings which were formerly fastened under the fingerboard of the viola d'amore, beneath the bridge, and, being tuned to the strings above, vibrated with them and strengthened the tone.
Symphonia (sĭm-fō-nī-ä), *Gr.* Agreement of sounds. The name was applied at one time to a stringed instrument of the hurdygurdy variety. A symphony.
Symphonic. In the style, or manner, of a symphony; harmonious; agreeing in sound.
Symphonie (sänh-fō-nē), *Fr.* } A form of com-
Symphonie (sĭm-fō-nē), *Ger.* } position for
Symphony (sĭm fō-ny), *Eng.* } orchestra (somewhat enlarged), of an elevated and noble style. There is no settled order of movements in a symphony, but in general (with or without a slow introduction) the first movement is allegro, in the form of a sonata-piece; the second is a slow movement; the third a scherzo or other playful movement, and the fourth a finale, which is more often a sonata-piece. The variety of instruments in a modern orchestra affords the symphony unlimited opportunities for poetical and pleasing effects of tone color and contrast. The greatest masters of symphony are Beethoven, Schubert, Schumann, and Brahms.
The name symphony is applied in England to orchestral or other interludes and preludes of songs. In this sense Handel

ä *arm*, ă *add*, ä *ale*, ĕ *end*, ē *eve*, ĭ *ill*, ī *isle*, ŏ *old*, ŏ *odd*, oo *moon*, ŭ *but*, ü *Fr. sound*, kh *Ger. ch*, nh *nasal.*

uses it in the "Messiah" as "Pastoral Symphony," which would now be called an intermezzo.

Symphonienseser (sĭm-fō-nĭ-ĕn-sĕ-sĕr), *Ger.* Symphonist; a composer of symphonies.

Symphonious. Harmonious; agreeing in sound.

Symphonische Dichtung (sĭm-fō'nĭ-shĕ dĭkh'-toong), *Ger.* A symphonic poem. An orchestral composition with a poetic basis (a program) and of a free form—the latter being determined by the subject, not by rule and custom. Liszt is the originator of the kind and the name. Before him Berlioz had written symphonies with a poetic basis and differing more or less from the orthodox compositions of that appellation. Nevertheless Liszt was an originator of more than the name, for his symphonic p ems are peculiar in various ways, especially in these two: their continuity (they are not broken up into separate divisions) and the extensive employment of transformation of themes (melodic, harmonic, and rhythmic, modification of themes for the purpose of changing their expression). This latter serves to give unity to the various constituents of the composition.

Symphonist. A composer of symphonies. In France the term symphonist is also applied to a composer of church-music.

Symposia. An epithet generally applicable to cheerful and convivial compositions, as catches, glees, rounds, etc.

Syncopate (sĭn-kō-pā'tä)
Syncopate (sĭn-kō-pä'tĕ), *It.* } Syncopated.
Syncopato (sĭn-kō-pä'tō),

Syncopatio (sĭn-kō-pä'tsĭ-ō), *Lat.* } A rhythmic disturbance consisting essentially of concealing the true accent by the device of beginning a tone on the weak pulse or part of a pulse, and prolonging it across the strong pulse or part of a pulse, thus depriving the strong rhythmic place of its proper accent. The note so begun, and prolonged across a point where an accent would be expected, is said to be syncopated.
Syncopation, *Eng.*
Syncope (säuh-kŏp), *Fr.*

In pianoforte-music, when one hand has syncopation, the other generally has the true accent. Syncopated notes are accented, the accent being anticipated from the strong pulse across which they sync pate. There are a few examples, in modern music, of syncopating forms in the accompaniment where no accent is implied. (For instance in Schumann's "Warum.")

Syncoper (sänh-kō-pā), *Fr.* } To syn-
Syncopiren (sĭn-kō-pē'r'n), *Ger.* } copate.

Système (sĭs-tăm), *Fr.* A system.

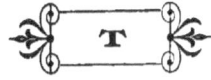

T. Abbreviation of Tempo; also of Tenor.
Taballó (tä-bäl'lō), *It.* A kettledrum.
Tabar (tä-bär), *It.* A small drum; a tabor.
Tablatura (täb-lä-too'rä), *It.* } A term for-
Tablature (tä-blä-tür), *Fr.* } merly ap-
Tablature (täb'lä-tshŭr), *Eng.* } plied to the
Tabulatur (tä' boo-lä-toor), *Ger.* } totality or general assemblage of the signs used in music; so that to understand the notes, clefs, and other necessary marks, and to be able to sing at sight, was to be skilled in the tablature. More particularly applied, however, to a curious notation for the lute, viols, and wind instruments invented between A. D. 1400 and 1500. It consisted of lines and bars, with signs in the spaces and above the staff. There were as many lines as strings upon the instrument noted. The lute had six frets, which the tablatura indicated by letters, *a* for open string, *b* for first fret, *c* for second, etc. The tablature had these letters for all the stopping required, bars for measure, and signs of value for duration. The tablature for wind instruments was different, but upon similar principles, indicating the mechanism of performing the tones rather than the tones themselves.

Table d'harmonie (tăbl d'är-mō-nē), *Fr.* A table or diagram of chords, intervals, etc.
Table d'instrument (tăbl d'änh-strü-mänh), *Fr.* The belly of an instrument.
Table songs. Songs for male voices formerly much in vogue in German glee clubs.
Tabor. A small drum, generally used to accompany the pipe or fife in dances. Probably a tambourine without jingles.
Taboret. A small tabor.
Tabourin (tä-boo-rănh), *Fr.* A tabor, or tambourine—a shallow drum with but one head.
Tabret. A kind of drum used by the ancient Hebrews.
Tacet (tä'sĕt), *or,* **Tacent** (tä-tsĕnt), *Lat.* }
Tace (tä'tshĕ), *It.*
Taci (tä'tshĭ), *It.*
Taciasi (tä-tshĭ-ä'zĭ), *It.*
Be silent; meaning that certain instruments are not to play; as, *violino tacet*, the violin is not to play; *oboe tacet*, let the oboe be silent.
Tact (täkt), *Ger.* See *Takt*.
Tactus (täk'toos), *L-t.* In the ancient music the stroke of the hand by which the time was measured or beaten.

Tafelmusik (tä'f'l-moo-sĭk'), *Ger.* Table-music; music sung at the table, as part-songs, glees, etc.

Taille (tä-ŭh), *Fr.* The tenor part; the viola.

Taille de violon (tä-ŭh dŭh vē-ō-lōnh), *Fr.* The viola, or tenor violin.

Tailpiece. That piece of ebony to which the violin, viola, etc., are fastened.

Takt (täkt), *Ger.* Time, measure.

Taktart (täkt'ärt), *Ger.* Species of time, common or triple.

Taktfest (täkt'fĕst), *Ger.* Steadiness in keeping time.

Taktführer (läkt-füh-rĕr), *Ger.* A conductor; leader.

Taktieren (läk'tĕr-ĕn), *Ger.* To direct in measure.

Taktlinie (täkt'lē-nĭ-ĕ), *Ger.* } A bar-line;
Taktstrich (täkt'strĭkh), *Ger.* } the lines which mark the bars.

Taktmässig (täkt'mä'sĭg), *Ger.* Conformable to the time.

Taktzeichen (täkt'tsī'kh'n), *Ger.* The figures, or signs, at the beginning of a piece, to show the time.

Talabalacco (tä-lä-bä-läk'kō), *It.* A species of Moorish drum.

Talon (tä-lōnh), *Fr.* The heel of the bow; that part nearest the nut.

Tambour (tänh-boor), *Fr.* Drum; the great drum; also a drummer.

Tamboura. An ancient instrument of the guitar kind used in the East.

Tambour de basque (tänh-boor dŭh bäsk), *Fr.* A tabour, or tabor; a tambourine.

Tambouret (tänh-boo-rā), *Fr.* } A timbrel, a
Tambourine, *Eng.* } small instrument of percussion, like the head of a drum, with little bells placed round its rim to increase the noise.

Tambourine (tänh-boo-rēn). *Fr.* A species of dance, accompanied by the tambourine; also a tambourine.

Tamboureur (tänh-boo-rē-nŭr), *Fr.* Drummer, tambourine-player.

Tambour major. See *Drum major.*

Tambourello (täm-boo-rāl'lō), *It.* } A tam-
Tambouretto (üm-boo-rāt'to), } bourine; a little drum.

Tambourone (täm-boo-rō'nĕ), *It.* The great drum.

Tamburaccio (täm-boo-rät'tshĭ-ō), *It.* A large old drum; a tabor.

Tamburino (täm-boo-rē'nō), *It.* A little drum; also a drummer.

Tamburo (täm-boo'rō), *It.* A drum.

Tamtam. An Indian instrument of percussion; a species of drum, or tambourine.

Tändelnd (tän'dĕlnd), *Ger.* In a playful manner.

Tanedor (tä-nĕ-thōr'), *Sp.* Player on a musical instrument.

Tangent (tän'ghĕnt), *Ger.* The jack of a harpsichord.

Tantino (tän-tē'nō), *It.* A little.

Tanto (tän'tō), *It.* So much; as much; *allegro non tanto*, not so quick, not too quick.

Tantum ergo (tän'toom är'gō), *Lat.* A hymn sung at the Benediction in the Roman Catholic service.

Tanz (tŭnts), *Ger.* A dance.

Tänze (tän'tsĕ), *Ger. pl.* Dances.

Tänzer (tän'tsĕr), *Ger.* A dancer.

Tänzerin (tän'tsĕ-rĭn), *Ger.* A female dancer.

Tanzkunst (tänts'koonst), *Ger.* The art of dancing.

Tanzstück (tans-stük), *Ger.* A dance tune.

Tap. A drum-beat of a single note.

Tarabouk. A musical instrument used by the Turks, formed by drawing a parchment over the bottom of a large earthen vessel.

Tarantella (tär-rän-tĕl'lä), *It.* A swift, delirious sort of Italian dance in 6-8 time. The form has been adopted by many of the modern composers, as Liszt, Chopin, etc. So called because long regarded by the peasantry as a remedy for the bite of the tarantula spider.

Tardamente (tär-dä-mĕn'tĕ), *It.* Slowly.

Tardando (tär-dän'dō), *It.* Lingering, retarding the time.

Tardo (tär'dō), *It.* Tardy, slow.

Tartini's tones. The resultant or combination tones, which are formed when two notes are sounded together upon the violin. Tartini first observed them, and as they always represent the natural root of the tones which sound them, he made them serve him as guides to the correct stopping of double touches in the high positions.

Tastame (täs-tä-mĕ), *It.* } The keys or
Tastatur (täs'tä-toor), *Ger.* } keyboard of a
Tastatura (täs-tä-too'rä), *Ger.* } pianoforte, or-
Tastiera (täs-tī-ā'rä), *It.* } gan, etc.

Taste. A sympathetic appreciation of the refined, intelligent, and noble in any art.

Taste (täs'tĕ), *Ger.* } The touch of any instru-
Tasto (täs'tō), *It.* } ment; hence, also, a key, or thing, touched.

Tastenbrett (täs't'n-brĕt), *Ger.* Keyboard of a pianoforte, etc.

Tasto solo (täs'tō sō'lō), *It.* One key alone; in organ or pianoforte music this means a note without harmony, the bass notes over or under which it is written are not to be accompanied with chords.

Tatto (tä'tō), *It.* The touch.

Tattoo. The beat of a drum at night calling the soldiers to their quarters.

Teatro (tä-ä'trō), *It.* A theater, playhouse.

Teatro di gran cartello (tä-ä'trō dē grän kär-tĕl'lō), *It.* Lyric theater of the first rank.

Technic. That part of the art of playing, performing, or working which can be taught. Upon instruments the technic includes the application of the fingers, their expertness, and the means for making them expert, and the mechanism of producing tones of different qualities. In composition the technic includes all the practical principles, and expertness in applying them. With reference to piano-playing, the term technic was formerly restricted to finger-facility merely, whereas at present it applies to all parts of the mechanism of playing, including every sort of movement and the art of differentiating tones.

Technik (těkh'nĭk), *Ger.* Technic.

Technisch (těkh'nĭsh), *Ger.* Technical; this word is also used to indicate mechanical proficiency, as regards execution.

Tedesca (tĕ-dĕs'kä), } *It.* } German; *alla tedesca*, in the German style.
Tedesco (tĕ-dĕs'kō),

Te Deum laudamus (tĕ dā'oom lou-dä'moos), *Lat.* We praise Thee; a canticle, or hymn of praise, often attributed to St. Ambrosius.

Telltale. A movable piece of metal, bone, or ivory, attached to an organ, indicating by its position the amount of wind supplied by the bellows.

Tema (tā'mä), *It.* A theme or subject; a melody.

Temperament. The system of compromise, in accordance with which the octave is divided into twelve equal intervals (sometimes called semitones) for the purpose of simplifying the music and permitting many relations of chords which would not be possible upon instruments producing fifths and thirds in perfectly accurate accoustical relation. In order to play in perfect tune upwards of fifty intervals in the octave would be necessary, and many tones which are identical upon the tempered instrument would then be found different and incapable of substitution for each other. An equal temperament is one in which the imperfections are equally distributed; an unequal temperament is one in which a few keys are nearly perfect, while all others are very bad. In correct temperaments the fifths are a twelfth of a comma flat; the fourths the same amount too sharp; the major third is a fourth of a comma too sharp, and so on. All intervals are incorrect except the octave and unison. But the differences are so small that, except in slow chords, the ear is quite well satisfied.

Temperatur (těm'pĕ-rä-toor), *Ger.* Temperament.

Tempestosamente (těm'pĕs-tō-zä-měn'tĕ), *It.* Furiously, impetuously.

Tempestoso (těm-pĕs-tō'zō), *It.* Tempestuous, stormy, boisterous.

Tempete (tänh-pāt'), *Fr.* A boisterous dance in 2-4 time.

Tempo (těm'pō), *It.* Time, rate of movement. Tempo is classified from very slow to moderate, fast, and very fast, the grades being the following: Grave, lento, adagio, andante, moderato, allegro, presto, prestissimo, the latter being as fast as possible; *a tempo*, in time.

Tempo alla breve (těm'pō äl'lä brā'vĕ), *It.* In a quick species of common time.

Tempo a piacere (těm'pō ä pē-ä-tshā'rĕ), *It.* The time at pleasure.

Tempobezeichnung (těm'pō-bĕ-tsīkh'noong), *Ger.* Measure-marking. The signs indicating the variety of measure.

Tempo comodo (těm'pō kŏ-mō'dō), *It.* Convenient time; an easy, moderate degree of movement.

Tempo di ballo (těm'pō dē bäl'lō), *It.* In dance time; rather quick.

Tempo di bolero (těm'pō dē bō-lĕ'rō), *It.* In time of a bolero.

Tempo di cappella (těm'pō dē käp-pĕl'lä), *It.* In the church time. See *Alla breve.*

Tempo di gavotta (těm'pō dē gä-vŏt'tä), *It.* In the time of a gavot.

Tempo di marcia (těm'pō dē mär'tshĭ-ä), *It.* In the time of a march.

Tempo di menuetto (těm'pō dē mĕ-noo-ĕt'tō), *It.* In the time of a minuet.

Tempo di polacca (těm'pō dē pō-läk'kä), *It.* In the time of a polacca.

Tempo di prima parte (těm'pō dē prē'mä pär'tĕ), *It.* In the same time as the first part.

Tempo di valse (těm'pō dē väl'se), *F.* In waltz time.

Tempo debole (těm'pō dā-bō'lĕ), *It.* The unaccented part of the measure.

Tempo frettevole (těm'pō frĕt-tā'vō-lĕ), } *It.*
Tempo frettoloso (těm'pō frĕt-tō-lō'zō), }
In quicker time; hurrying, hastily.

Tempo giusto (těm'pō joos'tō), *It.* In just, exact, strict time.

Tempo maggiore (těm'pō mäd-jĭ-ō'rĕ), *It.* In a quick species of common time.

Tempo ordinario (těm'pō ŏr-dĭ-nä'rĭ-ō), *It.* Ordinary or moderate time.

Tempo primo (těm'pō prē'mō), *It.* First, or original, time.

Tempo rubato (těm'pō roo-bä'tō), *It.* Robbed or stolen time; irregular time; meaning a slight deviation to give more expression, by retarding one note, and quickening another, but so that the time of each measure is not altered in the whole. Rubato is of several grades: Applied to a single tone, and so relating to the movement of the tones in one or two beats, or (2) within the measure as a whole, or (3) applied to a group of measures within which certain motives or tones are retarded and others accelerated.

Tempo wie vorher (těm'pō wē fōr'hār), *Ger.* The time as before.

ä *arm*, ă *add*, â *ale*, ĕ *eve*, ĭ *ill*, ī *isle*, ō *old*, ŏ *odd*, oo *moon*, u *but*, ü *Fr. sound*, kh *Ger. ch*, nh *nasal*.

Temps (tänh), **Tems** (tänh), *Fr.* } Time; also the various parts, or divisions, of a bar.

Temps foible (tänh fwäbl), *Fr.* The weak, or unaccented, parts of a measure.

Temps fort (tänh fōr), *Fr.* The strong, or accented, parts of a measure.

Temps levé (tänh lĕ-vä), *Fr.* The upbeats, or unaccented parts.

Temps trappé (tänh träp-pä), *Fr.* The downbeats, or accented parts.

Tempus imperfectum (tĕm'poos Im-pĕr-fĕk'tŏŏm), *Lat.* Imperfect time; a term used by old writers, meaning common time of two in a measure.

Tempus perfectum (tĕm'poos pĕr-fĕk'tŏŏm), *Lat.* Perfect time; a term used by old writers, meaning time of three in a measure.

Tendrement (tänhdr'-mänh), *Fr.* Tenderly, affectionately.

Tenebræ (tĕn'ĕ-bra), *Lat.* Darkness; a name given to the Roman Catholic evening service during Holy Week, in commemoration of the darkness which attended the crucifixion.

Teneramente (tĕ-nĕ'rä-mĕn'tĕ), *It.* Tenderly, delicately.

Tenerezza (tĕ-nĕ-rĕt'tsä), *It.* Tenderness, softness, delicacy.

Tenero (tā'nĕ-rō), *It.* Tenderly, softly, delicately.

Tenor. That species of male voice next above the baritone, and extending from the C upon the second space in the bass, to G on the second line in the treble.

Tenor C. The lowest C in the tenor voice; the lowest string of the viola, or tenor violin. One octave below middle C.

Tenor clef. The C clef when placed upon the fourth line.

Tenore (tĕ-nō'rĕ), *It.* Tenor voice; a tenor singer. See also *Viola*.

Tenore buffo (tĕ-nō'rĕ boof'fō), *It.* The second tenor singer of an opera company for comic parts.

Tenore di grazia (tĕ-nō'rĕ dē grä'tsĭ-ä), *It.* A delicate and graceful tenor.

Tenore leggiero (tĕ-nō'rĕ lĕd-jĭ-ā'rō), *It.* A tenor voice of a light quality of tone.

Tenore primo (tĕ-nō'rĕ prē'mō), *It.* First tenor.

Tenore robusto (tĕ-nō'rĕ rō-boos'tō), *It.* A strong tenor voice.

Tenore secondo (tĕ-nō'rĕ sĕ-kŏn'dō), *It.* Second tenor.

Tenore viola (tĕ-nō'rĕ vē-ō'lä), *It.* Tenor viol.

Tenorist (tĕn'ō-rĭst), *Ger.* } A tenor singer.
Tenorista (tĕn-ō-rēs'tä), *It.* }

Tenoroon. The old tenor hautboy, the compass of which extended downward to tenor C. The name is sometimes applied to an organ-stop.

Tenorposaune (tĕ-nōr'pō-zou'nĕ), *Ger.* The tenor trombone.

Tenorschlüssel (tĕ-nōr'shlüs's'l), *Ger.* The tenor clef.

Tenor, second. Low tenor.

Tenorstimme (tĕ-nōr'stĭm'mĕ), *Ger.* Tenor voice; a tenor.

Tenor trombone. A trombone having a compass from the small c to the one-lined g, and noted in the tenor clef.

Tenor viole (tĕ-nōr fī-ō'lĕ), *Ger.* } The viola.
Tenor violin, *Eng.* }

Tenorzeichen (tĕ-nōr'tsī'kh'n), *Ger.* The tenor clef.

Tensile. A term applied to all stringed instruments, on account of the tension of their strings.

Tenth. An interval comprising an octave and a third; also an organ-stop tuned a tenth above the diapasons, called, also, decima and double tierce; obsolete.

Tenue (tä-nü), *Fr.* See *Tenuto*.

Tenute (tä-noo'tĕ), *It.* } Held on, sustained
Tenuto (tä-noo'tō), *It.* } or kept down the full time.

Téorbe (tā-ōrb), *Fr.* See *Theorbo*.

Teoretico (tā-ō-rä'tĭ-kō), *It.* Theoretical.

Teoria (tā-ō-rē'ä), *It.* Theory.

Teoria del canto (tā-ō-rē'ä dĕl kän'tō), *It.* The theory, or art, of singing.

Tepidamente (tā-pĭ-dä-mĕn'tĕ), *It.* Coldly, with indifference; lukewarm.

Tepidita (tā-pĕ-dĭ-tä'), *It.* Coldness, indifference.

Ter (tĕr), *Lat.* Thrice, three times.

Tercero (tĕr-thä'rō), *Sp.* Third.

Tercet (tĕr-sā), *Fr.* A triplet.

Terms, musical. Words and sentences applied to passages of music for the purpose of indicating the style in which they should be performed.

Ternario (tĕr-nä'rĭ-ō), *It.* Ternario.

Ternario tempo (tĕr-nä'rĭ-ō tĕm'pō), *It.* Triple time.

Ternary measure. Threefold measure; triple time.

Terpodion. An instrument invented by Buschmann, of Hamburg, resembling the harmonium in appearance, the tone being produced from sticks of wood; the name is also given to an organ-stop of 8-feet tone.

Terpsichore. In classical mythology the muse of choral dance and song.

Tertia (tĕr'tsĭ-ä), *Lat.* } Third, tierce; also
Tertzia (tĕr'tsĭ-ĕ), *Ger.* } an organ-stop, sounding a third or tenth above the foundation stops.

Ter unca (tĕr oon'kä), *Lat.* Three-hooked; the old name of the demisemiquaver.

Terz ('ărts), *Ger.* ⎫ A third, the inter-
Terza (tăr'tsä), *It.* ⎪ val of a third; also
Terze (tär'tsĕ), *Ger.* ⎬ an organ-stop sound-
Terzie (tär'tsĭ-ĕ), *Ger.* ⎪ ing a third above the
Terzo (tär'tsŏ), *It.* ⎭ fifteenth. See *Tierce.*

Terz decimole (tărts dā-tsĭ-mō'lĕ), *Ger.* A group of thirteen notes, having the value of eight similar ones.

Terza maggiore (tär'tsä mäd-jĭ-ŏ'rĕ), *It.* Major third.

Terza minore (tär'tsä mē-nō'rĕ), *It.* Minor third.

Terzen (tär'ts'n), *Ger.* Thirds.

Terzetto (tĕr-tsĕt'tō), *It.* A short piece, or trio, for three voices.

Terzflöte (tärts'flö'tĕ), *Ger.* A flute sounding a minor third above; also an organ-stop.

Terzina (tär-tsē'nä), *It.* A triplet.

Testo (tĕs'tō), *It.* The text, subject, or theme of any composition. A word applied by the Italians to the poetry of a song; when the words are well written the song is said to have a good testo.

Testudo (tĕs-too'dō), *Lat.* Name given by the Romans, in imitation of the Greeks, to the lyre of Mercury, because it was made of the back or hollow of a sea tortoise.

Tetrachord (tĕt'rä-kŏrd), *Gr.* ⎫ A fourth; also
Tetracorde (tĕt'rä-kŏrd), *Fr.* ⎬ a system of
Tetracordo (tĕt-rä-kŏr'dō), *It.* ⎭ four sounds among the ancients, the extremes of which were fixed, but the middle sounds were varied according to the mode.

Tetrachords, conjoint. Two tetrachords, or fourths, where the same note is the highest of one and the lowest of the other.

Theile (tī'lĕ), *Ger. pl.* Parts, divisions of the bar; also strains, or component parts of a movement or piece.

Thema (thā'mä), *Gr.* ⎫
Thema (tä'mä), *Ger.* ⎬ A theme or subject.
Theme (tâm), *Fr.* ⎭

Thematic. Derived from appertaining to a theme. This style of music is illustrated by the Inventions of Bach, many pieces of Schumann (the Novellettes, etc.) and the middle part of the sonata-piece. It is opposed to lyric.

Theme. The subject of a composition.

Theorbe (tĕ-ŏr'bĕ), *Ger.* ⎫ An ancient in-
Theorbo (thĕ ŏr'bō), *Eng.* ⎬ strument of the lute species. See *Archlute.*

Theoretical musician. One who is acquainted with the essence, nature, and properties of music, considered as science, and as art.

Theoretiker (tĕ-ō-rĕ'tĭ-kĕr), *Ger.* ⎫ A theoret-
Théoricien (tā-ō-rē'sĭ-änh), *Fr.* ⎬ ical musician, a theorist.

Theoria (tĕ-ō'rĭ-ä), *Lat.* ⎫ The science of mu-
Théorie (tā'ō-rĕ'), *Fr.* ⎬ sic; the principles
Theory (thē'ō-ry), *Eng.* ⎭ of sound, as regards concords and discords; the system of harmonical and melodial arrangement for the purpose of musical expression.

Thesis (thā'sĭs), *Gr.* Downbeat; the accented part of the bar.

Theurgic hymns. Songs of incantation, such as those ascribed to Orpheus, performed in the mysteries upon the most solemn occasions. These hymns were the first of which we have any account in Greece.

Third. The interval between any tone of a scale and the next but one above or below. The major third is equal to four half-steps; the minor to three half-steps; the diminished to two half-steps. The latter is of rare occurrence.

Third shift. The double shift in violin-playing.

Thirteenth. An interval comprising an octave and a sixth. It contains twelve diatonic degrees, *i. e.*, thirteen sounds.

Thirty-second note. A demisemiquaver.

Thirty-second rest. A rest, or pause, equal to the length of a thirty-second note.

Thoroughbass. A system of indicating the chords by means of figures written over or under the notes of the bass. In this system 3, 5, or 8 indicated the common chord; 7, 6 5, 4-3, 4-2, or 2, various forms of the seventh. All intervals were indicated by writing their figural number, reckoning from the actual bass note (not necessarily the root). Hence the term "thoroughbass" is often employed as synonymous with "harmony." This notation was first invented for accompanying recitative, and afterwards used in scores for facilitating reading.

Three-eighth measure. A measure having the value of three eighth notes, marked 3-8.

Threefold. A chord consisting of three tones, comprising a tone combined with its third and fifth.

Threnodia (thrē-nō'dĭ-ä), *Lat.* ⎫ An elegy, a
Threnodie (thrĕ nō'dĕ), *Ger.* ⎬ funeral-song.

Threnody. Lamentation, a song of lamentation.

Thrice-marked octave. The name given in Germany to the notes between the C on the second added line above the treble staff and the next B above, inclusive; these notes are expressed by small letters, with three short strokes.

Tibia (tē'bĭ-ä), *Lat.* The ancient name of all wind instruments with holes, such as the flute, pipe, and fife; originally the term was applied to the human leg-bone made into a flute.

Tibia major (tē'bĭ-ä mä-yŏr), *Lat.* An organ-stop of 16-feet tone, the pipes of which are stopped or covered.

Tibiæ pares (tē'bĭ-ā pä'rĕs), *Lat. pl.* Two flutes, one for the right hand and the other for the left, which were played on by the same performer.

Tibia utricularia (tē'bĭ-ä oot-rĭ-koo-lā'rĭ-ä), *Lat.* Name by which the bagpipe was known among the ancient Romans.

Tibicen (tē'bĭ-tsĕn), *Lat.* The ancient fluteplayer, or piper.

Tie. A slur; a curved line placed over notes on the same degree of staff requiring a connected note.

Tief (tēf), *Ger.* Deep, low, profound.

Tiefer (tē'fĕr), *Ger.* Deeper, lower; *8va tiefer*, octave below.

Tieftönend (tēf'tö'nĕnd), *Ger.* Deep-toned.

Tierce (tērs), *Fr.* A third; also the name of an organ-stop tuned a major third higher than the fifteenth.

Tierce de picardie (tērs dŭh pĭ-kär'dē), *Fr.* Tierce of Picardy; a term applied to a major third, when introduced in the last chord of a composition in a minor mode; the custom was supposed to have originated in Picardy, and formerly was quite common.

Timbale (tănh-bäl'), *Fr.*
Timballo (tĕm-bäl'lō), *It.* } A kettledrum.

Timbalier (tănh-bä-lǐ-ā), *Fr.* A kettledrummer.

Timballes (tănh-bäl), *Fr. pl.* Kettledrums.

Timbre (tănh-br), *Fr.* Quality of tone or sound.

Timbrel. An ancient Hebrew instrument, supposed to have been like a tambourine.

Time. That in which duration exists. The measure of sounds in regard to their continuance or duration. Often used, inelegantly, in place of measure.

Time-table. A representation of the several notes in music, showing their relative lengths or durations.

Timidezza, con (tē-mĭ-dĕt'sä kōn), *It.* With timidity.

Timorosamente (tē - mō-rō - zä - mĕn' tĕ), *It.* Timidly, with fear.

Timoroso (tē-mō-rō'zō), *It.* Timorous, with hesitation.

Timpani (tĭm-pä'nē), *It. pl.* } The kettle-
Timpani (tĭm-pä'nē), *Sp. pl.* } drums.

Timpano (tĭm'pä-nō), *It.* Drum, timbrel, labor.

Tintement (tănh-t'-mänh), *Fr.* Tingling of a bell; vibration, or ringing sound.

Tintermell. An old dance.

Tintinnabulary. Having, or making, the sound of a bell.

Tintinnabulum (tĭn-tĭn-nä'bro-loom), *Lat.* }
Tintinnabolo (tĭn-tĭn-nä'bō-lō), *It.*
Tintinnabulo (tĭn-tĭn-nä'boo-lō), *It.* } A little bell.

Tintinnamento (tĭn-tĭn-nä-mĕn'tō), *It.* Tinkling of small bells.

Tiorba (tē-ōr'bä), *It.* Theorbo.

Tipping. A distinct articulation given to the tones of a flute by placing the end of the tongue on the roof of the mouth. See *Double-tonguing*.

Tirasse (tĭ-räss'), *Fr.* The pedals of an organ which act on the manual keys by pulling or drawing them down.

Tirata (tē-rä'tä), *It.* A term formerly applied to any number of notes of equal value or length, and moving in coujoint degrees.

Tirato (tē-rä'tō), *It.* Drawn, pulled, stretched out; a downbow. See, also, *Tirasse.*

Tira tutto (tē'rä toot'tō), *It.* A pedal or mechanism in an organ, which, acting upon all the stops, enables the performer to obtain at once the full power of the instrument.

Tiré (tē-rā), *Fr.* Drawn, pulled; a downbow.

Tiré-lirer (tĕ-rä lē-rā), *Fr.* To sing like a lark.

Toccata (tŏk-kä'tä), *It.* A purely instrumental form, of which we hear already in the latter part of the sixteenth century. The name is derived from *tocare*, to touch, to play. In its older form the toccata is a prelude consisting of a few chords and coloratore, or a something between a prelude and a fantasia, made up of runs, arpeggios, and short aperçus. A characteristic of the toccata is that it has the appearance of an improvisation. Although very different, the modern toccata shares yet to a greater or less extent the chief characteristics of its predecessor. It is generally constructed out of a nimble figure which is kept up throughout; melodic effusions are excluded, and technical display and rhythmical movement are mainly aimed at. In short, the modern toccata partakes of the nature of the prelude, study, and improvisation.

Toccatina (tŏk-kä-tē'nä), *It.* A short toccata.

Tocsin. An alarm-bell; ringing of a bell for the purpose of alarm.

Todesgesang (tō'dĕs-gĕ-zäng), *Ger.* } A dirge,
Todeslied (tō'dĕs-lēd), } a funeral-song.

Todtenglöckchen (tōd' t'n - glŏk' kh'n), *Ger.* Funeral-bell.

Todtenlied (tōd't'n-lēd'), *Ger.* Funeral-song or anthem.

Todtenmarsch (tōd't'n-märsh'), *Ger.* Funeral march.

Tolling. The act of ringing a church bell in a slow, measured manner.

Tome (tōm), *Fr.* Volume, book.

Tomtom. A sort of drum used by the natives in the East Indies.

Ton (tōnh), *Fr.* } Tone, sound, voice,
Ton (tōn), *Ger.* } melody; also accent,
Töne (tō'nē), *Ger. pl.* } stress; also the pitch
Tono (tō'nō), *Sp.* } of any note as to its
Tons *Fr. pl.* } acuteness or gravity;
also the key or mode. *Le ton d'ut*, the key of C. See, also, *Tone*.

Tonadica (to-nä-dē'kä), *Sp.* } A song of a lively and cheerful
Tonadilla (tō-nä-dĕl'yä), } character, generally with guitar accompaniment.

Tonæ fichti (tō'nĕ fĭch'tē), *Lat.* The transposed ecclesiastical modes.

Tonalität (tōn'ül-ĭ-tät'), *Ger.* } Tonality.
Tonalité (tōn-äl-ĭ-tā), *Fr.* }

Tonality. Relation in key.

ä *arm*, ă *add*, ā *ale*, ĕ *end*, ē *eve*, ĭ *ill*, ī *isle*, ŏ *old*, ŏ *odd*, oo *moon*, ŭ *but*, ü *Fr. sound*, kh *Ger. ch*, nh *nasal*.

Tonart (tōn'ärt), *Ger.* Mode, scale, key.

Tonbildung (tōn-bĭl'doong), *Ger.*

Ton de voix (tŏnh dŭh vwä), *Fr.* Tone of voice.

Tondichter (tŏn-dĭkh'tĕr), *Ger.* Poet of sound, a composer of music.

Tondichtung (tŏn'dĭkh-toong), *Ger.* Musical composition of a high character.

Tondo (tŏn'dō), *It.* Round, or full, as regards tone.

Tone. A musical sound. Its characteristic is the possession of a determinate pitch. In this it differs from noise. Sometimes improperly employed as a name for the interval of the whole step, or a major second.

Tönen (tö'nen), *Ger.* To sound, to resound.

Tönend (tö'nĕnd), *Ger.* Sounding.

Tonfall (tōn'fäll), *Ger.* A cadence.

Tonfarbe (tōn'fär-bĕ), *Ger.* Tone-color. Timbre.

Tonfolge (tōn'fōl'ghĕ), *Ger.* A succession of sounds.

Tonführung (tōn'fü'roong), *Ger.* Tone-carrying. Melodic and harmonic progression.

Tonfuss (tōn'foos), *Ger.* Metre.

Tongang (tōn'gäng), *Ger.* Tune, melody.

Tongattung (tōn'gät'toong), } *Ger.*
Tongeschlecht (tōn'gĕ-shlĕkht'), }
The division of the octave. The selection of tones for use in a particular strain. Hence the key and mode. Tongeschlecht is the more correct term.

Ton-générateur (tŏnh zhā-nā-rā-tür), *Fr.* The ruling, or principal, key in which a piece is written.

Tongue. In the reed pipe of an organ a thin, elastic slip of metal, somewhat bent, and placed near the reed.

Tonguing, double. A mode of articulating quick notes, used by flutists and players upon brass instruments.

Tonic. The tone, the keytone, from which all others are determined.

Tonica (tō'nĭ-kä), *It.* }
Tonica (tō'nĭ-kä), *Ger.* } Tonic.
Tonique (tŏnh-ēk'), *Fr.* }

Tonic pedal. A continued bass note on which chords foreign to its harmony are given.

Tonic section. A section closing on the common chord of the tonic.

Tonic solfa. A system of teaching music (principally vocal) which has attained wide success in England. It consists essentially of two elements: First an analysis of musical effects, in which everything is referred to relations in key. Hence the training addresses itself to the correct apprehension of the relations of tones to a central tone, the tonic, or, as they say it, "tones in key." This part of the work has been carried out in a highly ingenious manner in a multitude of textbooks and by thousands of well-trained teachers, and has exerted an appreciable influence upon the growth of musical taste by educating musical perceptions in people who, without this training, would rarely have arrived at them. The second element in the system is a notation, consisting of the letters indicating the solfa, d for do, r for re, m for mi, f for fa, etc., changing si to te for seven, in order to remove the ambiguity of s for sol and s for si. These initials take the place of notes, and are all written upon the same plane. Without additional marks they are to indicate the current octave. When a higher or lower octave is desired an index mark is written at the top or bottom of the initial letter. Time-values are indicated by means of bars and time-spaces, of which there are as many as the measure requires. When one initial occupies a time-space, the tone extends one beat; when two initials occupy the space, the tones are half-beats. When a tone is prolonged through a second time-space a dash is written in the second time-space, which means prolong it. Rests are indicated by vacant time-spaces. Example:

d : d | m : m | s :— | : | e : e | t, : t, | d :—| —||

This notation, being simplicity itself, and equally valid for all keys, has proven extremely valuable in elementary instruction and for children. It also has uses for advanced students as a generalized statement of relations in key. The tonic solfa was invented by Miss Glover, of Norwich, and greatly perfected by the late Rev. John Curwen, and his son, John Spencer Curwen, who is the present head of the movement.

Tonkunst (tōn'koonst), *Ger.* Music: the art and science of music.

Tonkünstler (tōn'künst'lĕr), *Ger.* Musician.

Tonkunstschule (tōn' koonst - shoo' lĕ), *Ger.* School of music.

Tonlehre (tōn'lā'rĕ), *Ger.* Acoustics; tones.

Tonleiter (tōn-lī'tĕr), *Ger.* Scale, gamut.

Ton majeur (tŏnh mäzhür), *Fr.* Major key.

Tonmalerei (tōn-mä'lĕ-rī'), *Ger.* Tone-painting.

Tonmass (tōn'mäs), *Ger.* Measure, time.

Tonmesser (tōn-mĕs'sĕr), *Ger.* A monochord.

Ton mineur (tŏnh mē-nūr), *Fr.* Minor key.

Tonos (tō'nŏs), *Gr.* Tone.

Tonsatz (tōn'säts), *Ger.* A musical composition.

Tonschluss (tōn-shloos'), *Ger.* A cadence.

Tonschlüssel (tōn-shlüs's'l), *Ger.* The key; keynote.

Tonschrift (tōn' shrĭft), *Ger.* Musical notes.

Tons de l'eglise (tŏnh dŭh l'ā-glēz), *Fr.* Church modes, or tones.

Tons de la trompette (tŏnh dŭh lä trŏm-pät'), } *Fr.*
Tons du cor (tŏnh dü kŏr), }
The additional crooks of the trumpet, and horn for raising or lowering the pitch.

ă *arm*, ă *add*, ā *ale*, ĕ *end*, ē *eve*, ĭ *ill*, ī *isle*, ŏ *old*, ŏ *odd*, oo *moon*, ŭ *but*, ü *Fr. sound*, kh *Ger. ch*, nh *nasal*

Tonsetzer (tōn-sĕt'tsĕr), *Ger.* A composer; a less flattering term than tondichter.

Tonsetzérkoonst (tōn-sĕt'tsĕr-koonst), *Ger.* The art of musical composition.

Tonsetzung (tōn-sĕt'tsoong), *Ger.*
Tonstück (tōn-stük), } A musical piece, or composition.

Tonsilbe (tōn-sĭl'bĕ), *Ger.* Accented syllable.

Tons overt (tōns ŏ-vār), *Fr.* Open tones.

Tonspiel (tōn'spĕl), *Ger.* Music, a concert.

Tonspieler (tōn-spē'lĕr), *Ger.* Musical performer.

Tonstufe (tōn-stoo'fĕ), *Ger.* Tone-step.

Tonsystem (tōn'sĭs-tām'), *Ger.* System of tones or sounds; the science of harmony; the systematic arrangement to musical tones or sounds in their regular order.

Tonumfang (tōn-oom'fäng), *Ger.* Tone compass.

Tonveränderung (tōn'vĕr-än'dĕ-roong), *Ger.* Modulation.

Tonverhalt (tōn'vĕr-hält'), *Ger.* Rhythm.

Tonwerk (tōn'wärk), *Ger.* A musical composition.

Tonwerkzeug (tōn-värk'zoig), *Ger.* A musical apparatus; an instrument; the human voice.

Tonzeichen (tōn'tsī'kh'n), *Ger.* Accent.

Tonwissenschaft (tōn'vĭs's'n-shäft), *Ger.* The science of tones.

Toph (tōf), *Heb.* An instrument like the tambourine, which was known to the Jews before they left Syria.

Torch dance. A dance of former times, in which the dancers carried torches.

Tosto (tōs'tō), *It.* Quick, swift, rapid. See, also, *Piu tosto*.

Touch. Style of striking, or pressing, the keys of an organ, pianoforte, or similar instrument; the resistance made to the fingers by the keys of any instrument, as when the keys are put down with difficulty, an instrument is said to have a hard, or heavy, touch; when there is little resistance the touch is said to be soft, or light. In speaking of the mechanism and results of touch, several compounds are of frequent occurrence: Finger touch, a touch made by the fingers only; staccato touch, a touch in which the tones are not connected, but separated; legato touch, a touch in which the fingers cling to the keys, so that the successive tones are fully connected. A similar effect can also be made by using the pedal discreetly. Organ touch is one in which the pressure quality is prominent. Piano touch is one in which the hammer element is important.

Touche (toosh), *Fr.* The touch: also a key of the pianoforte, etc.

Toucher (too-shā), *Fr.* To play upon an instrument.

Touquet (too-kā), *Fr.* A term formerly given to the lowest trumpet part.

Tourne boute (toorn boot). *Fr.* A musical instrument similar to the flute.

Tours de force (toor dŭh fŏrs), *Fr.* Bravura passages, roulades, divisions, etc.

Tout ensemble (toot änh-sänhbl), *Fr.* The whole together; the general effect.

Town pipers. Performers on the pipe, formerly retained by most of the principal towns in Scotland to assist in the celebration of particular holidays, festivals, etc.

Toys. A name formerly given to little trifling airs or dance tunes.

Tp. Abbreviation of Timpani.

Tr. Abbreviation for trumpet.

Trachea (trä'kä-ä), *Lat.* The windpipe.

Trackers. Thin strips of wood connecting organ-keys and valves.

Tractus (träk'toos), *Lat.* Tracts are melodies of sorrowful expression sung between the Graduale and Allelujah, during Lent, in the requiem mass, and upon some other occasions. The words are taken from the Psalms.

Tradolce (trä-dōl'tshĕ), *It.* Very soft; sweet.

Tradotto (trä-dōt'tō), *It.* Translated, arranged, adapted, fitted to.

Tragédie en musique (trä-zhā'dē änh mü-zēk) *Fr.* A serious, or tragic, opera.

Tragedy. A dramatic poem, representing some signal action performed by illustrious persons, and generally having a fatal issue.

Tragedy, lyric. A tragedy accompanied by singing; tragic opera.

Trainé (trä-nā), *Fr.* Slurred, bound, lingering, drawn along.

Trait (trā), *Fr.* Passage, run; a phrase.

Trait de chant (trä dŭh shänh), *Fr.* A melodic passage, or phrase.

Trait d'harmonie (trä där-mō-nē), *Fr.* Succession of chords; a sequence.

Traité (trä-tā'), *Fr.* A treatise on the practice, or the theory, of music.

Tranquillamente (trän-kwīl-lä-mĕn'tĕ), *It.* Quietly, calmly, tranquilly.

Tranquillezza (trän-kwīl-lĕ'tsä), } Tran-
Tranquillita (trän-kwīl-lī-tä'), *It.* } quillity,
Tranquillo (trän-kwīl'lō), } calmness, quietness.

Transcription. An arrangement for the pianoforte, or other instrument, of a song or other composition not originally designed for that instrument; an adaptation.

Transient. An epithet applied to those chords of whose harmony no account is meant to be taken, but which are used as passing chords.

Transitio (trän sē'tsī-ō), *Lat.* } Passing sud-
Transition. } denly out of one key into another without preparation for or hinting at another key; or without making use of chords common to both keys.

Transitus (trän'sĭ-toos), *Lat.* A passing note.

Transitus irregularis (trän'sĭ-toos Ir'rĕg-oo-lā'ris), *Lat.* Irregular passing notes. See *Changing notes.*

Transitus regularis (trän-sĭ-toos rĕ-goo-lā'ris), *Lat.* Passing notes placed on the unaccented parts of the bar.

Transpose. To change the pitch of a composition into a higher or lower key. This is done by substituting for each of the tones of the composition the corresponding scale tone of the desired key. Thus the tone do is answered by the do of the new key, re by re, etc. Accidentals are sometimes changed, sharps in some cases being changed to naturals, and naturals to flats. But in every correct transposition the melodic and harmonic effects are unchanged.

Transposed. Removed, or changed into another key.

Transposer (tränhs-pō-zā), *Fr.* } Change
Transponiren (träns-pō-nē'ren), *Ger.* } of key; removing a piece into another key.

Transposing instruments. The orchestral instruments which are not written in scores as they sound, but upon some other pitch. To this class belong the clarinets, horns, and trumpets; an instrument "in A," as it is called, sounds a minor third lower than written; an instrument "in B" sounds one degree lower than written; one "in E♭" a minor third higher than written.

Transverse flute. The German flute; the flauto traverso.

Traquenard (trä-kĕ-närd), *Fr.* A brisk sort of dance.

Trascinando (trä-shĭ-nän'dō), *It.* Dragging the time.

Trascritto (trä-skrĕt'tō), *It.* Copied, transcribed.

Trattato (trät-tä'tō), *It.* See *Traité.*

Trauergesang (trou'ĕr-gĕ-säng'), *Ger.* Mourning song, dirge.

Trauermarsch (trou'ĕr-märsh'), *Ger.* Funeral march.

Traurig (trou'rĭg), *Ger.* Heavily, sadly, mournfully.

Traversiere (trä-vĕr-sĭ-ār'), *Fr.* } Cross, across;
Traverso (trä-vĕr'sō), *It.* } applied to the transverse, or German, flute, to distinguish it from the flûte à bec.

Travestie (trä'fĕs-tē'), *Ger.* Parody.

Travestiren (trä'fĕs-tīr'ĕn), *Ger.* To parody.

Tre (trā), *It.* Three; *a tre,* for three voices or instruments.

Treble. The upper part, the highest voice, the soprano, that which generally contains the melody.

Treble clef. The G clef, the soprano clef.

Treble, first. The highest treble, or soprano.

Treble forte stop. A stop recently applied to cabinet organs, by means of which the treble part of the instrument may be increased in power, while the bass remains subdued.

Treble, second. Low soprano.

Treble staff. The staff upon which the treble clef is placed.

Treble viol. An instrument invented before the modern viol, furnished with six strings tuned chiefly by fourths.

Treble voice. The highest species of the female voice.

Tre corde (trā kŏr'dĕ), *It.* Three strings; in pianoforte music this means that the soft pedal must no longer be pressed down.

Treibend (trī'bĕnd), *Ger.* Hurrying, pressing, urging.

Tremando (trā-män'dō), *It.* See *Tremolando.*

Tremblant (tränh-blänh), *Fr.* Shaking. See *Tremulant.*

Tremblement (tränhbl-mänh), *Fr.* A trill, or shake.

Tremolando (trĕm-ō-län'dō), } Trembling,
Tremolate (trĕm-ō-lā'tĕ), *It.* } quivering;
Tremolo (trĕ'mō-lō), } a note, or
Tremulo (trā'moo-lō), } chord, reiterated with great rapidity, producing a tremulous kind of effect.

Tremolant. } An organ-stop which gives to
Tremulant. } the tone a waving, trembling, or undulating effect, resembling the vibrato in singing and the tremolando in violin-playing; also a harmonium stop of the same kind.

Tremore (trā-mō'rĕ), *It.* } Tremor,
Tremoroso (trā-mō-rō'zō), } trembling. See, also, *Tremolando.*

Trenchmore. An old dance, supposed to have been of a lively species.

Trenise (trā-nēz), *Fr.* One of the movements of a quadrille.

Trenodia (trā-nō'dĭ-ä), *It.* A funeral dirge.

Très (trā), *Fr.* Very, most.

Très-animé (trā sän-ĭ-mā), *Fr.* Very animated, very lively.

Tresca (trĕs'kä), *It.* A country dance.

Trescone (trĕs-kō'nĕ), *It.* A species of dance.

Très fort (trā fōr), *Fr.* Very loud.

Très lentement (trā länht-mänh), *Fr.* Very slow.

Très piano (trā pĕ-ä-nō), *Fr.* Very soft.

Très vif (trā vēf), *Fr.* Very lively, very brisk.

Très vite et impétueux (trā vēt ā änh-pĕt-oo-üz), *Fr.* Very quick and impetuous.

Treter (trā'tĕr), *Ger.* Treader of the bellows in German organs. The blower.

Tre volte (trā vŏl'tĕ), *It. pl.* Three times.

Triad. A "three-er." A chord of three tones, consisting of a root, its third and fifth. According to recent theorists all triads are either of the natural harmony triad, which corresponds with the partial tones of a fundamental, having a major third and a per-

ä arm, ă ada, ā ale, ĕ end, ē eve, ĭ ill, ī isle, ŏ old, ō odd, oo moon, ŭ but, ü Fr.sound, kh Ger. ch, nh nasal.

(223)

fect fifth, and imitations of it upon other degrees of the scale, where many strange intervals arise. For instance, in the major scale the triads of the tonic, fourth, and fifth are natural and complete. Those of the second, third, and sixth are minor, having a minor third and a perfect fifth, and that of the seventh degree having a minor third and diminished fifth, is called diminished. In the minor scale several other triads arise: Upon the first and fourth, minor triads; upon the second and seventh, diminished triads; upon the third an augmented triad, and upon the fifth and sixth, major triads.

A triad is said to be inverted when its bass is not the root but one of the other members of the chord. Hence two inversions, the first, in which the third of the triad is bass, and the second, in which the fifth of the triad is bass.

The root of a triad is its greatest common measure. In other words the root of the natural triad is exactly the natural bass tone which contains the third and fifth among its partials. In all other varieties of triad contradictory elements are present, at least two roots being represented. The absence of easy agreement is the source of the appealing effect in minor and all other less agreeable triads.

The proper fundamentals of any two tones sounding together are the combination tones generated in the low bass. Thus, C and E♭ together generate A♭ in the bass; C and E or E and C generate C; G and B♭ generate E♭. In general, minor thirds generate roots a twelfth below the upper of the two notes; major thirds generate the octave below the lower tone. Every two tones sounding together above treble clef G generate combination tones, which, when the tones are sounded loudly upon an organ in good tune, can always be heard.

Triad, augmented. Consisting of a root, major third, and augmented fifth. Its natural place is upon the third degree of the minor scale.

Triangle. A small three-sided steel frame, which is played upon by being struck with a rod.

Triangolo (trē-än-gō-lō), *It.* }
Triangulo (trē än-goo-lō), *Sp.* } A triangle.
Triangulus (trī-än'goo-loos), *Lat.* }

Trias deficiens (trē-ås dĕ-fē-sĭ-ĕns), *Lat.* The imperfect chord, or triad.

Tribrach (trē-bräk), *Lat.* A trisyllabic musical foot, comprising three short notes or syllables, ⌣ ⌣ ⌣.

Trichord. The name given to the three-stringed lyre, supposed to have been the invention of Mercury.

Tricinium (trē-tsī'nĭ-oom), *Lat.* A composition in three parts.

Tridiapason (trē'dĭ-ä-pä'sōn), *Gr.* A triple octave, or twenty-second.

Trigon. A three-stringed instrument resembling the lyre used by the ancient Greeks.

Trigonum, or triangular harp. An instrument supposed to have been of Phrygian invention, resembling the Theban harp.

Trill. A shake.

Trillando (trēl-län'dō), *It.* A succession, or chain, of shakes on different notes.

Trille (trēll), *Fr.* }
Triller (trĭl'lĕr), *Ger.* } A shake; a trill.
Trillo (trēl'lō), *It.* }

Trillerkette (trĭl'lĕr-kĕt'tĕ), *Ger.* A chain, or succession, of shakes.

Trillern (trĭl'lĕrn), *Ger.* To trill; to shake; to warble.

Trillette (trĭl-lĕt'tĕ), *Fr.* } A short trill, or
Trilletta (trēl-lĕt'tä), *It.* } shake; a short
Trilletto (trēl-lĕt'tō), *It.* } warble.

Trillettino (trēl-lĕt-tē'nō), *It.* A soft shake, a soft trilling.

Trill, imperfect. A trill, or shake, without a turn at the close.

Trillo caprino (trēl'-lō kä-prē'nō), *It.* A false shake.

Trimeters. Ancient lyrical verses of a six-feet measure.

Trinkgesang (trĭnk-gĕ-zäng), *Ger.* } A bac-
Trinklied (trĭnk-lēd), } chanalian, or drinking, song.

Trinona. An organ-stop of open eight-feet small scale, and pleasant, gamba-like tone.

Trio (trē'ō), *It.* A piece for three instruments. In England the word is also applied to a piece for three voices, but incorrectly, terzetto being the proper appellation. A trio is also the second movement to a menuetto, march, waltz, etc., and always leads back to a repetition of the first, or principal, movement.

Triole (trī ō'lĕ), *Ger.* } A triplet; a group of
Triolet (trī-ō-lā), *Fr.* } three notes to be played in the time of two.

Triomphale (trē-ōnh-fäl), *Fr.* }
Trionfale (trē-ōn-fä'lĕ), *It.* } Triumphal.

Triomphant (trē-ōnh-fänh), *Fr.* } Triumph-
Trionfante (trē-ōn-fän'tĕ), *It.* } ant.

Tripartite. Divided into three parts; scores in three parts are said to be tripartite.

Tripeltakt (trī'p'l-täkt), *Ger.* Triple measure.

Triphony. Three sounds heard together.

Tripla (trī'plä), *It.* Triple measure.

Triple. Threefold, treble.

Triple concerto. A concerto for three solo instruments with accompaniment. (Very unusual.)

Triple counterpoint. Counterpoint in three parts, invertible; that is, so contrived that each part will serve indifferently for either bass, middle or upper part.

Triple croche (trĭpl krōsh), *Fr.* A demisemiquaver.

ŭ *arm*, ă *add*, ā *ale*, ĕ *end*, ē *eve*, ĭ *ill*, ī *isle*, ŏ *old*, ō *odd*, oo *moon*, ū *but*, ü *Fr. sound*, kh *Ger. ch.* nh *nasal.*

(224)

Triple-dotted note. A note whose length is increased seven eighths of its original value by three dots placed after it.

Triple fugue. A fugue with three subjects, which after being worked separately are all worked together. This is possible only when the second and third subjects have been invented as counterpoints to the first subject.

Triplet. A group of three notes, played in the usual time of two similar ones.

Triplet, double. A sextole.

Triple time. Such as has an odd, or uneven, number of parts in a bar, as three, nine.

Triplum (trĭp'loom), *Lat.* Formerly the name of the treble, or highest, part.

Trisagion (trī sä'ghĭ-ŏn), *Gr.* } The same.
Trisagium (trī-sä-ghī-oom), *Lat.* } us.

Trisemitonium (trĕ'sĕmĭ-tŏ'nĭ-oom), *Lat.* The lesser, or minor, third.

Tristezza (trĭs-tĕt'sä), *It.* Sadness, heaviness, pensiveness.

Triton (trē-tōnh), *Fr.* } A superfluous,
Tritone (trī tōn), *Eng.* } or augmented,
Tritono (trē-tō'nŏ), *It.* } fourth, contain-
Tritonus (trī-tō'noos), *Lat.* } ing three whole steps.

Triton avis (trē'tŏn ä'vĭs), *Lat.* The name of a West-Indian bird remarkable for its musical powers, having three distinct notes—its tonic, or lower, note, and the twelfth and seventeenth of that note—and capable of sounding them all at the same time.

Tritt (trĭtt), *Ger.* Step, tread, treadle.

Trittbrett (trĭtt-brĕtt), *Ger.* } The board upon
Trittholz (trĭtt-hōlts), } which the bellows-treader steps in blowing an organ.

Triumphirend (trĭ-oom-fē'rĕnd), *Ger.* Triumphant.

Triumphlied (trĭ-oomf'lēd), *Ger.* Song of triumph.

Trochäisch (trŏ-khä'ĭsh), *Ger.* Trochaic.

Trochäus (trŏ-khä'oos), *Ger.* Trochee.

Trochee (trŏ' kā), *Lat.* A dissyllabic musical foot containing one long and one short syllable, — ˘.

Trois (trwä), *Fr.* Three.

Tromba (trŏm'bä), *It.* A trumpet; also an 8-feet reed organ-stop.

Trombacellociyde. A B♭ ophicleide.

Tromba cromatica (trŏm'bä krō-mä'tĭ-kä), *It.* The modern valve trumpet, upon which semitones can be produced.

Tromba di basso (trŏm'bä dē bäs'sō), *It.* The bass trumpet.

Trombadore (trŏm-bä-dō'rĕ), *It.* A trumpeter.

Tromba marina (trŏm'bä mä-rē'nä), *It.* See *Trumpet, marine.*

Tromba prima (trŏm'bä prē'mä), *It.* First trumpet.

Tromba seconda (trŏm'bä sā-kŏn'dä), *It.* Second trumpet.

Tromba spezzato (trŏm'bä spĕ-tsä'tō), *It.* An obsolete name for the bass trombone.

Trombe sorde (trŏm'bĕ sŏr'dĕ), *It. pl.* Trumpets having dampers.

Trombetta (trŏm-bĕt'tä), *It.* A small trumpet.

Trombettino (trŏm-bĕt-tē'nō), *It.* A trumpeter.

Trombone (trŏm-bō'nĕ), *It.* } A very powerful
Trombone (trŏnh-bōn), *Fr.* } instrument of the trumpet species, but much larger and with a sliding-tube; also a very powerful and full-toned reed-stop in an organ, of 8-feet scale on the manual, and 16- or 32-feet on the pedal.

Trombone, alto. A trombone having a compass from the small c or e to the one-lined a or two-lined c, and noted in the alto clef.

Trombone, bass. A trombone with a compass from the great C to the one-lined c, and noted in the F clef.

Trombone, tenor. A trombone having a compass from the small c to the one-lined g, and noted in the tenor clef.

Tromboni (trŏm-bō'nĭ), *It. pl.* Trombones.

Trommel (trŏm'm'l), *Ger.* The military drum.

Trommelboden (trŏm'm'l-bŏ'd'n), *Ger.* Bottom of a drum.

Trommelkasten (trŏm'm'l-käs-t'n), *Ger.* The body of a drum.

Trommelklöpfel (trŏm'm'l-klöp-fĕl), } *Ger.*
Trommelschlägel (trŏm'm'l-shlä'gĕl), } Drumsticks.

Trommeln (trŏm'mĕln), *Ger.* To drum; drumming; beating the drum.

Trommelstück (trŏm'm'l-stük'), *Ger.* A tambourine; a tabor.

Trompe (trōnhp), *Fr.* A trumpet; also a reed stop in an organ.

Trompe de béarn (trōnhp duh bā-ärn), *Fr.* The jew's-harp.

Trompete (trŏm-pā'tĕ), *Ger.* A trumpet; also a reed stop in an organ.

Trompetenzug (trŏm - pā' t'n - tsoog'), *Ger.* Trumpet stop, or register, in an organ.

Trompeter (trŏm-pā'tĕr), *Ger.* } A trum-
Trompeteur (trōnh-pā-tŭr), *Fr.* } peter.

Trompette (trōnh-pāt), *Fr.* A trumpet; also a trumpeter; also a reed-stop in an organ.

Trompette à clefs (trōnh-pāt ä klā), *Fr.* The keyed trumpet.

Trompette à pistons (trōnh-pāt ä pēs-tōnh), *Fr.* The valve trumpet.

Trompette harmonique (trōnh-pāt här-mŏnh-ĕk), *Fr.* Harmonic trumpet, a reed-stop in an organ of 8 or 16 feet. See *Harmonic flute.*

Troppo (trŏp'pō), *It.* Too much; *non troppo allegro*, not too quick.

ä *arm,* ă *add,* ä *ale,* ĕ *end,* ē *eve,* ĭ *ill,* ī *isle,* ŏ *old,* ō *odd,* oo *moon,* ŭ *but,* ü *Fr. sound,* kh *Ger. ch,* nh *nasal.*

15   (225)

Troubadours (troo-bä-door), ⎫ The
Trouveres (troo-vär),   *Fr. pl.* ⎬ bards,
Trouveurs (troo-vär), ⎭ and
poet-musicians of Provence about the tenth century.

Troupe, opera. A company of musicians associated for the purpose of giving operas, generally traveling from place to place.

Trovatore (trō-vä-tō'rĕ), *It.* A minstrel.

Trugschluss (troogh-shloos'), *Ger.* Interrupted, or deceptive, cadence; an unexpected, or interrupted, resolution of a discord.

Trumpet. The loudest of all portable wind instruments, consisting of a folded tube, generally made of brass, but sometimes of silver; it is used chiefly in martial and orchestral music.

Trumpeter. One who sounds, or plays, the trumpet.

Trumpet, harmonical. An instrument, the sounds of which resemble those of a trumpet, differing from that instrument only in being longer and having more branches; the sackbut.

Trumpet, marine. An ancient species of monochord, played with a bow, and producing a sound resembling that of a trumpet.

Trumpet, reed. An instrument consisting of a trumpet within which were inclosed thirty-six brass-reeded pipes, arranged in a circle, so that in turning the circle each pipe could, in turn, be brought between the mouth-piece and the bell of the instrument.

Trumpet stop. A stop in an organ having a tone similar to that of a trumpet.

Trumpet, valve. A trumpet the tones of which are changed by the use of valves.

Trumscheit (troom'shīt), *Ger.* A rude musical instrument with one or more chords. A sort of rude bass fiddle.

T. S. The initials of Tasto Solo. Unison.

Tuba (too'bä), *Lat.* A trumpet; also the name of a powerful reed-stop in an organ. See *Ophicleide.*

Tuba clarion (too'bä klä'rĭ-ŏn), *Lat.* A 4-feet reed-stop of the tuba species.

Tuba communis (too'bä kŏm-moo'nis), *Lat.* An ancient instrument of the trumpet kind so called in contradistinction to the tuba ductilis.

Tuba ductilis (too'bä dook-tĕ'lĭs), *Lat.* An ancient trumpet of the curvilinear form.

Tubare (too-bä'rĕ), *Lat.* To blow the trumpet.

Tu ba major (too'bä mä'yŏr) ⎫ *Lat.* An
Tuba mirabilis (too'bä mĭ-rä'bē-lĭs), ⎬ 8-feet
reed-stop, on a high pressure of wind, first introduced into the Birmingham Town Hall organ, and invented by William Hill. See *Ophicleide.*

Tuba stentorofonica (too'bä stĕn-to-rō-fō'nĭ-kä), *It.* The name given by Sir Samuel Morehead and other writers to his invention of the speaking-trumpet.

Tubicen (too'bĭ-tsĕn), *Lat.* A trumpeter; one who plays on the trumpet.

Tubular instruments. Instruments formed of tubes, straight or curved, of wood or metal.

Tucket. A flourish of trumpets.

Tuiau d'orgue (twē-ō dŏrg), *Fr.* See *Tuyau d'orgue.*

Tumultuoso (too-mool'too-ō'zō), *It.* Tumultuous, agitated.

Tunable. An epithet given to those pipes, strings, and other sonorous bodies which, from the equal density of their parts, are capable of being perfectly tuned.

Tune. An air, a melody; a succession of measured sounds agreeable to the ear, and possessing a distinct and striking character; to bring into harmony.

Tuned. Put in tune.

Tuneful. Harmonious, melodious, musical; as, tuneful notes, tuneful birds.

Tuneless. Unmelodious, unmusical.

Tuner. One whose occupation is to tune musical instruments.

Tuning. Putting in tune; rendering the tones of an instrument accordant.

Tuning-cone. A cone of metal or horn used in tuning organ-pipes. By pressing it in the end of the pipe the pitch is slightly lowered, or by pressing it over the end of the pipe it is slightly contracted, whereby the tone is sharpened.

Tuning-fork. A small steel instrument having two prongs, which, upon being struck, gives a certain fixed tone, used for tuning instruments, and for ascertaining, or indicating, the pitch of tunes.

Tuning-hammer. A steel or iron utensil used by harpsichord and pianoforte-tuners.

Tuning-key. A tuning-hammer.

Tuning-slide. An English instrument for pitching the keynote, producing thirteen semitones—from C to C.

Tuoni ecclesiastici (too-o'nĭ ĕk-klä-zĭ-äs-tĭ'-tshĭ), *It. pl.* Ecclesiastical modes or tones.

Tuoni transportati (too-ō'nĭ träns-pŏr-tä'tĭ), *It. pl.* Transposed tones or melodies.

Tuorbe (twŏrb), *Fr.* See *Theorbo.*

Turbo (tŭr'bō), *Gr.* A seashell anciently employed as a trumpet.

Turca (toor kä), ⎫ Turkish; *alla*
Turchesco (toor'-kä-skō), *It.* ⎬ *Turca*, in the
Turco (toor'kō) ⎭ style of Turkish music.

Turdion (toor-dĭ-ŏn'), *Sp.* An ancient Spanish dance.

Türkish (tür'kĭsh), *Ger.* See *Turca.*

Turkish music. See *Janitscharenmusik.*

ä *arm*, ă *add*, ā *ale*, ĕ *end*, ē *eve*, I *ill*, ī *isle*, ō *old*, ŏ *odd*, oo *moon*, ŭ *but*, ü *Fr. sound*, kh *Ger. ch.* ih *nasal.*

(226)

Turn. An embellishment formed of appoggiaturas, consisting of the note on which the turn is made, the note above, and the semitone below it.

Turn, common. A turn commencing on the note above the note on which the turn is made.

Turn, inverted. An embellishment formed by prefixing three notes to a principal note, viz.: the semitone below the principal note, the principal note, and the note above it.

Turn, regular. A turn consisting of the note above the principal note, the principal note, and the semitone below it.

Tusch (toosh), *Ger.* A flourish of trumpets and kettledrums.

Tute (too'tĕ), *Ger.* A cornet.

Tutta (toot'tä), *It.*) All, the whole; entirely,
Tutto (toot'tŏ), ∫ quite.

Tutta forza (toot-tä fōr'tsä), *It.*) The
Tutta la forza (toot'tä lä fōr'tsä), ∫ whole power; as loud as possible; with the utmost force and vehemence.

Tutte (toot'tĕ), *It.*) All, the entire band or
Tutti (toot'tī), ∫ chorus; in a solo or concerto it means that the full orchestra is to come in.

Tutte corde (toōt'tĕ kōr'dĕ), *It.* All the strings; in pianoforte music this means that the pedal, which shifts the action, or movement, must no longer be pressed down.

Tutti unisoni (toot'tī oo-nē-zo'uī), *It. pl.* All in unison.

Tutto arco (toot'tō är'kō), *It.* With the whole length of the bow.

Tuyau d'orgue (tü-yō dōrg), *Fr.* An organ-pipe.

Twelfth. An interval comprising eleven conjunct degrees, or twelve sounds; also an organ-stop tuned twelve notes above the diapasons.

Twice-marked octave. The name given in Germany to the notes between  inclusive; these are expressed by small letters with two short strokes.

Twitter. To make a succession of small, tremulous, intermitted tones.

Tympani (tĭm'pä-nē), *It. pl.* Kettledrums.

Tympanista. See *Timpanista*.

Type, music. Notes of music cast in metal, or cut in word for the purpose of printing.

Tyrolienne (tī-rō-li-ĕn), *Fr.* Songs or dances peculiar to the Tyrolese.

U

Ueberblasen (ü'b'r-blä-s'n), *Ger.* To overblow.

Uebergang (ü'bĕr-gäng), *Ger.* Transition, change of key.

Ueberleitung (ü'b'r-lī-toong), *Ger.* Leading over. A passage leading across to something else of greater importance.

Uebermässig (ü'bĕr-mäs'sĭg), *Ger.* Augmented, superfluous.

Ueberschlagen (ü'bĕr-shlä'g'n), *Ger.* Crossing over (the hands in piano-performance).

Uebersetzen (ü'b'r-sĕt-z'n), *Ger.* Setting over. The passing of a finger over the thumb, or of one foot over the other, in pedal-playing.

Uebung (ü'boong), *Ger.* An exercise; a study for the practice of some peculiar difficulty.

Uebungen (ü'boon-gĕn), *Ger. pl.* Exercises.

Ugab (oo-gäb), *Heb.* An organ.

Uguale (oo-gwä'lĕ), *It.* Equal, like, similar.

Ugualita (oo-gwäl'ī-tä), *It.* Equality.

Ugualmente (oo-gwäl-mĕn'tĕ), *It.* Equality, alike.

Umana (oo-mä'nä), *It.*) Human; *voce umana*,
Umano (oo-mä'nŏ), ∫ the human voice.

Umfang (oom'fäng), *Ger.* Compass, extent.

Umfang der Stimme (oom'fäng dĕr stĭm'mĕ), *Ger.* Compass of the voice.

Umkehrung (oom'kä-roong), *Ger.* Inversion.

Umore (oo-mō'rĕ), *It.* Humor, caprice.

Umschreibung (oom'shrī-boong), *Ger.* Circumscription, limitation.

Umstimmung (oom'stĭm-moong), *Ger.* Retuning, a change of tuning.

Un. Abbreviation of Unison.

Un (oon),)
Una (oo'nä), *It.* } A, an, one.
Uno (oo'nŏ),)

Una altera volta (oo'nä äl'tĕ-rä vōl'tä), *It.* Play it over again.

Unaccented. A term applied to those parts of a measure which have no accent.

Unaccompanied. A song or other vocal composition without instrumental accompaniment.

Una corda (oo'nä kōr'dä), *It.* One string, on one string only; in pianoforte music it means that the soft pedal is to be used.

Unca (oon'kä), *Lat.* The old name for a quaver.

Un canto spianato (oon kän'tō spē-ä-nä'tō), *It.* A vocal composition, the notes of which are peculiarly distinct from one another.

Und (oond), *Ger.* And; *Aria und Chor*, air and chorus.

Unda maris (oon'dä mä'rĭs), *Lat.* Wave of the sea; an organ-stop tuned rather sharper than the others, and producing an undulating, or waving, effect, when drawn in conjunction with another stop; this effect is sometimes produced by means of a pipe with two mouths, the one a little higher than the other.

Undecima (oon-dä'tsĭ-mä), *Lat.* The eleventh.

Undecimole (oon-dĕ-tshĭ-mō'lĕ), *It.* A group of eleven notes, occupying a unit of time or an aliquot part thereof.

Under part. The part beneath, or subordinate to, the other part or parts.

Under song. In very old English music this was a kind of ground or drone accompaniment to a song, and which was sustained by another singer; called, also, burden and foot.

Undulation. That agitation in the air caused by the vibration of any sonorous body. So called because it resembles the motion of waves.

Unendlicher Canon (oon-ĕnd'lĭ-kh'r kä'nōn), *Ger.* Endless canon, a canon which goes on indefinitely; a round.

Unequal Temperament. That method of tuning the twelve sounds included in an octave, which renders some of the scales more in tune than the others. See *Equal temperament*.

Ungar (oon'gär),
Ungarisch (oon-gä'rĭsh), *Ger.* } Hungarian; in the Hungarian style.

Ungeduldig (oon'gĕ-dool'dĭgh), *Ger.* Impatient.

Ungerade Taktart (oon-gĕ-rä'dĕ täkt'ärt), *Ger.* Triple time; uneven time.

Ungestüm (oon'gĕ-stüm), *Ger.* Impetuous.

Ungezwungen (oon'gĕ-tswoon-gh'n), *Ger.* Easy, natural.

Ungleicher Contrapunkt (oon'glī-kh'r kōn'-trä-poonkt'), *Ger.* Unequal counterpoint; counterpoint in which the notes are not of the same value as those of the cantus fermus.

Ungleichschwebende Temperatur (oon'glīkh-shwä'b'n-dĕ tĕm'pĕ-rä-toor'), *Ger.* Unequal temperament.

Unharmonischer Querstand (oon'här-mō'nĭ-shĕr kwär'ständ), *Ger.* A false relation.

Unichordum (oo-nĭ-kŏr'doom), *Lat.* A monochord. The marine trumpet.

Unison (oon-ĭ-sŏnh), *Fr.* One sound; unison.

Unison. An accordance, or coincidence, of one sound.

Unisonant.
Unisonous. } Being in unison; having the same degree of gravity or acuteness.

Unison, augmented. A semitone on same degree of staff.

Unisoni (oo'nē-zō'nĭ), *It. pl.* Unisons; two, three or more parts are to play or sing in unison with each other, or, if this be not practicable, in octaves.

Unisono (oo-nĭ-sō'nō), *It.*
Unisonus (oo-nĭ-sō'noos), *Lat.* } A unison; in unison, two or more sounds having the same pitch.

Unita (oo'nĭ-tä),
Unito (oo'uĭ-tō), *It.* } United, joined.

Unitamente (oo-nĭ-tä-mĕn'tĕ), *It.* Together jointly, unitedly.

Unite (ü-nēt), *Fr.* Unity.

Unity. Oneness, the agreement of all parts of a composition, or idea, in such manner that a whole is expressed. In essay unity depends upon the preponderance of a single idea, in composition, upon the preponderance of a single motive.

Unmeasured recitative. Recitative without definite measure.

Unmusical. Not musical, not harmonious or agreeable to the ear. Unmusical sounds are those produced by irregular vibrations.

Uno (oo'nō),
Una (oo'nä), *It.* } One.

Uno a uno (oo'no ä oo'no), *It.* One by one; one after another.

Un peu (ŭnh pŭh), *Fr.* A little.

Un peu lent (ŭnh pŭh länh), *Fr.* Rather slow.

Un peu plus vite qu'andante (ŭnh pŭh plü vēt k'änh-dänht), *Fr.* A little quicker than andante.

Un pochettino (oon pō-kĕt-tē'nō), *It.* } A little,
Un pochina (oon pō-kē'nä), a very little.

Un pochina piu mosso (oon pō-kē'nä pē'oo mōs'sō), *It.* A very little more lively.

Un poco (oon pō'kō), *It.* A little.

Un poco allegro (oon pō'kō al-lä'grō), *It.* A little quick, rather quick.

Un poco piu (oon pō'kō pē'oo), *It.* A little more.

Un poco piu presto (oon pō'kō pē'oo prĕs'tō), *It.* A little quicker.

Un poco ritenuto (oon pō'kō rē-tĕ-noo'tō), *It.* Gradually slower.

Un recitativo spianato (oon rĕ-tshĭ-tä-tē'vo spĭ-ä-nä'tō), *It.* A recitative having notes distinct from each other.

Unrein (oon'rīn), *Ger.* Impure; out of tune.

Unruhig (oon'roo-hĭg), *Ger.* Restless; inquiet. (Manifested mainly in nuances of the tempo rubato.)

Unschuldig (oon'shool'dĭgh), *Ger.* Innocent, simply.

Unsingbar (oon-sĭng'bär), *Ger.* Impossible to be sung.

Unstrung. Relaxed in tension; an intrument from which the strings have been taken.

ä *arm*, ă *add*, â *ale*, ĕ *end*, ē *eve*, ĭ *ill*, ī *isle*, ō *old*, ŏ *odd*, oo *moon*, ŭ *but*, ü *Fr. sound*, kh *Ger. ch*, nh *nasal.*

Un style aisé (ün stēl ā-zā), *Fr.* A free, easy style.
Unter (oon'tĕr), *Ger.* Under, below.
Unterbass (oon'tĕr-bäss), *Ger.* The double bass.
Unterbrechung (oon'ter-brĕ'khoong), *Ger.* Interruption.
Unterbrochene Cadenz (oon-tĕr-brō'kh'nĕ kä-dĕnz), *Ger.* Interrupted cadence.
Unterdominante (oon'tĕr-dō-mi-nän'tĕ), *Ger.* Under dominant. The subdominant.
Unterhalbton (oon'tĕr-hülb'tōn), *Ger.* A half-step below.
Unterhaltungsstück (oon'tĕr-häl'toongs-stük), *Ger.* Entertainment, short play, short piece of music.
Untermediant (oon'tĕr-mā'dĭ-änt), *Ger.* The submediant; the third below the tonic.
Unterricht (oon'tĕr-rĭkht), *Ger.* Instruction, information.
Untersatz (oon'tĕr-sätz), *Ger.* Supporter, stay; a pedal register, double-stopped bass of 32-feet tone, in German organs. See *Subbourdon.*
Untersetzen (oon'tĕr-sĕt-z'n), *Ger.* Passing the thumb under a finger in piano-playing; passing one foot under another in pedal-playing.
Unterstimme (oon'tĕr-stĭm-mĕ), *Ger.* The under voice; lowest voice in a composition.
Untertasten (oon'tĕr-täs-t'n), *Ger.* The lower, or white, keys of the pianoforte or organ.
Un terzo di battuta (oon tĕr'zō dē bät-too'tä), *It.* A third part of the bar.
Untönend (oon-tö'nĕnd), *Ger.* Not sonorous; void of tone.
Untunable. Incapable of being tuned.
Untune. To put out of tune; to make discordant.
Untuned. Not tuned; discordant.
Unverziert (oon'fĕr-zērt), *Ger.* Unornamented.

Unvollkommen (oon'vŏll-kŏm-mĕn), *Ger.* Incomplete. Applied generally to cadences and closes.
Uomo (oo-ō-mō), *It.* A man. *Primo uomo,* a male soprano.
Up beat. The raising of the hand, or baton, in beating, or marking, time.
Up-bow sign. A mark used in violin music, showing that the bow is to be carried up, >.
Upinge (oo-pĭn-ghĕ), *Ger.* The name of a song consecrated by the ancient Greeks to Diana.
Upper voice. A designation applied to the person who sings the higher part.
Upright pianoforte. A pianoforte, the strings of which are placed obliquely or vertically upward.
Uranion. An instrument in make similar to a harpsichord, or pianoforte.
Uscir di tuono (oos-tshĕr dē too-ō'nō), *It.* To get out of tune.
Usus (oo'sŭs), *Gr.* That branch of the ancient meloposia which comprehended the rules for so regulating the order, or succession, of the sounds as to produce an agreeable melody.
Ut (oot), *Fr.* The note C; the syllable originally applied by Guido to the note C, or do.
Ut bémol (oot bā'mōl), *Fr.* The note C♭.
Ut diese (oot dĭ-āz), *Fr.* The note C♯.
Ut diese mineur (oot dĭ-āz mē-nŭr), *Fr.* The key of C♯ minor.
Ut mineur (oot mē-nŭr), *Fr.* C minor.
Ut queant laxis (oot kwā'änt läx'ĭs), *Lat.* The commencing words of the hymn to St. John the Baptist, from which Guido is said to have taken the syllables ut, re, mi, fa, sol, la for his system of solmisation. It was composed about the year 770.
Utricularis tibia (oo-trĭk'oo-lä'rĭs tē'bē-ä), *Lat.* The name given by the Romans to the bagpipe. See that word.
Ut supra (oot soo-prä), *Lat.* As above, as before. See *Come sopra.*

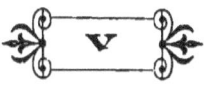

V., or **Vi.** Abbreviations for Violini.
Va (vä), *It.* Go on.
Vacillando (vät-tshĭ-län'dō), *It.* Wavering, uncertain, irregular in the time.
Va con spirito (vä kōn spē'rĭ-tō), *It.* Continue in a spirited style.
Va crescendo (vä krĕ-shĕn'dō), *It.* Go on increasing the tone.
Vagans (vä'gäns), *Lat.* Vague. A term applied by the old composers to the last part of a five-part composition, because, being written after the remaining voices, it had only the least significant opportunities, and could be written as second alto or second tenor.
Vago (vä'gō), *It.* Vague, rambling, uncertain, as to the time or expression.
Valce (väl'tshĕ), *It.* } A waltz, a dance in 3-4
Valse (väls), *Fr.* } time.
Valeur (vä-lŭr), *Fr.* } The value, length, or
Valore (vä-lō'rĕ), *It.* } duration, of a note.

ä *arm,* ā *add,* â *ale,* ĕ *end,* ē *eve,* ĭ *ill,* ī *isle,* ŏ *odd,* ō *old,* oo *moon,* ŭ *but,* ü *Fr. sound,* kh *Ger. ch,* nh *nasal.*

Valse à deux temps (väls ä dü tänh), *Fr.* A modern quick waltz, in which the dancers make two steps in each measure.

Valves. Contrivances for admitting or shutting off wind. Found in organs, reed organs, and especially in brass instruments, where they serve to admit air or cut it off from what are called "crooks," or additional lengths of tube. Horns and instruments of this class have three valves, one lowering the pitch a half step, one a full step, and one a step and a half. They may be used separately or together. Each of these valves opens a tube affording a complete set of harmonics like that of the natural tube, only as much lower as the tube affords additional length. Hence, by means of them a complete chromatic scale may be obtained, and many notes can be obtained in either one of several ways.

Valve trumpets, whose tones are varied by the use of valves.

Variamente (vä-rē-ä-mĕn'tĕ), *It.* } In a varied,
Variamento (vä-rē-ä-mĕn'tō), } free style of performance or execution.

Variationen (fä-rē-ä-tsē-ō'nĕn), *Ger. pl.* } Varia-
Variazioni (vä-rē-ä-tsē-ō'nĕ), *It. pl.* } tions.

Variations. A musical form consisting of characteristic treatments of a musical theme or air. The diversification of a theme in thematic work differs from that in variation work in the following particulars: In thematic work (sonata and fugue) the rhythm of the theme is not varied, but the harmony and melodic outline are; in variation writing there are two principles of proceeding. In the older one, called formal variations, the harmony of the theme is not varied, or if varied, only so much as to transfer it from major to minor mode; but the melody is amplified and ornamented to any extent. In the more modern method of writing, called character variations, the theme is sometimes varied in harmony to a very unusual degree. The limits of this method of diversification rest upon the fact that a musical theme consists of three elements, its melody, harmony, and rhythm. Its complete identity resides in the three combined, but either one or even two of these may be modified and still the theme contain enough of its original character to permit us to refer the modified forms to the original as their source. In thematic transformation the rhythm, being the ruling element, is rarely changed; in variation writing the melody (and its harmony) being the ruling element, these are less changed than the rhythm, and most variations are essentially amplifications of an idea rather than transformations. Of character variations those in the sonata of Beethoven, Opus 26, are strong examples; of formal variations those in the second movement of Beethoven's Sonata Appassionata are notable.

Variato (vä-rē-ä'tō), *It.* } Varied, diversified,
Varié (vä-rē-ā'), *Fr.* } with variations.

Variazione (vä-rē-ä-tsē-ō'nĕ), *It.* Variation.
Varsovienne (vär-sō-vĭ-änh), *Fr.* A slow Polish dance in ¾ measure.
Vaudevil. A ballad, a song, a vaudeville.
Vaudeville (vō-dĕ-vēl'), *Fr.* A country ballad, or song, a roundelay; also a simple form of operetta; a comedy, or short drama, interspersed with songs.
Vc. Abbreviation for Violoncello.
Veemente (vā-mĕn'tĕ), *It.* Vehement, forcible.
Veemenza (vā-mĕn'tsä), *It.* Vehemence, force.
Velata (vā-lä'tä), *It.* } Veiled; a voice sounding as if it were covered with a veil.
Velato (vā-lä'tō), }

Vellutata (vĕl-loo-tä'tä), *It.* } In a velvety
Vellutato (vĕl-loo-tä'tō), } manner; in a soft, smooth, and velvety style.
Veloce (vĕ-lō'tshĕ), } *It.*
Velocemente (vĕ-lō-tshĕ-mĕn'tĕ), } Swiftly, quickly, in a rapid time.
Velocissimamente (vĕ-lō-tshĕs-sē-mä-mĕn'tĕ), } *It.*
Velocissimo (vĕ-lō-tshĕs'sĭ-mō), } Very swiftly, with extreme rapidity.
Velocita (vĕ-lō-tshē'tä), *It.* Swiftness, rapidity.
Veneziana (vĕ-nä-tsĭ-ä'nä), *It.* Venetian, the Venetian style.
Ventil (fĕn'tĭl), *Ger.* } Valve, in modern
Ventile (vĕn-tē'lĕ), *It.* } wind instruments, for producing the semitones; also a valve for shutting off the wind in an organ.
Vepres (väpr), *Fr.* Vespers, evening prayer.
Veränderungen (fĕr-än'dĕr-oong-ĕn), *Ger. pl.* Variations.
Verbindung (fĕr-bĭn'doong), *Ger.* Combination, union, connection.
Verbindungszeichen (fĕr-bĭnd'oongs-tsī'kh'n), *Ger.* Binding-marks, *i.e.*, ties.
Verdeckt (fĕr-dĕkt), *Ger.* Hidden. (Octaves, fifths, etc.)
Verdoppelt (fĕr-dŏp'pĕlt), *Ger.* Doubled.
Verdoppelung (fĕr-dŏp'pĕl-oong), *Ger.* Doubling.
Vergellen (fĕr-gĕl'l'n), *Ger.* To diminish gradually.
Verger. The chief officer of a cathedral; a pew-opener or attendant at a church.
Vergliedern (fĕr-glē'dĕrn), *Ger.* To articulate.
Vergrösserung (fĕr-grös'sĕr-oong), *Ger.* Augmentation.
Verhallen (fĕr-häl'l'n), *Ger.* To diminish gradually.
Verhallend (fĕr-häl'lĕnd), *Ger.* Dying away.
Verilay. Rustic ballad, a roundelay. See *Vaudeville*, and, also, *Freemen's songs.*
Verkehrung (fĕr-kā'roong), *Ger.* Inversion; contrary motion in imitation.
Verkleinerung (fĕr-klī'nĕr-oong), *Ger.* Diminution.
Verlagsrecht (fĕr-lägs'rĕkht'), *Ger.* Copyright.

Verlöschend (fĕr-lö'shĕnd), *Ger.* Extinguishing.
Vermindert (fĕr-mĭn'dĕrt), *Ger.* Diminished; diminished interval.
Vers (fĕrs), *Ger.* Verse, strophe, stanza.
Verschiebung (fĕr-shē'boong), *Ger.* A "shift." The soft pedal of a piano.
Verschwindend (fĕr-shwĭn-dĕnd), *Ger.* Dying away.
Verse. That portion of an anthem, or service, intended to be sung by one singer to each part, and not by the full choir in chorus. In secular music, as a song or ballad, each stanza of the words is a verse.
Verse, hexameter. A verse having six feet, of which the first four may be either dactyls or spondees; the fifth must be a dactyl, and the sixth a spondee.
Verse, iambic. A verse consisting of a short syllable followed by a long one, or of an unaccented syllable followed by an accented one.
Verser (vär-sā), *Fr.* A verse.
Versetta (vĕr-sĕt'tä), *It.* } A short, or little,
Versetto (vĕr-sĕt'tō), verse; a strophe.
Versette (fĕr-sĕt'tĕ), *Ger.* } Short pieces for
Versetten (fĕr-sĕt't'n), the organ, intended as preludes, interludes, or postludes.
Versetzen (fĕr-sĕt'tsĕn), *Ger.* To transpose.
Versetzung (fĕr-sĕt'tsoong), *Ger.* Transposition.
Versetzungszeichen (fĕr-sĕt'tsoongs-tsī'kh'n), *Ger.* The marks of transposition, the sharp, the flat and the natural.
Versicle. A little verse.
Versikel (fĕr-sĭk'l), *Ger.* A versicle.
Versmass (fĕrs-mäss), *Ger.* The measure of the verse; the metre.
Verso (vĕr'sō), *It.* Verse.
Verspätung (fĕr-spä'toong), *Ger.* Retardation, delay.
Verstimmt (fĕr-stĭmt'), *Ger.* Out of tune.
Verte (vĕr'tĕ), *Lat.* Turn over.
Verte subito (vĕr'tĕ soo'bĭ-tō), *Lat.* Turn the leaf quickly.
Vertönen (fĕr-tö'nĕn), *Ger.* To cease sounding, to die away.
Verwandt (fĕr-wäudt'), *Ger.* Related, relative keys, etc.
Verwechselung (fĕr-wĕkh'sĕl-oong), *Ger.* Changing, mutation, as to key, tone, etc.
Verwellend (fĕr-wĭ'lĕnd), *Ger.* Delaying, retarding the time.
Verwerfung (fĕr-wĕrf'oong), *Ger.* Transposing.
Verziert (fĕr-tsĭrt'), *Ger.* Embellished, decorated.
Verzierung (fĕr-tsē'roong), *Ger.* Embellishment, ornament.
Verzögerung (fĕr-tsö'gĕ-roong), *Ger.* Retardation.

Verzweiflungsvoll (fĕr-tswī'floongs-fōl), *Ger.* Full of despair.
Vesper (fĕs'pĕr), *Ger.* }
Vespero (vĕs'pĕ-rō), *It.* } Vespers.
Vespro (vĕs'prō), *It.* }
Vesperæ (vĕs'pĕ-rä), *Lat.* Vespers, or the evening service in the Roman Catholic Church.
Vesper bell. The sounding of a bell about half an hour after sunset in Roman Catholic countries, calling to Vespers.
Vesper hymn. A hymn sung in the evening service of the Roman Catholic Church.
Vespers. Name of the last evening service in the Roman Catholic Church, consisting chiefly of singing.
Vespertini psalmi (vĕs-pĕr-tē'nĭ psäl'mĭ), *It. pl.* Evening psalms, or hymns.
Vezzosamente (vĕt-tsō zä-měn'tĕ), *It.* Tenderly, softly, gracefully.
Vezzoso (vĕt-tsō'zō), *It.* Graceful, sweet, tender.
Vibrante (vē-brän'tĕ), *It.* Vibrating, a tremulous, quivering touch, full resonance of tone.
Vibrate (vē-brä'tĕ), *It.* } A strong, vibrating,
Vibrato (vē-brä'tō), full quality of tone; resonant.
Vibration. The tremulous or undulatory motion of any sonorous body by which the sound is produced, the sound being grave or acute as the vibrations are fewer or more numerous in a given time.
Vibratissimo (vē-brä-tēs'sī-mō), *It.* Extremely vibrating and tremulous.
Vibrato molto (vē-brä'tō mŏl'tō), *It.* Extremely rapid.
Vibrazione (vē-brä-tsī-ō'nĕ), *It.* Vibration, tremulousness.
Vicenda (vē-tshĕn'dä), *It.* Alternation, change.
Vicendevole (vē-tshĕn-dä'vō-lĕ), *It.* Alternately, by turns.
Vide (vēd), *Fr.* } See *Vuide*.
Vido (vē'dō), *It.* }
Videl (fīd'ĕl), *Ger.* A fiddle.
Viel. An old name for instruments of the violin species.
Viel (fēl), *Ger.* Much, a great deal; *mit vielem Tone*, with much tone.
Vielchörig (fēl'kör-ĭgh), *Ger.* Many-choired. For several choirs.
Vielfacher kontrapunkt (fēl'fä-kh'r kön-trä-poonkt), *Ger.* Polymorphous counterpoint.
Vielle (vēl), *Fr.* The hurdygurdy.
Vielleur (vŏ-yŭr), *Fr.* Hurdygurdy-player.
Vielstimmig (fēl'stĭm'mĭg), *Ger.* For many voices.
Vielstimmiges Tonstück (fēl'stĭm'mĭ-gĕs tön-stük), *Ger.* A piece for several voices, a choral piece, a glee.
Vieltönig (fēl-tö'nĭgh), *Ger.* Multisonous, manysounding.

arm, å add, ä ale, ĕ end, ē eve, ĭ ill, ī isle, ŏ old, ŏ odd, oo moon, ŭ but, ü Fr. sound, kh Ger. ch, nh nasal.

Vier (fēr), *Ger.* Four.

Vierfach (fēr'fäkh), *Gcr.* Fourfold; of four ranks of pipes, etc.

Vierfüssig (fēr'füs-sĭg), *Ger.* Four-feet (of organ-pipes and pitch).

Viergesang (fēr'gĕ-zäng), *Ger.* Song for four voices.

Viergestrichene Note (fēr-gĕ-strī'kh'nĕ nō'tĕ), *Ger.* A demisemiquaver.

Viergestrichene Octave (fēr'gĕ-strī'kh'nĕ ŏk-tä'vĕ), *Ger.* The four-marked octave.

Vierhändig (fēr-hän'dĭgh), *Ger.* For four hands.

Vierhändiges Tonstück (fēr-hän'dĭ-ghĕs tŏn'-stük), *Ger.* A piece for four hands.

Vierklang (fēr'kläng), *Ger.* A chord of four tones.

Viermässig (fēr-mä'sĭgh), *Ger.* Containing four measures.

Viersaitig (fēr'säī-tĭgh), *Ger.* Four-stringed.

Vierstimmig (fēr'stĭm-mĭgh), *Ger.* Four-voiced; in four parts; for four voices or instruments.

Vierstimmiges Tonstück (fēr'stĭm-mĭ-ghĕs tŏn'stük), *Ger.* A quartet.

Vierstück (fēr-stük), *Ger.* Quartet; for four performers.

Vierte (fēr'tĕ), *Ger.* Fourth.

Viertelnote (fēr't'l-nō'tĕ), *Ger.* Quarter note; a crotchet, the fourth part of a semibreve.

Viertelton (fēr't'l-tōn), *Ger.* A quarter tone.

Vierundsechzigstel (fēr-oond-sĕkh'tsĭgh-stĕl), *Ger.* Hemidemisemiquavers.

Viervierteltakt (fēr-fēr'tl-täkt), *Ger.* Common time of four crotchets.

Vierzehn (fēr-tsān), *Ger.* Fourteen.

Vierzehnte (fēr'tsān-tĕ), *Ger.* Fourteenth.

Vierzweiteltact (fēr-zwī'tĕl-täkt'), *Ger.* Time of four minims. A measure composed of half notes, Four-two measure.

Vietato (vē-ā-tä'tō), *It.* Forbidden, prohibited; a term applied to such intervals and modulations as are not allowed by the laws of harmony.

Vif (vēf), *Fr.* Lively, brisk, quick, sprightly.

Vigorosamente (vē-gō-rō-zä-měn'tĕ), *It.* Vigorously, with energy.

Vigoróso (vē-gō-rō'zō), *It.* Vigorous, bold, energetic.

Viguela (vē-goo-ā'lä), *Sp.* A species of lute or guitar.

Vihuela (vē-hoo-ā'lä), *Sp.* Guitar.

Villageois (vē-lä-zhwä), *Fr.* Rustic; *à la villageoise*, in a rustic style.

Villancico (vĭl-yän-thĭ'kō), } *Sp.* } A species
Villancio (vĕl-yän'thĭ-ō), } of pastoral poem or song.

Villanella (vĕl-lä-nĕl'lä), *It.* } An old rustic
Villanelle (vĕl-yä-nĕl), *Fr.* } Italian dance, accompanied with singing.

Villareccio (vĭl-lä-rŏ'tshī-ō), *It.* Rustic, rural.

Vina. A Hindoo instrument, of the plucked-string variety. It consists of a sounding-body of bamboo, with two gourds as resonance-bodies. There are seven strings of fine wire or of silk. The instrument is furnished with frets. It is now obsolete. It dates from about a thousand years before the Christian era.

Vinata (vē-nä'tä), *It.* A vintage-song.

Vinetta (vē-nĕt'tä), *It.* Diminutive of Vinata.

Viol. An old instrument somewhat resembling the violin, of which it was the origin, but with a flat back; it had six strings, with frets, and was played with a bow. The contra bass is the only surviving representative.

Viola. A tenor violin; an instrument similar in tone and formation to the violin, but larger in size and having a compass a fifth lower.

Viola bardone (vē-ō'lä bär-dō'nĕ), *It.* A kind of baritone viol. This was a stringed instrument, approximately of the same size as the violoncello, mounted with six or seven catgut strings, tuned to C, E, A, D, g, b, e'. There were also a large number of wire strings, not passing over the bridge but lying along the belly. These were tuned diatonically, beginning with C, and resounded by resonation. Haydn wrote about sixty compositions for this instrument.

Viola bastada (vē-ō'lä bäs-tä'dä), *It.* Bastard viol. A kind of viol da gamba.

Viola da braccio (vē-ō'lä dä brät'tshī-ō), *It.* The viola; thus named because it rested on the arm.

Viola d'amore (vē-ō'lä dä-mō'rĕ), *It.* } An in-
Viola d'amour (vē-ōl' dä-moor'), *Fr.* } strument a little larger than the viola, furnished with frets and a greater number of strings, some above the fingerboard and some below. The name is also given to an organ-stop of similar quality to the gamba or salcional.

Viola pomposa (vē-ō'lä pŏm-pō'zä), *It.* An enlarged viol or viola of the same compass as the violoncello, but with the addition of a fifth string. It is said to have been invented by J. S. Bach. It is no longer used. The viola pomposa was one of many forms of viol tried in the period between the decadence of the lute and the certainty that four strings were sufficient for all demands.

Viol, bass. The violoncello; a stringed instrument in the form of a violin, but much larger, having four strings, and is performed on with a bow.

Viol da gamba (vē-ōl dä gäm'bä), *It.* } Leg
Viol di gamba (vē-ōl dē gäm'bä), } viol; an instrument formerly much used in Germany, but nearly obsolete. It was a little

---

ĭ *arm,* ă *add,* ä *ale,* ŏ *end,* ē *eve,* ĭ *ill,* ī *isle,* ŏ *old,* ō *odd,* oo *moon,* ü *but,* ü *Fr. sound,* kh *Ger. ch,* nh *nasal.*

smaller than the violoncello, furnished with frets and five or six strings, and held between the knees in playing, hence its name.

Viol, double-bass. The largest and deepest toned of stringed instruments.

Viole (fē ō'lĕ), *Ger.* } The viola.
Viole (vĕ ōl'), *Fr.* }

Viole alt (fē-ō'lĕ ält), *Ger.* The tenor violin.

Violentemente (vē-ō-lĕn-tĕ-mĕn'tĕ), *It.* Violently, with force.

Violento (vē-ō-lĕn'tō), *It.* Violent, vehement, boisterous.

Violenza (vē-ō-lĕn'tsä), *It.* Violence, force, vehemence.

Violin. A well-known stringed instrument, having four strings, and played with a bow. It is the most perfect musical instrument known, of brilliant tone, and capable of every variety of expression. When, or by what nation, this important instrument was first invented is not at present known.

Violinbogen (fē-ō-lĭn'bō'g'n), *Ger.* A violin-bow.

Violine (fē-ō-lē'nĕ), *Ger.* The violin; also an organ-stop of eight, four, or two feet.

Violinier (vē-ō-lĭ-nēr), *Fr.* A violinist.

Violinist. A performer on the violin.

Violinista (vē-ō-lē-nēs'tä), *It.* A violinist.

Violini unisoni (vē-ō-lē'nē oo-nē'zō-nī), *It.* The violins in unison.

Violino (vē-ō-lē'nō), *It.* The violin; it attained its present shape, with four strings, in the sixteenth century.

Violino alto (vē-ō-lē'nō äl'tō), *It.* Counter tenor viol, or small tenor viol, on which the alto may be played.

Violino picciolo (vē-ō-lē'nō pĕt'tshī-ō-lō), }
Violino piccolo (vē-ō-lē'nō pĕk'kō-lō), } *It.*
Violino pochetto (vē-ō-lē'nō pō-khĕt'tō), }
A small violin, tuned a fifth higher than the common violin.

Violino pomposo (vē-ō-lē'nō pŏm-pō'zō), *It.* A viola with an additional higher string. It was tuned c, g, d, a, e.

Violino primo (vē-ō-lē'nō prē'mō), }
Violino principale (vē-ō-lē'nō prēn-tshī-pä'lĕ), } *It.*
The first, or principal, violin part; the leading violin, or chef d'attaque.

Violin-principal. An eight- or four-feet organ-stop, with an agreeable and violin-like tone.

Violinsaite (fē-ō-līn'sī'tĕ), *Ger.* Violin string.

Violinschlüssel (fē-ō-līn'shlüs's'l), }
Violinzeichen (fē ō-līn'tsī'kh'n), } *Ger.*
The treble clef used for the violin.

Violino secondo (vē-ō-lē'nō sä-kŏn'dō), *It.* Second violin.

Violinschule (fē-ō-līn'shoo'lĕ), *Ger.* School for the violin.

Violinspieler (fē-ō-līn'spē'lĕr), *Ger.* A violin-player.

Violinsteg (fē-ō-līn'stĕgh), *Ger.* Violin bridge.

Violinstimme (fē-ō-līn'stĭm'mĕ), *Ger.* Part for the violin.

Violin-tenor. A violin of low tone.

Violinvirtuosin (fē-ō-līn'fīr-too-ō'zīn), *Ger.* A first-class violinist; a virtuoso on the violin.

Viol, leg. The viola di gamba; the bass viol.

Violon (vī-ō-lōnh), *Fr.* The French name for the violin.

Violon (fē-ō-lōn), *Ger.* The double bass. See also, *Violone.*

Violoncell (fē-ō-lōn'tsĕll), *Ger.* } The large,
Violoncelle (vī-ō-lōnh-sāl), *Fr.* } or bass, vi-
Violoncello (vē-ō-lōn-tshĕl'lō), *It.* } olin; the name is also applied to an organ-stop of small scale and crisp tone.

Violoncellist. A player on the violoncello.

Violone (vē-ō-lō'nĕ), } *It.* } The name originally given to the violoncello but afterward transferred to the double bass. Its pitch is an octave below that of the violoncello, and its true use is to sustain the harmony; the name is also applied to an open wood stop, of much smaller scale than the diapason, on the pedals of an organ.

Viols, chest of. An expression formerly applied to a set of viols, consisting of six, the particular use of which was to play fantasias in six parts, generally two each of bass, tenor, and treble.

Virelay. A rustic song, or ballad, in the fourteenth century; nearly the same as the roundel, but with this difference: the roundel begins and ends with the same sentence, or strain, but the virelay is under no such restriction. The name is derived from the Vaux de Vire, in Normandy; the subjects of the songs were generally love, drinking, and passing events. Vaudeville comes from the same source.

Virginal. A small-keyed instrument much used about the time of Queen Elizabeth, and placed upon a table when played upon. It is supposed to have been the origin of the spinet as the latter was of the harpsichord.

Virtuose (fēr-too-ō'zĕ), *Ger.* } A skillful per-
Virtuoso (vēr-too-ō'zō), *It.* } former upon some instrument.

Virtuosität (fīr' too- ō- zī- tät'), *Ger.* Remarkable proficiency, fine execution; applied both to singers and players.

Vis-à-vis (vīz-ä-vē'), *Fr.* Face to face. The name given a large double grand piano, with keyboards at opposite ends.

Vista (vēs' tä), *It.* Sight. *A prima vista,* at first sight.

Vistamente (vēs-tä-mĕn'tĕ), } *It.* } Quickly,
Vitamente (vē-tä-män'tĕ), } swiftly, briskly, immediately.

Vite (vĕt), } *Fr.* } Quickly, swiftly;
Vitement (vĕt-mänh), } *un peu plus vite,* a little more quickly.

ă *arm,* ä *add,* ā *ale,* ĕ *end,* ē *eve,* ĭ *ill,* ī *isle,* ŏ *old,* ō *odd,* oo *moon,* ŭ *but,* ü *Fr. sound,* kh *Ger. ch,* nh *nasal.*

Vitesse (vĕ-tĕss), *Fr.* Swiftness, quickness.
Vivace (vē-vä-tshĕ),
Vivacemente vē-vä-tshä-mĕn'tŏ), *It.* } Lively, briskly, quickly.
Vivace ma non troppo presto (vē-vä-tshĕ mä nôn trôp'pŏ prĕs'tŏ), *It.* Lively, but not too quick.
Vivacetto (vē-vä-tshĕt'tŏ), *It.* A little lively, somewhat quick.
Vivacezza (vē-vä-tshĕt'sä),
Vivacita (vē-vä-tshī-tä), *It.* } Vivacity, liveliness.
Vivacissimo (vē-vä-tshēs'sĭ-mō), *It.* Very lively, extreme vivacity.
Vivamente (vē-vä-mĕn'tĕ), *It.* In a lively, brisk manner.
Vive (vēv), *Fr.* Lively, brisk, quick, sprightly.
Vivente (vē-vĕn'tĕ), *It.* Animated, lively.
Vivezza (vē-vĕt'tsä), *It.* Vivacity, liveliness.
Vivido (vē'vĭ-dō), *It.* Lively, brisk.
Vivo (vē'vō), *It.* Animated, lively, brisk.
Via. Abbreviation for Viola.
Vocal. Belonging, or relating, to the human voice.
Vocal apparatus. The various organs which are employed in the formation and production of vocal sounds.
Vocale (vō-kä'lĕ), *It.* Vocal, belonging to the voice.
Vocalezzo (vō-kä-lĕt'tsō), *It.* A vocal exercise.
Vocalist. A singer.
Vocality. Quality of being utterable by the voice.
Vocalization. The practice and art of singing on vowels.
Vocalize. To practice vocal exercises, using the vowels and the letter A sounded in the Italian manner, for the purpose of developing the voice and of acquiring skill and flexibility.
Vocalizes. Solfeggios; exercises for the voice.
Vocalizzare (vō-kä-lĕt-tsä'rĕ), *It.* To vocalize; to sing exercises for the voice.
Vocalizzo (vō-kä-lĕt'tsō), *It.* Vocal exercises, to be sung on the vowels.
Vocal music. Music composed for the voice.
Vocal score. An arrangement of all the separate voice parts, placed in their proper order under each other.
Voce (vō-tshĕ), *It.* The voice.
Voce angelica (vō-tshĕ än-jĕl'ĭ-kä), *It.*
Vox angelica (vŏx än-gĕl'ĭ-kä), *Lat.* } Angel voice. The name of an organ-stop of delicate reed tone.
Voce di bianca (vō'tshĕ dē bē-än'kä), *It.* "White voice." Applied to pure and colorless tones, such as the voices of young women and children.

Voce di camera (vō'tshĕ dē kä'mĕ-rä), *It.* Voice for the chamber; one suited for private rather than public singing.
Voce di gola (vō'tshĕ dē gō'lä), *It.* The throat voice; also a gutteral voice.
Voce di petto (vō'tshĕ dē pĕt'tō), *It.* The chest voice, the lowest register of the voice.
Voce di ripenlo (vō'tshĕ dē rē-pē-nē'ŏ), *It.* A voice-part written in to fill up the harmony.
Voce di testa (vō'tshĕ dē tĕs'tä), *It.* The head voice, the falsetto, or feigned voice; the upper register of the voice.
Voce flebile (vō'tshĕ flä'bĭ-lĕ), *It.* A doleful voice.
Voce granita (vō'tshĕ grä-nē'tä), *It.* A firm, massive voice, round and full.
Voce intonata (vō'tshĕ ĭn-tō-nä'tä), *It.* A pure-toned voice.
Voce mezza (vō'tshĕ mĕt'tsä), *It.* Half the power of the voice; a moderate, subdued tone, rather soft than loud.
Voce pastosa (vō'tshĕ päs-tō'zä), *It.* A soft, flexible voice.
Voce piacente (vō'tshĕ pē-ä-tshĕn'tĕ), *It.* A pleasing voice.
Voce principale (vō'tshĕ prĭn-tshĭ-pä'lĕ), *It.* Principal voice.
Voce rauca (vō'tshĕ rä'oo-kä), *It.* A hoarse, rough voice.
Voce sola (vō'tshĕ sō'lä), *It.* The voice alone.
Voce spianata (vō'tshĕ spē-ä-nä'tä), *It.* Drawn out; an even, smooth, sustained voice.
Voce spiccata (vō'tshĕ spĕk-kä'tä), *It.* A clear, distinct voice, well articulated.
Voce umana (vō'tshĕ oo-mä'nä),' *It.* The human voice.
Vociaccia (vō-tshĭ-ä-tshĭ-ä), *It.* A bad, disagreeable voice.
Vocina (vō-tshē-nä), *It.* A little, thin voice.
Vogelflöte (fō-g'l-flö'te), *Ger.* Bird-flute.
Vogelgesang (fō'g'l-gē-zäng), *Ger.* Singing of birds; an accessory stop in some very old German organs, producing a chirping effect by some little pipes standing in a vessel with water, through which the wind passes to them.
Vogelpfeife (fō-g'l-pfī'fĕ), *Ger.* Bird-call, flageolet.
Voglia (vōl'yĭ-ä), *It.* Desire, longing, ardor, fervor.
Voice. The sound, or sounds, produced by the vocal organs in singing; applied also to the tuning, and quality of tone, of organ-pipes, the voicing being a most important part of the organ-builder's work. To voice also means writing the voice-parts, regard being had to the nature and capabilities of each kind of voice.
Voice, alto. The lowest female voice.
Voice, baritone. A male voice, intermediate in respect to pitch, between the bass and

tenor, the compass usually extending from B♭ to C.

Voice, bass. The gravest, or deepest, of the male voices.

Voice, chamber. A voice suited to the performance of parlor music.

Voice, chest. The register of the chest tones.

Voice, falsetto. Head-voice, feigned voice; certain notes in a man's voice which are above its natural compass, and which can only be produced in an artificial, or feigned, tone.

Voice, head. The highest register of the female voice; the falsetto in male voices.

Voice parts. The vocal parts, chorus parts.

Voices, accessory. Accompanying voices.

Voicing. The adjustment of the parts of an organ-pipe for the purpose of giving it its proper pitch and its peculiar character of sound.

Voix (vwä), *Fr.* The voice.

Voix aigre (vwü sägr), *Fr.* Harsh voice.

Voix angelique (vwäsün-jěl-ěk). See *Vox Angelica*.

Voix argentine (vwü sär-zhänh-tēn), *Fr.* A clear-toned voice, a silvery voice.

Voix celestes (vwä sä-lěst), *Fr.* Celestial voice, an organ-stop of French invention, formed of two dulcianas, one of which has the pitch slightly raised, which gives to the stop a waving, undulating character; also a soft stop on the harmonium.

Voix de poitrine (vwü dūh pwä-trěnn), *Fr.* Chest voice, natural voice.

Voix de tete (vwü dūh tät), *Fr.* Head voice, falsetto voice.

Voix éclatante (vwü sä-klä-tänht), *Fr.* Loud, piercing voice.

Voix glapissante (vwü glä-pē-sünht), *Fr.* A shrill voice.

Voix grele (vwü gräl), *Fr.* A sharp, thin voice.

Voix humaine (vwä hū-mänh), *Fr.* See *Vox humana*.

Voix percante (vwä pěr-sünht), *Fr.* Shrill voice.

Voix perlée (vwä pěr-lä'), *Fr.* A pearly voice.

Voix ronde (vwü rōnhd), *Fr.* A round, full voice.

Voix trainante (vwä trä-nänht), *Fr.* A drawling voice.

Volante (vō-län-tě), *It.* Flying; a light and rapid series of notes.

Volata (vō-lä'tä), *It.* A flight, run, rapid series of notes, a roulade, or division.

Volate (vō-lä'tě), *It. pl.* See *Volata*.

Volatina (vō-lä-tē'nä), *It.* A little flight, etc. See *Volata*.

Volatine (vō-lä-tē'ně), *It. pl.* Short runs. See *Volata*.

Volée (vō-lä'), *Fr.* A rapid flight of notes.

Volksgesang (fōlks'gě-säng'), \
Volkslied (folks'lēd), } *Ger.* \
Volksstückchen (fōlks'stük'kh'n),

Folksong. The simple and natural melodies which common people find for themselves, or those which good musicians compose for them, within the limits proper to this kind of composition. The qualities of good folks-melody are simplicity, diatonic progression, symmetry, and easy rhythm. In addition to these it should possess individuality, making it agreeable to sing and easy to remember. In America the melodies of Stephen C. Foster and Dr. Geo. F. Root best fulfill these conditions. The native songs of the negroes in the South are folksongs peculiar to the race. Every race and stock acquires, by heredity and historical association, aptitudes for certain kinds of musical progression, and especially of certain rhythms, which are common to their verse and their music.

Volkston (fōlks-tōn), *Ger.* Resembling people's songs.

Voll (fōll), *Ger.* Full; *mit vollem Werde*, with the full organ.

Völler (fōl'lěr), *Ger.* Fuller, louder.

Volles Werk (fōl'lěs wärk), *Ger.* The full organ.

Vollgesang (fōll'gě-säng'), *Ger.* Chorus.

Vollkommen (fōll'kōm'měn), *Ger.* Perfect, complete.

Vollstimmig (fōll'stĭm'mĭg), *Ger.* Full-toned, full-voiced.

Vollstimmigkeit (fōll-stĭm'mĭg-kīt), *Ger.* Fullness of tone.

Volltönend (fōll'tö'něnd), *Ger.* Full-sounding, sonorous.

Volltönige Stimme (fōll'tö'nĭ-gě stĭm'mě), *Ger.* Full-toned, sonorous voice.

Volonté (vō-lōnh-tā), *Fr.* Will, pleasure; *à volanté*, at will.

Volta (vōl'tä), *It.* Time; also an old three-timed air, peculiar to an Italian dance of the same name, and forming a kind of galliard.

Volta prima (vōl'tä prē'mä), *It.* First time.

Voltare (vōl-tä'rě), *It.* To turn, to turn over.

Volta seconda (vōl'tä sě-kōn'dä), *It.* The second time.

Volte (vōl'tě), *It.* } An obsolete dance in 3-4 \
Volte (vōlt), *Fr.* } measure, resembling the galliard, and with a rising and leaping kind of motion.

Volteggiando (vōl-těd-jĭ-än'dō), *It.* Crossing the hands, on the pianoforte.

Volti (vōl'tě), *It.* The plural of Volta.

Volteggiare (vōl-těd-jĭ-ä'rě), *It.* To cross the hands in playing.

Volti (vōl'tĭ), *It.* Turn over.

ä *arm*, ă *add*, ā *ale*, ĕ *end*, ē *eve*, ĭ *ill*, ī *isle*, ŏ *old*, ō *odd*, oo *moon*, ŭ *but*, ü *Fr. sound*, kh *Ger. ch*, nh *nasal*.

Volti, segue la seconda parte (võl'tĭ sä-gwĕ lä sĕ-kŏn'dä pär'tĕ), *It.* Turn over, the second part follows.

Volti subito (võl'tĭ soo'bĭ-tō), *It.* Turn over quickly.

Volubilita (vō-loo-bē'lĭ-tä), *It.*
Volubilmente (vō-loo-bĕl mĕn'tĕ), } Volubility, freedom of performance, fluency in delivery.

Volume. The quantity of fullness of the tone of a voice or instrument.

Voluntary. An introductory performance upon the organ, either extemporaneous or otherwise; also a species of toccata, generally in two or three movements, calculated to display the capabilities of the instrument and the skill of the performer.

Volver a la misma cancion (võl'vär ä lä mĕs'mä kän-thĭ-ōn'), *Sp.* To return to the old tune.

Vom Anfang (fŏm än'fäng), *Ger.* From the beginning.

Vom Blatte (fŏm blät'tĕ), *Ger.* From the page; at first sight.

Von (fŏn), *Ger.* By, of, from, on.

Vorausnahme (fōr-ous'nä-mĕ), *Ger.* Anticipation.

Vorbereitung (fōr'bĕ-rī-toong), *Ger.* Preparation, of discords, etc.

Vorbereitungsunterricht (fōr'bĕ-rī'toongsoon'tĕr-rĭkht'), *Ger.* Preparatory lesson, elementary instruction.

Vorgeiger (fōr'gī-ghĕr), *Ger.* The first violin, the leader of the violins.

Vorgreifung (fōr'grī-fooung), *Ger.*
Vorgriff (fōr'grĭff), } Anticipation.

Vorhalt (fōr'hält), *Ger.* A suspension, or syncopation.

Vorher (fōr'hĕr), *Ger.* Before. *Tempo wie vorher*, the time as before.

Vorig (fō'rĭgh), *Ger.* Former, preceding. *Voriges Zeitmaas*, in the preceding tempo.

Vorsang (fōr'säng), *Ger.* Leading off in the song; act of beginning the tune.

Vorsänger (fōr'sĕn-gĕr), *Ger.* The leading singer in a choir; a precentor.

Vorschlag (fōr'shläg), *Ger.* Appoggiatura, beat.

Vorspiel (fōr'spēl), *Ger.* Prelude; introductory movement.

Vorspieler (fōr'spē-l'r), *Ger.* Leader of the band; the principal, primo performer upon any orchestral instrument.

Vorsteller (fōr'stĕl-l'r), *Ger.* Performer, player.

Vortrag (fōr'träg), *Ger.* Execution, mode of executing a piece; delivery, elocution, diction; the act of uttering, or pronouncing.

Vortragsbezeichnungen ('ōr'trägs-bĕ-tsīkh'noon-gĕn), *Ger.* Marks of expression.

Vorzeichnung (fōr'tsīkh-noong), *Ger.* The signature; also a sketch, or outline, of a composition.

Vox (vŏx), *Lat.* Voice.

Vox acuta (vŏx ä-koo'tä), *Lat.* A shrill, or high voice. In the ancient music, the highest note in the bisdiapason, or double octave.

Vox angelica (vŏx än-gĕ'lĭ-kä), *Lat.* Angelic voice. See *Vox celestes*.

Vox antecedens (vŏx än'tĕ-tsä'dĕns), *Lat.* The antecedent voice. The voice proposing a subject for another voice to imitate.

Vox consequens (vŏx kŏn-sĕ'kwĕus), *Lat.* The consequent voice. The voice performing the imitation.

Vox gravis (vŏx grä'vĭs), *Lat.* A grave, or low voice.

Vox humana (vŏx hoo-mä'nä), *Lat.* Human voice. An organ reed stop of 8-feet tone, intended to imitate the human voice; which it sometimes does, though very imperfectly.

Vox nasalis (vŏx nä-sä'lĭs), *Lat.* A nasal voice.

Vox retusa (vŏx rĕ-too'sä), *Lat.* An 8-feet organ-stop.

Vuide (vwēd), *Fr.* Open. On the open string.

Vuoto (voo-ō'tō), *It.* Open, *e. g.*, an open string.

V. S. Abbreviation for Volti subito.

Waits. An old word, meaning hautboys; also players on the hautboys. See, also, *Wayghtes*.

Waldflöte (wäld'flö'tĕ), *Ger.* Forest-flute, shepherd's flute; an organ-stop with a full and powerful tone.

Waldhorn (wäld-hōrn), *Ger.* Forest-horn; also winding-horn.

Wals (wäls), *Dut.* A waltz.
Walz (wälts), *Ger.* } The name of a modern
Waltz. } dance originally used in Suabia. The measure of its music is triple, usually in 3-4 or 3-8 time, and performed moderately slow, or, at the quickest, in allegretto.

Walzer (wäl-tsĕr), *Ger.* Waltz, national German dance.

ä *arm*, ă *add*, ā *ale*, ĕ *end*, ē *eve*, ĭ *ill*, ī *isle*, ō *old*, ŏ *odd*, oo *moon*, û *but*, ü *Fr. sound*, kh *Ger. ch*, nh *nasal*

Wankend (wän'kĕnd), *Ger.* Wavering, unsteady, hesitating.

Warble. To quaver the sound; to sing in a manner imitating that of birds.

Würme (wär'mĕ), *Ger.* Warmth.

Wassail. An old term signifying a merry or convivial song.

Wasserorgel (wäs'sĕr-ör'g'l), *Ger.* Hydraulic organ.

Water music. A term applied by Handel to certain airs composed by him and performed on the water by the first band of wind instruments instituted in England.

Water organ. The hydraulicon.

Wayghtes. Persons who play hymn tunes, etc., in the streets during the night, about Christmas. See, also, *Waits*.

Way, lyra. One of the two modes of notation in the ancient Greek system.

Weber chronometer. An instrument similar to a metronome, but simpler in its construction, invented by Weber. It consists of a piece of twine about five feet in length, on which are fifty-five inch spaces, and a small weight at the lower end, the degree of motion being determined by the length of string swinging with the weight. Web. Chron. ♩=38″ Rh., (39½ Eng.)

Wechselchor (wĕk's'l-khör'), *Ger.* Alternate chorus or choir.

Wechselgesang (wĕk's'l-gĕ-säng'), *Ger.* Alternative, or antiphonal, song.

Wechselnoten (wĕk's'l - nō' t'n), *Ger. pl.* Changing notes; passing notes, notes of irregular transition, appoggiaturas.

Wehmuth (wā'moot), *Ger.* Sadness.

Wehmüthig (wā-mü'tĭgh), *Ger.* Sad, sorrowful.

Weiberstimme (wī'bĕr-stĭm'mĕ), *Ger.* A female voice, a treble voice.

Weich (wīkh), *Ger.* Minor, in respect to keys and mode.

Weihnachtslied (wī-näkhts-lēd'), *Ger.* Canticle at Christmas; Christmas hymn or carol.

Weinend (wī'nĕnd), *Ger.* Weeping.

Weise (wī'zĕ), *Ger.* Melody, air, song.

Weisse Note (wī'sĕ nō'tĕ), *Ger.* White note; minim.

Weite Harmonie (wī'tĕ här-mō-nē'), *Ger.* Dispersed or open harmony.

Welsh harp. See *Harp*.

Weltlich (wĕlt'lĭkh), *Ger.* Secular.

Weltliche Lieder (wĕlt'lĭkh-ĕ lē'dĕr), *Ger.* Secular songs.

Wenig (wā'nĭgh), *Ger.* Little; *ein wenig stark*, a little strong, rather loud.

Werk (wărk), *Ger.* Work, movement, action. See *Hauptwerk* and *Oberwerk*.

Wesentlich (wā'sĕnt-lĭkh), *Ger.* Essential.

Wesentliche Septime (wā'sĕnt-lĭkh-ĕ sĕp-tē'mĕ), *Ger.* Dominant seventh.

Wettgesang (wĕt'gĕ-säng), *Ger.* A singing-match.

Whistle. A small, shrill wind instrument, in tone resembling a fife, but blown at the end like an old English flute.

Whole note. A semibreve.

Whole rest. A pause equal in length to a whole note.

Whole shift. A violin shift on the eighth line, or A. See *Violin shift*.

Whole tone. Inelegant and unscientific term for a large second; a whole step.

Wieder anfangen (wē'dĕr än'fän-g'n), *Ger.* To begin again, to recommence.

Wiederholung (wē'dĕr-hō'loong), *Ger.* Repeating, repetition.

Wiederholungszeichen (wē'dĕr-hō'loongs-tsī'khĕn), *Ger.* Signs of repetition.

Wiederklang (wē'dĕr-kläng'), *Ger.* Echo, re-
Wiederschall (wē'dĕr-shäll'), } sounding.

Wieder schnell (wē'd'r schnĕll), *Ger.* Again quick.

Wieder zurückhalten (wē'd'r tzoo-rück'hält'n), *Ger.* Again retarding.

Wie oben (wē ō'b'n), *Ger.* Again as above.

Wind. To give a prolonged and varied sound, as, to wind a horn.

Wind band. A band composed of wind instruments.

Windchest. An airtight box under the soundboard of an organ, into which the wind passes from the bellows, and from which it passes to the pipes.

Wind instruments. A general name for all instruments the sounds of which are produced by the breath or by the wind of bellows.

Windharfe (wĭnd'här'fĕ), Æolian harp.

Windlade (wĭnd-lä'dĕ), *Ger.* Windchest in an organ.

Windmesser (wĭnd-mĕs'sĕr), *Ger.* Anemometer, windgauge.

Windstock (wĭnd'stŏk), *Ger.* Cover of organ-pipes.

Windtrunk. A large passage in an organ through which air is conveyed from the bellows to the windchest.

Windzunge (wĭnd'tsoon'ghĕ), *Ger.* Tongue of an organ-pipe.

Winselig (wĭn'sĕ-lĭg), *Ger.* Plaintive.

Winselstimme (wĭn's'l-stĭm'mĕ), *Ger.* A plaintive voice.

Wirbel (wĭr'b'l), *Ger.* Peg of a violin, viola, etc.; the stopper in an organ-pipe.

Wirbelkasten (wĭr-b'l-käs't'n), *Ger.* That part of the neck of a violin, etc., which contains the pegs.

ă arm, ă add, â ale, ĕ end, ē eve, ĭ ill, ī isle, ŏ old, ŏ odd, oo moon, ŭ but, ü *Fr.* sound, kh *Ger.* ch, nh *nasal.*

Wirbelstock (wĭr-b'l-stŏk'), *Ger.* A sound-board.
Wogend (wō'ghĕnd), *Ger.* Waving.
Wohlklang (wōl'kläng), *Ger.* Agreeable sound, harmony.
Wohlklingend (wōl'klīng-ĕnd), *Ger.* Harmonious, sonorous.
Wohllaut (wōl-lout), *Ger.* Euphony, harmony.
Wolf. Name commonly applied to the disagreeable beating and snarling of two organ-pipes when almost in perfect tune. The dissonances of the tempered scale are equally distributed in equal temperament, and there is no wolf; but in the old method some keys were tuned almost perfect, and the dissonances concentrated into one or two of the less used keys, where the wolf was very bad.
Word painting. Musical coloring aimed at the words individually more than to the general idea of a passage of poetry.
Wortklang (wört-kläng), *Ger.* Accent, tone.

Wrest. An old name for a tuning-key.
Wrestpins. Movable pins in a piano, about which one end of the string is wound, and by turning which the instrument is tuned.
Wrestplank. The plank into which the tuning-pins are driven. A wrestplank is glued up of several layers of wood, and must be very solid.
Wristguide. A contrivance for steadying the wrists of young piano-players in order to prevent unbecoming oscillation. While accomplishing the result intended, these apparatuses are unnecessary.
Wüchtig (wükh'tĭgh), *Ger.* Weighty.
Wunderlich (woon'd'r-lĭkh), *Ger.* Odd, capricious.
Wunderstimme (woon-d'r-stĭm'mĕ), *Ger.* A wonderful, extraordinary voice.
Würde (wür'dĕ), *Ger.* Dignity.
Würdevoll (wür'dĕ-fōl), **Würdig** (wür'dĭgh), *Ger.* } Dignified.
Wuth (woot), *Ger.* Madness, rage.

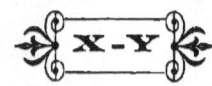

Xanorphika (ksän-ōr'fĭ-kä), *Ger.* A German instrument having a violin-bow and keys; a keyed violin.
Xenorphica. An instrument of the harpsichord and pianoforte class.
Xylharmonicon (ksĭl-här-mō'nĭ-kōn), *Gr.* The wooden harmonica, invented in 1810 by Uthe, an organ-builder at Saugerhausen.
Xylorganon (ksĭl'ōr-gŭ-nōn), **Xylophone** (ksĭl'ō-fōn), *Gr.* } An instrument composed of bars of wood lying upon bands of straw. Each piece of wood is tuned to a certain note, and tunes are played by striking the bars with wooden mallets. Called, also, in Germany, the *Strohfiedel*, straw fiddle.

Yabal (yä-bäl), *Heb.* The blast of a trumpet.
Yo. The Indian flute.

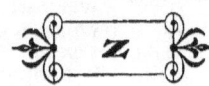

Za. A syllable formerly applied by the French, in their church music, to B♭, to distinguish it from B♮, called Si.
Zampogna (tsäm-pōn'yä), **Zampugna** (tsäm-poon'yä), *It.* } pipe, or bagpipe, now nearly extinct, with a reedy tone, resembling, but much inferior to, the clarinet. See *Cornamusa* and *Chalumeau*.
Zampognare (tsäm-pōn-yä're), *It.* To play on the pipes.
Zampognatore (tsäm-pōn-yä-tō'rĕ), *It.* A piper.
Zampognetta (tsäm-pōn-yĕt'tä), **Zampognino** (tsäm-pōn-yē'nō), *It.* } A small bagpipe.

Zapfenstreich (tsä'pf'n-strīkh'), *Ger.* The tattoo.
Zarge (tsär'ghĕ), *Ger.* The sides of a violin, guitar, etc.
Zart (tsärt), **Zärtlich** (tsärt'lĭkh), *Ger.* } Tenderly, softly, delicately.
Zarte Stimmen (tsär'tĕ stĭm'mĕn), *Ger.* Delicate stops; *mit zarten Stimmen*.
Zartflöte (tsärt'flö-tĕ), *Ger.* Soft-flute; an organ-stop of the flute species.
Zarzuela (thär-thoo-ā'lä), *Sp.* A short drama with incidental music, something similar to the vaudeville.
Zauber (tsou'b'r), *Ger.* Magic.

ŭ *arm*, ä *add*, ā *ale*, ĕ *end*, ē *eve*, ĭ *ill*, ī *isle*, ŏ *old*, ō *odd*, oo *moon*, ŭ *but*, ü *Fr. sound*, kh *Ger. ch*. nh *nasal*.

Zauberlied (tsou'b'r-lēd), *Ger.* A charming song.
Zauberstimme (tsou'b'r-stĭm'mĕ), *Ger.* A charming voice.
Zehn (tsān), *Ger.* Ten.
Zehnte (tsān'tĕ), *Ger.* Tenth.
Zeitmass (tsīt'mäs), *Ger.* Time measure.
Zeitmesser (tsīt'mĕs-sĕr), *Ger.* Time-measure, metronome.
Zele (zhāl), *Fr.* } Zeal, ardor, energy.
Zelo (tsā'lō), *It.* }
Zelosamente (tsā-lō-zä-mĕn'tĕ), *It.* Zealously, ardently.
Zeloso (tsā-lō'zō), *It.* Zealous, ardent, earnest.
Zeng (tsĕng), *Per.* The Persian cymbals.
Zerstreut (tsĕr-stroit'), *Ger.* Dispersed, scattered, with respect to the notes of arpeggios or chords, the situation of the different parts of a composition, etc.
Zeze. An African instrument similar to a guitar.
Zie Harmonica (tsē här-mō'nĭ-kä), *Ger.* The accordion.
Ziemlich (tsĕm'lĭkh), *Ger.* Tolerably, moderately.
Ziemlich langsam (tsĕm'lĭkh läng'säm), *Ger.* Tolerably slow.
Zierathen (tsē-rä'tĕn), *Ger.* Ornaments.
Zierliches Singen (tsēr-lĭkh-ĕs sĭng'ĕn), *Ger.* Modulation.
Ziffern (tsĭf'f'rn), *Ger.* Figures, namely, Arabic numerals.
Zigeunerartig (tsē-goin'ĕr-är'tĭgh), *Ger.* In gypsy style.
Zigeunermusik (tsē-goin'ĕr-moo-sĕk'), *Ger.* Gypsy music.
Zillo (tsĕl'lō), *It.* Chirp, chirping.
Zimbel (tsĕm'bĕl), *Ger.* Cymbal.
Zincke (tsĭnk'ĕ), *Ger.* See *Zinke*.
Zinfonia (tsĕn-fō-nē'ä), *It.* A symphony.
Zingana (tsĕn-gä'nä), *It.* Ballad; Bohemian song.
Zingaresa (tsĕn-gä-rä'zä), *It.* In the style of gypsy music.
Zingaresca (tsĕn-gä-rĕs'kä), *It.* A song or dance in the style of the gypsies.
Zingaro (tsĕn'gä-rō), *It.* Gypsy, in the gypsy style.
Zingen (tsĭn-g'n), *Dut.* To sing; singing.
Zinkbläser (tsĭnk'blä'zĕr), *Ger.* Cornet-player.
Zinke (tsĭnk'ĕ), *Ger.* } Small cornet,
Zinken (tsĭn'k'n), *pl.* } species of horn or trumpet of very ancient date, now almost obsolete. It was made either of wood or the small branches on the head of the deer. Also the name of a treble stop in German organs, which is sometimes a reed and at others a mixture stop.

Zither tsĭt'ĕr, *Ger.* A cither. (1) The old German zither was an instrument consisting of a soundbox, a neck with a fretted fingerboard, and eight, ten, twelve, or more strings, two and two tuned in unison, which were plucked with a quill or piece of whalebone (2) The modern zither consists of a low, flat soundbox without a neck, over which are stretched thirty-six or fewer or more strings of various material—steel wire, brass wire, catgut—some of them overspun. Under four or five of the strings on one side of the soundbox is a fretted fingerboard; on them the melody is played. These four or five strings the performer, who has the instrument lying before him on a table, stops with his left hand and plucks with a plectrum attached to his right-hand thumb; the rest of the strings he plucks with the other fingers of the same hand.
Zitherspieler (tsĭt'ĕr-spē'lĕr), } *Ger.*
Zitherschläger (tsĭt'ĕr-shlä'gĕr), } Guitar-player.
Zitternde Stimme (tsĭt'tĕrn-dĕ stĭm'mĕ), *Ger.* A trembling voice.
Zittino (tsĭt-tē'nō), *It.* Silence.
Zögernd (tsŏ'ghĕrnd), *Ger.* A continual retarding of the time.
Zolfa (tsōl'fä), *It.* See *Solfa*.
Zoppa (tsŏp'pä), } Lame, halting. See *Syn-*
Zoppe (tsŏp'pĕ), *It.* } *copation*.
Zoppo (tsŏp'pō), }
Zornig (tsōr'nĭgh), *Ger.* Angry, wrathful.
Zu (tsoo), *Ger.* At, by, in, to, unto.
Zufällig (tsoo-făl'lĭg), *Ger.* Accidental sharp, flat, etc.
Zufolo (tsoo-fō'lō), *It.* Flageolet, small flute, or whistle.
Zufolone (tsoo-fō-lō'nĕ), *It.* A flute, a large whistle.
Zug (tsoog), *Ger.* Draw-stop, or register, in an organ.
Züge (tsü'ghĕ), *Ger. pl.* See *Zug*.
Zügeglöckchen (tsü'ghĕ-glŏk'khĕn), *Ger.* The passing bell; a knell.
Zugtrompete (tsoogh'trŏm-pä'tĕ), *Ger.* Slide-trumpet. The soprano trombone.
Zugwerke (tsoog-wär'kĕ), *It.* Organ mechanism.
Zuklang (tsoo'-kläng), *Ger.* Unison, harmony, concord.
Zum (tsoom'), *Ger.* To the.
Zummarah. An Egyptian musical instrument, very harsh and discordant in its tone, formed of reeds.
Zunehmend (tsoo-nä'mĕnd), *Ger.* Increasing.
Zunge (tsoon'ghĕ), *Ger.* The tongue of a reed pipe.
Zungenblatt (tsoon'ghĕn-blät'), *Ger.* The clarinet reed.
Zurückblasen (tsoo-rük'blä'zĕn), *Ger.* To blow a retreat.

---

arm, ä add, ā ale, ĕ end, ē eve, ĭ ill, ī isle, ŏ old, ŏ odd, oo moon, ŭ but, ü Fr. sound, kh Ger. ch, nh nasal.

Zurückgehend (tsoo-rük'gä-ĕnd), *Ger.* Going back to the original tempo, after an accelerando or ritardando.

Zurückhaltung (tsoo-rük'häl'toong), *Ger.* Retardation; keeping back.

Zurücktönen (tsoo-rük-tö'něn), *Ger.* } To
Zurücktreiben (tsoo-rük'trī-b'n), } resound, to reverberate.

Zusammen (tsoo-zäm'm'n), *Ger.* Together.

Zusammengesetzt (tsoo-zäm'm'n-gĕ-sĕtst'), *Ger.* Compound, condensed, compound time.

Zusammenklang (tsoo-säm'm'n-kläng), *Ger.* Harmony, consonance.

Zusammenlaut (tsoo-säm'm'n-lout), *Ger.* Harmony, consonance.

Zusammenschlag (tsoo-säm'm'n-shläg), *Ger.*

Zusammensingen (tsoo-säm'm'n-sīn'gĕn), *Ger.* To sing together.

Zusammenstimmig (tsoo-säm'měn-stǐm'mǐgh), *Ger.* Harmonious, concordant.

Zusammenstimmung (tsoo-säm'měn-stǐm'-moong), *Ger.* Harmony, concord, consonance.

Zutraulich (tsoo-trou'lǐkh), *Ger.* Confidently.

Zuversicht (tsoo'fĕr-sǐkht'), *Ger.* Confidence.

Zwanzig (tswän'tsǐgh), *Ger.* Twenty.

Zwanzigste (tswän'tsǐgh-stĕ), *Ger.* Twentieth.

Zwei (tswī), *Ger.* Two.

Zweichörig (tswī'khö-rīgh), *Ger.* Two-choired.

Zweifach (tswī'fäkh), *Ger.* } Two-fold, of
Zweifältig (tswī'fäl'tǐgh), } two ranks, in organ pipes; compound, speaking of intervals, such as exceed the octave, as the 9th, 16th, etc.

Zweifüssig (tswī-füs'sǐg), *Ger.* Of two feet (organ-pipe and pitch.)

Zweigesang (tswī'gĕ-zäng'), *Ger.* For two voices; a duet.

Zweigestrichen (tswī-gĕ-strī'kh'n), *Ger.* With two strokes; applied to C on the third space in the treble, and the six notes above. See *Twice-marked octave*.

Zweiglied (tswīg'lēd), *Ger.* A sequence of two links or chords.

Zweihalbertakt (tswī'häl-bĕr-täkt'), *Ger.* Two half-note measure, 2-2 measure.

Zweihändige Uebungsstücke (tswī-hän'dīghĕ ü-boongs-stük'ĕ), *Ger.* Exercises for two hands.

Zweiklang (tswī'kläng), *Ger.* A chord of two sounds.

Zweimal (tswī'mäl), *Ger.* Twice.

Zweistimmig (tswī'stǐm'mǐg), *Ger.* For two voices, or parts; a duet.

Zweispiel (tswī'spēl), *Ger.* A duet.

Zweite (tswī'tĕ), *Ger.* Second.

Zweites Mal (tswī'tĕs mäl), *Ger.* Second time.

Zweites Manual (tswī'tĕs mä-noo-äl), *Ger.* The second manual.

Zweiunddreissigstel (tswī'oond-drī'sīgs-tĕl), *Ger.* A demisemiquaver.

Zweiunddreissigstel Pause (tswī'oond-drī'sīg-stĕl pow'zĕ), *Ger.* A demisemiquaver rest.

Zweiviertelnote (tswī-fěr'těl-nō'tĕ), *Ger.* A minim.

Zweiviertelpause (tswī-fěr'těl-pow'zĕ), *Ger.* A minim rest.

Zweivierteltakt (tswī-fěr'těl-täkt), *Ger.* Time of two crotchets, 2-4.

Zweizweiteltakt (tswī-tswī't'l-täkt), *Ger.* Time of two minims, 2-2.

Zwerchflöte (tswěrkh'flö-tĕ), *Ger.* Transverse flute, the German flute.

Zwerchpfeife (tswärkh'pfī-fĕ), *Ger.* Transverse pipe, the fife.

Zwey (tswī), *Ger.* See *Zwei*.

Zwischenakt (tswī'shěn-äkt'), *Ger.* Between acts; an intermezzo.

Zwischengesang (tswī'shěn-gĕ-zäng'), }
Zwischenhandlung (tswī'shěn-händ'-loong), } *Ger.* An episode.

Zwischenharmonie (tswī'shěn-här'mō-nē'), *Ger.* Between harmony; the connecting harmony in a fugue.

Zwischenräume (tswī'shěn-roy'mĕ), *Ger. pl* The spaces between the lines of the staff.

Zwischensatz (tswī'shěn-säts), *Ger.* Intermezzo, parenthesis, episode.

Zwischenspiel (tswī'shěn-spēl), *Ger.* Interlude played between the verses of a hymn

Zwischenstille (tswī'shěn-stǐl'lĕ), *Ger.* A pause.

Zwischenstimme (tswī'shěn-stǐm'mĕ), *Ger* Middle voice; high tenor or alto.

Zwischenton (tswī'shěn-tōn), *Ger.* Intermediate tone.

Zwölf (tswölf), *Ger.* Twelve.

Zwölfachteltakt (tswölf-äkh't'l-täkt'), *Ger.* 12-8 measure.

Zymbel (tsǐm'b'l), *Ger.* Cymbal.

ă *arm*, ă *add*, ā *ale*, ĕ *end*, ē *eve*, ĭ *ill*, ī *isle*, ŏ *old*, ō *odd*, oo *moon*, ü *but*, ü *Fr. sound*, kh *Ger. ch*, nh *nasal*.

HOW TO PRONOUNCE MUSICIANS' NAMES.

THEIR NATIVITY AND DATES OF BIRTH AND DEATH.

ABERT (ä-bär')—Bohemian composer, born September 21, 1832.
ABT (äbt), FRANZ—German composer, born December 22, 1819; died March 31, 1885.
ACCOLAY (ä'kō-lä)—
ACHENBACH (äkh'ĕn-bäkh)—
ADAM—French, born 1803; died 1856.
AHLSTROM (äl'strŏm)—
ALARY (ä-lä'rē)—French composer, born 1814; died 1891.
ALBERTI (äl-bär'tē)—
ALBRECHTSBERGER (äl'brĕkhts-bär'gĕr)—German composer, born February 3, 1736; died March 7, 1809.
ANDRE (än'drä)—German composer, born March 28, 1741; died June 18, 1799.
ARBAN (är-bä')—French composer, born February 28, 1825; died April 8, 1889.
ARDITI (är-dē'tē)—Italian composer, born July 22, 1822.
ASANTSCHEWSKY (ä sänt-shĕv'skī)—Russian composer, born 1838.
ASCHER (ä'shĕr)—German composer, born 1831; died June 3, 1869.
ATTENHOFER (ä'tĕn-hō'fĕr)—Swiss composer, born May 5, 1837.
AUBER (ō-bär')—French composer, born January 29, 1782; died May 12, 1870.
ALARD (ä-lär')—French violinist, born March 8, 1815; died February 22, 1888.
ARNE—English composer, born 1710; died 1778.
BACH (bäkh)—German composer, born March 21, 1685; died July 28, 1750.
BADARZEWSKA (bä-därt-sĕv'skī)—Polish female composer, born 1838; died 1862.
BAERMAN (bär'män)—German composer, born February 17, 1784; died June 11, 1847.
BAILLOT (bä-ē-ō')—French composer, born October 1, 1771; died September 15, 1842.
BALFE—English, born 1808; died 1870.
BARGIEL (bär-zhē'ĕl)—German composer, born October 3, 1828.
BARNBY—English composer, born 1838; died 1896.
BATTMAN (bät'män)—French composer, born August 25, 1818.
BAUMFELDER (boum'fĕl-dĕr)—German composer, born May 28, 1836,
BAZIN (bä-zä')—French composer, born September 4, 1816; died July, 1878.
BAZZINI (bät-zē'nī)—Italian composer, born November 11, 1818.

ä *arm*, ă *add*, ā *ale*, ĕ *end*, ē *eve*, ĭ *ill*, ī *isle*, ō *old*, ŏ *odd*, oo *moon*, ou *our*, **kh** Ger. *ch*, nh *nasa'*.

BEETHOVEN (bāt'hō·vĕn)—German composer, born December 16, 1770; died March 26, 1827.
BEHR (bār)—German composer, born July 22, 1837.
BERENS (bĕr'ĕnz)—German composer, born 1826; died May 9, 1880.
BERG (bārg)- Pianist, born 1785; died 1852.
BERGER (bār'gĕr)—German composer, born April 18, 1777; died February 16, 1839.
BERICT (bār'ĭ ō)—Belgian composer, born February 20, 1802; died April 8, 1870.
BERLIOZ (bār'lĭ ō)—French composer, born December 11, 1803; died March 9, 1869.
BERTINI (bār-tē'nĭ)—French composer, born October 28, 1798; died October 1, 1876.
BEVIGNANI (bĕv ĭn-yä'nĭ)—Italian composer and conductor.
BEYER (bī'ĕr)—German composer, born July 25, 1803; died May 14, 1863.
BIAL (bē'äl)—
BIEDERMANN (bē'dĕr·mäu)—
BIEHL (bēl)—German composer, born August 16, 1833.
BILLEMA (bē'yĕ·mä)—
BIZET (bē-zā')—French composer, born October 25, 1838; died June 3, 1875.
BLOMBERG (blŏm bārg)—
BLUMENTHAL (bloo'mĕn-täl)—German composer, born October 4, 1829.
BOCCHERINI (bŏk'kĕ·rē'nĭ)—Italian composer, born February 19, 1743; died May 28, 1805.
BOIELDIEU (bwŏl'dĭ-û)—French composer, born December 16, 1775; died October 8, 1834.
BOITO (bō'ĭ-tō)—Italian composer, born February 24, 1842.
BONAWITZ (bō'nä vītz)—German composer born December 4, 1839.
BORDESE (bŏr-dā'zā)—Italian composer, born 1815; died March, 1886.
BORDOGNI (bŏr-dŏn'yē)—Italian composer, born 1788; died 1856.
BRADSKY (bräd'skĭ)—Bohemian composer, born January 17, 1833; died August 9, 1881.
BRAGA (brä'gä)—Italian composer, born June 9, 1829.
BRAHMS (brämz)—German composer, born May 7, 1833; died April 3, 1897.
BRASSIN (brä-sā')—German composer, born June 24, 1840; died May 17, 1884.
BRUCH (brookh)—German composer, born January 6, 1838.
BRÜLL (brēl)—German composer, born November 7, 1846.
BUCK, DUDLEY – American composer, born 1839.
BÜLOW (bē'lō)–German composer, born January 8, 1830; died, 1894.
BURGMÜLLER (boorg'mĭl-lĕr)—German composer, born 1806; died February 13, 1874.
BELLINI (bĕl-lē'nĭ)—Italian composer, born November 1, 1801; died September 24, 1835.
BENDEL (bĕn'dĕl)—German composer, born March 23, 1833; died July 3, 1874.
BOHM (bōm)—German composer, born September 11, 1844.
BOTTESINI (bŏt-tĕ-zē'nĭ)—Italian composer, born December 24, 1823; died April 7, 1890.
CAMPAGNOLI (käm-pän-yō'lĭ)—Italian composer, born September 10, 1751; died November 6, 1827.
CAMPANA (käm-pän'ä)—Italian composer, born January 14, 1819; died February 2, 1882.
CARISSIMI (kär-ĭs'sĭ-mē)—Italian composer, born about 1604; died 1674.
CARULLI (kä-rool'lĭ)—Italian guitar-player, born February 10, 1770; died 1841.
CHADWICK, GEO. W.—American composer, born November 13, 1854.
CHAMINADE (shäm-ĭ-nä'dĕ), CECILE—French contemporary composer, born August 8, 1861.

ä *arm*, ā *add*, ă *ale*, ĕ *end*, ē *eve*, I *ill*, ī *isle*, ō *old*, ŏ *odd*, oo *moon*, ou *our*, kh Ger. *ch*, nh *nasal*.

CHE   DICTIONARY OF MUSIC.   EGG

CHERUBINI (kā-roo-bē'nĭ) — Italian composer, born September 14, 1760; died March 15, 1842.
CHOPIN (shŏ-pā') — Polish composer, born March 1, 1809; died October 17, 1849.
CHWATAL (shvä-täl') — Bohemian composer, born June 19, 1808; died June 14, 1879.
CIMAROSA (tshē-mä-rō-zä) — Italian composer, born December 17, 1749; died January 11, 1801.
CLAUSS (klouss), WILHELMINE — German pianist, born December 13, 1834.
CLEMENTI (klä-měn'tĭ) — Italian composer, born 1752; died March 10, 1832.
COENEN (kō'ĕ-něn), FRANZ — Dutch composer, born December 26, 1826.
"   "   WILLEM — Dutch composer, born November 17, 1837.
CONCONE (kōn-kō'nä) — Italian composer, born 1810; died June, 1861.
COSTA (koss'tä), SIR MICHAEL — Italian composer and conductor, born February, 1810; died 1884.
COUPERIN (koo-pĕ-rä') — French composer, born November 10, 1668; died 1733.
COURVOISIER (koor-vwä'zĭ-ä) — Swiss composer, born November 12, 1846.
CRAMER (krä'měr) — German composer, born February 24, 1771; died April 16, 1858
CRISTOFORI (krĭs'tō-fō'rĭ) — Italian; inventor of the piano; born 1651; died 1731.
CURSCHMAN (koorsh'män) — German composer, born June 21, 1805; died August 24, 1841.
CZERNY (tsăr'nĭ) — German composer, born February 21, 1791; died July 15, 1857.
CZERWINSKI (zăr-vĭn'shĭ).
CZIBULKA (zē-hool'kä) — Hungarian composer, born May 14, 1842.
DAMM (däm) — German composer, born January 25, 1830.
DANCLA (dänk'lä) — French composer, born December 19, 1818.
DAVID (dä'vĭd'), F. C. — French composer, born April 13, 1810; died August 29, 1876.
"   "   F. — German composer, born January 19, 1810; died July 18, 1873.
DELAHAYE (dĕl-ä-hä')
DELIBES (dĕl-ēb') — French composer, born 1836; died January 16, 1891.
DEPROSSE (dĕ-prŏs') — German composer, born May 18, 1838; died June 23, 1878.
DESORMES (däz-ōrm').
DESSAUER (dĕs-sour') — Bohemian composer, born May 28, 1798; died July, 1876.
DIABELLI (dē-ä-běl'lĭ) — German composer, born September 6, 1781; died April 7, 1858.
DOHLER (dō'lěr) — Italian pianist, born 1814; died 1856.
DONIZETTI (dōn-ĭ-tsĕt'tĭ) — Italian composer, born November 28, 1795; died April 8, 1848.
DOPPLER (dŏp'plěr) — German composer, born October 16, 1821; died July 27, 1883.
DOTZAUER (dŏt-sour') — German composer, born January 20, 1783; died March 6, 1860.
DREYSCHOCK (drī'shŏk), ALEX. — Bohemian composer, born October 15, 1818; died April 1, 1868.
DREYSCHOCK (drī'shŏk), FELIX — German composer, born December 27, 1860.
DROUET (droo'ā) — Dutch composer, born 1792; died September 30, 1873.
DULCKEN (dool'kĕn) — German composer, born 1837.
DUPONT (doo-pü') — Belgian composer, born February 9, 1828; died December 17, 1890.
DURAND (doo-rä') — French composer, born July 18, 1830.
DUSSEK (doo'sĕk) — Bohemian composer, born February 9, 1761; died March 20, 1812.
DUVERNOY (doo-văr-nwä) — French composer, born 1802; died 1880.
DVORAK (dĕv-ōr-zhäk) — Bohemian composer, born September 8, 1841.
ECCARD (ĕk-kär') — German composer, born 1553; died 1611.
EGGHARD (ĕg'gärd) — German composer, born April 24, 1834; died March 22, 1867.

ä *arm*, ă *add*, ā *ale*, ĕ *end*, ē *eve*, ĭ *ill*, ī *isle*, ō *old*, ŏ *odd*, oo *moon*, ou *our*, kh *Ger.*, ch, nh *nasal.*

EICHBERG (ikh'bărg)—German composer, born 1828; died January 19, 1893.
ENCKHAUSEN (ĕnk'hou-zĕn)—German composer, born August 28, 1799; died January 15, 1885.
FAHRBACH (fär'bäkh)—German composer, born August 25, 1804; died 1883.
FAURE (fō'ĕr)—French composer, born January 15, 1830.
FAUST (foust)—German composer, born February 18, 1825; died 1892.
FAVARGER (fä-vär-zhā')—French composer, born 1815; died 1868.
FLOTOW (flō'tŏ)—German opera composer, born 1812; died 1883.
FRANZ (fränts)—German composer, born June 28, 1815; died October 24, 1892.
FETIS (fā'tĭ)—French composer, born 1784; died 1871.
FOOTE—American composer, born 1853.
FORMES (fŏr'měs)—German basso, born 1810; died 1889.
FOSTER—American songwriter, born 1826; died 1864.
FRESCOBALDI (frĕs'cō-bäl'dī)—Italian composer, born 1583; died 1644.
GADE (gä'dā)—Danish composer, born February 22, 1817; died December 21, 1890.
GANSBACHER (günz'bükh-ĕr)—German composer, born 1778; died 1844.
GANZ (gänts)—German composer, born 1830.
GARCIA (gür'thī äh)—Spanish teacher, born 1805.
GENEE (zhā-nā')—German composer, born February 7, 1823.
GENEÉ (zhā-nā') DANTZIG—Born 1824; died 1896.
GILCHRIST—American composer, born 1846.
GILMORE—Irish, conductor, born 1829; died 1890.
GIORDANI (jŏ-ŏr-dä'nī)—Italian composer, born 1744; died 18—.
GLUCK (glook)—German opera composer, born 1714; died 1787.
GODARD (gō-dähr')—French composer, born 1849; died 1895.
GODDARD—English pianist, born 1836.
GOUDIMEL (goo'dĭ-mel)—French composer, born 1510; died 1572
GOUNOD (goo'nŏ')—French composer, born 1818; died 1893.
GRETRY (grā'trē)—Belgian composer, born 1741; died 1813.
GRIEG (grēg)—Swedish composer, born 1843.
GRISI (grē'sī)—Italian soprano, born 1812; died 1869.
GUARNERIUS (gwär-neh'rī-oos)—Italian, born 1683; died 1745.
GUIDO (gwē'dŏ)—Italian theorist, eleventh century.
GUILMANT (gēl'mong)—French organist, born 1837.
HABERBIER (hä'bĕr-beer), ERNST—German composer, born October 5, 1813; died March 12, 1869.
HALEVY (häl'lā-vē)—French composer, born May 27, 1799; died March 17, 1862.
HALLE (häl'lā), CHARLES—German conductor, born April 11, 1819; died 1896.
HÄNDEL, GEORG FRIEDRICH—German composer, born February 23, 1685; died April 14, 1759.
HATTON, J. L.—English composer, born October 12, 1809; died 1886.
HAUPT (houpt)—German organist, born August 12, 1810; died July 4, 1891.
HAUPTMANN (houpt-män), MORITZ—German teacher, born October 13, 1792; died January 3, 1868.
HAYDN (hīgh'dn), FRANCIS JOSEPH—Austrian composer, born March 31, 1732; died May 31, 1809.
HELLER, STEPHEN—Hungarian composer, born May 15, 1814; died January 14, 1888.
HENNES, ALOYSIUS—German teacher, born September 8, 1827; died June 8, 1889.
HENSCHEL, GEO.—German composer, born February 18, 1850.
HENSELT, ADOLF—German composer, born May 12, 1814; died October 10, 1889.

ā *arm*, ă *add*, ä *ale*, ĕ *end*, ē *eve*, ĭ *ill*, ī *isle*, ō *old*, ŏ *odd*, oo *moon*, ou *our*, kh Ger. *ch*, nh *nasal*.

HÉROLD (hā'rōld)—French composer, born January 28, 1791; died January 19, 1833.
HILLER, FERD.—German composer, born October 24, 1811; died May 10, 1885.
HÜNTEN, (hēn'tĕn) FRANCÔIS—German composer, born December 26, 1793; died February 22, 1878.
JACOBSOHN (yä'cōb-sōu)—German violinist, born 1839.
JADASSOHN (yä'däs-sōn)—German composer, born August 13, 1831.
JAELL (yä'ĕl)—Austrian pianist, born March 5, 1832; died February 22, 1882.
JENSEN (yĕn'sĕn), ADOLF—German composer, born January 12, 1837; died January 23, 1879.
JOACHIM (yō'ä-khǐm), JOSEF—Hungarian violinist, born June 28, 1831.
JOMELLI (yō-mĕl'lī)—Italian composer, born September 10, 1714; died August 25, 1774.
JOSEFFY (yō-sĕf'fī)—Hungarian pianist, born 1852.
JULLIEN (zhool'lĭ-änh)—French composer, born June 1, 1812; died 1860.
JUNGMANN (yoong'män)—German composer, born November 14, 1824; died September, 1892.
KALKBRENNER (kälk'brĕn-nĕr)—German composer, born 1784; died June 10, 1849.
KALLIWODA (käl-lǐ-vō'dä)—Bohemian composer, born March 21, 1800; died December 3, 1866.
KELER BÉLA (kā'lĕr bā'lä)—German composer, born February 13, 1820; died November 20, 1881.
KJERULF, HALFDAN (kē-roolf, häf'dän)—Norwegian composer, born 1815; died 1868.
KLINDWORTH (klĭnt'wŏrt), C.—German pianist, born September 25, 1830.
KÖHLER, (kā'lĕr) LOUIS—German composer, born September 5, 1820; died February 16, 1886.
KOSCHAT (kō'shät), THOMAS—German composer, born August 8, 1845.
KRAUSE (krou'sĕ), ANTON—German composer, born November 9, 1834.
KREHBIEL (krā-bēl), H. E.—American critic, born March 10, 1854.
KREUTZER (kroy'tzĕr), KONRADIN—German composer, born November 22, 1780; died December 14, 1849.
KRUG (kroogh), D.—German composer, born May 25, 1821; died April 7, 1880.
KULLAK (koo'läk), THEO.—German composer, born September 12, 1818; died March 1, 1882.
LABITSKY (lä-bĭt'skī), JOSEF—Bohemian composer, born July 4, 1802; died August 18, 1881.
LABLACHE (lä-bläsh'), LUIGI—Neapolitan basso, born December 4, 1794; died January 23, 1858.
LACHNER (läkh'nĕr), FRANZ—Bavarian composer, born April 2, 1804; died January 20, 1890.
LAMBILLOTE (läm-bĭ-yōte), LOUIS—French composer, born March 27, 1797; died February 27, 1855.
LAMOUREUX (lä-moo-rō'), CH.—French conductor, born September 21, 1834.
LAMPERTI (läm-pĕr'tī), F.—Italian singer, born March 11, 1813; died May 6, 1892.
LANGE (läng'ĕ), GUSTAV—German composer, born August 13, 1830; died July 20, 1889.
LANNER (län'nĕr), JOS. F. R.—Austrian composer, born April 12, 1801; died April 14, 1843.
LASSEN, (läs'sĕn) EDUARD—Danish composer, born April 13, 1830.
LAVALEE (lä-vä-lĕ), CALIXA—American pianist, born 1842; died 1888.

LEFÉBURE-WELY (lā-fā'boor-vā'lī), L. J. A.—French composer and organist, born November 13, 1817; died December 31, 1869.

LESCHETITZKY (lā-shŏ-tĭt'skĭ), THEODORE—Polish composer, pianist and teacher, born 1831.

LEYBACH (lā-bükh), IGNACE—French (Alsace) composer, born July 17, 1817; died May 23, 1891.

LICHNER (lĭkh'nĕr), HEINRICH—German composer, born March 6, 1829.

LIEBLING (lēb'lĭng), EMIL—American pianist and composer, born 1851.

LINDPAINTER, PETER JOSEF VON—German composer, born December 8, 1791; died August 21, 1856.

LISZT (lĭst), FRANZ—Hungarian pianist and composer, born October 22, 1811; died July 31, 1886.

LORTZING (lŏrt'sĭng), GUSTAV A.—German composer, born October 23, 1803; died January 21, 1851.

LÖW (lā-vĕ), JOSEF—Bohemian composer, born January 23, 1834; died October, 1886.

LULLY, JEAN BAPTISTE DE—Italian composer, born 1633; died March 22, 1687.

LWOFF, ALEXIS VON—Russian composer, born May 25, 1799; died December 28, 1870. Author of the "Russian National Hymn."

LYSBERG (lĭs'bärg), CHARLES—Swiss composer, born March 1, 1821; died February 15, 1873.

MACDOWELL, E. A.—American composer, born December 18, 1860.

MACFARREN, SIR GEO. ALEXANDER—English composer, born March 2, 1813; died November 2, 1887.

MACKENZIE, ALEX. C.—Scottish composer, born August 22, 1847.

MAELZEL (mĕl'tsĕl), J. N.—German musician and inventor of the metronome, born August 15, 1772; died July 21, 1838.

MALIBRAN (mā'lĭ-brän), MARIA F.—Singer, born 1808; died 1836.

MARCHESI (mär-kā'sĭ), MATHILDE DE C.—German teacher and singer, born March 26, 1826.

MARETZEK (mä-rĕts'ĕk), MAX—German composer and conductor, born 1821; died 1897.

MARPURG, (mür'poorg) FRED. WILHELM—German theorist, born October 1, 1718; died May 22, 1795.

MARIO (mü'rī-ō), G.—Italian tenor, born 1812; died 1883.

MARSCHNER (märsh'nĕr), H.—German composer, born August 16, 1796; died December 14, 1861.

MARTINI, GIOVANNI BATTISTA (mär-tē'nĭ, gē'ō-vä-nĭ bäp-tĭs'tä)—Italian composer, born April 25, 1706; died October 4, 1784.

MARX, A. B.—German composer and theorist, born May 15, 1799; died May 17, 1866.

MARZO (mär'tsō), EDUARD—Italian composer, born 1850.

MASCAGNI (mäs-kän'yĭ), PIETRO—Italian composer, born 1864.

MASON, DR. LOWELL—American composer and teacher, born January 8, 1792; died August 11, 1872.

MASON, DR. WILLIAM—American pianist and teacher, born January 24, 1829.

MASSENET (mäs'sĕ-nā'), J. F. E.—French composer, born May 12, 1842.

MATHEWS, W. S. B.—American pianist, teacher and writer, born May 8, 1837.

MATTEI, TITO (mät-tā'ĭ, tē'tō)—Italian composer, born 1841.

MAUREL, (mô-rĕl) VICTOR—French baritone.

MAYSEDER (mī'sĕh-dĕr), J.—Austrian violinist, born 1789; died 1863.

MAZZINGHI (mät-tsĭn'gĭ), J.—English composer, born 1765; died 1844.

MEHLIG (mā'lĭgh), ANNA—German pianist, born 1846.

MEHUL (mā-ool), E. N.—French composer, born 1763; died 1817.

MENDELSSOHN, J. L. FELIX B.—German composer and pianist, born 1809; died 1847.
MERCADANTE (měr-kä-dän'tě), S.—Italian composer, born 1795; died 1870.
MERKEL, (měr'kěl) GUSTAV—German composer and organist, born 1827; died 1885.
MERZ (měrts), CARL—German composer and writer, born 1834; died 1893.
MEYER, LEOPOLD VON—Austrian pianist, born 1811; died 1883.
MEYERBEER, G.—German composer, born 1791; died 1864.
MEYER-HELMUND, ERIK—Russian composer, born April 13 (25), 1861.
MILLS, S. B.—American composer and pianist, born 1839.
MOLLOY, J. L.—Irish composer, born 1837.
MONTEVERDE (mŏn-tĕ-věr'dě), C.—Italian composer, born 1568; died 1643.
MOSCHELES (mŏsh'ĕ-lĕhs), IGNAZ—German composer, born 1794; died 1870.
MOSZKOWSKI (mŏsh-kŏv'skĭ), M.—Polish composer, born 1854.
MOZART (mō'tsärt), WOLFGANG A.—German composer, born 1756; died 1791.
MURSKA, ILMA DE—Soprano, Croatia, born 1835; died 1889.
NÄGELI (nä'gĕ-lĭ), J. G.—Swiss composer, born 1768; died 1836.
NAUMANN (nou-männ), EMIL—German composer, born 1827; died 1888.
NEUKOMM (noy'kŏm), S. CHEV.—Austrian composer, born 1778; died 1858.
NICODE (nĭ-kŏ-dā), J. L.—Polish Silesia composer, born 1853.
NICOLAI (nĭ-kŏ-lä-ĭ), OTTO—German composer, born 1810; died 1849.
NICOLINI (nĭ-kŏ-lē'nĭ), E.—French tenor, born 1834.
NIECKS, (nĕks) FREDERIC—German musician, born 1845.
NIKISCH, ARTHUR—Hungarian composer, born 1855.
NOSKOWSKY (nŏs-kŏvs-kĭ), SIGISMUND—Polish composer, born 1846.
NOVELLO, VINCENT—English composer, born 1781; died 1861.
OBERTHÜR (ō'běr-těr), CH.—German composer, born 1819.
OESTEN (äs'těn), THEODOR—German composer, born 1813; died 1870.
OFFENBACH, JACQUES (ŏf'ĕn-bäh, zhäck)—French composer, born 1819; died 1880.
ONSLOW, G.—English composer, born 1784; died 1853.
PACHMANN, VLADIMIR DE (päsh-mäng, flä'dĭ-mĭr dā)—Russian pianist, born 1848.
PACINI (pä-chē'nĭ), G.—Italian composer, born 1796; died 1867.
PADEREWSKI (pä-děr-ěvs'kĭ), IGNATZ JOHANN—Polish composer, born 1859.
PAER (pä'ěr), F.—Italian composer, born 1771; died 1839.
PAGANINI (pä-gä-nē'nĭ), N.—Italian violinist, born 1784; died 1840.
PAINE, J. K.—United States composer, born 1839.
PAISIELLO (pä-ĭ-sĭ-ĕl'lō), G.—Italian composer, born May 9, 1741; died June 5, 1816.
PALADILHE (pä-lä-dēl'), EMILE—French composer, born June 3, 1844.
PALESTRINA (pä-lěs-trē'nä), G. P. DA—Italian composer, born 1515; died February 2, 1594.
PALMER, H. R.—American composer, born April 26, 1834.
PANSERON (pän-sĕ-rong), A.—French composer and vocalist, born April 26, 1796; died July 29, 1859.
PAPE (pä'pěh), WM. B.—American composer and pianist, born February 27, 1850.
PARADIES (pä-rä-dēs'), MARIA T. VON—Austrian pianist, born 1759; died 1824.
PAREPA, ROSA—Scottish soprano, born 1836; died 1874.
PARKER, J C. D.—American composer and organist, born June 2, 1828.
PASDELOUP (pä-dě-loo'), J. E.—French conductor, born September 15, 1819; died August 13, 1887.
PATTI, ADELINA—Spanish soprano, born 1843
PATTI, CARLOTTA (sister of A.)—Italian soprano, born 1840; died 1889.
PAUER (pou'ěr), ERNST—Austrian composer, pianist and writer, born 1826.

PERGOLESI (pĕr-gō-lĕh'sĭ), G. B.—Italian, born January 4, 1710; died March 16, 1736.
PIATTI (pē'ät-tĭ), A.—Italian composer and 'cellist, born January 8, 1822.
PICCINI (pĭt-chē'nĭ), N.—Italian composer, born January 16, 1728; died May 7, 1800.
PINSUTI, CIRO (pĭn-soo'tĭ, chē'rō)—Italian composer, born May 9, 1829; died March 10, 1888.
PLAIDY (play'dĭ), LOUIS—German pianist and writer, born November 28, 1810; died March 3, 1874.
PLANQUETTE, ROBERT—French composer, born July 21, 1850.
PLEYEL, IGNAZ (plī'ĕl, ĭg'näts), J.—German composer, born June 1, 1757; died November 14, 1831.
PONCHIELLI (pŏn-kĭ-ĕl'lĭ), A.—Italian composer, born September, 1834; died January 17, 1886.
PONIATOWSKI (pŏn-yä-tŏw'skĭ), PRINCE J. M. F. X. J.—Polish composer, born February 20, 1816; died July 3, 1873.
PRESSEL, G. A.—German composer, born June 11, 1827; died July 30, 1890
PORPORA (pŏr-pō-rä), NICCOLO—Italian composer, born August 19, 1686; died February, 1767.
PROCH (prŏkh), HEINRICH—German composer and violinist, born July 22, 1809; died December 18, 1878.
PROKSCH (prŏksh), J.—Bohemian teacher, born 1794; died 1864.
PRUDENT (proo-dong), E. B.—French composer, born February 3, 1817; died May 14, 1863.
PRUME (proom), F. H.—Belgian composer, born June 3, 1816; died July 14, 1849.
PURCELL, HENRY—English composer, born 1658: died November 21, 1695.
QUEDANT (kä-dong), JOSEPH—French composer, born December 7, 1815.
RAFF (räff), J. J.—German composer, born May 27, 1822; died June 25, 1882.
RAMEAU (rä-mō), J. P.—French composer, born September 26, 1683; died September 12, 1764.
REINECKE (rī'nĕ kŏ), CARL—German composer, born June 23, 1824.
REISSIGER (rīs'sĭ-gĕr), C. G.—German composer, born January 31, 1798; died November 7, 1859.
REMENYI (rĕ-mĕn-yĭ), ED.—Hungarian violinist, born 1830.
RHEINBERGER (rīn'bĕr-gĕr), J—German composer, born March 17, 1839.
RICCI (rĭt'chĭ), F.—Italian composer, born October 22, 1809; died December 10, 1877.
RICHARDS, BRINLEY—Welsh composer, born November 13, 1817; died May 1, 1859
RICHTER, HANS (rĭkh'tĕr, häns)—Hungarian composer, born April 4, 1843.
RIEMANN, HUGO (rē'män, hoo'gō)—German theorist, born July 18, 1849.
RIES (rēs), F.—German composer, born November 29, 1784; died January 13, 1838.
RIGHINI (rē-ghē'nĭ), V.—Italian composer, born January 22, 1756; died August 19, 1812.
RIMBAULT, ED. F.—English composer, born June 13, 1816; died September 26, 1876.
RINK, J. C. H.—German composer, born February 18, 1770; died August 7, 1846.
RITTER, FRED L—Alsatian composer, born 1831; died 1892.
ROECKEL (rĕk'ĕl), J. A.—German tenor, born 1783; died 1870.
ROMBERG, ANDREAS (rŏm-bärg, än'drĕ-äs)—German composer, born April 27, 1767; died November 10, 1821.
RONCONI, SEBASTIAN (rŏn-kō'nĭ, sĕ-bäs'tĭ-än)—Italian baritone, born 1814.
ROOT, GEO F.—American composer, born August 30, 1820; died 1895.
SACCHINI (säk-kē'nĭ), A. M. L.—Italian composer, born July 23, 1734; died October 7, 1786.
SAINT-SAËNS (sänh-sä-onh), CAMILLE—French composer, born October 9, 1835.

ä *arm*, ă *add*, ā *ale*, ĕ *end*, ē *eve*, ĭ *ill*, ī *isle*, ō *old*, ŏ *odd*, oo *moon*, ou *our*, kh Ger. *ch*, nh *nasal*.

SAINTON (säng-tong), P. P. C.—French composer, born June 5. 1813 ; died October 17, 1890.
SALIERI (sä-li-ä'rĭ), A.—Italian composer, born August 19, 1750; died May 7, 1825.
SCALCHI, SOFIA (skäl'kĭ, sō'fĭ-ä)—Italian alto, born 1850.
SCARLATTI (skär-lät'tĭ), A.—Italian composer, born 1659; died October 24, 1725.
SCHARWENKA (shär-věn'kä), PHILIP—German composer, born February 16, 1847.
SCHARWENKA, XAVER—German composer, born January 6, 1850.
SCHINDLER (shĭnt'lěr), ANTON—Germany, born 1796; died January 16, 1864.
SCHMIDT, ALOYS—German composer, born August 26, 1789; died July 25, 1866.
SCHUBERT, FRANZ PETER—Austrian composer, born January 31, 1797; died November 19, 1828.
SCHUMANN, ROBT. A.—German composer, born June 8, 1810; died July 29, 1856.
SCHUMANN, CLARA (WIECK), (wife of Robt.)—German pianist, born September 13, 1819; died 1896.
SGAMBATI (sgäm-bä'tĭ), G.—Italian composer, born May 18, 1843.
SHERWOOD, W. H.—American composer, born January 31, 1854.
SMART, HENRY—English organist, born 1813, died 1879.
SMETANA (smě-tä'nä), FR.—Hungarian composer, born March 2, 1824; died May 12, 1884.
SMITH, SIDNEY—English composer, born July 13, 1839; died 1889.
SÖDERMAN (sood'ěr-män), J. A.—Swedish composer, born July 17, 1832; died February 10, 1876.
SPOHR, LUDWIG—German violinist, born April 5, 1784; died October 22, 1859.
STAUDIGL (stou'dĭgl), JOS.—German basso, born 1807; died 1861.
STEFFANI (stěf-fä'nĭ), A.—Italian composer, born 1655; died 1730.
STEIBELT (stī'bělt), DAN.—German composer, born 1765; died September 20, 1823.
STIGELLI (stē-jěl'lĭ), G.—German composer, born 1819; died 1868.
STRADIVARI (strä-dĭ-vä'rĭ), A.—Italian violin-maker, born 1644 ; died December 18, 1737.
STRAUSS (strouss), ED.—Austrian composer, born February 14, 1835.
STRAUSS, JOS.—Austrian composer, born August, 1827 ; died July 22, 1870.
SULLIVAN, SIR A. S.—English composer, born May 13, 1842.
SUPPE (soop'pē), F. VON—German composer, born April 18, 1820.
TARTINI (tär-tē'nĭ), G.—Italian composer, born April 12, 1692; died February 16, 1770.
TAUSIG (tous'ĭg), CARL—Polish composer, born November 4, 1841 ; died July 17, 1871.
THALBERG (täl-běrg), S.—Swiss composer, born January 7, 1812; died April 27, 1871.
THOMAS, C. AMBROISE (tō-mä, äm-brō-äz)—French composer, born August 5, 1811.
THOMÉ (tō-mä), F. L. J.—Mauritius composer, born 1850.
TITJENS (tět'yěns), T. C. J.—German soprano, born 1831; died 1877.
TOSTI (tōs'tĭ), F. P.—Italian composer, born April 7, 1846.
TREBELLI (trē-běl'lĭ), LELIA—French alto, born 1838; died 1893.
TSCHAIKOWSKY (chī-kow'skĭ), P. I.—Russian composer, born April 25, 1840; died 1893.
VERDI (vär'dĭ), G.—Italian composer, born October 9, 1813.
VIARDOT-GARCIA (vē-är'dō gär'shĭ-ä), M. F. P.—French composer, born July 18, 1821.
VIEUXTEMPS (vee-oo-tom'), H.—French composer, born February 20, 1820; died June 6, 1881.

ärm, ă add, ā ale, ĕ end, ē eve, ĭ ill, ī isle, ŏ old, ô odd, oo moon, ou our, kh Ger. ch, nh nasal

VIOTTI (vē-ŏt'tĭ), G. B.—Italian composer, born May 23, 1753; died March 10, 1824.
VIVIER (vē-vī-ā'), E. L.—Corsican horn-player, born 1821.
VOLCKMAR (fōlk'mär), WIL.—German composer, born December 26, 1812; died August 27, 1887.
VOLKMANN (fōlk-män), F. R.—German composer, born April 6, 1815; died October 29, 1883.
WAGNER (väg-nĕr), W. RICHARD—German composer, born May 23, 1813; died February 13, 1883.
WEBER (vā'bĕr), CARL M. VON—German composer, born December 18, 1786; died 1826.
WEHLE (vā'lĕ), CARL—Bohemian pianist, born March 17, 1825; died June 2, 1883.
WIDOR (vē-dōr), CH. M.—French composer, born February 24, 1845.
WIENIAWSKI (vē-nĭ-äv'skĭ), H.—Polish composer, born July 10, 1835; died April 2, (March 31) 1880.
WILHELMJ (wĭl-hĕl'mĭ), A. E. D. F. V.—German violinist, born September 21, 1845.
YSAYE (ē-sä'ē), E.—Belgian violinist, born 1858.
ZACHAU (tsä'khou), F. W.—German composer, born November 19, 1663; died August 14, 1712.
ZARLINO (tsär-lē'nō), G.—Italian composer, born March 22, 1517; died February 14, 1590.
ZEUNER (tsoy'nĕr), CH.—German organist, born 1797; died 1857.
ZINGARELLI (tsĭn-gä-rĕl'lĭ), N. A.—Italian composer, born April 4, 1752; died May 5, 1837.
ZUNDEL, JOHANN (tsoon'dĕl, yō'hän)—German composer, born 1815; died 1882.

ä *arm*, a *add*, ā *ale*, ĕ *end*, ē *eve*, ĭ *ill*, ī *isle*, ō *old*, ŏ *odd*, oo *moon*, ou *our*, kh *Ger. ch*, uh *nasal*.

www.ingramcontent.com/pod-product-compliance
Lightning Source LLC
Chambersburg PA
CBHW032110220426
43664CB00008B/1200